REA's Test Prep Books Are The Best!
(a sample of the <u>hundreds of letters</u> REA receives each year)

" This book is a really good review and gives you quality questions similar to the AP exam. I got a 5 on the AP U.S. History exam. "
Student, New Orleans, LA

" This is absolutely the best test prep for AP U.S. History! Having read only four chapters of the comprehensive review, I took the test and scored a 4....I believe that if I had not picked up this book I would have scored a 2 or a 3. "
Student, San Andreas, CA

" The [REA AP U.S. History] review book I am using for my course has proven to be an excellent tool in furthering my comprehension of American history. Not only does the course review succeed in reinforcing the information I learn in class, but the book's practice tests are helping me properly prepare for the AP exam. "
Student, Putnam Valley, NY

" The [AP U.S. History practice tests] helped me quite a bit....
I found the book very helpful. "
Student, Seattle, WA

" Your book was responsible for my success on the exam, which helped me get into the college of my choice... I will look for REA the next time I need help. "
Student, Chesterfield, MO

" Just a short note to say thanks for the great support your book gave me in helping me pass the test... I'm on my way to a B.S. degree because of you! "
Student, Orlando, FL

(more on next page)

(continued from front page)

" I just wanted to thank you for helping me get a great score
on the AP U.S. History exam... Thank you for making great test preps! "
Student, Los Angeles, CA

" Your *Fundamentals of Engineering Exam* book was the absolute best
preparation I could have had for the exam, and it is one of the major
reasons I did so well and passed the FE on my first try. "
Student, Sweetwater, TN

" I used your book to prepare for the test and found that the advice and the
sample tests were highly relevant... Without using any other material, I earned
very high scores and will be going to the graduate school of my choice. "
Student, New Orleans, LA

" What I found in your book was a wealth of information sufficient to shore up
my basic skills in math and verbal... The section on analytical ability was
excellent. The practice tests were challenging and the answer explanations most
helpful. It certainly is the *Best Test Prep for the GRE*! "
Student, Pullman, WA

" I really appreciate the help from your excellent book. Please keep up
the great work. "
Student, Albuquerque, NM

" I am writing to thank you for your test preparation... your book helped me
immeasurably and I have nothing but praise for your *GRE* preparation."
Student, Benton Harbor, MI

(more on back page)

The Best Test Preparation for the

AP
United States History Exam

7ᵗʰ Edition

Gregory Feldmeth
Assistant Head of School
Instructor, AP United States History
Polytechnic School
Pasadena, CA

Gary Piggrem, Ph.D.
Professor of History
DeVry Institute of Technology
Columbus, OH

Jerome McDuffie, Ph.D.
Professor of History
University of North Carolina at Pembroke
Pembroke, NC

Steven E. Woodworth, Ph.D.
Assistant Professor of History
Toccoa Falls College
Toccoa, GA

Research & Education Association
Visit our website at
www.rea.com

Research & Education Association
61 Ethel Road West
Piscataway, New Jersey 08854
E-mail: info@rea.com

The Best Test Preparation for the
AP UNITED STATES HISTORY EXAM

Published 2008

Copyright © 2006 by Research & Education Association, Inc.
Prior editions copyright © 2001, 2000, 1998, 1997, 1994 by
Research & Education Association, Inc. All rights reserved.
No part of this book may be reproduced in any form without
permission of the publisher.

Printed in the United States of America

Library of Congress Control Number 2006922390

ISBN-13: 978-0-7386-0218-9
ISBN-10: 0-7386-0218-3

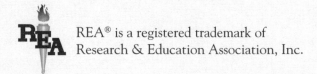 REA® is a registered trademark of
Research & Education Association, Inc.

CONTENTS

About Research & Education Association xiii

Staff Acknowledgments xiii

Preparing with Confidence:
Excelling on the AP United States History Exam xv
About the Exam xvi
About the Review Section xvii
Scoring the Exam xviii
Contacting the AP Program xix
AP United States History Study Schedule xx

AP UNITED STATES HISTORY COURSE REVIEW

Chapter 1
Pre-Columbian Cultures (12,000 B.C.E–1492 C.E.) 1
2,000 Separate Cultures 1
Highly Organized Society 2
Some Native Tribes Rendered Nearly Extinct 4
Historical Timeline 6

Chapter 2
European Exploration and the Colonial Period (1492–1763) 7
The Age of Exploration 7
The Beginnings of Colonization 11
The Colonial World 19
The 18th Century 24
Historical Timeline 28

Chapter 3

The American Revolution (1763–1787) **31**

The Coming of the American Revolution 31

The War for Independence 36

The Creation of New Governments 43

Historical Timeline 48

Chapter 4

The United States Constitution (1785–1789) **49**

Development and Ratification 49

Outline of the United States Constitution 52

Separation and Limitation of Powers 55

Historical Timeline 57

Chapter 5

The New Nation (1789–1824) **59**

The Federalist Era 59

The Establishment of the Executive Departments 60

Washington's Administration, 1789–1797 60

Foreign and Frontier Affairs 61

Internal Problems 62

John Adams' Administration, 1797–1801 63

Repression and Protest 64

The Revolution of 1800 64

The Jeffersonian Era 65

Conflict with the Judges 66

Domestic Affairs 67

International Involvement 69

Madison's Administration, 1809–1817 70

Postwar Developments 73

Internal Development, 1820–1830 74

The Marshall Court 75

Statehood: A Balancing Act 76

The Expanding Economy 77

The Transportation Revolution 78

Industrialization 79

Educational Development 80

Developments in Religious Life 82

Historical Timeline 84

Chapter 6
Jacksonian Democracy and Westward
Expansion (1824–1850) 87
The Jacksonian Democracy, 1829–1841 87
The Election of 1824 87
The Webster-Hayne Debate (1830) 91
The War on the Bank 92
The Election of 1840 93
The Meaning of Jacksonian Politics 94
Ante-bellum Culture: An Age of Reform 95
The Flowering of Literature 95
The Fine Arts 96
The Transcendentalists 97
The Utopians 97
The Mormons 98
Remaking Society: Organized Reform 98
Diverging Societies—Life in the North 101
The Role of Women and Minorities 103
The Northeast Leads the Way 104
Everyday Life in the North 106
Diverging Societies—Life in the South 106
Commerce and Industry 110
Life in the Southern States 111
Manifest Destiny and Westward Expansion 112
Tyler, Polk, and Continued Westward Expansion 115
Historical Timeline 124

Chapter 7
Sectional Conflict and the Causes of the
Civil War (1850–1860) 125
The Crisis of 1850 and America at Mid-century 125
The Return of Sectional Conflict 131
The Coming of the Civil War 137
Historical Timeline 141

Chapter 8
The Civil War and Reconstruction (1860–1877) 143
Hostilities Begin 143
The Union Preserved 146
The Ordeal of Reconstruction 154
Historical Timeline 165

Chapter 9
Industrialism, War, and the Progressive Era (1877–1912) 167

The New Industrial Era, 1877–1882 167
Politics of the Period, 1877–1882 167
The Economy, 1877–1882..168
Social and Cultural Developments, 1877–1882 170
Foreign Relations, 1877–1882...171
The Reaction to Corporate Industrialism, 1882–1887............................174
Politics of the Period, 1882–1887 174
The Economy, 1882–1887..175
Social and Cultural Developments, 1882–1887 176
Foreign Relations, 1882–1887...178
The Emergence of Regional Empire, 1887–1892 179
Politics of the Period, 1887–1892 179
The Economy, 1887–1892..180
Social and Cultural Developments, 1887–1892 181
Foreign Relations, 1887–1892...181
Economic Depression and Social Crisis, 1892–1897.............................183
The Economy, 1892–1897..185
Social and Cultural Developments, 1892–1897 186
Foreign Relations, 1892–1897...187
War and the Americanization of the World, 1897–1902 189
Politics of the Period, 1897–1902 189
The Economy, 1897–1902..190
Social and Cultural Developments, 1897–1902 191
Foreign Policy, 1897–1902 193
Theodore Roosevelt and Progressive Reforms, 1902–1907 197
Politics of the Period, 1902–1907 197
The Economy, 1902–1907..199
Social and Cultural Developments, 1902–1907 200
Foreign Relations, 1902–1907...202
The Regulatory State and the Ordered Society, 1907–1912...................203
Politics of the Period, 1907–1912 204
The Economy, 1907–1912..207
Social and Cultural Developments, 1907–1912 209
Foreign Relations, 1907–1912...210
Historical Timeline 213

Chapter 10
Wilson and World War I (1912–1920)... 215

Implementing the New Freedom: The Early Years of the
    Wilson Administration...215
The Triumph of New Nationalism 217

The Election of 1916.. 219
Social Issues in the First Wilson Administration.............................. 220
Wilson's Foreign Policy and the Road to War 221
The Road to War in Europe 223
World War I: The Military Campaign.. 226
Mobilizing the Home Front 227
Wartime Social Trends.. 231
Peacemaking and Domestic Problems, 1918–1920 232
Domestic Problems and the End of the Wilson Administration 236
Historical Timeline 239

Chapter 11
The Roaring Twenties and Economic
Collapse (1920–1929) 241

The Election of 1920.. 241
The Twenties: Economic Advances and Social Tensions.................. 242
American Society in the 1920s.. 246
Social Conflicts 251
Government and Politics in the 1920s:
      The Harding Administration.. 256
The Election of 1924.. 259
The Coolidge Administration.. 260
The Election of 1928.. 261
Foreign Policy in the Twenties... 262
The Great Depression: The Crash 263
Historical Timeline 264

Chapter 12
The Great Depression and the New Deal (1929–1941) 265

Reasons for the Depression 265
Hoover's Depression Policies.. 266
The Election of 1932.. 269
The First New Deal 270
Legislation of the First New Deal.. 271
The Second New Deal: Opposition from the Right and Left 275
The Second New Deal Begins... 276
The Election of 1936.. 278
The Last Years of the New Deal 280
Social Dimensions of the New Deal Era.. 282
Labor Unions.. 283
Cultural Trends of the 1930s 284
New Deal Diplomacy and the Road to War...................................... 286
United States Neutrality Legislation 288

Threats to World Order 289
The American Response to the War in Europe 290
The Election of 1940 292
American Involvement with the European War 293
The Road to Pearl Harbor 294
Historical Timeline 298

Chapter 13
World War II and the Postwar Era (1941–1960) **301**
Declared War Begins 301
The Home Front 301
The North African and European Theatres 303
The Pacific Theatre 304
The Atomic Bomb 306
Diplomacy 306
The Emergence of the Cold War and Containment 308
International Cooperation 310
Containment in Asia 310
Eisenhower-Dulles Foreign Policy 311
The Politics of Affluence: Demobilization and Domestic Policy 314
The Fair Deal 316
Anticommunism 317
Eisenhower's Dynamic Conservatism 318
Civil Rights 320
The Election of 1960 322
Society and Culture 322
Demographic Trends 323
Conformity and Security 324
Seeds of Rebellion 325
Historical Timeline 327

Chapter 14
The New Frontier, Vietnam, and Social
   Upheaval (1960–1972) **329**
Kennedy's "New Frontier" and the Liberal Revival 329
Civil Rights 329
The Cold War Continues 331
Johnson and the Great Society 332
Emergence of Black Power 334
Ethnic Activism 336
The New Left 336
The Counterculture 337
Women's Liberation 338

Vietnam..338
Election of 1968...339
The Nixon Conservative Reaction 340
Vietnamization 341
Foreign Policy..343
Election of 1972...343
Historical Timeline 345

Chapter 15
Watergate, Conservatism's Rise, and
Post–Cold War Challenges (1972–2005) **347**

The Watergate Scandal 347
The Ford Presidency 350
Carter's Moderate Liberalism 351
Carter's Foreign Policy 352
The Iranian Crisis...353
The Election of 1980...353
The Reagan Presidency: Attacking Big Government 354
Asserting American Power 356
Election of 1984..356
Second-Term Foreign Concerns 357
Second-Term Domestic Affairs 358
Election of 1988..359
Bush Abandons Reaganomics..360
Other Domestic Issues Under Bush...362
Bush's Activist Foreign Policy 363
Collapse of East European Communism 364
Persian Gulf Crisis...364
Breakup of the Soviet Union 366
The Election of 1992...366
The Clinton Presidency 366
The Election of 1996...368
The Election of 2000...369
American Society at the Dawn of the Twenty-first Century....................369
Historical Timeline 374

AP UNITED STATES HISTORY PRACTICE TESTS

Practice Test 1 .... **377**
Answer Key 409
Detailed Explanations of Answers.. 410

Practice Test 2 .... **437**
Answer Key 469
Detailed Explanations of Answers.. 470

Practice Test 3 .... **495**
Answer Key 528
Detailed Explanations of Answers.. 529

Practice Test 4 .... **579**
Answer Key 613
Detailed Explanations of Answers.. 614

Practice Test 5 .... **665**
Answer Key 695
Detailed Explanations of Answers.. 696

Practice Test 6 .... **721**
Answer Key 752
Detailed Explanations of Answers.. 753

ANSWER SHEETS.. **783**

INDEX **803**

ABOUT RESEARCH & EDUCATION ASSOCIATION

Founded in 1959, Research & Education Association is dedicated to publishing the finest and most effective educational materials—including software, study guides, and test preps—for students in middle school, high school, college, graduate school, and beyond.

REA's Test Preparation series includes books and software for all academic levels in almost all disciplines. Research & Education Association publishes test preps for students who have not yet entered high school, as well as high school students preparing to enter college. Students from countries around the world seeking to attend college in the United States will find the assistance they need in REA's publications. For college students seeking advanced degrees, REA publishes test preps for many major graduate school admission examinations in a wide variety of disciplines, including engineering, law, and medicine. Students at every level, in every field, with every ambition can find what they are looking for among REA's publications.

REA's practice tests are always based upon the most recently administered exams, and include every type of question that you can expect on the actual exams.

REA's publications and educational materials are highly regarded and continually receive an unprecedented amount of praise from professionals, instructors, librarians, parents, and students. Our authors are as diverse as the fields represented in the books we publish. They are well-known in their respective disciplines and serve on the faculties of prestigious high schools, colleges, and universities throughout the United States and Canada.

Today, REA's wide-ranging catalog is a leading resource for teachers, students, and professionals.

STAFF ACKNOWLEDGMENTS

We would like to thank Larry B. Kling, Vice President, Editorial, for his overall direction; Pam Weston, Vice President, Publishing, for setting the quality standards for production integrity and managing the publication to completion; Christine Reilley and Anne Winthrop Esposito, Senior Editors, for their editorial contributions; Diane Goldschmidt, Senior Editor, for post-production coordination; Molly Solanki, Associate Editor, for coordinating revisions; Christine Saul, Senior Graphic Designer, for designing the cover; Jeff LoBalbo, Senior Graphic Designer, for coordinating pre-press electronic file mapping; Kathy Caratozzolo, for typesetting revisions; and Aquent Publishing Services, for typesetting the manuscript.

PREPARE WITH CONFIDENCE
Excelling on the AP U.S. History Exam

If you're looking for a true edge on Test Day...

And if you're not willing to settle for second best...

...then this new edition of REA's AP U.S. History test prep is for you.

REA gives you **all the tools** you'll need to master the Advanced Placement Examination in United States History:

■ Unrivaled detailed review of all the facts in a context that will sharpen classroom discussion and keep you from having to continually check your textbook for citations as you study.

■ Handy timelines that clearly summarize each period's major events.

■ Photographs and other carefully chosen artwork that bring critical events and personalities to life.

■ Sidebars that highlight key historical figures and issues.

■ Comprehensive index that speeds specific referencing.

■ Six full-length, true-to-format practice exams—with 480 multiple-choice items in all—that prepare you for the actual AP exam like no other book.

■ Full explanations of every practice-exam answer.

■ Complete array of sample essay questions and answers.

Beginning with the 2006 exam, the AP Program's U.S. History Development Committee has embraced the trend on college and university campuses to view United States history through the prism of social change on the one hand, and cultural and intellectual developments on the other. Our book does likewise.

In choosing REA, you're putting yourself in the company of tens of thousands of AP students who have benefited from our total preparation package year after year. Moreover, teachers across the nation and beyond find that this book offers a clear-eyed, no-nonsense perspective on the history of the United States of America. In fact, many AP instructors use it to supplement their classroom text and lectures precisely because it so comprehensively supports specific curriculum objectives for the AP course and exam.

ABOUT THE EXAM

The Advanced Placement Program is designed to allow high school students to pursue college-level studies while attending high school. The three-hour five-minute AP U.S. History exam is usually given to high school students who have completed a year's study in a college-level U.S. History course. The test results are then used to determine the awarding of course credit and/or advanced course placement in college.

According to the College Board, students taking this exam are called upon to demonstrate "systematic factual knowledge" and bring to bear critical, persuasive analysis of the full sweep of U.S. history. This is why we make every effort to establish and build upon context for you, rather than encouraging rote memorization of disconnected facts.

FORMAT. The AP U.S. History Exam is divided into two sections as follows:

1) **Multiple-Choice Items:** This section is composed of 80 multiple-choice questions designed to gauge your ability to understand and analyze U.S. history from the Pre-Columbian period to the present. The majority of the questions, however, are based on nineteenth- and twentieth-century history. This section tests factual knowledge, scope of preparation, and knowledge-based analytical skills. You'll have 55 minutes to complete this section, which accounts for 50 percent of your final grade.

2) **Free-Response Items:** This section is composed of three essay questions designed to measure your ability to write coherent, intelligent, well-organized essays on historical topics. The essays require you to demonstrate mastery of historical interpretation and the ability to express views and knowledge in writing. The essays may relate documents to different areas, analyze common themes of different time periods, or compare individual and group experiences that reflect socioeconomic, racial, gender, and ethnic differences. Part A consists of a mandatory 15-minute reading period, followed by 45 minutes during which you must answer a document-based question (DBQ), which changes from year to year. In Part B and Part C, you'll be directed to answer one of two questions presented in each section. You will have 70 minutes to write your essays. The free-response section counts for 50 percent of your final grade.

CONTENT. Subject coverage and time-period allotments are shown below.

Topics covered on the exam*	Approx. %
Political institutions, behavior, and public policy	35%
Social change and cultural and intellectual developments	40%
Diplomacy and international relations	15%
Economic developments	10%

Time periods covered on the exam*	Approx. %
Pre-Columbian through 1789	20%
1790–1914	45%
1915–present	35%

*Multiple-choice section only

ABOUT THE REVIEW SECTION

This book begins with REA's 375-page review of U.S. history designed to acquaint you with the exam's scope of coverage. Our review covers these topics and historical time periods, with handy historical timelines at the end of each chapter to serve as a ready reference for each period's key events:

Pre-Columbian Cultures (12,000 B.C.E. –1492 C.E.)

European Exploration and the Colonial Period (1492–1763)

The American Revolution (1763–1787)

The United States Constitution (1787–1789)

The New Nation (1789–1824)

Jacksonian Democracy and Westward Expansion (1824–1850)

Sectional Conflict and the Causes of the Civil War (1850–1860)

The Civil War and Reconstruction (1860–1877)

Industrialism, War, and the Progressive Era (1877–1912)

Wilson and World War I (1912–1920)

The Roaring Twenties and Economic Collapse (1920–1929)

The Great Depression and the New Deal (1929–1941)

World War II and the Postwar Era (1941–1960)

The New Frontier, Vietnam, and Social Upheaval (1960–1972)

Watergate, Conservatism's Rise, and Post–Cold War Challenges (1972-2005)

SCORING THE EXAM

The multiple-choice section of the exam is scored by crediting each correct answer with one point and deducting one-fourth of a point for each incorrect answer. *You will neither receive a credit nor suffer a deduction for unanswered questions.* The free-response essays are graded by instructors and professors from across the country who come together each June for a week of nonstop AP essay grading. Each essay booklet is read and scored by several graders. Each grader provides a score for the individual essays. The DBQ is scored on a scale from 0 to 15, 0 being the lowest and 15 the highest. Each topic-based essay receives a score from 0 to 9. These scores are concealed so that each grader is unaware of the previous graders' assessments. When the essays have been graded completely, the scores are averaged—one score for each essay—so that the free-response section generates three scores.

The total weight of the free-response section is 50 percent of the total score. Your work in the multiple-choice section counts for the other 50 percent. Each year, grades fluctuate slightly because the grading scale is adjusted to take into account the performance of the total AP U.S. History test-taker population. When used with the corresponding chart, the scoring method we present here will *strongly approximate* the score you would receive if you were sitting for the actual AP U.S. History exam.*

SCORING THE MULTIPLE-CHOICE SECTION

For the multiple-choice section, use this formula to calculate your raw score:

_____ – (_____ × 1/4) = _____ (round to the nearest whole number)

number   number   raw
right   wrong   score

SCORING THE FREE-RESPONSE SECTION

For the free-response section, use this formula to calculate your raw score:

_____ + _____ + _____ = _____ (round to the nearest whole number)

DBQ   essay #1   essay #2   raw score

You may want to give your essays three different grades, such as a 13, a 10, and an 8, and then calculate your score three ways: as if you did well, average, and poorly. This will give you a safe estimate of how you will do on the actual exam. Try to be objective about grading your own essays. If possible, have a friend, teacher, or parent grade them for you. Make sure your essays follow all of the AP requirements before you assess the score.

---

* The statistical formulations used by the AP Program preclude our REA practice-test scoring system from precisely replicating the procedures and determinations of the AP Program. Bear in mind that the cut-off point between each of the five AP grades typically shifts slightly from year to year. This occurs both because one year's exam cannot be expected to be exactly as difficult as another year's and because no two test-taker groups can be expected to be equally strong.

THE COMPOSITE SCORE

To obtain your composite score, use this method:

$1.13 \times$ _____ = _____ (weighted multiple-choice score—**do not round**)
              multiple-choice
              raw score

$2.73 \times$ _____ = _____ (weighted free-response score—**do not round**)
              free-response
              raw score

Now add the two weighted sections together and round to the nearest whole number. The result is your total composite score. See the range within which your score falls on this table to *approximate* your final grade:

AP Grade	Composite Score Range
5	114–180
4	91–113
3	74–90
2	49–73
1	0–48

These overall scores are interpreted as follows: **5**–extremely well qualified; **4** well qualified; **3**–qualified; **2**–possibly qualified; and **1**–no recommendation. *Most* colleges grant students who earn a 3 or better either college credit or advanced placement. Check with your high school's guidance office about specific requirements.

CONTACTING THE AP PROGRAM

Prospective examinees should download from the College Entrance Examination Board's website or request by phone the free bulletin offering a general description of the AP Program, including policies and procedures as well as instructions on how to register for the AP Examination in United States History. Here's how to contact the College Board:

AP Services
P.O. Box 6671
Princeton, NJ 08541-6671
Phone: (609) 771-7300
Website: *http://apcentral.collegeboard.com*
E-mail: *apexams@info.collegeboard.org*

AP UNITED STATES HISTORY STUDY SCHEDULE

Here is REA's suggested eight-week study schedule to guide your prep for the AP U.S. History Exam. Depending on how soon you will be taking the exam, you can expand or condense this timetable. If time is especially short, each two-week period devoted to the practice tests can be compressed into one week. The key to gaining a firm command of the subject matter and the test itself is to set aside time each day for study. Once you commit to an activity, stick with it to the end. This will help ensure that you cover everything you need to be completely in control of the material—and the exam—come test day.

Week	Activity
1	**Day 1:** Acquaint yourself with the exam by reading our introduction, "Prepare with Confidence." If you have a computer with an Internet connection, check the College Board website (*http://apcentral. collegeboard.com*) to be sure you're completely in tune with all the procedural details. This way, you can walk into the test center with a clear mind and be able to focus exclusively on the task at hand. **Day 2:** Now it's time to dive into our course review. You'll have 14 days to get through 15 chapters. To build up a good head of steam, read **Chapters 1 and 2** today. That will leave you with 13 chapters to tackle in 13 days—*perfect!* **Days 3–7:** Read **Chapters 3–7**—that's one chapter per day. Take notes as you proceed, and then review them in light of the end-of-the-chapter timelines.
2	**Days 8–14:** Welcome to week 2! Read **Chapters 8–14**—yes, that's one chapter per day. Be sure you are taking adequate notes as you proceed— they will be valuable to you later on, during the testing phase. And make your end-of-the-chapter review work count, as well.
3	**Day 15:** Read and review **Chapter 15**. **Day 16: Reflect and review.** Reflect upon what you've read and learned, and study the notes you've made. **Day 17: Take Practice Test 1** as a diagnostic to gauge your strengths and weaknesses. After comparing your answers against the answer key and reading the detailed explanations, flag any test items that were difficult for you. Review your problem areas by using the appropriate textbooks, classroom notes, and this book's AP U.S. History course review. When done, you will be ready to take Practice Test 2.

From this point onward, it's no longer a day-by-day affair. Give yourself the freedom to choose the time that's most convenient for you during the course of the remaining four and a half weeks. It's critical that you make each practice test session as realistic as possible, which means that you should sit and take the test without interruption or distraction.

Measure your progress from test to test. Take note of where your performance improves, remains static, or falls off. Allow extra time to address the latter two categories.

4	**Take Practice Test 2.** When done, thoroughly read all the detailed explanations—not just those for the test items you answered incorrectly—and flag any sections that pose difficulty for you. Use appropriate textbooks, classroom notes, and our course review to go over those areas for which you need clarification.
5	**Take Practice Test 3.** By now, you may be feeling a bit more confident. Even so, keep the momentum going by reading the answer explanations and flagging your problem areas, and then review your resources.
6	**Take Practice Test 4.** Follow the same course as for week 5, and demand the most from yourself. Review your areas of weakness, and approach the next test optimistically.
7	**Take Practice Test 5.** Now try to raise the bar even higher. Redouble your effort to strengthen those unclear areas. One more Practice Test to go—approach it seriously, like the real thing.
8	**Take Practice Test 6.** Focus on the answers you got wrong, and read through the explanations very carefully; then review and review again.

Chapter 1

PRE-COLUMBIAN CULTURES (12,000 B.C.E.–1492 C.E.)

While historians disagree as to when the first Americans reached the Western Hemisphere, there is no disagreement as to where: the Bering Strait between Siberia and Alaska. Most scholars place the arrival at between 15,000 and 30,000 years ago; it appears that the receding waters exposed enough of a land bridge over the 56 miles that separate North America and Asia for groups to migrate across on at least two occasions. The Asian immigrants probably followed large game animals, such as mammoths, bison, and giant ground sloths. The small groups gradually spread across North and South America, and there is evidence that some reached the tip of South America by 9000 B.C.E.

2,000 SEPARATE CULTURES

The three most advanced civilizations of the more than 2,000 separate cultures that developed in the New World were the Incas, the Mayas, and the Aztecs.

Around 1000 C.E. the Incas successfully conquered neighboring tribes and eventually controlled an area more than 2,500 miles in length. By 1500 the Incas were the largest and richest of the ancient empires of the Americas. The Incas built palaces surrounded by high walls in Peru and connected a series of mountain towns and villages with an elaborate network of roads. They developed a system of terraces to effectively farm on the steep hillsides and used canals and aqueducts to irrigate crops. The potato and the tomato were two of the Incan contributions to world diets. Despite the lack of a written language, the Incan governmental system was well-organized when Spanish conquistador Francisco Pizarro and his brothers Juan, Gonzalo, and Hernando arrived in 1532 with fewer than 200 soldiers. The Pizarros defeated the Incan army and executed their king, Atahualpa, who had allowed the Spaniards to enter the city because he did not sense a threat from their small force against his 80,000-member army. The Pizarros then captured the capital of Cuzco and looted its wealth of silver and gold.

The Mayas built temples and pyramids surrounding broad plazas in the mountains, deserts, and rain forests of what is now Guatemala, Belize, Honduras, and the Yucatán region of Mexico. The Mayas also constructed observatories, developed accurate calendars, knew of the mathematical concept of zero, and invented their own writing system, which used both syllables and single written characters, known as glyphs. Most of the written record of the Mayas was destroyed by Spanish invaders. The first ceremonial buildings appear to have been constructed about 1000 B.C.E. The Mayas were sophisticated farmers and used raised fields to plant maize, the cereal grain that is the ancestor of modern corn. The Mayas went into a decline in around 800 C.E. and were ruled as smaller city-states when the Spanish conquest began in the 1520s.

HIGHLY ORGANIZED SOCIETY

The Aztecs were the latest of the three advanced civilizations to develop, having arrived at what is now Mexico City (Tenochtitlán) in the thirteenth century C.E. The city, featuring elaborate temples and canals and boasting a population of over 100,000, was the center of a large empire. The Aztecs developed a highly organized society ruled by a king and included a class of priests and tax collectors, a warrior elite, and an active merchant class. The Aztecs were a warlike people, exacting tribute from other tribes and capturing prisoners for the human sacrifice that was central to their religion. The Aztecs were conquered shortly after the arrival of Spaniard Hernán Cortés in 1519, and their king, Moctezuma, was killed. The Spaniards' accounts say that Moctezuma's attempts to address his subjects, who took a dim view of their leader's submission to Spanish forces, resulted in his being attacked with stones and arrows that inflicted fatal wounds. But the Aztecs' belief that their king had been murdered at the hand of the Spaniards caused the Cortés force heavy loss of life and treasure as it tried to leave the Aztec capital under cover of darkness.

By the time the Aztecs were conquered by the Spanish, the population of Mexico may have numbered 25 million people. Farther north, in what is now the United States and Canada, there were only about 1 million Indians. Most of the inhabitants were nomadic tribes subsisting as hunters or gatherers. Very few, mostly in the American Southwest, settled in one location as farmers.

The Anasazi built five-story pueblos in Chaco Canyon and cliff dwellings in what is now Arizona and New Mexico, and created a system of roads that reached villages 400 miles away. They watered their crops with a system of irrigation canals. But their canals, even combined with other techniques to counter lengthy dry seasons, were not enough to overcome the prolonged drought of the thirteenth century. This drought, the effects of which were compounded by attacks by neighboring tribes, contributed to their decline.

Pueblo peoples also used cliff dwellings (some survive to this day at Mesa Verde, Colorado) that were built during the fourteenth and fifteenth centuries. The Pueblos adopted architectural and religious practices from the Anasazi and, in addition, used plants that were more drought-resistant.

Indian tribes that lived in the Mississippi Valley found conditions that were much less harsh and thus more favorable to continued settlement. The area provided rich soil and a network of rivers that allowed for fishing, hunting, and trade. Beginning about 800 C.E., immigrants to the area, perhaps from the Yucatán Peninsula, planted new strains of maize and beans. The largest settlement, Cahokia, near present-day St. Louis, may have included as many as 40,000 people in the thirteenth century. Even though, as for almost all other New World groups, no written records exist, huge earthen pyramids reveal a sophisticated religious system. Cahokia featured more than 100 of these temple mounds. The main pyramid at Cahokia covers over 15 acres and extended over 35 feet high. Residents traded with groups throughout the eastern half of what is now the United States, including tribes on the Atlantic coastline. As with the Anasazi, the people of Cahokia disappeared for unknown reasons sometime in the fourteenth century, though it is thought that overpopulation, warfare, and urban diseases such as tuberculosis took huge tolls.

One group of Mississippi Valley residents that survived well past the arrival of whites were those known as the Natchez. Their ruler, known as the Great Sun, presided over a class-based society. Advisors to the Great Sun comprised the noble class and served as chiefs of villages. The mass of peasants, called Stinkards, cultivated the land. The Natchez were warlike and practiced torture and human sacrifice. Organized into confederacies of local farming villages, they proved unable to resist the diseases and conquests of the invading Europeans.

The Eastern Woodland Indians of North America occupied the lands east of the Mississippi River. They usually lived in small, self-governing clans of related families and were governed by clan elders. Unlike the Aztec or Mayan rulers, however, these kinship-based systems used consensus, rather than coercion, to govern. The peoples of this region spoke a wide variety of languages belonging

Cahokia Mounds
Cahokia Mounds, the site of the largest pre-Columbian Indian city north of Mexico. This painting, by L. K. Townsend, shows central Cahokia circa 1150 to 1200 B.C.E. Courtesy Cahokia Mounds Historic Site.

to a few language groups. Most of the Indians living between the St. Lawrence River and Chesapeake Bay (Pequots and Delaware, for example) spoke Algonquian languages. The area between the Hudson River and the Great Lakes was home to the Five Nations of the Iroquois (Seneca, Cayuga, Oneida, Onondaga, and Mohawk), who spoke Iroquoian languages. The tribes in the Southeast, such as the Choctaw and Creek, spoke Muskhogean language dialects.

Most Eastern Woodland tribes did not live in permanent settlements, though tribes claimed territorial lands as their own. Groups moved about seasonally, gathering berries and seeds, fishing and hunting, and settling in the summer on fertile lands. While men were responsible for hunting and fishing, women controlled agricultural production. In some tribes, such as the Iroquois, the eldest women selected the clan chief, and inheritance of goods was matrilineal, with rights to land and other property passing to daughters from mothers. The economic nature of Eastern Woodland life was primarily one of subsistence agriculture, and these groups never developed large urban centers that the Native Americans of Mexico inhabited.

The arrival of Europeans on the American continent greatly affected Native American cultures. The tribes along the Atlantic Coast were pressured almost immediately to adapt to the white settlers and traders. Some very early contact was peaceful. Trade seemed to be the main interest of many. Whites provided metal tools and weapons in exchange for beaver and other pelts, which were in abundant supply to the Indians.

Often, trading encounters led to efforts of the Europeans to civilize the Indians, attempting to persuade them to live in permanent houses, learn to read and write, and, almost always, to accept Christianity. Jesuits and Franciscan priests and missionaries accompanied Spanish explorers in the American Southwest, and French fur traders in what is now Canada were closely followed by Jesuits who sought to convert the Indians they encountered.

SOME NATIVE TRIBES RENDERED NEARLY EXTINCT

The interaction between the natives and the new immigrants was largely, but not always, negative. Horses, which had first evolved in the New World, returned with the Spanish in the 1500s and became central to the lives of many peoples, particularly those who lived in the Great Plains. While nomadic before the horse's re-introduction to the continent, they now could range much farther and develop new means of hunting and fighting other tribes. In sum, however, the benefits of the contact with whites were drastically outweighed by the devastation caused by conquest and disease. Superior European weapons resulted in many decisive defeats for Indian groups throughout the Americas. In addition, illnesses such as measles, typhus, and smallpox ravaged Indian groups that had developed no immunities. Within 50 years of Columbus's arrival in the Caribbean, some native tribes on the islands were virtually extinct. On the island of Hispaniola, the population dropped from approximately 1 million to just *500* by 1600. In Peru the population dropped from 9 million in 1530 to 500,000 in 1630. Some historians estimate that in some regions as much as 95 percent of Indian groups died of European diseases in the first century after contact.

In this Columbian exchange, whites fared much better than Indians. While sexually transmitted diseases were carried by sailors returning to Europe, other New World contributions were of great positive value. New agricultural techniques and new crops, such as tomatoes, potatoes, pumpkins, beans, and squash, enriched European diets. Maize (corn), which Columbus brought back to Spain after his first voyage, became an important part of European diets.

In sum, the contact with European civilizations proved disastrous for the Indian residents of the New World. They were devastated by conquering armies and by disease, and made to work as slaves. While vestiges of their cultures have survived to the present day, most of their traditions, cities and villages, and populations have been wiped out.

◄─── HISTORICAL TIMELINE ───►
Pre-Columbian Cultures (12,000 B.C.E.–1492 C.E.)

ca. 12,000 B.C.E.	Asians begin several migrations over Bering Strait
5000 B.C.E.	Maize cultivation begins in southern Mexico
700 B.C.E.	Olmec people flourish along Gulf of Mexico
100 C.E.	Hopewell culture sets up massive trading network
300	Mayan city of Tikal features 20,000 residents and many temples
500	Teotihuacán's population reaches 100,000 at peak of culture
600	Hohokam civilization develops in present Arizona and New Mexico
800	Collapse of many Mayan cities
900	Anasazi build cliff villages in American southwest
1000	Leif Ericson and Norsemen settle Vinland in current Newfoundland
1125	City of Cahokia (near present-day St. Louis) has 15,000 residents and 100 temple mounds
1325	Aztecs build Tenochtitlán on site of current Mexico City
1438	Incas begin conquest of Andean region of South America
1492	Columbus lands at San Salvador in Bahamas

Chapter 2

EUROPEAN EXPLORATION AND THE COLONIAL PERIOD (1492–1763)

THE AGE OF EXPLORATION

The Treaty of Tordesillas

Excited by the gold Columbus had brought back from America (after Amerigo Vespucci, an Italian member of a Portuguese expedition to South America whose widely reprinted report suggested a new world had been found), Ferdinand and Isabella, joint monarchs of Spain, sought formal confirmation of their ownership of these new lands. They feared the interference of Portugal, which was at that time a powerful seafaring nation and had been active in overseas exploration. In 1493, at Spain's urging, the pope drew a "Line of Demarcation" 100 leagues west of the Cape Verde Islands, dividing the heathen world into two equal parts—that east of the line for Portugal and that west of it for Spain.

Because this line tended to be unduly favorable to Spain, and because Portugal had the stronger navy, the two countries worked out the Treaty of Tordesillas (1494), by which the line was moved farther west. As a result, Brazil eventually became a Portuguese colony, while Spain maintained claims to the rest of the Americas. As other European nations joined the hunt for colonies, they tended to ignore the Treaty of Tordesillas.

The Spanish Conquistadores

To conquer the Americas the Spanish monarchs used their powerful army, led by independent Spanish adventurers known as *conquistadores*. At first the conquistadores confined their attentions to the Caribbean islands, where the European diseases they unwittingly carried with them devastated the local Indian populations, who had no immunities against such diseases.

Juan Ponce de León. Courtesy State Library and Archives of Florida.

After about 1510 the conquistadores turned their attention to the American mainland. In 1513 Vasco Núñez de Balboa crossed the isthmus of Panama and became the first European to see the Pacific Ocean. The same year Juan Ponce de León explored Florida in search of gold and a fabled fountain of youth. He found neither, but claimed Florida for Spain. In 1519 Hernando (Hernán) Cortés led his dramatic expedition against the Aztecs of Mexico. Aided by the fact that the Indians at first mistook him for a god, as well as by firearms, armor, horses, and (unbeknown to him) smallpox germs, all previously unknown in America, Cortés destroyed the Aztec empire and won enormous riches. By the 1550s other such fortune seekers had conquered much of South America.

In North America the Spaniards sought in vain for riches. In 1528 Panfilio de Narvaez led a disastrous expedition through the Gulf Coast region from which only four of the original four hundred men returned. One of them, Cabeza de Vaca, brought with him a story of seven great cities full of gold (the "Seven Cities of Cibola") somewhere to the north. In response to this, two Spanish expeditions explored the interior of North America. Hernando de Soto led a six hundred-man expedition (1539–1541) through what is now the southeastern United States, penetrating as far west as Oklahoma and discovering the Mississippi River, on whose banks de Soto was buried. Francisco Vasquez de Coronado led an expedition (1540–1542) from Mexico, north across the Rio Grande and through New Mexico, Arizona, Texas, Oklahoma, and Kansas. Some of Coronado's men were the first Europeans to see the Grand Canyon. While neither expedition discovered rich Indian civilizations to plunder, both increased Europe's knowledge of the interior of North America and asserted Spain's territorial claims to the continent.

New Spain

Spain administered its new holdings as an autocratic, rigidly controlled empire in which everything was to benefit the parent country. Tight control of even mundane matters was carried out by a suffocating bureaucracy run directly from Madrid. Annual treasure fleets carried the riches of the New World to Spain for the furtherance of its military-political goals in Europe.

As population pressures were low in 16th-century Spain, only about 200,000 Spaniards came to America during that time. To deal with the consequent labor shortages—and as a reward to successful conquistadores—the Spaniards developed a system of large manors or estates (*encomiendas*), with Indian slaves ruthlessly managed for the benefit of the conquistadores. The encomienda system was later replaced by the similar but somewhat milder *hacienda* system. As the Indian population died from overwork and European diseases, Spaniards began importing African slaves to supply their labor needs. Society in New Spain was rigidly stratified, with the highest level reserved for natives of Spain (*peninsulares*) and the next for those of Spanish parentage born in the New World (*creoles*). Those of mixed or Indian blood occupied lower levels.

English and French Beginnings

In 1497 the Italian John Cabot (Giovanni Caboto), sailing under the sponsorship of the king of England in search of a Northwest Passage (a water route to the Orient through or around the North American continent), became the first European since the Viking voyages more than four centuries earlier to reach the mainland of North America, which he claimed for England.

In 1524 the king of France authorized another Italian, Giovanni da Verrazzano, to undertake a mission similar to Cabot's. Endeavoring to duplicate the achievement of Portuguese Ferdinand Magellan, who had five years earlier found a way around the southern tip of South America, Verrazzano followed the American coast from present-day North Carolina to Maine.

Beginning in 1534, Jacques Cartier, also authorized by the king of France, mounted three expeditions to the area of the St. Lawrence River, which he believed might be the hoped-for Northwest Passage. He explored up the river as far as the site of Montreal, where—as he saw it—rapids prevented him from continuing to China. He claimed the area for France before abandoning his last expedition and returning to France in 1542. France made no further attempts to explore or colonize in America for sixty-five years.

England showed little interest in America as well during most of the 16th century. But when the English finally did begin colonization, commercial capitalism in England had advanced to the point that the English efforts were supported by private rather than government funds, allowing the English colonists to enjoy a greater degree of freedom from government interference.

Partially as a result of the New World rivalries and partially through differences between Protestant and Catholic countries, the 16th century was a violent time both in Europe and in America. French Protestants, called Huguenots, who attempted to escape persecution in Catholic France by settling in the New World were massacred by the Spaniards. One such incident led the Spaniards, nervous about any possible encroachment on what they considered to be their exclusive holdings in America, to build a fort that became the beginning of a settlement at St. Augustine, Florida, the first city in North America. Spanish priests ventured north from St. Augustine, but no permanent settlements were built in the interior.

French and especially English sea captains made great sport of—and considerable profit from—plundering the Spaniards of the wealth they had first plundered from the Indians. One of the most successful English captains, Francis Drake, sailed around South America and raided the Spanish settlements on the Pacific coast of Central America before continuing on to California, which he claimed for England and named Nova Albion. Drake then returned to England by sailing around the world. England's Queen Elizabeth, sister and Protestant successor to Mary, had been quietly investing in Drake's highly profitable voyages. On Drake's return from his round-the-world voyage, Elizabeth openly showed her approval.

Angered by this, as well as by Elizabeth's support of the Protestant cause in Europe, Spain's King Philip II in 1588 dispatched a mighty fleet, the Spanish Armada, to conquer England. Instead, the Armada was defeated by the English navy and largely destroyed by storms in the North Sea. This victory established England as a great power and moved it a step closer to overseas colonization, although the war with Spain continued until 1604.

Gilbert, Raleigh, and the First English Attempts at Colonization

English nobleman Sir Humphrey Gilbert believed England should found colonies and find a Northwest Passage. In 1576 he sent English sea captain Martin Frobisher to look for such a passage. Frobisher scouted along the inhospitable northeastern coast of Canada and brought back large amounts of a yellow metal that turned out to be fool's gold. In 1578 Gilbert obtained a charter allowing him to found a colony with his own funds and guaranteeing the prospective colonists all the rights of those born and residing in England, thus setting an important precedent for future colonial charters. His attempts to found a colony in New-foundland failed, and while pursuing these endeavors he was lost at sea.

With the queen's permission, Gilbert's work was taken up by his half-brother, Sir Walter Raleigh. Raleigh turned his attention to a more southerly portion of the North American coastline, which he named Virginia, in honor of England's unmarried queen. He selected as a site for the first settlement Roa-noke Island just off the coast of present-day North Carolina.

After one abortive attempt, a group of 114 settlers—men, women, and children—landed in July 1587. Shortly thereafter, Virginia Dare became the first English child born in America. Later that year the expedition's leader, John White, returned to England to secure additional supplies. Delayed by the war with Spain, he did not return until 1590, when he found the colony deserted. It is not known what became of the Roanoke settlers. After this failure, Raleigh was forced by financial constraints to abandon his attempts to colonize Virginia. Hampered by unrealistic expectations, inadequate financial resources, and the ongoing war with Spain, English interest in American colonization was sub-merged for fifteen years.

THE BEGINNINGS OF COLONIZATION

Virginia

In the first decade of the 1600s, Englishmen, exhilarated by the recent vic-tory over Spain and influenced by the writings of Richard Hakluyt (who urged American colonization as the way to national greatness and the spread of the gospel), once again undertook to plant colonies.

Two groups of merchants gained charters from James I, Queen Elizabeth's successor. One group of merchants was based in London and received a charter to North America between what are now the Hudson and the Cape Fear rivers. The other was based in Plymouth and was granted the right to colonize in North America from the Potomac to the northern border of present-day Maine. They were called the Virginia Company of London and the Virginia Company of Plym-outh, respectively. These were joint-stock companies, which raised their capital by the sale of shares of stock. Companies of this sort had already been used to finance and carry on English trade with Russia, Africa, and the Middle East.

The Plymouth Company, in 1607, attempted to plant a colony in Maine, but after one winter the colonists became discouraged and returned to Britain. Thereafter the Plymouth Company folded.

The Virginia Company of London, in 1607, sent out an expedition of three ships with 104 men to plant a colony some forty miles up the James River from

Chesapeake Bay. Like the river on which it was located, the new settlement was named Jamestown in honor of England's king. It became the first permanent English settlement in North America, but for a time it appeared to be going the way of the earlier attempts. During the early years of Jamestown, the majority of the settlers died of starvation, various diseases, or hostile action by Indians. Though the losses were continuously replaced by new settlers, the colony's survival remained in doubt for a number of years.

There were several reasons for these difficulties. The entire colony was owned by the company, and all members shared the profits regardless of how much or how little they worked; thus, there was a lack of incentive. Many of the settlers were gentlemen, who considered themselves too good to work at growing the food the colony needed to survive. Others were simply unambitious and little inclined to work in any case. Furthermore, the settlers had come with the expectation of finding gold or other quick and easy riches and wasted much time looking for these while they should have been providing for their survival.

For purposes of defense, the settlement had been sited on a peninsula formed by a bend in the river; but this low and swampy location proved to be a breeding ground for all sorts of diseases and, at high tide, even contaminated the settlers' drinking supply with sea water. To make matters worse, relations with Powhatan, the powerful local Indian chief, were at best uncertain and often openly hostile, with disastrous results for the colonists.

In 1608 and 1609 the dynamic and ruthless leadership of John Smith kept the colony from collapsing. Smith's rule was, "He who works not, eats not." After Smith returned to England in late 1609, the condition of the colony again became critical.

In 1612, a Virginia resident named John Rolfe discovered that a superior strain of tobacco, native to the West Indies, could be grown in Virginia. There was a large market for this tobacco in Europe, and Rolfe's discovery gave Virginia a major cash crop.

To secure more settlers and boost Virginia's shrinking labor force, the company moved to make immigration possible for Britain's poor, who were without economic opportunity at home or financial means to procure transportation to America. This was achieved by means of the indenture system, by which a poor worker's passage to America was paid by an American planter (or the company itself), who in exchange, was indentured to work for the planter (or the company) for a specified number of years. The system was open to abuse and often resulted in the mistreatment of the indentured servants.

To control the workers thus shipped to Virginia, as well as the often lazy and unruly colonists already present, the company gave its governors in America dictatorial powers. Governors such as Lord De La Warr, Sir Thomas Gates, and Sir Thomas Dale made use of such powers, imposing a harsh rule.

For such reasons, and its well-known reputation as a death trap, Virginia continued to attract inadequate numbers of immigrants. To solve this, a reform-minded faction within the company proposed a new approach, and under its leader, Edwin Sandys, made changes designed to attract more settlers. Colonists were promised the same rights they had in England. A representative assembly, the House of Burgesses, was founded in 1619—the first in America. Additionally, private ownership of land was instituted.

Despite these reforms, Virginia's unhealthy reputation kept many Englishmen away. Large numbers of indentured servants were brought in, especially young, single men. The first Africans were brought to Virginia in 1619 but were treated as indentured servants rather than slaves.

Virginia's Indian relations remained difficult. In 1622 an Indian massacre took the lives of 347 settlers. In 1644 the Indians struck again, massacring another 300 settlers. Shortly thereafter, the coastal Indians were subdued and no longer presented a serious threat.

Impressed by the potential profits from tobacco growing, King James I determined to have Virginia for himself. Using the high mortality and the 1622 massacre as a pretext, he revoked the London Company's charter in 1624 and made Virginia a royal colony. This pattern was followed throughout colonial history; both company colonies and proprietary colonies tended eventually to become royal colonies. Upon taking over Virginia, James revoked all political rights and the representative assembly—he did not believe in such things—but fifteen years later his son, Charles I, was forced, by constant pressure from the Virginians and the continuing need to attract more settlers, to restore these rights.

New France

Shortly after England returned to the business of colonization, France renewed its interest in the areas previously visited by such French explorers as Jacques Cartier. The French opened with the Indians a lucrative trade in furs, plentiful in America and much sought after in Europe.

The St. Lawrence River was the French gateway to the interior of North America. In 1608 Samuel de Champlain established a trading post in Quebec, from which the rest of what became New France eventually spread.

Relatively small numbers of Frenchmen came to America, and, partially because of this, they were generally able to maintain good relations with the Indians. French Canadians were energetic in exploring and claiming new lands for France.

French exploration and settlement spread through the Great Lakes region and the valleys of the Mississippi and Ohio rivers. In 1673 Jacques Marquette explored the Mississippi Valley, and in 1682 Sieur de la Salle followed the river to its mouth. French settlements in the Midwest were not generally real towns, but rather forts and trading posts serving the fur trade.

Throughout its history, New France was handicapped by an inadequate population and a lack of support from the parent country.

New Netherlands

Other countries also took an interest in North America. In 1609 Holland sent an Englishman named Henry Hudson to explore for them in search of a Northwest Passage. In this endeavor Hudson discovered the river that bears his name.

Arrangements were made to trade with the Iroquois for furs, especially beaver pelts for the hats then popular in Europe. In 1624 Dutch trading outposts were established on Manhattan Island (New Amsterdam) and at the site of present-day Albany (Fort Orange). A profitable fur trade was carried on and became the main source of revenue for the Dutch West India Company, the joint-stock company that ran the colony.

To encourage enough farming to keep the colony supplied with food, the Dutch instituted the patroon system, by which large landed estates would be given to wealthy men who transported at least fifty families to New Netherlands. These families would then become tenant farmers on the estate of the patroon who had transported them. As Holland's home economy was healthy, few Dutch felt desperate enough to take up such unattractive terms.

New Netherlands was, in any case, internally weak and unstable. It was poorly governed by inept and lazy governors, and its population was a mixture of people from all over Europe as well as many African slaves, forming what historians have called an "unstable pluralism."

Pilgrims Landing at Plymouth Rock
Saromy & Major, The Landing of the Pilgrims on Plymouth Rock, Dec. 11th, 1620. 1846.
U.S. Library of Congress.

The Pilgrims at Plymouth

Many Englishmen came from England for religious reasons. For the most part, these fell into two groups, Puritans and Separatists. Though similar in many respects to the Puritans, the Separatists believed the Church of England was beyond saving and so felt they must separate from it.

One group of Separatists, suffering government harassment, fled to Holland. Dissatisfied there, they decided to go to America and, thus, became the famous Pilgrims.

Led by William Bradford, they departed in 1620, having obtained from the London Company a charter to settle just south of the Hudson River. Driven by storms, their ship, the Mayflower, made landfall at Cape Cod in Massachusetts. They decided it was God's will for them to settle in that area. This, however, put them outside the jurisdiction of any established government, and so, before going ashore, they drew up and signed the *Mayflower Compact*, establishing a foundation for orderly government based on the consent of the governed. After a difficult first winter that saw many die, the Pilgrims went on to establish a quiet and modestly prosperous colony. After a number of years of hard work they were able to buy out the investors who had originally financed their voyage and thus gain greater autonomy.

The Massachusetts Bay Colony

The Puritans were far more numerous than the Separatists. Contrary to stereotype, they did not dress in drab clothes and were not ignorant or bigoted. They did, however, take the Bible and their religion seriously and felt the Anglican Church still retained too many unscriptural practices left over from Roman Catholicism.

King James I had no use for the Puritans but, mindful of their growing political power, refrained from bringing on a confrontation. His son, Charles I, determined in 1629 to persecute the Puritans aggressively and to rule without the Puritan-dominated Parliament. This course would lead eventually (ten years later) to civil war, but in the meantime some of the Puritans decided to set up a community in America.

To accomplish their purpose, they sought in 1629 to charter a joint-stock company to be called the Massachusetts Bay Company. Whether because Charles was glad to be rid of the Puritans or because he did not realize the special nature of this joint-stock company, the charter was granted. Further, the charter neglected to specify where the company's headquarters should be located. Taking advantage of this unusual omission, the Puritans determined to make their headquarters in the colony itself, three thousand miles from meddlesome royal officials.

Under the leadership of John Winthrop, who taught that a new colony should provide the whole world with a model of what a Christian society ought to be, the Puritans carefully organized their venture and, upon arriving in Massachusetts in 1630, did not undergo the "starving time" that had often plagued other first-year colonies.

The government of Massachusetts developed to include a governor and a representative assembly (called the General Court) selected by the "freemen"— adult male church members. As Massachusetts' population increased (20,000 Puritans had come by 1642 in what came to be called the Great Migration), new towns were chartered, each town being granted a large tract of land by the Massachusetts government. As in European villages, these towns consisted of a number of houses clustered around the church house and the village green. Farmland was located around the outside of the town. In each new town the elect—those who testified of having experienced saving grace—covenanted together as a church.

Rhode Island, Connecticut, and New Hampshire

Puritans saw their colony not as a place to do whatever might strike one's fancy, but as a place to serve God and build His kingdom. Dissidents would be tolerated only insofar as they did not interfere with the colony's mission.

One such dissident was Roger Williams. A Puritan preacher, Williams was received warmly in Massachusetts in 1631; but he had a talent for carrying things to their logical (or sometimes not so logical) extreme. When his activities became disruptive he was asked to leave the colony. To avoid having to return to England—where he would have been even less welcome—he fled to the wilderness around Narragansett Bay, bought land from the Indians, and founded the settlement of Providence (1636), soon populated by his many followers.

Another dissident was Anne Hutchinson, who openly taught things contrary to Puritan doctrine. Called before the General Court to answer for her teachings, she claimed to have had special revelations from God superseding the Bible. This was unthinkable in Puritan theology and led to Hutchinson's banishment from the colony. She also migrated to the area around Narragansett Bay and with her followers founded Portsmouth (1638). She later migrated still farther west and was killed by Indians.

In 1644 Roger Williams secured from Parliament a charter combining Providence, Portsmouth, and other settlements that had sprung up in the area into the colony of Rhode Island. Through Williams' influence the colony granted complete religious toleration. Rhode Island tended to be populated by such exiles and troublemakers as could not find welcome in the other colonies or in Europe. It suffered constant political turmoil.

Connecticut was founded by Puritans who had slight religious disagreements with the leadership of Massachusetts. In 1636 Thomas Hooker led a group of settlers westward to found Hartford. (Hooker, though a good friend of Massachusetts Governor John Winthrop, felt he was exercising somewhat more authority than was prudent.) Others also moved into Connecticut from Massachusetts. In 1639 the *Fundamental Orders of Connecticut*, the first written constitution in America, were drawn up, providing for representative government.

In 1637 a group of Puritans led by John Davenport founded the neighboring colony of New Haven. Davenport and his followers felt that Winthrop, far from being too strict, was not being strict enough. In 1662 a new charter combined both New Haven and Connecticut into an officially recognized colony of Connecticut.

New Hampshire's settlement did not involve any disagreement at all among the Puritans. It was simply settled as an overflow from Massachusetts. In 1677 King Charles II chartered the separate royal colony of New Hampshire. It remained economically dependent on Massachusetts.

Maryland

By the 1630s, the English crown was taking a more direct interest in exercising control over the colonies, and therefore turned away from the practice of granting charters to joint-stock companies, and towards granting such charters to single individuals or groups of individuals known as proprietors. The proprietors would actually own the colony, and would be directly responsible for it to the king, in an arrangement similar to the feudalism of medieval Europe. Though this was seen as providing more opportunity for royal control and less for autonomy on the part of the colonists, in practice proprietary colonies turned out much like the company colonies because settlers insisted on self-government.

The first proprietary colony was Maryland, granted in 1632 to George Calvert, Lord Baltimore. It was to be located just north of the Potomac River and to be at the same time a reward for Calvert's loyal service to the king as well as a refuge for English Catholics, of whom Calvert was one. George Calvert died before the colony could be planted, but the venture was carried forward by his son Cecilius.

From the start, more Protestants than Catholics came. To protect the Catholic minority Calvert approved an Act of Religious Toleration (1649) guaranteeing political rights to Christians of all persuasions. Calvert also allowed a representative assembly. Economically and socially, Maryland developed as a virtual carbon copy of neighboring Virginia.

The Carolinas

In 1663 Charles II, having recently been restored to the throne after a twenty-year Puritan revolution that had seen his father beheaded, moved to reward eight of the noblemen who had helped him regain the crown by granting them a charter for all the lands lying south of Virginia and north of Spanish Florida.

The new colony was called Carolina, after the king. In hopes of attracting settlers, the proprietors came up with an elaborate plan for a hierarchical, almost feudal, society. Not surprisingly this proved unworkable, and despite offers of generous land grants to settlers, the Carolinas grew slowly.

The area of North Carolina developed as an overflow from Virginia with similar economic and cultural features. South Carolina was settled by English planters from the island of Barbados; they founded Charles Town (Charleston) in 1670. These planters brought with them their black slaves; thus, unlike the Chesapeake colonies of Virginia and Maryland, South Carolina had slavery as a fully developed institution from the outset.

New York and New Jersey

Charles II, though immoral and dissolute, was cunning and had an eye for increasing Britain's power. The Dutch colony of New Netherlands, lying between the Chesapeake and the New England colonies, caught his eye as a likely target for British expansion. In 1664 Charles gave his brother, James, Duke of York, title to all the Dutch lands in America, provided James conquered them first. To do this James sent an invasion fleet under the command of Colonel Richard Nicols. New Amsterdam fell almost without a shot and became New York.

James was adamantly opposed to representative assemblies and ordered that there should be none in New York. To avoid unrest Nicols shrewdly granted as many other civil and political rights as possible; but residents, particularly Puritans who had settled on Long Island, continued to agitate for self-government. Finally, in the 1680s, James relented, only to break his promise when he became king in 1685.

To add to the confusion in the newly renamed colony, James granted a part of his newly acquired domain to John Lord Berkeley and Sir George Carteret (two of the Carolina proprietors) who named their new proprietorship New Jersey. James neglected to tell Colonel Nicols of this, with the result that both Nicols, on the one hand, and Carteret and Berkeley, on the other, were granting title to the same land—to different settlers. Conflicting claims of land ownership plagued New Jersey for decades, being used by the crown in 1702 as a pretext to take over New Jersey as a royal colony.

THE COLONIAL WORLD

Life in the Colonies

New England grew not only from immigration but also from natural increase during the 17th century. The typical New England family had more children than the typical English or Chesapeake family, and more of those children survived to have families of their own. A New Englander could expect to live 15 to 20 years longer than his counterpart in the parent country and 25 to 30 years longer than his fellow colonist in the Chesapeake. Because of the continuity provided by these longer lifespans, because the Puritans had migrated as intact family units, and because of the homogeneous nature of the Puritan New England colonies, New England enjoyed a much more stable and well-ordered society than did the Chesapeake colonies.

Puritans placed great importance on the family, which in their society was highly patriarchal. Young people were generally subject to their parents' direction in the matter of when and whom they would marry. Few defied this system, and illegitimate births were rare. Puritans also placed great importance on the ability to read, since they believed everyone should be able to read the Bible, God's word, himself. As a result, New England was ahead of the other colonies educationally and enjoyed extremely widespread literacy.

Since New England's climate and soil were unsuited to large-scale farming, the region developed a prosperous economy based on small farming, home industry, fishing, and especially trade and a large shipbuilding industry. Boston became a major international port.

Life in the Chesapeake colonies was drastically different. The typical Chesapeake colonist lived a shorter, less healthy life than his New England counterpart and was survived by fewer children. As a result the Chesapeake's population steadily declined despite a constant influx of settlers. Nor was Chesapeake society as stable as that of New England. Most Chesapeake settlers came as indentured servants; and since planters desired primarily male servants for work in the tobacco fields, men largely outnumbered women in Virginia and Maryland. This hindered the development of family life. The short lifespans also contributed to the region's unstable family life, as few children reached adulthood without experiencing the death of one or both parents. Remarriage resulted in households that contained children from several different marriages.

The system of indentured servitude was open to serious abuse, with masters sometimes treating their servants brutally or contriving through some technicality to lengthen their terms of indenture. In any case, 40 percent of Chesapeake region indentured servants failed to survive long enough to gain their freedom.

By the late 17th century life in the Chesapeake was beginning to stabilize, with death rates declining and life expectancies rising. As society stabilized, an elite group of wealthy families such as the Byrds, Carters, Fitzhughs, Lees, and Randolphs, among others, began to dominate the social and political life of the region. Aping the lifestyle of the English country gentry, they built lavish manor houses from which to rule their vast plantations. For every one of these, however, there were many small farmers who worked hard for a living, showed deference to the great planters, and hoped someday they, or their children, might reach that level.

On the bottom rung of Southern society were the black slaves. During the first half of the 17th century, blacks in the Chesapeake made up only a small percentage of the population and were treated more or less as indentured servants. In the decades between 1640 and 1670 this gradually changed, and blacks came to be seen and treated as lifelong chattel slaves whose status would be inherited by their children. Larger numbers of them began to be imported and with this and rapid natural population growth they came by 1750 to compose 30 to 40 percent of the Chesapeake population.

While North Carolina tended to follow Virginia in its economic and social development (although with fewer great planters and more small farmers), South Carolina developed a society even more dominated by large plantations and chattel slavery. By the early decades of the 18th century, blacks had come to outnumber whites in that colony. South Carolina's economy remained dependent on the cultivation of its two staple crops, rice and, to a lesser extent, indigo.

Mercantilism and the Navigation Acts

Beginning around 1650, British authorities began to take more interest in regulating American trade for the benefit of the mother country. A key idea that underlay this policy was the concept of mercantilism. Mercantilists believed the world's wealth was sharply limited, and therefore one nation's gain was automatically another nation's loss. Each nation's goal was to export more than it imported (i.e., to have a "favorable balance of trade"). The difference would be made up in gold and silver, which, so the theory ran, would make the nation strong both economically and militarily. To achieve their goals, mercantilists believed economic activity should be regulated by the government. Colonies could fit into England's mercantilist scheme by providing staple crops, such as rice, tobacco, sugar, and indigo, and raw materials, such as timber, that England would otherwise have been forced to import from other countries.

To make the colonies serve this purpose, Parliament passed a series of Navigation Acts (1651, 1660, 1663, and 1673). These were the foundation of England's worldwide commercial system and some of the most important pieces of imperial legislation during the colonial period. They were also intended as weapons in England's on-going struggle against its chief seventeenth-century maritime rival, Holland. The system created by the Navigation Acts stipulated that trade with the colonies was to be carried on only in ships made in Britain or America and with at least 75 percent British or American crews. Additionally, when certain "enumerated" goods were shipped from an American port, they were to go only to Britain or to another American port. Finally, almost nothing could be imported to the colonies without going through Britain first.

Mercantilism's results were mixed. Though ostensibly for the benefit of all subjects of the British Empire, its provisions benefited some at the expense of others. It boosted the prosperity of New Englanders, who engaged in large-scale shipbuilding (something Britain's mercantilist policy-makers chose to encourage), while it hurt the residents of the Chesapeake by driving down the price of tobacco (an enumerated item). On the whole, the Navigation Acts, as intended, transferred wealth from America to Britain by increasing the prices Americans had to pay for British goods and lowering the prices Americans received for the goods they produced. Mercantilism also helped bring on a series of three wars between England and Holland in the late 1600s.

Charles II and his advisors worked to tighten up the administration of colonies, particularly the enforcement of the Navigation Acts. In Virginia tempers grew short as tobacco prices plunged as a result. Virginians were also angry at Royal Governor Sir William Berkeley, whose high-handed, high-taxing ways they despised and whom they believed was running the colony for the benefit of himself and his circle of cronies.

When, in 1674, an impoverished nobleman of shady past by the name of Nathaniel Bacon came to Virginia and failed to gain admittance to Berkeley's inner circle with its financial advantages, he began to oppose Berkeley at every turn and came to head a faction of like-minded persons. In 1676 disagreement over Indian policy brought the matter to the point of armed conflict. Bacon and his men burned Jamestown, but then the whole matter came to an anticlimactic ending when Bacon died of dysentery.

The British authorities, hearing of the matter, sent ships, troops, and an investigating commission. Berkeley, who had had twenty-three of the rebels hanged in reprisal, was removed. Thenceforth Virginia's royal governors had strict instructions to nun the colony for the benefit of the mother country. In response, Virginia's gentry, who had been divided over Bacon's Rebellion, united to face this new threat to their local autonomy. By political means they consistently obstructed the governors' efforts to increase royal control.

The Half-Way Covenant

By the latter half of the seventeenth century many Puritans were coming to fear that New England was drifting away from its religious purpose. The children and grandchildren of the first generation were displaying more concern for making money than creating a godly society.

To deal with this, some clergymen in 1662 proposed the "Half-Way Covenant," providing a sort of half-way church membership for the children of members, even though those children, having reached adulthood, did not profess saving grace as was normally required for Puritan church membership. Those who embraced the Half-Way Covenant felt that in an increasingly materialistic society it would at least keep church membership rolls full and might preserve some of the church's influence in society.

Some communities rejected the Half-Way Covenant as an improper compromise, but in general the shift toward secular values continued, though slowly.

King Philip's War

As New England's population grew, local Indian tribes felt threatened, and conflict sometimes resulted. Puritans endeavored to convert Indians to Christianity. The Bible was translated into Algonquian; four villages were set up for converted Indians, who by 1650 numbered over a thousand. Still, most Indians remained unconverted.

In 1675 a Wampanoag chief named King Philip (Metacomet) led a war to exterminate the whites. Some 2,000 settlers lost their lives before King Philip was killed and his tribe subdued. New England continued to experience Indian troubles from time to time, though not as severe as those suffered by Virginia.

The Dominion of New England

The trend toward increasing imperial control of the colonies continued. In 1684 the Massachusetts charter was revoked in retaliation for that colony's large-scale evasion of the restrictions of the Navigation Acts.

The following year Charles II died and was succeeded by his brother, James II. James was prepared to go even farther in controlling the colonies, favoring the establishment of a unified government for all of New England, New York, and New Jersey. This was to be called the Dominion of New England, and the fact that it would abolish representative assemblies and facilitate the imposition of the Church of England on Congregationalist (Puritan) New England made it still more appealing to James.

To head the Dominion, James sent the obnoxious and dictatorial Sir Edmond Andros. Arriving in Boston in 1686, Andros quickly alienated the New Englanders. When news reached America of England's 1688 Glorious Revolution, replacing the Catholic James with his Protestant daughter Mary and her husband, William of Orange, New Englanders cheerfully shipped Andros back to England.

Similar uprisings occurred in New York and Maryland. William and Mary's new government generally accepted these actions, though Jacob Leisler, leader of Leisler's Rebellion in New York, was executed for hesitating to turn over power to the new royal governor. This unfortunate incident poisoned the political climate of New York for many years.

The charter of Massachusetts, now including Plymouth, was restored in 1691, this time as a royal colony, though not as tightly controlled as others of that type.

The Salem Witch Trials

In 1692 Massachusetts was shaken by an unusual incident in which several young girls in Salem Village (now Danvers) claimed to be tormented by the occult activities of certain of their neighbors. Before the resulting Salem witch trials could be stopped by the intervention of Puritan ministers such as Cotton Mather, some twenty persons had been executed (nineteen by hanging and one crushed under a pile of rocks).

Pennsylvania and Delaware

Pennsylvania was founded as a refuge for Quakers. One of a number of radical religious sects that had sprung up about the time of the English Civil War, the Quakers held many controversial beliefs. They believed all persons had an "inner light" which allowed them to commune directly with God. They believed human institutions were, for the most part, unnecessary and, since they believed they could receive revelation directly from God, placed little importance on the Bible. They were also pacifists and declined to show customary deference to those who were considered to be their social superiors. This and their aggressiveness in denouncing established institutions brought them trouble in both Britain and America.

William Penn, a member of a prominent British family, converted to Quakerism as a young man. Desiring to found a colony as a refuge for Quakers, in 1681 he sought and received from Charles II a grant of land in America as payment of a large debt the king had owed Penn's late father.

Penn advertised his colony widely in Europe, offered generous terms on land, and guaranteed a representative assembly and full religious freedom. He personally went to America to set up his colony, laying out the city of Philadelphia. He succeeded in maintaining peaceful relations with the Indians.

In the years that followed, settlers flocked to Pennsylvania from all over Europe. The colony grew and prospered and its fertile soil made it not only attractive to settlers, but also a large exporter of grain to Europe and the West Indies.

Delaware, though at first part of Pennsylvania, was granted by Penn a separate legislature, but until the American Revolution, Pennsylvania's proprietary governors also functioned as governor of Delaware.

THE 18TH CENTURY

Economy and Population

British authorities continued to regulate the colonial economy, though usually without going so far as to provoke unrest. An exception was the Molasses Act of 1733, which would have been disastrous for New England merchants. In this case, trouble was averted by the customs agents wisely declining to enforce the act stringently.

The constant drain of wealth from America to Britain, created by the mother country's mercantilistic policies, led to a corresponding drain in hard currency (gold and silver). The artificially low prices that this shortage of money created for American goods was even more advantageous to British buyers. When colonial legislatures responded by endeavoring to create paper money, British authorities blocked such moves. Despite these hindrances, the colonial American economy remained for the most part extremely prosperous.

America's population continued to grow rapidly, both from natural increases due to prosperity and a healthy environment, and from large-scale immigration, not only of English but also of such other groups as Scots-Irish and Germans.

The Germans were prompted to migrate because of wars, poverty, and religious persecution in their homeland. They found Pennsylvania especially attractive and settled there fairly close to the frontier, where land was more readily available. They eventually came to be called the "Pennsylvania Dutch."

The Scots-Irish, Scottish Presbyterians who had been living in northern Ireland for several generations, left their homes because of high rent and economic depression. In America they settled even farther west than the Germans, on or beyond the frontier in the Appalachians.

The Early Wars of the Empire

Between 1689 and 1763 Britain and its American colonies fought a series of four wars with Spain, France, and France's Indian allies, in part to determine who would dominate North America.

Though the first war, known in America as King William's War (1689–1697) but in Europe as the War of the League of Augsburg, was a limited conflict involving no major battles in America, it did bring a number of bloody and terrifying border raids by Indians. It was ended by the Treaty of Ryswick, which made no major territorial changes.

The second war was known in America as Queen Anne's War (1702–1713), but in Europe as the War of the Spanish Succession, and brought America twelve years of sporadic fighting against France and Spain. It was ended by the Treaty of Utrecht, the terms of which gave Britain major territorial gains and trade advantages.

In 1739 war once again broke out with France and Spain. Known in America as King George's war, it was called the War of Jenkins' Ear in Europe (since Captain Robert Jenkins had claimed to have lost an ear to the Spanish coast guards in the Caribbean) and later the War of the Austrian Succession. American troops played an active role, accompanying the British on several important expeditions and suffering thousands of casualties. In 1745 an all-New England army, led by William Pepperrell, captured the powerful French fortress of Louisbourg at the mouth of the St. Lawrence River. To the Americans' disgust, the British in the 1748 Treaty of Aix-la-Chapelle gave Louisbourg back to France in exchange for lands in India.

Georgia

With this almost constant imperial warfare in mind, it was decided to found a colony as a buffer between South Carolina and Spanish-held Florida. A group of British philanthropists, led by General James Oglethorpe, obtained a charter for such a colony in 1732, to be located between the Savannah and Altamaha rivers and to be populated by such poor as could not manage to make a living in Great Britain.

The philanthropist trustees, who were to control the colony for twenty-one years before it reverted to royal authority, made elaborate and detailed rules to mold the new colony's society as they felt best. As a result, relatively few settlers came, and those who did complained endlessly. By 1752 Oglethorpe and his colleagues were ready to acknowledge their efforts a failure.

The Enlightenment

As the eighteenth century progressed, Americans came to be more or less influenced by European ways of thought, culture, and society. Some Americans embraced the European intellectual movement known as the "Enlightenment."

The key concept of the Enlightenment was rationalism—the belief that human reason was adequate to solve all of mankind's problems and, correspondingly, much less faith was needed in the central role of God as an active force in the universe.

A major English political philosopher of the Enlightenment was John Locke. Writing partially to justify England's 1688 Glorious Revolution, he strove to find in the social and political world the sort of natural laws Isaac Newton had recently discovered in the physical realm. He held that such natural laws included the rights of life, liberty, and property; that to secure these rights people submit to governments; and that governments which abuse these rights may justly be overthrown. His writings were enormously influential in America, though usually indirectly, by way of early eighteenth-century English political philosophers. Americans tended to equate Locke's law of nature with the universal law of God.

The most notable Enlightenment man in America was Benjamin Franklin. While Franklin never denied the existence of God, he focused his attention on human reason and what it could accomplish.

The Great Awakening

Of much greater impact on the lives of the common people in America was the movement known as the Great Awakening. It consisted of a series of religious revivals occurring throughout the colonies from the 1720s to the 1740s. Preachers such as the Dutch Reformed Theodore Frelinghuysen, the Presbyterians William and Gilbert Tennent, and the Congregationalist Jonathan Edwards—best known for his sermon "Sinners in the Hands of an Angry God"—proclaimed a message of personal repentance and faith in Jesus Christ for salvation from an otherwise certain eternity in hell. The most dynamic preacher of the Great Awakening was the Englishman George Whitefield, who traveled through the colonies several times, speaking to crowds of up to 30,000.

The Great Awakening had several important results. America's religious community came to be divided between the "Old Lights," who rejected the great Awakening, and the "New Lights," who accepted it—and sometimes suffered persecution because of their fervor. A number of colleges were founded (many of them today's "Ivy League" schools), primarily for the purpose of training New-Light ministers. The Great Awakening also fostered a greater readiness to lay the claims of established authority (in this case religious) alongside a fixed standard (in this case the Bible) and to reject any claims it found wanting.

The French and Indian War

The Treaty of Aix-la-Chapelle (1748), ending King George's War, provided little more than a breathing space before the next European and imperial war.

England and France continued on a collision course as France determined to take complete control of the Ohio Valley and western Pennsylvania.

British authorities ordered colonial governors to resist this, and Virginia's Robert Dinwiddie, already involved in speculation on the Ohio Valley lands, was eager to comply. George Washington, a young major of the Virginia militia, was sent to western Pennsylvania to request the French to leave. When the French declined, Washington was sent in 1754 with 200 Virginia militiamen to expel them. After success in a small skirmish, Washington was forced by superior numbers to fall back on his hastily built Fort Necessity and then to surrender.

The war these operations initiated spread to Europe two years later, where it was known as the Seven Years' War. In America it later came to be known as the French and Indian War.

While Washington skirmished with the French in western Pennsylvania, delegates of seven colonies met in Albany, New York, to discuss common plans for defense. Delegate Benjamin Franklin proposed a plan for an intercolonial government. While the other colonies showed no support for the idea, it was an important precedent for the concept of uniting in the face of a common enemy.

To deal with the French threat, the British dispatched Major General Edward Braddock with several regiments of British regular troops. Braddock marched overland toward the French outpost of Fort Duquesne, at the place where the Monongahela and Allegheny rivers join to form the Ohio. About eight miles short of his goal he was ambushed by a small force of French and Indians. Two-thirds of the British regulars, including Braddock himself, were killed. However, Britain bounced back from this humiliating defeat and several others that followed, and under the leadership of its capable and energetic prime minister, William Pitt, had by 1760 taken Quebec and Montreal and virtually liquidated the French empire in North America.

By the Treaty of Paris of 1763, which officially ended hostilities, Britain gained all of Canada and all of what is now the United States east of the Mississippi River. France lost all of its North American holdings.

Americans at the end of the French and Indian War were proud to be part of the victorious British Empire and proud of the important role they had played in making it so. They felt affection for Great Britain, and thoughts of independence would not have crossed their minds.

HISTORICAL TIMELINE
The Colonial Period (1500–1763)

1517	Martin Luther challenges Roman Catholic authority, beginning Protestant Reformation in Europe
1521	Cortés conquers Aztecs in Mexico Magellan circumnavigates the globe
1533	Pizarro captures Inca capital in Peru
1539	De Soto explores southeastern U.S.
1540	Coronado explores southwestern U.S.
1555	Elizabeth I takes throne in England
1585	Roanoke Island colony established off Virginia coast, then disappears
1607	Jamestown colony founded
1608	Champlain founds Quebec
1611	First Virginia tobacco crop harvested
1619	First Africans arrive in Virginia
1620	Plymouth Colony founded House of Burgesses established in Virginia
1622	Powhatan Confederacy attacks Virginia settlers
1630	Massachusetts Bay Colony founded
1635	Roger Williams establishes Rhode Island colony
1636	Harvard College founded

1660	Anne Hutchinson expelled from Massachusetts Bay Colony
1642–1648	English Civil War
1647	Massachusetts law requires a public school in every town
1649	King Charles I executed
1660	Charles II becomes king
1662	Halfway Covenant established in New England
1676	Bacon's Rebellion in Virginia
1681	Pennsylvania established by William Penn
1688	Glorious Revolution in England William and Mary succeed James II
1692	Witchcraft trials begin in Salem
1714	George I takes throne, beginning Hanover dynasty
1734	Great Awakening begins
1739	Stono Rebellion in North Carolina George Whitefield begins preaching in America
1743	Benjamin Franklin sets up the American Philosophical Society
1754	French and Indian War begins Albany Plan of Union
1759	Britain captures Quebec
1763	Regulator movement in the Carolinas Pontiac's Revolt Treaty of Paris

Chapter 3

THE AMERICAN REVOLUTION (1763–1787)

THE COMING OF THE AMERICAN REVOLUTION

Writs of Assistance

While Americans' feelings toward Great Britain were pride and affection, British officials felt contemptuous of Americans and were eager to increase imperial control over them beyond anything that had previously been attempted. This drive to gain new authority over the colonies, beginning in 1763, led directly to American independence.

Even before that time the Writs of Assistance cases had demonstrated that Americans would not accept a reduction of their freedom.

In 1761 a young Boston lawyer named James Otis argued before a Massachusetts court that Writs of Assistance (general search warrants issued to help royal officials stop evasion of Britain's mercantilist trade restrictions) were contrary to natural law. He made his point though he lost his case, and others in the colonies joined in protesting against the Writs.

Grenville and the Stamp Act

In 1763 the strongly anti-American George Grenville became prime minister and set out to solve some of the empire's more pressing problems. Chief among these was the large national debt incurred in the recent war.

Of related concern was the cost of defending the American frontier, recently the scene of a bloody Indian uprising led by an Ottawa chief named Pontiac. Goaded by French traders, Pontiac had aimed to drive the entire white population into the sea. While failing in that endeavor, he had succeeded in killing a large number of settlers along the frontier.

Grenville created a comprehensive program to deal with these problems and moved energetically to put it into effect. He sent the Royal Navy to suppress American smuggling and vigorously enforce the Navigation Acts. He also issued the Proclamation of 1763, forbidding white settlement west of the crest of the Appalachians, in hopes of keeping the Indians happy and the settlers close to the coast and thus easier to control.

In 1764, Grenville pushed through Parliament the Sugar Act (also known as the Revenue Act) aimed at raising revenue by taxes on goods imported by the Americans. It halved the duties imposed by the Molasses Act but was intended to raise revenue rather than control trade. Unlike the Molasses Act, it was stringently enforced, with accused violators facing trial in admiralty courts without benefit of jury or the normal protections of due process.

Grenville determined to maintain up to 10,000 British regulars in America to control both colonists and Indians and secure passage of the Quartering Act, requiring the colonies in which British troops were stationed to pay for their maintenance. Americans had never before been required to support a standing army in their midst.

Grenville also saw through the passage of his Currency Act of 1764, which forbade once and for all any colonial attempts to issue currency not redeemable in gold or silver, making it more difficult for Americans to avoid the constant drain of money that Britain's mercantilist policies were designed to create in the colonies.

Most important, however, Grenville got Parliament to pass the Stamp Act (1765), imposing a direct tax on Americans for the first time. The Stamp Act required Americans to purchase revenue stamps on everything from newspapers to legal documents and would have created an impossible drain on hard currency in the colonies. Because it overlooked the advantage already provided by Britain's mercantilist exploitation of the colonies, Grenville's policy was shortsighted and foolish; but few in Parliament were inclined to see this.

Americans reacted first with restrained and respectful petitions and pamphlets, in which they pointed out that "taxation without representation is tyranny." From there resistance progressed to stronger and stronger protests that eventually became violent and involved intimidation of those Americans who had contracted to be the agents for distributing the stamps.

Resistance was particularly intense in Massachusetts, where it was led first by James Otis and then by Samuel Adams, who formed the organization known as the Sons of Liberty.

Other colonies copied Massachusetts' successful tactics while adding some of their own. In Virginia, a young Burgess named Patrick Henry introduced seven resolutions denouncing the Stamp Act. Though only the four most moderate of them were passed by the House of Burgesses, newspapers picked up all seven and circulated them widely through the colonies, giving the impression all seven had been adopted. By their denial of Parliament's authority to tax the colonies they encouraged other colonial legislatures to issue strongly worded statements.

In October 1765, delegates from nine colonies met as the Stamp Act Congress. Called by the Massachusetts legislature at the instigation of James Otis, the Stamp Act Congress passed moderate resolutions against the act, asserting that Americans could not be taxed without their consent, given by their representatives. They pointed out that Americans were not, and because of their location could not practically be, represented in Parliament and concluded by calling for the repeal of both the Stamp and Sugar Acts. Most important, however, the Stamp Act Congress showed that representatives of the colonies could work together and gave political leaders in the various colonies a chance to become acquainted with each other.

Most effective in achieving repeal of the Stamp Act was colonial merchants' nonimportation (boycott) of British goods. Begun as an agreement among New York merchants, the boycott spread throughout the colonies and had a powerful effect on British merchants and manufacturers, who began clamoring for the act's repeal.

Meanwhile, the fickle King George III had dismissed Grenville over an unrelated disagreement and replaced him with a Cabinet headed by Charles Lord Rockingham. In March 1766, under the leadership of the new ministry, Parliament repealed the Stamp Act. At the same time, however, it passed the Declaratory Act, claiming power to tax or make laws for the Americans "in all cases whatsoever."

Though the Declaratory Act denied exactly the principle Americans had just been at such pains to assert—that of no taxation without representation—the Americans generally ignored it in their exuberant celebration of the repeal of the Stamp Act. Americans continued to eagerly proclaim their loyalty to Great Britain.

The Townshend Acts

The Rockingham ministry proved to be even shorter lived than that of Grenville. It was replaced with a Cabinet dominated by Chancellor of the Exchequer Charles Townshend. Townshend had boasted that he could successfully tax the colonies, and in 1766 Parliament gave him his chance by passing his program of taxes on items imported into the colonies. These taxes came to be known as the Townshend Duties. Townshend mistakenly believed the Americans would accept this method while rejecting the use of direct internal taxes. The Townshend Acts also included the use of admiralty courts to try those accused of violations, the use of writs of assistance, and the paying of customs officials out of the fines they levied. Townshend also had the New York legislature suspended for noncompliance with the Quartering Act.

American reaction was at first slow. Philadelphia lawyer John Dickinson wrote an anonymous pamphlet entitled "Letters from a Farmer in Pennsylvania," in which he pointed out in moderate terms that the Townshend Acts violated the principle of no taxation without representation and that if Parliament could suspend the New York legislature it could do the same to others. At the same time he urged a restrained response on the part of his fellow Americans.

In February 1768 the Massachusetts legislature, at the urging of Samuel Adams, passed the Massachusetts Circular Letter, reiterating Dickinson's mild arguments and urging other colonial legislatures to pass petitions calling on Parliament to repeal the acts. Had the British government done nothing, the matter might have passed quietly.

Instead, British authorities acted. They ordered that if the letter was not withdrawn, the Massachusetts legislature should be dissolved and new elections held. They forbade the other colonial legislatures to take up the matter, and they also sent four regiments of troops to Boston to prevent intimidation of royal officials and intimidate the populace instead.

The last of these actions was in response to the repeated pleas of the Boston customs agents. Corrupt agents had used technicalities of the confusing and poorly written Sugar and Townshend Acts to entrap innocent merchants and line their own pockets. Mob violence had threatened when agents had seized the ship *Liberty*, belonging to Boston merchant John Hancock. Such incidents prompted the call for troops.

The sending of troops, along with the British authority's repressive response to the Massachusetts Circular Letter, aroused the Americans to resistance. Non-importation was again instituted, and soon British merchants were calling on Parliament to repeal the acts. In March 1770, Parliament, under the new prime minister, Frederick Lord North, repealed all of the taxes except that on tea, which was retained to prove Parliament had the right to tax the colonies if it so desired.

By the time of the repeal, however, friction between British soldiers and Boston citizens had led to an incident in which five Bostonians were killed. Although the British soldiers had acted more or less in self-defense, Samuel Adams labeled the incident the "Boston Massacre" and publicized it widely. At their trial the British soldiers were defended by prominent Massachusetts lawyer John Adams and were acquitted on the charge of murder.

The Return of Relative Peace

Following the repeal of the Townshend duties a period of relative peace set in. The tax on tea remained as a reminder of Parliament's claims, but it could be easily avoided by smuggling.

Much good will had been lost and colonists remained suspicious of the British government. Many Americans believed the events of the previous decade to have been the work of a deliberate conspiracy to take their liberty.

Occasional incidents marred the relative peace. One such was the burning, by a seagoing mob of Rhode Islanders disguised as Indians, of the *Gaspee*, a British customs schooner that had run aground offshore. The *Gaspee's* captain and crew had alienated Rhode Islanders by their extreme zeal for catching smugglers as well as by their theft and vandalism when ashore.

In response to this incident British authorities appointed a commission to find the guilty parties and bring them to England for trial. Though those responsible for the burning of the *Gaspee* were never found, this action on the part of the British prompted the colonial legislatures to form committees of correspondence to communicate with each other regarding possible threats from the British government.

The Tea Act

The relative peace was brought to an end by the Tea Act of 1773.

In desperate financial condition—partially because the Americans were buying smuggled Dutch tea rather than the taxed British product—the British East India Company sought and obtained from Parliament concessions allowing it to ship tea directly to the colonies rather than only by way of Britain. The result would be that East India Company tea, even with the tax, would be cheaper than smuggled Dutch tea. The colonists would thus, it was hoped, buy the tea, tax and all. The East India Company would be saved and the Americans would be tacitly accepting Parliament's right to tax them.

The Americans, however, proved resistant to this approach, and, rather than seem to admit Parliament's right to tax, they vigorously resisted the cheaper tea. Various methods, including tar and feathers, were used to prevent the collection of the tax on tea. In most ports Americans did not allow the tea to be landed.

In Boston, however, pro-British Governor Thomas Hutchinson forced a confrontation by ordering Royal Navy vessels to prevent the tea ships from leaving the harbor. After twenty days this would, by law, result in the cargoes being sold at auction and the tax paid. The night before the time was to expire, December 16, 1773, Bostonians thinly disguised as Indians boarded the ships and threw the tea into the harbor.

Many Americans felt this—the destruction of private property—was going too far, but the reaction of Lord North and Parliament quickly united Americans in support of Boston and opposition to Britain.

The Intolerable Acts

The British responded with four acts collectively titled the Coercive Acts. First, the Boston Port Act closed the port of Boston to all trade until local citizens would agree to pay for the lost tea (they would not). Secondly, the Massachusetts Government Act greatly increased the power of Massachusetts' royal governor at the expense of the legislature. Thirdly, the Administration of Justice Act provided that royal officials accused of crimes in Massachusetts could be tried elsewhere, where chances of acquittal might be greater. Finally, a strengthened Quartering Act allowed the new governor, General Thomas Gage, to quarter his troops anywhere, including unoccupied private homes.

A further act of Parliament also angered and alarmed Americans. This was the Quebec Act, which extended the province of Quebec to the Ohio River, established Roman Catholicism as Quebec's official religion, and set up for Quebec a government without a representative assembly.

For Americans this was a denial of the hopes and expectations of westward expansion for which they had fought the French and Indian War. Also, New Englanders especially saw it as a threat that in their colonies too, Parliament could establish autocratic government and the hated Church of England.

Americans lumped the Quebec Act together with the Coercive Acts and referred to them all as the Intolerable Acts.

In response to the Coercive Acts, the First Continental Congress was called and met in Philadelphia in September 1774. It once again petitioned Parliament for relief but also passed the Suffolk Resolves (so called because they were first passed in Suffolk County, Massachusetts), denouncing the Intolerable Acts and calling for strict nonimportation and rigorous preparation of local militia companies in case the British should resort to military force.

The Congress then narrowly rejected a plan, submitted by Joseph Galloway of Pennsylvania, calling for a union of the colonies within the empire and a rearrangement of relations with Parliament. Most of the delegates felt matters had already gone too far for such a mild measure. Finally, before adjournment, it was agreed that there should be a Second Continental Congress to meet in May of the following year if the colonies' grievances had not been righted by then.

THE WAR FOR INDEPENDENCE

Lexington and Concord

The British government paid little attention to the First Continental Congress, having decided to teach the Americans a military lesson. More troops were sent to Massachusetts, which was officially declared to be in a state of rebellion. Orders were sent to General Gage to arrest the leaders of the resistance or, failing that, to provoke any sort of confrontation that would allow him to turn British military might loose on the Americans.

Gage decided on a reconnaissance-in-force to find and destroy a reported stockpile of colonial arms and ammunition at Concord. Seven hundred British troops set out on this mission on the night of April 18, 1775. Their movement was detected by American surveillance and news was spread throughout the countryside by dispatch riders Paul Revere and William Dawes.

At the little village of Lexington, Captain John Parker and some seventy Minutemen (militiamen trained to respond at a moment's notice) awaited the British on the village green. As the British approached, a British officer shouted at the Minutemen to lay down their arms and disperse. The Minutemen did not lay down their arms but did turn to file off the green. A shot was fired, and then the British opened fire and charged. Eight Americans were killed and several others wounded, most shot in the back.

The British continued to Concord only to find that nearly all of the military supplies they had expected to find had already been moved. Attacked by growing numbers of Minutemen, they began to retreat toward Boston. As the British retreated, Minutemen, swarming from every village for miles around, fired on the column from behind rocks, trees, and stone fences. Only a relief force of additional British troops saved the first column from destruction.

Open warfare had begun, and the myth of British invincibility was destroyed. Militia came in large numbers from all the New England colonies to join the force besieging Gage and his army in Boston.

Bunker Hill

In May 1775, three more British generals, William Howe, Henry Clinton, and John Burgoyne, arrived in Boston urging Gage to further aggressive action. The following month the Americans tightened the noose around Boston by fortifying Breed's Hill (a spur of Bunker Hill), from which they could, if necessary, bombard Boston.

The British determined to remove them by a frontal attack that would demonstrate the awesome power of British arms. Twice the British were thrown back and finally succeeded as the Americans ran out of ammunition. Over a thousand British soldiers were killed or wounded in what turned out to be the bloodiest battle of the war (June 17, 1775). Yet the British had gained very little and remained bottled up in Boston.

Meanwhile in May 1775, American forces under Ethan Allen and Benedict Arnold took Fort Ticonderoga on Lake Champlain.

Congress, hoping Canada would join in resistance against Britain, authorized two expeditions into Quebec. One, under General Richard Montgomery took Montreal and then turned toward the city of Quebec. It was met there by the second expedition under Benedict Arnold. The attack on Quebec (December 31, 1775) failed. Montgomery was killed, Arnold wounded, and American hopes for Canada ended.

The Second Continental Congress

While these events were taking place in New England and Canada, the Second Continental Congress met in Philadelphia in May 1775. Congress was divided into two main factions. One was composed mostly of New Englanders and leaned toward declaring independence from Britain. The other drew its strength primarily from the Middle Colonies and was not yet ready to go that far. It was led by John Dickinson of Pennsylvania.

Congress took action to deal with the difficult situation facing the colonies. It adopted the New England army around Boston, calling on the other colonies to send troops and sending George Washington to command it, adopted a "Declaration of the Causes and Necessity for Taking up Arms" and adopted the "Olive Branch Petition" pleading with King George III to intercede with Parliament to restore peace.

This last overture was ignored in Britain, where the king gave his approval to the Prohibitory Act, declaring the colonies in rebellion and no longer under his protection. Preparations were made for full-scale war against America.

Throughout 1775, Americans remained deeply loyal to Britain and King George III despite the king's proclamations declaring them to be in revolt. In Congress moderates still resisted independence.

In January 1776, Thomas Paine published a pamphlet entitled *Common Sense*, calling for immediate independence. Its arguments were extreme and sometimes illogical and its language intemperate, but it sold largely and may have had much influence in favor of independence. Continued evidence of Britain's intention to carry on the war throughout the colonies also weakened the moderates' resistance to independence. The Prohibitory Act, with its virtual declaration of war against America, convinced many that no further moral scruples need stand in the way of such a step.

On June 7, 1776, Richard Henry Lee of Virginia introduced a series of formal resolutions in Congress calling for independence and a national government. Accepting these ideas, Congress named two committees. One, headed by John Dickinson, was to work out a framework for a national government. The other was to draft a statement of the reasons for declaring independence. This statement, the Declaration of Independence, was primarily the work of Thomas Jefferson of Virginia. It was a restatement of political ideas by then commonplace in America, showing why the former colonists felt justified in separating from Great Britain. It was formally adopted by Congress on July 4, 1776.

Washington Takes Command

Britain, meanwhile, was preparing a massive effort to conquer the United States. Gage was removed for being too timid, and top command went to Howe. To supplement the British army, large numbers of troops were hired from various German principalities. Since many of these Germans came from the state of Hesse-Kassel, Americans referred to all such troops as Hessians.

Although the London authorities desired a quick and smashing campaign, General Howe and his brother, British naval commander Richard, Admiral Lord Howe, intended to move slowly, using their powerful force to cow the Americans into signing loyalty oaths.

In March 1776, Washington placed on Dorchester Heights, overlooking Boston, some of the large cannon that had been captured at Ticonderoga, forcing the British to evacuate the city.

The British shipped their troops to Nova Scotia and then, together with large reinforcements from Britain, landed that summer at New York City. They hoped to find many loyalists there and make that city the key to their campaign to subdue America.

Washington anticipated the move and was waiting at New York, which Congress had ordered should be defended. However, the under-trained,

WASHINGTON, CROSSING THE DELAWARE.

Washington preparing to cross the Delaware. Currier and Ives print.

under-equipped, and badly outnumbered American army was no match for the powerful forces under the Howes. Defeated at the Battle of Long Island (August 27, 1776), Washington narrowly avoided being trapped there (an escape partially due to the Howes' slowness). Defeated again at the Battle of Washington Heights (August 29–30, 1776) on Manhattan, Washington was forced to retreat across New Jersey with the aggressive British General Lord Cornwallis, a subordinate of Howe, in pursuit. By December, what was left of Washington's army had made it into Pennsylvania.

With his victory almost complete, Howe decided to wait till spring to finish annihilating Washington's army. Scattering his troops in small detachments so as to hold all of New Jersey, he went into winter quarters.

Washington, with his small army melting away as demoralized soldiers deserted, decided on a bold stroke. On Christmas night 1776, his army crossed the Delaware River and struck the Hessians at Trenton. The Hessians, still groggy from their hard-drinking Christmas party, were easily defeated. A few days later Washington defeated a British force at Princeton (January 3, 1777).

Howe was so shocked by these two unexpected defeats that he pulled his outposts back close to New York. Much of New Jersey was regained. Those who had signed British loyalty oaths in the presence of Howe's army were now at the mercy of their patriot neighbors. And Washington's army was saved from disintegration.

Early in the war France began making covert shipments of arms to the Americans. This it did, not because the French government loved freedom (it did not), but because it hated Britain and saw the war as a way to weaken Britain by depriving it of its colonies. Arms shipments from France were vital for the Americans.

Saratoga and Valley Forge

For the summer of 1777 the British home authorities adopted an elaborate plan of campaign urged on them by General Burgoyne. According to the plan, Burgoyne himself would lead an army southward from Canada along the Lake Champlain corridor while another army under Howe moved up the Hudson River to join hands with Burgoyne at Albany. This, it was hoped, would cut off New England and allow the British to subdue that region, which they considered the hotbed of the "rebellion."

Howe had other ideas and shipped his army by sea to Chesapeake Bay, hoping to capture the American capital, Philadelphia, and destroy Washington's army at the same time. At Brandywine Creek (September 1, 1777) Washington tried but failed to stop Howe's advance. Yet the American army, though badly beaten, remained intact. Howe occupied Philadelphia as the Congress fled westward to York, Pennsylvania.

In early October, Washington attempted to drive Howe out of Philadelphia; but his attack at Germantown, though at first successful, failed at least partially due to thick fog and the still imperfect level of training in the American army, both of which contributed to confusion among the troops. Thereafter Howe settled down to comfortable winter quarters in Philadelphia, and Washington and his army to very uncomfortable ones at nearby Valley Forge, while far to the north, the British strategy that Howe had ignored was going badly awry.

Burgoyne's advance began well but slowed as the Americans placed obstructions on the rough wilderness trails by which his army, including numerous cannon and much bulky baggage, had to advance. A diversionary force of British troops and Iroquois Indians under the command of Colonel Barry St. Leger swung east of Burgoyne's column, but although it defeated and killed American General Nicholas Herkimer at the Battle of Oriskany (August 6, 1777), it was finally forced to withdraw to Canada.

In mid-August, a detachment of Burgoyne's force was defeated by New England militia under General John Stark near Bennington in what is now Vermont. By autumn Burgoyne found his way blocked by an American army: continentals (American regular troops such as those that made up most of Washington's army, paid, in theory at least, by Congress); and New England militia, under General Horatio Gates, at Saratoga, about thirty miles north of Albany. Burgoyne's two attempts to break through (September 19 and October 7, 1777) were turned back by the Americans under the brilliant battlefield leadership of Benedict Arnold. On October 17, 1777, Burgoyne surrendered to Gates.

The American victory at Saratoga convinced the French to join openly in the war against England. Eventually the Spanish (1779) and the Dutch (1780) joined as well, and England was faced with a world war.

The British Move South

The new circumstances brought a change in British strategy. With fewer troops available for service in America, the British would have to depend more on loyalists, and since they imagined that larger numbers of these existed in the South than elsewhere, it was there they turned their attention.

Howe was relieved and replaced by General Henry Clinton, who was ordered to abandon Philadelphia and march to New York. In doing so, he narrowly avoided defeat at the hands of Washington's army—much improved after a winter's drilling at Valley Forge under the direction of Prussian nobleman Baron von Steuben—at the Battle of Monmouth, New Jersey (June 28, 1778).

Clinton was thenceforth to maintain New York as Britain's main base in America while detaching troops to carry out the new Southern strategy. In November 1778 the British easily conquered Georgia. Late the following year

Clinton moved on South Carolina with a land and naval force, and in May 1780, U.S. General Benjamin Lincoln surrendered Charleston. Clinton then returned to New York, leaving Cornwallis to continue the Southern campaign.

Congress, alarmed at the British successes, sent General Horatio Gates to lead the forces opposing Cornwallis. Gates blundered to a resounding defeat at the Battle of Camden, in South Carolina (August 16, 1780).

The general outlook seemed bad for America at that point in the war. Washington's officers grumbled about their pay in arrears. The army was understrength and then suffered successive mutinies among the Pennsylvania and New Jersey troops. Benedict Arnold went over to the British. In short, the British seemed to be winning the contest of endurance. This outlook was soon to change.

In the West, George Rogers Clark, acting under the auspices of the state of Virginia, led an expedition down the Ohio River and into the area of present-day Illinois and Indiana, defeating a British force at Vincennes, Indiana, and securing the area north of the Ohio River for the United States.

In the South, Cornwallis began to move northward toward North Carolina, but on October 7, 1780, a detachment of his force under Major Patrick Ferguson was defeated by American frontiersmen at the Battle of Kings Mountain in northern South Carolina. To further increase the problems facing the British, Cornwallis had unwisely moved north without bothering to secure South Carolina first. The result was that the British would no sooner leave an area than American militia or guerilla bands, such as that under Francis Marion ("the Swamp Fox"), were once again in control and able to deal with those who had expressed loyalty to Britain in the presence of Cornwallis's army.

To command the continental forces in the South, Washington sent his most able subordinate, military genius Nathaniel Greene. Greene's brilliant strategy led to a crushing victory at Cowpens, South Carolina (January 17, 1781), by troops under Greene's subordinate, General Daniel Morgan of Virginia. It also led to a near victory by Greene's own force at Guilford Court House, North Carolina (March 15, 1781).

Yorktown

The frustrated and impetuous Cornwallis now abandoned the Southern strategy and moved north into Virginia. Clinton, disgusted at this departure from plan, sent instructions for Cornwallis to take up a defensive position and await further orders. Against his better judgment Cornwallis did so, selecting Yorktown, Virginia, on a peninsula that reaches into Chesapeake Bay between the York and James rivers.

Washington now saw and seized the opportunity this presented. With the aid of a French fleet which took control of Chesapeake Bay and a French army that joined him in sealing off the land approaches to Yorktown, Washington succeeded in trapping Cornwallis. After three weeks of siege, Cornwallis surrendered on October 17, 1781.

The War at Sea

Britain had other problems as well. Ships of the small but daring U.S. Navy as well as privateers (privately owned vessels outfitted with guns and authorized by a warring government to capture enemy merchant ships for profit) preyed on the British merchant marine. John Paul Jones, the most famous of American naval leaders, captured ships and carried out audacious raids along the coast of Britain itself. French and Spanish naval forces also struck against various outposts of the British Empire.

The Treaty of Paris of 1783

News of the debacle at Yorktown brought the collapse of Lord North's ministry, and the new Cabinet opened peace negotiations. The extremely able American negotiating team was composed of Benjamin Franklin, John Adams, and John Jay. The negotiations continued for some time, delayed by French and Spanish maneuvering. When it became apparent that France and Spain were planning to achieve an agreement unfavorable to the United States, the American envoys negotiated a separate treaty with Britain.

The final agreement became known as the Treaty of Paris of 1783. Its terms stipulated the following: 1) The United States was recognized as an independent nation by the major European powers, including Britain; 2) Its western boundary was set at the Mississippi River; 3) Its southern boundary was set at 31° north latitude (the northern boundary of Florida); 4) Britain retained Canada but had to surrender Florida to Spain; 5) Private British creditors would be free to collect any debts owed by U.S. citizens; and 6) Congress was to recommend that the states restore confiscated loyalist property.

THE CREATION OF NEW GOVERNMENTS

The State Constitutions

After the collapse of British authority in 1775, it became necessary to form new state governments. By the end of 1777 ten new state constitutions had been formed.

Connecticut and Rhode Island kept their colonial charters, which were republican in nature, simply deleting references to British sovereignty. Massachusetts waited until 1780 to complete the adoption of its new constitution.

The constitutions ranged from such extremely democratic models as the virtually unworkable Pennsylvania constitution (soon abandoned), in which a unicameral legislature ruled with little check or balance, to more reasonable frameworks such as those of Maryland and Virginia, which included more safeguards against popular excesses.

Massachusetts voters set an important example by insisting that a constitution should be made by a special convention rather than the legislature. This would make the constitution superior to the legislature and, it was hoped, assure that the legislature would be subject to the constitution.

Most state constitutions included bills of rights—lists of things the government was not supposed to do to the people.

The Articles of Confederation

In the summer of 1776, Congress appointed a committee to begin devising a framework for national government. When completed, this document was known as the Articles of Confederation. John Dickinson, who had played a leading role in writing the Articles, felt a strong national government was needed; but by the time Congress finished revising them, the Articles went to the opposite extreme of preserving the sovereignty of the states and creating a very weak national government.

The Articles of Confederation provided for a unicameral Congress in which each state would have one vote, as had been the case in the Continental Congress. Executive authority under the Articles would be vested in a committee of thirteen, one member from each state. In order to amend the Articles, the unanimous consent of all the states was required.

The Articles of Confederation government was empowered to make war, make treaties, determine the amount of troops and money each state should contribute to the war effort, settle disputes between states, admit new states to the Union, and borrow money. More importantly, however, was that it was not empowered to levy taxes, raise troops, or regulate commerce.

Ratification of the Articles of Confederation was delayed by a disagreement over the future status of the lands that lay to the west of the original thirteen states. Some states, notably Virginia, held extensive claims to these lands based on their original colonial charters. Maryland, which had no such claim, withheld ratification until in 1781 Virginia agreed to surrender its western claims to the new national government.

Meanwhile, the country was on its way to deep financial trouble. Unable to tax, Congress resorted to printing large amounts of paper money to finance the war; but these inflated "Continentals" were soon worthless. Other financial schemes fell through, and only grants and loans from France and the Netherlands

Declaration of Independence

staved off complete financial collapse. A plan to amend the Articles to give Congress power to tax was stopped by the lone opposition of Rhode Island. The army, whose pay was far in arrears, threatened mutiny. Some of those who favored a stronger national government welcomed this development and in what became known as the Newburgh Conspiracy (1783) consulted with army second-in-command Horatio Gates as to the possibility of using the army to force the states to surrender more power to the national government. This movement was stopped by a moving appeal to the officers by Washington himself.

The Trans-Appalachian West and the Northwest Ordinance

For many Americans the enormous trans-Appalachian frontier represented an opportunity to escape the economic hard times that followed the end of the war.

In 1775, Daniel Boone opened the "Wilderness Road" through the Cumberland Gap and on to the "Bluegrass" region of Kentucky. Others scouted down the Ohio River from Pittsburgh. By 1790, over 100,000 had settled in Kentucky and Tennessee, despite the risk of violent death at the hands of Indians. This risk was made worse by the presence of the British in northwestern military posts that should have been evacuated at the end of the war. From these posts they supplied the Indians with guns and encouraged them to use them on Americans. The Spaniards on the Florida frontier behaved in much the same way.

The settlement of Kentucky and Tennessee increased the pressure for the opening of the lands north of the Ohio River. To facilitate this, Congress passed three land ordinances in the years from 1784 to 1787.

The Land Ordinance of 1784 provided for territorial government and an orderly system by which each territory could progress to full statehood (this ordinance is sometimes considered part of the Land Ordinance of 1785).

The Land Ordinance of 1785 provided for the orderly surveying and distribution of land in townships six miles square, each composed of thirty-six one-square-mile (640 acre) sections, of which one should be set aside for the support of education. (This ordinance is sometimes referred to as the "Northwest Ordinance of 1785").

The Northwest Ordinance of 1787 provided a bill of rights for settlers and forbade slavery north of the Ohio River.

These ordinances were probably the most important legislation of the Articles of Confederation government.

The Jay-Gardoqui Negotiations

Economic depression followed the end of the war as the United States remained locked into the disadvantageous commercial system of the British Empire but without the trade advantages that this system had provided.

One man who thought he saw a way out of the economic quagmire was Congress's secretary of foreign affairs, John Jay. In 1784, Jay began negotiating with Spanish minister Gardoqui a treaty that would have granted lucrative commercial privileges—benefiting large east-coast merchants such as Jay—in exchange for U.S. acceptance of Spain's closure of the Mississippi River as an outlet for the agricultural goods of the rapidly growing settlements in Kentucky and Tennessee. This the Spanish desired because they feared that extensive settlement in what was then the western part of the United States might lead to American hunger for Spanish-held lands.

When Jay reported this to Congress in the summer of 1786, the West and South were outraged. Negotiations were broken off. Some, angered that Jay could show so little concern for the other sections of the country, talked of dissolving the Union; this helped spur to action those who desired not the dissolution but the strengthening of the Union.

Shays' Rebellion

Nationalists were further stimulated to action by Shays' Rebellion (1786). Economic hard times coupled with high taxes intended to pay off the state's war debt drove western Massachusetts farmers to desperation. Led by war veteran Daniel Shays, they shut down courts to prevent judges from seizing property or condemning people to debtors' prison for failing to pay their taxes.

The unrest created a disproportionate amount of panic in the rest of the state and the nation. The citizens of Boston subscribed money to raise an army to suppress the rebels. The success of this army together with timely tax relief caused the "rebellion" to fizzle out fairly quickly.

Amid the panic caused by the news of the uprising, many came to feel that a stronger government was needed to control such violent public outbursts as those of the western Massachusetts farmers.

◄────────── **HISTORICAL TIMELINE** ──────────►
The American Revolution (1763–1783)

1763	Proclamation Line of 1763
1764	Sugar Act Currency Act
1765	Stamp Act Sons of Liberty formed
1767	Townshend Duties Dickinson's "Letters of a Pennsylvania Farmer"
1770	Boston Massacre Lord North becomes British prime minister
1772	H.M.S. *Gaspee* burned off coast of Rhode Island
1773	Tea Act Boston Tea Party
1774	Intolerable Acts First Continental Congress
1775	Lexington and Concord Battle of Bunker Hill
1776	*Common Sense* published by Thomas Paine Declaration of Independence Battle of New York City Battle of Trenton
1777	British surrender 5,800 men at Saratoga American army at Valley Forge
1778	French-American alliance established British begin Southern strategy and capture Savannah
1780	British capture Charleston French army lands in Connecticut
1781	Articles of Confederation approved Gen. Cornwallis surrenders at Yorktown
1783	Treaty of Paris ends war, grants American independence Newburgh Conspiracy of American army officers

Chapter 4

THE UNITED STATES CONSTITUTION (1785–1789)

DEVELOPMENT AND RATIFICATION

Toward a New Constitution

As time went on, the inadequacy of the Articles of Confederation became increasingly apparent. Congress could not compel the states to comply with the terms of the Treaty of Paris of 1783 regarding debts and loyalists' property. The British used this as an excuse for not evacuating their Northwestern posts, hoping to be on hand to make the most of the situation when, as they not unreasonably expected, the new government fell to pieces. In any case, Congress could do nothing to force them out of the posts, nor to solve any of the nation's other increasingly pressing problems.

In these dismal straits, some called for disunion, others for monarchy. Others felt that republican government could still work if given a better constitution, and they made it their goal to achieve this.

In 1785 a meeting of representatives of Virginia, Maryland, Pennsylvania, and Delaware was held at George Washington's residence, Mt. Vernon, for the purpose of discussing current problems of interstate commerce. At their suggestion the Virginia legislature issued a call for a convention of all the states on the same subject, to meet the following summer in Annapolis, Maryland.

The Annapolis Convention met in September of 1786, but only five states were represented. Among those present, however, were such nationalists as Alexander Hamilton, John Dickinson, and James Madison. With so few states represented it was decided instead to call for a convention of all the states to meet the following summer in Philadelphia for the purpose of revising the Articles of Confederation.

The Constitutional Convention

The men who met in Philadelphia in 1787 were remarkably able, highly educated, and exceptionally accomplished. For the most part they were lawyers, merchants and planters. Though representing individual states, most thought in national terms. Prominent among them were James Madison, Alexander Hamilton, Gouverneur Morris, Robert Morris, John Dickinson, and Benjamin Franklin.

George Washington was unanimously elected to preside, and the enormous respect that he commanded helped hold the convention together through difficult times (as it had the Continental Army) and make the product of the convention's work more attractive to the rest of the nation. The delegates then voted that the convention's discussions should be secret, to avoid the distorting and confusing influence of the press and publicity.

The delegates shared a basic belief in the innate selfishness of man, which must somehow be kept from abusing the power of government. For this purpose the document that they finally produced contained many checks and balances, designed to prevent the government, or any one branch of the government, from gaining too much power.

Madison, who has been called the "father of the Constitution," devised a plan of national government and persuaded fellow Virginian Edmund Randolph, who was more skilled at public speaking, to introduce it. Known as the "Virginia Plan," it called for an executive branch and two houses of Congress, each based on population.

Smaller states, who would thus have seen their influence decreased, objected and countered with William Paterson's "New Jersey Plan," calling for the continuation of a unicameral legislature with equal representation for the states as well as sharply increased powers for the national government.

A temporary impasse developed that threatened to break up the convention. At this point Benjamin Franklin played an important role in reconciling the often wrangling delegates, suggesting that the sessions of the convention henceforth begin with prayer (they did) and making various other suggestions that eventually helped the convention arrive at the "Great Compromise." The Great Compromise provided for a Presidency, a Senate with all states represented equally (by two Senators each), and a House of Representatives with representation according to population.

Another crisis involved North-South disagreement over the issue of slavery. Here also a compromise was reached. Slavery was neither endorsed nor condemned by the Constitution. Each slave was to count as three-fifths of a person for purposes of apportioning representation and direct taxation on the states (the Three-Fifths Compromise). The federal government was prohibited from stopping the importation of slaves prior to 1808.

The third major area of compromise was the nature of the Presidency. This was made easier by the virtual certainty that George Washington would be the first president and the universal trust that he would not abuse the powers of the office or set a bad example for his successors. The result was a strong Presidency with control of foreign policy and the power to veto Congress's legislation. Should the president commit an actual crime, Congress would have the power to impeach him. Otherwise the president would serve for a term of four years and be re-electable without limit. As a check to the possible excesses of democracy, the president was to be elected by an Electoral College, in which each state would have the same number of electors as it did Senators and Representatives combined. The person with the second highest total in the Electoral College would be Vice-President. If no one gained a majority in the Electoral College, the President would be chosen by the House of Representatives.

The new Constitution was to take effect when nine states, through special state conventions, had ratified it.

The Struggle for Ratification

As the struggle over ratification got under way, those favoring the Constitution astutely took for themselves the name Federalists (i.e., advocates of centralized power) and labeled their opponents Antifederalists. The Federalists were effective in explaining the convention and the document it had produced. *The Federalist Papers*, written as a series of eighty-five newspaper articles by Alexander Hamilton, James Madison, and John Jay, brilliantly expounded the Constitution and demonstrated how it was designed to prevent the abuse of power from any direction. These essays are considered to be the best commentary on the Constitution by those who helped write it.

At first, ratification progressed smoothly, with five states approving in quick succession. In Massachusetts, however, a tough fight developed. By skillful maneuvering, Federalists were able to win over to their side such popular opponents of the Constitution as Samuel Adams and John Hancock. Others were won over by the promise that a bill of rights would be added to the Constitution, limiting the federal government just as the state governments were limited by their bills of rights. With such promises, Massachusetts ratified by a narrow margin.

By June 21, 1788, the required nine states had ratified, but the crucial states of New York and Virginia still held out. In Virginia, where George Mason and Patrick Henry opposed the Constitution, the influence of George Washington and the promise of a bill of rights finally prevailed and ratification was achieved there as well. In New York, where Alexander Hamilton led the fight for ratification, *The Federalist Papers*, the promise of a bill of rights, and the news of Virginia's ratification were enough to carry the day.

Only North Carolina and Rhode Island still held out, but they both ratified within the next fifteen months.

In March 1789, George Washington was inaugurated as the nation's first president.

OUTLINE OF THE UNITED STATES CONSTITUTION

Articles of the Constitution

Preamble

"We the People of the United States, in order to form a more perfect Union, establish justice, insure domestic tranquility, provide for the common defense, promote the general welfare, and secure the blessings of liberty to ourselves and our posterity, do ordain and establish this Constitution for the United States of America."

Article I – Legislature

The legislature is divided into two parts—the House of Representatives (435 members currently; determined by proportional representation of the population) and the Senate (100 members currently; two from each state).

The House of Representatives may bring impeachment charges. All bills which concern money must originate in the House. Because of the size of the body, debate is limited except in special cases, where all representatives may meet as the Committee of the Whole. The Speaker of the House presides over the proceedings. Terms of representatives are two years, re-electable without limit, to persons who are at least 25 years of age.

The Senate, originally elected by state legislatures but now by direct election (17th Amendment), approves or rejects presidential nominations and treaties, and serves as the court and jury in impeachment proceedings. Debate within the Senate is unlimited. The President pro tempore usually presides, but the Vice-President of the United States is the presiding officer, and may vote to break a tie. Senate elected terms are for six years, re-electable without limit, to persons who are at least 30 years of age.

Article II – Executive

The President of the United States is elected for a four-year term, originally electable without limit (the 22nd Amendment limits election to two terms), and must be at least 35 years old.

Responsibilities for the President as outlined in the Constitution include acting as the Chief of State, the Chief Executive, Commander-in-Chief of the Armed Forces, the Chief Diplomat, and Chief Legislature.

Article III – Judiciary

While the Constitution describes the Supreme Court in Article 111, the actual construction of the court system was accomplished by the Judiciary Act of 1789. The Supreme Court has jurisdiction for federal courts and appellate cases on appeal from lower courts.

Article IV – Interstate Relations

This article guarantees that court decisions and other legal actions (marriage, incorporation, etc.) valid in one state are valid in another. Extradition of criminals (and, originally, runaway slaves) and the exchange of citizenship benefits are likewise guaranteed. Article IV also provides for the admission of new states and guarantees federal protection against invasion and violence for each state. States admitted maintain the same status as the original states. All states are guaranteed a republican form of government.

Article V – Amendment Process

Amendments are proposed by a two-thirds vote of each house of Congress or by a special convention called by Congress upon the request of two-thirds of the state legislatures. Amendments are ratified by three-fourths of the state legislatures or state conventions.

Article VI – Supremacy Clause

Article VI sets up the hierarchy of laws in the United States. The Constitution is the "supreme law of the land," and supersedes treaties. Treaties supercede federal laws, federal laws (later to include federal regulatory agency directives) supercede state constitutions, state laws and local laws, respectively. All federal and state officials, including judges, must take an oath to support and defend the Constitution.

Article VII – Ratification

This article specified the ratification process necessary for the Constitution to take effect. Nine of the original thirteen states had to ratify the Constitution before it became operative.

Amendments to the Constitution

The Amendments to the Constitution guarantee certain individual rights and amend original dictates of the Constitution. The first ten amendments are known as the Bill of Rights, for which Thomas Jefferson provided the impetus.

1 – protects the freedom of religion, speech, press, assembly, as well as the right to petition the government for the redress of grievances (1791)
2 – protects the right to bear arms in a regulated militia (on a state basis; it was not intended to guarantee an individual's rights) (1791)

3 – ensures that troops will not be housed in private citizens' homes (1791)

4 – protects against unreasonable search and seizure (need for search warrant) (1791)

5 – protects the rights for the accused, including required indictments, double jeopardy, self-incrimination, due process, and just compensation (1791)

6 – guarantees a speedy and public trial, the confrontation by witnesses, and the right to call witnesses on one's own behalf (1791)

7 – guarantees a jury trial (1791)

8 – protects against excessive bail and cruel and unusual punishment (1791)

9 – says that all rights not enumerated are nonetheless retained by the people (1791)

10 – says that all powers not specifically delegated to the federal government are retained by the states (1791)

11 – states may not be sued by individuals (1798)

12 – dictates that electors will cast separate ballots for President and Vice-President; in the event of no clear winner, the House will select the President and the Senate the Vice-President (1804)

13 – abolished slavery (1865)

14 – extends citizenship to all persons; made Confederate debt void and Confederate leaders ineligible for public office; states which denied voting rights to qualified citizens (blacks) would have their representation in Congress reduced; conferred "dual" citizenship (both of the United States and of a specific state) on all citizens (1868)

15 – extends voting rights to blacks (1870)

16 – legalized the income tax (1913)

17 – provides for the direct election of senators (1913)

18 – prohibited the general manufacture, sale and use of alcoholic beverages (1919)

19 – extends voting rights to women (1920)

20 – changed inauguration date from March 4 to January 20; eliminated the "lame duck" session of Congress (after the November elections) (1933)

21 – repealed the 18th Amendment (1933)

22 – limits presidents to two terms (1951)

23 – gives presidential electoral votes to the District of Columbia (1961)

24 – prohibits poll taxes (1964)

25 – changed the order of the presidential line of succession and provides guidelines for presidential disability (1967)

26 – extends voting rights to eighteen-year-olds (1971)

27 – restricts the practice of congressional salary adjustment (1992)

SEPARATION AND LIMITATION OF POWERS

Powers Reserved for the Federal Government Only

- Regulate foreign commerce regulation
- Regulate interstate commerce regulation
- Mint money
- Create and establish post offices
- Regulate naturalization and immigration
- Grant copyrights and patents
- Declare and wage war, declare peace
- Admit new states
- Fix standards for weights and measures
- Raise and maintain an army and a navy
- Govern the federal city (Washington, D.C.)
- Conduct relations with foreign powers
- Universalize bankruptcy laws

Powers Reserved for the State Governments Only

- Conduct and monitor elections
- Establish voter qualifications
- Provide for local governments
- Ratify proposed amendments to the Constitution
- Regulate contracts and wills
- Regulate intrastate commerce
- Provide education for its citizens
- Levy direct taxes (the 16th Amendment permits the federal government to levy direct taxes)
- Maintain police power over public health and safety
- Maintain integrity of state borders

Powers Shared by Federal and State Governments

- Taxing, borrowing and spending money
- Controlling the militia
- Acting directly on individuals

Restrictions on the Federal Government

- No ex post facto laws
- No bills of attainder
- Two-year limit on appropriation for the military
- No suspension of habeas corpus (except in a crisis)
- One port may not be favored over another
- All guarantees as stated in the Bill of Rights

Restrictions on State Governments

- Treaties, alliances, or confederations may not be entered into
- Letters of marque and reprisal may not be granted
- Contracts may not be impaired
- Money may not be printed or bills of credit emitted
- No import or export taxes
- May not wage war (unless invaded)

Required Percentages of Voting

Actions which require a simple majority include raising taxes, requesting appropriations, declaring war, increasing the national debt, instituting a draft, and introducing impeachment charge (House).

Actions which require a two-thirds majority include overriding a presidential veto, proposing amendments to the Constitution, expelling a member of Congress (in the individual house only), ratifying treaties (Senate), acting as a jury for impeachment (Senate), ratifying presidential appointments (Senate).

The action which requires a three-fourths majority is approving a proposed constitutional amendment (states).

HISTORICAL TIMELINE

The United States Constitution (1785–1789)

1785	Land Ordinance provides for orderly development of territories Spain closes the Mississippi River to American shipping
1786	Annapolis Convention Virginia adopts Jefferson's "Statute of Religious Freedom" Shays' Rebellion
1787	Northwest Ordinance prohibits slavery in new territories Constitutional Convention meets in Philadelphia
1788	*Federalist Papers* published New Hampshire is ninth state to ratify Constitution, making it the law of the land
1789	Washington elected and inaugurated as president French Revolution begins as Bastille is stormed French National Assembly issues "Declaration of Rights of Man"

Chapter 5

THE NEW NATION (1789–1824)

THE FEDERALIST ERA

The results of the first elections held under the new Constitution made it clear that the fledgling government was going to be managed by those who had drawn up the document and by their supporters. Few Antifederalists were elected to Congress, and many of the new legislators had served as delegates to the Philadelphia Convention two years before. This Federalist majority immediately set about to draft legislation which would fill in the gaps left by the convention and to erect the structure of a strong central government.

The New Executive

There had never been any doubt as to who would be the first president. George Washington received virtually all the votes of the presidential electors, and John Adams received the next highest number, thus becoming the vice president. After a triumphal journey from Mount Vernon, Washington was inaugurated in New York City, the temporary seat of government, on April 30, 1789.

Congress Erects the Structure of Government

The new national legislature immediately acted to honor the Federalist pledge of a bill of rights made to those voters who had hesitated to ratify the new Constitution. Twelve amendments were drafted which embodied the guarantees of personal liberties, most of which had been traditionally enjoyed by English citizens. Ten of these were ratified by the states by the end of 1791, and they became our Bill of Rights. The first nine spelled out specific guarantees of personal freedoms, such as religion, speech, press, assembly, petition, and a speedy trial by one's peers, and the 10th Amendment reserved to the states all those powers not specifically withheld, or granted to the federal government. This last was a concession to those who feared the potential of the central government to usurp the sovereignty of the individual states.

The Establishment of the Federal Court System

The Judiciary Act of 1789 provided for a Supreme Court, with six justices, and invested it with the power to rule on the constitutional validity of state laws. It was to be the interpreter of the "supreme law of the land." A system of district courts was established to serve as courts of original jurisdiction, and three courts of appeal were also provided for.

THE ESTABLISHMENT OF THE EXECUTIVE DEPARTMENTS

The Constitution had not specified the names or number of the departments of the executive branch. Congress established three—state, treasury, and war—and also the offices of attorney general and postmaster general. President Washington immediately appointed Thomas Jefferson, Alexander Hamilton, and Henry Knox, respectively, to fill the executive posts, and Edmund Randolph became attorney general. These four men were called upon regularly by the president for advice, and they later formed the nucleus of what became known as the Cabinet, although no provision for such was made in the Constitution.

WASHINGTON'S ADMINISTRATION, 1789–1797

Hamilton's Financial Program

Treasury Secretary Alexander Hamilton, in his "Report on the Public Credit," proposed the funding of the national debt at face value, federal assumption of state debts, and the establishment of a national bank. In his "Report on Manufactures," Hamilton proposed an extensive program for federal stimulation of industrial development, through subsidies and tax incentives. The money needed to fund these programs, proposed Hamilton, would come from an excise tax on distillers and from tariffs on imports.

Opposition to Hamilton's Program

Jefferson and others objected to the funding proposal because it obviously would benefit speculators who had bought up state and confederation obligations at depressed prices, and who would profit handsomely by their redemption at face value. The original purchasers, they claimed, should at least share in the windfall. They opposed the tax program because it would fall primarily on the small farmers. They saw Hamilton's entire program as enriching a small elite group at the expense of the more worthy common citizen.

The Appearance of Political Parties

Political parties had been considered a detrimental force by the founding fathers, since they were seen as contributing to the rise of "factions." Thus, no mention of such was made in the Constitution. But differences in philosophy very quickly began to drive the leaders of government into opposing camps—the Federalists and the Republicans.

Alexander Hamilton and the Federalists

Hamilton, as the theorist of the group who favored a strong central government, interpreted the Constitution as having vested extensive powers in the federal government. This "implied powers" stance claimed that the government was given all powers that were not expressly denied to it. This is the "broad" interpretation.

Thomas Jefferson and the Republicans

Jefferson and Madison held the view that any action not specifically permitted in the Constitution was thereby prohibited. This is the "strict" interpretation, and the Republicans opposed the establishment of Hamilton's national bank on this view of government. The Jeffersonian supporters, primarily under the guidance of James Madison, began to organize political groups in opposition to the Federalist program, and called themselves Republicans.

Sources of Partisan Support

The Federalists received their strongest support from the business and financial groups in the commercial centers of the Northeast and in the port cities of the South. The strength of the Republicans lay primarily in the rural and frontier areas of the South and West.

FOREIGN AND FRONTIER AFFAIRS

The French Revolution

When revolutionary France went to war with the European powers in 1792, Washington's response was a Proclamation of Neutrality. Citizen Genet violated that policy by trying to encourage popular support in this country for the French government, and embarrassed the president. American merchants traded with both sides, though the most lucrative business was carried on with the French West Indies. This brought retaliation by the British, who began to seize American merchant ships and force their crews into service with the British navy.

Jay's Treaty with Britain (1794)

John Jay negotiated a treaty with the British which attempted to settle the conflict at sea, as well as to curtail English agitation of their Indian allies on the western borders. The agreement actually settled few of the issues and merely bought time for the new nation in the worsening international conflict. Jay was severely criticized for his efforts, and was even hanged in effigy, but the Senate accepted the treaty as the best possible under the circumstances.

The Treaty with Spain (1795)

Thomas Pinckney was invited to the Spanish court to strengthen what Madrid perceived to be her deteriorating position on the American frontier. The result was the Pinckney Treaty, ratified by the Senate in 1796, in which the Spanish opened the Mississippi River to American traffic, including the right of deposit in the port city of New Orleans, and recognized the 31st parallel as the northern boundary of Florida.

Frontier Problems

Indian tribes on the Northwest and Southwest borders were increasingly resisting the encroachments on their lands by the American settlers. British authorities in Canada were encouraging the Indians in their depredations against frontier settlements.

In 1794, General Anthony Wayne decisively defeated the Indians at the Battle of Fallen Timbers, and the resulting Treaty of Greenville cleared the Ohio territory of Indian tribes.

INTERNAL PROBLEMS

The Whiskey Rebellion (1794)

Western farmers refused to pay the excise tax on whiskey which formed the backbone of Hamilton's revenue program. When a group of Pennsylvania farmers terrorized the tax collectors, President Washington sent out a federalized militia force of some 15,000 men, and the rebellion evaporated, thus strengthening the credibility of the young government.

Land Policy

As the original 13 states ceded their Western land claims to the new federal government, new states were organized and admitted to the Union, thus strengthening the ties of the Western farmers to the central government (Vermont, 1791; Kentucky, 1792; and Tennessee, 1796).

JOHN ADAMS' ADMINISTRATION, 1797–1801

The Election of 1796

John Adams was the Federalist candidate, and Thomas Jefferson ran under the opposition banner of the Republicans. John Adams was elected president. Since Jefferson received the second highest number of electoral votes, he became vice-president. Thus, a Federalist president and a Republican vice president served together, an obviously awkward arrangement. Adams was a brilliant lawyer and statesman, but too dogmatic and uncompromising to be an effective politician, and he endured a very frustrating and unproductive term in office.

The XYZ Affair

A three-man delegation was sent to France in 1798 to persuade the French to stop harassing American shipping. When they were solicited for a bribe by three subordinates of the French Minister Talleyrand, they indignantly refused, and their report of this insult produced outrage at home. The cry "millions for defense, but not one cent for tribute" was raised, and public feelings against the French ran high. Since Talleyrand's officials were unnamed in the dispatches, the incident became known as the "XYZ Affair."

Quasi-War, 1798–1799

This uproar moved Adams to suspend all trade with the French, and American ship captains were authorized to attack and capture armed French vessels. Congress created the Department of the Navy, and war seemed imminent. In 1800, the new French government, now under Napoleon, signed a new treaty, and the peace was restored.

REPRESSION AND PROTEST

The Alien and Sedition Acts

The elections in 1798 had increased the Federalists' majorities in both houses of Congress and they used their "mandate" to enact legislation to stifle foreign influences. The Alien Act raised new hurdles in the path of immigrants trying to obtain citizenship, and the Sedition Act widened the powers of the Adams administration to muzzle its newspaper critics. Both bills were aimed at actual or potential Republican opposition, and a number of editors were actually jailed for printing critical editorials.

The Kentucky and Virginia Resolutions

Republican leaders were convinced that the Alien and Sedition Acts were unconstitutional, but the process of deciding on the constitutionality of federal laws was as yet undefined. Jefferson and Madison decided that the state legislatures should have that power, and they drew up a series of resolutions which were presented to the Kentucky and Virginia legislatures, respectively. They proposed that John Locke's "compact theory" be applied, which would empower the state bodies to "nullify" federal laws within those states. These resolutions were adopted, but only in these two states, and so the issue died. A principle, however, had now been set forth which would later bear fruit in the nullification controversy of the 1830s and ultimately in the secession crisis of 1860–61.

THE REVOLUTION OF 1800

The Election

Thomas Jefferson and Aaron Burr ran on the Republican ticket, though not together, against John Adams and Charles Pinckney for the Federalists. All ran for the presidency; the candidate winning the second-highest number of votes would become vice-president. Jefferson and Burr received the same number of electoral votes, so the selection went to the House of Representatives. After a lengthy deadlock, Alexander Hamilton threw his support to Jefferson, and Burr had to accept the vice presidency, the result obviously intended by the electorate. This increased the ill will between Hamilton and Burr and helped set the stage for their famous duel in 1804.

Packing the Judiciary

The Federalist Congress passed a new Judiciary Act early in 1801 and President Adams filled the newly created vacancies with party supporters, many of them with last-minute commissions. John Marshall was then appointed Chief Justice of the U.S. Supreme Court, thus guaranteeing continuation of Federalist policies from the bench of the high court.

THE JEFFERSONIAN ERA

Thomas Jefferson and his Republican followers envisioned a society in vivid contrast to that of Hamilton and the Federalists. They dreamed of a nation of independent farmers, living under a central government that exercised a minimum of control over their lives and served merely to protect the individual liberties guaranteed by the Constitution. This agrarian paradise would be free from the industrial smoke and urban blight of Europe, and would serve as a beacon light of Enlightenment rationalism to a world searching for direction. That vision was to prove a mirage, and Jefferson was to preside over a nation that was growing more industrialized and urban, and which seemed to need an ever stronger hand at the presidential tiller.

The New Federal City

The city of Washington had been designed by Pierre L'Enfant and was briefly occupied by the Adams administration. When Jefferson moved in, it was still a straggling provincial town, with muddy streets and muggy summers. Most of its inhabitants moved out when Congress was not in session.

Jefferson the President

The new president tried to project an image of democratic simplicity,

Lewis and Clark and the Corps of Discovery

—Courtesy U.S. Mint, Philadelphia

Obverse of 2004 Lewis & Clark Bicentennial Silver Dollar shows captains Lewis and Clark on a stream bank, planning another day of exploration.

Napolean's decision to sell the massive Louisiana Purchase to the United States in 1803 provided President Thomas Jefferson with a major challenge: how to determine exactly what was in this vast, largely unexplored region of North America between the Mississippi River and the headwaters of the Missouri River. A British explorer, Alexander Mackenzie, had ventured across Canada and reached the Pacific Coast in 1793, but no European-American had made the trek up the Missouri River, over the Rockies, and then down the Columbia River to the Pacific Ocean.

Soon after the purchase, Jefferson asked the Congress for $2,500, "to send intelligent officers with ten or twelve men, to explore even to the western ocean." While commissioned to study and map the terrain, make contact with the Indian tribes living there, and collect scientific specimens, Jefferson was most interested in the possibility of a Northwest Passage by water to the Pacific. The expedition was also an attempt to gain information about the activities of British and French

cont'd on next page

sometimes appearing so casually dressed as to appear slovenly. But he was a brilliant thinker and a shrewd politician. He appointed men to his Cabinet who agreed with his political philosophy: James Madison as Secretary of State and Albert Gallatin to the Treasury.

CONFLICT WITH THE JUDGES

Marbury vs. Madison

William Marbury, one of Adams' "midnight appointments," sued Secretary of State Madison to force delivery of his commission as a justice of the peace in the federal district. John Marshall, as Supreme Court justice, refused to rule on the request, claiming that the law which gave the Supreme Court jurisdiction over such matters had exceeded the Constitutional grant of powers and thus was unconstitutional. Marshall thus asserted the power of judicial review over federal legislation, a power which has become the foundation of the Supreme Court's check on the other two branches of government.

The Impeachment Episodes

Jefferson began a campaign to remove Federalist judges by impeachment. One district judge was removed, and proceedings were begun to impeach Supreme Court Justice Samuel Chase. That effort failed, but the threat had encouraged the judiciary to be less blatantly political.

fur-trappers, who had been in the area for years.

Jefferson chose Captain Meriwether Lewis as the leader of this Corps of Discovery and Lewis immediately asked an old friend, William Clark, to be his co-commander. While officially still a second lieutenant, Lewis from the start treated Clark as an equal and referred to him as "Captain" with the men of the Corps, which consisted of 33 members. The Corps left from Camp River Dubois, near present-day Hartford, Illinois, on May 14, 1804. They traveled up the Missouri and passed the last white settlement at La Charrette. On August 20, 1804, the Corps of Discovery lost one member, Sergeant Charles Floyd, who apparently died from acute appendicitis. That was their only fatality of the nearly three-year journey. They spent the winter of 1804–1805 at Fort Mandan, in present-day North Dakota. They hired a French Canadian, Toussaint Charbonneau, as a guide. Charbonneau's Shoshone wife, Sacagawea, also accompanied the Corps and proved to be an invaluable guide and source of information. She had a son, Jean Baptiste (or Pomp, as he was called by Clark), who was born just before the expedition left the Mandans. Because the Corps traveled with a woman and a child, the Indian tribes they encountered recognized that this strange group of whites (and one African-American, York, Clark's slave) was not a war party and mostly aided the voyage.

The journey up the Missouri River was difficult because of heat, injuries, mosquitoes, and the river itself, which was difficult to navigate. The Corps employed a keelboat and two smaller boats, called pirogues, on the voyage and averaged 15 miles per day. The expedition followed the Missouri

cont'd on next page

DOMESTIC AFFAIRS

Enforcement of the Alien and Sedition Acts was immediately suspended, and the men convicted under those laws were released.

The federal bureaucracy was reduced and expenses were drastically cut. The size of the army was reduced and the expansion program of the Navy was cancelled.

The excise taxes were repealed and federal income was limited to land sale proceeds and customs duties. Federal land sale policy was liberalized, smaller parcels were authorized, and less cash was required—policies which benefitted small farmers.

The 12th Amendment was adopted and ratified in 1804, ensuring that a tie vote between candidates of the same party could not again cause the confusion of the Jefferson-Burr affair.

Following the Constitutional mandate, the importation of slaves was stopped by law in 1808.

The Louisiana Purchase

Napoleon, in an effort to regain some of France's New World empire, had obtained the old French trans-Mississippi territory from Spain by political pressure. Jefferson sent a delegation to Paris to try to buy New Orleans, lest the new French officials close it to American traffic. Napoleon's defeat in Santo Domingo persuaded him that Louisiana could not be exploited, and indeed was now subject to potential American incursions. So he offered to sell the entire territory to the United States for $15 million. The American delegation

through what are now the states of Missouri, Nebraska, North Dakota, and Montana, where they discovered the Missouri's headwaters. They then crossed the Rocky Mountains and reached the West Coast of North America by paddling down the Clearwater River, the Snake River, and the Columbia River through what is now Oregon until they reached the Pacific Ocean in December 1805. The trip ran into several huge obstacles, such as the need for horses to cross the Rockies, but the expedition was aided in that quest by the chance encounter of Sacagawea with her brother, Kamahweit, and his tribe of Shoshones, from whom she had been kidnapped as a girl years earlier. It was from the Shoshones that the expedition was able to purchase the horses it needed. When the Corps reached the Pacific, they camped on the south side of the Columbia River and built Fort Clatsop near the modern town of Astoria, Oregon. When a hoped-for European ship never showed up during their rain-soaked wait, they started a return trip across the continent on March 23, 1806, and arrived back in St. Louis on September 23.

The Corps of Discovery traveled over 8,000 miles, lost only one member of their party, and cost the government the small sum of $40,000. The Lewis and Clark expedition made a major contribution in mapping a vastly unexplored segment of the North American continent. The journals of Lewis and Clark documented valuable information about the natural history of the area and the Native Americans living there. Hundreds of new plant and animal species were identified. Perhaps most importantly, they focused the attention of the nation on the West and paved the way for the many emigrants who would follow on the Oregon Trail to the Pacific Northwest.

accepted the offer in April 1803, even though they had no authority to buy more than the city of New Orleans.

The Constitutional Dilemma

Jefferson's stand on the strict interpretation of the Constitution would not permit him to purchase land without Congressional approval. But he accepted his advisors' counsel that his treaty-making powers included the authority to buy the land. Congress concurred, after the fact, and the purchase price was appropriated, thus doubling the territory of the nation overnight.

Exploring the West

Even before Napoleon's offer, Jefferson had authorized an expedition to explore the Western territory to the Pacific. The Lewis and Clark group, with 48 men, left St. Louis in 1804, and returned two years later with a wealth of scientific and anthropological information, and having strengthened the United States' claim to the Oregon territory. At the same time, Zebulon Pike and others had been traversing the middle parts of Louisiana and mapping the land.

The Essex Junto (1804)

Some New England Federalists saw the Western expansion as a threat to their position in the Union, and they tried to organize a secessionist movement. They courted Aaron Burr's support by offering to back him in a bid for the governorship of New York. Hamilton led the opposition to that campaign and

The Louisiana Purchase, in 1803, doubled the size of the U.S.

when Burr lost the election, he challenged Hamilton to a duel, which resulted in Hamilton's death.

The Burr Conspiracy

Aaron Burr was now a fugitive, without a political future. He became involved in a scheme to take Mexico from Spain and establish a new nation in the West.

In the fall of 1806, he led a group of armed men down the Mississippi River system toward New Orleans. He was arrested in Natchez and tried for treason in Richmond, Virginia. Judge John Marshall's decision for acquittal helped to narrow the legal definition of treason. Jefferson's attempts to influence and prejudice the trial were justified by his claims of "executive privilege," but they were fruitless.

John Randolph and the Yazoo Claims

Jefferson's Republican opponents, under the leadership of his cousin John Randolph of Roanoke, called themselves the "Quids." They accused the president of complicity in the Yazoo Land controversy which had followed Georgia's cession of her western lands to the federal government. This created serious strife within the Republican party and weakened Jefferson's effectiveness in his second term.

INTERNATIONAL INVOLVEMENT

The Barbary War

In 1801 Jefferson sent a naval force to the Mediterranean to break the practice of the North African Muslim rulers of exacting tribute from Western merchant ships. Intermittent undeclared war dragged on until 1805, with no decisive settlement.

The Napoleonic Wars

War continued in Europe between France under Napoleon and the European powers led by Britain. Both sides tried to prevent trade with their enemies by neutral powers, especially the United States. Napoleon's "Continental System" was answered by Britain's "Orders in Council." American ships were seized by both sides and American sailors were "impressed" into the British navy.

The Chesapeake-Leopard Affair (1807)

The British ship *H.M.S. Leopard* stopped the *U.S.S. Chesapeake* off the Chesapeake Bay, and four alleged British deserters were taken off. Public outcry for war followed, and Jefferson was hard pressed to remain neutral.

The Embargo of 1807

Jefferson's response to the cry for war was to draft a law prohibiting American ships from leaving port for any foreign destination, thus avoiding contact with vessels of either belligerent. The result was economic depression, particularly in the heavily commercial Northeast. This proved to be his most unpopular policy of both terms in office.

MADISON'S ADMINISTRATION, 1809–1817

The Election of 1808

Republican James Madison won the election over Federalist Charles Pinckney, but the Federalists gained seats in both houses of the Congress. The embargo-induced depression was obviously a heavy political liability, and Madison was to face growing pressures to deal with the international crisis. He was a brilliant man but with few social or political skills. His greatest asset was probably his wife, the vivacious and energetic Dolley.

The War of 1812

Congress had passed a modified embargo just before Madison's inauguration, known as the Non-Intercourse Act, which opened trade to all nations except France and Britain. When it expired in 1810, it was replaced by Macon's Bill No. 2, which gave the president power to prohibit trade with any nation that violated our neutrality.

The Indian tribes of the Northwest and the Mississippi Valley were resentful of the government's policy of pressured removal to the West, and the British authorities in Canada were exploiting their discontent by encouraging border raids against the American settlements.

The Shawnee chief Tecumseh set out to unite the Mississippi Valley tribes and reestablish Indian dominance in the Old Northwest. With the help of his brother, the Prophet, and the timely New Madrid earthquake, he persuaded a sizeable force of warriors to join him. On November 11, 1811, General William Henry Harrison destroyed Tecumseh's village on Tippecanoe Creek and dashed his hopes for an Indian confederacy.

Southern frontiersmen coveted Spanish Florida, which included the southern ranges of Alabama, Mississippi and Louisiana. They resented Spanish support of Indian depredations against the borderlands, and since Spain was Britain's ally, they saw Britain as the background cause of their problems.

The Congress in 1811 contained a strong pro-war group called the War Hawks, led by Henry Clay and John C. Calhoun. They gained control of both houses and began agitating for war with the British. On June 1, 1812, President Madison asked for a declaration of war, and Congress complied.

A three-pronged invasion of Canada met with disaster on all three fronts, and the Americans fell back to their own borders. At sea, American privateers and frigates, including "Old Ironsides," scored early victories over British warships, but were soon driven back into their home ports and blockaded by the powerful British ships-of-the-line.

Admiral Oliver Hazard Perry constructed a fleet of ships on Lake Erie and on September 10, 1813, defeated a British force at Put-In Bay and established control of the lake. His flagship flew the banner, "Don't Give Up the Ship." This victory opened the way for William Henry Harrison to invade Canada in October and defeat a combination British and Indian force at the Battle of the Thames.

The War in the Southwest

Andrew Jackson led a force of frontier militia into Alabama in pursuit of Creek Indians who had massacred the white inhabitants of Fort Mims. On March 27, 1814, he crushed the Indians at Horseshoe Bend, and then seized the Spanish garrison at Pensacola.

British Strategy Changes, 1814

A British force came down Lake Champlain and met defeat at Plattsburgh, New York, in September. A British armada sailed up the Chesapeake Bay and sacked and burned Washington, D.C. It then proceeded toward Baltimore, which was guarded by Fort McHenry. That fort held firm through the British bombardment, inspiring Key's "Star Spangled Banner."

The Battle of New Orleans

The most serious British threat came at the port of New Orleans. A powerful invasion force was sent there to close the mouth of the Mississippi River, but Andrew Jackson decisively defeated it with a polyglot army of frontiersmen, blacks, creoles and pirates. The battle was fought on January 8, 1815, two weeks after a peace treaty had been signed at the city of Ghent, in Belgium.

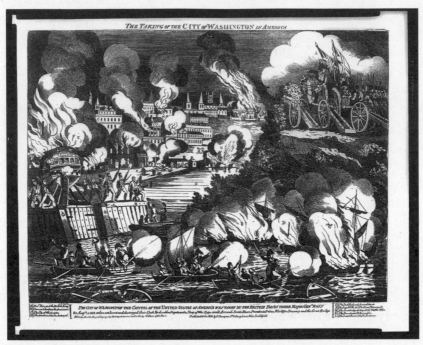

The War of 1812 forced the President and the Congress to flee from Washington as the British set public buildings ablaze. From Reginald Horsman, *The War of 1812*, 1969, London, Eyre & Spottiswoode Ltd.

The Treaty of Ghent, Christmas Eve, 1814

With the European wars ended, the major causes for the dispute with Britain had ceased to be important, so both sides were eager for peace. The treaty provided for the acceptance of the status quo at the beginning of hostilities and so both sides restored their wartime conquests to the other.

The Hartford Convention, December 1814

The Federalists had become increasingly a minority party. They vehemently opposed the war and Daniel Webster and other New England congressmen consistently blocked the Administration's efforts to prosecute the war effort. On December 15, 1814, delegates from the New England states met in Hartford, Connecticut, and drafted a set of resolutions suggesting nullification—and even secession—if their interests were not protected against the growing influence of the South and the West.

Soon after the convention adjourned the news of the victory at New Orleans was announced and their actions were discredited. The Federalist party ceased to be a political force from this point on.

POSTWAR DEVELOPMENTS

Protective Tariff (1816)

The first protective tariff in the nation's history was passed in 1816 to slow the flood of cheap British manufactures into the country.

Rush-Bagot Treaty (1817)

An agreement was reached in 1817 between Britain and the United States to stop maintaining armed fleets on the Great Lakes. This first "disarmament" agreement is still in effect.

Jackson's Florida Invasion (1817)

Indian troubles in the newly acquired areas of western Florida prompted General Andrew Jackson, acting under dubious authority, to invade Spanish East Florida and to hang two British subjects whom he suspected of selling guns and supplies to the Indians. Then he reoccupied Pensacola and raised the American flag, a clear violation of international law. Only wide public support prevented his arrest and prosecution by the government.

Indian Policy

The government began to systematically pressure all the Indian tribes remaining in the East to cede their lands and accept new homes west of the Mississippi, a policy which met with disappointing results. Most declined the offer.

The Barbary Wars (1815)

In response to continued piracy and extortion in the Mediterranean, Congress declared war on the Muslim state of Algiers in 1815, and dispatched a naval force to the area under Stephen Decatur. He quickly defeated the North African pirates and forced them to pay indemnities for past tribute they had exacted from American ship captains. This action finally gained the United States free access to the Mediterranean basin.

The Adams-Onis Treaty (1819)

Spain had decided to sell the remainder of the Florida territory to the Americans before they took it anyway. Under this agreement, the Spanish surrendered all their claims to the territory and drew the boundary of Mexico all the way to the Pacific. The United States in exchange agreed to assume $5 million in debts owed to American merchants.

The Monroe Doctrine

Around 1810, national revolutions had begun in Latin America, so the colonial populations refused to accept the rule of the new Napoleonic governments in Europe. Leaders like San Martin and Bolivar had declared independence for their countries and, after Napoleon's fall in 1814, were defying the restored Hapsburg and Bourbon rulers of Europe.

British and American leaders feared that the new European governments would try to restore the former New World colonies to their erstwhile royal owners.

In December 1823, President Monroe included in his annual message to Congress a statement that the American hemisphere was "henceforth not to be considered as subjects for future colonization by any European powers." Thus began a thirty-year period of freedom from serious foreign involvement for the United States.

INTERNAL DEVELOPMENT, 1820–1830

The years following the War of 1812 were years of rapid economic and social development. Too rapid, in fact, and they were followed by a severe depression in 1819. But this slump was temporary, and it became obvious that the country was moving rapidly from its agrarian origins toward an industrial, urban future. Westward expansion accelerated, and the mood of the people became very positive. In fact, these years were referred to as the "Era of Good Feelings."

The Monroe Presidency, 1817–1825

James Monroe, the last of the "Virginia Dynasty," had been hand-picked by the retiring Madison and he was elected with only one electoral vote opposed: a symbol of national unity.

Postwar Boom

The years following the war were characterized by a high foreign demand for American cotton, grain and tobacco; commerce flourished. The Second National Bank, through its overly liberal credit policies, proved to be an inflationary influence, and the price level rose rapidly.

The Depression of 1819

Inventories of British manufactured goods had built up during the war, and English merchants began to dump their products on the American market at cut-rate prices. American manufacturers suffered from this influx of imports. The U.S. Bank tried to slow the inflationary spiral by tightening credit, and a sharp business slump resulted.

This depression was most severe in the newly expanding West, partly because of its economic dependency, partly because of heavy speculation in Western lands.

THE MARSHALL COURT

John Marshall delivered the majority opinions in a number of critical decisions in these formative years, all of which served to strengthen the power of the federal government and restrict the powers of state governments.

Marbury v. Madison (1803)

This case established the Supreme Court's power of judicial review over federal legislation.

Fletcher v. Peck (1810)

The Georgia legislature had issued extensive land grants in a shady deal with the Yazoo Land Company. A subsequent legislative session repealed that action because of the corruption that had attended the original grant. The Court decided that the original action by the Georgia Assembly had constituted a valid contract which could not be broken regardless of the corruption which had followed. This was the first time a state law was voided on the grounds that it violated a principle of the U.S. Constitution.

Dartmouth College v. Woodward (1819)

The quarrel between the president and the trustees of the New Hampshire college became a political issue when the Republicans backed the president and the Federalists supported the trustees. The president tried to change Dartmouth from a private to a public institution by having its charter revoked. The Court ruled that the charter, though issued by the king during colonial days, still constituted a contract, and thus could not be arbitrarily changed or revoked without the consent of both parties. The result of this decision was to severely limit the power of state governments to control the corporation, which was the emerging form of business organization.

McCulloch v. Maryland (1819)

The state of Maryland had tried to levy a tax on the Baltimore branch of the Bank of the United States, and so protect the competitive position of its own state banks. Marshall's ruling declared that no state has the right to control an agency of the federal government. Since "the power to tax is the power to destroy," such state action violated Congress' "implied powers" to establish and operate a national bank.

Gibbons v. Ogden (1824)

The State of New York had granted a monopoly to Ogden to operate a steamboat between New York and New Jersey. Gibbons obtained a Congressional permit to operate a steamboat line in the same waters. When Ogden sued to maintain his monopoly, the New York courts ruled in his favor. Gibbons' appeal went to the Supreme Court. John Marshall ruled that commerce included navigation, and that only Congress has the right to regulate commerce among states. Thus the state-granted monopoly was void.

STATEHOOD: A BALANCING ACT

The Missouri Compromise (1820)

The Missouri Territory, the first to be organized from the Louisiana Purchase, applied for statehood in 1819. Since the Senate membership was evenly divided between slave-holding and free states at that time, the admission of a new state was obviously going to give the voting advantage either to the North or to the South. Slavery was already well-established in the new territory, so the Southern states were confident in their advantage, until Representative Tallmadge of New York proposed an amendment to the bill which would prohibit slavery in Missouri.

The Southern outcry was immediate, and the ensuing debate grew hot. The Senate was dead-locked.

Henry Clay's Compromise Solution

As the debate dragged on, the northern territory of Massachusetts applied for admission as the state of Maine. This offered a way out of the dilemma, and House Speaker Clay formulated a package that both sides could accept. The two admission bills were combined, with Maine coming in free and

Missouri as a slave state. To make the package palatable for the House, a provision was added to prohibit slavery in the remainder of the Louisiana Territory, north of the southern boundary of Missouri (latitude 36° 30'). Clay guided this bill through the House and it became law, thus maintaining the balance of power.

The debates in Congress had reminded everyone of the deep division between the sections, and some saw it as evidence of trouble to come. Thomas Jefferson, in retirement at Monticello, remarked that the news from Washington was like a "fire-ball in the night."

THE EXPANDING ECONOMY

The Growing Population

Population continued to double every 25 years. The migration of people to the West increased in volume and by 1840 over one-third of all Americans lived west of the Alleghenies. Immigration from abroad was not significant until 1820; then it began to increase rapidly, mostly from the British Isles.

The Farming Sector

The growth of markets for farm products in the expanding cities, coupled with liberal land sale policies by the federal government, made the growing of staple agricultural crops more profitable. More and more land was put into cultivation, and the prevailing system of clearing and planting became more wasteful of timber as well as of the fertility of the land.

The Cotton Kingdom

The new lands in the Southwest, then constituting Alabama, Mississippi, Louisiana and Texas, proved ideal for the production of short-staple cotton. Eli Whitney's invention of the cotton gin solved the problem of separating the seeds from the fibers, and the cotton boom was under way.

The growing market for food and work animals in the cotton South provided the opportunity for the new Western farmers to specialize in those items and further stimulated the westward movement.

Fishing

New England and Chesapeake fishing proved very profitable. Deep-sea whaling became a significant enterprise, particularly from the Massachusetts/ Rhode Island ports.

Lumbering

The expanding population created a need for building materials, and timber remained a profitable export item. Shipbuilding thrived in a number of Eastern Seaboard and Gulf Coast ports.

Fur Trade

John Jacob Astor and others opened up business all the way to the Northwest coast. "Mountain men" probed deeper and deeper into the Rocky Mountain ranges in search of the beaver.

Trade with the Spanish

The Santa Fe Trail, which ran from New Mexico northeast to Independence, Missouri, became an active trading corridor, opening up the Spanish territories to American migration and influence, and also providing the basis for future territorial claims.

THE TRANSPORTATION REVOLUTION

The first half of the 19th century witnessed an extraordinary sequence of inventions and innovations which produced a true revolution in transport and communications.

River Traffic

The steamboats built by Robert Fulton, the *Clermont* in 1807 and the *New Orleans* in 1811, transformed river transport. As shipment times and freight rates both plummeted, regular steam service was established on all the major river systems.

Road Building

By 1818, the National Road, which was built with federal funds, had been completed from Cumberland, Maryland, to Wheeling, Virginia, linking the Potomac with the Ohio River. A network of privately owned toll roads (turnpikes) began to reach out from every sizeable city. They were usually built for only a few miles out, and they never accounted for a significant share of the total freight tonnage moved, but they formed the nucleus of a growing road system in the new nation.

The Canal Era

The Erie Canal, linking the Hudson River at Albany, New York, with Lake Erie, was completed in 1825 and became the first and most successful example of an artificial waterway. It was followed by a rash of construction until canals linked every major waterway system east of the Mississippi River.

Canals were the first development projects to receive large amounts of public funding. They ran east-west and so tied the new West to the old East, with later implications for sectional divisions.

The Rise of New York City

Its location as a transport hub, coupled with innovations in business practices, boosted New York City into a primary trade center, and made it America's largest city by 1830. One such innovation was the packet boats, which operated on a guaranteed schedule and helped to rationalize commerce, both internal and international.

New York soon dominated the domestic market for cotton, a situation which progressively reduced the South to the status of an economic colony.

INDUSTRIALIZATION

The Rise of the Factory System

Samuel Slater had migrated from Britain in 1789, having served as an apprentice under inventor Richard Arkwright and then as a mill manager. He used his knowledge to build the first successful cotton-spinning mill in this country. The first cotton manufacturing plant in the world to include all the elements of manufacturing under one roof was built in Boston in 1813.

Eli Whitney's development and application of the principle of interchangeable parts, first used in his firearms factories, helped to speed the growth of mass-production operations.

The expansion of markets in Latin America and the Far East, as well as domestic markets, both resulted from and helped to develop the factory system.

Manufacturers and industrialists found it necessary to organize banks, insurance companies, and real estate firms to meet the needs of their growing business organizations.

The Corporation

The corporate form, with its limited liability and its potential for raising and utilizing large amounts of capital, became the typical type of business organization. By the 1830s, most states had enacted general laws for incorporating.

The Labor Supply

In the early days, the "Lowell System" became a popular way to staff the New England factories. Young women were hired from the surrounding countryside, brought to town and housed in dormitories in the mill towns. They were paid low wages for hard work under poor conditions, but they were only working for a short time, to earn a dowry or help out with the family income, so they soon went back home. This "rotating labor supply" was ideal for the owners, since the girls were not motivated to agitate for better wages and conditions.

Labor was always in short supply in this country, so the system depended on technology to increase production. This situation always placed a premium on innovation in machinery and technique.

The Growth of Unions

The factory system separated the owners from the workers and thus depersonalized the workplace. It also made the skilled artisan less important, since the repetitive processes of the mill could be performed by relatively unskilled laborers.

Although the first organized strike took place in 1828, in Paterson, New Jersey, by child workers, periodic economic downturns helped keep workers relatively dependent and passive until the 1850s.

A major goal of early unions was the 10-hour day, and this effort sparked a period of growth in organized labor which was later effectively quenched by the depression of 1837.

EDUCATIONAL DEVELOPMENT

The Growth of Public Schools

Before 1815, there were no public schools to speak of in this country. Some states had endorsed the idea of free schools for the people, but they shrank from the task of financing such a system. Jefferson had outlined such a plan for Virginia, but it came to nothing.

Schools were primarily sponsored by private institutions—corporate academies in the Northeast and religious institutions in the South and mid-Atlantic states. Most were aristocratic in orientation, training the nation's leaders, and few had any interest in schooling the children of the poor.

Women were likewise considered unfit for academic training, and those female schools which existed concentrated on homemaking skills and the fine arts which would make "ornaments" of the young ladies enrolled.

The New York Free School, one of those rare examples of a school for the poor, experimented for a time with the Lancastrian system, in which older students tutored the younger ones, thus stretching scarce budget dollars.

Higher Education

Although the numbers of institutions of higher learning increased sharply in the early years of the nineteenth century, none was truly public. All relied upon high tuition rates for survival, so less than one in ten young men, and no women, ever attended a college or university.

The training these schools provided was very limited as well. The only professional training was in theology, and only a scattering of colleges offered brief courses of study in law or medicine. The University of Pennsylvania, for example, offered one year of medical schooling, after which a person could obtain a license to practice the healing arts. Needless to say, medical practice was quite primitive.

The Growth of Cultural Nationalism

Jeffersonian Americans tried to demonstrate their newly-won independence by championing a strong sense of cultural nationalism, a feeling that their young republic represented the "final stage" of civilization, the "last great hope of mankind."

Literary Nationalism

Although most Americans had access to one or more newspapers, the market for native authors was quite limited. Publishers preferred to print works from British authors or to import books from Europe. A few Americans who were willing to pay the costs of publishing their own works found a growing number of readers.

Significant American Authors

Washington Irving was by far the best-known native writer in America. He excelled in the telling of folk tales and local color stories, and is best remembered for his portraits of Hudson River characters.

Mercy Otis Warren, the revolutionary pamphleteer, published a multivolume *History of the Revolution* in 1805.

"Parson" Mason Weems wrote the best-seller *Life of Washington* in 1806, which was short on historical accuracy but long on nationalistic hero-worship.

Educational Literature

Early schoolbooks, like Noah Webster's *Blue Backed Speller*, as well as his dictionary of the "American" language, reflected the intense desire to promote patriotism and a feeling of national identity.

DEVELOPMENTS IN RELIGIOUS LIFE

The Post-Revolution Years

The Revolutionary War weakened the position of the traditional, established churches. The doctrines of the Enlightenment became very popular, and its religious expression, deism, gained a considerable following among the educated classes. Rationalism, Unitarianism, and Universalism all saw a period of popularity. Thomas Paine's exposition of the rationalist posture, *The Age of Reason*, attacked the traditional Christian values and was read widely.

The Second Great Awakening

The reaction to the trend toward rationalism, the decline in church membership, and the lack of piety, was a renewal of personal, heart-felt evangelicalism. A second Great Awakening began in 1801 at Cane Ridge, Kentucky, in the first "camp meeting."

As the revival spread, its characteristics became more uniform—an emphasis on personal salvation, an emotional response to God's grace, an individualistic

**Lithograph of a religious revival meeting in a western forest.
Lippincott, Grambo & Co., 1854. U.S. Library of Congress.**

faith. Women took a major part in the movement. Blacks were also heavily involved, and the individualistic emphasis created unrest among their ranks, particularly in the slave-holding South.

The revival produced strong nationalistic overtones, and the Protestant ideas of a "called nation" were to flourish later in some of the Manifest Destiny doctrines of expansionism. The social overtones of this religious renewal were to spark the great reform movements of the 1830s and 1840s.

◄───── HISTORICAL TIMELINE ─────►
The New Nation (1789–1824)

1789	Judiciary Act sets up federal court system
1791	Bill of Rights approved First Bank of United States chartered
1793	Washington issues Proclamation of Neutrality Louis XVI executed in France Cotton gin patented by Eli Whitney
1794	Whiskey Rebellion
1795	Jay Treaty Pinckney Treaty Treaty of Greenville
1796	Adams defeats Jefferson for presidency
1798	XYZ Affair Alien and Sedition Acts Virginia and Kentucky Resolutions
1800	Jefferson defeats Adams for presidency Prosser's Rebellion
1801	John Marshall becomes Chief Justice Midnight judges appointed by Adams
1803	*Marbury v. Madison* decision Louisiana Purchase
1804	Lewis and Clark Expedition
1807	Chesapeake-Leopard incident Embargo Act Robert Fulton builds *Clermont*, first steamboat
1811	Battle of Tippecanoe
1812	Congress declares war on Britain

1814	British burn Washington, D.C. Treaty of Ghent ends War of 1812 Hartford Convention
1815	Jackson defeats British at New Orleans
1819	First section of Erie Canal is opened Panic of 1819 *McCullough v. Maryland* decision
1820	Missouri Compromise
1823	Monroe Doctrine
1824	Congress sets protective tariffs *Gibbons v. Ogden* decision promotes interstate trade

Chapter 6

JACKSONIAN DEMOCRACY AND WESTWARD EXPANSION (1824–1850)

THE JACKSONIAN DEMOCRACY, 1829–1841

While the "Age of Jackson" did not bring perfect political, social or economic equality to all Americans, it did mark a transformation in the political life of the nation that attracted the notice of European travelers and observers. Alexis de Tocqueville observed an "equality of condition" here that existed nowhere else in the world, and an egalitarian spirit among the people that was unique. Certainly the electorate had become broadened so that all white males had access to the polls, even if blacks and women were still outside the system. It was, in that sense, the "age of the common man." As to whether Andrew Jackson and his party were actually working for the good of those common men is another matter.

THE ELECTION OF 1824

The Expansion of the Electorate

Most states had already eliminated the property qualifications for voting before the campaigns for this election began. The new Massachusetts state constitution of 1820 had led the way in this liberalization of the franchise, and most Northern states followed soon after, usually with some conservative opposition, but not violent reactions. In Rhode Island, Thomas Dorr led a bloodless "rebellion" in an effort to expand the franchise in that state, and though he was briefly imprisoned for his efforts, the incident led the conservative legislature to relent and grant the vote to non-property owners. The movement for reform was much slower in the Southern states.

Free blacks were excluded from the polls across the South, and in most of the Northern states. In those areas where they had held the franchise, they were gradually excluded from the social and economic mainstream—as well as from the political arena—in the early years of this period.

National elections had never attracted much enthusiasm until 1824. Legislative caucuses had made the presidential nominations and kept the ruling cliques in power by excluding the voters from the process. But this year the system failed, and the caucuses were bypassed.

The members of the electoral college were now being almost universally elected by the people, rather than by the state legislatures, as in the early days.

The Candidates

Secretary of the Treasury William H. Crawford of Georgia was the pick of the Congressional caucus. Secretary of State John Quincy Adams held the job which traditionally had been the stepping-stone to the executive office. Speaker of the House Henry Clay presented the only coherent program to the voters, the "American System," which provided a high tariff on imports to finance an extensive internal improvement package. Andrew Jackson of Tennessee presented himself as a war hero from the 1812 conflict. All four candidates claimed to be Republicans.

The Election

Jackson won 43 percent of the popular vote, but the four-way split meant that he only received 38 percent of the electoral votes. Under the provisions of the 12th Amendment, the top three candidates were voted on by the House of Representatives. This left Henry Clay out of the running, and he threw his support to Adams. The votes had no sooner been counted when the new president, Adams, appointed Henry Clay his Secretary of State.

Andrew Jackson and his supporters immediately cried "foul!" and accused Clay of making a deal for his vote. The rallying cry of "corrupt bargain" became the impetus for their immediate initiation of the campaign for the 1828 election.

The Adams Administration

The new president pushed for an active federal government in areas like internal improvements and Native American affairs. These policies proved unpopular in an age of increasing sectional jealousies and conflicts over states' rights.

Adams was frustrated at every turn by his Jacksonian opposition, and his unwillingness, or inability, to compromise further antagonized his political enemies. For example, his refusal to endorse and enforce the Creek Native Americans' land cession to the state of Georgia was negated by their re-cession of their lands under pressure from Georgia's Jacksonian government.

John C. Calhoun and Nullification

In 1828, Congress passed a new tariff bill which was originally supported by Southern congressmen in order to embarrass the administration. The finished bill, however, included higher import duties for many goods which were bought by Southern planters, so they bitterly denounced the law as the "Tariff of Abominations."

John C. Calhoun was serving as Adams' vice president, so to protest the tariff and still protect his position, he anonymously published the "South Carolina Exposition and Protest," which outlined his theory of the "concurrent majority"; that a federal law which was deemed harmful to the interests of an individual state could be declared null and void within that state by a convention of the people. Thus, a state holding a minority position could ignore a law enacted by the majority which they considered unconstitutional (shades of Thomas Jefferson).

The Election of 1828

Adams' supporters now called themselves the National Republicans, and Jackson's party ran as the Democratic Republicans. Andrew Jackson had aggressively campaigned since his defeat in the House in 1825.

It was a dirty campaign. Adams' people accused Jackson of adultery and of the murder of several militiamen who had been executed for desertion during the War of 1812. Jackson's followers in turn defamed Adams and his programs and accused him of extravagance with public funds.

When the votes were counted, Jackson had won 56 percent of the popular vote and swept 178 of the 261 electoral votes. John C. Calhoun was elected vice president.

Andrew Jackson as President

Jackson was popular with the common man. He seemed to be the prototype of the self-made Westerner: rough-hewn, violent, vindictive, with few ideas but strong convictions. He ignored his appointed Cabinet officers and relied instead

Andrew Jackson's Inauguration, March 4, 1829. U.S. Library of Congress.

on the counsel of his "Kitchen Cabinet," a group of partisan supporters who had the ear and the confidence of the president.

Jackson expressed the conviction that government operations could be performed by untrained, common folk, and he threatened the dismissal of large numbers of government employees, to replace them with his supporters. Actually, he talked more about this "spoils system" than he acted on it.

He exercised his veto power more than any other president before him. A famous example was the Maysville Road, a project in Kentucky which would require a federal subsidy. Jackson opposed it because it would exist only within the boundaries of a single state.

Jacksonian Indian Policy

Jackson supported the removal of all Indian tribes to west of the Mississippi River. The Indian Removal Act in 1830 provided for federal enforcement of that process.

The portion of the Cherokee Nation which occupied northern Georgia claimed to be a sovereign political entity within the boundaries of that state. The Supreme Court supported that claim in its decision in *Worcester v. Georgia* (1832), but President Jackson refused to enforce the court's decision.

The result of this policy was the Trail of Tears, the forced march, under U.S. Army escort, of thousands of Cherokees to the West. A quarter or more of the Indians, mostly women and children, perished on the journey.

THE WEBSTER-HAYNE DEBATE (1830)

Federal Land Policy

The method of disposing of government land raised sectional differences. Westerners wanted cheap lands available to the masses. Northeasterners opposed this policy because it would lure away their labor supply and drive up wages. Southerners supported the West, hoping to weaken the ties between East and West.

The Senate Confrontation

Senator Robert Hayne of South Carolina made a speech in support of cheap land and he used Calhoun's anti-tariff arguments to support his position. In his remarks, he referred to the possibility of nullification.

Daniel Webster's famous replies to this argument moved the debate from the issue of land policy to the nature of the Union and states' rights within it. Webster argued for the Union as indissoluble and sovereign over the individual states. His concluding statements have become a part of our rhetorical heritage: "It is, Sir, the people's Constitution, the people's government, made for the people, made by the people, and answerable to the people....Liberty and Union, now and for ever, one and inseparable!"

The Second Nullification Crisis

The final split between Andrew Jackson and his vice president, John C. Calhoun, came over the new Tariff of 1832, and over Mrs. Calhoun's snub of Peggy Eaton, the wife of Secretary of War John Eaton.

Mrs. Eaton was a commoner, and the aristocratic Mrs. Calhoun refused to include her on the guest lists for the Washington parties. Jackson, no doubt remembering the slights to his own dear Rachel, defended his friends Peggy and John, and demanded that they be included in the social life of the capital.

Jackson was a defender of states' rights, but within the context of a dominant Union. When he supported the higher rates of the new tariff, Calhoun resigned his office in a huff and went home to South Carolina. There he composed an Ordinance of Nullification, which was duly approved by a special convention, and the customs officials were ordered to stop collecting the duties at the port of Charleston.

Jackson's response was immediate and decisive. He obtained a Force Bill from Congress (1833), which empowered him to use federal troops to enforce the collection of the taxes. And he suggested the possibility of hanging Calhoun.

At the same time, he offered a gradual reduction in the levels of the duties. Calhoun backed down, both sides claimed victory, and the crisis was averted.

THE WAR ON THE BANK

The Controversy

The Bank of the United States had operated under the direction of Nicholas Biddle since 1823. He was a cautious man, and his conservative economic policy enforced conservatism among the state and private banks—which many bankers resented. Many of the Bank's enemies opposed it simply because it was big and powerful. Many still disputed its constitutionality.

The Election of 1832

Andrew Jackson freely voiced his antagonism toward the Bank and his intention to destroy it. During the campaign for the presidency in 1832, Henry Clay and Daniel Webster promoted a bill to recharter the Bank, even though its charter did not expire until 1836. They feared that Jackson would gain support over time and could kill the Bank as a parting shot as he retired. The Congress passed the recharter bill, but Jackson vetoed it. This left that institution a lame duck agency.

Jackson soundly defeated Henry Clay in the presidential race and he considered his victory a mandate from the people to destroy the Bank. His first move was to remove the federal government's deposits from Biddle's vaults and distribute the funds to various state and local banks, called by his critics the "pet banks." Biddle responded by tightening up on credit and calling in loans, hoping to embarrass the government and force a withdrawal by Jackson. Jackson stood firm and the result was a financial recession.

The Panic of 1837

When Biddle was forced to relent through pressure from business interests, the economy immediately rebounded. With credit policies relaxed, inflation began to pick up. The government contributed to this expansion by offering millions of acres of western land for sale to settlers at low prices.

In 1836, Jackson ordered a distribution of surplus funds and thus helped to further fuel the inflationary rise in prices. Finally, even Jackson recognized the danger, and tried to slow the spiral by issuing the Specie Circular, which required payment for public land in hard money; no more paper or credit. Depression quickly followed this move.

The business recession lasted well into the 1840s. Our national economy was by this time so tied in with international business and finance that the downturn affected the entire Atlantic community, and was in turn worsened by the global impact. But most Americans blamed everyone in power, including Jackson, and our institutions and business practices. This disillusionment helped to initiate and intensify the reform movement which so occupied this nation in the 19th century's second quarter.

The Election of 1836

Jackson had handpicked his Democratic successor, Martin Van Buren of New York. The Whigs ran three regional candidates in hopes of upsetting the Jacksonians. The Whig Party had emerged from the ruins of the National Republicans and other groups who opposed Jackson's policies. The name was taken from the British Whig tradition, which simply refers to the "opposition."

Van Buren's Presidency

Van Buren, known as Old Kinderhook (O.K.), inherited all the problems and resentments generated by his mentor. He spent most of his term in office dealing with the financial chaos left by the death of the Second Bank. The best he could do was to eventually persuade Congress to establish an Independent Treasury to handle government funds. It began functioning in 1840.

THE ELECTION OF 1840

The Candidates

The Whigs nominated William Henry Harrison, "Old Tippecanoe," Western Indian fighter. Their choice for vice president was John Tyler, a former Democrat from Virginia. The Democrats put up Van Buren again, but they could not agree on a vice presidential candidate, so they ran no one.

The Campaign

This election saw the largest voter turnout to date. The campaign was a dramatic one. The Whigs stressed the depression and the opulent lifestyle of the incumbent in contrast to the simple "log cabin" origins of their candidate.

Harrison won a narrow popular victory, but swept 80 percent of the electoral vote. Unfortunately for the Whigs, President Harrison died only a month after the inauguration, having served the shortest term in presidential history.

THE MEANING OF JACKSONIAN POLITICS

The Party System

The Age of Jackson was the beginning of the modern party system. Popular politics, based on emotional appeal, became the accepted style. The practice of meeting in mass conventions to nominate national candidates for office was established during these Jackson years.

The Strong Executive

Jackson, more than any president before him, used his office to dominate his party and the government to such an extent that he was called "King Andrew" by his critics.

The Changing Emphasis Towards States' Rights

Andrew Jackson supported the authority of the states against the national government, but he drew the line at the concept of nullification. He advocated a strong union made up of sovereign states, and this created some dissonance in his political thinking.

The Supreme Court reflected this shift in thinking in its decision on the *Charles River Bridge* case in 1837, delivered by Jackson's new Chief Justice, Roger Taney. He ruled that a state could abrogate a grant of monopoly if that original grant had ceased to be in the best interests of the community. This was clearly a reversal of the *Dartmouth College* principle of the sanctity of contracts, in a case where the general welfare was perceived as being involved.

Party Philosophies

The Democrats opposed big government and the requirements of modernization: urbanization and industrialization. Their support came from the working classes, small merchants, and small farmers.

The Whigs promoted government participation in commercial and industrial development, the encouragement of banking and corporations, and a cautious approach to westward expansion. Their support came largely from Northern business and manufacturing interests, and from large Southern planters. Calhoun, Clay, and Webster dominated the Whig party during these early decades of the nineteenth century.

Tocqueville's Democracy in America

Alexis de Tocqueville, a French civil servant, traveled to this country in the early 1830s to study the American prison system, which was one of the more innovative systems in the world. His book, *Democracy in America*, published in 1835, was the result of his observations, and it reflected a broad interest in the entire spectrum of the American democratic process and the society in which it had developed. His insightful commentary on the American way of life has proven to be almost prophetic in many respects, and provides the modern reader with an outsider's objective view of what this country was like in the Age of Jackson.

ANTE-BELLUM CULTURE: AN AGE OF REFORM

The American people in 1840 found themselves living in an era of transition and instability. The society was changing and traditional values were being challenged. The responses to this uncertainty were two-fold: a movement toward reform and a rising desire for order and control.

We have a fairly vivid picture of what Americans were like in this period of time, from accounts by hundreds of foreign visitors who came to this country to observe our society-in-the-making. These observers noted a restless population, always on the move, compulsive joiners of associations, committed to progress, hard-working and hard-playing, driven relentlessly by a desire for wealth. They believed in and talked about equality, but the reality was that the system was increasingly creating a class society. Americans seemed to lean toward violence, and mob incidents were common.

The Reform Impulse: Major Sources of Reform

Romanticism held a belief in the innate goodness of man, thus in his improvability. This movement had its roots in turn-of-the-century Europe, and it emphasized the emotions and feelings over rationality. It appeared as a reaction against the excesses of the Enlightenment which had put strong emphasis on reason, to the exclusion of feelings.

There was also a growing need perceived for a stable social order, and control over the forces which were threatening the traditional values.

Both of these major streams of reform activity were centered in the Northeast, especially in New England.

THE FLOWERING OF LITERATURE
Northern Writers and Themes

James Fenimore Cooper's *Leatherstocking Tales* emphasized the independence of the individual, and also the importance of a stable social order.

Walt Whitman's *Leaves of Grass* likewise celebrated the importance of individualism.

Henry Wadsworth Longfellow's epic poems *Evangeline* and *Hiawatha* spoke of the value of tradition, and the impact of the past on the present.

Herman Melville's classic stories—*Typee, Billy Budd, Moby Dick*—all lashed out at the popular optimism of his day. He believed in the Puritan doctrine of original sin and his characters spoke of the mystery of life.

Historian and nationalist Francis Parkman vividly portrayed the struggle for empire between France and Britain in his *Montcalm and Wolfe. The Oregon Trail* described the opening frontier of the Rocky Mountains and beyond.

James Russell Lowell, poet and editor, wrote the *Bigelow Papers* and the *Commemoration Ode*, honoring Civil War casualties of Harvard.

A writer of romances and tales, Nathaniel Hawthorne is best remembered for his criticism of Puritan bigotry in *The Scarlet Letter*.

Southern Writers and Themes

Author of *The Raven, Tamerlane* and many tales of terror and darkness, Edgar Allan Poe explored the world of the spirit and the emotions.

South Carolina poet William Gilmore Simms changed from a staunch nationalist to a defender of the slave system and the uniqueness of the Southern way of life.

A Georgia storyteller, Augustus Longstreet used vulgar, earthy language and themes to paint the common folk of the South.

THE FINE ARTS

Artists and Themes

The Hudson River School was a group of landscape painters who portrayed the awesomeness of nature in America, the new world. George Catlin painted the American Indian, whom he saw as a vanishing race. John James Audubon painted the wide array of American birds and animals.

Music and the Theatre

The theatre was popular, but generally condemned by the church and conservatives as a "vagabond profession." The only original American contribution was the blackface minstrel show.

THE TRANSCENDENTALISTS

Major Themes

This movement had its origins in Concord, Massachusetts. The basic objective of these thinkers was to transcend the bounds of the intellect and to strive for emotional understanding, to attain unity with God, without the help of the institutional church, which they saw as reactionary and stifling to self-expression.

Major Writers

Ralph Waldo Emerson, essayist and lecturer, authored "Nature" and "Self-Reliance." Henry David Thoreau, best known for his *Walden*, repudiated the repression of society, and preached civil disobedience to protest unjust laws.

THE UTOPIANS

Their Purpose

The cooperative community was their attempt to improve the life of the common man in the face of increasing impersonal industrialism.

The Utopian Communities

Brook Farm, in Massachusetts, was the earliest commune in America, and it was short-lived. Nathaniel Hawthorne was a short-term resident, and his *Blithedale Romance* was drawn from that experience. This work and *The Scarlet Letter* were both condemnations of the life of social isolation.

New Harmony, Indiana, was founded by Robert Owen, of the New Lanark experiment in Wales, but it failed after two years. He attacked religion, marriage, and the institution of private property, so he encountered resistance from neighboring communities.

Nashoba was in the environs of Memphis, Tennessee, established by the free thinking Englishwoman Frances Wright as a communal haven for freed slaves. Needless to say, her community experiment encountered fierce opposition from her slaveholding neighbors and it survived only briefly.

Oneida Community in New York was based on free love and open marriages.

The Shakers were directed by Mother Ann Lee. The communities were socialistic experiments which practiced celibacy, sexual equality and social discipline. The name was given them by onlookers at their community dancing sessions.

Amana Community, in Iowa, was another socialist experiment, with a rigidly ordered society.

THE MORMONS
The Origins of the Religion

Joseph Smith received the "sacred" writings in New York state in 1830, and organized the Church of Jesus Christ of Latter Day Saints. They were not popular with their neighbors, primarily because of their practice of polygamy, and so were forced to move about, first to Missouri, then to Nauvoo, Illinois. There Smith was killed by a mob, and in 1847 the community was led to the valley of the Great Salt Lake by their new leader, Brigham Young, in one of the great epic migrations to the West.

The Church

They established a highly organized, centrally controlled system, which provided security and order for the faithful. They held a strong belief in human perfectability, and so were in the mainstream of romantic utopians.

REMAKING SOCIETY: ORGANIZED REFORM
Sources of Inspiration

Transcendentalism, as a branch of European Romanticism, spawned a great deal of interest in remaking society into more humane forms.

Protestant Revivalism was a powerful force for the improvement of society. Evangelist Charles G. Finney, through his "social gospel," offered salvation to all. A strong sectarian spirit split the Protestant movement into many groups (e.g., the Cumberland Presbyterians). Also evident was a strong anti-Catholic element, which was strengthened by the new waves of immigration from Catholic Ireland and southern Germany after 1830.

Temperance

The American Society for Promotion of Temperance was organized in 1826. It was strongly supported by Protestants, but just as strongly opposed by the new Catholic immigrants.

Public Schools

The motivations for the free school crusade were mixed. Some wanted to provide opportunity for all children to learn the skills for self-fulfillment and success in a republic. Others wanted to use schools as agencies for social control—to Americanize the new immigrant children as well as to Protestantize the Catholics, and to defuse the growing problems of urbanization. The stated purpose of the public schools was to instill social values: thrift, order, discipline, democracy.

Public apathy and even opposition met the early reformers: Horace Mann, the first secretary of the Massachusetts Board of Education, and Henry Barnard, his counterpart in Connecticut and Rhode Island.

The movement picked up momentum in the 1830s, but progress was very spotty. Few public schools were available in the West, fewer still for Southern whites, and none at all for Southern blacks.

Higher Education

In 1839, the first state supported school for women, Troy Female Seminary, was founded in Troy, New York. Oberlin College in Ohio was the nation's first coeducational college. The Perkins School for the Blind in Boston was the first of its kind in the United States.

Asylums for the Mentally Ill

Dorothea Dix (see sidebar) led the fight for these institutions, advocating more humane treatment for the mentally incompetent.

Prison Reform

The purpose of the new penitentiaries was not to just punish, but to rehabilitate. The first was built in Auburn, New York, in 1821.

Feminism

The Seneca Falls, New York, meeting in 1848, and its "Declaration of Sentiments

Dorothea Dix: America's Mental Health Pioneer

"In a world where there is so much to be done, I felt strongly impressed that there must be something for me to do."
—Dorothea Dix

National Library of Medicine

At a time when most American women could not vote, attend college, or in many states even own property, Dorothea Dix was a young woman who overcame an unhappy childhood and serious depression to become

cont'd on next page

and Resolutions," was the beginning of the modern feminist movement. The Grimké sisters, Elizabeth Cady Stanton, and Harriet Beecher Stowe were active in these early days. The movement was linked with that of the abolitionists, but suffered because it was considered to be of secondary importance.

The Abolitionist Movement

The early anti-slavery movement was benign, advocating only the purchase and transportation of slaves to free states in Africa. The American Colonization Society was organized in 1817 and established the colony of Liberia in 1830, but by that time the movement had reached a dead end.

In 1831, William Lloyd Garrison started his paper, *The Liberator*, and began to advocate total and immediate emancipation, thus giving new life to the movement. He founded the New England Anti-slavery Society in 1832, and the American Antislavery Society in 1833. Theodore Weld pursued the same goals, but advocated more gradual means.

Frederick Douglass, having escaped from his Maryland owner, became a fiery orator for the movement, and published his own newspaper, the *North Star*.

There were frequent outbursts of anti-abolition violence in the 1830s, against the fanaticism of the radicals. Abolitionist editor Elijah Lovejoy was killed by a mob in Illinois.

The movement split into two wings: Garrison's radical followers, and the moderates who favored "moral suasion" and petitions to Congress. In 1840, the Liberty

one of America's important early social reformers of the 19th century. In her quest to establish insane asylums throughout the United States, Dix became the first woman to speak before the U.S. Congress. During the Civil War, she became Superintendent of Female Nurses for the Union Army and convinced the Army that women could take on tasks normally handled by male nurses.

Dix began her career as a teacher and writer. Entering a period of severe illness (either depression or tuberculosis) in the mid-1830s, she was sent in 1836 by friends to England to recover on the family estate of the Rathbones, wealthy Quaker reformers. She spent a year in England, emerged from her depression, and noticed the humane and effective programs Quakers had developed in institutions for the mentally ill. She studied these asylums, such as York Retreat, and noted the family-type setting that rehabilitated the mentally ill.

Upon returning to America in 1841, she began teaching a Sunday school class to women in a Boston jail where—in addition to criminals—drunkards, prostitutes, and the retarded, mentally ill, and insane were often sent by their families. She asked to see how the mentally ill were treated and was shown their quarters, which amounted to a cold, damp, smelly room with straw on the floor. The patients, half-clothed, were huddled together for warmth. Dix began visiting jails and almshouses throughout Massachusetts, observing conditions and taking extensive notes. It was assumed at the time that mental illness was incurable and that money spent trying to improve institutional conditions was wasted. Dix argued that, in fact, improving conditions

cont'd on next page

Party, the first national anti-slavery party, fielded a presidential candidate on the platform of "free soil," non-expansion of slavery into the new western territories.

The literary crusade continued with Harriet Beecher Stowe's *Uncle Tom's Cabin* being the most influential among the many books which presented the abolitionist message.

Educating the Public

This was the golden age of oratory. Speechmaking drew huge and patient crowds, and four-hour-long orations were not uncommon, especially at public events like Fourth of July celebrations.

Newspapers and magazines multiplied and were available to everyone.

Women more and more became the market for magazines oriented to their interests. Periodicals like *Godey's Ladies Book* reached mass circulation figures.

Colleges sprang up everywhere, the products of religious sectarianism as well as local pride, which produced "booster colleges" in every new community as population moved west. Many of these were poorly funded and managed, and thus did not survive.

DIVERGING SOCIETIES— LIFE IN THE NORTH

Although the United States was a political entity, with all of the institutions of government and society shared among the peoples of the various states, there had always been a wide diversity of cultural and economic goals among the various states of the union. As the nineteenth

would provide an opportunity for the mentally ill to get better and be productive. She assembled a report, which she then delivered to the Massachusetts legislature. After a long debate, the state legislature approved financing for institutions for the mentally ill.

Following this initial success in Massachusetts, Dix visited every state east of the Mississippi, observing conditions, lobbying state legislatures, and raising awareness about mental illness. She traveled over 80,000 miles, visiting more than 9,000 mentally ill individuals in a wide variety of facilities. In Rhode Island in 1843, she reported to the state legislature about a patient in a poorhouse named Abram Simmons. Simmons, though ill and covered with sores, was confined in a cage for 30 years. Her report shocked the Rhode Island legislators into action. Dix went on to found 32 hospitals, a number of schools for the mentally retarded, and a number of nursing training facilities. Despite her own poor health, she tirelessly advocated for the mentally ill and insane. In 1848 she submitted a request to the U.S. Congress for five million acres to be set aside to take care of the mentally ill and addressed Congress herself, the first woman to do so. Despite its passage by both houses, the bill was vetoed by President Franklin Pierce in 1854.

Exhausted and discouraged, Dix returned to Europe to investigate conditions and recommend improvement for the treatment of the mentally ill there. She visited Russia, Denmark, Sweden, Holland, England, France, Scotland, Germany, and Belgium. Dix's efforts resulted in improvements in many nations.

At the start of the Civil War she volunteered to be Superintendent of Union Army Nurses. While she was

cont'd on next page

century progressed, that diversity seemed to grow more pronounced, and the collection of states seemed to polarize more into the two sections we call the North and the South, with the expanding West becoming ever more identified with the North.

Population Growth, 1790–1860

The new West was the fastest growing area of the country, with population tending to move along parallels westward. From four million in 1790, population had reached 32 million in 1860 with one-half living in states and territories which did not even exist in Washington's administration.

Increase in Median Age

Birth rates began to drop after 1800, more rapidly in the cities than in the rural areas. Families who had averaged six children in 1800 only had five in 1860. Some

not as successful in this effort, her efforts did convince the Army that women nurses could effectively serve in field hospitals.

In the years following the Civil War, Dix returned to her mental health reform work, though her work by now was mainly confined to letter-writing. Unfortunately the family-type care that she advocated in asylums became increasingly rare as the mental hospitals grew into overcrowded, impersonal establishments.

Dix was one of the most effective advocates for the mentally ill in the nineteenth century, yet she was incredibly humble, refusing to put her names on many publications and insisting that hospitals she helped found not be named after her. She spent her last six years in a New Jersey hospital and died at the age of 85 in 1887. Her life work is best summarized by her own words: "If I am cold, they are cold; if I am weary, they are distressed; if I am alone, they are abandoned."

of the reasons were economic: children were becoming liabilities rather than assets. The new "cult of domesticity" reflected a shift in family responsibilities. Father was out of the home working, and the burden of child-rearing fell more heavily on mother. Primitive birth control methods were used, and abortion was becoming common enough that several states passed laws restricting it. One result of all this was an aging population, with the median age rising from 16 to 20 years.

Immigration

The influx of immigrants had slowed during the conflicts with France and England, but the flow increased between 1815 and 1837, when the economic downturn again sharply reduced their numbers. Thus the overall rise in population during these years was due more to incoming foreigners than to natural increase. Most of the newcomers were from Britain, Germany and southern Ireland. The Germans usually fared best, since they brought more money and more skills. Discrimination was common in the job market, primarily directed against the Catholics. "Irish Need Not Apply" signs were common. However, the persistent labor shortage prevented the natives from totally excluding the foreign elements. These newcomers huddled in ethnic neighborhoods in the cities, or those who could moved west to try their hand at farming.

Growth of the Cities

In 1790 5 percent of the U.S. population lived in cities of 2,500 or more. By 1860, that figure had risen to 25 percent. This rapid urbanization created an array of problems.

Problems of Urbanization

The rapid growth in urban areas was not matched by the growth of services. Clean water, trash removal, housing and public transportation all lagged behind, and the wealthy got them first. Bad water and poor sanitation produced poor health, and epidemics of typhoid fever, typhus and cholera were common. Police and fire protection were usually inadequate and the development of professional forces was resisted because of the cost and the potential for political patronage and corruption.

Social Unrest

Rapid growth helped to produce a wave of violence in the cities. In New York City in 1834, the Democrats fought the Whigs with such vigor that the state militia had to be called in. New York and Philadelphia witnessed race riots in the mid-1830s, and a New York mob sacked a Catholic convent in 1834. In the 1830s, 115 major incidents of mob violence were recorded. Street crime was common in all the major cities.

THE ROLE OF WOMEN AND MINORITIES

Women

Women were treated as minors before the law. In most states a woman's property became her husband's with marriage. Political activity was limited to the formation of associations in support of various pious causes, such as abolition, and religious and benevolent activity. Professional employment was largely limited to schoolteaching; that occupation became dominated by women. The women's rights movement focused on social and legal discrimination, and women like Lucretia Mott and Sojourner Truth became well-known figures on the speakers' circuit.

Blacks

By 1850, 200,000 free blacks lived in the North and West. Their lives were restricted everywhere by prejudice, and "Jim Crow" laws separated the races. Black citizens organized separate churches and fraternal orders. The African Methodist Episcopal Church, for example, had been organized in 1794 in Philadelphia, and flourished in the major Northern cities. Black Masonic and Odd Fellows lodges were likewise established. The economic security of the free blacks was constantly threatened by the newly-arrived immigrants, who were willing to work at the least desirable jobs for less wages. Racial violence was a daily threat.

THE NORTHEAST LEADS THE WAY

The Growth of Industry

By 1850, the value of industrial output had surpassed that of agricultural production. The Northeastern states led the way in this movement. Over one-half of the manufacturing establishments were located there, and most of the larger enterprises. Seventy percent of the workers who were employed in manufacturing lived in New England and the middle states, and the Northeast produced more than two-thirds of the manufactured goods.

Inventions and Technology

The level of technology used in American manufacturing already exceeded that of European industry. Eli Whitney's applications of interchangeable parts were being introduced into a wide variety of manufacturing processes. Coal was replacing water as the major source of industrial power. Machine tools were reaching a high level of sophistication. Much of this progress was due to the contributions of America's inventors. Between 1830 and 1850 the number of patents issued for industrial inventions almost doubled. Charles Goodyear's process of vulcanizing rubber was put to 500 different uses and formed the basis for an entire new industry. Elias Howe's sewing machine was to revolutionize the clothing industry. The mass production of iron, with its new techniques and uses, created a new array of businesses, of which the new railroad industry was the largest consumer. Samuel B. Morse's new electric telegraph was first used in 1840 to transmit business news and information.

The Rise of Unions

The growth of the factory system was accompanied by the growth of the corporate form of business ownership, which in turn further separated the owners from the workers. One result was the organization of worker groups to fight for benefits, an early example of which was the 10-hour day. In 1835, Boston construction craftsmen struck for seven months to win a 10-hour work day, and Paterson, New Jersey, textile workers became the first factory workers to strike for shorter hours. The federal government's introduction of the 10-hour day for federal projects, in 1840, helped to speed the acceptance of this goal. The influx of immigrants who were willing to work for low wages helped to spur the drive for unions, and in turn their numbers helped to weaken the bargaining position of union members.

The Revolution in Agriculture

Farm and industry reinforced each other and developed simultaneously. As more urban workers became dependent on food grown by others, the potential profits of farming increased. Many of the technological developments and inventions were applied to farm machinery, which in turn enabled farmers to produce more food more cheaply for the urban workers. As in industry, specialization and mechanization became the rule in agriculture, particularly on the newly opening western prairies of Illinois, Iowa, and Kansas.

Inventions and Technology

Large-scale farming on the prairies spurred critical inventions. McCormick's mechanical reaper, patented in 1834, enabled a crew of six men to harvest in one day as much wheat as 15 men could using older methods. John Deere's steel plow, patented in 1837, provided a more durable tool to break the heavy prairie sod. Jerome Case's threshing machine multiplied the bushels of grain that could be separated from the stalk in a day's time.

The New Market Economy

These developments not only made large-scale production possible—they also shifted the major emphasis from corn to small grain production, and made farming for the international market feasible, which in turn made the Western farmer dependent on economic forces over which he had no control. This dependence produced the rising demand for government provision of free land and the agricultural colleges which later were provided by the Homestead and Morrill bills during the Civil War.

In the East, the trend was toward truck farming for the nearby burgeoning urban areas, and the production of milk, fruits, and berries. Here, as in the West, there was much interest in innovative practices which could increase production efficiency and profits.

The Revolution in Commerce

Before the coming of the railroad, coastal sailing ships practically monopolized domestic trade. The canal construction boom of the 1830s had taken commercial traffic from the river systems, but by 1840 the railroad had begun to emerge as the carrier of the future. Pennsylvania and New York State contained most of the 3,328 miles of track, but the rail system was rapidly expanding across the northern tier of states, tying the industrializing East to the expanding, agricultural West.

EVERYDAY LIFE IN THE NORTH

Between 1800 and 1860 output of goods and services increased twelve fold and the purchasing power of the average worker doubled. The household labor system was breaking down, and the number of wage-earners exceeded for the first time the numbers of independent, self-employed Americans. Even so, everyday living was still quite primitive. Most people bathed only infrequently, washed clothes and dishes even less. Housing was primitive for most, consisting of one- or two-room cabins heated by open fireplaces, with water carried in from springs or public faucets. For the working man, rural or urban, life was hard.

DIVERGING SOCIETIES—LIFE IN THE SOUTH

The Southern states experienced dramatic growth in the second quarter of the nineteenth century. The economy grew more productive and more prosperous, but still the section called the South was basically agrarian, with few important cities and scattered industry. The plantation system, with its cash crop production driven by the use of slave labor, remained the dominant institution. In the words of one historian, "The South grew, but it did not develop." The South grew more unlike the North, and it became more defensive of its distinctive way of life.

The Cotton Kingdom

The most important economic phenomenon of the early decades of the nineteenth century was the shift in population and production from the old "upper South" of Virginia and the Carolinas to the "lower South" of the newly opened Gulf States of Alabama, Mississippi, and Louisiana. This shift was the direct result of the increasing importance of cotton. In the older Atlantic states, tobacco retained its importance, but had shifted westward to the Piedmont, and was replaced in the east by food grains. The southern Atlantic coast continued to produce rice and southern Louisiana and east Texas retained their emphasis on sugar cane. But the rich black soil of the new Gulf states proved ideal for the production of short-staple cotton, especially after the invention of the gin, and cotton became the center of the Southern economy. Nearly three million bales were being produced annually by 1850.

By 1860, cotton was to account for two-thirds of the value of U.S. exports. In the words of a Southern legislator of that era, "Cotton is King!"

Classes in the South

Although the large plantation with its white-columned mansion and its aristocratic owners is frequently seen as typical of Southern life, the truth is quite different.

The Planter Class

Owners of large farms who also owned 50 or more slaves actually formed a small minority of the Southern population. Three-fourths of Southern whites owned no slaves at all, almost half of slave-owning families owned fewer than six, and 12 percent owned 20 or more. But this minority of large slave owners exercised political and economic power far beyond what their numbers would indicate. They became a class to which all others paid deference, and they dominated the political and social life of their region.

The Yeoman Farmers

The largest group of Southern whites was the independent small farmers who worked their land with their family, sometimes side-by-side with one or two slaves, to produce their own food, with sometimes enough surplus to sell for a little extra cash. These simple folk predominated in the upland South and constituted a sizeable element even in the lower cotton-producing states. Their major crop was corn, and indeed the South's corn crop was more valuable than its cotton. The corn was used at home for dinner tables and for animal feed, however, and so ranked behind cotton as an item of export. These people were generally poorer than their Northern counterparts.

The Poor Whites

Perhaps a half-million white Southerners lived on the edge of the agrarian economy, in varying degrees of poverty. These "crackers," or "sandhillers," occupied the barren soils of the red hills or sandy bottoms, and they lived in squalor worse than the slaves. They formed a true underclass.

The Institution of Slavery

As the necessary concomitant of this expanding plantation system, the "Peculiar Institution" of black slavery fastened itself upon the Southern people, even as it isolated them from the rest of the world.

Slavery as a Labor System

The utilization of slave labor varied according to the region and the size of the growing unit. The large plantations growing cotton, sugar or tobacco used the gang system, in which white overseers directed black drivers, who supervised large groups of workers in the fields, all performing the same operation. In the culture of rice, and on the smaller farms, slaves were assigned specific tasks, and when those tasks were finished, the worker had the remainder of the day to himself.

House servants usually were considered the most favored since they were spared the hardest physical labor and enjoyed the most intimate relationship with the owner's family. This could be considered a drawback, since they were frequently deprived of the social communion of the other slaves, enjoyed less privacy, and were more likely to suffer the direct wrath of a dissatisfied master or mistress.

It is still debated as to whether the living conditions of the Southern plantation slaves were better or worse than the Northern wage laborers. Certainly their lot was better than their counterparts in South America and the Carribean.

Urban Slavery in the Southern City

A sizeable number of black slaves worked in the towns, serving as factory hands, domestics, artisans, and construction workers. They lived fairly independent lives and indeed a good number purchased their freedom with their savings, or quietly crossed the color line and disappeared into the general population. As the 19th century progressed, these people were increasingly seen as a bad model and a threat to the institution, and so urban slavery practically disappeared.

The Slave Trade

The most significant demographic shift in these decades was the movement of blacks from the Old South to the new Southwest. Traders shipped servants by the thousands to the newly opened cotton lands of the gulf states. A prime field hand fetched an average price of $800, as high as $1,500 in peak years. Families were frequently split apart by this miserable traffic. Planters freely engaged in this trade, but assigned very low status to the traders who carried it out.

Although the importation of slaves from abroad had been outlawed by Congress since 1808, they continued to be smuggled in until the 1850s. The import ban kept the price up and encouraged the continuation of the internal trade.

Slaves' Reaction to Slavery

Blacks in bondage suffered varying degrees of repression and deprivation. The harsh slave codes were comprehensive in their restrictions on individual freedom, but they were unevenly applied, and so there was considerable variety in the severity of life. The typical slave probably received a rough but adequate diet and enjoyed crude but sufficient housing and clothing.

But the loss of freedom and the injustice of the system produced a variety of responses. Many "soldiered" on the job, and refused to work hard, or they found ways to sabotage the machinery or the crops. There was an underground system of ridicule toward the masters which was nurtured, as reflected in such oral literature as the "Br'er Rabbit" tales.

Violent reaction to repression was not uncommon. Gabriel Prosser in Richmond (1800), Denmark Vesey in Charleston (1822), and Nat Turner in coastal Virginia (1831) all plotted or led uprisings of blacks against their white masters. Rumors of such uprisings kept whites in a state of constant apprehension.

The ultimate rebellion was to simply leave, and many tried to run away, some successfully. Especially from the states bordering the North, an ever increasing number of slaves fled to freedom, many with the aid of the "underground railroad" and smugglers such as Harriet Tubman, who led over 300 of her family and friends to freedom after she herself had escaped.

Most of those in bondage, however, were forced simply to adapt, and they did. A rich culture was developed within the confines of the system, and included distinctive patterns of language, music and religion.

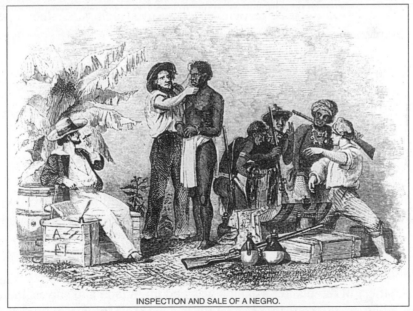

INSPECTION AND SALE OF A NEGRO.

**"Inspection and Sale of a Negro," an 1854 engraving by Whitney, Jocelyn & Annin, depicts an African man being inspected for sale into slavery.
U.S. Library of Congress.**

COMMERCE AND INDUSTRY

The lack of manufacturing and business development has frequently been blamed for the South's losing its bid for independence in 1861–1865. Actually the South was highly industrialized for its day, and compared favorably with most European nations in the development of manufacturing capacity. Obviously, it trailed far behind the North, so much so that when war erupted in 1861, the Northern states owned 81 percent of the factory capacity in the United States.

Manufacturing

The Southern states saw considerable development in the 1820s and 1830s in textiles and iron production and in flour milling. Richmond's Tredegar Iron Works compared favorably with the best in the North. Montgomery Bell's forges in Tennessee produced a good proportion of the ironware used in the upper South. Even so, most of the goods manufactured in these plants were for plantation consumption rather than for export, and they never exceeded two percent of the value of the cotton crop.

Commercial Activity

The businessmen of the South worked primarily with the needs and products of the plantation and the factors of New Orleans and Charleston had to serve as bankers and insurance brokers as well as the agents for the planters. An organized network of commerce never developed in the South, even though the planters themselves must be recognized as businessmen, since they operated large, complex staple-producing units.

Voices for Change

There were those who saw their native South sinking ever more into the position of dependency upon Northern bankers and businessmen, and they cried out for reform. James B.D. DeBow's *Review* advocated commercial development and agricultural diversification, but his cries fell largely on deaf ears.

Why were Southerners so wedded to the plantation system, in the face of much evidence that it was retarding development? Certainly one reason is that cotton was profitable. Over the long run, capital return on plantation agriculture was at least as good as on Northern industrial capital. Even though skilled slaves abounded and could have manned factories, they were more profitable in the field.

Since most of the planter's capital was tied up in land and slaves, there was little left to invest in commerce or manufacturing. Most important, perhaps, was the value system of the Southern people, who put great store in traditional rural ideals: chivalry, leisure, genteel elegance. Even the yeoman farmer held these values, and hoped someday to attain to the position the planters held.

LIFE IN THE SOUTHERN STATES

The Role of Women

The position of the Southern woman was similar in many ways to her Northern counterpart, but also very different. She had fewer opportunities for anything but home life. The middle-class wife was heavily involved in the operation of the farm, and served as supervisor and nurse for the servants, as well as manager of the household, while the upper class women served merely as ornaments. Education was rare, and centered on the "domestic arts." High birth and death rates took their toll on childbearing women, and many men outlived several wives. The half-breed slave children were constant reminders of the planters' dalliances and produced constant tension and frustration among plantation wives.

Education

Schooling beyond literacy training was available only to the sons of the well-to-do. Academies and colleges abounded, but not for the working classes, and what public schools there were were usually inferior and ill-supported. By 1860, one-half of all the illiterates in the United States lived in the South.

Daily Life in the South

The accounts of travelers in the Southern states provide us with vivid pictures of living conditions on the average homestead. Housing was primitive, one- or two-room cabins being the rule. Corn, sweet potatoes, and pork formed the staples of the Southern diet and health problems reflected the resulting vitamin deficiencies. Rickets and pellagra were common ailments.

Although the prevalence of violence has probably been overstated, it certainly existed and the duel remained an accepted avenue for settling differences well into the nineteenth century.

Southern Response to the Anti-Slavery Movement

As the crusade for abolition intensified in the North, the South assumed an ever more defensive position. Biblical texts were used to justify the enslavement of an "inferior race." Scientific arguments were advanced to prove the inherent inferiority of the black African. Southern postal authorities refused to deliver any mail that contained information antagonistic to the slave system. Any kind of dissent was brutally suppressed, and the South became more and more a closed society. Literature and scholarship shriveled, and creative writers like Edgar Allan Poe and William Gilmore Simms became the rare exception.

The last serious Southern debate over the institution of slavery took place in the Virginia legislature in 1832, in the aftermath of Nat Turner's revolt. That discussion squelched any move toward emancipation. In 1836 Southern members of the U.S. House of Representatives pushed through the infamous "gag rule," which forbade any discussion on the question of slavery on the floor of the House. That rule remained in effect until 1844.

The most elaborate product of this ferment was John C. Calhoun's theory of the "concurrent majority," in which a dual presidency would insure a South independent of Northern dominance, and would forever keep majority rule at bay.

Beginning in 1837, regular conventions were held across the South to discuss ways to escape Northern economic and political hegemony.

As the decade of the 1840s opened, the two sections were becoming more and more estranged, and the channels of compromise were becoming more and more poisoned by the emotional responses to black slavery. The development which contributed most to keeping the sore festering was westward expansion.

MANIFEST DESTINY AND WESTWARD EXPANSION

Although the term "Manifest Destiny" was not actually coined until 1844, the belief that the American nation was destined to eventually expand all the way to the Pacific Ocean, and to possibly embrace Canada to the North, and Mexico to the South, had been voiced for years by many who believed that American liberty and ideals should be shared with everyone possible, by force if necessary. The rising sense of nationalism which followed the War of 1812 was fed by the rapidly expanding population, the reform impulse of the 1830s, and the desire to acquire new markets and resources for the burgeoning economy of "Young America."

Louisiana and the Far West Fur Trade

The Lewis and Clark expedition had scarcely filed its reports before a variety of adventurous entrepreneurs began to penetrate the newly acquired territory and the lands beyond. "Mountain men" like Jim Bridges trapped the Rocky Mountain streams and the headwaters of the Missouri River system for the greatly prized beaver pelts, while explorers like Jedediah Smith mapped the vast territory which stretched from the Rockies to the Sierra Nevada range and on into California. John Jacob Astor established a fur post at the mouth of the Columbia River which he named Astoria, and challenged the British claim to the northwest. Though he was forced to sell out his establishment to the British, he lobbied Congress to pass trade restrictions against British furs, and eventually became the first American millionaire from the profits of the American Fur Company. The growing trade with the Orient in furs and other specialty goods was sharpening the desire of many businessmen for American ports on the Pacific coast.

"Fur Traders Descending the Missouri," 1845, a painting by George Caleb Bingham. This image characterized the impact of the opening of new territory following the Lewis and Clark expedition. Metropolitan Museum of Art.

The Oregon Country

The Adams-Onis Treaty of 1819 had set the northern boundary of Spanish possessions near the present northern border of California. The territory north of that line and west of the vague boundaries of the Louisiana Territory had been claimed over the years by Spain, England, Russia, France, and the United States. By the 1820s, all these claims had been yielded to Britain and the United States. The Hudson's Bay Company had established a fur trading station at Fort Vancouver, and claimed control south to the Columbia. The United States claimed all the way north to the 54° 40' parallel. Unable to settle the dispute, they had agreed on a joint occupation of the disputed land.

In the 1830s American missionaries followed the traders and trappers to the Oregon country, and began to publicize the richness and beauty of the land, sending back official reports on their work which were published in the new, inexpensive "penny press" papers. Everyone read these reports, and the result was the "Oregon Fever" of the 1840s, as thousands of settlers trekked across the Great Plains and the Rocky Mountains to settle the new Shangri-La.

The Texas Question: 1836–1845

Texas had been a state in the Republic of Mexico since 1822, following the Mexican revolution against Spanish control. The United States had offered to buy the territory at the time, since it had renounced its claim to the area in the Adams-Onis agreement of 1819. The new Mexican government indignantly refused to sell, but immediately began to invite immigration from the north by offering land grants to Stephen Austin and other Americans. They needed to increase the population of the area and to produce revenue for the infant government. The Americans responded in great numbers, and by 1835 approximately 35,000 "gringos" were homesteading on Texas land.

The Mexican officials saw their power base eroding as the foreigners flooded in, and so they moved to tighten control, through restrictions on new immigration, and through tax increases. The Texans responded in 1836 by proclaiming independence and establishing a new republic. The ensuing war was short-lived. The Mexican dictator Antonio López de Santa Anna advanced north and annihilated the Texan garrisons at the Alamo and at Goliad. On April 23, 1836, Sam Houston defeated him at San Jacinto, and the Mexicans were forced to let Texas go its way.

Houston immediately asked the American government for recognition and annexation, but President Andrew Jackson feared the revival of the slavery issue since the new state would come in on the slave-holding side of the political balance, and he also feared war with Mexico, so he did nothing. When Van Buren followed suit, the new republic sought foreign recognition and support, which the European nations eagerly provided, hoping thereby to create a counterbalance to rising American power and influence in the Southwest. France and England both quickly concluded trade agreements with the Texans.

New Mexico and California

The district of New Mexico had, like Texas, encouraged American immigration, and for the same reasons. Soon that state was more American than Mexican. The Santa Fe Trail—from Independence, Missouri, to the town of Santa Fe—created a prosperous trade in mules, gold and silver, and furs which moved north in exchange for manufactured goods which went south. American settlements sprung up all along the route.

Though the Mexican officials in California had not encouraged it, American immigration nevertheless had been substantial. First traders and whaling crews, then merchants, arrived to set up stores and developed a brisk trade. As the decade of the 1830s passed, the number of newcomers increased. Since the Missouri Compromise had established the northern limits for slavery at the 36° 30' parallel, most of this Mexican territory lay in the potential slave-holding domain, and many of the settlers had carried their bondsmen with them.

Manifest Destiny and Sectional Stress

The question of expansion was universally discussed. Although the strongest sentiment was found in the North and West, the South had its own ambitions, and they usually involved the extension of their "peculiar institution."

The Democrats generally favored the use of force, if necessary, to extend American borders. The Whigs favored more peaceful means, through diplomacy. Some Whigs, like Henry Clay, feared expansion under any circumstances, because of its potential for aggravating the slavery issue.

Clay was closest to the truth. As the decade of the 1840s opened, the questions of Texas, California and the New Mexican territory were increasingly prominent, and the sectional tension which they produced was destined to light the fires of civil war.

TYLER, POLK, AND CONTINUED WESTWARD EXPANSION

Tyler and the Whigs

When William Henry Harrison became president, he immediately began to rely on Whig leader Henry Clay for advice and direction, just as Clay had planned and expected he would. He appointed to his Cabinet those whom Clay suggested, and at Clay's behest he called a special session of Congress to vote the Whig legislative program into action. To the Whigs' dismay, Harrison died of pneumonia just one month into his term, to be replaced by Vice President John Tyler.

A states' rights Southerner and a strict constitutionalist who had been placed on the Whig ticket to draw Southern votes, Tyler rejected the entire Whig program of a national bank, high protective tariffs, and federally funded internal improvements (roads, canals, etc.). Clay stubbornly determined to push the program through anyway. In the resulting legislative confrontations, Tyler vetoed a number of Whig-sponsored bills.

The Whigs were furious. Every Cabinet member but one resigned in protest. Tyler was officially expelled from the party and made the target of the first serious impeachment attempt. (It failed.) In opposition to Tyler over the next few years the Whigs, under the leadership of Clay, transformed themselves from a loose grouping of diverse factions to a coherent political party with an elaborate organization.

One piece of important legislation that did get passed during Tyler's administration was the Preemption Act (1841), allowing settlers who had squatted on unsurveyed federal lands first chance to buy the land (up to 160 acres at low prices) once it was put on the market.

The Webster-Ashburton Treaty

The member of Tyler's Cabinet who did not immediately resign in protest was Secretary of State Daniel Webster. He stayed on to negotiate the Webster-Ashburton Treaty with Great Britain.

There were at this time several causes of tension between the U.S. and Great Britain:

1) The Canada-Maine boundary in the area of the Aroostook Valley was disputed. British efforts to build a military road through the disputed area led to reaction by Maine militia in a bloodless confrontation known as the "Aroostook War" (1838).

2) The Caroline Affair (1837) involved an American ship, the *Caroline*, that had been carrying supplies to Canadian rebels. It was burned by Canadian loyalists who crossed the U.S. border in order to do so.

3) In the Creole Incident, Britain declined to return escaped slaves who had taken over a U.S. merchant ship, the *Creole*, and sailed to the British-owned Bahamas.

4) British naval vessels, patrolling the African coast to suppress slave-smuggling, sometimes stopped and searched American ships.

The Webster-Ashburton Treaty (1842) dealt with these problems in a spirit of mutual concession and forbearance:

1) Conflicting claims along the Canada-Maine boundary were compromised.

2) The British expressed regret for the destruction of the *Caroline*.

3) The British promised to avoid "officious interference" in freeing slaves in cases such as that of the *Creole*.

4) Both countries agreed to cooperate in patrolling the African coast to prevent slave-smuggling.

The Webster-Ashburton Treaty was also important in that it helped create an atmosphere of compromise and forebearance in U.S.-British relations.

After negotiating the treaty, Webster too resigned from Tyler's Cabinet.

The Texas Issue

Rejected by the Whigs and without ties to the Democrats, Tyler was a politician without a party but not without ambitions. Hoping to gather a political following of his own, he sought an issue with powerful appeal and believed he had found it in the question of Texas annexation.

The Republic of Texas had gained its independence from Mexico in 1836 and, since most of its settlers had come from the U.S., immediately sought admission as a state. It was rejected because anti-slavery forces in Congress resented the presence of slavery in Texas and because Mexico threatened war should the U.S. annex Texas.

To excite American jealousy and thus hasten annexation, Texas President Sam Houston made much show of negotiating for closer relations with Great Britain. Southerners feared that Britain, which opposed slavery, might bring about its abolition in Texas and then use Texas as a base from which to undermine slavery in the American South. Other Americans were disturbed at the possibility of a British presence in Texas because of the obstacle it would present to what many Americans were coming to believe—and what New York journalist John L. O'Sullivan would soon express—as America's "manifest destiny to overspread the continent."

Tyler's new secretary of state, John C. Calhoun, negotiated an annexation treaty with Texas. Calhoun's identification with extreme pro-slavery forces and his insertion in the treaty of pro-slavery statements brought the treaty's rejection by the Senate (1844). Nevertheless, the Texas issue had been injected into national politics and could not be made to go away.

The Election of 1844

Democratic front-runner Martin Van Buren and Whig front-runner Henry Clay agreed privately that neither would endorse Texas annexation and that it would not become a campaign issue, but expansionists at the Democratic convention succeeded in dumping Van Buren in favor of James K. Polk. Polk, called "Young Hickory" by his supporters, was a staunch Jacksonian who opposed protective tariffs and a national bank but, most important, favored territorial expansion, including not only annexation of Texas but also occupation of all the Oregon country (up to latitude 54° 40') hitherto jointly occupied by the U.S. and Britain. The latter claim was expressed in his campaign slogan, "Fifty-four forty or fight."

Tyler, despite his introduction of the issue that was to decide that year's presidential campaign, was unable to build a party of his own and withdrew from the race.

The Whigs nominated Clay, who continued to oppose Texas annexation but, sensing the mood of the country was against him, began to equivocate. His wavering cost him votes among those Northerners who were extremely sensitive to the issue of slavery and believed that the settlement, independence, and proposed annexation of Texas was a gigantic plot to add slave states to the Union. Some of these voters shifted to the Liberty party.

The anti-slavery Liberty party nominated James G. Birney. Apparently because of Clay's wavering on the Texas issue, Birney was able to take enough votes away from Clay in New York to give that state, and thus the election, to Polk.

Tyler, as a lame-duck president, made one more attempt to achieve Texas annexation before leaving office. By means of a joint resolution, which unlike a treaty required only a simple majority rather than a two-thirds vote, he was successful in getting the measure through Congress. Texas was finally admitted to the Union (1845).

Polk as President

Though a relatively unknown "dark horse" at the time of his nomination for the Presidency, Polk had considerable political experience within his home state of Tennessee and was an adept politician. He turned out to be a skillful and effective president.

As a good Jacksonian, Polk favored a low, revenue-only tariff rather than a high, protective tariff. This he obtained in the Walker Tariff (1846). He also opposed a national debt and a national bank and re-established Van Buren's Independent Sub-Treasury system, which then remained in effect until 1920.

The Settlement of Oregon

A major issue in the election campaign of 1844, Oregon at this time comprised all the land bounded on the east by the Rockies, the west by the Pacific, the south by latitude 42°, and the north by the boundary of Russian-held Alaska at 54° 40'. Oregon had been visited by Lewis and Clark and in later years by American fur traders and especially missionaries such as Jason Lee and Marcus Whitman. Their reports sparked interest in Oregon's favorable soil and climate. During the first half of the 1840s, some 6,000 Americans had taken the 2,000-mile, six-month journey on the Oregon Trail, from Independence, Missouri, across the plains along the Platte River, through the Rockies at South Pass, and down the Snake River to their new homesteads. Most of them settled in the Willamette Valley, south of the Columbia River.

The area had been under the joint occupation of the U.S. and Great Britain since 1818, but Democrats in the election of 1844 had called for U.S. ownership of all of Oregon. Though this stand had helped him win the election, Polk had little desire to fight the British for land he considered unsuitable for agriculture and unavailable for slavery, which he favored. This was all the more so since trouble seemed to be brewing with Mexico over territory Polk considered far more desirable.

The British, for their part, hoped to obtain the area north of the Columbia River, including the natural harbor of Puget Sound (one of only three on the Pacific coast), with its adjoining Strait of Juan de Fuca.

By the terms of the Oregon Treaty (1846), a compromise solution was reached. The existing U.S.-Canada boundary east of the Rockies (49°) was extended westward to the Pacific, thus securing Puget Sound and shared use of the Strait of Juan de Fuca for the U.S. Some northern Democrats were angered and felt betrayed by Polk's failure to insist on all of Oregon, but the Senate readily accepted the treaty.

The Mormon Migration

Aside from the thousands of Americans who streamed west on the Oregon Trail during the early 1840s, and the smaller number who migrated to what was then Mexican-held California, another large group of Americans moved west but to a different destination and for different reasons. These were the Mormons.

Mormonism is a unique religion founded in 1832 by Joseph Smith at Palmyra, New York. Mormons were often in trouble with their neighbors, and had been forced to migrate to Kirtland, Ohio, then Clay County, Missouri; and finally, Nauvoo, Illinois. There, on the banks of the Mississippi River, they built the largest city in the state, had their own militia, and were a political force to be reckoned with.

In 1844 Mormon dissidents published a newspaper critical of church leader Smith and his newly announced doctrine of polygamy. Smith had their printing press destroyed. Arrested by Illinois authorities, Smith and his brother were confined to a jail in Carthage, Illinois, but later killed by a crowd of hostile non-Mormons who forced their way into the jail.

The Mormons then decided to migrate to the Far West, preferably someplace outside U.S. jurisdiction. Their decision to leave was hastened by pressure from their non-Mormon neighbors, among whom anti-Mormon feeling ran high as a response to polygamy and the Mormons' monolithic social and political structure.

Under the leadership of new church leader Brigham Young, some 85,000 Mormons trekked overland in 1846 to settle in the valley of the Great Salt Lake in what is now Utah (but was then owned by Mexico). Young founded the Mormon republic of Deseret and openly preached (and practiced) polygamy.

After Deseret's annexation by the U.S. as part of the Mexican Cession, Young was made territorial governor of Utah. Nevertheless, friction developed with the federal government. By 1857 public outrage over polygamy prompted then-President James Buchanan to replace Young with a non-Mormon governor. Threats of Mormon defiance led Buchanan to send 2500 army troops to compel Mormon obedience to federal law. Young responded by calling out the Mormon militia and blocking the passes through which the army would have to advance. This standoff, known as the "Mormon War," was resolved in 1858, with the Mormons accepting the new governor and Buchanan issuing a general pardon.

The Coming of War with Mexico

For some time American interest had been growing in the far western lands then held by Mexico:

1) Since the 1820s Americans had been trading with Santa Fe and other Mexican settlements along the Rio Grande by means of the Santa Fe Trail. Though not extensive enough to be of economic importance the trade aroused further American interest in the area.
2) Also, since the 1820s, American "mountain men," trappers who sought beaver pelts in the streams of the Rockies, had explored the mountains of the Far West, opening new trails and discovering fertile lands. They later served as guides for settlers moving west.
3) At the same time whaling ships and other American vessels had carried on a thriving trade with the Mexican settlements on the coast of California.
4) Beginning in 1841, American settlers came overland to California by means of the California Trail, a branch from the Oregon Trail that turned southwest in the Rockies and crossed Nevada along the Humboldt River. By 1846 several hundred Americans lived in California.

The steady flow of American pioneers into Mexican-held areas of the Far West led to conflicting territorial desires and was thus an underlying cause of the Mexican War. Several more immediate causes existed:

1) Mexico's ineffective government was unable to protect the lives and property of American citizens in Mexico during the country's frequent and recurring revolutions and repeatedly declined to pay American claims for damages even when such claims were supported by the findings of mutually agreed upon arbitration.

2) Mexico had not reconciled itself to the loss of Texas and considered its annexation by the U.S. a hostile act.

3) The southern boundary of Texas was disputed. Whereas first the independent Republic of Texas and now the U.S. claimed the Rio Grande as the boundary, Mexico claimed the Nueces River, 130 miles farther north, because it had been the boundary of the province of Texas when it had been part of Mexico.

4) Mexican suspicions had been aroused regarding U.S. designs on California when, in 1842, a U.S. naval force under Commodore Thomas Catsby Jones had seized the province in the mistaken belief that war had broken out between the U.S. and Mexico. When the mistake was discovered, the province was returned and apologies made.

5) Mexican politicians had so inflamed the Mexican people against the U.S. that no Mexican leader could afford to take the risk of appearing to make concessions to the U.S. for fear of being overthrown.

Though Mexico broke diplomatic relations with the U.S. immediately upon Texas' admission to the Union, there still seemed to be some hope of a peaceful settlement. In the fall of 1845 Polk sent John Slidell to Mexico City with a proposal for a peaceful settlement of the differences between the two countries. Slidell was empowered to cancel the damage claims and pay $5 million for the disputed land in southern Texas. He was also authorized to offer $25 million for California and $5 million for other Mexican territory in the Far West. Polk was especially eager to obtain California because he feared the British would snatch it from Mexico's extremely weak grasp.

Nothing came of these attempts at negotiation. Racked by coup and countercoup, the Mexican government refused even to receive Slidell.

Polk thereupon sent U.S. troops into the disputed territory in southern Texas. A force under General Zachary Taylor (who was nicknamed "Old Rough and Ready") took up a position just north of the Rio Grande. Eight days later, on April 5, 1846, Mexican troops attacked an American patrol. When news of the clash reached Washington, Polk sought and received from Congress a declaration of war against Mexico, on May 13, 1846.

The Mexican War

Americans were sharply divided about the war. Some favored it because they felt Mexico had provoked the war or because they felt it was the destiny of America to spread the blessings of freedom to oppressed peoples. Others opposed the war. Some, primarily Polk's political enemies the Whigs, accused the president of having provoked it. Others, generally Northern abolitionists, saw in the war the work of a vast conspiracy of Southern slaveholders greedy for more slave territory.

In planning military strategy, Polk showed genuine skill. American strategy consisted originally of a three-pronged attack, consisting of a land movement westward through New Mexico into California, a sea movement against California, and a land movement southward into Mexico.

The first prong of this three-pronged strategy, the advance through New Mexico and into California, was led by Colonel Stephen W. Kearny. Kearny's force easily secured New Mexico, entering Santa Fe on August 16, 1846, before continuing west to California. There American settlers, aided by an Army exploring party under John C. Fremont, had already revolted against Mexico's weak rule in what was called the Bear Flag Revolt.

As part of the second prong of U.S. strategy, naval forces under Commodore John D. Sloat had seized Monterey and declared California to be part of the United States. Forces put ashore by Commodore Robert Stockton joined with Kearny's troops to defeat the Mexicans at the Battle of San Gabriel in January 1847, and complete the conquest of California.

The third prong of the American strategy, an advance southward into Mexico, was itself divided into two parties:

1) Troops under Colonel Alexander W. Doniphan defeated Mexicans at El Brazito (December 25–28, 1846) to take El Paso, and then proceeded southward, winning the Battle of Sacramento (February 28, 1847) to take the city of Chihuahua, capital of the Mexican province of that name.

2) The main southward thrust, however, was made by a much larger American army under General Zachary Taylor. After badly defeating larger Mexican forces at the battles of Palo Alto (May 7, 1846) and Resaca de la Palma (May 8, 1846), Taylor advanced into Mexico and defeated an even larger Mexican force at the Battle of Monterey (September 20–24, 1846). Then, after substantial numbers of his troops had been transferred to other sectors of the war, he successfully withstood, though badly outnumbered, an attack by a Mexican force under Antonia Lopez de Santa Anna at the Battle of Buena Vista, February 22–23, 1847.

Despite the success of all three parts of the American strategy, the Mexicans refused to negotiate. Polk therefore ordered U.S. forces under General Winfield Scott to land on the east coast of Mexico, march inland, and take Mexico City.

Scott landed at Veracruz March 9, 1847, and by March 27 had captured the city with the loss of only twenty American lives. He advanced from there, being careful to maintain good discipline and avoid atrocities in the countryside. At Cerro Cord (April 18, 1847), in what has been called "the most important single battle of the war," Scott outflanked and soundly defeated a superior enemy force in a seemingly impregnable position. After beating another Mexican army at Churubusco (August 19–20, 1847), Scott paused outside Mexico City to offer the Mexicans another chance to negotiate. When they declined, U.S. forces stormed the fortress of Chapultepec (September 13, 1847) and the next day entered Mexico City. Still Mexico refused to negotiate a peace and instead carried on guerilla warfare.

Negotiated peace finally came about when the State Department clerk Nicholas Trist, though his authority had been revoked and he had been ordered back to Washington two months earlier, negotiated and signed the Treaty of Guadalupe-Hidalgo (February 2, 1848), ending the Mexican War. Under the terms of the treaty Mexico ceded to the U.S. the territory Polk had originally sought to buy, this time in exchange for a payment of $15 million and the assumption of $3.25 million in American citizens' claims against the Mexican government. This territory, the Mexican Cession, included the natural harbors at San Francisco and San Diego, thus giving the U.S. all three of the major west-coast natural harbors.

Despite the appropriation of vast territories, many, including Polk, felt the treaty was far too generous. There had been talk of annexing all of Mexico or of forcing Mexico to pay an indemnity for the cost of the war. Still, Polk felt compelled to accept the treaty as it was, and the Senate subsequently ratified it.

On the home front many Americans supported the war enthusiastically and flocked to volunteer. Some criticized the war, among them Henry David Thoreau, who, to display his protest, went to live at Walden Pond and refused to pay his taxes. Jailed for this, he wrote "Civil Disobedience."

Although the Mexican War increased the nation's territory by one-third, it also brought to the surface serious political issues that threatened to divide the country, particularly the question of slavery in the new territories.

◄─────── HISTORICAL TIMELINE ───────►
Jacksonian Democracy and Westward Expansion (1824–1850)

1825	John Quincy Adams wins Corrupt Bargain presidential election
1828	Tariff of Abominations Jackson wins presidency
1830	Jackson vetoes Maysville Road extension Baltimore & Ohio becomes first railroad company Joseph Smith publishes *Book of Mormon*
1831	*Cherokee Nation v. Georgia* denies Indian claim of nationhood Nat Turner's Rebellion
1832	Jackson vetoes U.S. Bank re-charter Nullification crisis in South Carolina
1834	Women workers at Lowell, Massachusetts, stage first strike
1836	Texas independence fight Gag rule prevents discussion of slavery in Congress
1837	Panic of 1837
1838	Trail of Tears
1842	*Commonwealth v. Hunt* legalizes unions
1845	Annexation of Texas
1846	U.S. declares war on Mexico Oregon Treaty
1847	Winfield Scott captures Mexico City
1848	Gold discovered in northern California Treaty of Guadalupe Hidalgo Seneca Falls statement of women's rights
1849	California gold rush

Chapter 7

SECTIONAL CONFLICT AND THE CAUSES OF THE CIVIL WAR (1850–1860)

THE CRISIS OF 1850 AND AMERICA AT MID-CENTURY

The Wilmot Proviso

The Mexican War had no sooner started when, on August 8, 1846, freshman Democratic Congressman David Wilmot of Pennsylvania introduced his Wilmot Proviso as a proposed amendment to a war appropriations bill. It stipulated that "neither slavery nor involuntary servitude shall ever exist" in any territory to be acquired from Mexico. It was passed by the House, and though rejected by the Senate it was reintroduced again and again amid increasingly acrimonious debate.

The Wilmot Proviso aroused intense sectional feelings. Southerners, who had supported the war enthusiastically, felt they were being treated unfairly. Northerners, some of whom had been inclined to see the war as a slaveholders' plot to extend slavery, felt they saw their worst suspicions confirmed by the Southerners' furious opposition to the Wilmot Proviso. There came to be four views regarding the status of slavery in the newly acquired territories.

The Southern position was expressed by John C. Calhoun, now serving as senator from South Carolina. He argued that the territories were the property not of the U.S. federal government, but of all the states together, and therefore Congress had no right to prohibit in any territory any type of "property" (by which he meant slaves) that was legal in any of the states.

Anti-slavery Northerners, pointing to the Northwest Ordinance of 1787 and the Missouri Compromise of 1820 as precedents, argued that Congress had the right to make what laws it saw fit for the territories, including, if it so chose, laws prohibiting slavery.

A compromise proposal favored by President Polk and many moderate Southerners called for the extension of the 36° 30' line of the Missouri Compromise westward through the Mexican Cession to the Pacific, with territory north of the line to be closed to slavery and territory south of it open to slavery.

Another compromise solution, favored by Northern Democrats such as Lewis Case of Michigan and Stephen A. Douglas of Illinois, was known as "squatter sovereignty" and later as "popular sovereignty." It held that the residents of each territory should be permitted to decide for themselves whether or not to allow slavery, but it was vague as to when they might exercise that right.

The Election of 1848

Both parties sought to avoid as much as possible the hot issue of slavery in the territories as they prepared for the 1848 election campaign.

The Democrats nominated Lewis Cass, and their platform endorsed his middle-of-the-road popular sovereignty position with regard to slavery in the territories.

The Whigs dodged the issue even more effectively by nominating General Zachary Taylor, whose fame in the Mexican War made him a strong candidate. Taylor knew nothing of the current political issues, had never voted, and liked to think of himself as above politics. He took no position at all with respect to slavery in the territories.

Some anti-slavery Northern Whigs and Democrats, disgusted with their parties' failure to take a clear stand against the spread of slavery, deserted the party ranks to form another antislavery third party. They were known as "Conscience" Whigs (because they voted their conscience) and "Barnburner" Democrats (because they were willing to burn down the whole Democratic "barn" to get rid of the pro-slavery "rats"). Their party was called the Free Soil Party, since it stood for keeping the soil of new western territories free of slavery. Its candidate was Martin Van Buren.

The election excited relatively little public interest. Taylor won a narrow victory, apparently because Van Buren took enough votes from Cass in New York and Pennsylvania to throw those states into Taylor's column.

Gold in California

The question of slavery's status in the Western territories was made more immediate when, on January 24, 1848, gold was discovered at Sutter's Mill, not far from Sacramento, California. The next year gold-seekers from the eastern U.S. and from many foreign countries swelled California's population from 14,000 to 100,000.

Once in the gold fields these "forty-niners" proved to contain some rough characters, and that fact, along with the presence, or at least the expectation, of quick and easy riches, made California a wild and lawless place. No territorial government had been organized since the U.S. had received the land as part of the Mexican Cession, and all that existed was an inadequate military government. In September 1849, having more than the requisite population and being much in need of better government, California petitioned for admission to the Union as a state.

Since few slaveholders had chosen to risk their valuable investments in human property in the turbulent atmosphere of California, the people of the area not surprisingly sought admission as a free state, touching off a serious sectional crisis back east.

The Compromise of 1850

President Zachary Taylor, though himself a Louisiana slaveholder, opposed the further spread of slavery. Hoping to sidestep the dangerously divisive issue of slavery in the territories, he encouraged California as well as the rest of the Mexican Cession to organize and seek admission directly as states, thus completely bypassing the territorial stage.

Southerners were furious. They saw admission of a free-state California as a backdoor implementation of the hated Wilmot Proviso they had fought so hard to turn back in Congress. They were also growing increasingly alarmed at what was becoming the minority status of their section within the country. Long outnumbered in the House of Representatives, the South would now find itself, should California be admitted as a free state, also outvoted in the Senate.

Other matters created friction between North and South. A large tract of land was disputed between Texas, a slave state, and the as-yet-unorganized New Mexico Territory, where slavery's future was at best uncertain. Southerners were angered by the small-scale but much-talked-of efforts of Northern abolitionists' "underground railroad" to aid escaped slaves in reaching permanent freedom in Canada. Northerners were disgusted by the presence of slave pens and slave markets in the nation's capital. Radical southerners talked of secession and scheduled an all-Southern convention to meet in Nashville in June 1850 to propose ways of protecting Southern interests, inside or outside the Union.

At this point the aged Henry Clay attempted to compromise the various matters of contention between North and South. He proposed an eight-part package deal that he hoped would appeal to both sides.

For the North, the package contained these aspects: California would be admitted as a free state; the land in dispute between Texas and New Mexico would go to New Mexico; New Mexico and Utah Territories (all of the Mexican Cession outside of California) would not be specifically reserved for slavery, but its status there would be decided by popular sovereignty; and, the slave trade would be abolished in the District of Columbia.

For the South, the package offered the following: A tougher Fugitive Slave Law would be enacted; the federal government would pay Texas' $10,000,000 pre-annexation debt; Congress would declare that it did not have jurisdiction over the interstate slave trade; and, Congress would promise not to abolish slavery itself in the District of Columbia.

What followed the introduction of Clay's compromise proposal was eight months of heated debate, during which Clay, Calhoun, and Daniel Webster, the three great figures of Congress during the first half of the 19th century— all three aged and none of them with more than two years to live—made some of their greatest speeches. Clay called for compromise and "mutual forbearance." Calhoun gravely warned that the only way to save the Union was for the North to grant all the South's demands and keep quiet on the issue of slavery. Webster abandoned his previous opposition to the spread of slavery (as well as most of his popularity back in his home state of Massachusetts) to support the Compromise in an eloquent speech.

The opponents of the Compromise were many and powerful and ranged from President Taylor, who demanded admission of California without reference to slavery, to Northern extremists such as Senator William Seward of New York, who spoke of a "higher law" than the Constitution, forbidding the spread of slavery, to Southern extremists such as Calhoun or Senator Jefferson Davis of Mississippi. By mid-summer all seemed lost for the Compromise, and Clay left Washington exhausted and discouraged.

Then the situation changed dramatically. President Taylor died (apparently of gastroenteritis) July 9, 1850, and was succeeded by Vice President Millard Fillmore, a quiet but efficient politician and a strong supporter of compromise. In Congress the fight for the Compromise was taken up by Senator Stephen A. Douglas of Illinois. Called the "Little Giant" for his small stature and large political skills, Douglas broke Clay's proposal into its component parts so that he could use varying coalitions to push each part through Congress. This method proved successful, and the Compromise was adopted.

The Compromise of 1850 was received with joy by most of the nation. Sectional harmony returned, for the most part, and the issue of slavery in the territories seemed to have been permanently settled. That this was an illusion became apparent within a few years.

The Election of 1852

The 1852 Democratic convention deadlocked between Cass and Douglas and so instead settled on dark horse Franklin Pierce of New Hampshire. The Whigs, true to form, chose General Winfield Scott, a war hero of no political background.

The result was an easy victory for Pierce, largely because the Whig Party, badly divided along North-South lines as a result of the battle over the Compromise of 1850, was beginning to come apart. The Free Soil Party's candidate, John P. Hale of New Hampshire, fared poorly, demonstrating the electorate's weariness with the slavery issue.

Pierce and "Young America"

Americans eagerly turned their attention to railroads, cotton, clipper ships, and commerce. The world seemed to be opening up to American trade and influence.

President Pierce expressed the nation's hope that a new era of sectional peace was beginning. To assure this he sought to distract the nation's attention from the slavery issue to an aggressive program of foreign economic and territorial expansion known as "Young America."

In 1853 Commodore Matthew Perry led a U.S. naval force into Tokyo Bay on a mission to open Japan—previously closed to the outside world—to American diplomacy and commerce.

By means of the Reciprocity Treaty (1854) Pierce succeeded in opening Canada to greater U.S. trade. He also sought to annex Hawaii, increase U.S. interest in Central America, and acquire territories from Mexico and Spain.

From Mexico he acquired in 1853 the Gadsden Purchase, a strip of land in what is now southern New Mexico and Arizona along the Gila River. The purpose of this purchase was to provide a good route for a trans-continental railroad across the southern part of the country.

Pierce sought to buy Cuba from Spain. When Spain declined, three of Pierce's diplomats, meeting in Ostend, Belgium, sent him the Ostend Manifesto urging military seizure of Cuba should Spain remain intransigent.

Pierce was the first "doughface" president—"a northern man with southern principles"—and his expansionist goals, situated as they were in the South, aroused suspicion and hostility in anti-slavery northerners. Pierce's administration appeared to be dominated by southerners, such as Secretary of War Jefferson Davis, and whether in seeking a southern route for a trans-continental railroad or seeking to annex potential slave territory such as Cuba, it seemed to be working for the good of the South.

Economic Growth

The chief factor in the economic transformation of America during the 1840s and 1850s was the dynamic rise of the railroads. In 1840 America had less than 3000 miles of railroad track. By 1860 that number had risen to over

30,000 miles. Railroads pioneered big-business techniques, and by improving transportation helped create a nationwide market. They also helped link the Midwest to the Northeast rather than the South, as would have been the case had only water transportation been available.

Water transportation during the 1850s saw the heyday of the steamboat on inland rivers and the clipper ship on the high seas. The period also saw rapid and sustained industrial growth. The factory system began in the textile industry, where Elias Howe's invention of the sewing machine (1846) and Isaac Singer's improved model (1851) aided the process of mechanization, and spread to other industries.

Agriculture varied according to region. In the South, large plantations and small farms existed side by side for the most part, and both prospered enormously during the 1850s from the production of cotton. Southern leaders referred to the fiber as "King Cotton," an economic power that no one would dare fight against.

In the North the main centers of agricultural production shifted from the Middle Atlantic states to the more fertile lands of the Midwest. The main unit of agriculture was the family farm, and the main products were grain and livestock. Unlike the South, where 3.5 million slaves provided abundant labor, the North faced incentives to introduce labor-saving machines. Cyrus McCormick's mechanical reaper came into wide use, and by 1860 over 100,000 were in operation on Midwestern farms. Mechanical threshers also came into increasing use.

Decline of the Two-Party System

Meanwhile, ominous developments were taking place in politics. America's second two-party system, which had developed during the 1830s, was in the process of breaking down. The Whig Party, whose dismal performance in the election of 1852 had signaled its weakness, was now in the process of complete disintegration. Partially this was the result of the issue of slavery, which tended to divide the party along North-South lines. Partially, though, it may have been the result of the nativist movement.

The nativist movement and its political party, the American, or, as it was called, the Know-Nothing Party, grew out of alarm on the part of native-born Americans at the rising tide of German and Irish immigration during the late 1840s and early 1850s. The Know-Nothing Party, so called because its members were told to answer "I know nothing" when asked about its secret proceedings, was anti-foreign and, since many of the foreigners were Catholic, also anti-Catholic. It surged briefly to become the country's second-largest party by 1855 but faded even more quickly due to the ineptness of its leaders and the growing urgency of the slavery question, which, though ignored by the

Know-Nothing Party, was rapidly coming to overshadow all other issues. To some extent the Know-Nothing movement may simply have benefitted from the already progressing disintegration of the Whig Party, but it may also have helped to complete that disintegration.

All of this was ominous because the collapse of a viable nationwide two-party system made it much more difficult for the nation's political process to contain the explosive issue of slavery.

THE RETURN OF SECTIONAL CONFLICT
Continuing Sources of Tension

While Americans hailed the apparent sectional harmony created by the Compromise of 1850 and enjoyed the rapid economic growth of the decade that followed, two items which continued to create tension centered on the issue of slavery.

The Strengthened Fugitive Slave Law

The more important of these was a part of the Compromise itself, the strengthened federal Fugitive Slave Law. The law enraged Northerners, many of whom believed it little better than a legalization of kidnapping. Under its provisions blacks living in the North and claimed by slave catchers were denied trial by jury and many of the other protections of due process. Even more distasteful to anti-slavery Northerners was the provision that required all U.S. citizens to aid, when called upon, in the capture and return of alleged fugitives. So violent was Northern feeling against the law that several riots erupted as a result of attempts to enforce it. Some Northern states passed personal liberty laws in an attempt to prevent the working of the Fugitive Slave Law.

The effect of all this was to polarize the country even further. Many Northerners who had not previously taken an interest in the slavery issue now became opponents of slavery as a result of having its injustices forcibly brought home to them by the Fugitive Slave Law. Southerners saw in Northern resistance to the law further proof that the North was determined to tamper with the institution of slavery.

Uncle Tom's Cabin

One Northerner who was outraged by the Fugitive Slave Act was Harriet Beecher Stowe. In response, she wrote *Uncle Tom's Cabin*, a fictional book depicting what she perceived as the evils of slavery. Furiously denounced in the South, the book became an overnight best-seller in the North, where it turned many toward active opposition to slavery. This, too, was a note of harsh discord among the seemingly harmonious sectional relations of the early 1850s.

The Kansas-Nebraska Act

All illusion of sectional peace ended abruptly when in 1854 Senator Stephen A. Douglas of Illinois introduced a bill in Congress to organize the area west of Missouri and Iowa as the territories of Kansas and Nebraska. Douglas, who apparently had no moral convictions on slavery one way or the other, hoped organizing the territories would facilitate the building of a trans-continental railroad on a central route, something that would benefit him and his Illinois constituents.

Though he sought to avoid directly addressing the touchy issue of slavery, Douglas was compelled by pressure from Southern senators such as David Atchison of Missouri to include in the bill an explicit repeal of the Missouri Compromise (which banned slavery in the areas in question) and a provision that the status of slavery in the newly organized territories be decided by popular sovereignty.

The bill was opposed by most Northern Democrats and a majority of the remaining Whigs, but with the support of the Southern-dominated Pierce administration it was passed and signed into law.

The Republican Party

The Kansas-Nebraska Act aroused a storm of outrage in the North, where the repeal of the Missouri Compromise was seen as the breaking of a solemn agreement. It hastened the disintegration of the Whig Party and divided the Democratic Party along North-South lines.

In the North, many Democrats left the party and were joined by former Whigs and Know-Nothings in the newly created Republican Party. Springing to life almost overnight as a result of Northern fury at the Kansas-Nebraska Act, the Republican party included diverse elements whose sole unifying principle was the firm belief that slavery should be banned from all the nation's territories, confined to the states where it already existed, and allowed to spread no further.

Though its popularity was confined almost entirely to the North, the Republican Party quickly became a major power in national politics.

Bleeding Kansas

With the status of Kansas (Nebraska was never in much doubt) to be decided by the voters there, North and South began competing to see which could send the greatest number. Northerners formed the New England Emigrant Aid Company to promote the settling of anti-slavery men in Kansas, and Southerners responded in kind. Despite these efforts the majority of Kansas settlers were Midwesterners who were generally opposed to the spread of slavery but were more concerned with finding good farm land than deciding the national debate over slavery in the territories.

Despite this large anti-slavery majority, large-scale election fraud, especially on the part of heavily armed Missouri "border ruffians" who crossed into Kansas on election day to vote their pro-slavery principles early and often, led to the creation of a virulently pro-slavery territorial government. When the presidentially-appointed territorial governor protested this gross fraud, Pierce removed him from office.

Free-soil Kansans responded by denouncing the pro-slavery government as illegitimate and forming their own free-soil government in an election which the pro-slavery faction boycotted. Kansas now had two rival governments, each claiming to be the only lawful one.

Both sides began arming themselves and soon the territory was being referred to in the Northern press as "Bleeding Kansas" as full-scale guerilla war erupted. In May 1856, Missouri border ruffians sacked the free-soil town of Lawrence, killing two, and destroying homes, businesses, and printing presses. Two days later a small band of antislavery zealots under the leadership of fanatical abolitionist John Brown retaliated by killing and mutilating five unarmed men and boys at a pro-slavery settlement on Pottawatomie Creek. In all, some 200 died in the months of guerilla fighting that followed.

Meanwhile, violence had spread even to Congress itself. In the same month as the Sack of Lawrence and the Pottawatomie Massacre, Senator Charles Sumner of Massachusetts made a two-day speech entitled "The Crime Against Kansas," in which he not only denounced slavery but also made degrading personal references to aged South Carolina Senator Andrew Butler. Two days later Butler's nephew, Congressman Preston Brooks, also of South Carolina, entered the Senate chamber and, coming on Sumner from behind, beat him about the head and shoulders with a cane, leaving him bloody and unconscious.

Once again the North was outraged, while in the South, Brooks was hailed as a hero. New canes were sent to him to replace the one he had broken over Sumner's head. Denounced by Northerners, he resigned his seat and was overwhelmingly re-elected. Northerners were further incensed and bought thousands of copies of Sumner's inflammatory speech.

The Election of 1856

The election of 1856 was a three-way contest that pitted Democrats, Know-Nothings, and Republicans against each other.

The Democrats dropped Pierce and passed over Douglas to nominate James Buchanan of Pennsylvania. Though a veteran of forty years of politics, Buchanan was a weak and vacillating man whose chief qualification for the nomination was that during the slavery squabbles of the past few years he had been out of the country as American minister to Great Britain and therefore had not been forced to take public positions on the controversial issues.

The Know-Nothings, including the remnant of the Whigs, nominated Millard Fillmore. However, choice of a Southerner for the nomination of vice president so alienated Northern Know-Nothings that many shifted their support to the Republican candidate.

The Republicans nominated John C. Frémont of California. A former officer in the army's Corps of Topographical Engineers, Frémont was known as "the Pathfinder" for his explorations in the Rockies and the Far West. The Republican platform called for high tariffs, free Western homesteads (160 acres) for settlers, and, most important, no further spread of slavery. Their slogan was "Free Soil, Free Men, and Frémont." Southerners denounced the Republican Party as an abolitionist organization and threatened secession should it win the election.

Against divided opposition Buchanan won with apparent ease. However, his victory was largely based on the support of the South, since Frémont carried most of the Northern states. Had the Republicans won Pennsylvania and either Illinois or Indiana, Frémont would have been elected. In the election the Republicans demonstrated surprising strength for a political party only two years old and made clear that they, and not the Know-Nothings, would replace the moribund Whigs as the other major party along with the Democrats.

The *Dred Scott* Case

Meanwhile, there had been, rising through the court system, a case that would give the Supreme Court a chance to state its opinion on the question of slavery in the territories. The case was *Dred Scott v. Sanford*, which involved a Missouri slave, Dred Scott, who had been encouraged by abolitionists to sue for his freedom on the basis that his owner, an Army doctor, had taken him for a stay of several years in a free state, Illinois, and then in a free territory, Wisconsin. By 1856 the case had made its way to the Supreme Court, and by March of the following year the Court was ready to render its decision.

The justices were at first inclined to rule simply that Scott, as a slave, was not a citizen and could not sue in court. Buchanan, however, shortly before his inauguration, urged the justices to go farther and attempt to settle the whole slavery issue once and for all, thus removing it from the realm of politics where it might prove embarrassing to the president.

The Court obliged. Under the domination of aging pro-Southern Chief Justice Roger B. Taney of Maryland, it attempted to read the extreme Southern position on slavery into the Constitution, ruling not only that Scott had no standing to sue in federal court, but also that temporary residence in a free state, even for several years, did not make a slave free, and that the Missouri Compromise (already a dead letter by that time) had been unconstitutional all along because Congress did not have the authority to exclude slavery from any territory whatsoever. Nor did territorial governments, which were considered to receive their power from Congress, have the right to prohibit slavery.

Far from settling the sectional controversy, the *Dred Scott* case only made it worse. Southerners were encouraged to take an extreme position and refuse compromise, while anti-slavery Northerners became more convinced than ever that there was a pro-slavery conspiracy controlling all branches of government, and expressed an unwillingness to accept the Court's dictate as final.

Buchanan and Kansas

Later in 1857 the pro-slavery government in Kansas, through largely fraudulent means, arranged for a heavily pro-slavery constitutional convention to meet at the town of Lecompton. The result was a state constitution that allowed slavery. To obtain a pretense of popular approval for this constitution the convention provided for a referendum in which the voters were to be given a choice only to prohibit the entry of additional slaves into the state.

Disgusted free-soilers boycotted the referendum, and the result was a constitution that put no restrictions at all on slavery. Touting this Lecompton constitution, the pro-slavery territorial government petitioned Congress for admission to the Union as a slave state. Meanwhile the free-soilers drafted a constitution of their own and submitted it to Congress as the legitimate one for the prospective state of Kansas.

Eager to appease the South, which had started talking of secession again, and equally eager to suppress anti-slavery agitation in the North, Buchanan vigorously backed the Lecompton constitution. Douglas, appalled at this travesty of popular sovereignty, broke with the administration to oppose it. He and Buchanan became bitter political enemies, with the president determined to use all the power of the Democratic organization to crush Douglas politically.

After extremely bitter and acrimonious debate the Senate approved the Lecompton constitution, but the House insisted that Kansans be given a chance to vote on the entire document. Southern congressmen did succeed in managing to apply pressure to the Kansas voters by adding the stipulation that, should the Lecompton constitution be approved, Kansas would receive a generous grant of federal land, but should it be voted down, Kansas would remain a territory.

Nevertheless, Kansas voters, when given a chance to express themselves in a fair election, turned down the Lecompton constitution by an overwhelming margin, choosing to remain a territory rather than become a slave state. Kansas was finally admitted as a free state in 1861.

The Panic of 1857

In 1857 the country was struck by a short but severe depression. There were three basic causes for this "Panic of 1857": several years of overspeculation in railroads and lands, faulty banking practices, and an interruption in the flow of European capital into American investments as a result of the Crimean War. The North blamed the Panic on low tariffs, while the South, which had suffered much less than the industrial North, saw the Panic as proof of the superiority of the Southern economy in general and slavery in particular.

The Lincoln-Douglas Debates

The 1858 Illinois senatorial campaign produced a series of debates that got to the heart of the issues that were threatening to divide the nation. In that race incumbent Democratic Senator and front-runner for the 1860 presidential nomination Stephen A. Douglas was opposed by a Springfield lawyer, little known outside the state, by the name of Abraham Lincoln.

Though Douglas had been hailed in some free-soil circles for his opposition to the Lecompton constitution, Lincoln, in a series of seven debates that the candidates agreed to hold during the course of the campaign, stressed that Douglas's doctrine of popular sovereignty failed to recognize slavery for the moral wrong it was. Again and again Lincoln hammered home the theme that Douglas was a secret defender of slavery because he did not take a moral stand against it.

Douglas, for his part, maintained that his guiding principle was democracy, not any moral standard of right or wrong with respect to slavery. The people could, as far as he was concerned, "vote it up or vote it down." At the same time he strove to depict Lincoln as a radical and an abolitionist who believed in racial equality and race mixing.

At the debate held in Freeport, Illinois, Lincoln pressed Douglas to reconcile the principle of popular sovereignty with the Supreme Court's decision in the *Dred Scott* case. How could the people "vote it up or vote it down," if, as the Supreme Court said, no territorial government could prohibit slavery? Douglas, in what came to be called his "Freeport Doctrine," replied that the people of any territory could exclude slavery simply by declining to pass any of the special laws that slave jurisdictions usually passed for their protection.

Douglas's answer was good enough to win him re-election to the Senate, although by the narrowest of margins, but hurt him in the coming presidential campaign. The Lecompton fight had already destroyed Douglas's hopes of uniting the Democratic Party and defusing the slave issue. It had also damaged his 1860 presidential hopes by alienating the South. Now his Freeport Doctrine hardened the opposition of Southerners already angered by his anti-Lecompton stand.

For Lincoln, despite the failure to win the Senate seat, the debates were a major success, propelling him into the national spotlight and strengthening the backbone of the Republican Party to resist compromise on the free-soil issue.

THE COMING OF THE CIVIL WAR

John Brown's Raid

On the night of October 16, 1859, John Brown, the Pottawatomie Creek murderer, led eighteen followers in seizing the federal arsenal at Harpers Ferry, Virginia (now West Virginia), taking hostages, and endeavoring to incite a slave uprising. Brown, supported and bankrolled by several prominent Northern

Abolitionist John Brown. From a daguerreotype; Levin C. Handy, photographer. U.S. Library of Congress.

abolitionists (later referred to as "the Secret Six"), planned to arm local slaves and then spread his uprising across the South. His scheme was ill-conceived and had little chance of success. Quickly cornered by Virginia militia, he was eventually captured by a force of U.S. Marines under the command of Army Colonel Robert E. Lee. Ten of Brown's eighteen men were killed in the fight, and Brown himself was wounded.

Charged under Virginia law with treason and various other crimes, Brown was quickly tried, convicted, sentenced, and, on December 2, 1859, hanged. Throughout his trial and at his execution he conducted himself with fanatical resolution, making eloquent and grandiose statements that convinced many Northerners that he was a martyr rather than a criminal. His death was marked in the North by signs of public mourning.

Though responsible Northerners such as Lincoln denounced Brown's raid as a criminal act that deserved to be punished by death, many Southerners became convinced that the entire Northern public approved of Brown's action and that the only safety for the South lay in a separate Southern confederacy. This was all the more so because Brown, in threatening to create a slave revolt, had touched on the foremost fear of white Southerners.

Hinton Rowan Helper's Book

The second greatest fear of Southern slaveholders was that Southern whites who did not own slaves, by far the majority of the Southern population, would come to see the continuation of slavery as not being in their best interest. This fear was touched on by a book, *The Impending Crisis in the South*, by a North Carolinian named Hinton Rowan Helper. In it Helper argued that slavery was economically harmful to the South and that it enriched the large planter at the expense of the yeoman farmer.

Southerners were enraged, and more so when the Republicans reissued a condensed version of the book as campaign literature. When the new House of Representatives met in December 1859 for the first time since the 1858 elections, angry Southerners determined that no Republican who had endorsed the book should be elected speaker.

The Republicans were the most numerous party in the House although they did not hold a majority. Their candidate for speaker, John Sherman of Ohio, had endorsed Helper's book. A rancorous two-month battle ensued in which the House was unable even to organize itself, let alone transact any business. Secession was talked of openly by Southerners, and as tensions rose congressmen came to the sessions carrying revolvers and Bowie knives. The matter was finally resolved by the withdrawal of Sherman and the election of a moderate Republican as speaker. Tensions remained fairly high.

The Election of 1860

In this mood the country approached the election of 1860, a campaign that eventually became a four-man contest.

The Democrats met in Charleston, South Carolina. Douglas had a majority of the delegates, but at that time a party rule required a two-thirds vote for the nomination. Douglas, faced with the bitter opposition of the Southerners and the Buchanan faction, could not gain this majority. Finally, the convention split up when Southern "fire-eaters" led by William L. Yancey walked out in protest of the convention's refusal to include in the platform a plank demanding federal protection of slavery in all the territories.

A second Democratic convention several weeks later in Baltimore also failed to reach a consensus, and the sundered halves of the party nominated separate candidates. The Southern wing of the party nominated Buchanan's vice president, John C. Breckinridge of Kentucky, on a platform calling for a federal slave code in all the territories. What was left of the national Democratic Party nominated Douglas on a platform of popular sovereignty.

A third presidential candidate was added by the Constitutional Union Party, a collection of aging former Whigs and Know Nothings from the southern and border states as well as a handful of moderate Southern Democrats. It nominated John Bell of Tennessee on a platform that sidestepped the issues and called simply for the Constitution, the Union, and the enforcement of the laws.

The Republicans met in Chicago, confident of victory and determined to do nothing to jeopardize their favorable position. Accordingly they rejected as too radical front-running New York Senator William H. Seward in favor of Illinois favorite son Abraham Lincoln. The platform was designed to have something for all Northerners, including the provisions of the 1856 Republican platform as well as a call for federal support of a trans-continental railroad. Once again its centerpiece was a call for the containment of slavery.

Douglas, believing only his victory could reconcile North and South, became the first U.S. presidential candidate to make a vigorous nationwide speaking tour. In his speeches he urged support for the Union and opposition to any extremist candidates that might endanger its survival, by which he meant Lincoln and Breckinridge.

On election day the voting went along strictly sectional lines. Breckinridge carried the Deep South; Bell, the border states; and Lincoln, the North. Douglas, although second in popular votes, carried only a single state and part of another. Lincoln led in popular votes, and though he was short of a majority in that category, he did have the needed majority in electoral votes and was elected.

The Secession Crisis

Lincoln had declared he had no intention of disturbing slavery where it already existed, but many Southerners thought otherwise. They also feared further raids of the sort John Brown had attempted and felt their pride injured by the election of a president for whom no Southerner had voted.

On December 20, 1860, South Carolina, by vote of a special convention made up of delegates elected by the people of the state, declared itself out of the Union. By February 1, 1861, six more states (Alabama, Georgia, Florida, Mississippi, Louisiana, and Texas) had followed suit.

Representatives of the seven seceded states met in Montgomery, Alabama, in February 1861 and declared themselves to be the Confederate States of America. They elected former Secretary of War and U.S. Senator Jefferson Davis of Mississippi as president, and Alexander Stephens of Georgia as vice president. They also adopted a constitution for the Confederate States which, while similar to the U.S. Constitution in many ways, contained several important differences:

1) Slavery was specifically recognized, and the right to move slaves from one state to another was guaranteed.
2) Protective tariffs were prohibited.
3) The president was to serve for a single non-renewable six-year term.
4) The president was given the right to veto individual items within an appropriations bill.
5) State sovereignty was specifically recognized.

In the North reaction was mixed. Some, such as prominent Republican Horace Greeley of the *New York Tribune*, counseled, "Let erring sisters go in peace." President Buchanan, now a lame duck, seemed to be of this mind, since he declared secession to be unconstitutional but at the same time stated his belief that it was unconstitutional for the federal government to do anything to stop states from seceding. Taking his own advice, he did nothing.

Others, led by Senator John J. Crittenden of Kentucky, strove for a compromise that would preserve the Union. Throughout the period of several weeks as the Southern states one by one declared their secession, Crittenden worked desperately with a congressional compromise committee in hopes of working out some form of agreement.

The compromise proposals centered on the passage of a constitutional amendment forever prohibiting federal meddling with slavery in the states where it existed as well as the extension of the Missouri Compromise line (36° 30') to the Pacific, with slavery specifically protected in all the territories south of it.

Some Congressional Republicans were inclined to accept this compromise, but President-elect Lincoln urged them to stand firm for no further spread of slavery. Southerners would consider no compromise that did not provide for the spread of slavery, and talks broke down.

HISTORICAL TIMELINE

Sectional Conflict and the Causes of the Civil War (1850–1860)

1850	Compromise of 1850 Fugitive Slave Law passed
1852	*Uncle Tom's Cabin* published
1854	Ostend Manifesto Kansas-Nebraska Act Republican Party formed
1856	"Bleeding Kansas"
1857	*Dred Scott* decision Lecompton Constitution in Kansas
1858	Lincoln-Douglas debates
1859	John Brown's raid
1860	Lincoln elected president

Chapter 8

THE CIVIL WAR AND RECONSTRUCTION (1860–1877)

HOSTILITIES BEGIN

Fort Sumter

Lincoln did his best to avoid angering the slave states that had not yet seceded. In his inaugural address he urged Southerners to reconsider their actions but warned that the Union was perpetual, that states could not secede, and that he would therefore hold the federal forts and installations in the South.

Of these only two remained in federal hands: Fort Pickens, off Pensacola, Florida; and Fort Sumter, in the harbor of Charleston, South Carolina. Lincoln soon received word from Major Robert Anderson, commanding the small garrison at Sumter, that supplies were running low. Desiring to send in the needed supplies, Lincoln informed the governor of South Carolina of his intention but promised that no attempt would be made to send arms, ammunition, or reinforcements unless Southerners initiated hostilities.

Not satisfied, Southerners determined to take the fort. Confederate General P. G. T. Beauregard, acting on orders from President Davis, demanded Anderson's surrender. Anderson said he would if not resupplied. Knowing supplies were on the way, the Confederates opened fire at 4:30 a.m. on April 12, 1861. The next day the fort surrendered.

The day following Sumter's surrender Lincoln declared the existence of an insurrection and called for the states to provide 75,000 volunteers to put it down. In response to this, Virginia, Tennessee, North Carolina, and Arkansas declared their secession.

The remaining slave states, Delaware, Kentucky, Maryland, and Missouri, wavered to varying degrees but stayed with the Union. Delaware, which had few slaves, gave little serious consideration to the idea of secession. Kentucky declared itself neutral and then sided with the North when the South failed to respect this neutrality. Maryland's incipient secession movement was crushed by Lincoln's timely imposition of martial law. Missouri was saved for the Union by the quick and decisive use of federal troops as well as the sizeable population of pro-Union, anti-slavery German immigrants living in St. Louis.

Relative Strengths at the Outset

An assessment of available assets at the beginning of the war would not have looked favorable for the South.

The North enjoyed at least five major advantages over the South. It had overwhelming preponderance in wealth and thus was better able to finance the enormous expense of the war. The North was also vastly superior in industry and thus capable of producing the needed war materials; the South, as a primarily agricultural society, often had to improvise or do without.

The North furthermore had an advantage of almost three-to-one in manpower, and over one-third of the South's population was composed of slaves, whom Southerners would not use as soldiers. Unlike the South, the North received large numbers of immigrants during the war. The North retained control of the U.S. Navy, and thus would command the sea and be able, by blockading, to cut the South off from outside sources of supply.

Finally, the North enjoyed a far superior system of railroads, while the South's relatively sparse railroad net was composed of a number of smaller railroads, often not interconnected and with varying gauges of track. They were more useful for carrying cotton from the interior to port cities than for moving large amounts of war supplies or troops around the country.

The South did, however, have several advantages of its own. It was vast in size, and this would make it difficult to conquer; it did not need to conquer the North, but only resist being conquered itself. Its troops would also be fighting on their own ground, a fact that would give them the advantage of familiarity with the terrain, as well as the added motivation of defending their homes and families. Its armies would often have the opportunity of fighting on the defensive, a major advantage in the warfare of that day.

At the outset of the war the South drew a number of highly qualified senior officers, such as Robert E. Lee, Joseph E. Johnston, and Albert Sidney Johnston, from the U.S. Army. By contrast, the Union command structure was already set when the war began, with the aged Winfield Scott, of Mexican War fame, at the top. It took young and talented officers, such as Ulysses S. Grant and William T. Sherman, time to work up to high rank. Meanwhile, Union armies were often led by inferior commanders as Lincoln experimented while in search of good generals.

At first glance, the South might also have seemed to have an advantage in its president. Jefferson Davis had extensive military and political experience and was acquainted with the nation's top military men and, presumably, with their relative abilities. On the other hand, Lincoln had been, up until his election to the presidency, less successful politically and had virtually no military experience. In fact, Lincoln was much superior to Davis as a war leader, showing firmness, flexibility, mental toughness, great political skill, and, eventually, an excellent grasp of strategy.

Opposing Strategies

Both sides were full of enthusiasm for the war. In the North the battle cry was "On to Richmond," the new Confederate capital established after the secession of Virginia. In the South it was "On to Washington." Yielding to popular demand, Lincoln ordered General Irvin McDowell to advance on Richmond with his army. At a creek called Bull Run near the town of Manassas Junction, Virginia, just southwest of Washington, D.C., they met a Confederate force under generals P. G. T. Beauregard and Joseph E. Johnston, July 21, 1861. In the First Battle of Bull Run (called First Battle of Manassas in the South) the Union army was forced to retreat in confusion back to Washington.

Bull Run demonstrated the unpreparedness and inexperience of both sides. It also demonstrated that the war would be long and hard, and, particularly in the North, that greater efforts would be required. Lincoln would need an overall strategy. To supply this, Winfield Scott suggested his Anaconda Plan to squeeze the life out of the Confederacy. This plan included a naval blockade to shut out supplies from Europe, a campaign to take the Mississippi River, thereby splitting the South in two, and the taking of several strategic points, then waiting for pro-Union sentiment in the South to overthrow the secessionists. Lincoln liked the first two points of Scott's strategy but considered the third point unrealistic.

He ordered a naval blockade, an overwhelming task considering the South's long coastline. Yet under Secretary of the Navy Gideon Welles the Navy was expanded enormously and the blockade, derided in the early days as a "paper blockade," became increasingly effective.

Lincoln also ordered a campaign to take the Mississippi River. A major step in this direction was taken when naval forces under Captain David G. Farragut took New Orleans in April 1862.

Rather than waiting for pro-Unionists in the South to gain control, Lincoln hoped to raise huge armies and apply overwhelming pressure from all sides at once until the Confederacy collapsed. The strategy was good; the problem was finding good generals to carry it out.

THE UNION PRESERVED

Lincoln Tries McClellan

To replace the discredited McDowell, Lincoln chose General George B. McClellan. McClellan was a good trainer and organizer and was loved by the troops, but was unable to effectively use the powerful army (now called the Army of the Potomac) he had built up. Despite much prodding from Lincoln, McClellan hesitated to advance, badly overestimating his enemy's numbers.

Finally, in the spring of 1862, he took the Army of the Potomac by water down Chesapeake Bay to land between the York and James rivers in Virginia. His plan was to advance up the peninsula formed by these rivers directly to Richmond.

The operations that followed were known as the Peninsula Campaign. McClellan advanced slowly and cautiously toward Richmond, while his equally cautious Confederate opponent, General Joseph E. Johnston, drew back to the outskirts of the city before turning to fight at the Battle of Seven Pines. May 31–June 1, 1862. In this inconclusive battle Johnston was wounded. To replace him Jefferson Davis appointed his military advisor, General Robert E. Lee.

Lee summoned General Thomas J. "Stonewall" Jackson and his army from the Shenandoah Valley (where Jackson had just finished defeating several superior federal forces, causing consternation in Washington) and with the combined forces attacked McClellan.

After two days of bloody but inconclusive fighting, McClellan lost his nerve and began to retreat. In the remainder of what came to be called the Battle of the Seven Days, Lee continued to attack McClellan, forcing him back to his base, though at great cost in lives. McClellan's army was loaded back onto its ships and taken back to Washington.

Before McClellan's army could reach Washington and be completely deployed in northern Virginia, Lee saw and took an opportunity to thrash Union General John Pope, who was operating in northern Virginia with another Northern army, at the Second Battle of Bull Run.

Union Victories in the West

In the western area of the war's operations, (essentially everything west of the Appalachian Mountains,) matters were proceeding in a much different fashion. The Northern commanders there, Henry W. Halleck and Don Carlos Buell, were no more enterprising than McClellan, but Halleck's subordinate, Ulysses S. Grant, definitely was.

Seeking and obtaining permission from Halleck, Grant mounted a combined operation—army troops and navy gunboats—against two vital Confederate strongholds, Forts Henry and Donelson, which guarded the Tennessee and Cumberland rivers in northern Tennessee, and which were the weak point of the thin-stretched Confederate line under General Albert Sidney Johnston. When Grant captured the forts in February 1862, Johnston was forced to retreat to Corinth in northern Mississippi.

Grant pursued but, ordered by Halleck to wait until all was in readiness before proceeding, Grant halted his troops at Pittsburg Landing on the Tennessee River, twenty-five miles north of Corinth. On April 6, 1862, Johnston, who had received reinforcements and been joined by General P. G. T. Beauregard, surprised Grant there, but in the two-day battle that followed (Shiloh) failed to defeat him. Johnston himself was among the many killed in what was, up to this point, the bloodiest battle in American history.

Grant was severely criticized in the North for having been taken by surprise. Yet with other Union victories and Farragut's capture of New Orleans, the North had taken all of the Mississippi River except for a 110-mile stretch between the Confederate fortresses of Vicksburg, Mississippi, and Port Hudson, Louisiana.

The Success of Northern Diplomacy

Many Southerners believed Britain and France would rejoice in seeing a divided and weakened America. The two countries would likewise be driven by the need of their factories for cotton and thus intervene on the Confederacy's behalf. So strongly was this view held that during the early days of the war, when the Union blockade was still too weak to be very effective, the Confederate government itself prohibited the export of cotton in order to hasten British and French intervention.

This view proved mistaken for several reasons. Britain already had on hand large stocks of cotton from the bumper crops of the years immediately prior to the war. During the war the British were successful in finding alternative sources of cotton, importing the fiber from India and Egypt. British leaders may also have weighed their country's need to import wheat from the northern United States against its desire for cotton from the Southern states. Finally, British public opinion opposed slavery.

Skillful Northern diplomacy had a great impact. In this, Lincoln had the extremely able assistance of Secretary of State William Seward, who took a hard line in warning Europeans not to interfere, and of Ambassador to Great Britain Charles Francis Adams. Britain therefore remained neutral and other European countries, France in particular, followed its lead.

One incident nevertheless came close to fulfilling Southern hopes for British intervention. In November 1861 Captain Charles Wilkes of the U.S.S.

San Jacinto stopped the British mail and passenger ship *Trent* and forcibly removed Confederate emissaries James M. Mason and John Slidell. News of Wilkes' action brought great rejoicing in the North but outrage in Great Britain, where it was viewed as a violation of Britain's rights on the high seas. Lincoln and Seward, faced with British threats of war at a time when the North could ill afford it, wisely chose to release the envoys and smooth things over with Britain.

The Confederacy was able to obtain some loans and to purchase small amounts of arms, ammunition, and even commerce-raiding ships such as the highly successful C.S.S. *Alabama*. However, Union naval superiority kept such supplies to a minimum.

The War at Sea

The Confederacy's major bid to challenge the Union's naval superiority was based on the employment of a technological innovation, the ironclad ship. The first and most successful of the Confederate ironclads was the C.S.S. *Virginia*. Built on the hull of the abandoned Union frigate *Merrimac*, the *Virginia* was protected from cannon fire by iron plates bolted over her sloping wooden sides. In May 1862 she destroyed two wooden warships of the Union naval force at Hampton Roads, Virginia, and was seriously threatening to destroy the rest of the squadron before being met and fought to a standstill by the Union ironclad U.S.S. *Monitor*.

The Home Front

The war on the home front dealt with the problems of maintaining public morale, supplying the armies of the held, and resolving constitutional questions regarding authority and the ability of the respective governments to deal with crises.

For the general purpose of maintaining public morale but also as items many Republicans had advocated even before the war, Congress in 1862 passed two highly important acts dealing with domestic affairs in the North.

The Homestead Act granted 160 acres of government land free of charge to any person who would farm it for at least five years. Much of the West was eventually settled under the provisions of this act. The Morrill Land Grant Act offered large amounts of the federal government's land to states that would establish "agricultural and mechanical" colleges. Many of the nation's large state universities were founded in later years under the provisions of this act.

Keeping the people relatively satisfied was made more difficult by the necessity, apparent by 1863, of imposing conscription in order to obtain adequate manpower for the huge armies that would be needed to crush the South. Especially hated by many working class Northerners was the provision of the conscription act that allowed a drafted individual to avoid service by hiring a substitute or paying $300. Resistance to the draft led to riots in New York City in which hundreds were killed.

The Confederacy, with its much smaller manpower pool on which to draw, had instituted conscription in 1862. Here, too, it did not always meet with cooperation. Some Southern governors objected to it on doctrinaire states' rights grounds, doing all they could to obstruct its operation. A provision of the Southern conscription act allowing one man to stay home as overseer for every twenty slaves led the non-slaveholding whites who made up most of the Southern population to grumble that it was a "rich man's war and a poor man's fight." Draft-dodging and desertion became epidemic in the South by the latter part of the war.

Scarcity of food and other consumer goods in the South as well as high prices led to further desertion as soldiers left the ranks to care for their starving families. Discontent also manifested itself in the form of a "bread riot" in Richmond.

Supplying the war placed an enormous strain on both societies, but one the North was better able to bear.

To finance the Northern side of the war, high tariffs and an income tax (the nation's first) were resorted to, yet even more money was needed. The Treasury Department, under Secretary of the Treasury Salmon P. Chase, issued "greenbacks," an unbacked fiat currency that nevertheless fared better than the Southern paper money because of greater confidence in Northern victory. To facilitate the financing of the war through credit expansion, the National Banking Act was passed in 1863.

The South, with its scant financial resources, found it all but impossible to cope with the expense of war. Excise and income taxes were levied and some small loans were obtained in Europe, yet the Southern Congress still felt compelled to issue paper money in such quantities that it became virtually worthless. That, and the scarcity of almost everything created by the war and its disruption of the economy, led to skyrocketing prices.

The Confederate government responded to the inflation it created by imposing taxes-in-kind and impressment, the seizing of produce, livestock, etc., by Confederate agents in return for payment according to an artificially set schedule of prices. Since payment was in worthless inflated currency, this amounted to confiscation and soon resulted in goods of all sorts becoming even scarcer than otherwise when a Confederate impressment agent was known to be in the neighborhood.

Questions of constitutional authority to deal with crises plagued both presidents.

To deal with the emergency of secession, Lincoln stretched the presidential powers to the limit, or perhaps beyond the limit, of the Constitution. To quell the threat of secession in Maryland, Lincoln suspended the writ of *habeas corpus* and imprisoned numerous suspected secessionists without charges or trial, ignoring the insistence of pro-Southern Chief Justice Roger B. Taney in *ex Parte Merryman* (1861) that such action was unconstitutional.

"Copperheads," Northerners such as Clement L. Vallandigham of Ohio who opposed the war, denounced Lincoln as a tyrant and would-be dictator but remained a minority. Though occasionally subject to arrest and/or deportation for their activities, they were generally allowed a considerable degree of latitude.

Davis encountered obstructionism from various state governors, the Confederate Congress, and even his own vice president, who denounced him as a tyrant for assuming too much power and failing to respect states' rights. Hampered by such attitudes, the Confederate government proved less effective than it might have been.

The Emancipation Proclamation

By mid-1862, Lincoln, under pressure from radical elements of his own party and hoping to create a favorable impression on foreign public opinion, determined to issue the Emancipation Proclamation, declaring free, as of January 1, 1863, all slaves in areas still in rebellion. In order that this not appear an act of panic and desperation in view of the string of defeats the North had recently suffered on the battlefields of Virginia, Lincoln, at Seward's recommendation, waited to announce the proclamation until the North should win some sort of victory. This was provided by the Battle of Antietam, September 17, 1862.

Though the Radical Republicans, pre-war abolitionists for the most part, had for some time been urging Lincoln to take such a step, Northern public opinion as a whole was less enthusiastic, as the Republicans suffered major losses in the November 1862 congressional elections.

The Turning Point in the East

After his victory of the Second Battle of Bull Run, August 27–30, 1862, Lee moved north and crossed into Maryland, where he hoped to win a decisive victory that would force the North to recognize Southern independence.

He was confronted by the Army of the Potomac, once again under the command of General George B. McClellan. Through a stroke of good fortune early in the campaign, detailed plans for Lee's entire audacious operation fell into McClellan's hands, but the Northern general, by extreme caution and slowness, threw away this incomparable chance to annihilate Lee and win—or at least shorten—the war.

The armies finally met along Antietam Creek, just east of the town of Sharpsburg in western Maryland. In a bloody but inconclusive day-long battle, known as Antietam in the North and as Sharpsburg in the South, McClellan's timidity led him to miss another excellent chance to destroy Lee's cornered and badly outnumbered army. After the battle Lee retreated to Virginia, and Lincoln, besides issuing the Emancipation Proclamation, removed McClellan from command.

To replace him, Lincoln chose General Ambrose E. Burnside, who promptly demonstrated his unfitness for command by blundering into a lopsided defeat at Fredericksburg, Virginia, December 13, 1862.

Lincoln then replaced Burnside with General Joseph "Fighting Joe" Hooker. Handsome and hard-drinking, Hooker had bragged of what he would do to "Bobby Lee" when he got at him; but when he took his army south, "Fighting Joe" quickly lost his nerve. He was out-generaled and soundly beaten at the Battle of Chancellorsville, May 5–6, 1863. At this battle the brilliant Southern General "Stonewall" Jackson was accidentally shot by his own men and died several days later.

Lee, anxious to shift the scene of the fighting out of his beloved Virginia, sought and received permission from President Davis to invade Pennsylvania. He was pursued by the Army of the Potomac, now under the command of General George G. Meade, whom Lincoln had selected to replace the discredited Hooker. They met at Gettysburg, and in a three-day battle (July 1–3, 1863) that was the bloodiest of the entire war, Lee, who sorely missed the services of Jackson and whose cavalry leader, the normally reliable J. E. B. Stuart, failed to provide him with timely reconnaissance, was defeated. However, he was allowed by the victorious Meade to retreat to Virginia with his army intact if battered, much to Lincoln's disgust. Still, Lee would never again have the strength to mount such an invasion.

Lincoln Finds Grant

Meanwhile, Grant undertook to take Vicksburg, one of the two last Confederate bastions on the Mississippi River. In a brilliant campaign, he bottled up the Confederate forces of General John C. Pemberton inside the city and placed them under siege. After six weeks of siege, the defenders surrendered, July 4, 1863. Five days later Port Hudson surrendered as well, giving the Union complete control of the Mississippi.

After Union forces under General William Rosecrans suffered an embarrassing defeat at the Battle of Chickamauga in northwestern Georgia, September 19–20, 1863, Lincoln named Grant overall commander of Union forces in the West.

Grant went to Chattanooga, Tennessee, where Confederate forces under General Braxton Bragg were virtually besieging Rosecrans, and immediately took control of the situation. Gathering Union forces from other portions of the western theater and combining them with reinforcements from the East, Grant won a resounding victory at the Battle of Chattanooga (November 23–25, 1863), in which federal forces stormed seemingly impregnable Confederate positions on Lookout Mountain and Missionary Ridge. This victory put Union forces in position for a drive into Georgia, which began the following spring.

Early in 1864 Lincoln made Grant commander of all Union armies. Grant devised a coordinated plan for constant pressure on the Confederacy. General William T. Sherman would lead a drive toward Atlanta, Georgia, with the goal of destroying the Confederate army under General Joseph E. Johnston (who had replaced Bragg). Grant himself would accompany Meade and the Army of the Potomac in advancing toward Richmond with the goal of destroying Lee's Confederate army.

In a series of bloody battles (the Wilderness, Spotsylvania, Cold Harbor) in May and June of 1864, Grant drove Lee to the outskirts of Richmond. Still unable to take the city or get Lee at a disadvantage, Grant circled around to try to take both by way of the back door, attacking Petersburg, Virginia, an important railroad junction just south of Richmond and the key to that city's—and Lee's—supply lines. Once again turned back by entrenched Confederate troops, Grant settled down to besiege Petersburg and Richmond in a stalemate that lasted some nine months.

Sherman had been advancing simultaneously in Georgia. He maneuvered Johnston back to the outskirts of Atlanta with relatively little fighting. At that point Confederate President Davis lost patience with Johnston and replaced him with the aggressive General John B. Hood. Hood and Sherman fought three fierce but inconclusive battles around Atlanta in late July, then settled down to a siege of their own during the month of August.

The Election of 1864 and Northern Victory

In the North discontentment grew with the long casualty lists and seeming lack of results. Yet the South could stand the grinding war even less. By late 1864 Jefferson Davis had reached the point of calling for the use of blacks in the Confederate armies, though the war ended before black troops could see action for the Confederacy. The South's best hope was that Northern war-weariness would bring the defeat of Lincoln and the victory of a peace candidate in the election of 1864.

Lincoln ran on the ticket of the National Union Party, essentially the Republican party with loyal or "War" Democrats. His vice-presidential candidate was Andrew Johnson, a loyal Democrat from Tennessee.

The Democratic Party's presidential candidate was General George B. McClellan, who, with some misgivings, ran on a platform labeling the war

As the industrial and political capital of the Confederacy, Richmond, Virginia, found itself caught in the bloody crossfire between two mighty American armies. Here, the Petersburg Railway Depot lies in ruins in 1865. AP Photo.

a failure and calling for a negotiated peace settlement even if that meant Southern independence.

The outlook was bleak for a time, and even Lincoln himself believed that he would be defeated. Then in September 1864 came word that Sherman had taken Atlanta. The capture of this vital Southern rail and manufacturing center brought an enormous boost to northern morale. Along with other Northern victories that summer and fall, it insured a resounding election victory for Lincoln and the continuation of the war to complete victory for the North.

To speed that victory, Sherman marched through Georgia from Atlanta to the sea, arriving at Savannah in December 1864 and turning north into the Carolinas, leaving behind a 60-mile-wide swath of destruction. His goal was to impress on southerners that continuation of the war could mean only ruin for all of them. He and Grant planned that his army should press on through the Carolinas and into Virginia to join Grant in finishing off Lee.

Before Sherman's troops could arrive, Lee abandoned Richmond (April 3, 1865) and attempted to escape with what was left of his army. Pursued by Grant, he was cornered and forced to surrender at Appomattox, Virginia, on April 9, 1865. Other Confederate armies still holding out in various parts of the South surrendered over the next few weeks.

Lincoln did not live to receive news of the final surrenders. On April 14, 1865, he was shot in the back of the head while watching a play at Ford's Theater in Washington. His assassin, pro-Southern actor John Wilkes Booth, injured his ankle in making his escape. Hunted down by Union cavalry several days later, he died of a gunshot wound, apparently self-inflicted. Several other individuals were tried, convicted, and hanged by a military tribunal for participating with Booth in a conspiracy to assassinate not only Lincoln, but also Vice President Johnson and Secretary of State Seward.

THE ORDEAL OF RECONSTRUCTION

Lincoln's Plan of Reconstruction

Reconstruction began well before the fighting of the Civil War came to an end. It brought a time of difficult adjustments in the South.

Among those who faced such adjustments were the recently freed slaves, who flocked into Union lines, followed advancing Union armies, or whose plantations were part of the growing area of the South that came under Union military control. Some slaves had left their plantations, and thus their only means of livelihood, in order to obtain freedom within Union lines. Many felt they had to leave their plantations in order to be truly free, and some sought to find relatives separated during the days of slavery. Some former slaves also seemed to misunderstand the meaning of freedom, thinking they need never work again.

To ease the adjustment for these recently freed slaves, Congress in 1865 created the Freedman's Bureau, to provide food, clothing, and education, and generally look after the interests of former slaves.

Even before the need to deal with this problem had forced itself on the Northern government's awareness, steps had been taken to deal with another major adjustment of Reconstruction, the restoration of loyal governments to the seceded states. By 1863 substantial portions of several Southern states had come under Northern military control, and Lincoln had set forth a policy for re-establishing governments in those states.

Lincoln's policy, known as the Ten Percent Plan, stipulated that Southerners, except for high-ranking rebel officials, could take an oath promising future loyalty to the Union and acceptance of the end of slavery. When the number of those who had taken this oath within any one state reached ten percent of the number who had been registered to vote in that state in 1860, a loyal state government could be formed. Only those who had taken the oath could vote or participate in the new government.

Tennessee, Arkansas, and Louisiana met the requirements and formed loyal governments but were refused recognition by Congress, which was dominated by Radical Republicans.

The Radical Republicans, such as Thaddeus Stevens of Pennsylvania, believed Lincoln's plan did not adequately punish the South, restructure Southern society, and boost the political prospects of the Republican Party. The loyal southern states were denied representation in Congress and electoral votes in the election of 1864.

Instead, the Radicals in Congress drew up the Wade-Davis Bill. Under its stringent terms a majority of the number who had been alive and registered to vote in 1860 would have to swear an "ironclad" oath stating that they were now loyal and had never been disloyal. This was obviously impossible in any former Confederate state unless blacks were given the vote, something Radical Republicans desired but Southerners definitely did not. Unless the requisite number swore the "ironclad" oath, Congress would not allow the state to have a government.

Lincoln killed the Wade-Davis bill with a "pocket veto," and the Radicals were furious. When Lincoln was assassinated the Radicals rejoiced, believing Vice President Andrew Johnson would be less generous to the South or at least easier to control.

Johnson's Attempt at Reconstruction

To the dismay of the Radicals, Johnson followed Lincoln's policies very closely, making them only slightly more stringent by requiring ratification of the 13th Amendment (officially abolishing slavery), repudiation of Confederate debts, and renunciation of secession. He also recommended the vote be given to blacks.

Southern states proved reluctant to accept these conditions, some declining to repudiate Confederate debts or ratify the 13th Amendment (it nevertheless received the ratification of the necessary number of states and was declared part of the Constitution in December 1865). No Southern state extended the vote to blacks (at this time no Northern state did, either). Instead the Southern states promulgated Black Codes, imposing various restrictions on the freedom of the former slaves.

Foreign Policy Under Johnson

On coming into office Johnson had inherited a foreign policy problem involving Mexico and France. The French Emperor, Napoleon III, had made Mexico the target of one of his many grandiose foreign adventures. In 1862, while the U.S. was occupied with the Civil War and therefore unable to prevent this violation of the Monroe Doctrine, Napoleon III had Archduke Maximilian of Austria installed as a puppet emperor of Mexico, supported by French troops. The U.S. had protested but for the time could do nothing.

With the war over, Johnson and Secretary of State Seward were able to take more vigorous steps. General Philip Sheridan was sent to the Rio Grande with a military force. At the same time Mexican revolutionary leader Benito Juarez was given the tacit recognition of the U.S. government. Johnson and Seward continued to invoke the Monroe Doctrine and to place quiet pressure on Napoleon III to withdraw his troops. In May 1866, facing difficulties of his own in Europe, the French emperor did so, leaving the unfortunate Maximilian to face a Mexican firing squad.

Johnson's and Seward's course of action in preventing the extension of the French Empire into the Western Hemisphere strengthened America's commitment to and the rest of the world's respect for the Monroe Doctrine.

In 1866 the Russian minister approached Seward with an offer to sell Alaska to the U.S. The Russians desired to sell Alaska because its fur resources had been largely exhausted and because they feared that in a possible war with Great Britain (something that seemed likely at the time) they would lose Alaska anyway.

Seward, who was an ardent expansionist, pushed hard for the purchase of Alaska, known as "Seward's Folly" by its critics, and it was largely through his efforts that it was pushed through Congress. It was urged that purchasing Alaska would reward the Russians for their friendly stance toward the U.S. government during the Civil War, at a time when Britain and France had seemed to favor the Confederacy.

In 1867 the sale went through and Alaska was purchased for $7.2 million.

Congressional Reconstruction

Southern intransigence in the face of Johnson's relatively mild plan of Reconstruction manifested in the refusal of some states to repudiate the Confederate debt and ratify the 13th Amendment. The refusal to give the vote to blacks, the passage of black codes, and the election of many former high-ranking Confederates to Congress and other top positions in the Southern states, played into the hands of the Radicals, who were anxious to impose harsh rule on the South. They could now assert that the South was refusing to accept the verdict of the war.

Once again Congress excluded the representatives of the Southern states. Determined to reconstruct the South as it saw fit, Congress passed a Civil Rights Act and extended the authority of the Freedman's Bureau, giving it both quasi-judicial and quasi-executive powers.

Johnson vetoed both bills, claiming they were unconstitutional; but Congress overrode the vetoes. Fearing that the Supreme Court would agree with Johnson and overturn the laws, Congress approved and sent on to the states for ratification (June 1866) the 14th Amendment, making constitutional the laws Congress had just passed. The 14th Amendment defined citizenship and forbade

A brilliant orator and writer, Frederick Douglass became one of the leading
human-rights champions of the nineteenth century.

states to deny various rights to citizens, reduced the representation in Congress of states that did not allow blacks to vote, forbade the paying of the Confederate debt, and made former Confederates ineligible to hold public office.

With only one Southern state, Tennessee, ratifying, the amendment failed to receive the necessary approval of three-fourths of the states. But the Radicals in Congress were not finished. Strengthened by victory in the 1866 elections, they passed, over Johnson's veto, the Military Reconstruction Act, dividing the South into five military districts to be ruled by military governors with almost dictatorial powers. Tennessee, having ratified the 14th Amendment, was spared the wrath of the Radicals. The rest of the Southern states were ordered to produce constitutions giving the vote to blacks and to ratify the 14th Amendment before they could be "readmitted." In this manner the 14th Amendment was ratified.

Realizing the unprecedented nature of these actions, Congress moved to prevent any check or balance from the other two branches of government. Steps were taken toward limiting the jurisdiction of the Supreme Court so that it could not review cases pertaining to congressional Reconstruction policies. This proved unnecessary as the Court, now headed by Chief Justice Salmon P. Chase in place of the deceased Taney, readily acquiesced and declined to overturn the Reconstruction acts.

To control the president, Congress passed the Army Act, reducing the president's control over the Army. In obtaining the cooperation of the Army the Radicals had the aid of General Grant, who already had his eye on the 1868 Republican presidential nomination. Congress also passed the Tenure of Office Act, forbidding Johnson to dismiss Cabinet members without the Senate's permission. In passing the latter act, Congress was especially thinking of Radical Secretary of War Edwin M. Stanton, a Lincoln holdover whom Johnson desired to dismiss.

Johnson obeyed the letter but not the spirit of the Reconstruction acts, and Congress, angry at his refusal to cooperate, sought in vain for grounds to impeach him until in August 1867, Johnson violated the Tenure of Office Act (by dismissing Stanton) in order to test its constitutionality. The matter was not tested in the courts, however, but in Congress, where Johnson was impeached by the House of Representatives and came within one vote of being removed by the Senate. For the remaining months of his term he offered little further resistance to the Radicals.

The Election of 1868 and the 15th Amendment

In 1868 the Republican convention, dominated by the Radicals, drew up a platform endorsing Radical Reconstruction. For president, the Republicans nominated Ulysses S. Grant, who had no political record and whose views—if any—on national issues were unknown. The vice-presidential nominee was Schuyler Colfax.

Though the Democratic nomination was sought by Andrew Johnson, the party knew he could not win and instead nominated former Governor Horatio Seymour of New York for president and Francis P. Blair, Jr. of Missouri for vice president. Both had been Union generals during the war. The Democratic platform mildly criticized the excesses of Radical Reconstruction and called for continued payment of the war debt in greenbacks, although Seymour himself was a hard-money man.

Grant, despite his enormous popularity as a war hero, won by only a narrow margin, drawing only 300,000 more popular votes than Seymour. Some 700,000 blacks had voted in the Southern states under the auspices of Army occupation, and since all of these had almost certainly voted for Grant, it was clear that he had not received a majority of the white vote.

The narrow victory of even such a strong candidate as Grant prompted Republican leaders to decide that it would be politically expedient to give the vote to all blacks, North as well as South. For this purpose the 15th Amendment was drawn up and submitted to the states. Ironically, the idea was so unpopular in the North that it won the necessary three-fourths approval only with its ratification by Southern states required to do so by Congress.

Postwar Life in the South

Reconstruction was a difficult time in the South. During the war approximately one in ten Southern men had been killed. Many more were maimed for life. Those who returned from the war found destruction and poverty. Property of the Confederate government was confiscated by the federal government, and dishonest Treasury agents confiscated private property as well. Capital invested in slaves or in Confederate war bonds was lost. Property values fell to one-tenth of their pre-war level. The economic results of the war stayed with the South for decades.

The political results were less long-lived but more immediately disturbing to Southerners. Southerners complained of widespread corruption in governments sustained by federal troops and composed of "carpetbaggers," "scalawags" (the Southern names for Northerners who came to the South to participate in Reconstruction governments and for southerners who supported the Reconstruction regimes, respectively), and recently freed blacks.

Under the Reconstruction governments, social programs were greatly expanded, leading to higher taxes and growing state debts. Some of the financial problems were due to corruption, a problem in both North and South in this era when political machines, such as William Marcy "Boss" Tweed's Tammany Hall machine in New York, dominated many Northern city governments and grew rich.

Southern whites sometimes responded to Reconstruction governments with violence, carried out by groups such as the Ku Klux Klan, aimed at intimidating blacks and white Republicans out of voting. The activities of these organizations were sometimes a response to those of the Union League, an organization used by Southern Republicans to control the black vote. The goal of Southerners not allied with the Reconstruction governments, whether members of the Ku Klux Klan or not, was "redemption" (i.e., the end of the Reconstruction governments).

By 1876 Southern whites had been successful, by legal means or otherwise, in "redeeming" all but three Southern states.

Reconstruction ended primarily because the North lost interest. Corruption in government, economic hard times brought on by the Panic of 1873, and general weariness on the part of Northern voters with the effort to remake Southern society all sapped the will to continue. Diehard Radicals such as Thaddeus Stevens and Charles Sumner were dead.

Corruption Under Grant

Having arrived in the presidency with no firm political positions, Grant found that the only principle he had to guide his actions was his instinctive loyalty to his old friends and the politicians who had propelled him into office. This principle did not serve him well as president. Though personally of unquestioned integrity, he naively placed his faith in a number of thoroughly dishonest men. His administration was rocked by one scandalous revelation of government corruption after another. Not every scandal involved members

"Man with the (Carpet) Bags," Thomas Nast, 1872. This caricature of Carl Schurz appeared in *Harper's Weekly*. U.S. Library of Congress.

of the executive branch, but together they tended to taint the entire period of Grant's administration as one of unparalleled corruption.

The "Black Friday" Scandal

In the "Black Friday" scandal, two unscrupulous businessmen, Jim Fiske and Jay Gould, schemed to corner the gold market. To further their designs, they got Grant's brother-in-law to persuade the president that stopping government gold sales would be good for farmers. Grant naively complied, and many businessmen were ruined as the price of gold was bid up furiously on "Black Friday." By the time Grant realized what was happening, much damage had already been done.

The Credit Mobilier Scandal

In the Credit Mobilier scandal, officials of the Union Pacific Railroad used a dummy construction company called Credit Mobilier to skim off millions of dollars of the subsidies the government was paying the Union Pacific for building a transcontinental railroad. To ensure that Congress would take a benevolent attitude toward all this, the officials bribed many of its members lavishly. Though much of this took place before Grant came into office, its revelation in an 1872 congressional investigation created a general scandal.

The "Salary Grab Act"

In the "Salary Grab Act" of 1873, Congress voted a 100 percent pay raise for the president and a 50 percent increase for itself and made both retroactive two years. Public outrage led to a Democratic victory in the next congressional election and the law was repealed.

The Sanborn Contract Fraud

In the Sanborn Contract fraud, a politician named Sanborn was given a contract to collect $427,000 in unpaid taxes for a 50 percent commission. The commission found its way into Republican campaign funds.

The Whiskey Ring Fraud

In the Whiskey Ring fraud, distillers and treasury officials conspired to defraud the government of large amounts of money from the excise tax on whiskey. Grant's personal secretary was in on the plot, and Grant himself naively accepted gifts of a questionable nature. When the matter came under investigation, Grant endeavored to shield his secretary.

The Bribing of Belknap

Grant's secretary of war, W. W. Belknap, accepted bribes from corrupt agents involved in his department's administration of Indian affairs. When the matter came out, he resigned to escape impeachment.

The Liberal Republicans

Discontentment within Republican ranks with regard to some of the earlier scandals as well as with the Radicals' vindictive Reconstruction policies led a faction of the party to separate and constitute itself as the Liberal Republicans. Besides opposing corruption and favoring sectional harmony, the Liberal Republicans favored hard money and a laissez-faire approach to economic issues. For the election of 1872 they nominated *New York Tribune* editor Horace Greeley for president. Eccentric, controversial, and ineffective as a campaigner, Greeley proved a poor choice. Though nominated by the Democrats as well as the Liberal Republicans, he was easily defeated by Grant, who was again the nominee of the Radicals.

Economic Issues Under Grant

Many of the economic difficulties the country faced during Grant's administration were caused by the necessary readjustments from a wartime back to a peacetime economy.

Indian prisoners, from Black Kettle's camp, captured by General Custer, traveling through snow. Illustrated by Theodore R. Davis, *Harper's Weekly*, v. 12, 1868. p. 825. U.S. Library of Congress.

The central economic question was deflation versus inflation or, more specifically, whether to retire the unbacked paper money, greenbacks, printed to meet the wartime emergency, or to print more.

Economic conservatives, creditors, and business interests usually favored retirement of the greenbacks and an early return the gold standard.

Debtors, who had looked forward to paying off their obligations in depreciated paper money worth less than the gold-backed money they had borrowed, favored a continuation of currency inflation through the use of more greenbacks. The deflation that would come through the retirement of existing greenbacks would make debts contracted during or immediately after the war much harder to pay.

Generally, Grant's policy was to let the greenbacks float until they were on par with gold and could then be retired without economic dislocation.

Early in Grant's second term the country was hit by an economic depression known as the Panic of 1873. Brought on by the overexpansive tendencies of railroad builders and businessmen during the immediate post-war boom, the Panic was triggered by economic downturns in Europe and, more immediately, by the failure of Jay Cooke and Company, a major American financial firm.

The financial hardship brought on by the Panic led to renewed clamor for the printing of more greenbacks. In 1874 Congress authorized a small new issue of greenbacks, but it was vetoed by Grant. Pro-inflation forces were further enraged when Congress in 1873 demonetized silver, going to a straight gold standard. Silver was becoming more plentiful due to Western mining and was seen by some as a potential source of inflation. Pro-inflation forces referred to the demonetization of silver as the "Crime of '73."

In 1875 Congress took a further step toward retirement of the greenbacks and return to a working gold standard when, under the leadership of John Sherman, it passed the Specie Resumption Act, calling for the resumption of specie payments (i.e., the redeemability of the nation's paper money in gold) by January 1, 1879.

Disgruntled proponents of inflation formed the Greenback Party and nominated Peter Cooper for president in 1876. However, they gained only an insignificant number of votes.

The Disputed Election of 1876

In the election of 1876, the Democrats campaigned against corruption and nominated New York Governor Samuel J. Tilden, who had broken the Tweed political machine of New York City.

The Republicans passed over Grant, who was interested in another term and had the backing of the remaining hard-core Radicals, and turned instead to Governor Rutherford B. Hayes of Ohio. Like Tilden, Hayes was decent, honest, in favor of hard money and civil service reform, and opposed to government regulation of the economy. In their campaigning, the Republicans resorted to a tactic known as "waving the bloody shirt." Successfully used in the last two presidential elections, this meant basically playing on wartime animosities, urging Northerners to vote the way they had shot, and suggested that a Democratic victory and a Confederate victory would be about the same thing.

This time the tactic was less successful. Tilden won the popular vote and led in the electoral vote 184 to 165. However, 185 electoral votes were needed for election, and 20 votes, from the three Southern states still occupied by Federal troops and run by Republican governments, were disputed.

Though there had been extensive fraud on both sides, Tilden undoubtedly deserved at least the one vote he needed to win. Congress created a special commission to decide the matter. It was to be composed of five members each from the Senate, the House, and the Supreme Court. Of these, seven were to be Republicans, seven Democrats, and one an independent. The Republicans arranged, however, for the independent justice's state legislature to elect him to the Senate. When the justice resigned to take his Senate seat, it left all the remaining Supreme Court justices Republican. One of them was chosen, and in a series of eight-to-seven votes along straight party lines, the commission voted to give all 20 disputed votes—and the election—to Hayes.

When outraged congressional Democrats threatened to reject these obviously fraudulent results, a compromise was worked out. In the Compromise of 1877, Hayes promised to show consideration for Southern interests, end Reconstruction, and withdraw the remaining Federal troops from the South in exchange for Democratic acquiescence in his election.

Reconstruction would probably have ended anyway, since the North had already lost interest in it.

◄——— HISTORICAL TIMELINE ———►
THE CIVIL WAR AND RECONSTRUCTION (1860–1877)

1860	Crittenden Compromise proposed South Carolina secedes
1861	Confederacy formed Firing on Ft. Sumter First Battle of Bull Run
1862	Shiloh Antietam Homestead Act Emancipation Proclamation announced
1863	Vicksburg Gettysburg New York City draft riots
1864	Grant takes command of all Union armies Sherman captures Atlanta
1865	Lee surrenders at Appomattox Lincoln assassinated 13th Amendment ends slavery Freedmen's Bureau established
1867	Alaska purchased from Russia Grange founded
1868	President Johnson impeached 14th Amendment passed Grant elected president
1869	Transcontinental railroad completed Knights of Labor formed
1873	Slaughterhouse case Panic of 1873

1875	Dwight L. Moody begins urban revivalism movement
1876	Custer defeated by Sioux at Little Big Horn
1877	Compromise of 1877 Reconstruction ends

Chapter 9

INDUSTRIALISM, WAR, AND THE PROGRESSIVE ERA (1877–1912)

THE NEW INDUSTRIAL ERA, 1877–1882

The structure of modern American society was erected by democratic, capitalistic and technological forces in the post–Civil War era. Between the 1870s and 1890s, "Gilded Age" America emerged as the world's leading industrial and agricultural producer.

POLITICS OF THE PERIOD, 1877–1882

The presidencies of Abraham Lincoln and Theodore Roosevelt mark the boundaries of a half century of relatively weak executive leadership, and legislative domination by Congress and the Republican Party.

The Compromise of 1877

With Southern Democratic acceptance of Rutherford B. Hayes' Republican presidency, the last remaining Union troops were withdrawn from the Old Confederacy (South Carolina, Florida, Louisiana), and the country was at last reunified as a modern nation-state led by corporate and industrial interests. The Hayes election arrangement also marked the government's abandonment of its earlier vague commitment to African-American equality.

Republican Factions

"Stalwarts" led by New York Senator Roscoe Conkling favored the old spoils system of political patronage. "Half-Breeds" headed by Maine Senator James G. Blaine pushed for civil service reform and merit appointments to government posts.

Election of 1880

James A. Garfield of Ohio, a Half-Breed, and his vice presidential running mate, Chester A. Arthur of New York, a Stalwart, defeated the Democratic candidate, General Winfield S. Hancock of Pennsylvania and former Indiana congressman William English. Tragically, the Garfield administration was but an interlude, for the president was assassinated in 1881 by a mentally disturbed patronage seeker, Charles Guiteau. Although without much executive experience, the Stalwart Arthur had the courage to endorse reform of the political spoils system by supporting passage of the Pendleton Act (1883) which established open competitive examinations for civil service positions.

The Greenback-Labor Party

The Greenback-Labor Party movement polled over one million votes in 1878, and elected 14 members to Congress in an effort to promote the inflation of farm prices, and the cooperative marketing of agricultural produce. In 1880, the party's presidential candidate, James Weaver of Iowa, advocated public control and regulation of private enterprises such as railroads in the common interest of more equitable competition. Weaver theorized that because railroads were so essential, they should be treated as a public utility. He polled only 3 percent of the vote.

THE ECONOMY, 1877–1882

Industrial expansion and technology assumed mayor proportions in this period. Between 1860 and 1894 the United States moved from the fourth-largest manufacturing nation to the world's leader through capital accumulation, natural resources (especially in iron, oil and coal) an abundance of labor helped by massive immigration, railway transportation and communications (the telephone was introduced by Alexander Graham Bell in 1876), and major technical innovations such as the development of the modern steel industry by Andrew Carnegie, and electrical energy by Thomas Edison. In the petroleum industry, John D. Rockefeller controlled 95 percent of the U.S. oil refineries by 1877.

The New South

By 1880, Northern capital erected the modern textile industry in the New South by bringing factories to the cotton fields. Birmingham, Alabama, emerged as the South's leading steel producer, and the introduction of machine-made cigarettes propelled the Duke family to prominence as tobacco producers.

Standard of Living

An elite class rose during this period which accumulated vast family fortunes, while many Americans, especially immigrants and newly freed slaves, suffered crushing poverty.

Social Darwinism

Many industrial leaders used the doctrines associated with the "Gospel of Wealth" to justify the unequal distribution of national wealth. Self-justification by the wealthy was based on the notion that God had granted wealth as He had given grace for material and spiritual salvation of the select few. These few, according to William Graham Sumner, relied heavily on the survival-of-the-fittest philosophy associated with Charles Darwin.

Labor Unrest

When capital over-expansion and over-speculation led to the economic panic of 1873, massive labor disorders spread through the country leading to the paralyzing railroad strike of 1877. Unemployment and salary reductions caused major class conflict. President Hayes used federal troops to restore order after dozens of workers were killed. Immigrant workers began fighting among themselves in California where Irish and Chinese laborers fought for economic survival.

Labor Unions

The depression of the 1870s undermined national labor organizations. The National Labor Union (1866) had a membership of 600,000 but failed to withstand the impact of economic adversity. The Knights of Labor (1869) managed to open its membership to not only white native American workers, but immigrants, women and African-Americans as well. Although they claimed one million members, they too could not weather the hard times of the 1870s, and eventually went under in 1886 in the wake of the bloody Haymarket Riot in Chicago.

Agricultural Militancy

Agrarian discontent expressed through the activities of the National Grange and the Farmers' Alliances in the West and South showed greater lasting power. During the Civil War, many farmers had over-expanded their operations, purchased more land and machinery, and gone heavily into debt. When the relatively high wartime agricultural prices collapsed in the decades after the war, farmers worked collectively to promote currency inflation, higher farm prices, silver and gold bimetalism, debt relief, cooperative farm marketing ventures, and regulation of monopolies and railroads by the federal and state governments. Although not very successful in the 1870s, farmer militancy continued to be a powerful political and economic force in the decades of the 1880s and 1890s.

SOCIAL AND CULTURAL DEVELOPMENTS, 1877–1882

Urbanization was the primary social and cultural phenomenon of the period. Both internal and external migrations contributed to an industrial urban state that grew from 40 million people in 1870 to almost 80 million in 1900. New York, Chicago, and Philadelphia emerged as cities of over 1 million people.

Skyscrapers and Immigrants

Cities grew both up and out as the skyscraper made its appearance after the introduction of the mechanical elevator by Elisha Otis. The city also grew outward into a large, impersonal metropolis divided into various business, industrial and residential sectors, usually segregated by ethnic group, social class and race. Slums and tenements sprang up within walking distance of department stores and townhouses. Two million immigrants from northern Europe poured into the U.S. during the 1870s. In the 1880s another 5 million entered the country, but by this time they were coming from southern and eastern Europe.

Lack of Government Policy

There were few programs to deal with the vast influx of humanity other than the prohibition of the criminal and the insane. City governments soon developed the primary responsibility for immigrants—often trading employment, housing and social services for political support.

Social Gospel

In time, advocates of the "social gospel" such as Jane Addams and Washington Gladden urged the creation of settlement houses and better health and education services to accommodate the new immigrants. New religions also appeared, including the Salvation Army, and Mary Baker Eddy's Church of Christian Science in 1879.

Education

Public education continued to expand, especially on the secondary level. Private Catholic parochial schools and teaching colleges grew in number as well. Adult education and English instruction became important functions of both public and private schooling.

African-American Leaders

Booker T. Washington emerged in 1881 as the president of Tuskegee Institute in Alabama, a school devoted to teaching and vocational education for African-Americans with a mission to encourage self-respect and economic equality of the races. It was at Tuskegee that George Washington Carver emerged in subsequent years as an agricultural chemist who did much to find industrial applications for agricultural products.

Feminism

The new urban environment encouraged feminist activism. Millions of women worked outside the home, and continued to demand voting rights. Many women became active in social reform movements such as the prohibitionist Women's Christian Temperance Movement, planned parenthood, humane societies, anti-prostitution crusades, and equal rights for all regardless of gender, race, or class.

Literature

Important books appeared such as Henry George's *Progress and Poverty* (1879), a 3-million-copy seller that advocated one single tax on land as the means to redistribute wealth for greater social and economic justice. In fiction Lew Wallace's *Ben Hur* (1880), and the many Horatio Alger stories promoting values such as hard work, honesty, and a touch of good fortune sold many millions of copies. Other famous works of the era included Mark Twain's *The Gilded Age* (1873), and *The Adventures of Tom Sawyer* (1876), Bret Harte's stories of the Old West, William Dean Howell's social commentaries, and Henry James's *Daisy Miller* (1879) and *Portrait of a Lady* (1881).

FOREIGN RELATIONS, 1877–1882

The United States gradually became involved in the "new imperialism" of the 1870s geared to finding markets for surplus industrial production, access to needed raw materials, and opportunities for overseas investment during a time of domestic economic depression. Unlike European territorial colonialism, however, the United States preferred market expansion without the political liability of military occupation.

Latin America

President Hayes recognized the government of dictator Porfirio Diaz in Mexico, thus encouraging not only trade expansion, but U.S. investment in railroads, mines, agriculture and oil.

Pan Americanism

In 1881 Secretary of State James G. Blaine advocated the creation of an International Bureau of American Republics to promote a customs union of trade and political stability for the Western Hemisphere. The assassination of President Garfield temporarily kept Blaine from forming this organization until 1889. The Bureau subsequently evolved into the Pan American Union in 1910, and the Organization of American States in 1948.

Mediation of Border Disputes

The United States offered its good offices to promote the peaceful resolution of border conflicts between a number of states: in 1876 between Argentina and Paraguay; in 1880 between Colombia and Chile; and in 1881 between Mexico and Guatemala, Argentina and Chile, and Peru and Chile. The United States also worked to bring an end to the War of the Pacific (1879–1884) fought between Chile and the alliance of Peru and Bolivia.

Canal Project

In 1876 the Interoceanic Canal Commission recommended a Nicaraguan route for a canal to link the Atlantic and Pacific oceans. In the 1880s, the U.S. officially took a hostile position against the French Panama Canal project.

The Pacific

In 1878, the United States ratified a treaty with Samoa giving the U.S. trading rights and a naval base at Pago Pago.

Japan

In 1878, the United States was the first country to negotiate a treaty granting tariff autonomy to Japan, and set a precedent for ending the practice by Western nations of controlling customs house collections in Asian states.

Geronimo, Apache leader who rose to prominence in mounting
an offensive against U.S. forces' forcible displacement of 4,000 Apaches
to a barren wasteland in the Southwest. Undated. AP Photo.

Korea

Commodore Robert Wilson Shufeldt opened trade and diplomatic relations with the Hermit Kingdom in 1882. The United States promoted the principles of equal opportunity of trade, and the sovereignty of Korea (later known as open door policies) which had earlier been advocated as desirable in China.

Native Americans

Westward expansion and the discovery of gold in South Dakota in the early 1870s led to the Sioux War, 1876–1877, and George A. Custer's "last stand." In 1877 the Nez Perce War in Idaho resulted from similar causes. The Apache in Arizona and New Mexico fought as well.

Reservations

The Indian tribes were eventually vanquished and compelled to live on isolated reservations. In addition to superior U.S. military force, disease, railway construction, alcoholism, and the virtual extermination of the bison contributed to their defeat. In 1881 Helen Hunt Jackson's *A Century of Dishonor* chronicled the tragic policy pursued against Native Americans.

THE REACTION TO CORPORATE INDUSTRIALISM, 1882–1887

The rise of big business and monopoly capitalism—especially in banking, railroads, mining, and the oil and steel industries—generated a reaction on the part of working class Americans in the form of new labor organizations and collective political action. Most Americans, however, were not opposed to free enterprise economics, but simply wanted an opportunity to share in the profits.

POLITICS OF THE PERIOD, 1882–1887

The only Democrat elected president in the half century after the Civil War was Grover Cleveland.

Election of 1884

The Republicans nominated James G. Blaine (Maine) for president and John Logan (Illinois) for vice president. The Democrats chose New York governor Grover Cleveland and Thomas A. Hendricks (Indiana). The defection of Independent Republicans supporting civil service reforms, known as "Mugwumps" (such as E.L. Godkin and Carl Schurz) to the Cleveland camp cost Blaine, the former Speaker of the House, the election. The Democrats held control of the House and the Republicans controlled the Senate.

Presidential Succession Act of 1886

The death of Vice President Hendricks in 1885 led to a decision to change the line of succession (established in 1792) from the president *pro tempore* of the Senate to the Cabinet officers in order of creation of their departments to maintain party leadership. This system lasted until 1947 when the Speaker of the House was declared third in line.

Executive Appointments

President Cleveland insisted that executive appointments and removals were the prerogative of the executive and not the Senate. This was the first time since Andrew Johnson that a president had strengthened the independence of his office.

THE ECONOMY, 1882–1887

Large, efficient corporations prospered. Captains of industry, or robber barons, such as John D. Rockefeller in oil, J. P. Morgan in banking, Gustavus Swift in meat processing, Andrew Carnegie in steel, and E. H. Harriman in railroads, put together major industrial empires.

Big Business

The concentration of wealth and power in the hands of a relatively small number of giant firms in many industries led to monopoly capitalism that minimized competition. This process, in turn, led to a demand by smaller businessmen, farmers and laborers for government regulation of the economy in order to promote capital competition for the salvation of free enterprise economics.

The Interstate Commerce Act (1887)

Popular resentment of railroad abuses such as price fixing, kickbacks, and discriminatory freight rates created demands for state regulation of the railway industry. When the Supreme Court ruled individual state laws unconstitutional (*Wabash* case, 1886) because only Congress had the right to control interstate commerce, the Interstate Commerce Act was passed providing that a commission be established to oversee fair and just railway rates, prohibit rebates, end discriminatory practices, and require annual reports and financial statements. The Supreme Court, however, remained a friend of special interests, and often undermined the work of the I.C.C.

Expanding Cultivation

Agrarians and ranchers continued their westward expansion. The amount of land under cultivation between 1870 and 1890 more than doubled from 408 to 840 million acres. Transcontinental railroads, modem farm machinery, and soil conservation practices contributed to national prosperity.

Low Farm Prices

Despite success many farmers were concerned about capital indebtedness, low farm prices resulting from surplus production, railroad rate discrimination, and the lack of sufficient silver currency to promote price inflation. Agrarian groups such as the National Grange and the Farmers' Alliances called for government of the economy to redress their grievances. To a certain extent, however, many of these problems were determined by participation of American agriculture in global markets. Farmers did not completely understand all the risks in an international free market economy.

American Federation of Labor, 1886

Confronted by big business, Samuel Gompers and Adolph Strasser put together a combination of national craft unions to represent the material interests of labor in the matter of wages, hours, and safety conditions. The American Federation of Labor philosophy was pragmatic and not directly influenced by the dogmatic Marxism of some European labor movements. Although militant in its use of the strike and its demand for collective bargaining in labor contracts with large corporations such as those in railroads, mining and manufacturing, the American Federation of Labor did not intend violent revolution or political radicalism.

Scientific Management

Frederick W. Taylor, an engineer credited as the father of scientific management, introduced modern concepts of industrial engineering, plant management, and time and motion studies. This gave rise to efficiency experts and a separate class of managers in industrial manufacturing.

SOCIAL AND CULTURAL DEVELOPMENTS, 1882–1887

The continued growth of urban America contributed to the dissemination of knowledge and information in many fields.

Newspapers and Magazines

The linotype machine (1886) invented by Otto Mergenthaler cut printing costs dramatically. Press associations flourished and publishing became big business. In 1884, Joseph Pulitzer, a Hungarian-born immigrant, was the first publisher to reach a mass audience selling 100,000 copies of the *New York World*. New magazines such as *Forum* appeared in 1886 with a hard-hitting editorial style that emphasized investigatory journalism and controversial subjects.

Higher Education

Colleges and universities expanded and introduced a more modern curriculum. Graduate study emphasized meticulous research and the seminar method as pioneered in the United States at Johns Hopkins University.

Women's Colleges

Bryn Mawr (1885) was established and soon found a place among such schools as Vassar, Wellesley, and Mount Holyoke in advancing education for women.

Natural Science

Albert Michelson at the University of Chicago, working on measuring the speed of light, contributed in the 1880s to theories which helped prepare the way for Einstein's Theory of Relativity. In 1907, Michelson was the first American to win a Nobel Prize.

The New Social Science

Richard T. Ely studied the ethical implications of economic problems. Henry C. Adams and Simon Patten put forth theories to justify government regulation and planning in the economy. In sociology, Lester Frank Ward's *Dynamic Sociology* (1883) stressed intelligent planning and decision making over genetic determinism as promoted by Social Darwinists such as William Graham Sumner. Woodrow Wilson's *Congressional Government* was a critique of the committee system in Congress and called for a better working relationship between the executive and legislative branches of government. After winning the presidency in 1912, Wilson would be in a position to put his ideas into practice.

Literary Realism

Romanticism declined in favor of a more realistic approach to literature. Novelists explored social problems such as crime and political corruption, urban ghetto life, class conflict, evolution, and the environment. Mark Twain's masterpiece *Huckleberry Finn* appeared in 1884. In 1885, William Dean Howell's *The*

Rise of Silas Lapham presented the theme of business ethics in a competitive society. *The Bostonians* (1886) by Henry James attempted a complex psychological study of female behavior.

Art

Realism could also be seen in the artistic works of Thomas Eakins, Mary Cassatt, Winslow Homer, and James Whistler. Museums and art schools expanded. Wealthy patrons spent fortunes on personal art collections.

FOREIGN RELATIONS, 1882–1887

Contrary to popular belief, the United States was not an isolationist nation in the 1880s. Trade expansion and the protection of markets were primary concerns.

Modern Navy

In 1883 Congress authorized the construction of new steel ships that would take the U.S. Navy in a 20-year period from twelfth to third in world naval ranking. In 1884, the U.S. Naval War College was established in Newport, Rhode Island—the first of its kind.

Europe

Problems existed with Britain over violence in Ireland and England. In 1886, the U.S. refused to extradite an Irish national accused of terrorist activity in London.

Diseased meat products in the European market led to British and German bans against uninspected American meat exports. Congress soon provided for government regulation and inspection of meat for export. This action would set a precedent for systematic food and drug inspection in later years.

Africa

The United States participated in the Berlin Conference (1884) concerning trade in the Congo. The U.S. also took part in the Third International Red Cross Conference.

Asia and the Pacific

In 1882, Congress passed a law suspending Chinese immigration to the U.S. for ten years. The act reflected racist attitudes and created friction with China.

In 1886, the U.S. obtained by treaty with Hawaii the Pearl Harbor Naval Base.

Missionaries

American Christian missionaries were active in the Pacific, Asia, Africa, Latin America and the Middle East. Missionaries not only brought religion to many third world regions, but also Western education, exposure to science and technology, and commercial ventures. Some missionaries also took with them racist concepts of white supremacy.

Latin America

In 1884, the U.S. signed a short lived pact with Nicaragua for joint ownership of an isthmian canal in Central America.

THE EMERGENCE OF REGIONAL EMPIRE, 1887–1892

Despite a protective tariff policy, the United States became increasingly international as it sought to export surplus manufactured and agricultural goods. Foreign markets were viewed as a safety valve for labor employment problems and agrarian unrest. The return of Secretary of State James G. Blaine in 1889 marked a major attempt by the United States to promote a regional empire in the Western Hemisphere and reciprocal trade programs.

POLITICS OF THE PERIOD, 1887–1892

National politics became more controversial and turbulent in this era.

Election of 1888

Although the Democrat Grover Cleveland won the popular vote by about 100,000 over the Republican Benjamin Harrison, Harrison carried the electoral college 233 to 168, and was declared president after waging a vigorous campaign to protect American industrial interests with a high protective tariff. In Congress, Republicans won control of both the House and Senate.

House Rules of Operation

Republican Thomas B. Reed became Speaker of the House in 1890, and changed the rules of operation to make himself a veritable tsar with absolute control in running the House.

Force Bill (1890)

Senate objections kept Congress from protecting African-American voters in the South through federal supervision of state elections.

Dependent Pensions Act (1890)

Congress granted service pensions to Union veterans and their dependents for the first time.

THE ECONOMY, 1887–1892

Anti-monopoly measures, protective tariffs and reciprocal trade, and a billion dollar budget became the order of the day.

Sherman Anti-Trust Act, 1890

Corporate monopolies (trusts) which controlled whole industries were subject to federal prosecution if they were found to be combinations or conspiracies in restraint of trade. Although supported by smaller businesses, labor unions and farm associations, the Sherman Anti-Trust Act was in time interpreted by the Supreme Court to apply to labor unions and farmers' cooperatives as much as to large corporate combinations.

Sherman Silver Purchase Act, 1890

Pro-silver interests passed legislation authorizing Congress to buy 4.5 million ounces of silver each month at market prices, and issue Treasury notes redeemable in gold and silver. This act created inflation and lowered gold reserves.

McKinley Tariff, 1890

This compromise protective tariff promised by the Republicans in 1888, and introduced by William McKinley of Ohio was passed and extended to industrial and agricultural goods. The act also included reciprocal trade provisions that allowed the president to retaliate against nations that discriminated against U.S. products, and reward states that opened their markets to American goods. Subsequent price increases led to a popular backlash, and a Democratic House victory in the 1890 congressional elections.

Billion-Dollar Budget

Congress depleted the Treasury surplus with the first peacetime billion-dollar appropriation of funds for state tax refunds, infrastructure improvements, Navy modernization, and pension payments. The loss of Treasury reserves put the economy in a precarious position when an economic panic occurred in 1893.

SOCIAL AND CULTURAL DEVELOPMENTS, 1887–1892

Entertainment for the masses became increasingly differentiated.

Popular Amusements

In addition to the legitimate stage, vaudeville shows presenting variety acts became immensely popular. The circus expanded when Barnum and Bailey formed a partnership to present "the greatest show on earth." Distinctively American Wild West shows toured North America and Europe. To record these activities, George Eastman's newly invented roll-film camera became popular with spectators.

Sports

In 1888, professional baseball sent an all-star team to tour the world. Boxing adopted leather gloves in 1892. Croquet and bicycle racing were new crazes. Basketball was invented in 1891 by James Naismith, a Massachusetts Y.M.C.A. instructor. Organized inter collegiate sports such as football, basketball, and baseball created intense rivalries between colleges that attracted mass spectator interest.

Childrearing Practices

Parents became more supportive and sympathetic to their children and less authoritarian and restrictive. The 1880s were something of a golden age in children's literature. Mary Wells Smith depicted an agrarian ideal; Sidney Lanier wrote tales of heroic boys and girls; Howard Pyle's *Robin Hood* gained wide readership and Joel Chandler Harris' characters Br'er Rabbit, Br'er Fox, and Uncle Remus became very popular.

Religion

Many churches took issue with the growing emphasis on materialism in American society. Dwight Lyman Moody introduced Urban revivalism comparable to earlier rural movements among Protestant denominations. In addition, the new immigrants generated significant growth for Roman Catholicism and Judaism. By 1890, there were about 150 religious denominations in the United States.

FOREIGN RELATIONS, 1887–1892

Following in the footsteps of William Seward as a major architect of American foreign policy, James G. Blaine promoted hemispheric solidarity with Latin America and economic expansionism.

Pan Americanism

As Secretary of State, Blaine was concerned with international trade, political stability and excessive militarism in Latin America. His international Bureau of American Republics was designed to promote a Pan American customs union and peaceful conflict resolution. To achieve his aims, Blaine opposed U.S. military intervention in the hemisphere. To a certain extent, his policies were in the tradition of President James Monroe and his Secretary of State, John Quincy Adams.

Haiti

After the Haitian revolution of 1888–1889, Blaine resisted pressure for U.S. intervention to establish a naval base near Port-au-Prince. The noted African-American Frederick Douglass played a key role in advising Blaine as U.S. minister to Haiti.

Chilean Revolution

When American sailors from the U.S.S. *Baltimore* were killed in Valparaiso (1891), President Harrison threatened war with the anti-American revolutionary government of President Balmaceda. Secretary Blaine helped to bring about a Chilean apology and preserve his Pan American policy.

Asia and the Pacific

The medical missionary/diplomat Horace Allen promoted peaceful American investment and trade with Korea.

In 1889, the United States upheld its interests against German expansion in the Samoan Islands by establishing a three-party protectorate over Samoa with Britain and Germany. The United States retained the port of Pago Pago.

In 1891, Queen Lydia Kamekeha Liliuokalani resisted American attempts to promote a protectorate over Hawaii. By 1893, pro-American sugar planters overthrew the native Hawaiian government and established a new government friendly to the United States.

Africa

The United States refused (1890) naval bases in the Portuguese colonies of Angola and Mozambique when Portugal was looking for allies against British expansion in Africa. Blaine opposed territorial expansion for the U.S. in Africa, but favored the development of commercial markets.

Theoretical Works

In 1890, naval Captain Alfred Thayer Mahan published *The Influence of Sea Power on History* which argued that control of the seas was the means to world power. Josiah Strong's *Our Country* presented the thesis that Americans had a mission to fulfill by exporting the word of God around the world, especially to non-white populations. Frederick Jackson Turner's "Frontier Thesis" (1893) justified overseas economic expansion as a way to secure political power and prosperity. In *The Law of Civilization and Decay* (1895), Brooks Adams postulated that a nation must expand or face inevitable decline.

Europe

The murders of eleven Italian citizens in New Orleans (1891) brought the United States and Italy into confrontation. The United States defused the situation by compensating the families of the victims.

ECONOMIC DEPRESSION AND SOCIAL CRISIS, 1892–1897

The economic depression that began in 1893 brought about a collective response from organized labor, militant agriculture and the business community. Each group called for economic safeguards, and a more humane free enterprise system that would expand economic opportunities in an equitable manner.

Election of 1892

Democrat Grover Cleveland (New York) and his vice presidential running mate, Adlai E. Stevenson (Illinois), regained the White House by defeating the Republican President Benjamin Harrison (Indiana) and Vice President Whitelaw Reid (New York). Voters generally reacted against the inflationary McKinley Tariff. Cleveland's conservative economic stand in favor of the gold standard brought him the support of various business interests. The Democrats won control of both houses of Congress.

Populist Party

The People's Party (Populist) nominated James Weaver (Iowa) for president and James Field (Virginia) for vice president in 1892. The party platform put together by such Populist leaders as Ignatius Donnally (Minnesota), Thomas Watson (Georgia), Mary Lease (Kansas), and "Sockless" Jerry Simpson (Kansas) called for the enactment of a program espoused by agrarians, but also for a coalition with urban workers and the middle class. Specific goals were the coinage of silver to gold at a ratio of 16 to 1; federal loans to farmers; a graduated income tax; postal savings banks; public ownership of railroads, telephone and telegraph systems; prohibition of alien land ownership; immigration restriction; a ban on private armies used by corporations to break up strikes; an 8-hour working day; a single six-year term for president, and direct election of senators; the right of initiative and referendum; and the use of the secret ballot.

Although the Populists were considered radical by some, they actually wanted to reform the system from within, and allow for a fairer distribution of wealth. In a society with vast differences in income and wealth, the Populists were able to garner about one million votes (out of 11 million votes cast), and 22 electoral votes. By 1894, Populists had elected 4 senators, 4 congressmen, 21 state executive officials, 150 state senators, and 315 state representatives, primarily in the West and South. After the 1893 depression, the Populists planned a serious bid for national power in the 1896 election.

Repeal of Sherman Silver Purchase Act (1893)

After the economic panic of 1893, Cleveland tried to limit the outflow of gold reserves by asking Congress to repeal the Sherman Silver Act which had provided for notes redemptive in either gold or silver. Congress did repeal the act, but the Democratic Party split over the issue.

Election of 1896

The Republicans nominated William McKinley (Ohio) for president and Garrett Hobart (New Jersey) for vice president on a platform calling for maintaining the gold standard and protective tariffs. The Democratic Party repudiated Cleveland's conservative economics and nominated William Jennings Bryan (Nebraska) and Arthur Sewell (Maine) for president and vice president on a platform similar to the Populists: 1) coinage of silver at a ratio of 16 to 1; 2) condemnation of monopolies, protective tariffs and anti-union court injunctions; 3) criticism of the Supreme Court's removal of a graduated income tax from the Wilson-Gorman tariff bill (1894). Bryan delivered one of the most famous speeches in American history when he declared that the people must not be "crucified upon a cross of gold."

The Populist Party also nominated Bryan, but chose Thomas Watson (Georgia) for vice president. Having been outmaneuvered by the Silver Democrats, the Populists lost the opportunity to become a permanent political force.

McKinley won a hard-fought election by only about one-half million votes as Republicans succeeded in creating fear among business groups and middle class voters that Bryan represented a revolutionary challenge to the American system. The manipulation of higher farm prices, and the warning to labor unions that they would face unemployment if Bryan won the election helped to tilt the vote in favor of McKinley. An often forgotten issue in 1896 was the Republican promise to stabilize the ongoing Cuban revolution. This pledge would eventually lead the U.S. into war with Spain (1898) for Cuban independence. The Republicans retained control over Congress which they had gained in 1894.

THE ECONOMY, 1892–1897

The 1890s was a period of economic depression and labor agitation.

Homestead Strike, 1892

Iron and steel workers went on strike in Pennsylvania against the Carnegie Steel Company to protest salary reductions. Carnegie employed strike-breaking Pinkerton security guards. Management-labor warfare led to a number of deaths on both sides.

Depression of 1893

The primary causes for the Depression of 1893 were the dramatic growth of the federal deficit; withdrawal of British investments from the American market and the outward transfer of gold; loss of business confidence. The bankruptcy of the National Cordage Company was the first among thousands of U.S. corporations that closed banks and businesses. As a consequence, 20 percent of the work force was eventually unemployed. The depression would last four years. Recovery would be helped by war preparation.

March of Unemployed (1894)

The Populist businessman Jacob Coxey led a march on Washington of hundreds of unemployed workers asking for a government work relief program. The government met the marchers with force and arrested their leaders.

Pullman Strike (1894)

Eugene V. Debs' American Railway Union struck the Pullman Palace Car Co. in Chicago over wage cuts and job losses. President Cleveland broke the violent strike with federal troops. Popular opinion deplored violence and militant labor tactics.

Wilson-Gorman Tariff (1894)

This protective tariff did little to promote overseas trade as a way to ease the depression. A provision amended to create a graduated income tax was stricken by the Supreme Court as unconstitutional (*Pollack v. Farmers' Loan and Trust Co., 1895*).

Dingley Tariff (1897)

The Dingley Tariff raised protection to new highs for certain commodities.

Surplus Production and Foreign Trade

Anxiety over domestic class warfare, and the desire to sell surplus manufactured goods overseas led many business interests to encourage the U.S. government to find new international markets. Carnegie Steel and Standard Oil lobbied the State Department for better trade promotion policies as a way to recover from the depression, and provide jobs for American workers. Ironically, special business interests often undercut efforts to establish reciprocal trade agreements and free trade in favor of politically motivated tariff protection.

SOCIAL AND CULTURAL DEVELOPMENTS, 1892–1897

Economic depression and war dominated thought and literature in the decade of the 1890s.

Literature

Lester Frank Ward of Brown University presented a critique of excessive competition in favor of social planning in *The Psychic Factors of Civilization,* 1893. William Dean Howells' *A Hazard of New Fortunes,* 1890, was a broad attack on urban living conditions in industrial America, and on the callous treatment of workers by wealthy tycoons. Stephen Crane wrote about society's abuse of women in *Maggie, A Girl of the Streets,* 1892, and the pain of war in *The Red Badge of Courage,* 1895. Edward Bellamy's *Looking Backward* presented a science fiction look into a prosperous, but regimented future.

Americans also began to read such European realists as Dostoevsky, Ibsen, Tolstoy and Zola.

William James' *Principles of Psychology* introduced the discipline to American readers as a modern science of the human mind.

Prohibition of Alcohol

The Anti-Saloon League was formed in 1893. Women were especially concerned about the increase of drunkenness during the depression.

Immigration

Immigration declined by almost 400,000 during the depression. Jane Addams' Hull House in Chicago continued to function as a means of settling poor immigrants from Greece, Germany, Italy, Poland, Russia and elsewhere into American society. Lillian Wald's Henry Street Settlement in New York, and Robert Wood's South End House in Boston performed similar functions. Such institutions also lobbied against sweatshop labor conditions, and for bans on child labor.

Chautauqua Movement

Home study courses growing out of the Chautauqua Movement in New York State became popular.

Chicago World's Fair (1893)

Beautifying the cities was the fair's main theme. One lasting development was the expansion of urban public parks.

Radio and Film

Nathan Stubblefield transmitted voice over the air without wires in 1892. Thomas Edison's kinetoscope permitted the viewing of motion pictures in 1893.

FOREIGN RELATIONS, 1892–1897

In addition to the economic depression, three international events in 1895 that propelled the United States foreign policy were the Cuban war for independence against Spain, Britain's boundary dispute with Venezuela, and the settlement of the Sino-Japanese War.

Cuba and Spain

The Cuban revolt against Spain in 1895 impacted on the U.S. in that Americans had about $50 million invested in the Cuban economy, and did an annual business of over $100 million in Cuba. During the election of 1896, McKinley promised to stabilize the situation and work for an end to hostilities. Sensational "yellow" journalism, and nationalistic statements from officials such as Assistant Secretary of the Navy Theodore Roosevelt encouraged popular support for direct American military intervention on behalf of Cuban independence. President McKinley, however, proceeded cautiously through 1897.

Britain and Venezuela (1895)

The dispute over the border of Britain's colony of Guiana threatened war with Venezuela, especially after gold was discovered in the area. Although initially at odds with Britain, the United States eventually came to support British claims against Venezuela when Britain agreed to recognize the Monroe Doctrine in Latin America. Britain also sought U.S. cooperation in its dispute with Germany in South Africa. This rivalry would in time lead to the Boer War. The realignment of the United States and Britain would play a significant role during World War I.

The Sino-Japanese War, 1894–1895

Japan's easy victory over China signaled to the United States and other nations trading in Asia that China's weakness might result in its colonization by industrial powers, and the closing of the China market. The U.S. resolved to seek a naval base in the Pacific to protect its interests. The opportunity to annex the Philippines after the war with Spain was in part motivated by the desire to protect America's trade and future potential in Asia. This concern would also lead the U.S. to announce the Open Door policy with China in 1899 and 1900 designed to protect equal opportunity of trade, and China's political independence.

Latin America

When revolutions broke out in 1894 in both Brazil and Nicaragua, the United States supported the existing governments in power to maintain political stability and favorable trade treaties. Secretaries of State Walter Q. Gresham, Richard Olney and John Sherman continued to support James G. Blaine's Pan American policy.

The Pacific

The United States intervened in the Hawaiian revolution (1893) to overthrow the anti-American government of Queen Liliuokalani. President Cleveland rejected American annexation of Hawaii in 1894, but President McKinley agreed to annex it in 1898.

WAR AND THE AMERICANIZATION OF THE WORLD, 1897–1902

In 1900 an Englishman named William T. Stead authored a book entitled *The Americanization of the World* in which he predicted that American productivity and economic strength would propel the United States to the forefront of world leadership in the twentieth century. The Spanish-American War and the events following it indicated that the U.S. would be a force in the global balance of power for years to come. Few, however, would have predicted that as early as 1920 the U.S. would achieve the pinnacle of world power as a result of the debilitating policies pursued by European political leaders during World War I (1914–1919). One question remained: Would the American people be prepared to accept the responsibility of world leadership?

POLITICS OF THE PERIOD, 1897–1902

President McKinley's wartime leadership and tragic assassination closed one door in American history, but opened another door to the leadership of Theodore Roosevelt, the first "progressive" president.

Election of 1900

The unexpected death of Vice President Garrett Hobart led the Republican Party to choose the war hero and reform governor of New York, Theodore Roosevelt, as President William McKinley's vice presidential running mate. Riding the crest of victory against Spain, the G.O.P. platform called for upholding the gold standard for full economic recovery, promoting economic expansion and power in the Caribbean and the Pacific, and building a canal in Central America. The Democrats once again nominated William Jennings Bryan and Adlai Stevenson on a platform condemning imperialism and the gold standard. McKinley easily won reelection by about 1 million votes (7.2 million to 6.3 million), and the Republicans retained control of both houses of Congress.

Other Parties

The fading Populists nominated Wharton Barker (Pennsylvania) and Ignatius Donnelly (Minnesota) on a pro-inflation platform but only received 50,000 votes. The Socialist Democratic Party nominated Eugene V. Debs (Indiana) and Job Harriman (California) on a platform urging the nationalization of major industries. Debs received 94,000 votes. The Prohibition Party nominated John Woolley (Illinois) and Henry Metcalf (Rhode Island) and called for a ban on alcohol production and consumption. They received 209,000 votes.

McKinley Assassination (1901)

While attending the Pan American Exposition in Buffalo, New York, the president was shot on September 6 by Leon Czolgosz, an anarchist sworn to destroy all governments. The president died on September 14 after many officials had said they thought he would recover. Theodore Roosevelt became the nation's twenty-fifth president and—at age 42—its youngest to that time.

THE ECONOMY, 1897–1902

The war with Spain provided the impetus for economic recovery. President Roosevelt promised a "square deal" for all Americans, farmers, workers, consumers and businessmen. Progressive economic reform was geared to the rejuvenation of free enterprise capitalism following the 1893 depression, and the destruction of illegal monopolies. In this way, radicals would be denied an audience for more revolutionary and violent change.

War with Spain (1898)

The financial cost of the war was $250 million. Eastern and Midwestern industrial cities tended to favor war and benefit from it. Northeastern financial centers were more cautious about war until March 1898, and questioned the financial gains of wartime production at the expense of peacetime expansion and product/market development.

Federal Bankruptcy Act (1898)

This act reformed and standardized procedures for bankruptcy, along with the responsibilities of creditors and debtors.

Erdman Act (1898)

This act provided for mediation by the chair of the Interstate Commerce Commission and the commissioner of the Bureau of Labor in unresolved railroad labor controversies.

Currency Act (1900)

The United States standardized the amount of gold in the dollar at 25.8 grains $9/10$ fine. A separate gold reserve was set apart from other general funds, and government bonds were sold to maintain the reserve.

Technology

Between 1860 and 1900 railroad trackage grew from 36,800 miles to 193,350 miles. U.S. Steel Corp. was formed in 1901, Standard Oil Company of New Jersey in 1899.

SOCIAL AND CULTURAL DEVELOPMENTS, 1897–1902

Debates about the war and territorial acquisitions, and the state of the economy, tended to dominate thought and literature.

Yellow Journalism

Joseph Pulitzer's *New York World* and William Randolph Hearst's *New York Journal* competed fiercely to increase circulation through exaggeration of Spanish atrocities in Cuba. Such stories whipped up popular resentment of Spain, and helped to create a climate of opinion receptive to war.

DeLôme Letter and Sinking of the *Maine*

On February 9, 1898, the newspapers published a letter written by the Spanish minister in Washington, Depuy de Lôme, personally criticizing President McKinley in insulting terms. On February 15, the Battleship U.S.S. *Maine* was blown up in Havana harbor with a loss of 250 Americans. The popular demand for war with Spain grew significantly even though it was likely that the *Maine* was blown up by accident when spontaneous combustion in a coal bunker caused a powder magazine to explode.

U.S. Military

Facing its first war since the Civil War, the U.S. Army was not prepared for a full-scale effort in 1898. Although 245,000 men served in the war (with over 5,000 deaths), the Army at the outset consisted of only 28,000 troops. The volunteers who signed up in the early stages were surprised to be issued winter uniforms to train in the tropics for war in Cuba. Cans of food stockpiled since the Civil War were reissued. After getting past these early problems, the War Department settled down to a more effective organizational procedure. Sadly, more deaths resulted from disease and food poisoning than from battlefield casualties. The U.S. Navy (26,000 men) was far better prepared for war as a result of past years of modernization.

"The Rough Riders" of the U.S. Army's 1st Volunteer Cavalry commanded by Lt. Col. Theodore Roosevelt, atop San Juan Hill. U.S. National Archives and Records Administration.

Territories

After the United States had defeated Spain (see "Foreign Policy"), it was faced with the issue of what to do with such captured territories as the Philippines, Puerto Rico, the Isle of Pines, and Guam. A major public debate ensued with critics of land acquisition forming the Anti-Imperialist League with the support of Mark Twain, William James, William Jennings Bryan, Grover Cleveland, Charles Francis Adams, Carl Schurz, Charles W. Eliot, David Starr Jordan, Andrew Carnegie and Samuel Gompers among others. Supporters of colonialism included Theodore Roosevelt, Mark Hanna, Alfred Thayer Mahan, Henry Cabot Lodge, Albert Beveridge, President McKinley and many others. Ironically, many individuals in both camps favored U.S. economic expansion, but had difficulty with the idea that a democracy would actually accept colonies and overseas armies of occupations.

Literature

Thorstein Veblen's *Theory of the Leisure Class* (1899) attacked the "predatory wealth" and "conspicuous consumption" of the new rich in the gilded age. Veblen added evidence and argument to a critique begun by Jacob Riis in *How*

**One of the most celebrated examples of early skyscrapers,
the 21-story Flatiron Building rose in New York in 1902. AP Photo.**

the Other Half Lives (1890), documenting the gnawing poverty, illness, crime and despair of New York's slums. Frank Norris's *McTeague* (1899) chronicled a man's regression to brutish animal behavior in the dog-eat-dog world of unbridled and unregulated capitalist competition. His novel *The Octopus* (1901) condemned monopoly.

FOREIGN POLICY, 1897–1902

The summer war with Spain, and the expansion of American interests in Asia and the Caribbean were dominant factors.

Decision for War (1898)

Loss of markets, threats to Americans in Cuba, and the inability of both Spain and Cuba to resolve the Cuban revolution either by force or diplomacy led to McKinley's request of Congress for a declaration of war. The sinking of the *Maine* in February 1898, and the return of Vermont Senator Redfield Proctor from a fact-finding mission on March 17, 1898, revealed how poor the situation was in Cuba.

U.S.S. *Maine* on February 16, 1898, the day after an explosion sank the battleship in Havana Harbor, killing 266 crew members.
AP Photo/Key West Art/Historical Society.

McKinley's Ultimatum

On March 27, President McKinley asked Spain to call an armistice, accept American mediation to end the war, and end the use of concentration camps in Cuba. When Spain refused to comply, McKinley requested Congress declare war. On April 21, Congress declared war on Spain with the objective of establishing Cuban independence (Teller Amendment).

Cuba

After the first U.S. forces landed in Cuba on June 22, 1898, the United States proceeded to victories at El Caney and San Juan Hill. By July 17, Admiral Sampson's North Atlantic Squadron destroyed the Spanish fleet, Santiago surrendered, and American troops quickly went on to capture Puerto Rico.

The Philippines

As early as December 1897, Commodore Perry's Asiatic Squadron was alerted to possible war with Spain. On May 1, 1898, the Spanish fleet in the Philippines was destroyed and Manila surrendered on August 13. Spain agreed to a peace conference to be held in Paris in October 1898.

Treaty of Paris

Secretary of State William Day led the American negotiating team, which secured Cuban independence, the ceding of the Philippines, Puerto Rico and Guam to the U.S., and the payment of $20 million to Spain for the Philippines. The treaty was ratified by the Senate February 6, 1900.

Philippines Insurrection

Filipino nationalists under Emilio Aguinaldo rebelled against the United States (February 1899) when they learned the Philippines would not be given independence. The United States used 70,000 men to suppress the revolutionaries by June 1902. A special U.S. commission recommended eventual self-government for the Philippines.

Hawaii and Wake Island

During the war with Spain, the U.S. annexed Hawaii on July 7, 1898. In 1900 the U.S. claimed Wake Island, 2,000 miles west of Hawaii.

China

Fearing the break-up of China into separate spheres of influence, Secretary of State John Hay called for acceptance of the Open Door Notes by all nations trading in the China market to guarantee equal opportunity of trade (1899), and the sovereignty of the Manchu government of China (1900). With Manila as a base of operations, the United States was better able to protect its economic and political concerns in Asia. Such interests included the American China Development Co. (1898), a railway and mining concession in south China, and various oil, timber, and industrial investments in Manchuria.

Boxer Rebellion (1900)

Chinese nationalists ("Boxers") struck at foreign settlements in China, and at the Ch'ing dynasty Manchu government in Beijing for allowing foreign industrial nations such as Britain, Japan, Russia, France, Germany, Italy, Portugal, Belgium, The Netherlands, and the United States large concessions within Chinese borders. An international army helped to put down the rebellion, and aided the Chinese government to remain in power.

Platt Amendment (1901)

Although Cuba was granted its independence, the Platt Amendment provided that Cuba become a virtual protectorate of the United States. Cuba could not 1) make a treaty with a foreign state impairing its independence, or 2) contract an excessive public debt. Cuba was required to 1) allow the U.S. to preserve order on the island, and 2) lease a naval base for 99 years to the U.S. at Guantanamo Bay.

Hay-Pauncefote Treaty (1901)

This treaty between the U.S. and Britain abrogated an earlier agreement (1850, Clayton-Bulwer Treaty) to build jointly an isthmian canal. The United States was free unilaterally to construct, fortify and maintain a canal that would be open to all ships.

Insular Cases (1901–1903)

The Supreme Court decided that constitutional rights did not extend to territorial possessions, thus the Constitution did not follow the flag. Congress had the right to administer each island possession without constitutional restraint. Inhabitants of those possessions did not have the same rights as American citizens.

THEODORE ROOSEVELT AND PROGRESSIVE REFORMS, 1902–1907

As a Republican progressive reformer committed to honest and efficient government designed to serve all social classes in America, Theodore Roosevelt restored the presidency to the high eminence it had held through the Civil War era, and redressed the balance of power with old guard leaders in Congress.

POLITICS OF THE PERIOD, 1902–1907

President Roosevelt did much to create a bipartisan coalition of liberal reformers whose objective was to restrain corporate monopoly and promote economic competition at home and abroad. Roosevelt won the support of enlightened business leaders, the middle class, consumers, and urban and rural workers with his promise of a "square deal" for all.

Roosevelt's Anti-Trust Policy, 1902

The president pledged strict enforcement of the Sherman Anti-Trust Act (1890) to break up illegal monopolies and regulate large corporations for the public good through honest federal government administration.

Progressive Reform in the States

Taking their cue from Washington, many states enacted laws creating honest and efficient political and economic regulatory standards. Political reforms included enacting laws establishing primary elections (Mississippi, Wisconsin), initiative and referendum (South Dakota, Oregon), and the rooting out of political bosses on the state and municipal levels (especially in New York, Ohio, Michigan, and California).

Commission Form of Government, 1903

After a hurricane and tidal wave destroyed much of Galveston, Texas, progressive businessmen and Texas state legislators removed the ineffective and corrupt mayor and city council and established a city government of five elected commissioners who were experts in their fields to rebuild Galveston. Numerous other cities adopted the commission form of government to replace the mayor/council format.

State Leaders

Significant state reformers in the period were Robert LaFollette of Wisconsin, Albert Cummins of Iowa, Charles Evans Hughes of New York, James M. Cox of Ohio, Hiram Johnson of California, William S. Wren of Oregon, Albert Beveridge of Indiana, and Woodrow Wilson of New Jersey.

City Reformers

Urban leaders included John Purroy Mitchell of New York City, Tom L. Johnson and Newton Baker of Cleveland, Hazen Pingree of Detroit, Sam Jones of Toledo, and Joseph Folk of St. Louis.

Election of 1904

Having assured Republican Party leaders that he wished to reform corporate monopolies and railroads, but not interfere with monetary policy or tariffs, Roosevelt was nominated for president along with Charles Fairbanks (Indiana) for vice president. The Democratic Party nominated New York judge Alton B. Parker for president and Henry G. Davis (West Virginia) for vice president on a platform that endorsed Roosevelt's "trust-busting," which called for even greater power for such regulatory agencies as the Interstate Commerce Commission, and accepted the conservative gold standard as the basis for monetary policy. Roosevelt easily defeated Parker by about two million votes, and the Republicans retained control of both houses of Congress.

Hepburn Act, 1906

Membership of the Interstate Commerce Commission was increased from five to seven. The I.C.C. could set its own fair freight rates, had its regulatory power extended over pipelines, bridges, and express companies, and was empowered to require a uniform system of accounting by regulated transportation companies. This act and the Elkins Act (1903—reiterated illegality of railroad rebates) gave teeth to the original interstate Commerce Act of 1887.

Pure Food and Drug Act (1906)

Prohibited the manufacture, sale and transportation of adulterated or fraudulently labeled foods and drugs in accordance with consumer demands to which Theodore Roosevelt was especially sensitive.

Meat Inspection Act (1906)

Provided for federal and sanitary regulations and inspections in meat packing facilities. Wartime scandals in 1898 relating to spoiled canned meats were a powerful force for reform.

Immunity of Witness Act (1906)

Corporate officials could no longer make a plea of immunity to avoid testifying in cases dealing with their corporation's illegal activities.

Conservation Laws

From 1902 to 1908 a series of laws and executive actions were enacted to create federal irrigation projects, national parks and forests, develop water power (Internal Waterways Commission), and establish the National Conservation Commission to oversee the nation's resources.

THE ECONOMY, 1902–1907

Anti-trust policy and government regulation of the economy gave way to a more lenient enforcement of federal laws after the panic of 1907. Recognition of the rights of labor unions was enhanced.

Anti-Trust Policy (1902)

In order to restore free competition, President Roosevelt ordered the Justice Department to prosecute corporations pursuing monopolistic practices. Attorney General P.C. Knox first brought suit against the Northern Securities Company, a railroad holding corporation put together by J. P. Morgan; then he moved against Rockefeller's Standard Oil Company. By the time he left office in 1909, Roosevelt brought indictments against 25 monopolies.

Department of Commerce and Labor (1903)

A new Cabinet position was created to address the concerns of business and labor. Within the department, the Bureau of Corporations was empowered to investigate and report on the illegal activities of corporations.

Coal Strike (1902)

Roosevelt interceded with government mediation to bring about negotiations between the United Mine Workers union and the anthracite mine owners after a bitter strike over wages, safety conditions and union recognition. This was the first time that the government intervened in a labor dispute without automatically siding with management.

Panic of 1907

A brief economic recession and panic occurred in 1907 as a result, in part, of questionable bank speculations, a lack of flexible monetary and credit policies, and a conservative gold standard. This event called attention to the need for banking reform which would lead to the Federal Reserve System in 1913. Although Roosevelt temporarily eased the pressure on anti-trust activity, he made it clear that reform of the economic system to promote free-enterprise capitalism would continue.

St. Louis World's Fair (1904)

The World's Fair of 1904 celebrated the centennial of the Louisiana Purchase, and brought the participation of Asian nations to promote foreign trade.

SOCIAL AND CULTURAL DEVELOPMENTS, 1902–1907

Debate and discussion over the expanding role of the federal government commanded the attention of the nation.

Progressive Reforms

There was not one unified progressive movement, but a series of reform causes designed to address specific social, economic, and political problems. Middle-class men and women were especially active in attempting to correct the excessive powers of giant corporations, and the radical extremes of Marxist revolutionaries and radicals among intellectuals and labor activists. However, mainstream of business and labor leaders were moderate in their desire to preserve economic opportunities and the free enterprise system.

Varieties of Reform

Progressive reform goals included not only honest government, economic regulation, environmental conservation, labor recognition, and new political structures. Reformers also called for gender equality for men and women in the work force (Oregon Ten Hour Law), an end to racial segregation (National Association for the Advancement of Colored People), child labor laws, prison reform, regulation of the stock market, direct election of senators, and a more efficient foreign service among other reform activities.

Muckrakers

Muckrakers (a term coined by Roosevelt) were investigative journalists and authors who were often the publicity agents for reforms. Popular magazines included *McClure's, Collier's, Cosmopolitan*, and *Everybody's*. Famous articles that led to reforms included "The Shame of the Cities" by Lincoln Steffens,

A Chicago stockyard around the time of Upton Sinclair's muckraking book *The Jungle* (1906), which exposed in vivid detail the sordid conditions of the meat-packing industry. Photo courtesy of Dover Publications, Inc.

"History of Standard Oil Company" by Ida Tarbell, "The Treason of the Senate" by David Phillips, and "Frenzied Finance" by Thomas Lawson.

Literature

Works of literature with a social message included *Following the Color Line* by Ray Stannard Baker, *The Bitter Cry of the Children* by John Spargo, *Poverty* by Robert Hunter, *The Story of Life Insurance* by Burton Hendrick, *The Financier* by Theodore Dreiser, *The Jungle* by Upton Sinclair, *The Boss* by Henry Lewis, *Call of the Wild, The Iron Heel* and *The War of the Classes* by Jack London, *A Certain Rich Man* by William Allen White, and *The Promise of American Life* by Herbert Croly.

Inventions

The Wright brothers made the first piloted flight of a heavier-than-air machine at Kitty Hawk, North Carolina, in 1903. News of their feat traveled slowly and was widely doubted.

FOREIGN RELATIONS, 1902–1907

Theodore Roosevelt's "Big Stick" diplomacy and economic foreign policy were characteristics of the administration.

Panama Canal

Roosevelt used executive power to engineer the separation of Panama from Colombia, and the recognition of Panama as an independent country. The Hay-Bunau-Varilla Treaty of 1903 granted the United States control of the canal zone in Panama for $10 million and an annual fee of $250,000 beginning nine years after ratification of the treaty by both parties. Construction of the canal began in 1904 and was completed in 1914.

Roosevelt Corollary to the Monroe Doctrine

The U.S. reserved the right to intervene in the internal affairs of Latin American nations to keep European powers from using military force to collect debts in the Western Hemisphere. The U.S. eventually intervened in the affairs of Venezuela, Haiti, the Dominican Republic, Nicaragua, and Cuba by 1905 as an international policeman brandishing the "big stick" against Europeans and Latin Americans.

Rio de Janeiro Conference (1906)

Secretary of State Elihu Root attempted to de-emphasize U.S. military and political intervention in order to promote political goodwill, economic development, trade and finances in Latin America. President Roosevelt was actually moving away from "big stick" diplomacy and toward "dollar diplomacy" before he left office. The United States also promoted the Pan American Railway project at this meeting of the International Bureau of American Republics.

China

In pursuit of the Open Door policy of equal opportunity of trade and the guaranteed independence of China, the United States continued to promote its trade interests in Asia. Segregation and restrictions of Chinese immigrants in California and other states led Chinese national leaders to call for a boycott in 1905 of U.S. goods and services in both China and the United States. The boycott ended in 1906 without significant changes in state laws.

Russo-Japanese War (1904–1905)

With American encouragement and financial loans, Japan pursued and won a war against tsarist Russia. Roosevelt negotiated the Treaty of Portsmouth,

New Hampshire, which ended the war, and for which the President ironically received the Nobel Peace Prize in 1906. Japan, however, was disappointed at not receiving more territory and financial compensation from Russia and blamed the United States.

Taft-Katsura Memo, 1905

The United States and Japan pledged to maintain the Open Door principles in China. Japan recognized American control over the Philippines and the United States granted a Japanese protectorate over Korea.

Gentleman's Agreement with Japan, 1907

After numerous incidents of racial discrimination against Japanese in California, Japan agreed to restrict the emigration of unskilled Japanese workers to the U.S.

Great White Fleet, 1907

In order to show American strength to Japan and China, Roosevelt sent the great white naval fleet to Asian ports.

Algeciras Conference, 1906

The United States participated in the Algeciras Conference with eight European states to guarantee equal opportunity of trade for Morocco. The independence granted the sultan of Morocco was reminiscent of the Open Door policy initiated by the U.S. with China at the turn of the century. The conference (held at Algeciras, Spain, January 16–April 7, 1906), however, created tension between Germany and France, which would end up at war in the next decade.

The Second Hague Conference, 1907

Forty-six nations, including the United States, met in the Netherlands to discuss disarmament and the creation of an international court of justice. Little was accomplished except for the adoption of a resolution banning the use of military force for the collection of foreign debts.

THE REGULATORY STATE AND THE ORDERED SOCIETY, 1907–1912

The progressive presidencies of Roosevelt, Taft and Wilson brought the concept of big government to fruition. A complex corporate society needed rules and regulations as well as powerful agencies to enforce those measures necessary to maintain and enhance democratic free enterprise competition. The search for political, social and economic standards designed to preserve order in American society while still guaranteeing political, social and economic freedom was a difficult, but primary task. The nation increasingly looked to Washington to protect the less powerful segments of the republic from the special interests that had grown up in the late 19th century. A persistent problem for the federal government was how best to preserve order and standards in a complex technological society while not interfering with the basic liberties Americans came to cherish in the Constitution and throughout their history. The strain of World War I after 1914 would further complicate the problem.

POLITICS OF THE PERIOD, 1907–1912

The continuation of progressive reforms by both Republican and Democratic leaders helped to form a consensus for the establishment of regulatory standards.

Election 1908

Deciding not to run for re-election, Theodore Roosevelt opened the way for William H. Taft (Ohio) and James S. Sherman (New York) to run on a Republican platform calling for a continuation of anti-trust enforcement, environmental conservation, and a lower tariff policy to promote international trade. The Democrats nominated William Jennings Bryan for a third time with John Kern (Indiana) for vice president on an anti-monopoly and low tariff platform. The Socialists once again nominated Eugene V. Debs. Taft easily won by over a million votes, and the Republicans retained control of both houses of Congress. For the first time, the American Federation of Labor entered national politics officially with an endorsement of Bryan. This decision began a long alliance between organized labor and the Democratic Party in the 20th century.

Taft's Objectives

The president had two primary political goals in 1909. One was the continuation of Roosevelt's trust-busting policies, and the other was the reconciliation of the old guard conservatives and young progressive reformers in the Republican Party.

Anti-Trust Policy

In pursuing anti-monopoly law enforcement, Taft chose as his Attorney General George Wickersham, who brought 44 indictments in anti-trust suits.

Political Rift

Taft was less successful in healing the Republican split between conservatives and progressives over such issues as tariff reform, conservation, and the almost dictatorial power held by the reactionary Republican Speaker of the House, Joseph Cannon (Illinois). Taft's inability to bring both wings of the party together led to the hardened division which would bring about a complete Democratic victory in the 1912 elections.

The Anti-Cannon Crusade

In 1910, Republican progressives joined with Democrats to strip Speaker Cannon of his power to appoint the Committee on Rules and serve on it himself. Critical of Cannon, Taft failed to align himself with the progressives. Democrats gained control of the House in the 1910 elections, and a Republican Democratic coalition ran the Senate.

Ballinger-Pinchot Dispute (1909–1910)

Progressives backed Gifford Pinchot, chief of the U.S. Forest Service, in his charge that the conservative Secretary of the Interior, Richard Ballinger, was giving away the nation's natural resources to private corporate interests. A congressional investigatory committee found that Ballinger had done nothing illegal, but did act in a manner contrary to the government's environmental policies. Taft had supported Ballinger through the controversy, but negative public opinion forced Ballinger to resign in 1911. Taft's political standing with progressive Republicans was hurt going into the election of 1912.

The Sixteenth Amendment

Congress passed in 1909 a graduated income tax amendment to the Constitution which was ratified in 1913.

Mann-Elins Act (1910)

This act extended the regulatory function of the Interstate Commerce Commission over cable and wireless companies, and telephone and telegraph lines; gave the I.C.C. power to begin its own court proceedings and suspend questionable rates; and set up a separate but temporary commerce court to handle rate-dispute cases.

Election of 1912

This election was one of the most dramatic in American history. President Taft's inability to maintain party harmony led Theodore Roosevelt to return to national politics. When denied the Republican nomination, Roosevelt and his supporters formed the Progressive Party (Bull Moose) and nominated Roosevelt for president and Hiram Johnson (California) for vice president on a political platform nicknamed "The New Nationalism." It called for stricter regulation on large corporations, creation of a tariff commission, women's suffrage, minimum wages and benefits, direct election of senators, initiative, referendum and recall, presidential primaries, and prohibition of child labor. Roosevelt also called for a Federal Trade Commission to regulate the broader economy, a stronger executive, and more government planning. Theodore Roosevelt did not see big business as evil, but a permanent development that was necessary in a modern economy.

The Republicans

President Taft and Vice President Sherman retained control of the Republican Party after challenges by Roosevelt and Robert LaFollette, and were nominated on a platform of "Quiet Confidence" calling for a continuation of progressive programs pursued by Taft over the past four years.

The Democrats

After forty-five ballots without a nomination, the Democratic convention finally worked out a compromise whereby William Jennings Bryan gave his support to New Jersey Governor Woodrow Wilson on the forty-sixth ballot. Thomas Marshall (Indiana) was chosen as the vice presidential candidate. Wilson called his campaign the "New Freedom" based on progressive programs similar to those in the Progressive and Republican parties. Wilson, however, did not agree with Roosevelt on the issue of big business, which Wilson saw as morally evil. Therefore, Wilson called for breaking up large corporations rather than just regulating them. He differed from the other two party candidates by favoring independence for the Philippines, and the exemption from prosecution of labor unions under the Sherman Anti-Trust Act. Wilson also supported such measures as lower tariffs, a graduated income tax, banking reform, and direct election of senators. Philosophically, Wilson was skeptical of big business and big government. In some respects, he hoped to return to an earlier and simpler concept of a free enterprise republic. After his selection, however, he would modify his views to conform more with those of Theodore Roosevelt.

Election Results

The Republican split clearly paved the way for Wilson's victory. Wilson received 6.2 million votes, Roosevelt 4.1 million, Taft 3.5 million, and the Socialist Debs 900,000 votes. In the electoral college, Wilson received 435 votes, Roosevelt 88, Taft 8. Although a minority president, Wilson garnered the largest electoral majority in American history to that time. Democrats won control of both houses of Congress.

The Wilson Presidency

The Wilson administration brought together many of the policies and initiatives of the previous Republican administrations, and reform efforts in Congress by both parties. Before the outbreak of World War I in 1914, President Wilson, working with cooperative majorities in both houses of Congress, achieved much of the remaining progressive agenda including lower tariff reform (Underwood-Simmons Act, 1913), the 16th Amendment (graduated income tax, 1913), the 17th Amendment (direct election of senators, 1913), Federal Reserve Banking System (which provided regulation and flexibility to monetary policy, 1913), Federal Trade Commission (to investigate unfair business practices, 1914), and the Clayton Anti-Trust Act (improving the old Sherman Act and protecting labor unions and farm cooperatives from prosecution, 1914).

Other goals such as the protection of children in the work force (Keating-Owen Act, 1916), credit reform for agriculture (Federal Farm Loan Act, 1916), and an independent tariff commission (1916) came later. By the end of Wilson's presidency, the New Freedom and the New Nationalism merged into one government philosophy of regulation, order and standardization in the interest of an increasingly diverse and pluralistic American nation.

THE ECONOMY, 1907–1912

The short-lived panic of 1907 revealed economic weaknesses in U.S. banking and currency policy addressed by Presidents Roosevelt, Taft, and Wilson, and by Congress. Fortunately, the American economy was strengthened just in time to meet the challenges of World War I.

National Monetary Commission, 1908

Chaired by Senator Nelson Aldrich of Rhode Island, the 18-member National Monetary Commission recommended what later became the basis for the Federal Reserve System in 1913 with a secure Treasury reserve and branch banks to add and subtract currency from the monetary supply to accommodate the needs of the economy.

Payne-Aldrich Tariff, 1909

Senate amendments added to the Payne-Aldrich Tariff of 1909 turned the bill, originally intended to lower the tariff, into a protective measure. Progressive reformers felt betrayed by special interests opposed to consumer-price concerns. President Taft made the political mistake of endorsing the tariff.

Postal Savings Banks, 1910

On the recommendation of President Taft, certain U.S. post offices were authorized to receive deposits and pay interest. This was an idea that had been championed early on by the Populist Party.

New Battleship Contract, 1910

The State Department arranged for Bethlehem Steel Corporation to receive a large contract to build battleships for Argentina. This was an example of Taft's "dollar diplomacy" in action.

Anti-Trust Proceedings

Although a friend to the business community, President Taft ordered 90 legal proceedings against monopolies, and 44 anti-trust suits including the one which broke up the American Tobacco Trust (1911). It was also under Taft that the government succeeded with its earlier suit against Standard Oil.

Canadian Reciprocity, 1911

A reciprocal trade agreement between the United States and Canada was repudiated by the Canadian legislature which feared economic and political domination by the United States.

New Cabinet Posts, 1913

The Department of Commerce and Labor was divided into two separate autonomous Cabinet-level positions.

Automobiles

In 1913 Henry Ford introduced the continuous-flow process on the automobile assembly line.

SOCIAL AND CULTURAL DEVELOPMENTS, 1907–1912

Progressive reform and government activism were important themes in American society.

Social Programs

States led the way with programs such as public aid to mothers of dependent children (Illinois, 1911), and the first minimum wage law (Massachusetts, 1912).

Race and Ethnic Attitudes

Despite the creation of the NAACP in 1909, many progressive reformers tended to be Anglo-Saxon elitists critical of the lack of accomplishments of Native American Indians, African-Americans, and Asian, Southern and Eastern European immigrants. In 1905, the African-American intellectual militant W. E. B. DuBois founded the Niagara Movement calling for federal legislation to protect racial equality, and full rights of citizenship.

Radical Labor

Although moderate labor unions as represented by the A.F. of L. functioned within the American system, a radical labor organization called the Industrial Workers of the World (I.W.W. or Wobblies, 1905–1924) was active in promoting violence and revolution. Led by colorful figures such as Carlo Tresca, Elizabeth Gurley Flynn (the Red Flame), Daniel DeLeon, "Mother" Mary Harris Jones, the maverick priest Father Thomas Hagerty, and "Big Bill" Haywood, among others, the I.W.W. organized effective strikes in the textile industry in 1912, and among a few Western miners groups, but generally had little appeal to the average American worker. After the Red Scare of 1919, the government worked to smash the I.W.W. and deport many of its immigrant leaders and members.

White Slave Trade

In 1910, Congress made interstate prostitution a federal crime with passage of the Mann Act.

Literature

Enthused by the self-confidence exuded by political reformers, writers remained optimistic in their realism, and put their faith in the American people to solve social and economic problems with honest and efficient programs.

Motion Pictures

By 1912 Hollywood had replaced New York and New Jersey as the center for silent film production. There were 13,000 movie houses in the United States and Paramount Pictures had just been formed as a large studio resembling other large corporations. Serials, epic features and Mack Sennett comedies were in production. All of these developments contributed to the "star system" in American film entertainment.

Science

The X-ray tube was developed by William Coolidge in 1913. Robert Goddard patented liquid rocket fuel in 1914. Plastics and synthetic fibers such as rayon were developed in 1909 by Arthur Little and Leo Baekeland, respectively. Adolphus Busch applied the Diesel engine to the submarine in 1912.

FOREIGN RELATIONS, 1907–1912

The expansion of American international interests through Taft's "dollar diplomacy," and world tensions foreshadowing the First World War were dominant themes.

Dollar Diplomacy

President Taft sought to avoid military intervention, especially in Latin America, by replacing "big stick" policies with "dollar diplomacy" in the expectation that American financial investments would encourage economic, social and political stability. This idea proved an illusion as investments never really filtered through all levels of Latin American societies, nor did such investments generate democratic reforms.

Mexican Revolution (1910)

Francisco I. Madero overthrew the dictator Porfirio Diaz (1911) declaring himself a progressive revolutionary akin to reformers in the United States. American and European corporate interests (especially oil and mining) feared national interference with their investments in Mexico. President Taft recognized Madero's government, but stationed 10,000 troops on the Texas border (1912) to protect Americans from the continuing fighting. In 1913 Madero was assassinated by General Victoriano Huerta. Wilson urged Huerta to hold democratic elections and adopt a constitutional government. When Huerta refused his advice, Wilson invaded Mexico with troops at Vera Cruz in 1914. A second U.S. invasion came in northern Mexico in 1916. War between the U.S. and Mexico might have occurred had not World War I intervened.

Latin American Interventions

Although Taft and Secretary of State P. C. Knox created the Latin American Division of the State Department in 1909 to promote better relations, the United States kept a military presence in the Dominican Republic and Haiti, and intervened militarily in Nicaragua (1911) to quiet fears of revolution and help manage foreign financial problems.

Arbitration Treaties

Taking a page from Roosevelt's book, Taft promoted arbitration agreements as an alternative to war in Latin America and in Asia.

Lodge Corollary to the Monroe Doctrine, 1911

When a Japanese syndicate moved to purchase a large tract of land in Mexico's Lower California, Senator Lodge introduced a resolution to block the Japanese investment. The Corollary went further to exclude non-European powers from the Western Hemisphere under the Monroe Doctrine.

Bryan's Arbitration Treaties (1913–1915)

Wilson's Secretary of State, William Jennings Bryan, continued the policies of Roosevelt and Taft to promote arbitration of disputes in Latin America and elsewhere. Bryan negotiated about 30 such treaties.

Root-Takahira Agreement (1908)

This agreement reiterated the status quo in Asia established by the United States and Japan by the Taft-Katsura Memo (1905).

China Consortium (1909)

American bankers and the State Department demanded entry into an international banking association with Britain, France, and Germany to build a railway network (Hukuang) in southern and central China. Wilson withdrew the U.S. from participation in 1913 as the Chinese revolution deteriorated into greater instability.

Manchuria

President Taft and Secretary Knox attempted to force the sale of Japanese and Russian railroad interests in Manchuria to American investment interests. When this diplomacy failed, Knox moved to construct a competing rail system. The Chinese government, however, refused to approve the American plan. Both Japan and Russia grew more suspicious of United States interests in Asia.

Chinese Revolution, 1911

Chinese nationalists overthrew the Manchu Dynasty and the last emperor of China, Henry Pu Yi. Although the military war lord Yuan Shih-Kai seized control, decades of factionalism, revolution, and civil war destabilized China and its market potential for American and other foreign investors.

◄─── HISTORICAL TIMELINE ───►
Industrialism, War, and the Progressive Era (1877–1912)

1877	San Francisco anti-chinese riots
1878	Bland-Allison Act
1879	Edison invents the light bulb
1881	President Garfield assassinated Helen Hunt Jackson writes *A Century of Dishonor*
1882	Standard Oil Trust formed Chinese Exclusion Act
1883	Pendleton Civil Service Act
1885	First skyscraper built in Chicago
1886	Haymarket Square bombing in Chicago American Federation of Labor formed
1887	Dawes Act
1889	Jane Addams founds Hull House in Chicago
1890	Sioux massacred at Wounded Knee Sherman Antitrust Act Sherman Silver Purchase Act U.S. Census declares frontier's end Alfred Mahan writes *The Influence of Sea Power upon History*
1891	Populist Party formed
1892	Homestead Steel Strike
1893	Panic of 1893 Great Northern Railroad completed

1894	Pullman strike Coxey's Army
1895	Booker T. Washington's Atlanta Compromise speech
1896	*Plessy v. Ferguson* upholds separate but equal McKinley defeats Bryan for president
1898	U.S.S. *Maine* sinks in Havana Harbor Spanish-American War Dewey captures Philippine Islands Hawaii annexed by U.S.
1899	Aguinaldo leads Filipinos against Americans Treaty of Paris ends Spanish-American War Open Door Policy in China
1900	Boxer Rebellion in China
1901	Theodore Roosevelt becomes president
1902	Platt Amendment President Roosevelt settles coal strike
1903	U.S. recognizes Panama's independence
1904	Northern Securities Trust dissolved Roosevelt Corollary declared
1906	Upton Sinclair writes *The Jungle* Pure Food and Drug Act Hepburn Act passed President Roosevelt wins Nobel Peace Prize
1908	*Muller v. Oregon* limits women's working hours Taft elected president
1909	NAACP formed
1911	Triangle Shirtwaist Fire Mexican Revolution erupts
1912	Roosevelt forms Progressive Party to challenge Taft Wilson elected president

Chapter 10

WILSON AND WORLD WAR I (1912–1920)

IMPLEMENTING THE NEW FREEDOM: THE EARLY YEARS OF THE WILSON ADMINISTRATION

The New President

Woodrow Wilson was only the second Democrat (Cleveland was the first) elected president since the Civil War. He was born in Virginia in 1856, the son of a Presbyterian minister, and was reared and educated in the South. After earning a doctorate at Johns Hopkins University, he taught history and political science at Princeton, and in 1902 became president of that university. In 1910 he was elected governor of New Jersey as a reform or progressive Democrat.

The Cabinet

The key appointments were William Jennings Bryan as secretary of state and William Gibbs McAdoo as secretary of the treasury.

The Inaugural Address

Wilson called the Congress, now controlled by Democrats, into a special session beginning April 7, 1913, to consider three topics: Reduction of the tariff, reform of the national banking and currency laws, and improvements in the antitrust laws. On April 8 he appeared personally before Congress, the first president since John Adams to do so, to promote his program.

The Underwood-Simmons Tariff Act of 1913

Average rates were reduced to about 29 percent as compared with 37 to 40 percent under the previous Payne-Aldrich Tariff. A graduated income tax was included in the law to compensate for lost tariff revenue. It ranged from a tax of one percent on personal and corporate incomes over $4,000, a figure well above the annual income of the average worker, to seven percent on incomes over $500,000. The 16th Amendment to the Constitution, ratified in February 1913, authorized the income tax.

The Federal Reserve Act of 1913

Following the Panic of 1907, it was generally agreed that there was need for more stability in the banking industry and for a currency supply which would expand and contract to meet business needs.

Three points of view on the subject developed. Most Republicans backed the proposal of a commission headed by Senator Nelson W. Aldrich for a large central bank controlled by private banks. Bryanite Democrats, pointing to the Wall Street influence exposed by the 1913 Pujo Committee investigation of the money trust, wanted a reserve system and currency owned and controlled by the government. Conservative Democrats favored a decentralized system privately owned and controlled but free from Wall Street.

The bill which finally passed in December 1913 was a compromise measure. The law divided the nation into twelve regions with a Federal Reserve bank in each region. Commercial banks in the region owned the Federal Reserve Bank by purchasing stock equal to six percent of their capital and surplus, and elected the directors of the bank. National banks were required to join the system, and state banks were invited to join. The Federal Reserve Banks held the gold reserves of their members. Federal Reserve Banks loaned money to member banks by rediscounting their commercial and agricultural paper; that is, the money was loaned at interest less than the public paid to the member banks, and the notes of indebtedness of businesses and farmers to the member banks were held as collateral. This allowed the Federal Reserve to control interest rates by raising or lowering the discount rate.

The money loaned to the member banks was in the form of a new currency, Federal Reserve Notes, which was backed sixty percent by commercial paper and forty percent by gold. This currency was designed to expand and contract with the volume of business activity and borrowing. Checks on member banks were cleared through the Federal Reserve System.

The Federal Reserve System serviced the financial needs of the federal government. The system was supervised and policy was set by a national Federal Reserve Board composed of the secretary of the Treasury, the comptroller of the currency, and five other members appointed by the president of the United States.

The Clayton Antitrust Act of 1914

This law supplemented and interpreted the Sherman Antitrust Act of 1890. Under its provisions, stock ownership by a corporation in a competing corporation was prohibited. Interlocking directorates of competing corporations were prohibited; that is, the same persons could not manage competing corporations. Price discrimination (charging less in some regions than in others to undercut the competition) and exclusive contracts which reduced competition were prohibited. Officers of corporations could be held personally responsible for violations of antitrust laws. Lastly, labor unions and agricultural organizations were not to be considered "combinations or conspiracies in restraint of trade" as defined by the Sherman Antitrust Act.

The Federal Trade Commission Act of 1914

The law prohibited all unfair trade practices without defining them, and created a commission of Eve members appointed by the president. The commission was empowered to issue cease and desist orders to corporations to stop actions considered to be in restraint of trade, and to bring suit in the courts if the orders were not obeyed. Firms could also contest the orders in court. Under previous antitrust legislation, the government could act against corporations only by bringing suit.

Evaluation

The Underwood-Simmons Tariff, the Federal Reserve Act, and the Clayton Act were clearly in accord with the principles of the New Freedom, but the Federal Trade Commission reflected a move toward the kind of government regulation advocated by Roosevelt in his New Nationalism. Nonetheless, in 1914 and 1915 Wilson continued to oppose federal government action in such matters as loans to farmers, child labor regulation, and woman suffrage.

THE TRIUMPH OF NEW NATIONALISM

Political Background

The Progressive Party dissolved rapidly after the election of 1912. The Republicans made major gains in Congress and in the state governments in the 1914 elections, and their victory in 1916 seemed probable. Early in 1916 Wilson and the Democrats abandoned most of their limited government and states' rights positions in favor of a legislative program of broad economic and social reforms designed to win the support of the former Progressives for the Democratic Party in the election of 1916. The urgency of their concern was increased by the fact that Theodore Roosevelt intended to seek the Republican nomination in 1916.

The Brandeis Appointment

Wilson's first action marking the adoption of the new program was the appointment on January 28, 1916, of Louis D. Brandeis, considered by many to be the principal advocate of social justice in the nation, as an associate justice of the Supreme Court.

The Federal Farm Loan Act of 1916

The law divided the country into twelve regions and established a Federal Land Bank in each region. Funded primarily with federal money, the banks made farm mortgage loans at reasonable interest rates. Wilson had threatened to veto similar legislation in 1914.

The Child Labor Act of 1916

This law, earlier opposed by Wilson, forbade shipment in interstate commerce of products whose production had involved the labor of children under fourteen or sixteen, depending on the products. The legislation was especially significant because it was the first time that Congress regulated labor within a state using the interstate commerce power. The law was declared unconstitutional by the Supreme Court in 1918 on the grounds that it interfered with the powers of the states.

The Adamson Act of 1916

This law mandated an eight-hour day for workers on interstate railroads with time and a half for overtime and a maximum of sixteen hours in a shift. Its passage was a major victory for railroad unions, and averted a railroad strike in September 1916.

The Kerr-McGillicuddy Act of 1916

This law initiated a program of workmen's compensation for federal employees.

THE ELECTION OF 1916

The Democrats

The minority party nationally in terms of voter registration, the Democrats nominated Wilson and adopted his platform calling for continued progressive reforms and neutrality in the European war. "He kept us out of war" became the principal campaign slogan of Democratic politicians.

The Republicans

The convention bypassed Theodore Roosevelt, who had decided not to run as a Progressive and had sought the Republican nomination. On the first ballot it chose Charles Evans Hughes, an associate justice of the Supreme Court and formerly a progressive Republican governor of New York. Hughes, an ineffective campaigner, avoided the neutrality issue because of divisions among the Republicans, and found it difficult to attack the progressive reforms of the Democrats. He emphasized what he considered the inefficiency of the Democrats, and failed to find a popular issue.

Opening game 1916.   Bx 112

President Wilson throws out the first pitch on Opening Day, 1916.
U.S. Library of Congress.

The Election

Wilson won the election with 277 electoral votes and 9,129,000 popular votes, almost three million more than he received in 1912. Hughes received 254 electoral votes and 8,538,221 popular votes. The Democrats controlled Congress by a narrow margin. While Wilson's victory seemed close, the fact that he had increased his popular vote by almost fifty percent over four years previous was remarkable. It appears that most of his additional votes came from people who had voted for the Progressive or Socialist tickets in 1912.

SOCIAL ISSUES IN THE FIRST WILSON ADMINISTRATION

Blacks

In 1913 Treasury Secretary William G. McAdoo and Postmaster General Albert S. Burleson segregated workers in some parts of their departments with no objection from Wilson. Many Northern blacks and whites protested, especially black leader W. E. B. DuBois, who had supported Wilson in 1912. William Monroe Trotter, militant editor of the Boston Guardian, led a protest delegation to Washington and clashed verbally with the president. No further segregation in government agencies was initiated, but Wilson had gained a reputation for being inimical to civil rights.

Women

The movement for woman suffrage, led by the National American Woman Suffrage Association, was increasing in momentum at the time Wilson became president, and several states had granted the vote to women. Wilson opposed a federal woman suffrage amendment, maintaining that the franchise should be controlled by the states. Later he changed his view and supported the 19th Amendment.

Immigration

Wilson opposed immigration restrictions which were proposed by labor unions and some reformers. He vetoed a literacy test for immigrants in 1915, but in 1917 Congress overrode a similar veto.

WILSON'S FOREIGN POLICY AND THE ROAD TO WAR

Wilson's Basic Premise: New Freedom Policy

Wilson promised a more moral foreign policy than that of his predecessors, denouncing imperialism and dollar diplomacy, and advocating the advancement of democratic capitalist governments throughout the world.

Conciliation Treaties

Secretary Bryan negotiated treaties with 29 nations under which they agreed to submit disputes to international commissions for conciliation, not arbitration. They also included provisions for a cooling-off period, usually one year, before the nations would resort to war. While the treaties probably had no practical effect, they illustrated the idealism of the administration.

Dollar Diplomacy

Wilson signaled his repudiation of Taft's dollar diplomacy by withdrawing American involvement from the six-power loan consortium of China.

Japan

In 1913 Wilson failed to prevent passage of a California law prohibiting land ownership by Japanese aliens. The Japanese government and people were furious, and war seemed possible. Relations were smoothed over, but the issue was unresolved. In 1915 American diplomatic pressure made Japan back off from its 21 demands on China, but in 1917 the Lansing-Ishii Agreement was signed wherein Japan recognized the Open Door in China but the United States recognized Japan's special interest in that nation.

The Caribbean

Like his predecessors, Wilson sought to protect the Panama Canal, which opened in 1914, by maintaining stability in the area. He also wanted to encourage diplomacy and economic growth in the underdeveloped nations of the region. In applying his policy, he became as interventionist as Roosevelt and Taft.

In 1912 American marines had landed in Nicaragua to maintain order, and an American financial expert had taken control of the customs. The Wilson administration kept the marines in Nicaragua, and negotiated the Bryan-Chamorro Treaty of 1914 which gave the United States an option to build a canal through the country. In effect, Nicaragua became an American protectorate, although treaty provisions authorizing such action were not ratified by the Senate.

Claiming that political anarchy existed in Haiti, Wilson sent marines in 1915 and imposed a treaty making the country a protectorate, with American control of its finances and constabulary. The marines remained until 1934.

In 1916 Wilson sent marines to the Dominican Republic to stop a civil war, and established a military government under an American naval commander.

Wilson feared in 1915 that Germany might annex Denmark and its Caribbean possession, the Danish West Indies or Virgin Islands. After extended negotiations, the United States purchased the islands from Denmark by treaty on August 4, 1916 for $25 million, and took possession of them on March 31, 1917.

In 1913 Wilson refused to recognize the government of Mexican military dictator Victoriano Huerta, and offered unsuccessfully to mediate between Huerta and his Constitutionalist opponent, Venustiano Carranza. When the Huerta government arrested several American seamen in Tampico in April 1914, American forces occupied the port of Veracruz, an action condemned by both Mexican political factions. In July 1914 Huerta abdicated his power to Carranza, who was soon opposed by his former general Francisco "Pancho" Villa. Seeking American intervention as a means of undermining Carranza, Villa shot sixteen Americans on a train in northern Mexico in January 1916, and burned the border town of Columbus, New Mexico, in March 1916, killing 19 people. Carranza reluctantly consented to Wilson's request that the United States be allowed to pursue and capture Villa in Mexico, but did not expect the force of about six thousand Army troops under the command of General John J. Pershing which crossed the Rio Grande on March 18. The force advanced over three hundred miles into Mexico, failed to capture Villa, and became, in effect, an army of occupation. The Carranza government demanded an American withdrawal, and several clashes with Mexican troops occurred. War threatened, but in January 1917 Wilson removed the American forces.

Pan American Mediation, 1914

John Barrett, head of the Pan American Union (formerly Blaine's International Bureau of American Republics) called for multilateral mediation to bring about a solution to Mexico's internal problems, and extract the United States from its military presence in Mexico. Although Wilson initially refused, Argentina, Brazil, and Chile did mediate among the Mexican factions and Wilson withdrew American troops. Barrett hoped to replace the unilateral Monroe Doctrine with a multilateral Pan American policy to promote collective responses and mediation to difficult hemispheric problems. Wilson, however, refused to share power with Latin America.

THE ROAD TO WAR IN EUROPE

American Neutrality

When World War I broke out in Europe, Wilson issued a proclamation of American neutrality on August 4, 1914. Despite that action, the United States drifted toward closer ties with the Allies, especially Britain and France. While many Americans were sympathetic to the Central Powers, the majority, including Wilson, hoped for an Allied victory. Although British naval power effectively prevented American trade with the Central Powers and European neutrals, often in violation of international law, the United States limited itself to formal diplomatic protests. The value of American trade with the Central Powers fell from $169 million in 1914 to almost nothing in 1916, but trade with the Allies rose from $825 million to $3.2 billion during the same period. In addition, the British and French had borrowed about $3.25 billion from American sources by 1917. The United States had become a major supplier of Allied munitions, food, and raw materials.

The Submarine Crisis of 1915

The Germans began the use of submarines in 1915, announced a submarine blockade of the Allies on February 4, and began to attack unarmed British passenger ships in the Atlantic. Wilson insisted to the Germans that Americans had a right as neutrals to travel safely on such ships, and that international law required a war ship to arrange for the safe removal of passengers before attacking such a ship. The sinking of the British liner Lusitania off the coast of Ireland on May 7, 1915, with the loss of 1,198 lives, including 128 Americans, brought strong protests from Wilson. Secretary of State Bryan, who believed Americans should stay off belligerent ships, resigned rather than insist on questionable neutral rights, and was replaced by Robert Lansing. Following the sinking of another liner, the Arabic, on August 19, the Germans gave the "Arabic pledge" to stop attacks on unarmed passenger vessels.

The Gore-McLemore Resolution

During the latter part of 1915 the British began to arm their merchant ships. Many Americans thought it in the interest of United States neutrality that Americans not travel on the vessels of belligerents. Early in 1916 the Gore-McLemore Resolution to prohibit American travel on armed ships or on ships carrying munitions was introduced in Congress, but it was defeated in both houses after intensive politicking by Wilson.

The Sussex Pledge

When the unarmed French channel steamer Sussex was torpedoed but not sunk on March 24, 1916, with seven Americans injured, Wilson threatened to sever relations unless Germany ceased all surprise submarine attacks on all shipping, whether belligerent or neutral, armed or unarmed. Germany acceded with the "Sussex pledge" at the beginning of May, but threatened to resume submarine warfare if the British did not stop their violations of international law.

The House-Grey Memorandum

Early in 1915 Wilson sent his friend and adviser, Colonel Edward M. House, on an unsuccessful visit to the capitals of the belligerent nations on both sides to offer American mediation in the war. Late in the year House returned to London to propose that Wilson call a peace conference, and, if Germany refused to attend or was uncooperative at the conference, the United States would probably enter the war on the Allied side. An agreement to that effect, called the House-Grey Memorandum, was signed by the British foreign secretary, Sir Edward Grey, on February 22, 1916.

Preparedness

In November 1915 Wilson proposed a major increase in the Army and the abolition of the National Guard as a preparedness measure. Americans divided on the issue, with organizations like the National Security League proposing stronger military forces, and others like the League to Enforce Peace opposing. After opposition by Southern and Western antipreparedness Democrats, Congress passed a modified National Defense Act in June 1916 which increased the Army from about 90,000 to 220,000, and enlarged the National Guard under federal control. In August over $500 million was appropriated for naval construction. The additional costs were met by increased taxes on the wealthy.

The Election of 1916

Wilson took the leadership on the peace issue, charging that the Republicans were the war party and that the election of Charles Evans Hughes would probably result in war with Germany and Mexico. His position was popular with many Democrats and progressives, and the slogan "He kept us out of war" became the principal theme of Democratic campaign materials, presumably contributing to his election victory.

Wilson's Final Peace Efforts, 1916–1917

On December 12, 1916, the Germans, confident of their strong position, pro-posed a peace conference, a step which Wilson previously had advocated. When Wilson asked both sides to state their expectations, the British seemed agreeable to reasonable negotiations, but the Germans were evasive and stated that they did not want Wilson at the conference. In an address to Congress on January 22, 1917, Wilson made his last offer to serve as a neutral mediator. He proposed a "peace without victory," based not on a "balance of power" but on a "community of power," alluding to his proposal of May 1916 for an "association of nations."

Unlimited Submarine Warfare

Germany announced on January 31, 1917, that it would sink all ships, belligerent or neutral, without warning in a large war zone off the coasts of the Allied nations in the eastern Atlantic and the Mediterranean. The Germans realized that the United States might declare war, but they believed that, after cutting the flow of supplies to the Allies, they could win the war before the Americans could send any sizable force to Europe. Wilson broke diplomatic relations with Germany on February 3. During February and March several American merchant ships were sunk by submarines.

The Zimmerman Telegram

The British intercepted a secret message from the German foreign secretary, Arthur Zimmerman, to the German minister in Mexico, and turned it over to the United States on February 24, 1917. The Germans proposed that, in the event of a war between the United States and Germany, Mexico attack the United States. After the war, the "lost territories" of Texas, New Mexico, and Arizona would be returned to Mexico. In addition, Japan would be invited to join the alliance against the United States. When the telegram was released to the press on March 1, many Americans became convinced that war with Germany was necessary.

The Declaration of War

Wilson, on March 2, 1917, called Congress to a special session beginning April 2. When Congress convened, he requested a declaration of war against Germany. The declaration was passed by the Senate on April 4 by a vote of 82 to 6, by the House on April 6 by a vote of 373 to 50, and signed by Wilson on April 6.

Wilson's Reasons

Wilson's decision to ask for a declaration of war seems to have been based primarily on four considerations. He believed that the Zimmerman Telegram showed that the Germans were not trustworthy and would eventually go to war against the United States. He also felt that armed neutrality could not adequately protect American shipping. The democratic government established in Russia after the revolution in March 1917 also provided more acceptable as an ally than the Tsarist government. Finally, he was convinced that the United States could hasten the end of the war and insure for itself a major role in designing a lasting peace.

WORLD WAR I: THE MILITARY CAMPAIGN

Raising an Army

Despite the enlistment of many volunteers, it was apparent that a draft would be necessary. The Selective Service Act was passed on May 18, 1917, after bitter opposition in the House led by the speaker, "Champ" Clark. Only a compromise outlawing the sale of liquor in or near military camps secured passage. Originally including all males 21 to 30, the limits were later extended to 17 and 46. The first drawing of 500,000 names was made on July 20, 1917. By the end of the war 24,231,021 men had been registered and 2,810,296 had been inducted. In addition, about two million men and women volunteered.

Women and Minorities in the Military

Some women served as clerks in the Navy or in the Signal Corps of the Army. Originally nurses were part of the Red Cross, but eventually some were taken into the Army. About 400,000 black men were drafted or enlisted, despite the objections of Southern political leaders. They were kept in segregated units, usually with white officers, which were used as labor battalions or for other support activities. Some black units did see combat, and a few blacks became officers, but did not command white troops.

The War at Sea

In 1917 German submarines sank 6.5 million tons of Allied and American shipping, while only 2.7 million tons were built. German hopes for victory were based on the destruction of Allied supply lines. The American Navy furnished destroyers to fight the submarines, and, after overcoming great resistance from the British navy, finally began the use of the convoy system in July 1917.

Shipping losses fell from almost 900,000 tons in April 1917 to about 400,000 tons in December 1917, and remained below 200,000 tons per month after April 1918. The American Navy transported over 900,000 American soldiers to France, while British transports carried over 1 million. Only two of the well-guarded troop transports were sunk. The Navy had over 2,000 ships and over half a million men by the end of the war.

The American Expeditionary Force

The soldiers and marines sent to France under the command of Major General John J. Pershing were called the American Expeditionary Force, or the AEF. From a small initial force which arrived in France in June 1917, the AEF increased to over two million by November 1918. Pershing resisted efforts by European commanders to amalgamate the Americans with the French and British armies, insisting that he maintain a separate command. American casualties included 112,432 dead, about half of whom died of disease, and 230,024 wounded.

Major Military Engagements

The American force of about 14,500 which had arrived in France by September 1917 was assigned a quiet section of the line near Verdun. As numbers increased, the American role became more significant. When the Germans mounted a major drive toward Paris in the spring of 1918, the Americans experienced their first important engagements. In June they prevented the Germans from crossing the Marne at Chateau-Thierry, and cleared the area of Belleau Woods. In July, eight American divisions aided French troops in attacking the German line between Reims and Soissons. The American First Army with over half a million men under Pershing's immediate command was assembled in August 1918, and began a major offensive at St. Mihiel on the southern part of the front on September 12. Following the successful operation, Pershing began a drive against the German defenses between Verdun and Sedan, an action called the Meuse-Argonne offensive, and reached Sedan on November 7. During the same period the English in the north and the French along the central front also broke through the German lines. The fighting ended with the armistice on November 11, 1918.

MOBILIZING THE HOME FRONT

Industry

The Council of National Defense, comprised of six cabinet members and a seven-member advisory commission of business and labor leaders, was established in 1916 before American entry into the war to coordinate industrial mobilization, but it had little authority. In July 1917 the council created the War Industries Board to control raw materials, production, prices, and labor relations. The military forces refused to cooperate with the civilian agency in purchasing their supplies, and the domestic war effort seemed on the point of collapse in December 1917 when a Congressional investigation began. In 1918 Wilson took stronger action under his emergency war powers which were reinforced by the Overman Act of May 1918. In March 1918 Wilson appointed Wall Street broker Bernard M. Baruch to head the WIB, assisted by an advisory committee of 100 businessmen. The WIB allocated raw materials, standardized manufactured products, instituted strict production and purchasing controls, and paid high prices to businesses for their products. Even so, American industry was just beginning to produce heavy armaments when the war ended. Most heavy equipment and munitions used by the American troops in France were produced in Britain or France.

Food

The United States had to supply not only its own food needs but those of Britain, France, and some of the other Allies as well. The problem was compounded by bad weather in 1916 and 1917 which had an adverse effect on agriculture. The Lever Act of 1917 gave the president broad control over the production, price, and distribution of food and fuel. Herbert Hoover was appointed by Wilson to head a newly-created Food Administration. Hoover fixed high prices to encourage the production of wheat, pork, and other products, and encouraged the conservation of food through such voluntary programs as "Wheatless Mondays" and "Meatless Tuesdays." Despite the bad harvests in 1916 and 1917, food exports by 1919 were almost triple those of the pre-war years, and real farm income was up almost 30 percent.

Fuel

The Fuel Administration under Harry A. Garfield was established in August 1917. It was concerned primarily with coal production and conservation because coal was the predominant fuel of the time and was in short supply during the severe winter of 1917–1918. "Fuelless Mondays" in nonessential industries to conserve coal and "Gasless Sundays" for automobile owners to save gasoline were instituted. Coal production increased about 35 percent from 1914 to 1918.

Railroads

The American railroad system, which provided most of the inter-city transportation in the country, seemed near collapse in December 1917 because of the wartime demands and heavy snows which slowed service. Wilson created the United States Railroad Administration under William G. McAdoo, the secretary of the Treasury, to take over and operate all the railroads in the nation as one system. The government paid the owners rent for the use of their lines, spent over $500 million on improved tracks and equipment, and achieved its objective of an efficient railroad system.

Maritime Shipping

The United States Shipping Board was authorized by Congress in September 1916, and in April 1917 it created a subsidiary, the Emergency Fleet Corporation, to buy, build, lease, and operate merchant ships for the war effort. Edward N. Hurley became the director in July 1917, and the corporation constructed several large shipyards which were just beginning to produce vessels when the war ended. By seizing German and Dutch ships, and by the purchase and requisition of private vessels, the board had accumulated a large fleet by September 1918.

Labor

To prevent strikes and work stoppages in war industries, the War Labor Board was created in April 1918 under the joint chairmanship of former president William Howard Taft and attorney Frank P. Walsh with members from both industry and labor. In hearing labor disputes the WLB in effect prohibited strikes, but it also encouraged higher wages, the eight-hour day, and unionization. Union membership doubled during the war from about 2.5 million to about 5 million.

War Finance and Taxation

The war is estimated to have cost about $33.5 billion by 1920, excluding such future costs as veterans' benefits and debt service. Of that amount at least $7 billion was loaned to the Allies, with most of the money actually spent in the United States for supplies. The government raised about $10.5 billion in taxes, and borrowed the remaining $23 billion. Taxes were raised substantially in 1917, and again in 1918. The Revenue Act of 1918, which did not take effect until 1919, imposed a personal income tax of six percent on incomes up to $4,000, and twelve percent on incomes above that amount. In addition, a graduated surtax went to a maximum of 65 percent on large incomes, for a total of 77 percent. Corporations paid an excess profits tax of 65 percent, and excise taxes were levied on luxury items. Much public, peer, and employer pressure was exerted on citizens to buy Liberty Bonds which covered a major part of the borrowing. An inflation of about one hundred percent from 1915 to 1920 contributed substantially to the cost of the war.

The Committee on Public Information

The committee, headed by journalist George Creel, was formed by Wilson in April 1917. Creel established a successful system of voluntary censorship of the press, and organized about 150,000 paid and volunteer writers, lecturers, artists, and other professionals in a propaganda campaign to build support for the American cause as an idealistic crusade, and to portray the Germans as barbaric and beastial Huns. The CPI set up volunteer Liberty Leagues in every community, and urged their members, and citizens at large, to spy on their neighbors, especially those with foreign names, and to report any suspicious words or actions to the Justice Department.

War Hysteria

A number of volunteer organizations sprang up around the country to search for draft dodgers, enforce the sale of bonds, and report any opinion or conversation considered suspicious. Perhaps the largest such organization was the American Protective League with about 250,000 members, which claimed the approval of the Justice Department. Such groups publicly humiliated people accused of not buying war bonds and persecuted, beat, and sometimes killed people of German descent. As a result of the activities of the CPI and the vigilante groups, German language instruction and German music were banned in many areas, German measles became "liberty measles," pretzels were prohibited in some cities, and the like. The anti-German and anti-subversive war hysteria in the United States far exceeded similar public moods in Britain and France during the war.

The Espionage and Sedition Acts

The Espionage Act of 1917 provided for fines and imprisonment for persons who made false statements which aided the enemy, incited rebellion in the military, or obstructed recruitment or the draft. Printed matter advocating treason or insurrection could be excluded from the mails. The Sedition Act of May 1918 forbade any criticism of the government, flag, or uniform, even if there were not detrimental consequences, and expanded the mail exclusion. The laws sounded reasonable, but they were applied in ways which trampled on civil liberties. Eugene V. Debs, the perennial Socialist candidate for president, was given a ten-year prison sentence for a speech at his party's convention in which he was critical of American policy in entering the war and warned of the dangers of militarism. Movie producer Robert Goldstein released the movie *The Spirit of '76* about the Revolutionary War. It naturally showed the British fighting the Americans. Goldstein was fined $10,000 and sentenced to ten years in prison because the film depicted the British, who were now fighting on the same side as the United States, in an unfavorable light. The Espionage Act was upheld by the Supreme Court in the case of *Shenk v. United States* in 1919. The opinion, written by Justice Oliver Wendell Holmes Jr., stated that Congress could limit free speech when the words represented a "clear and present danger," and that, in effect, a person cannot cry "fire" in a crowded theater. The Sedition Act was similarly upheld in *Abrams v. United States* a few months later. Ultimately 2,168 persons were prosecuted under the laws, and 1,055 were convicted, of whom only ten were charged with actual sabotage.

WARTIME SOCIAL TRENDS

Women

With approximately 16 percent of the normal labor force in uniform and demand for goods at a peak, large numbers of women, mostly white, were hired by factories and other enterprises in jobs never before open to them. They were often resented and ridiculed by male workers. When the war ended, almost all returned to traditional "women's jobs" or to homemaking. Returning veterans replaced them in the labor market. Women continued to campaign for woman suffrage. In 1917 six states, including the large and influential states of New York, Ohio, Indiana, and Michigan, gave the vote to women. Wilson changed his position in 1918 to advocate woman suffrage as a war measure. In January 1918 the House of Representatives adopted a suffrage amendment to the constitution which was defeated later in the year by Southern forces in the Senate. The way was paved for the victory of the suffragists after the war.

Racial Minorities

The labor shortage opened industrial jobs to Mexican-Americans and to blacks. W. E. B. DuBois, among the most prominent black leaders of the time, supported the war effort in the hope that a war to make the world safe for democracy would bring a better life for blacks in the United States. About half a million rural Southern blacks migrated to cities, mainly in the North and Midwest, to obtain employment in war and other industries, especially in steel and meatpacking. Some white Southerners, fearing the loss of labor when cotton prices were high, tried forceably to prevent their departure. Some white Northerners, fearing job competition and encroachment on white neighborhoods, resented their arrival. In 1917 there were race riots in twenty-six cities North and South, with the worst in East St. Louis, Illinois. Despite the opposition and their concentration in entry-level positions, there is evidence that the blacks who migrated generally improved themselves economically.

Prohibition

Proponents of prohibition stressed the need for military personnel to be sober and the need to conserve grain for food, and depicted the hated Germans as disgusting beer drinkers. In December 1917 a constitutional amendment to prohibit the manufacture and sale of alcoholic beverages in the United States was passed by Congress and submitted to the states for ratification. While alcohol consumption was being attacked, cigarette consumption climbed from 26 billion in 1916 to 48 billion in 1918.

PEACEMAKING AND DOMESTIC PROBLEMS, 1918–1920

The Fourteen Points

From the time of the American entry into the war, Wilson had maintained that the war would make the world safe for democracy. He insisted that there should be peace without victory, meaning that the victors would not be vindictive toward the losers, so that a fair and stable international situation in the postwar world would insure lasting peace. In an address to Congress on January 8, 1918, he presented his specific peace plan in the form of the Fourteen Points. The first five points called for open rather than secret peace treaties, freedom of the seas, free trade, arms reduction, and a fair adjustment of colonial claims. The next eight points were concerned with the national aspirations of various European peoples and the adjustment of boundaries, as, for example, in the creation of an independent Poland. The fourteenth point, which he considered the most important and had espoused as early as 1916, called for a "general association of nations" to preserve the peace. The reception of the Fourteen Points was mixed in Europe, as there was a great desire to punish Germany. In the United States, however, many people opposed a peace plan that risked American involvement in another European war.

The Election of 1918

On October 25, 1918, a few days before the congressional elections, Wilson appealed to the voters to elect a Democratic Congress, saying that to do otherwise would be a repudiation of his leadership in European affairs.

Republicans, who had loyally supported his war programs, were affronted. The voters, probably influenced more by domestic and local issues than by foreign policy, gave the Republicans a slim margin in both houses in the election. Wilson's statement had undermined his political support at home and his stature in the eyes of world leaders.

The Armistice

The German Chancellor, Prince Max of Baden, on October 3, 1918, asked Wilson to begin peace negotiations based on his concepts of a just peace and the Fourteen Points. Wilson insisted that the Germans must evacuate Belgium and France and form a civilian government. By early November the Allied and American armies were advancing rapidly and Germany was on the verge of collapse. The German Emperor fled to the Netherlands and abdicated. Representatives of the new German republic signed the armistice on November 11, 1918, to be effective at 11:00 a.m. that day, and agreed to withdraw German forces to the Rhine and to surrender military equipment, including 150 submarines.

The Versailles or Paris Peace Conference

Wilson decided that he would lead the American delegation to the peace conference which opened in Paris on January 12, 1919. In doing so he became the first president to leave the country during his term of office. The other members of the delegation were Secretary of State Robert Lansing, General Tasker Bliss, Colonel Edward M. House, and attorney Henry White. Wilson made a serious mistake in not appointing any leading Republicans to the commission and in not consulting the Republican leadership in the Senate about the negotiations. In Paris, Wilson joined Prime Minister David Lloyd George of Great Britain, Premier Georges Clemenceau of France, and Prime Minister Vittorio Orlando of Italy to form the "Big Four" which dominated the conference. In the negotiations, which continued until May 1919, Wilson found it necessary to make many compromises in forging the text of the treaty.

The Soviet Influence

Russia was the only major participant in the war which was not represented at the peace conference. Following the Communist Revolution of 1917, Russia had made a separate peace with Germany in March 1918. Wilson had resisted Allied plans to send major military forces to Russia to oust the Communists and bring Russia back into the war. An American force of about five thousand was sent to Murmansk in the summer of 1918 in association with British and

French troops to prevent the Germans from taking military supplies, and was soon active in assisting Russian anti-Bolsheviks. It remained in the area until June 1919. In July 1918 Wilson also sent about ten thousand soldiers to Siberia where they took over the operation of the railroads to assist a Czech army which was escaping from the Germans by crossing Russia. They were also to counterbalance a larger Japanese force in the area, and remained until April 1920. Wilson believed that the spread of communism was the greatest threat to peace and international order. His concern made him reluctant to dispute too much with the other leaders at the Versailles Conference, and more agreeable to compromise, because he believed it imperative that the democracies remain united in the face of the communist threat.

Important Provisions of the Versailles Treaty

In the drafting of the treaty Wilson achieved some of the goals in the Fourteen Points, compromised on others, and failed to secure freedom of the seas, free trade, reduction of armaments, or the return of Russia to the society of free nations. Some major decisions were as follows:

1) The League of Nations was formed, implementing the point which Wilson considered the most important. Article X of the Covenant, or charter, of the League called on all members to protect the "territorial integrity" and "political independence" of all other members.

2) Germany was held responsible for causing the war, and required to agree to pay the Allies for all civilian damage and veterans' costs, which eventually were calculated at $33 billion; the German army and navy were limited to tiny defensive forces; and the west bank of the Rhine was declared a military-free zone forever and occupied by the French for fifteen years. These decisions were clearly contrary to the idea of peace without victory.

3) New nations of Yugoslavia, Austria, Hungary, Czechoslovakia, Poland, Lithuania, Latvia, Estonia, and Finland partially fulfilled the idea of self-determination for all nationalities, but the boundaries drawn at the conference left many people under the control of other nationalities.

4) German colonies were made mandates of the League of Nations, and given in trusteeship to France, Japan, and Britain and its Dominions.

Germany and the Signing of the Treaty

The German delegates were allowed to come to Versailles in May 1919 after the completion of the treaty document. They expected to negotiate on the basis of the draft, but were told to sign it "or else," probably meaning an economic boycott of Germany. They protested, but signed the Versailles Treaty on June 28, 1919.

The Senate and the Treaty

Following a protest by 39 senators in February 1919, Wilson obtained some changes in the League structure to exempt the Monroe Doctrine and domestic matters from League jurisdiction. Then, on July 26, 1919, he presented the treaty with the League within it to the Senate for ratification. Almost all of the 47 Democrats supported Wilson and the treaty, but the 49 Republicans were divided. About a dozen were "irreconcilables" who thought that the United States should not be a member of the League under any circumstances. The remainder included 25 "strong" and 12 "mild" reservationists who would accept the treaty with some changes. The main objection centered on Article X of the League Covenant, where the reservationists wanted it understood that the United States would not go to war to defend a League member without the approval of Congress. The leader of the reservationists was Henry Cabot Lodge of Massachusetts, the chairman of the Foreign Relations Committee. More senators than the two-thirds necessary for ratification favored the treaty either as written or with reservations.

Wilson and the Senate

On September 3, 1919, Wilson set out on a national speaking tour to appeal to the people to support the treaty and the League, and to influence their senators. He collapsed after a speech in Pueblo, Colorado, on September 25, and returned to Washington where he suffered a severe stroke on October 2 which paralyzed his left side. He was seriously ill for several months, and never fully recovered. In a letter to the Senate Democrats on November 18, Wilson urged them to oppose the treaty with the Lodge reservations. In votes the next day, the treaty failed to get a two-thirds majority either with or without the reservations.

The Final Vote

Many people, including British and French leaders, urged Wilson to compromise with Lodge on reservations, including the issue of Article X. Wilson, instead, wrote an open letter to Democrats on January 8, 1920, urging them to make the election of a Democratic president in 1920 a "great and solemn referendum" on the treaty as written. Such partisanship only acerbated the situation. Many historians think that Wilson's ill health impaired his judgment, and that he would have worked out a compromise had he not had the stroke. The Senate took up the treaty again in February 1920, and on March 19 it was again defeated both with and without the reservations. The United States officially ended the war with Germany by a resolution of Congress signed on July 2, 1921, and a separate peace treaty was ratified on July 25. The United States did not join the League.

Consequences of War

The impact of the war was far-reaching in the twentieth century. The United States emerged as the economic and political leader of the world—even if the American people were not prepared to accept the responsibility. The Russian revolution overthrew the tsar and inaugurated a communist dictatorship. Britain, France, Austria, and Turkey went into various states of decline. Germany was devastated at the Versailles Peace Conference. Revenge and bitterness would contribute to the rise of Adolf Hitler and the Nazi movement. The European industrial nations would never recover from the cost of the war. Lingering economic problems would contribute to the Crash of 1929 and the Great Depression of the 1930s. The seeds of World War II had been planted.

DOMESTIC PROBLEMS AND THE END OF THE WILSON ADMINISTRATION

Demobilization

The AEF was brought home as quickly as possible in early 1919, and members of the armed forces were rapidly discharged. Congress provided for wounded veterans through a system of veteran's hospitals under the Veteran's Bureau, and funded relief, especially food supplies, for war-torn Europe. The wartime agencies for the control of the economy, such as the War Industries Board, were soon disbanded. During 1919 Congress considered various plans to nationalize the railroads or continue their public operation, but then passed the Esch-Cummings or Transportation Act of 1920 which returned them to private ownership and operation. It did extend Interstate Commerce Commission control over their rates and financial affairs, and allowed supervised pooling. The fleet of ships accumulated by the Shipping Board during the war was sold to private owners at attractive prices.

Final Reforms of the Progressive Era

In January 1919 the 18th Amendment to the Constitution prohibiting the manufacture, sale, transportation, or importation of intoxicating liquors was ratified by the states, and it became effective in January 1920. The 19th Amendment providing for woman suffrage, which had been defeated in the Senate in 1918, was approved by Congress in 1919. It was ratified by the states in time for the election of 1920.

The Postwar Economy

Despite fear of unemployment with the return of veterans to the labor force and the end of war purchases, the American economy boomed during 1919 and the first half of 1920. Consumers had money from high wages during the war, and the European demand for American food and manufactured products continued for some months after the war. The demand for goods resulted in a rapid inflation. Prices in 1919 were 77 percent above the prewar level, and in 1920 they were 105 percent above that level.

Strikes

The great increase in prices prompted 2,655 strikes in 1919 involving about four million workers or twenty percent of the labor force. Unions were encouraged by the gains they had made during the war and thought they had the support of public opinion. However, the Communist Revolution in Russia in 1917 soon inspired in many Americans, including government officials, a fear of violence and revolution by workers. While most of the strikes in early 1919 were successful, the tide of opinion gradually shifted against the workers.

Four major strikes received particular attention. In January 1919 all unions in Seattle declared a general strike in support of a strike for higher pay by shipyard workers. The action was widely condemned, the federal government sent marines, and the strike was soon abandoned.

In September 1919 Boston police struck for the right to unionize. Governor Calvin Coolidge called out the National Guard and stated that there was "no right to strike against the public safety by anybody, anywhere, anytime." The police were fired and a new force was recruited.

The American Federation of Labor attempted to organize the steel industry in 1919. When Judge Elbert H. Gary, the head of U.S. Steel, refused to negotiate, the workers struck in September. After much violence and the use of federal and state troops, the strike was broken by January 1920.

The United Mine Workers of America under John L. Lewis struck for shorter hours and higher wages on November 1, 1919. Attorney General A. Mitchell Palmer obtained injunctions and the union called off the strike. An arbitration board later awarded the miners a wage increase.

The Red Scare

Americans feared the spread of the Russian Communist Revolution to the United States, and many interpreted the widespread strikes of 1919 as communist-inspired and the beginning of the revolution. Bombs sent through the mail to prominent government and business leaders in April 1919 seemed to confirm their fears, although the origin of the bombs has never been determined. The membership of the two communist parties founded in the United States in 1919 was less than one hundred thousand, but many Americans were sure that many workers, all foreign-born persons, radicals, and members of the International Workers of the World (also known as "Wobblies"), a radical union in the western states, were communists. The anti-German hysteria of the war years was transformed into the anti-communist and anti-foreign hysteria of 1919 and 1920, and continued in various forms through the twenties.

The Palmer Raids

Attorney General A. Mitchell Palmer was one of the targets of the anonymous bombers in the spring of 1919. He was also an aspirant for the Democratic nomination for president in 1920, and he realized that many Americans saw the threat of a communist revolution as a grave danger. In August 1919 he named J. Edgar Hoover to head a new Intelligence Division in the Justice Department to collect information about radicals. In November 1919 Palmer's agents arrested almost seven hundred persons, mostly anarchists, and deported forty-three of them as undesirable aliens. On January 2, 1920, Justice Department agents, local police, and vigilantes in thirty-three cities arrested about four thousand people accused of being communists. It appears that many people caught in the sweep were neither communists nor aliens. Eventually 556 were shown to be communists and aliens, and were deported. Palmer then announced that huge communist riots were planned for major cities on May Day, May 1, 1920. Police and troops were alerted, but the day passed with no radical activity. Palmer was discredited and the Red Scare subsided.

The Race Riots of 1919

During the war about half a million blacks had migrated from the South to industrial cities, mostly in the North and Midwest, to find employment. After the war, white hostility based on competition for lower-paid jobs and black encroachment into neighborhoods led to race riots in twenty-five cities with hundreds killed or wounded and millions of dollars in property damage. Beginning in Longview, Texas, the riots spread, among other places, to Washington, D.C., and Chicago. The Chicago riot in July was the worst, lasting 13 days and leaving 38 dead, 520 wounded, and 1,000 families homeless. Fear of resuming black veterans in the South lead to an increase of lynchings from 34 in 1917 to 60 in 1918 and 70 in 1919. Some of the victims were veterans still in uniform.

HISTORICAL TIMELINE

Wilson and World War I (1912–1920)

1912	Wilson elected president
1913	Underwood Tariff Federal Reserve Act 16th Amendment (income tax) ratified 17th Amendment (direct senator election) ratified
1914	Clayton Antitrust Act Panama Canal opens World War I begins
1915	Germans sink *Lusitania*
1916	Margaret Sanger organizes New York Birth Control League Gen. Pershing pursues Pancho Villa in Mexico
1917	Germany resumes unrestricted submarine warfare U.S. declares war on Germany War Industries Board established Espionage Act passed Russian Revolution Committee on Public Information established
1918	Wilson proposes Fourteen Points Armistice ends war U.S. troops intervene in Russia
1919	Treaty of Versailles Red Scare and Palmer raids Senate rejects U.S. role in League of Nations 18th Amendment (Prohibition) ratified Over 20 percent of U.S. labor force goes on strike *Schenck v. United States* Race riots and lynchings throughout U.S.
1920	19th Amendment (women's suffrage) ratified

Chapter 11

THE ROARING TWENTIES AND ECONOMIC COLLAPSE (1920–1929)

THE ELECTION OF 1920

The Political Climate

It seemed to many political observers in 1920 that the Republicans had an excellent chance of victory. The Wilson administration was blamed by many for the wartime civil liberties abuses, the League of Nations controversy, and the strikes and inflation of the postwar period.

The Republican Convention

The principal contenders for the nomination were General Leonard Wood, who had the support of the followers of the deceased Theodore Roosevelt, and Governor Frank O. Lowden of Illinois, the pick of many of the party bosses. When the convention seemed to deadlock, Henry Cabot Lodge, the convention chairman, and several other leaders arranged for the name of Senator Warren G. Harding of Ohio to be introduced as a dark-horse candidate. Harding was nominated on the tenth ballot, and Governor Calvin Coolidge of Massachusetts was chosen as the vice presidential nominee. The platform opposed the League, and promised low taxes, high tariffs, immigration restriction, and aid to farmers.

The Democratic Convention

The front-runners were William Gibbs McAdoo, the secretary of the Treasury and Wilson's son-in-law, and Attorney General A. Mitchell Palmer. Governor James Cox of Ohio was entered as a favorite son. Wilson expected the convention to deadlock, at which point his name would be introduced and he would be nominated for a third term by acclamation. His plan never materialized.

McAdoo and Palmer contended for thirty-seven ballots with neither receiving the two-thirds necessary for nomination. Palmer then released his delegates, most of whom turned to Cox. Cox was nominated on the forty-fourth ballot, and Franklin D. Roosevelt, an assistant secretary of the Navy and distant cousin of Theodore, was selected as his running mate. The platform endorsed the League, but left the door open for reservations.

The Campaign

Harding's managers decided that he should speak as little as possible, but he did address visiting delegations from his front porch in Marion, Ohio. It was impossible to tell where he stood on the League issue, but he struck a responsive chord in many people when he urged that the nation should abandon heroics, nostrums, and experiment, and return to what he called normalcy. Cox and Roosevelt travelled extensively, speaking mostly in support of the League. Many found neither presidential candidate impressive.

The Election

Harding received 16,152,200 popular votes, 61 percent of the total, for 404 electoral votes. Cox received 9,147,353 popular votes for 127 electoral votes. Socialist candidate Eugene V. Debs, in federal prison in Atlanta for an Espionage Act conviction, received 919,799 votes. The Democrats carried only states in the Solid South, and even there lost Tennessee. It appears that people voted Republican more as a repudiation of Wilson's domestic policies than as a referendum on the League. Wilson had alienated German-Americans, Irish-Americans, antiwar progressives, civil libertarians, and Midwestern farmers, all groups which had given the Democrats considerable support in 1916.

THE TWENTIES: ECONOMIC ADVANCES AND SOCIAL TENSIONS

The Recession of 1920–1921

The United States experienced a severe recession from mid-1920 until the end of 1921. Europe returned to normal and reduced its purchases in America, and domestic demand for goods not available in wartime was filled. Prices fell, and unemployment exceeded twelve percent in 1921.

Prosperity and Industrial Productivity

Though overall the economy was strong between 1922 and 1929, certain segments of the economy—notably agriculture—did not share in the nation's general prosperity. Improved industrial efficiency, which resulted in lower prices for goods, was primarily responsible. Manufacturing output increased about 65 percent, and productivity, or output per hour of work increased about forty percent. The number of industrial workers actually decreased from 9 million to 8.8 million during the decade. The increased productivity resulted from improved machinery, which in turn came about for several reasons. Industry changed from steam to electric power, allowing the design of more intricate machines which replaced the work of human hands. By 1929, 70 percent of industrial power came from electricity. The moving assembly line, first introduced by Henry Ford in the automobile industry in 1913 and 1914, was widely adopted. Scientific management, exemplified by the time and motion studies pioneered by Frederick W. Taylor before the war, led to more efficient use of workers and lower labor costs. Larger firms began, for the first time, to fund major research and development activities to find new and improved products, reduce production costs, and utilize by-products, and the like.

The Automobile

The principal driving force of the economy of the 1920s was the automobile. There were 8,131,522 motor vehicles registered in the United States in 1920, and 26,704,825 in 1929. Annual output of automobiles reached 3.6 million in 1923, and remained at about that level throughout the decade. By 1925 the price of a Ford Model T had been reduced to $290, less than three months' pay for an average worker. Ford plants produced nine thousand Model Ts per day, and Henry Ford cleared about $25,000 a day throughout the decade. Just as information technology has been credited with enhancing, and even driving, innovation and productivity growth in the economy of early-twenty-first-century America, Henry Ford's use of electric motors to power automobile assembly lines led to the reorganization of a major production process. In turn, automobile manufacturing stimulated supporting industries such as steel, rubber, and glass, as well as gasoline refining and highway construction. It was during the 1920s that the United States became a nation of paved roads. Mileage of paved roads increased from 387,000 miles in 1921, most of which was in urban areas, to 662,000 in 1929. Highway construction costs averaged over one billion dollars a year in the late 1920s, in part due to the Federal Highway Act of 1916 which started the federal highway system and gave matching funds to the states for construction. One estimate stated that the automobile industry directly or indirectly employed 3.7 million people in 1929.

Other Leading Industries

The electrical industry also expanded rapidly during the 1920s. The demand for power for industrial machinery as well as for business and some lighting increased dramatically, and a host of electrical appliances such as stoves, vacuum cleaners, refrigerators, toasters, and radios became available. About two-thirds of American homes had electricity by 1929, leaving only those in rural areas without it. Home and business construction also experienced a boom from 1922 until 1928. Other large industries which grew rapidly were chemicals and printing. The movie industry expanded rapidly, especially after the introduction of sound films, and employed about 325,000 people by 1930. New industries which began in the period were radio and commercial aviation.

Consumer Credit and Advertising

Unlike earlier boom periods which had involved large expenditures for capital investments such as railroads and factories, the prosperity of the 1920s depended heavily on the sale of consumer products. Purchases of "big ticket" items such as automobiles, refrigerators, and furniture were made possible by installment or time payment credit. The idea was not new, but the availability of consumer credit expanded tremendously during the 1920s. Consumer interest and demand was spurred by the great increase in professional advertising using newspapers, magazines, radio, billboards, and other media. By 1929 advertising expenditures reached $3.4 billion, more than was spent on education at all levels.

The Dominance of Big Business

There was a trend toward corporate consolidation during the 1920s. By 1929 the 200 largest corporations held 49 percent of the corporate wealth and received 43 percent of corporate income. The top 5 percent of the corporations in the nation received about 85 percent of the corporate income. Corporate profits and dividends increased about 65 percent during the decade. In most fields an oligopoly of two to four firms dominated, exemplified by the automobile industry, where Ford, General Motors, and Chrysler produced 83 percent of the nation's vehicles in 1929. Firms in many fields formed trade associations which represented their interests to the public and the government, and which claimed to stabilize each industry. Government regulatory agencies such as the Federal Trade Commission and the Interstate Commerce Commission were passive and generally controlled by persons from the business world. The public generally accepted the situation and viewed the businessmen with respect. Illustrating the attitudes of the time, *The Man Nobody Knows*, a book by advertising executive Bruce Barton published in 1925, became a best-seller. It described Jesus as the founder of modern business and his apostles as an exemplary business management team.

Banking and Finance

As with other industries, there was a trend toward consolidation in banking. Bank assets increased about 66 percent from 1919 to 1929. There was a growth in branch banking, and in 1929 the 3.2 percent of the banks with branch operations controlled 46 percent of the banking resources. Because corporations were raising much of their money through the sale of stocks and bonds, the demand for business loans declined. Commercial banks then put more of their funds into real estate loans, loans to brokers against stocks and bonds, and the purchase of stocks and bonds themselves. By doing so they made themselves vulnerable to economic disaster when the depression began in late 1929. Even during the prosperous 1920s, 5,714 banks failed, most of them in rural areas or in Florida. Banks in operation in 1929 numbered 25,568.

Labor

The National Association of Manufacturers and its state affiliates began a drive in 1920 to restore the "open shop," or nonunion, workplace. As an alternative, firms sought to provide job satisfaction so that the workers would not want a union. Company-sponsored pension and insurance plans, stock purchase plans, efforts to ensure worker safety and comfort, social and sporting events, and company magazines were undertaken. Company unions, designed to give workers some voice with management under company control, were organized by 317 firms. The American Federation of Labor and other unions, which had prospered during World War I, found themselves on the defensive. Leaders, especially William Green, president of the American Federation of Labor after 1924, were conservative and nonaggressive. Union membership dropped about twenty percent, from five million to about four million, during the decade. The most violent labor confrontations occurred in the mining and southern textile industries. The United Mine Workers of America, headed by John L. Lewis, was involved in bitter strikes in Pennsylvania, West Virginia, Kentucky, and Illinois, but by 1929 had lost most of its power. The United Textile Workers failed to organize southern textile workers in a campaign from 1927 to 1929, but violent strikes occurred in Tennessee, North Carolina, and Virginia.

The Farm Problem

Farmers did not share in the prosperity of the twenties. Farm prices had been high during World War I because of European demand and government price fixing. By 1920 the European demand had dropped considerably, and farm prices were determined by a free market. Farm income dropped from $10 billion annually in 1919 to about $4 billion in 1921, and then leveled off at

**Texas Guinan, an actress who is best remembered as a popular
nightclub hostess during Prohibition. AP Photo.**

about $7 billion a year from 1923 through 1929. During the same period farm
expenses rose with the cost of more sophisticated machinery and a greater use
of chemical fertilizers.

AMERICAN SOCIETY IN THE 1920s

Population

During the 1920s the population of the U.S. increased by 16.1 percent, from
105,710,620 in 1920 to 122,775,046 in 1930, a slower percentage of growth
than in previous decades. The birthrate was also lower than in former times,
dropping from 27.7 per 100,000 in 1920 to 21.3 per 100,000 in 1930. About
88 percent of the people were white.

Urbanization

In 1920 for the first time a majority of Americans, 51 percent, lived in an urban place with a population of 2,500 or more. By 1930 the figure had increased to 56 percent. In terms of Standard Metropolitan Areas, which are defined as areas with central cities of at least 50,000 population, 44 percent of the people lived in an SMA in 1920, and 50 percent in 1930. Farm residents dropped from 26 percent of the total population in 1920 to 21 percent in 1930. A new phenomenon of the 1920s was the tremendous growth of suburbs and satellite cities, which grew more rapidly than the central cities. Streetcars, commuter railroads, and automobiles contributed to the process, as well as the easy availability of financing for home construction. The suburbs had once been the domain of the wealthy, but the technology of the twenties opened them to working-class families.

The Standard of Living

Improved technology and urbanization led to a sharp rise in the standard of living. Urban living improved access to electricity, natural gas, telephones, and piped water. Two-thirds of American homes had electricity by 1929. The use of indoor plumbing, hot water, and central heating increased dramatically. Conveniences such as electric stoves, vacuum cleaners, refrigerators, washing machines, toasters, and irons made life less burdensome. Improved machinery produced better-fitting and more comfortable ready-made clothing and shoes. Diet improved as the consumption of fresh vegetables increased 45 percent and canned vegetables 35 percent. Sales of citrus fruit and canned fruit were also up. Correspondingly, per capita consumption of wheat, corn, and potatoes fell. Automobiles, radios, phonographs, and commercial entertainment added to the enjoyment of life. Yet enjoyment of the new standard of living was uneven. The one-third of the households which still did not have electricity in 1929 lacked access to many of the new products. For those who had access, the new standard of living required more money than had been necessary in former times. Despite heavy sales of appliances, by 1929 only 25 percent of American families had vacuum cleaners, and only 20 percent had electric toasters. The real income of workers increased about 11 percent during the decade, but the benefits of prosperity were not spread evenly across the nation. It is estimated that the bottom 93 percent of the population actually saw a 4 percent drop in real disposable per capita income from 1923 to 1929. In 1929 about 12 million families, or 43 percent of the total, had annual incomes under $1,500, which was considered by many to be the poverty line. About 20 million families, or 72 percent, had incomes under $2,500, the family income deemed necessary for a decent standard of living with reasonable comforts.

The Sexual Revolution

Traditional American moral standards regarding premarital sex and marital fidelity were widely questioned for the first time during the 1920s. There was a popular misunderstanding by people who had not read his works that Sigmund Freud had advocated sexual promiscuity. Movies, novels, and magazine stories were more sexually explicit and sensational. The "flaming youth" of the "Jazz Age" emphasized sexual promiscuity and drinking, as well as new forms of dancing considered erotic by the older generation. The automobile, by giving people mobility and privacy, was generally considered to have contributed to sexual license. Journalists wrote about "flappers," young women who were independent, assertive, and promiscuous. Birth control, though illegal, was promoted by Margaret Sanger and others, and was widely accepted. The sexual revolution occurred mostly among some urban dwellers, middle class people, and students, who were an economically select group at the time. Many continued to adhere to the old ways. Compared with the period from 1960 to the present, it was a relatively conservative time.

Women

Many feminists believed that the passage of the 19th Amendment in 1920 providing women suffrage would solve all problems for women. When it became apparent that women did not vote as a block, political leaders gave little additional attention to the special concerns of women. The sexual revolution brought some emancipation. Women adopted less bulky clothing with short skirts and bare arms and necks. They could smoke and socialize with men in public more freely than before. Birth control was more acceptable. Divorce laws were liberalized in many states at the insistence of women. In 1920 there was one divorce for every 7.5 marriages. By 1929 the ratio was 1 in 6. The number of employed women rose from 8.4 million in 1920 to 10.6 million in 1929, but the total work force increased in about the same proportion. Black and foreign-born women comprised 57 percent of the female work force, and domestic service was the largest job category. Most other women workers were in traditional female occupations such as secretarial and clerical work, retail sales, teaching, and nursing. Rates of pay were below those for men. Most women still pursued the traditional role of housewife and mother, and society accepted that as the norm.

Blacks

The migration of Southern rural blacks to the cities continued, with about 1.5 million moving during the 1920s. By 1930 about 20 percent of blacks lived in the North, with the largest concentrations in New York, Chicago, and Philadelphia. While they were generally better off economically in the cities than they had been as tenant farmers, they tended to hold low-paying jobs and were confined to segregated areas of the cities. The Harlem section of New York City, with a black population of 73,000 in 1920 and 165,000 in 1930, was the largest black urban community, and became the center for black writers, musicians, and intellectuals. Blacks throughout the country developed jazz and blues as music forms which enjoyed widespread popularity. W. E. B. DuBois, the editor of *The Crisis*, continued to call for integration and to attack segregation despite his disappointment with the lack of progress after World War I. The National Association for the Advancement of Colored People was a more conservative but active voice for civil rights, and the National Urban League concentrated on employment and economic advancement. Lynchings continued in the South, and the anti-black activities of the Ku Klux Klan are mentioned under Social Conflicts later in this chapter.

Marcus Garvey and the UNIA

A native of Jamaica, Marcus Garvey founded the Universal Negro Improvement Association there in 1914, and moved to New York in 1916. He advocated black racial pride and separatism rather than integration, and a return of blacks to Africa. Some of his ideas soon alienated the older black organizations. He developed a large following, especially among Southern blacks, but his claim of six million members in 1923 may be inflated. An advocate of black economic self-sufficiency, he urged his followers to buy only from blacks, and founded a chain of businesses, including grocery stores, restaurants, and laundries. In 1921 he proclaimed himself the provisional president of an African empire, and sold stock in the Black Star Steamship Line, which would take migrants to Africa. The line went bankrupt in 1923, Garvey was convicted and imprisoned for mail fraud in the sale of the line's stock, and then deported. His legacy was an emphasis on black pride and self-respect.

Mexicans and Puerto Ricans

Mexicans had long migrated to the southwestern part of the United States as agricultural laborers, but in the 1920s they began to settle in cities such as Los Angeles, San Antonio, and Denver. Like other immigrants, they held low-paying jobs and lived in poor neighborhoods, which they called *barrios*. The 1920s also saw the first large migration of Puerto Ricans to the mainland, mostly to New York City. There they were employed in manufacturing, in service industries such as restaurants, and in domestic work. They lived in barrios in Brooklyn and Manhattan.

Education

Free elementary education was available to most students in 1920, except for many black children. Growth of elementary schools in the 1920s reflected population growth and the addition of kindergartens. High school education became more available, and the number of public secondary schools doubled from 2.2 million in 1920 to 4.4 million in 1930. High school instruction shifted from an emphasis on college preparation to include vocational education, which was funded in part by the Smith-Hughes Act of 1917; this act provided federal funding for agricultural and technical studies, including home economics. There was also a substantial growth in enrollment in higher education from 600,000 in 1920 to 1.1 million in 1930.

Religion

Church and synagogue membership increased more rapidly than the population during the 1920s despite much religious tension and conflict. Most Protestants had been divided North and South since before the Civil War. By the 1920s, there was another major division between the modernists who accommodated their thinking with modern biblical criticism and evolution, and fundamentalists who stressed the literal truth of the Bible and creationism. There was also division on social issues such as support of labor. The only issue which united most Protestants, except Lutherans, was prohibition. The Roman Catholic Church and Jewish congregations were assimilating the large number of immigrants who had arrived prior to 1922. They also found themselves under attack from the Ku Klux Klan and the immigration restrictions.

Popular Culture

The trend whereby entertainment shifted from the home and small social groups to commercial profit-making activities had begun in the late nineteenth century and reached maturity in the 1920s. Spending for entertainment in 1929 was $4.3 billion. The movies attracted the most consumer interest and generated the most money. Movie attendance averaged 40 million a week in 1922 and 90 million a week in 1929. Introduction of sound with *The Jazz Singer* in 1927 generated even more interest. Stars like Douglas Fairbanks, Gloria Swanson, Rudolph Valentino, Clara Bow, and Charlie Chaplin were tremendously popular. Americans spent ten times more on movies than on all sports, the next attraction in popularity. It was called the golden age of major-league baseball, with an attendance increase of over 50 percent during the decade. Millions followed the exploits of George Herman "Babe" Ruth and other stars. Boxing was popular, and made Jack Dempsey and others famous. College football began to attract attention with Knute Rockne coaching at Notre Dame and Harold "Red" Grange playing for the University of Illinois.

When Grange signed with the Chicago Bears in 1926, professional football began to grow in popularity. Commercial radio began when station KDKA in Pittsburgh broadcasted the election results in November 1920. By 1929 over 10 million families, over one-third of the total, had radios. National network broadcasting began when the National Broadcasting Company was organized in 1926, followed by the Columbia Broadcasting System in 1927. Radio was free entertainment, paid for by advertising. Despite the many new diversions, Americans continued to read, and millions of popular magazines were sold each week. Popular books of the period included the Tarzan series and Zane Grey's Westerns, as well as literary works, some of which are mentioned under Literary Trends below.

Literary Trends

Many talented writers of the 1920s were disgusted with the hypocrisy and materialism of contemporary American society, and expressed their concern in their works. Often called the "Lost Generation," many of them, such as novelists Ernest Hemingway and F. Scott Fitzgerald and poets Ezra Pound and T.S. Eliot, moved to Europe. Typical authors and works include Hemingway's *The Sun Also Rises* (1926) and *A Farewell to Arms* (1929); Sinclair Lewis's *Babbitt* (1922), *Arrowsmith* (1925), and *Elmer Gantry* (1927); F. Scott Fitzgerald's *The Great Gatsby* (1925) and *Tender Is the Night* (1929); John Dos Passos' *Three Soldiers* (1921); and Thomas Wolfe's *Look Homeward, Angel* (1929). H. L. Mencken, a journalist who began publication of the *American Mercury* magazine in 1922, ceaselessly and vitriolicly attacked the "booboisie," as he called middle-class America, but his literary talent did not match that of the leaders of the period.

SOCIAL CONFLICTS

A Conflict of Values

The rapid technological changes represented by the automobile, the revolution in morals, and the rapid urbanization with many immigrants and blacks inhabiting the growing cities brought a strong reaction from white Protestant Americans of older stock who saw their traditional values gravely threatened. In many ways their concerns continued the emotions of wartime hysteria and the Red Scare. The traditionalists were largely residents of rural areas and small towns, and the clash of farm values with those of an industrial society of urban workers was evident. The conflict is often called a rural-urban conflict, and to a great extent it was, but some think the lines of division were not that neat. The traditionalist backlash against modern urban industrial society expressed itself primarily through intolerance.

The Ku Klux Klan

On Thanksgiving Day in 1915 the Knights of the Ku Klux Klan, modeled on the organization of the same name in the 1860s and 1870s, was founded near Atlanta by William J. Simmons. Its purpose was mainly to intimidate blacks, who were experiencing an apparent rise in status during World War I. The Klan remained small until 1920 when two advertising experts, Edward Y. Clark and Elizabeth Tyler, were hired by the leadership. Clark and Tyler used modern advertising to recruit members, charged a ten dollar initiation fee of which they received $2.50, and made additional money from the sale of regalia and emblems. By 1923 the Klan had about five million members throughout the nation. The largest concentrations of members were in the South, the Southwest, the Midwest, California, and Oregon. The use of white hoods, masks, and robes, and secret ritual and jargon, seemed to appeal mostly to lower middle class men in towns and small cities. The Klan stood for "100 percent pure Americanism" to preserve "native, white, Protestant supremacy." It opposed blacks and Catholics primarily. In addition, Jews and the foreign-born were often its targets. It also attacked bootleggers, drunkards, gamblers, and adulterers for violating moral standards. The Klan's methods of repression included cross burnings, tar and featherings, kidnappings, lynchings, and burnings. The Klan was not a political party, but it endorsed and opposed candidates, and exerted considerable control over elections and politicians in at least nine states. The Klan began to decline after 1925 when it was hit by scandals, especially the murder conviction of Indiana Grand Dragon David Stephenson. The main reason for its decline was the staunch opposition of courageous editors, politicians, and other public figures who exposed its lawlessness and terrorism in the face of great personal danger of violence. Many historians see the Klan as the American expression of fascism, which was making headway in Italy, Germany, and other European nations during the twenties.

Immigration Restriction

There had been calls for immigration restriction since the late nineteenth century. Labor leaders believed that immigrants depressed wages and impeded unionization. Some progressives believed that they created social problems. In June 1917 Congress, over Wilson's veto, had imposed a literacy test for immigrants and excluded many Asian nationalities. During World War I and the Red Scare, almost all immigrants were considered radicals and communists, and the tradition was quickly picked up by the Klan. With bad economic conditions in postwar Europe, over 1.3 million came to the United States during the three years from 1919 through 1921. As in the period before the war, they were mostly from southern and eastern Europe and mostly Catholics and Jews, the groups most despised by nativist Americans. In 1921 Congress quickly passed the Emergency Quota Act, which limited immigration by nation to three percent of the number of foreign-born persons from that nation in the United States in 1910. In practice, the law admitted about as many as wanted to come from such nations as Britain, Ireland, and Germany, while severely restricting Italians, Greeks, Poles, and eastern European Jews. It became effective in 1922 and reduced the number of immigrants annually to about 40 percent of the 1921 total. Congress then passed the National Origins Act of 1924 which set the quotas at two percent of the number of foreign-born persons of that nationality in the United States in 1890, excluded all Asians, and imposed an annual maximum of 164,000.

Immigration from Western Hemisphere nations, including Canada and Mexico, was not limited. The law further reduced the number of southern and eastern Europeans, and cut the annual immigration to 20 percent of the 1921 figure. In 1927 the annual maximum was reduced to 150,000. The quotas were not fully calculated and implemented until 1929. Objections to the law were not aimed at the idea of restriction, but at the designation of certain nationalities and religious groups as undesirable. The law was resented by such groups as Italian- and Polish-Americans.

Prohibition

The 18th Amendment, which prohibited the manufacture, sale, or transportation of intoxicating liquors, took effect in January 1920. It was implemented by the Volstead Act, signed into law in October 1919, which defined intoxicating beverages as containing one-half of 1 percent alcohol by volume and imposed criminal penalties for violations. Many states had authorized the sale of light beer, believing that it was not covered by the amendment, but Anti-Saloon League lobbyists pushed through the Volstead Act. Many historians believe that prohibition of hard liquor might have been successful if light wine and beer had been allowed. As things turned out, the inexpensive light beverages were less available while expensive illegal hard liquor was readily available. Prohibition was enforceable only if many people in the society accepted and supported it. Enforcement was reasonably effective in some rural Southern and Midwestern states that had been dry before the amendment. In urban areas where both foreign-born and native citizens often believed that their liberty had been infringed upon, neither the public nor their elected officials were interested in enforcement. Speakeasies, supposedly secret bars operated by bootleggers, replaced the saloons. Smuggled liquor flowed across the boundaries and coastlines of the nation, and the manufacture of "bathtub gin" and similar beverages was undertaken by thousands. Organized crime, which previously had been involved mainly with prostitution and gambling, grew tremendously to meet the demand. Al Capone of Chicago was perhaps the most famous of the bootlegging gangsters. The automobile was used both to transport liquor and to take customers to speakeasies. Women, who had not gone to saloons in the pre-prohibition period, frequented speakeasies and began to drink in public. By the mid-1920s, the nation was badly divided on the prohibition issue. Support continued from rural areas and almost all Republican office-holders. The Democrats divided between the urban Northerners who advocated repeal, and rural, especially Southern, Democrats who supported prohibition. Some people who originally favored prohibition changed their views because of the public hypocrisy and criminal activity which it caused.

Creationism and the Scopes Trial

Fundamentalist Protestants, under the leadership of William Jennings Bryan, began a campaign in 1921 to prohibit the teaching of evolution in the schools, and thus protect belief in the literal Biblical account of creation. The idea was especially well-received in the South. In 1925 the Tennessee legislature passed a law that forbade any teacher in the state's schools or colleges to teach evolution. The American Civil Liberties Union found a young high school biology teacher,

Clarence Darrow and William Jennings Bryan, 1925. AP Photo.

John Thomas Scopes, who was willing to bring about a test case by breaking the law. Scopes was tried in Dayton, Tennessee, in July 1925. Bryan came to assist the prosecution, and Chicago trial lawyer Clarence Darrow defended Scopes. The trial attracted national attention through newspaper and radio coverage. The judge refused to allow expert testimony, so the trial was a duel of words between Darrow and Bryan. As was expected, Scopes was convicted and fined one hundred dollars. Bryan died of exhaustion a few days after the trial. Both sides claimed a moral victory. The anti-evolution crusaders continued their efforts, and secured enactment of a statute in Mississippi in 1926. They failed after a bitter fight in North Carolina in 1927, and in several other states until Arkansas in 1928 passed an anti-evolution law by use of the initiative.

Sacco and Vanzetti

On April 15, 1920, two unidentified gunmen robbed a shoe factory and killed two men in South Braintree, Massachusetts. Nicola Sacco and Bartolomeo Vanzetti, Italian immigrants and admitted anarchists, were tried for murder. Judge Webster Thayer clearly favored the prosecution, which based its case on the political radicalism of the defendants. After they were convicted and sentenced to death in July 1921, there was much protest in the United States and in Europe that they had not received a fair trial. After six years of delays, they were executed on August 23, 1927. A debate on their innocence and the possible perversion of

The Scopes "Monkey" Trial

One of the most famous trials of the 20th century took place in the tiny rural town of Dayton, Tennessee, in the summer of 1925. The trial of John Scopes pitted two of America's leading lawyers in a test of the Butler Act, which forbade the teaching of "any theory that denies the story of the Divine Creation of man as taught in the Bible, and to teach instead that man has descended from a lower order of animals." William Jennings Bryan, a three-time losing candidate for President and former U.S. Secretary of State led the prosecution of Scopes, while Clarence Darrow, perhaps the most famous defense attorney of his time, provided the defense.

When the Tennessee state legislature passed the Butler Act in March 1925, it was seen by most as more of a statement of support for religious fundamentalism rather than a practical educational law that would be enforced. The fine for breaking the law was to be no more than $500. The American Civil Liberties Union, however, decided to test the law and sought a teacher to challenge it. They found him in John T. Scopes, a 24-year-old football coach in Dayton, who also sometimes taught biology, using Hunter's *Civic Biology* as his textbook. Scopes agreed to test the case, was arrested for violating the Butler Act, and the battle began.

Dayton, with a population of 1,800 residents, mostly farmers, became the focus of the nation that summer. Besides Bryan and Darrow, H. L. Mencken, a reporter for *The Baltimore Sun* and a leading cultural critic, covered the trial, as did more than 100 newspapers.

cont'd on next page

American justice continued long afterward. The men were ultimately vindicated by Governor Michael Dukakis in 1977.

GOVERNMENT AND POLITICS IN THE 1920s: THE HARDING ADMINISTRATION

Warren G. Harding

Harding was a handsome and amiable man of limited intellectual and organizational abilities. He had spent much of his life as the publisher of a newspaper in the small city of Marion, Ohio. He recognized his limitations, but hoped to be a much-loved president. He showed compassion by pardoning socialist Eugene V. Debs for his conviction under the Espionage Act and inviting him to dinner at the White House. He also persuaded U.S. Steel to give workers the eight-hour day. A convivial man, he liked to drink and play poker with his friends, and kept the White House stocked with bootleg liquor despite prohibition. He was accused of keeping a mistress, Nan Britton. His economic philosophy was conservative.

The Cabinet and Government Appointments

Harding appointed some outstanding persons to his Cabinet, including Secretary of State Charles Evans Hughes, a former Supreme Court justice and presidential candidate; Secretary of the Treasury Andrew Mellon, a Pittsburgh aluminum and banking magnate and reportedly the richest man in America; and Secretary of

Many saw the entire spectacle as a publicity stunt. Mencken referred to the residents of Dayton as "yokels" and "morons." This was the first trial ever broadcast on radio, with station WGN of Chicago providing coverage.

Bryan, however, took the issues of the Scopes trial very seriously. He was perhaps the leading spokesman for fundamentalism, which accepted a literal interpretation of the Bible. This included the account of creation in the book of Genesis, which describes all of the universe as having been created in six days. Bryan viewed the teaching of Charles Darwin—who in his landmark book *Origin of Species* proposed that all plant and animal life, including humans evolved over time—as an attack on the Bible and God.

Opposing Bryan was a team that included Darrow, a towering figure of the 20th century. An open agnostic, Darrow responded to an appeal by the American Civil Liberties Union to assist in Scopes' defense. The verdict was never in question: Scopes would be found guilty. After all, all but one of the jurors were church members. The town was firmly in opposition to Scopes, Darrow, and Darwin. Darrow's early strategy was to minimize the difference between evolution and the creation account in Genesis, using the written testimony of evolution experts.

As the trial progressed, however, the focus turned to Bryan. Defense counsel Darrow asked to cross-examine prosecution counsel Bryan, a very unorthodox procedure. Darrow's purpose was to suggest that belief in the historical accuracy and the miracles of the Bible was unreasonable in an age of modern science. Darrow questioned the story of Jonah and the whale, Joshua causing the earth to stand

cont'd on next page

Commerce Herbert Hoover, a dynamic multimillionaire mine owner who was famous for wartime relief efforts. Less impressive was his appointment of his cronies Albert B. Fall as Secretary of the Interior and Harry M. Daugherty as Attorney General. Other cronies, some dishonest, were appointed to other government posts.

Tax Reduction

Mellon believed in low taxes and government economy to free the rich from "oppressive" taxes and thus encourage investment. The farm bloc of Midwestern Republicans and Southern Democrats in Congress prevented cuts in the higher tax brackets as great as Mellon recommended. The Revenue Acts of 1921 and 1924 cut the maximum tax rates to 50 percent and then to 40 percent. Taxes in lower brackets were also reduced, but inheritance and corporate income taxes were retained. Despite the cuts, Mellon was able to reduce the federal debt by an average of $500 million a year.

The Fordney-McCumber Tariff

Mellon sought substantial increases in the tariffs, but again there was a compromise with the farm bloc. The Fordney-McCumber Tariff of September 1922 imposed high rates on farm products and protected such infant industries as rayon, china, toys, and chemicals. Most other items received moderate protection, and a few items including farm equipment, were duty-free. The president could raise or lower rates to a limit of 50 percent on recommendation of the Tariff Commission. The average

still, and Bishop Ussher's contention that creation occurred in 4004 B.C. Darrow accused Bryan of insulting "every man of science and learning in the world because he does not believe in your fool religion." Bryan shot back that the purpose of the defense attack was "to cast ridicule on anyone who believed in the Bible." The questioning of Bryan by Darrow lasted for two hours on the trial's seventh day. On the next morning the judge ruled the entire examination of Bryan irrelevant to the case and that it would be removed from the trial's records. Darrow then changed Scopes's plea to guilty, thus preventing Bryan from delivering a closing statement, which would amount to a speech opposing evolution. Scopes was found guilty after nine minutes of jury deliberation and fined $100. The defense team appealed the decision and the Tennessee Supreme Court overturned the conviction on a technicality, though it supported the constitutionality of the Butler Act, which remained on the books in Tennessee until 1967.

The Scopes trial was the first legal challenge to the teaching of evolution in public schools. Despite the Butler Act, evolution continued to be taught in biology classes in Tennessee. Scopes abandoned teaching after the trial and studied geology at the University of Chicago. While the Scopes trial was a 1925 Tennessee event, the evolution-versus-creation argument still rages across the nation. In 1968 the U.S. Supreme Court ruled in *Epperson v. Arkansas* that evolution can be taught in public schools because it is a science, but creationism cannot be taught, because it constitutes religious teaching. Bryan and Darrow provided the first major confrontation in a debate that continues today.

rate was about 33 percent, compared with about 26 percent under the previous tariff.

The Budget

As a result of the Budget and Accounting Act of 1921, the federal government had a unified budget for the first time. The law also provided for a director of the budget to assist in its preparation, and a comptroller general to audit government accounts.

The Harding Scandals

Harding apparently was completely honest, but several of his friends whom he appointed to office became involved in major financial scandals. Most of the information about the scandals did not become public knowledge until after Harding's death.

The "Teapot Dome" Scandal began when Secretary of the Interior Albert B. Fall in 1921 secured the transfer of several naval oil reserves to his jurisdiction. In 1922 he secretly leased reserves at Teapot Dome in Wyoming to Harry F. Sinclair of Monmouth Oil and at Elk Hills in California to Edward Doheny of Pan-American Petroleum. A Senate investigation later revealed that Sinclair had given Fall $305,000 in cash and bonds and a herd of cattle, while Doheny had given him a $100,000 unsecured loan. Sinclair and Doheny were acquitted in 1927 of charges of defrauding the government, but in 1929 Fall was convicted, fined, and imprisoned for bribery.

Another scandal involved Charles R. Forbes, appointed by Harding to head the new Veterans' Bureau. He seemed energetic and efficient in operating the new hospitals and services for veterans. It was later estimated that he had stolen or squandered about $250 million in bureau funds.

Scandal also tainted Attorney General Daugherty who, through his intimate friend Jesse Smith, took bribes from bootleggers, income tax evaders, and others in return for protection from prosecution. When the scandal began to come to light, Smith committed suicide in Daugherty's Washington apartment in May 1923. There was also evidence that Daugherty received money for using his influence in returning the American Metal Company, seized by the government during the war, to its German owners.

Harding's Death

Depressed by the first news of the scandals, Harding left in June 1923 for an extended trip that included a tour of Alaska. On his return to California, he died suddenly in San Francisco on August 2, 1923, apparently of a heart attack. Rumors of foul play or suicide persisted for years.

Coolidge Becomes President

Vice President Calvin Coolidge became president to complete Harding's term. As the scandals of the deceased president's administration came to light, Coolidge was able to avoid responsibility for them. He had a reputation for honesty, although he did not remove Daugherty from the Cabinet until March 1924.

THE ELECTION OF 1924

The Republicans

Progressive insurgents failed to capture the convention. Calvin Coolidge was nominated on the first ballot with Charles G. Dawes as his running mate. The platform endorsed business development, low taxes, and rigid economy in government. The party stood on its record of economic growth and prosperity since 1922.

The Democrats

The party had an opportunity to draw farmers and labor into a new progressive coalition. An attractive Democratic candidate would have had a good chance against the bland Coolidge and the Harding scandals. Instead, two wings of the party battled to exhaustion at the convention. The Eastern wing, led by Governor Alfred E. Smith of New York, wanted the platform to favor repeal of prohibition and to condemn the Ku Klux Klan. Southern and Western delegates, led by William G. McAdoo and William Jennings Bryan, narrowly defeated both proposals. Smith and McAdoo contested for 103 ballots with neither receiving the two-thirds necessary for nomination. John W. Davis, a conservative Wall Street lawyer, was finally chosen as a dark horse with Charles W. Bryan, brother of William Jennings, as the vice presidential candidate. The platform favored a lower tariff, but otherwise was similar to the Republican document.

The Progressives

Robert M. LaFollette, after failing in a bid for the Republican nomination, formed a new Progressive Party with support from Midwest farm groups, socialists, and the American Federation of Labor. The platform attacked monopolies and called for the nationalization of railroads, the direct election of the president, and other reforms.

The Campaign

Neither Coolidge nor Davis were active or effective campaigners. Republican publicity concentrated on attacking LaFollette as a communist. LaFollette campaigned vigorously, but he lacked money and was disliked by many for his 1917 opposition to entrance into World War I.

The Election

Coolidge received 15,725,016 votes and 382 electoral votes, more than his two opponents combined. Davis received 8,385,586 votes and 136 electoral votes, while LaFollette had 4,822,856 votes and 13 electoral votes from his home state of Wisconsin.

THE COOLIDGE ADMINISTRATION

Calvin Coolidge

Coolidge was a dour and taciturn man. Born in Vermont, his adult life and political career were spent in Massachusetts. "The business of the United States is business," he proclaimed, and "the man who builds a factory builds a temple." His philosophy of life was stated in the remark that "four-fifths of all our troubles in this world would disappear if only we would sit down and keep still." Liberal political commentator Walter Lippmann wrote that "Mr. Coolidge's genius for inactivity is developed to a very high point." He intentionally provided no presidential leadership.

The McNary-Haugen Bill

In 1921 George Peek and Hugh S. Johnson, farm machinery manufacturers in Illinois, developed a plan to raise prices for basic farm products. The government would buy and resell in the domestic market a commodity such as wheat at the world price plus the tariff. The surplus would be sold abroad at the world price, and the difference made up by an equalization fee on all farmers in proportion to the amount of the commodity they had sold. When farm conditions did not improve, the idea was incorporated in the McNary-Haugen Bill, which passed Congress in 1927 and 1928, but was vetoed both times by Coolidge. The plan was a forerunner of the agricultural programs of the 1930s.

Muscle Shoals

During World War I the government had constructed a dam and two nitrate plants on the Tennessee River at Muscle Shoals, Alabama. In 1925 Senator George W. Norris of Nebraska led the defeat of a plan to lease the property to private business, but his proposal for government operation was vetoed by

Coolidge in 1928. The facility was to become the nucleus of the Tennessee Valley Authority in the 1930s.

Veterans' Bonus

Legislation to give veterans of World War I 20-year endowment policies with values based on their length of service was passed over Coolidge's veto in 1924.

The Revenue Act of 1926

Mellon's tax policies were finally implemented by the Revenue Act of 1926, which reduced the basic income tax, cut the surtax to a maximum of 20 percent, abolished the gift tax, and cut the estate tax in half.

THE ELECTION OF 1928

The Republicans

Coolidge did not seek another term, and the convention quickly nominated Herbert Hoover, the secretary of commerce, for president, and Charles Curtis as his running mate. The platform endorsed the policies of the Harding and Coolidge administrations.

The Democrats

Governor Alfred E. Smith of New York, a Catholic and an anti-prohibitionist, controlled most of the non-Southern delegations. Southerners supported his nomination with the understanding that the platform would not advocate repeal of prohibition. Senator Joseph T. Robinson of Arkansas, a Protestant and a prohibitionist, was the vice presidential candidate. The platform differed little from that of the Republicans, except in advocating lower tariffs.

The Campaign

Hoover asserted that Republican policies would end poverty in the country. Smith was also economically conservative, but he attacked prohibition and bigotry. He was met in the South by a massive campaign headed by Bishop James Cannon Jr. of the Methodist Episcopal Church South, attacking him as a Catholic and a wet.

The Election

Hoover received 21,392,190 votes and 444 electoral votes, carrying all of the North except Massachusetts and Rhode Island, and seven states in the Solid South. Smith had 15,016,443 votes for 87 electoral votes in eight states.

FOREIGN POLICY IN THE TWENTIES

The Washington Conference

At the invitation of Secretary of State Charles Evans Hughes, representatives of the United States, Great Britain, France, Japan, Italy, China, the Netherlands, Belgium, and Portugal met in Washington in August 1921 to discuss naval limitations and Asian affairs. Three treaties resulted from the conference.

The Five Power Pact or Treaty, signed in February 1922, committed the United States, Britain, Japan, France, and Italy to end new construction of capital naval vessels, to scrap some ships, and to maintain a ratio of 5:5:3:1.67:1.67 for tonnage of capital or major ships in order of the nations listed. Hughes did not realize that the treaty gave Japan naval supremacy in the Pacific.

The Nine Power Pact or Treaty was signed by all of the participants at the conference. It upheld the Open Door in China by binding the nations to respect the sovereignty, independence, and integrity of China.

The Four Power Pact or Treaty bound the United States, Great Britain, Japan, and France to respect each other's possessions in the Pacific, and to confer in the event of disputes or aggression in the area.

War Debts, Reparations, and International Finance

The United States had lent the Allies about $7 billion during World War I and about $3.25 billion in the postwar period, and insisted on full payment of the debts. Meanwhile, Germany was to pay reparations to the Allies, but by 1923 Germany was bankrupt. The Dawes Plan, proposed by American banker Charles G. Dawes, was accepted in 1924. Under it, American banks made loans of $2.5 billion to Germany by 1930. Germany paid reparations of over $2 billion to the Allies during the same period, and the Allies paid about $2.6 billion to the United States on their war debts. The whole cycle was based on loans from American banks.

The Kellogg-Briand Pact

A group of American citizens campaigned during the 1920s for a treaty which would outlaw war. In 1927 the French foreign minister, Aristide Briand, proposed such a treaty with the United States. Frank B. Kellogg, Coolidge's secretary of state, countered by proposing that other nations be invited to sign. At Paris, in August 1928, almost all major nations signed the treaty, which renounced war as an instrument of national policy. It outlawed only aggression, not self-defense, and had no enforcement provisions.

Latin America

American investment in Latin America almost doubled during the 1920s to $5.4 billion, and relations with most nations in the region improved. Coolidge removed the Marines from Nicaragua in 1925, but a revolution erupted and the Marines were returned. Revolutionary General Augusto Sandino fought against the marines until they were replaced by an American-trained national guard under Anastasio Somoza. The Somoza family ruled Nicaragua until 1979 when they were overthrown by revolutionaries called the Sandinistas.

THE GREAT DEPRESSION: THE CRASH

Hoover Becomes President

Herbert Hoover, an Iowa farm boy and an orphan, graduated from Stanford University with a degree in mining engineering. He became a multimillionaire from mining and other investments around the world. After serving as the director of the Food Administration under Wilson, be became secretary of commerce under Harding and Coolidge. He believed that an associative economic system with voluntary cooperation of business and government would enable the United States to abolish poverty through continued economic growth.

The Stock Market Boom

Stock prices increased throughout the decade. The boom in prices and volume of sales was especially active after 1925, and was intensive during 1928–29. The Dow Jones Industrial Average finished the year 1924 at 120; for the month of September 1929 it was 381; and for the year 1932 it dropped to 41. Stocks were selling for more than 16 times their earnings in 1929, well above the rule of thumb at the time of ten times their earnings.

The Stock Market Crash

Careful investors, realizing that stocks were overpriced, began to sell to take their profits. During October 1929 prices declined as more stock was sold. On "Black Thursday," October 24, 1929, almost 13 million shares were traded, a large number for that time, and prices fell precipitously. Investment banks tried to boost the market by buying, but on October 29, "Black Tuesday," the market fell about 40 points, with 16.5 million shares traded. A long decline followed until early 1933, and with it, depression.

◄──────── HISTORICAL TIMELINE ────────►

The Roaring Twenties and Economic Collapse (1920–1929)

1920	Sacco and Vanzetti arrested Harding elected president First commercial radio broadcast
1921	Washington Naval Conference Emergency Quota Act restricts immigration
1923	Teapot Dome scandal Marcus Garvey claims 6 million followers Ku Klux Klan claims 5 million members
1924	National Origins Act sets 2 percent quotas for immigration
1925	*Scopes* Tennessee evolution trial Model T Ford drops to cost of $290 (three months' wages)
1927	Lindbergh's solo flight across the Atlantic Sacco and Vanzetti executed Babe Ruth hits 60 home runs for the Yankees Al Jolson stars in *The Jazz Singer*, the first talking film
1928	Hoover elected president Fifty-two nations sign Kellogg-Briand Pact renouncing war
1929	Stock Market crashes in October

Chapter 12

THE GREAT DEPRESSION AND THE NEW DEAL (1929–1941)

REASONS FOR THE DEPRESSION

A stock market crash does not mean that a depression must follow. A similar crash in October 1987, for example, did not lead to depression. In 1929 a complex interaction of many factors caused the decline of the economy.

Many people had bought stock on a margin of ten percent, meaning that they had borrowed ninety percent of the purchase through a broker's loan, and put up the stock as collateral. Broker's loans totaled $8.5 billion in 1929, compared with $3.5 billion in 1926. When the price of a stock fell more than ten percent, the lender sold the stock for whatever it would bring and thus further depressed prices. The forced sales brought great losses to the banks and businesses which had financed the broker's loans, as well as to the investors.

There were already signs of recession before the market crash in 1929. Because the gathering and processing of statistics was not as advanced then as it is now, some factors were not so obvious to people at the time. The farm economy, which involved almost twenty-five percent of the population, had been depressed throughout the decade. Coal, railroads, and New England textiles had not been prosperous. After 1927 new construction declined and auto sales began to sag. Many workers had been laid off before the crash of 1929.

Many scholars believe that there was a problem of underconsumption, meaning that ordinary workers and farmers, after using their consumer credit, did not have enough money to keep buying the products which were being produced. One estimate says that the income of the top one percent of the population increased at least 75 percent during the decade, while that of the bottom 93 percent increased only 6 percent. The process continued after the depression began. After the stock market crash, people were conservative and saved their money, thus reducing the demand for goods. As demand decreased, workers were laid off or had wage reductions, further reducing their purchasing power and bringing another decrease in demand.

With the decline in the economy, Americans had less money for foreign loans and bought fewer imported products. That meant that foreign governments and individuals were not able to pay their debts in the United States. The whole reparations and war debts structure collapsed. American exports dropped, further hurting the domestic economy. The depression eventually spread throughout the world.

Economic Effects of the Depression

During the early months of the depression most people thought it was just an adjustment in the business cycle which would soon be over. Hoover repeatedly assured the public that prosperity was just around the corner. As time went on, the worst depression in American history set in, reaching its bottom point in early 1932. The gross national product fell from $104.6 billion in 1929 to $56.1 billion in 1933. Unemployment reached about 13 million in 1933, or about 25 percent of the labor force excluding farmers. National income dropped 54 percent from $87.8 billion to $40.2 billion. Labor income fell about 41 percent, while farm income dropped 55 percent from $11.9 billion to $5.3 billion. Industrial production dropped about 51 percent. The banking system suffered as 5,761 banks, over 22 percent of the total, failed by the end of 1932.

The Human Dimension of the Depression

As the depression grew worse, more and more people lost their jobs or had their wages reduced. Many were unable to continue credit payments on homes, automobiles, and other possessions, and lost them. Families doubled up in houses and apartments. Both the marriage rate and the birth rate declined as people put off family formation. Hundreds of thousands became homeless and lived in groups of makeshift shacks called Hoovervilles in empty spaces around cities. Others traveled the country by foot and boxcar seeking food and work. State and local government agencies and private charities were overwhelmed in their attempts to care for those in need, although public and private soup kitchens and soup lines were set up throughout the nation. Malnutrition was widespread but few died of starvation, perhaps because malnourished people are susceptible to many fatal diseases.

HOOVER'S DEPRESSION POLICIES

The Agricultural Marketing Act

Passed in June 1929 before the market crash, the Agricultural Marketing Act, proposed by the president, created the Federal Farm Board with a revolving fund of $500 million to lend the agricultural cooperatives to buy commodities such as wheat and cotton, and hold them for higher prices. Until 1931 it did keep agricultural prices above the world level. Then world prices plummeted, the board's funds ran out, and there was no period of higher prices in which the cooperatives could sell their stored commodities.

The Hawley-Smoot Tariff

The Hawley-Smoot Tariff, passed in June 1930, raised duties on both agricultural and manufactured imports. It did nothing of significance to improve the economy, and historians argue over whether or not it contributed to the spread of the international depression.

Voluntarism

Hoover believed that voluntary cooperation would enable the country to weather the depression. He held meetings with business leaders at which he urged them to avoid lay-offs of workers and wage cuts, and he secured no-strike pledges from labor leaders. He urged all citizens to contribute to charities to help alleviate the suffering. While people were generous, private charity could not begin to meet the needs.

Public Works

In 1930 Congress appropriated $750 million for public buildings, river and harbor improvements, and highway construction in an effort to stimulate employment.

The Reconstruction Finance Corporation

Chartered by Congress in 1932, the RFC had an appropriation of $500 million and authority to borrow $1.5 billion for loans to railroads, banks, and other financial institutions. It prevented the failure of basic firms on which many other elements of the economy depended, but was criticized by some as relief for the rich.

The Federal Home Loan Bank Act

The Federal Home Loan Bank Act, passed in July 1932, injected $125 million of capital into newly created home loan banks so that loans could be made to building and loan associations, savings banks, and insurance companies to help them avoid foreclosures on homes.

A shantytown, or "Hooverville," in Seattle, Wash., March 20, 1933. AP Photo

Relief

Hoover staunchly opposed the use of federal funds for relief for the needy. In July 1932 he vetoed the Garner-Wagner Bill, which would have appropriated funds for relief. He did compromise by approving legislation authorizing the RFC to lend $300 million to the states for relief, and to make loans to states and cities for self-liquidating public works.

The Bonus Army

The Bonus Expeditionary Force, which took its name from the American Expeditionary Force of World War I, was a group of about fourteen thousand unemployed veterans who went to Washington in the summer of 1932 to lobby Congress for immediate payment of the bonus which had been approved in 1926 for payment in 1945. At Hoover's insistence, the Senate did not pass the bonus bill, and about half of the BEF accepted a congressional offer of transportation home. The remaining five or six thousand, many with wives and children, continued to live in shanties along the Anacostia River and to lobby for their cause. After two veterans were killed in a clash with the police, Hoover, calling them insurrectionists and communists, ordered the Army to remove them. On July 28, 1932, General Douglas MacArthur, the Army chief of staff, assisted by Majors Dwight D. Eisenhower and George S. Patton, personally commanded the removal operation. With machine guns, tanks, cavalry, infantry with fixed bayonets, and tear gas, MacArthur drove the veterans from Washington and burned their camp.

The Farm Holiday Association

Centered in Iowa, the Farm Holiday Association, headed by Milo Reno and others, called a farm strike in August 1932. They urged farmers not to take their products to market in an effort to raise farm prices. The picketing of markets led to violence, and the strike collapsed.

THE ELECTION OF 1932

The Republicans

At the Republican convention in Chicago, Hoover was nominated on the first ballot. The platform called for a continuation of his depression policies.

The Democrats

Franklin D. Roosevelt, the popular governor of New York, gained the support of many Southern and Western delegates through the efforts of his managers, Louis Howe and James Farley. When the Democratic convention opened in Chicago, he had a majority of delegates, but not the necessary two-thirds for nomination. House speaker John Nance Garner, a favorite son candidate from Texas, threw support to Roosevelt, who was nominated on the fourth ballot. Garner then became the vice presidential candidate. Roosevelt took the unprecedented step of flying to the convention to accept the nomination in person, declaring that he pledged a "new deal" for the American people. The platform called for the repeal of prohibition, government aid for the unemployed, and a twenty five percent cut in government spending.

The Campaign

Hoover declared that he would lead the nation to prosperity with higher tariffs and the maintenance of the gold standard. He warned that the election of Roosevelt would lead to grass growing in the streets of the cities and towns of America. Roosevelt called for "bold, persistent experimentation," and expressed his concern for the "forgotten man" at the bottom of the economic heap, but he did not give a clear picture of what he intended to do. Roosevelt had a broad smile and amiable disposition which attracted many people, while Hoover was aloof and cold in his personal style.

The Election

Roosevelt received 22,809,638 votes for 57.3 percent of the total, and 472 electoral votes, carrying all but six Northeastern states. Hoover had 15,758,901 votes and 59 electoral votes. Despite the hard times, Norman Thomas, the Socialist candidate, received only 881,951 votes. The Democrats also captured the Senate, and increased their majority in the House.

THE FIRST NEW DEAL

Franklin D. Roosevelt

The heir of a wealthy family and a fifth cousin of Theodore Roosevelt, Franklin was born in 1882 on the family estate at Hyde Park, New York. He graduated from Harvard and the Columbia Law School, married his distant cousin Anna Eleanor Roosevelt in 1905, and practiced law in New York City. He entered state politics, then served as assistant secretary of the Navy under Wilson, and was the Democratic vice-presidential candidate in 1920. In 1921 he suffered an attack of polio which left him paralyzed for several years and on crutches or in a wheelchair for the rest of his life. In 1928 he was elected governor of New York to succeed Al Smith, and was reelected in 1930. As governor, his depression programs for the unemployed, public works, aid to farmers, and conservation attracted national attention.

The Cabinet

Important Cabinet appointments included Senator Cordell Hull of Tennessee as secretary of state; Henry A. Wallace as secretary of agriculture; Harold L. Ickes as secretary of the interior; Frances Perkins, a New York social worker, as secretary of labor and the first woman appointed to a Cabinet post; and James A. Farley, Roosevelt's political manager, as postmaster general.

The Brain Trust

Roosevelt's inner circle of unofficial advisors, first assembled during the campaign, was more influential than the Cabinet. Prominent in it were agricultural economist Rexford G. Tugwell, political scientist Raymond Moley, lawyer Adolph A. Berle Jr., the originators of the McNary-Haugen Bill—Hugh S. Johnson and George Peek—and Roosevelt's personal political advisor, Louis Howe.

The New Deal Program

Roosevelt did not have a developed plan of action when he took office. He intended to experiment and to find that which worked. As a result, many programs overlapped or contradicted others, and were changed or dropped if they did not work.

Repeal of Prohibition

In February 1933, before Roosevelt took office, Congress passed the 21st Amendment to repeal prohibition, and sent it to the states. In March the new Congress legalized light (lower alcohol content) beer. The amendment was ratified by the states and took effect in December 1933.

The Banking Crisis

In February 1933, as the inauguration approached, a severe banking crisis developed. Banks could not collect their loans or meet the demands of their depositors for withdrawals, and runs occurred on many banks. Eventually banks in thirty-eight states were closed by the state governments, and the remainder were open for only limited operations. An additional 5,190 banks failed in 1933, bringing the depression total to 10,951.

The Inaugural Address

By the time Roosevelt was inaugurated on March 4, 1933, the American economic system seemed to be on the verge of collapse. Roosevelt assured the nation that "the only thing we have to fear is fear itself," called for a special session of Congress to convene on March 9, and asked for "broad executive powers to wage war against the emergency." Two days later, he closed all banks, and forbade the export of gold or the redemption of currency in gold.

LEGISLATION OF THE FIRST NEW DEAL

The Hundred Days and the First New Deal

The special session of Congress, from March 9 to June 16, 1933, passed a great body of legislation which has left a lasting mark on the nation, and the period has been referred to ever since as the "Hundred Days." Over the next two years legislation was added, but the basic recovery plan of the

Hundred Days remained in operation. Hence, the period from 1933 to 1935 is called the First New Deal. A new wave of programs beginning in 1935 is called the Second New Deal. The distinction was not known at the time, but is a device of historians to differentiate between two stages in Roosevelt's administration.

Economic Legislation of the Hundred Days

The banking crisis was the most immediate problem facing Roosevelt and the Congress. A series of laws were passed to deal with the crisis and to reform the American economic system.

Emergency Banking Relief Act was passed on March 9, the first day of the special session. The law provided additional funds for banks from the RFC and the Federal Reserve, allowed the Treasury to open sound banks after ten days and to merge or liquidate unsound ones, and forbade the hoarding or export of gold. Roosevelt on March 12 assured the public of the soundness of the banks in the first of many "fireside chats," or radio addresses. People believed him and most banks were soon open with more deposits than withdrawals.

The Banking Act of 1933, or the Glass-Steagall Act, established the Federal Deposit Insurance Corporation (FDIC) to insure individual deposits in commercial banks, and separated commercial banking from the more speculative activity of investment banking.

The Truth-in-Securities Act required that full information about stocks and bonds be provided by brokers and others to potential purchasers.

The Home Owners Loan Corporation (HOLC) had authority to borrow money to refinance home mortgages and thus prevent foreclosures. Eventually it lent over $3 billion to over 1 million home owners.

Gold was taken out of circulation following the president's order of March 6, and the nation went off the gold standard. Eventually, on January 31, 1934, the value of the dollar was set at $35 per ounce of gold, 59 percent of its former value. The object of the devaluation was to raise prices and help American exports.

Later Economic Legislation of the First New Deal

The Securities and Exchange Commission was created in 1934 to supervise stock exchanges and to punish fraud in securities trading.

The Federal Housing Administration (FHA) was created by Congress in 1934 to insure long-term, low-interest mortgages for home construction and repair.

Relief and Employment Programs of the Hundred Days

Roosevelt's relief and employment programs were intended to provide temporary relief for people in need, and to be disbanded when the economy improved.

The Federal Emergency Relief Act appropriated $500 million for aid to the poor to be distributed by state and local governments. Half of the funds were to be distributed on a one to three matching basis with the states. It also established the Federal Emergency Relief Administration under Harry Hopkins. Additional appropriations were made many times later.

The Civilian Conservation Corps enrolled 250,000 young men ages 18 to 24 from families on relief to go to camps where they worked on flood control, soil conservation, and forest projects under the direction of the War Department. A small monthly payment was made to the family of each member. By the end of the decade, 2.75 million young men had served in the corps.

The Public Works Administration, under Secretary of the Interior Harold Ickes, had $3.3 billion to distribute to state and local governments for building projects such as schools, highways, and hospitals. The object was to "prime the pump" of the economy by creating construction jobs. Additional money was appropriated later.

Later Relief Efforts

After the Hundred Days, in November 1933, Roosevelt established the Civil Works Administration under Harry Hopkins with $400 million from the Public Works Administration to hire four million unemployed workers. The temporary and makeshift nature of the jobs, such as sweeping streets, brought much criticism, and the experiment was terminated in April 1934.

Agricultural Programs of the Hundred Days

The Agricultural Adjustment Act of 1933 created the Agricultural Adjustment Administration (AAA), which was headed by George Peek. It sought to return farm prices to parity with those of the 1909 to 1914 period. Farmers agreed to reduce production of principal farm commodities and were paid a subsidy in return. The money came from a tax on the processing of the commodities. Farm prices increased, but tenants and sharecroppers were hurt when owners took land out of cultivation. The law was declared unconstitutional in January 1936 on the grounds that the processing tax was not constitutional.

The Federal Farm Loan Act consolidated all farm credit programs into the Farm Credit Administration to make low-interest loans for farm mortgages and other agricultural purposes.

Later Agricultural Programs

The Commodity Credit was established in October 1933 by the AAA to make loans to corn and cotton farmers against their crops so that they could hold them for higher prices.

The Frazier-Lemke Farm Bankruptcy Act of 1934 allowed farmers to defer foreclosure on their land while they obtained new financing, and helped them to recover property already lost through easy financing.

The National Industrial Recovery Act

The National Industrial Recovery Act, passed on June 16, 1933, the last day of the Hundred Days, was viewed as the cornerstone of the recovery program. It sought to stabilize the economy by preventing extreme competition, labor-management conflicts, and over-production. A board composed of industrial and labor leaders in each industry or business drew up a code for that industry which set minimum prices, minimum wages, maximum work hours, production limits, and quotas. The antitrust laws were temporarily suspended. The approach was based on the idea of many economists at the time; because a mature industrial economy produced more goods than could be consumed, it would be necessary to create a relative shortage of goods in order to raise prices and restore prosperity. The idea was proved wrong by the expansion of consumer goods after World War II. Section 7a of the law also provided that workers had the right to join unions and to bargain collectively. The National Recovery Administration (NRA) was created under the leadership of Hugh S. Johnson to enforce the law and generate public enthusiasm for it. In May 1935 the law was declared unconstitutional in the case of *Schechter v. United States*, on the grounds that Congress had delegated legislative authority to the code-makers, and that Schechter, who slaughtered chickens in New York, was not engaged in interstate commerce. It was argued later that the NRA had unintentionally aided big firms to the detriment of smaller ones because the representatives of the larger firms tended to dominate the code-making process. It was generally unsuccessful in stabilizing small businesses such as retail stores, and was on the point of collapse when it was declared unconstitutional.

The Tennessee Valley Authority

Different from the other legislation of the Hundred Days which addressed immediate problems of the depression, the Tennessee Valley Authority, a public corporation under a three-member board, was proposed by Roosevelt as the first major experiment in regional public planning. Starting from the nucleus of the government's Muscle Shoals property on the Tennessee River, the TVA built 20 dams in an area of 40,000 square miles to stop flooding and soil erosion, improve navigation, and generate hydroelectric power. It also manufactured nitrates for fertilizer, conducted demonstration projects for farmers, engaged in reforestation, and attempted to rehabilitate the whole area. It was fought unsuccessfully in the courts by private power companies. Roosevelt believed that it would serve as a yardstick to measure the true cost of providing electric power.

Effects of the First New Deal

The economy improved but remained far from recovered between 1933 and 1935. The gross national product rose from $74.2 billion in 1933 to $91.4 billion in 1935. Manufacturing salaries and wages increased from $6.24 billion in 1933 to over $9.5 billion in 1935, with average weekly earnings going from $16.73 to $20.13. Farm income rose from $1.9 billion in 1933 to $4.6 billion in 1935. The money supply, as currency and demand deposits, grew from $19.2 billion to $25.2 billion. Unemployment dropped from about 25 percent of nonfarm workers in 1933 to about 20.1 percent, or 10.6 million, in 1935. While the figure had improved, it was a long way from the 3.2 percent of pre-depression 1929, and suffering as a result of unemployment was still a major problem.

THE SECOND NEW DEAL: OPPOSITION FROM THE RIGHT AND LEFT

FDR Weathers Criticism

The partial economic recovery brought about by the first New Deal provoked criticism from the right for doing too much, and from the left for doing too little. Conservatives and businessmen criticized the deficit financing, which accounted for about half of the federal budget, federal spending for relief, and government regulation of business. They frequently charged that the New Deal was socialist or communist in form, and some conservative writers labeled the wealthy Roosevelt "a traitor to his class." People on the lower end of the economic scale thought that the New Deal, especially the NRA, was too favorable to big business. Small-business people and union members complained that the NRA codes gave control of industry to the big firms, while farmers complained that the NRA set prices too high. The elderly thought that nothing had been done to help them. Several million people who were or had been tenant farmers or sharecroppers were badly hurt. When the AAA paid farmers to take land out of production, the landowners took the money while the tenants and sharecroppers lost their livelihood. Several opposition organizations and persons were particularly active in opposing Roosevelt's policies.

The American Liberty League was formed in 1934 by conservatives to defend business interests and promote the open shop. While many of its members were Republicans and it was financed primarily by the Du Pont family, it also attracted conservative Democrats like Alfred E. Smith and John W. Davis. It supported conservative congressional candidates of both parties in the election of 1934 with little success.

The Old Age Revolving Pension Plan was advanced by Dr. Francis E. Townsend, a retired California physician. The plan proposed that every retired person over sixty receive a pension of $200 a month, about double the average worker's salary, with the requirement that the money be spent within the month. The plan would be funded by a national gross sales tax. Townsend claimed that it would end the depression by putting money into circulation, but economists thought it fiscally impossible. Some three to five million older Americans joined Townsend Clubs.

The Share Our Wealth Society was founded in 1934 by Senator Huey "The Kingfish" Long of Louisiana. Long was a populist demagogue who was elected governor of Louisiana in 1928, established a practical dictatorship over the state, and moved to the United States Senate in 1930. He supported Roosevelt in 1932, but then broke with him, calling him a tool of Wall Street for not doing more to combat the depression. Long called for the confiscation of all fortunes over five million dollars and a tax of one hundred percent on annual incomes over one million. With the money, the government would provide subsidies so that every family would have a "homestead" of house, car, and furnishings worth at least $5,000, a minimum annual income of $2,000, and free college education for those who wanted it. His slogan was "Every Man a King." Long talked of running for president in 1936, and published a book entitled My First Days in the White House. His society had over five million members when he was assassinated on the steps of the Louisiana Capitol on September 8, 1935. The Reverend Gerald L.K. Smith appointed himself Long's successor as head of the society, but he lacked Long's ability.

The National Union for Social Justice was headed by Father Charles E. Coughlin, a Catholic priest in Royal Oak, Michigan, who had a weekly radio program. Beginning as a religious broadcast in 1926, Coughlin turned to politics and finance, and attracted an audience of millions of many faiths. He supported Roosevelt in 1932, but then turned against him. He advocated an inflationary currency and was anti-Semitic, but beyond that his fascist-like program was not clearly defined.

THE SECOND NEW DEAL BEGINS

Roosevelt's Position

With millions of Democratic voters under the sway of Townsend, Long, and Coughlin, with the destruction of the NRA by the Supreme Court imminent, and with the election of 1936 approaching the next year, Roosevelt began to push through a series of new programs in the spring of 1935. Much of the legislation was passed during the summer of 1935, a period sometimes called the Second Hundred Days.

Legislation and Programs of the Second New Deal

The Works Progress Administration (WPA) was started in May 1935 following the passage of the Emergency Relief Appropriations Act of April 1935. Headed by Harry Hopkins, the WPA employed people from the relief rolls for thirty hours of work a week at pay double the relief payment but less than private employment. There was not enough money to hire all of the unemployed, and the numbers varied from time to time, but an average of 2.1 million people per month were employed. By the end of the program in 1941, 8.5 million people had worked at some time for the WPA at a total cost of $11.4 billion. Most of the projects undertaken were in construction. The WPA built hundreds of thousands of miles of streets and roads, and thousands of schools, hospitals, parks, airports, playgrounds, and other facilities. Hand work was emphasized so that the money would go for pay rather than equipment, provoking much criticism for inefficiency. Unemployed artists painted murals in public buildings; actors, musicians, and dancers performed in poor neighborhoods; and writers compiled guide books and local histories.

The National Youth Administration (NYA) was established as part of the WPA in June 1935 to provide part-time jobs for high school and college students to enable them to stay in school, and to help young adults not in school to find jobs.

The Rural Electrification Administration (REA) was created in May 1935 to provide loans and WPA labor to electric cooperatives to build lines into rural areas not served by private companies.

The Resettlement Administration (RA) was created in the Agriculture Department in May 1935 under Rexford Tugwell. It relocated destitute families from seemingly hopeless situations to new rural homestead communities or to suburban greenbelt towns.

The National Labor Relations or Wagner Act was passed in May 1935 to replace the provisions of Section 7a of the NIRA. It reaffirmed labor's right to unionize, prohibited unfair labor practices, and created the National Labor Relations Board (NLRB) to oversee and insure fairness in labor-management relations.

The landmark Social Security Act was passed in August 1935. It established a retirement plan for persons over age sixty-five funded by a tax on wages paid equally by employee and employer. The first benefits, ranging from $10 to $85 per month, were paid in 1942. Another provision of the act had the effect of forcing the states to initiate unemployment insurance programs. It imposed a payroll tax on employers which went to the state if it had an insurance program, and to the federal government if it did not. The act also provided matching funds to the states for aid to the blind, handicapped, and dependent children, and for public health services. The American Social Security system was limited compared with those of other industrialized nations, and millions of workers were not covered by it. Nonetheless, it marked a major change in American policy.

The Banking Act of 1935 created a strong central Board of Governors of the Federal Reserve System with broad powers over the operations of the regional banks.

The Public Utility Holding Company or Wheeler-Rayburn Act of 1935 empowered the Securities and Exchange Commission to restrict public utility holding companies to one natural region and to eliminate duplicate holding companies. The Federal Power Commission was created to regulate interstate electrical power rates and activities, and the Federal Trade Commission received the same kind of power over the natural gas companies.

The Revenue Act of 1935 increased income taxes on higher incomes, and also inheritance, large gift, and capital gains taxes.

The Motor Carrier Act of 1935 extended the regulatory authority of the Interstate Commerce Commission to cover interstate trucking lines.

THE ELECTION OF 1936

The Democrats

At the convention in Philadelphia in June, Roosevelt and Garner were renominated by acclamation on the first ballot. The convention also ended the requirement for a two-thirds vote for nomination. The platform promised an expanded farm program, labor legislation, more rural electrification and public housing, and enforcement of the antitrust laws. In his acceptance speech Roosevelt declared that "this generation of Americans has a rendezvous with destiny." He further proclaimed that he and the American people were fighting for democracy and capitalism against the "economic royalists," business people he charged with seeking only their own power and wealth, and opposing the New Deal.

The Republicans

Governor Alfred M. Landon of Kansas, a former progressive supporter of Theodore Roosevelt, was nominated on the first ballot at the convention in Cleveland in June. Frank Knox, a Chicago newspaper publisher, was chosen as his running mate. The platform criticized the New Deal for operating under unconstitutional laws, and called for a balanced budget, higher tariffs, and lower corporate taxes. It did not call for the repeal of all New Deal legislation, and

**Destitute pea pickers in California during the Great Depression.
Photo by Dorothea Lange. Courtesy of U.S. Library of Congress.**

promised better and less expensive relief, farm, and labor programs. In effect, Landon and the Republicans were saying that they would do about the same thing, but do it better.

The Union Party

Dr. Francis Townsend, Father Charles Coughlin, and the Reverend Gerald L. K. Smith, Long's successor in the Share Our Wealth Society, organized the Union Party to oppose Roosevelt. The nominee was Congressman William Lemke of North Dakota, an advocate of radical farm legislation but a bland campaigner. Vicious attacks by Smith and Coughlin on Roosevelt brought a backlash against them, and American Catholic leaders denounced Coughlin.

The Election

Roosevelt carried all of the states except Maine and Vermont with 27,757,333 votes, or 60.8 percent of the total, and 523 electoral votes. Landon received 16,684,231 votes and 8 electoral votes. Lemke had 891,858 votes for 1.9 percent of the total. Norman Thomas, the Socialist candidate, received 187,000 votes, only 21 percent of the 881,951 votes he received in 1932.

The New Deal Coalition

Roosevelt had put together a coalition of followers who made the Democratic Party the majority party in the nation for the first time since the Civil War. While retaining the Democratic base in the Solid South and among white ethnics in the big cities, Roosevelt also received strong support from Midwestern farmers. Two groups which made a dramatic shift into the Democratic ranks were union workers and blacks. Unions took an active political role for the first time since 1924, providing both campaign funds and votes. Blacks had traditionally been Republican since emancipation, but by 1936 about three-fourths of the black voters, who lived mainly in the Northern cities, had shifted into the Democratic Party.

THE LAST YEARS OF THE NEW DEAL

Court Packing

Frustrated by a conservative Supreme Court which had overturned much of his New Deal legislation, Roosevelt, after receiving his overwhelming mandate in the election of 1936, decided to curb the power of the court. In doing so, he overestimated his own political power and underestimated the force of tradition. In February 1937 he proposed to Congress the Judicial Reorganization Bill which would allow the president to name a new federal judge for each judge who did not retire by the age of 70 1/2. The appointments would be limited to a maximum of fifty, with no more than six added to the Supreme Court. At the time, six justices were over the proposed age limit. Roosevelt cited a slowing of the judicial process due to the infirmity of the incumbents, and the need for a modern outlook. The president was astonished by the wave of opposition from Democrats and Republicans alike, and uncharacteristically refused to compromise. In doing so, he not only lost the bill but he lost control of the Democratic Congress which he had dominated since 1933. Nonetheless, the Court changed its position as Chief Justice Charles Evans Hughes and Justice Owen Roberts began to vote with the more liberal members. The National Labor Relations Act was upheld in March 1937, and the Social Security Act in April. In June a conservative justice retired, and Roosevelt had the opportunity to make an appointment.

The Recession of 1937–1938

Most economic indicators rose sharply between 1935 and 1937. The gross national product had recovered to the 1930 level, and unemployment, if WPA workers were considered employed, had fallen to 9.2 percent. Average yearly earnings of the employed had risen from $1,195 in 1935 to $1,341 in 1937, and average hourly manufacturing earnings from 55 cents to 62 cents. During the same period there were huge federal deficits. In fiscal 1936, for example, there was a deficit of $4.4 billion in a budget of $8.5 billion. Roosevelt decided that the recovery was sufficient to warrant a reduction in relief programs and a move toward a balanced budget. The budget for fiscal 1938, from July 1937 to June 1938, was reduced to $6.8 billion, with the WPA experiencing the largest cut. During the winter of 1937–1938 the economy slipped rapidly and unemployment rose to 12.5 percent. In April 1938 Roosevelt requested and received from Congress an emergency appropriation of about $3 billion for the WPA, as well as increases for public works and other programs. In July 1938 the economy began to recover, and it regained the 1937 levels in 1939.

Legislation of the Late New Deal

With the threat of adverse Supreme Court rulings removed, Roosevelt rounded out his program during the late 1930s.

The Bankhead-Jones Farm Tenancy Act, passed in July 1937, created the Farm Security Administration (FSA) to replace the Resettlement Administration. The FSA continued the homestead projects, and loaned money to farmers to purchase farms, lease land, and buy equipment. It also set up camps for migrant workers and established rural health care programs.

The National Housing, or Wagner-Steagall Act, passed in September 1937, established the United States Housing Authority (USHA) which could borrow money to lend to local agencies for public housing projects. By 1941 it had loaned $750 million for 511 projects.

The Second Agricultural Adjustment Act of February 1938 appropriated funds for soil conservation payments to farmers who would remove land from production. The law also empowered the Agriculture Department to impose market quotas to prevent surpluses in cotton, wheat, corn, tobacco, and rice if two-thirds of the farmers producing that commodity agreed.

The Fair Labor Standards Act, popularly called the minimum wage law, was passed in June 1938. It provided for a minimum wage of 25 cents an hour which would gradually rise to 40 cents, and a gradual reduction to a work week of 40 hours, with time and a half for overtime. Workers in small businesses and in public and nonprofit employment were not covered. The law also prohibited the shipment in interstate commerce of manufactured goods on which children under 16 worked.

SOCIAL DIMENSIONS OF THE NEW DEAL ERA

Blacks and the New Deal

Blacks suffered more than other people from the depression. Unemployment rates were much higher than for the general population, and before 1933 they were often excluded from state and local relief efforts. Blacks did benefit from many New Deal relief programs, but about forty percent of black workers were sharecroppers or tenants who suffered from the provisions of the first Agricultural Adjustment Act. Roosevelt seems to have given little thought to the special problems of black people, and he was afraid to endorse legislation such as an anti-lynching bill for fear of alienating the southern wing of the Democratic party. Eleanor Roosevelt and Harold Ickes strongly supported civil rights, and a "Black Cabinet" of advisors was assembled in the Interior Department. More blacks were appointed to government positions by Roosevelt than ever before, but the number was still small. When government military contracts began to flow in 1941, A. Philip Randolph, the president of the Brotherhood of Sleeping Car Porters, proposed a black march on Washington to demand equal access to defense jobs. To forestall such an action, Roosevelt issued an executive order on June 25, 1941, establishing the Fair Employment Practices Committee to insure consideration for minorities in defense employment.

Native Americans and the New Deal

John Collier, the commissioner of the Bureau of Indian Affairs, persuaded Congress to repeal the Dawes Act of 1887 by passing the Indian Reorganization Act of 1934. The law restored tribal ownership of lands, recognized tribal constitutions and government, and provided loans to tribes for economic development. Collier also secured the creation of the Indian Emergency Conservation Program, a Native American CCC for projects on the reservations. In addition, he helped Native Americans secure entry into the WPA, NYA, and other programs.

Mexican Americans and the New Deal

Mexican Americans benefitted the least from the New Deal, for few programs covered them. Farm owners turned against them as farm workers after they attempted to form a union between 1933 and 1936. By 1940 most had been replaced by whites dispossessed by the depression. Many returned to Mexico, and the Mexican American population dropped almost forty percent from 1930 to 1940.

Women During the New Deal

The burden of the depression fell on women as much or more as it did on men. Wives and mothers found themselves responsible for stretching meager budgets by preparing inexpensive meals, patching old clothing, and the like. "Making do" became a slogan of the period. In addition, more women had to supplement or provide the family income by going to work. In 1930 there were 10.5 million working women comprising 29 percent of the work force. By 1940 the figures had grown to over 13 million and 35 percent. There was much criticism of working women based on the idea that they deprived men of jobs. Male job losses were greatest in heavy industry such as factories and mills, while areas of female employment such as retail sales were not hit as hard. Unemployed men seldom sought jobs in the traditional women's fields.

LABOR UNIONS

Unions During the First New Deal

Labor unions had lost members and influence during the twenties, and slipped further during the economic decline of 1929 to 1933. The National Industrial Recovery Act gave them new hope when Section 7a guaranteed the right to unionize, and during 1933 about 1.5 million new members joined unions. It soon became clear that enforcement of the industrial codes by the NRA was ineffective, and labor leaders began to call it the "National Run Around." As a result in 1934 there were many strikes, sometimes violent, including a general strike in San Francisco involving about 125,000 workers.

Craft Versus Industrial Unions

The passage of the National Labor Relations, or Wagner, Act in 1935 resulted in a massive growth of union membership, but only at the expense of bitter conflict within the labor movement. The American Federation of Labor was made up primarily of craft unions. Some leaders, especially John L. Lewis, the dynamic president of the United Mine Workers, wanted to unionize the mass production industries, such as automobiles and rubber, with industrial unions. In 1934 the AFL convention authorized such unions, but the older unions continued to try to organize workers in those industries by crafts. In November 1935 Lewis and others established the Committee for Industrial Organization to unionize basic industries, presumably within the AFL. President William Green of the AFL ordered the CIO to disband in January 1936. When the rebels refused, they were expelled by the AFL executive council in March 1937. The insurgents then reorganized the CIO as the independent Congress of Industrial Organizations to be composed of industrial unions.

The Growth of the CIO

During its organizational period the CIO sought to initiate several industrial unions, particularly in the steel, auto, rubber, and radio industries. In late 1936 and early 1937 it used a tactic called the sit-down strike, with the strikers occupying the workplace to prevent any production. There were 477 sit-down strikes involving about 400,000 workers. The largest was in the General Motors plant in Flint, Michigan, as the union sought recognition by that firm. In February 1937 General Motors recognized the United Auto Workers as the bargaining agent for its 400,000 workers. When the CIO established its independence in March 1937, it already had 1.8 million members, and it reached a membership of 3.75 million six months later. The AFL had about 3.4 million members at that time. By the end of 1941 the CIO had about 5 million members, the AFL about 4.6 million, and other unions about one million. Union members comprised about 11.5 percent of the work force in 1933, and 28.2 percent in 1941.

CULTURAL TRENDS OF THE 1930s

Literary Developments

The writers and intellectuals who had expressed disdain for the middle class materialism of the 1920s found it even more difficult to deal with the meaning of the crushing poverty in America and the rise of fascism in Europe during the 1930s. Some turned to communism, including the fifty-three writers who signed an open letter endorsing the Communist presidential candidate in 1932. Some turned to proletarian novels, such as Jack Conroy in *The Disinherited* (1933) and Robert Cantwell in *The Land of Plenty* (1934). Ernest Hemingway seemed to have lost his direction in *Winner Take All* (1933) and *The Green Hills of Africa* (1935), but in *To Have and Have Not* (1937), a strike novel, he turned to social realism, and *For Whom the Bell Tolls* (1941) expressed his concern about fascism. Sinclair Lewis also dealt with fascism in *It Can't Happen Here* (1935), but did not show the power of his works of the 1920s. John Dos Passos depicted what he saw as the disintegration of American life from 1900 to 1929 in his trilogy *U.S.A.* (1930–1936). William Faulkner sought values in Southern life in *Light in August* (1932), *Absalom! Absalom!* (1936), and *The Unvanquished* (1938). The endurance of the human spirit and personal survival were depicted in James T. Farrell's trilogy *Studs Lonigan* (1936) about the struggles of lower-middle-class Irish Catholics in Chicago, while Erskine Caldwell's *Tobacco Road* (1932) dealt with impoverished Georgia sharecroppers, and John Steinbeck's *The Grapes of Wrath* (1939) depicted "Okies" migrating from the dust bowl to California in the midst of the depression.

New Deal–era poster shows a man with a WPA shovel attacking a wolf called Rumor.

Popular Culture

The depression greatly reduced the amount of money available for recreation and entertainment. There was an increase in games and sports among family groups and friends. The WPA and the CCC constructed thousands of playgrounds, playing fields, picnic areas, and the like for public use. Roosevelt and Harry Hopkins, the director of the WPA, hoped to develop a mass appreciation of culture through the WPA murals in public buildings, with traveling plays, concerts, and exhibits, and with community arts centers. Beyond some revival of handicrafts, it is doubtful that the program had much effect. There were, however, several popular forms of entertainment.

Radio was the favorite form of daily entertainment during the depression because, after the initial cost of the instrument, it was free. There were about forty million radios in the United States by 1938. It provided comedy and mystery shows, music, sports and news. A study at the time indicated that radio tended to make Americans more uniform in their attitudes, taste, speech, and humor.

While radio was the form of entertainment most used, the movies were the most popular. By 1939 about 65 percent of the people went to the movies at least once a week. The movie industry was one of the few which did not suffer financially from the depression. Movies were the great means of escape, providing release from the pressures of the depression by transporting people to a make-believe world of beauty, mystery, or excitement. Spectacular musicals with dozens of dancers and singers, such as *Broadway Melody of 1936*, were popular. The dance team of Fred Astaire and Ginger Rogers thrilled millions in *Flying Down to Rio* and *Shall We Dance?* Shirley Temple charmed the public as their favorite child star. Judy Garland rose to stardom in *The Wizard of Oz*, while animated films like *Snow White* appealed to children of all ages. People enjoyed the triumph of justice and decency in *Mr. Smith Goes to Washington* and *You Can't Take It with You* with Jimmy Stewart. Dozens of light comedies starred such favorites as Cary Grant, Katharine Hepburn, Clark Gable, and Rosalind Russell, while Errol Flynn played in such larger-than-life roles as Robin Hood. A different kind of escape was found in gangster movies with Edward G. Robinson, James Cagney, or George Raft. Near the end of the decade *Gone with the Wind*, released in 1939 starring Clark Gable and Vivien Leigh, became a timeless classic, while *The Grapes of Wrath* in 1940 commented on the depression itself.

The popular music of the decade was swing, and the big bands of Duke Ellington, Benny Goodman, Glenn Miller, Tommy Dorsey, and Harry James vied for public favor. The leading popular singer was Bing Crosby. City African Americans refined the country blues to city blues, and interracial audiences enjoyed both city blues and jazz. African American musicians were increasingly accepted by white audiences.

Comic strips existed before the thirties, but they became a standard newspaper feature as well as a source of comic books during the decade. "Dick Tracy" began his war on crime in 1931, and was assisted by "Superman" after 1938. "Tarzan" began to swing through the cartoon jungles in 1929, and "Buck Rogers" began the exploration of space in 1930.

NEW DEAL DIPLOMACY AND THE ROAD TO WAR
The Good Neighbor Policy

Roosevelt and Secretary of State Cordell Hull continued the policies of their predecessors in endeavoring to improve relations with Latin American nations, and formalized their position by calling it the Good Neighbor Policy.

Nonintervention

At the Montevideo Conference of American Nations in December of 1933 the United States renounced the right of intervention in the internal affairs of Latin American countries. In 1936, in the Buenos Aires Convention, the United States further agreed to submit all American disputes to arbitration. Accordingly, the Marines were removed from Haiti, Nicaragua, and the Dominican Republic by 1934. The Haitian protectorate treaty was allowed to expire in 1936, the right of intervention in Panama was ended by treaty in 1936, and the receivership of the finances of the Dominican Republic ended in 1941.

Cuba

The United States did not intervene in the Cuban revolution in the spring of 1933, but it did back a coup by Fulgencio Batista to overthrow the liberal regime of Ramon Grau San Martin in 1934. Batista was given a favorable sugar import status for Cuba in return for establishing a conservative administration. In May 1934 the United States abrogated its Platt Amendment rights in Cuba except for control of the Guantanamo Naval Base.

Mexico

The Mexican government of Lazaro Cardenas began to expropriate American property, including oil holdings, in 1934. Despite calls for intervention, Roosevelt insisted only on compensation. A joint commission worked out a settlement which was formally concluded on November 19, 1941.

The London Economic Conference

An international conference in London in June 1933 tried to obtain tariff reduction and currency stabilization for the industrialized nations. Roosevelt would not agree to peg the value of the dollar to other currencies because he feared that it might impede his recovery efforts. The conference failed for lack of American cooperation.

Recognition of Russia

The United States had not had diplomatic relations with the Union of Soviet Socialist Republics since it was established after the 1917 revolution. In an effort to open trade with Russia, mutual recognition was negotiated in November 1933. The financial results were disappointing.

Philippine Independence

The Tydings-McDuffie Act of March 1934 forced the Philippines to become independent on July 4, 1946, rather than granting the dominion status which the Filipinos had requested.

The Reciprocal Trade Agreement Act

The Reciprocal Trade Agreement, the idea of Cordell Hull, was passed in June 1934. It allowed the president to negotiate agreements which could vary from the rates of the Hawley-Smoot Tariff up to 50 percent. By 1936 lower rates had been negotiated with 13 nations, and by 1941 almost two-thirds of all American foreign trade was covered by agreements.

UNITED STATES NEUTRALITY LEGISLATION

Isolationism

Belief that the United States should stay out of foreign wars and problems began in the 1920s and grew in the 1930s. It was fed by House and Senate investigations of arms traffic and the munitions industry in 1933 and 1934, especially an examination of profiteering by bankers and munitions makers in drawing the United States into World War I by Senator Gerald Nye of North Dakota. Books of revisionist history which asserted that Germany had not been responsible for World War I and that the United States had been misled were also influential during the 1930s. A Gallup poll in April 1937 showed that almost two-thirds of those responding thought that American entry into World War I had been a mistake. Such feelings were strongest in the Midwest and among Republicans, but were found in all areas and across the political spectrum. Leading isolationists included Congressman Hamilton Fish of New York, Senator William Borah of Idaho, and Senator George Norris of Nebraska, all Republicans. Pacifist movements, such as the Fellowship of Christian Reconciliation, were influential among college and high school students and the clergy.

The Johnson Act of 1934

When European nations stopped payment on World War I debts to the United States, the Johnson Act of 1934 prohibited any nation in default from selling securities to any American citizen or corporation.

The Neutrality Acts of 1935

Isolationist sentiment prompted Senator Key Pittman, a Nevada Democrat, to propose these laws. Roosevelt would have preferred more presidential flexibility, but Congress wanted to avoid flexibility and the mistakes of World War I. The laws provided that, on outbreak of war between foreign nations, all exports of American arms and munitions to them would be embargoed for six months. In addition, American ships were prohibited from carrying arms to any belligerent, and the president was to warn American citizens not to travel on belligerent ships.

The Neutrality Acts of 1936

The Neutrality Acts of 1936 gave the president authority to determine when a state of war existed, and prohibited any loans or credits to belligerents.

The Neutrality Acts of 1937

The Neutrality Acts of 1937 gave the president authority to determine if a civil war was a threat to world peace and covered by the Neutrality Acts, prohibited all arms sales to belligerents, and allowed the cash and carry sale of nonmilitary goods to belligerents.

THREATS TO WORLD ORDER

The Manchurian Crisis

In September 1931 the Japanese army invaded and seized the Chinese province of Manchuria. The action violated the Nine Power Pact and the Kellogg-Briand Pact. When the League of Nations sought consideration of some action against Japan, Hoover refused to consider either economic or military sanctions. The only American action was to refuse recognition of the action or the puppet state of Manchukuo which the Japanese created.

Ethiopia

Following a border skirmish between Italian and Ethiopian troops, the Italian army of Fascist dictator Benito Mussolini invaded Ethiopia from neighboring Italian colonies in October 1935. The League of Nations failed to take effective action, the United States looked on, and Ethiopia fell in May 1936.

Occupation of the Rhineland

In defiance of the Versailles Treaty, Nazi dictator Adolf Hitler sent his German army into the demilitarized Rhineland in March 1936.

The Rome-Berlin Axis

Germany and Italy, under Hitler and Mussolini, formed an alliance called the Rome-Berlin Axis on October 25, 1936.

The Sino-Japanese War

The Japanese launched a full-scale invasion of China in July 1937. When Japanese planes sank the American Gunboat *Panay* and three Standard Oil tankers on the Yangtze River in December 1937, the United States accepted a Japanese apology and damage payments while the American public called for the withdrawal of all American forces from China.

The "Quarantine the Aggressor" Speech

In a speech in Chicago in October 1937 Roosevelt proposed that the democracies unite to quarantine the aggressor nations. When public opinion did not pick up on the idea, he did not press the issue.

German Expansion

Hitler brought about a union of Germany and Austria in March 1938, took the German-speaking Sudetenland from Czechoslovakia in September 1938, and occupied the rest of Czechoslovakia in March 1939.

The Invasion of Poland and the Beginning of World War II

On August 24, 1939, Germany signed a nonaggression pact with Russia which contained a secret provision to divide Poland between them. German forces then invaded Poland on September 1, 1939. Britain and France declared war on Germany on September 3 because of their treaties with Poland. By the end of September Poland had been dismembered by Germany and Russia, but the war continued in the west along the French-German border.

THE AMERICAN RESPONSE TO THE WAR IN EUROPE

Preparedness

Even before the outbreak of World War II, Roosevelt began a preparedness program to improve American defenses. In May 1938 he requested and received a naval construction appropriation of about one billion dollars. In October, Congress provided an additional $300 million for defense, and in January 1939 a regular defense appropriation of $1.3 billion with an added $525 million for equipment, especially airplanes. Defense spending increased after the outbreak of war. In August 1939 Roosevelt created the War Resources Board to develop a plan for industrial mobilization in the event of war. The next month he established the

Office of Emergency Management in the White House to centralize mobilization activities.

The Neutrality Act of 1939

Roosevelt officially proclaimed the neutrality of the United States on September 5, 1939. He then called Congress into special session on September 21 and urged it to allow the cash-and-carry sale of arms. Despite opposition from isolationists, the Democratic Congress, in a vote that followed party lines, passed a new Neutrality Act in November. It allowed the cash-and-carry sale of arms and short-term loans to belligerents, but forbade American ships to trade with belligerents or Americans to travel on belligerent ships. The new law was helpful to the Allies because they controlled the Atlantic.

Changing American Attitudes

Hitler's armies invaded and quickly conquered Denmark and Norway in April 1940. In May, German forces swept through the Netherlands, Belgium, Luxembourg, and France. The British were driven from the continent, and France surrendered on June 22. Almost all Americans recognized Germany as a threat. They divided on whether to aid Britain or to concentrate on the defense of America. The Committee to Defend America by Aiding the Allies was formed in May 1940, and the America First Committee, which opposed involvement, was incorporated in September 1940.

Greenland

In April 1940 Roosevelt declared that Greenland, a possession of conquered Denmark, was covered by the Monroe Doctrine, and he supplied military assistance to set up a coastal patrol there.

Defense Mobilization

In May 1940 Roosevelt appointed a Council of National Defense chaired by William S. Knudson, the president of General Motors, to direct defense production and especially to build fifty thousand planes. The Council was soon awarding defense contracts at the rate of $1.5 billion a month. The Office of Production Management was created to allocate scarce materials, and the Office of Price Administration was established to prevent inflation and protect consumers. In June, Roosevelt made Republicans Henry L. Stimson and Frank Knox secretaries of war and the Navy, respectively, partly as an attempt to secure bipartisan support.

Selective Service

Congress approved the nation's first peacetime draft, the Selective Service and Training Act, in September 1940. Men ages 21 to 35 were registered, and many were called for one year of military training.

Destroyers for Bases

Roosevelt had determined that to aid Britain in every way possible was the best way to avoid war with Germany. He ordered the army and navy to turn over all available weapons and munitions to private dealers for resale to Britain. In September 1940 he signed an agreement to give Britain fifty American destroyers in return for a 99-year lease on air and naval bases in British territories in Newfoundland, Bermuda, and the Caribbean.

THE ELECTION OF 1940

The Republicans

Passing over their isolationist front-runners, Senator Robert A. Taft of Ohio and New York attorney Thomas E. Dewey, the Republicans nominated Wendell L. Willkie of Indiana, a dark horse candidate. Willkie was a liberal Republican who had been a Democrat most of his life, and the head of an electric utility holding company which had fought against the TVA. The platform supported a strong defense program, but severely criticized the New Deal domestic policies.

The Democrats

Roosevelt did not reveal his intentions regarding a third term, but he neither endorsed another candidate nor discouraged his supporters. When the convention came in July, he sent a message to the Democratic National Committee implying that he would accept the nomination for a third time if it were offered. He was then nominated on the first ballot, breaking a tradition which had existed since the time of Washington. Only with difficulty did Roosevelt's managers persuade the delegates to accept his choice of vice president, Secretary of Agriculture Henry A. Wallace, to succeed Garner. The platform endorsed the foreign and domestic policies of the administration.

The Campaign

Willkie's basic agreement with Roosevelt's foreign policy made it difficult for him to campaign. Willkie had a folksy approach which appealed to many voters, but he first attacked Roosevelt for the slowness of the defense program, and then, late in the campaign, called him a warmonger. Roosevelt, who lost the support of many Democrats, including his adviser James Farley, over the third term issue, campaigned very little. When Willkie began to gain on the warmongering issue, Roosevelt declared on October 30 that "your boys are not going to be sent into any foreign wars."

The Election

Roosevelt won by a much narrower margin than in 1936, with 27,243,466 votes, 54.7 percent, and 449 electoral votes. Willkie received 22,304,755 votes and 82 electoral votes. Socialist Norman Thomas had 100,264 votes, and Communist Earl Browder received 48,579.

AMERICAN INVOLVEMENT WITH THE EUROPEAN WAR

The Lend-Lease Act

The British were rapidly exhausting their cash reserves with which to buy American goods. In January 1941 Roosevelt proposed that the United States provide supplies to be paid for in goods and services after the war. The Lend-Lease Act was passed by Congress and signed on March 11, 1941, and the first appropriation of $7 billion was provided. In effect, the law changed the United States from a neutral to a nonbelligerent on the Allied side.

The Patrol of the Western Atlantic

The Germans stepped up their submarine warfare in the Atlantic to prevent the flow of American supplies to Britain. In April 1941 Roosevelt started the American Neutrality Patrol. The American navy would search out but not attack German submarines in the western half of the Atlantic, and warn British vessels of their location.

Greenland

In April 1941, United States forces occupied Greenland and in May the president declared a state of unlimited national emergency.

Occupation of Iceland

American Marines occupied Iceland, a Danish possession, in July 1941 to protect it from seizure by Germany. The American Navy began to convoy American and Icelandic ships between the United States and Iceland.

The Atlantic Charter

On August 9, 1941, Roosevelt and Winston Churchill, the British prime minister, met for the first time on a British battleship off Newfoundland. They issued the Atlantic Charter, which described a postwar world based on self-determination for all nations. It also endorsed the principles of freedom of speech and religion and freedom from want and fear, which Roosevelt had proposed as the Four Freedoms earlier that year.

Aid to Russia

Germany invaded Russia in June 1941, and in November the United States extended lend-lease assistance to the Russians.

The Shoot-on-Sight Order

The American destroyer *Greer* was attacked by a German submarine near Iceland on September 4, 1941. Roosevelt ordered the American military forces to shoot on sight at any German or Italian vessel in the patrol zone. An undeclared naval war had begun. The American destroyer *Kearny* was attacked by a submarine on October 16, and the destroyer *Reuben James* was sunk on October 30, with 115 lives lost. In November, Congress authorized the arming of merchant ships.

THE ROAD TO PEARL HARBOR

A Japanese Empire

Following their invasion of China in 1937, the Japanese began to speak of the Greater East Asia Co-Prosperity Sphere, a Japanese empire of undefined boundaries in east Asia and the western Pacific. Accordingly, they forced out American and other business interests from occupied China, declaring that the Open Door policy had ended. Roosevelt responded by lending money to China and requesting American aircraft manufacturers not to sell to Japan.

The Embargo of 1940

Following the fall of France, a new and more militant Japanese government in July 1940 obtained from the German-controlled Vichy French government the right to build air bases and to station troops in northern French Indochina. The United States, fearing that the step would lead to further expansion, responded in late July by placing an embargo on the export of aviation gasoline, lubricants, and scrap iron and steel to Japan, and by granting an additional loan to China. In December the embargo was extended to include iron ore and pig iron, some chemicals, machine tools, and other products.

The Tripartite Pact

Japan joined with Germany and Italy to form the Rome-Berlin-Tokyo Axis on September 27, 1940, when it signed the Tripartite Pact or Triple Alliance with the other Axis powers.

The Embargo of 1941

In July 1941 Japan extracted a new concession from Vichy France by obtaining military control of southern Indochina. Roosevelt reacted by freezing Japanese funds in the United States, closing the Panama Canal to Japan, activating the Philippine militia, and placing an embargo on the export of oil and other vital products to Japan.

Japanese-American Negotiations

Negotiations to end the impasse between the United States and Japan were conducted in Washington between Secretary Hull and Japanese Ambassador Kichisaburo Nomura. Hull demanded that Japan withdraw from Indochina and China, promise not to attack any other area in the western Pacific, and withdraw from the Tripartite Pact in return for the reopening of American trade. The Japanese offered to withdraw from Indochina when the Chinese war was satisfactorily settled, to promise no further expansion, and to agree to ignore any obligation under the Tripartite Pact to go to war if the United States entered a defensive war with Germany. Hull refused to compromise.

A Summit Conference Proposed

The Japanese proposed in August 1941 that Roosevelt meet personally with the Japanese prime minister, Prince Konoye, in an effort to resolve their differences. Such an action might have strengthened the position of Japanese moderates, but Roosevelt replied in September that he would do so only if Japan agreed to leave China. No meeting was held.

Final Negotiations

In October 1941 a new military cabinet headed by General Hideki Tojo took control of Japan. The Japanese secretly decided to make a final effort to negotiate, and to go to war if no solution was found by November 25. A new round of talks followed in Washington, but neither side would make a substantive change in its position, and on November 26, Hull repeated the American demand that the Japanese remove all their forces from China and Indochina immediately. The Japanese gave final approval on December 1 for an attack on the United States.

Japanese Attack Plans

The Japanese planned a major offensive to take the Dutch East Indies, Malaya, and the Philippines in order to obtain the oil, metals, and other raw materials which they needed. At the same time they would attack Pearl Harbor in Hawaii to destroy the American Pacific fleet to keep it from interfering with their plans.

American Awareness of Japanese Plans

The United States had broken the Japanese diplomatic codes, and knew that trouble was imminent. Between December 1 and December 6, 1941, it became clear to administration leaders that Japanese task forces were being ordered into battle. American commanders in the Pacific were warned of possible aggressive action there, but not forcefully. Apparently most American leaders thought that Japan would attack the Dutch East Indies and Malaya, but would avoid American territory so as not to provoke action by the United States. Some argue that Roosevelt wanted to let the Japanese attack so that the American people would be squarely behind the war.

The attack on Pearl Harbor by the Japanese pushed the United States into World War II. U.S. Naval Historical Center Photo.

The Pearl Harbor Attack

At 7:55 a.m. on Sunday December 7, 1941, the first wave of Japanese carrier-based planes attacked the American fleet in Pearl Harbor. A second wave followed at 8:50 a.m. American defensive action was almost nil, but by the second wave a few anti-aircraft batteries were operating and a few Army planes from another base in Hawaii engaged the enemy. The United States suffered the loss of two battleships sunk, six damaged and out of action, three cruisers and three destroyers sunk or damaged, and a number of lesser vessels destroyed or damaged. All of the 150 aircraft at Pearl Harbor were destroyed on the ground. Worst of all, 2,323 American servicemen were killed and about 1,100 wounded. The Japanese lost 29 planes, five midget submarines, and one fleet submarine.

The Declaration of War

On December 8, 1941, Roosevelt told a joint session of Congress that the day before had been a "date that would live in infamy." Congress declared war on Japan with one dissenting vote. On December 11, Germany and Italy declared war on the United States.

◄——— HISTORICAL TIMELINE ———►
The Great Depression and the New Deal (1929–1941)

1929	Agricultural Marketing Act attempts to support farm prices
1930	Hawley-Smoot Tariff raises duties on farm products and manufactured goods
1931	Japan invades Manchuria
1932	Reconstruction Finance Corporation attempts to support industry Bonus Expeditionary Force marches on Washington, D.C. Franklin Roosevelt wins presidency
1933	Prohibition repealed Hundred Days of legislation follows FDR's inauguration Banks closed after over 6,000 fail FDIC established by Glass-Steagall Act Agricultural Adjustment Act passed National Industrial Recovery Act passed Tennessee Valley Authority established Civilian Conservation Corps enrolls 250,000 young men Hitler becomes chancellor of Germany
1934	Securities and Exchange Commission established Huey Long begins Share Our Wealth clubs Dr. Francis Townsend promotes Old Age Revolving Pension Plan Nye Committee probes World War I profiteering by American industrialists
1935	*Schecter v. United States* rules NIRA unconstitutional Works Progress Administration established National Labor Relations (Wagner) Act protects workers' rights Social Security Act passed Congress passes first of annual Neutrality Acts

1936	FDR defeats Republican Landon and third-party Union Party for president General Motors sitdown strike Germany occupies the Rhineland Spanish Civil War begins Ethiopia falls to Italy
1937	FDR proposes court-packing plan, which fails Japan invades China U.S. gunship *Panay* sunk by Japanese in Yangtze River
1938	Appeasement at Munich by England's Chamberlain as Germany takes Sudetenland
1939	Czechoslovakia falls to Germany Austria votes to be annexed by Germany Germany invades Poland Neutrality Act allows cash-and-carry for military purchases Germany and Soviet Union sign nonaggression pact
1940	Germany conquers Denmark, Norway, the Netherlands, Belgium, and France Congress approves first peace-time draft U.S. and Great Britain sign destroyers for bases deal America First Committee established, urging U.S. neutrality Italy, Germany, and Japan form the Rome-Berlin-Tokyo Axis FDR wins unprecedented third term for president
1941	Lend-Lease Act allows U.S. to financially assist Allied nations FDR and Churchill sign Atlantic Charter, pledging self-determination for all nations Germany invades Soviet Union Japan attacks Pearl Harbor, Hawaii, on December 7, killing 2,323 U.S. servicemen U.S. declares war on Japan on December 8

Chapter 13

WORLD WAR II AND THE POSTWAR ERA (1941–1960)

DECLARED WAR BEGINS

Declaration of War

On December 8, Congress declared war on Japan. Three days later the Axis powers, Germany and Italy, declared war on the United States. Great Britain and the United States then established the Combined Chiefs of Staff, headquartered in Washington, to direct Anglo-American military operations.

Declaration of the United Nations

On January 1, 1942, representatives of 26 nations met in Washington, D.C., and signed the Declaration of the United Nations, pledging themselves to the principles of the Atlantic Charter and promising not to make a separate peace with their common enemies.

THE HOME FRONT

War Production Board

The War Production Board was established in 1942 by President Franklin D. Roosevelt for the purpose of regulating the use of raw materials.

Wage and Price Controls

In April 1942 the General Maximum Price Regulation Act froze prices and extended rationing. In April 1943 prices, wages, and salaries were all frozen.

Revenue Act of 1942

The Revenue Act of 1942 extended the income tax to the majority of the population. Payroll deduction for the income tax began in 1944.

Lula Barber, Meta Kres, and Meda Brendall (from left), outside welding shop at the Bethlehem-Fairfield Shipyards, 1942, Baltimore, Maryland. Women made a major contribution to the war effort without even leaving the States. Photo courtesy of Veterans History Project, American Folklife Center, Library of Congress.

Social Changes

Rural areas lost population while coastal areas increased rapidly. Women entered the work force in increasing numbers. Blacks moved from the rural South to Northern and Western cities with racial tensions often resulting, most notably in the June 1943 racial riot in Detroit.

Smith-Connolly Act

Passed in 1943, the Smith-Connolly Antistrike Act authorized government seizure of a plant or mine idled by a strike if the war effort was impeded. It expired in 1947.

Korematsu v. United States

In 1944 the Supreme Court upheld President Roosevelt's 1942 order that Issei (Japanese Americans who had emigrated from Japan) and Nisei (native-born Japanese Americans) be relocated to concentration camps. The camps were closed in March 1946.

Smith v. Allwright

In 1944 the Supreme Court struck down the Texas primary elections, which were restricted to whites, for violating the 15th Amendment.

Presidential Election of 1944

President Franklin D. Roosevelt, together with new vice-presidential candidate Harry S. Truman of Missouri, defeated his Republican opponent, Governor Thomas Dewey of New York.

Death of Roosevelt

Roosevelt died on April 12, 1945, at Warm Springs, Georgia. Harry S. Truman became president.

THE NORTH AFRICAN AND EUROPEAN THEATRES

Nearly 400 ships were lost in American waters of the Atlantic to German submarines between January and June 1942.

The United States joined in the bombing of the European continent in July 1942. Bombing increased during 1943 and 1944 and lasted to the end of the war.

The Allied army under Dwight D. Eisenhower attacked French North Africa in November, 1942. The French surrendered.

In the Battle of Kassarine Pass, February 1943, North Africa, the Allied army met General Erwin Rommel's Africa Korps. Although the battle is variously interpreted as a standoff or a defeat for the U.S., Rommel's forces were soon trapped by the British moving in from Egypt. In May 1943, Rommel's Africa Korps surrendered.

Allied armies under George S. Patton invaded Sicily from Africa in July 1943 and gained control by mid-August. Moving from Sicily, the Allied armies invaded the Italian mainland in September. Benito Mussolini had already fallen from power and his successor, Marshal Pietro Badoglio surrendered. The Germans, however, put up a stiff resistance with the result that Rome did not fall until June 1944.

In March 1944, the Soviet Union began pushing into Eastern Europe.

On "D-Day," June 6, 1944, Allied armies under Dwight D. Eisenhower, now commander in chief of Supreme Headquarters, Allied Expeditionary Forces, began an invasion of Normandy, France. Allied armies under General Omar Bradley took the transportation hub of St. Lo, France in July.

Allied armies liberated Paris in August. By mid-September they had arrived at the Rhine, on the edge of Germany.

Beginning December 16, 1944, at the Battle of the Bulge, the Germans counter-attacked, driving the Allies back about 50 miles into Belgium. By January the Allies were once more advancing toward Germany.

The Allies crossed the Rhine in March 1945. In the last week of April, Eisenhower's forces met the Soviet army at the Elbe.

On May 7, 1945, Germany surrendered.

THE PACIFIC THEATRE

By the end of December 1941, Guam, Wake Island, the Gilbert Islands, and Hong Kong had fallen to the Japanese. In January 1942, Raboul, New Britain fell, followed in February by Singapore and Java, and in March by Rangoon, Burma.

The U.S. air raids on Tokyo in April 1942 were militarily inconsequential but they raised Allied morale.

U.S. forces surrendered at Corregidor, Philippines, on May 6, 1942.

In the Battle of the Coral Sea, May 7–8, 1942 (northeast of Australia, south of New Guinea and the Solomon Islands), planes from the American carriers *Lexington* and *Yorktown* forced Japanese troop transports to turn back from attacking Port Moresby. The battle stopped the Japanese advance on Australia.

Unable to obtain a Japanese surrender and fearing a Japanese invasion that advisors said could take half a million American lives, President Truman authorized the dropping of two atomic bombs in August 1945—over Hiroshima, above, and Nagasaki. Truman's decision remains the subject of great scholarly debate. AP Photo.

At the Battle of Midway, June 4–7, 1942, American air power destroyed four Japanese carriers and about 300 planes while the U.S. lost the carrier Yorktown and one destroyer. The battle proved to be the turning point in the Pacific.

A series of land, sea, and air battles took place around Guadalcanal in the Solomon Islands from August 1942 to February 1943, stopping the Japanese.

The Allied strategy of island hopping, begun in 1943, sought to neutralize Japanese strongholds with air and sea power and then move on. General Douglas MacArthur commanded the land forces moving from New Guinea toward the Philippines, while Admiral Chester W. Nimitz directed the naval attack on important Japanese islands in the central Pacific.

U.S. forces advanced into the Gilberts (November 1943), the Marshalls (January 1944), and the Marianas (June 1944).

In the Battle of the Philippine Sea, June 19–20, 1944, the Japanese lost three carriers, two submarines, and over 300 planes while the Americans lost 17 planes. After the American capture of the Marianas, General Tojo resigned as premier of Japan.

The Battle of Leyte Gulf, October 25, 1944, involved three major engagements that resulted in Japan's loss of most of its remaining naval power. It also brought the first use of the Japanese kamikaze, or suicide, attacks by Japanese pilots who crashed into American carriers.

Forces under General Douglas MacArthur liberated Manila in March 1945.

Between April and June 1945, in the battle for Okinawa, nearly 50,000 American casualties resulted from the fierce fighting which virtually destroyed Japan's remaining defenses.

THE ATOMIC BOMB

The Manhattan Engineering District was established by the Army engineers in August 1942 for the purpose of developing an atomic bomb. The mission eventually became known as the Manhattan Project. J. Robert Oppenheimer directed the design and construction of a transportable atomic bomb at Los Alamos, New Mexico.

On December 2, 1942, Enrico Fermi and his colleagues at the University of Chicago produced the first atomic chain reaction.

On July 16, 1945, the first atomic bomb was exploded at Alamogordo, New Mexico.

The *Enola Gay* dropped an atomic bomb on Hiroshima, Japan, on August 6, 1945, killing about 78,000 people and injuring 100,000 more. On August 9, a second bomb was dropped on Nagasaki, Japan. Some 40,000 people were killed in the explosion. Thousands more died later from burns, injuries, and radiation exposure.

On August 8, 1945, the Soviet Union entered the war against Japan.

Japan surrendered on August 15, 1945. The formal surrender was signed on September 2.

DIPLOMACY

Casablanca Conference

On January 14–25, 1943, Franklin D. Roosevelt and Winston Churchill, prime minister of Great Britain, declared a policy of unconditional surrender for "all enemies."

Moscow Conference

In October 1943, Secretary of State Cordell Hull obtained Soviet agreement to enter the war against Japan after Germany was defeated and to participate in a world organization after the war was over.

Declaration of Cairo

Issued on December 1, 1943, after Roosevelt met with General Chiang Kai-shek in Cairo from November 22 to 26, the Declaration of Cairo called for Japan's unconditional surrender and stated that all Chinese territories occupied by Japan would be returned to China and that Korea would be free and independent.

Teheran Conference

The first "Big Three" (Roosevelt, Churchill, and Stalin) conference, met at Teheran from November 28 to December 1, 1943. Stalin reaffirmed the Soviet commitment to enter the war against Japan and discussed coordination of the Soviet offensive with the Allied invasion of France.

Yalta Conference

On February 4–11, 1945 the "Big Three" met to discuss post-war Europe. Stalin said that the Soviet Union would enter the Pacific war within three months after Germany surrendered and agreed to the "Declaration of Liberated Europe" which called for free elections. They called for a conference on world organization, to meet in the U.S. beginning on April 25, 1945, and agreed that the Soviets would have three votes in the General Assembly and that the

At the Yalta Conference in 1945, Churchill, Roosevelt, and Stalin planned for Nazi Germany's final defeat and occupation. Photo by ITAR—Tass/Sovfoto.

U.S., Great Britain, the Soviet Union, France, and China would be permanent members of the Security Council. Germany was divided into occupation zones, and a coalition government of communists and non-communists was agreed to for Poland. Roosevelt accepted Soviet control of Outer Mongolia, the Kurile Islands, the southern half of Sakhalin Island, Port Arthur (Darien), and partici-pation in the operation of the Manchurian railroads.

Potsdam Conference

From July 17 to August 2, 1945, Truman, Stalin, and Clement Atlee (who during the conference replaced Churchill as prime minister of Great Britain) met at Potsdam. During the conference, Truman ordered the dropping of the atomic bomb on Japan. The conference disagreed on most major issues but did establish a Council of Foreign Ministers to draft peace treaties for the Balkans. Approval was also given to the concept of war-crimes trials and the demilitarization and denazification of Germany.

THE EMERGENCE OF THE COLD WAR AND CONTAINMENT

Failure of U.S.–Soviet Cooperation

By the end of 1945 the Soviet Union controlled most of Eastern Europe, Outer Mongolia, parts of Manchuria, Northern Korea, the Kurile Islands, and Sakhalin Island. In 1946–47 it took over Poland, Hungary, Rumania, and Bulgaria.

Iron Curtain

In a speech in Fulton, Missouri, in 1946, Winston Churchill stated that an Iron Curtain had been spread across Europe separating the democratic from the authoritarian communist states.

Containment

In 1946, career diplomat and Soviet expert George F. Kennan warned that the Soviet Union had no intention of living peacefully with the United States. The next year, in July 1947 he wrote an anonymous article for Foreign Affairs in which he called for a counter-force to Soviet pressures for the purpose of "containing" communism.

Truman Doctrine

In February 1947 Great Britain notified the United States that it could no longer aid the Greek government in its war against communist insurgents. The next month President Harry S. Truman asked Congress for $400 million in military and economic aid for Greece and Turkey. He argued in what became known as the "Truman Doctrine" that the United States must support free peoples who were resisting communist domination.

Marshall Plan

Secretary of State George C. Marshall proposed in June 1947 that the United States provide economic aid to help rebuild Europe. Meeting in July, representatives of the European nations agreed on a recovery program jointly financed by the United States and the European countries. The following March, Congress passed the European Recovery Program, popularly known as the Marshall Plan, providing more than $12 billion in aid.

Czechoslovakia

In February 1948 the Soviets sponsored a coup d'état in Czechoslovakia, thereby extending communism in Europe.

Berlin Crisis

After the United States, France, and Great Britain announced plans to create a West German Republic out of their German zones, the Soviet Union in June 1948 blocked surface access to Berlin. The U.S. then instituted an airlift to transport supplies to the city until the Soviets lifted their blockade in May 1949.

The Berlin Airlift, 1948, became a powerful symbol of the Allies' interest in stemming further Soviet expansion in Europe. AP Photo.

NATO

In April 1949 the North Atlantic Treaty Organization was signed by the United States, Great Britain, France, Italy, Belgium, the Netherlands, Luxembourg, Denmark, Norway, Portugal, Iceland, and Canada. The signatories pledged that an attack against one would be considered an attack against all. Greece and Turkey joined the alliance in 1952 and West Germany in 1954. The Soviets formed the Warsaw Treaty Organization in 1955 to counteract NATO.

Atomic Bomb

The Soviet Union exploded an atomic device in September 1949.

INTERNATIONAL COOPERATION

Bretton Woods, New Hampshire

Representatives from Europe and the U.S. at a conference held July 1–22, 1944, signed agreements for an international bank and a world monetary fund to stabilize international currencies and rebuild the economies of war-torn nations.

Yalta Conference

In February 1945 Roosevelt, Churchill, and Stalin called for a conference on world organization to meet in April 1945 in the United States.

United Nations

From April to June 1945, representatives from 50 countries met in San Francisco to establish the United Nations. The U.N. charter created a General Assembly composed of all member nations which would act as the ultimate policy-making body. A Security Council, made up of 11 members, including the United States, Great Britain, France, the Soviet Union, and China as permanent members and six additional nations elected by the General Assembly for two-year terms, would be responsible for settling disputes among U.N. member nations.

CONTAINMENT IN ASIA

Japan

General Douglas MacArthur headed a four-power Allied Control Council which governed Japan, allowing it to develop economically and politically.

China

Between 1945 and 1948 the United States gave over $2 billion in aid to the Nationalist Chinese under Chiang Kai-shek and sent George C. Marshall to settle the conflict between Chiang's Nationalists and Mao Tse-tung's Communists. In 1949, however, Mao defeated Chiang and forced the Nationalists to flee to Formosa (Taiwan). Mao established the People's Republic of China on the mainland.

Korean War

On June 25, 1950, North Korea invaded South Korea. President Truman committed U.S. forces commanded by General MacArthur but under United Nations auspices. By October, the U.N. (mostly American) had driven north of the 38th parallel which divided North and South Korea. Chinese troops attacked MacArthur's forces on November 26, pushing them south of the 38th parallel, but by spring 1951, the U.N. forces had recovered their offensive. MacArthur called for a naval blockade of China and bombing north of the Yalu River, criticizing the president for fighting a limited war. In April 1951, Truman removed MacArthur from command.

Armistice

Armistice talks began with North Korea in the summer of 1951. In June 1953 an armistice was signed leaving Korea divided along virtually the same boundary that had existed prior to the war.

EISENHOWER-DULLES FOREIGN POLICY

John Foster Dulles

Dwight D. Eisenhower, elected president in 1952, chose John Foster Dulles as secretary of state. Dulles talked of a more aggressive foreign policy, calling for "massive retaliation" and "liberation" rather than containment. He wished to emphasize nuclear deterrents rather than conventional armed forces. Dulles served as secretary of state until ill health forced him to resign in April 1959. Christian A. Herter took his place.

Hydrogen Bomb

The U.S. exploded its first hydrogen bomb in November 1952 while the Soviets followed with theirs in August 1953.

Soviet Change of Power

Josef Stalin died in March 1953. After an internal power struggle that lasted until 1955, Nikita Khrushchev emerged as the Soviet leader. He talked of both "burying" capitalism and "peaceful coexistence."

Asia

In 1954 the French asked the U.S. to commit air forces to rescue French forces at Dien Bien Phu, Vietnam, as they were besieged by the nationalist forces led by Ho Chi Minh, but Eisenhower refused. In May 1954 Dien Bien Phu surrendered.

Geneva Accords

France, Great Britain, the Soviet Union, and China signed the Geneva Accords in July 1954, dividing Vietnam along the 17th parallel. The North would be under Ho Chi Minh and the South under Emperor Bao Dai. Elections were scheduled for 1956 to unify the country, but Ngo Dinh Diem overthrew Bao Dai and prevented the elections from taking place. The United States supplied economic aid to South Vietnam.

Southeast Asia Treaty Organization

Dulles attempted to establish a Southeast Asia Treaty Organization parallel to NATO but was able to obtain only the Philippine Republic, Thailand, and Pakistan as signatories in September 1954.

Quemoy and Matsu

The small islands of Quemoy and Matsu off the coast of China were occupied by the Nationalist Chinese under Chiang Kai-shek but claimed by the People's Republic of China. In 1955, after the mainland Chinese began shelling these islands, Eisenhower obtained authorization from Congress to defend Formosa (Taiwan) and related areas.

Middle East—The Suez Canal Crisis

The United States had agreed to lend money to Egypt, under the leadership of Colonel Gamal Abdul Nasser, to build the Aswan Dam but refused to give arms. Nasser then drifted toward the Soviet Union and in 1956 established diplomatic relations with the People's Republic of China. In July 1956 the U.S. withdrew its loan to Egypt. In response, Nasser nationalized the Suez Canal.

France, Great Britain, and Israel then attacked Egypt but Eisenhower demanded that they pull out. On November 6 a cease-fire was announced.

Eisenhower Doctrine

President Eisenhower announced in January 1957 that the U.S. was prepared to use armed force in the Middle East against communist aggression. Under this doctrine, U.S. marines entered Beirut, Lebanon in July 1958 to promote political stability during a change of governments. The Marines left in October.

Summit Conference with the Soviet Union

In July 1955 President Eisenhower met in Geneva with Anthony Eden, prime minister of Great Britain, Edgar Faure, premier of France, and Nikita Khrushchev and Nikolai Bulganin, at the time co-leaders of the Soviet Union. They discussed disarmament and reunification of Germany but made no agreements.

Atomic Weapons Test Suspension

Eisenhower and Khrushchev voluntarily suspended in October 1958 atmospheric tests of atomic weapons.

Soviet-American Visitations

Vice President Richard M. Nixon visited the Soviet Union and Soviet Vice-Premier Anastas I. Mikoyan came to the United States in the summer of 1959. In September Premier Khrushchev toured the United States and agreed to another summit meeting.

U-2 Incident

On May 1, 1960, an American U-2 spy plane was shot down over the Soviet Union and pilot Francis Gary Powers was captured. Eisenhower ultimately took responsibility for the spy plane and Khrushchev angrily called off the Paris summit conference which was to take place in a few days.

Latin America

The U.S. supported the overthrow of President Jacobo Arbenz Guzman of Guatemala in 1954 because he began accepting arms from the Soviet Union.

Vice President Nixon had to call off an eight nation goodwill tour of Latin America after meeting hostile mobs in Venezuela and Peru in 1958.

In January 1959 Fidel Castro overthrew Fulgencio Batista, dictator of Cuba. Castro soon began criticizing the United States and moved closer to the Soviet Union, signing a trade agreement with the Soviets in February 1960. The United States prohibited the importation of Cuban sugar in October 1960 and broke off diplomatic relations in January 1961.

THE POLITICS OF AFFLUENCE: DEMOBILIZATION AND DOMESTIC POLICY

Truman Becomes President

Harry S. Truman, formerly a senator from Missouri and vice president of the United States, became president on April 12, 1945. In September 1945 he proposed a liberal legislative program, including expansion of unemployment insurance, extension of the Employment Service, a higher minimum wage, a permanent Fair Employment Practices Commission, slum clearance, low-rent housing, regional TVA-type programs, and a public works program, but was unable to put it through Congress.

Employment Act of 1946

This act established a three member Council of Economic Advisors to evaluate the economy, advise the president, and set up a Congressional Joint Committee on the Economic Report. The act declared that the government was committed to maintaining maximum employment.

Atomic Energy

Congress created the Atomic Energy Commission in 1946, establishing civilian control over nuclear development and giving the president sole authority over the use of atomic weapons in warfare.

Price Controls

Truman vetoed a weak price control bill passed by Congress, thereby ending the wartime price control program. When prices quickly increased about 6 percent, Congress passed another bill in July 1946. Although Truman signed this bill, he used its powers inconsistently, especially when—bowing to pressure—he ended price controls on beef. In late 1946, he lifted controls on all items except rents, sugar, and rice.

Labor

In early 1946, the United Auto Workers, under Walter Reuther, struck General Motors, and steelworkers, under Philip Murray, struck U.S. Steel, demanding wage increases. Truman suggested an 18 cent-per-hour wage increase and in February allowed U.S. Steel to raise prices to cover the increase. This formula became the basis for settlements in other industries. After John L. Lewis's United Mine Workers struck in April 1946, Truman ordered the government to take over the mines and then accepted the union's demands, which included safety and health and welfare benefits. The president averted a railway strike by seizing the railroads and threatening to draft strikers into the Army.

Demobilization

By 1947 the total armed forces had been cut to 1.5 million. The Army fell to 600,000 from a WWII peak of 8 million. The Serviceman's Readjustment Act (G.I. Bill of Rights) of 1944, provided $13 billion in aid ranging from education to housing.

Taft-Hartley Act

The Republicans, who had gained control of Congress as a result of the 1946 elections, sought to control the power of the unions through the Taft-Hartley Act, passed in 1947. This act made the "closed-shop" illegal; labor unions could no longer force employers to hire only union members although it allowed the "union shop" in which newly hired employees were required to join the union. It established an 80 day cooling-off period for strikers in key industries; ended the practice of employers collecting dues for unions; forbade such actions as secondary boycotts, jurisdictional strikes, featherbedding, and contributing to political campaigns; and required an anti-communist oath of union officials. The act slowed down efforts to unionize the South and by 1954, 15 states had passed "right to work" laws, forbidding the "union shop."

Reorganization of Armed Forces

In 1947 Congress passed the National Security Act creating a National Military Establishment, National Security Council, Joint Chiefs of Staff, and Central Intelligence Agency (CIA). Together these organizations were intended to coordinate the armed forces and intelligence services.

Government Reorganization

Truman in 1947 appointed former President Herbert Hoover to head a Commission on Organization of the Executive Branch. The Commission's 1949 report led to the Organization Act of 1949 which allowed the president to make organizational changes subject to congressional veto.

Civil Rights

In 1946 Truman appointed the President's Committee on Civil Rights, which a year later produced its report *To Secure These Rights*. The report called for the elimination of all aspects of segregation. In 1948 the president banned racial discrimination in federal hiring practices and ordered desegregation of the armed forces.

Presidential Succession

The Presidential Succession Act of 1947 placed the speaker of the House and the president pro tempore of the Senate ahead of the secretary of state and after the vice president in the line of succession. The 22nd Amendment to the Constitution, ratified in 1951, limited the president to two terms.

Election of 1948

Truman was the Democratic nominee but the Democrats were split by the States' Rights Democratic Party (Dixiecrats) which nominated Governor Strom Thurmond of South Carolina and the Progressive Party which nominated former Vice-President Henry Wallace. The Republicans nominated Governor Thomas E. Dewey of New York. After traveling widely and attacking the "do-nothing Congress," Truman won a surprise victory.

THE FAIR DEAL

The Fair Deal Program

Truman sought to enlarge and extend the New Deal. He proposed increasing the minimum wage, extending Social Security to more people, maintaining rent controls, clearing slums and building public housing, and providing more money to TVA, rural electrification, and farm housing. He also introduced bills dealing with civil rights, national health insurance, federal aid to education, and repeal of the Taft-Hartley Act. A coalition of Republicans and Southern Democrats prevented little more than the maintenance of existing programs.

Farm Policy

Because of improvements in agriculture, overproduction continued to be a problem. Secretary of Agriculture Charles F. Brannan proposed a program of continued price supports for storable crops and guaranteed minimum incomes to farmers of perishable crops. It was defeated in Congress and surpluses continued to pile up.

ANTICOMMUNISM

Smith Act

The Smith Act of 1940, which made it illegal to advocate the overthrow of the government by force or to belong to an organization advocating such a position, was used by the Truman administration to jail leaders of the American Communist Party.

Loyalty Review Board

In response to criticism, particularly from the House Committee on Un-American Activities, that his administration was "soft on communism," Truman established this board in 1947 to review government employees.

The Hiss Case

In 1948 Whittaker Chambers, formerly a communist and then an editor of *Time,* charged Alger Hiss, a former State Department official and then president of the Carnegie Endowment for International Peace, with having been a communist who supplied classified American documents to the Soviet Union. In 1950 Hiss was convicted of perjury, the statute of limitations on his alleged spying having run out.

McCarran Internal Security Act

Passed in 1950, this act required communist-front organizations to register with the attorney general and prevented their members from defense work and travel abroad. It was passed over Truman's veto.

Rosenberg Case

In 1950 Julius and Ethel Rosenberg, as well as Harry Gold, were charged with giving atomic secrets to the Soviet Union. The Rosenbergs were convicted and executed in 1953.

Joseph McCarthy

On February 9, 1950, Senator Joseph R. McCarthy of Wisconsin stated that he had a list of known communists who were working in the State Department. He later expanded his attacks to diplomats and scholars and contributed to the electoral defeat of two senators. After making charges against the army, he was censured and discredited by the Senate in 1954 and died in 1957.

EISENHOWER'S DYNAMIC CONSERVATISM

1952 Election

The Republicans nominated Dwight D. Eisenhower, most recently NATO commander, for the presidency and Richard M. Nixon, senator from California, for the vice-presidency. The Democrats nominated Governor Adlai E. Stevenson of Illinois for president. Eisenhower won by a landslide; for the first time since Reconstruction the Republicans won some Southern states.

Conservatism

Eisenhower sought to balance the budget and lower taxes but did not attempt to roll back existing social and economic legislation. Eisenhower first described his policy as "dynamic conservatism" and then as "progressive moderation." The administration abolished the Reconstruction Finance Corporation, ended wage and price controls, and reduced farm price supports. It cut the budget and in 1954 lowered tax rates for corporations and individuals with high incomes; an economic slump, however, made balancing the budget difficult.

Social Legislation

Social Security was extended in 1954 and 1956 to an additional 10 million people, including professionals, domestic and clerical workers, farm workers, and members of the armed services. In 1959 benefits were increased 7 percent. In 1955 the minimum wage was raised from 75 cents to $1.00 an hour.

Public Power

Opposed to the expansion of TVA, the Eisenhower administration supported a plan to have a privately owned power plant (called Dixon-Yates) built to supply electricity to Memphis, Tennessee. After two years of controversy and discovery that the government consultant would financially benefit from Dixon-Yates, the administration turned to a municipally owned power plant. The Idaho Power Company won the right to build three small dams on the Snake River rather than the federal government establishing a single large dam at Hell's Canyon. The Atomic Energy Act of 1954 allowed the construction of private nuclear power plants under Atomic Energy Commission license and oversight.

Farm Policy

The Rural Electrification Administration announced in 1960 that 97 percent of American farms had electricity. In 1954 the government began financing the export of farm surpluses in exchange for foreign currencies and later provided surpluses free to needy nations, including milk to school children and to the poor in exchange for governmentally issued food stamps.

Public Works

In 1954 Eisenhower obtained congressional approval for joint Canadian-U.S. construction of the St. Lawrence Seaway, giving ocean-going vessels access to the Great Lakes. In 1956 Congress authorized construction of the Interstate Highway System, with the federal government covering 90 percent of the cost and the states 10 percent. The program further undermined the American railroad system.

Supreme Court

Eisenhower appointed Earl Warren, formerly governor of California, chief justice of the Supreme Court in 1953. That same year he appointed William J. Brennan associate justice. Although originally perceived as conservatives, both justices used the court as an agency of social and political change.

Election of 1956

The 1956 election once again pitted Eisenhower against Stevenson. The president won easily, carrying all but seven states.

Space and Technology

The launching of the Soviet space satellite Sputnik on October 4, 1957, created fear that America was falling behind technologically. Although the U.S.

launched Explorer I on January 31, 1958, the concern continued. In 1958 Congress established the National Aeronautics and Space Administration (NASA) to coordinate research and development and passed the National Defense Education Act to provide grants and loans for education.

Sherman Adams Scandal

In 1958 the White House chief of staff, Sherman Adams, resigned after it was revealed that he had received a fur coat and an oriental rug in return for helping a Boston industrialist deal with the federal bureaucracy. This became known as the Sherman Adams Scandal.

Labor

The Landrum-Griffen Labor-Management Act of 1959 sought to control unfair union practices by establishing rules such as penalties for misuse of funds.

New States

On January 3, 1959, Alaska became the forty-ninth state and on August 21, 1959, Hawaii became the fiftieth.

CIVIL RIGHTS

Initial Eisenhower Actions

Eisenhower completed the formal integration of the armed forces, desegregated public services in Washington, D.C., naval yards, and veteran's hospitals, and appointed a Civil Rights Commission.

Legal Background to *Brown*

In *Ada Lois Sipuel v. Board of Regents* (1948) and *Sweatt v. Painter* (1950) the Supreme Court ruled that African Americans must be allowed to attend integrated law schools in Oklahoma and Texas.

Brown v. Board of Education of Topeka

In *Brown v. Board of Education of Topeka*, a 1954 case, NAACP lawyer Thurgood Marshall challenged the doctrine of "separate but equal" (*Plessy v. Ferguson*, 1896). The Court declared that separate educational facilities were inherently unequal. In 1955 the Court ordered states to integrate "with all deliberate speed."

Southern Reaction

Although at first the South reacted cautiously, by 1955 there were calls for "massive resistance" and White Citizens Councils emerged to spearhead the resistance. State legislatures used a number of tactics to get around Brown. By the end of 1956 desegregation of the schools had advanced very little.

Little Rock

Although he did not personally support the Supreme Court decision, Eisenhower sent 10,000 National Guardsmen and 1,000 paratroopers to Little Rock, Arkansas, to control mobs and enable blacks to enroll at Central High in September 1957. A small force of soldiers was stationed at the school through out the year.

Emergence of Non-Violence

On December 1, 1955, in Montgomery, Alabama, Rosa Parks, a black woman, refused to give up her seat on a city bus to a white passenger and was arrested. Under the leadership of Martin Luther King Jr., a black pastor, blacks of Montgomery organized a bus boycott that lasted for a year, until in December 1956 the Supreme Court refused to review a lower court ruling that stated that separate but equal was no longer legal.

Civil Rights Acts

Eisenhower proposed the Civil Rights Act of 1957, that established a permanent Civil Rights Commission and a Civil Rights Division of the Justice Department which was empowered to prevent interference with the right to vote. The Civil Rights Act of 1960 gave the federal courts power to register African American voters.

Ending "Massive Resistance"

In 1959 state and federal courts nullified Virginia laws which prevented state funds from going to integrated schools. This proved to be the beginning of the end for "massive resistance."

Sit-Ins

In February 1960 four black students who had been denied service staged a sit-in at a segregated Woolworth lunch counter in Greensboro, North Carolina. This inspired sit-ins elsewhere in the South and led to the formation of the Student Nonviolent Coordinating Committee (SNCC). SNCC's primary aims included the end of segregation in public accommodations and winning voting rights.

THE ELECTION OF 1960

The Nominations

Vice President Richard M. Nixon won the Republican presidential nomination while the Democrats nominated Senator John F. Kennedy for the presidency with Lyndon B. Johnson, majority leader of the Senate, as his running mate.

Catholicism

Kennedy's Catholicism was a major issue until, on September 12, he told a gathering of Protestant ministers that he accepted the separation of church and state and that he would not allow Catholic leaders to tell him how to act as president.

Debates

A series of televised debates between Kennedy and Nixon helped create a positive image for Kennedy and may have been a turning point in the election.

Kennedy's Victory

Kennedy won the election by slightly over 100,000 popular votes and 94 electoral votes, based on majorities in New England, the Middle Atlantic, and the South.

SOCIETY AND CULTURE

Gross National Product

The GNP almost doubled between 1945 and 1960, growing at an annual rate of 3.2 percent from 1950 to 1960. Inflation meanwhile remained under 2 percent annually throughout the 1950s. Defense spending was the most important stimulant, and military-related research helped create or expand the new industries of chemicals, electronics, and aviation. The U.S. had a virtual monopoly over international trade, because of the devastation of the World War. Technological innovations contributed to productivity, which jumped 35 percent between 1945 and 1955. After depression and war, Americans had a great desire to consume. Between 1945 and 1960 the American population grew by nearly 30 percent, which contributed greatly to consumer demand.

Consumption Patterns

Home ownership grew by 50 percent between 1945 and 1960. These new homes required such appliances as refrigerators and washing machines, but the most popular product was television, which increased from 7,000 sets in 1946 to 50 million sets in 1960. *TV Guide* became the fastest-growing magazine and advertising found the TV medium especially powerful. Consumer credit increased 800 percent between 1945 and 1957 while the rate of savings dropped to about 5 percent of income. The number of shopping centers rose from 8 in 1945 to 3,840 in 1960. Teenagers became an increasingly important consumer group, making—among other things—a major industry of rock 'n' roll music, with Elvis Presley as its first star, by the mid-1950s.

DEMOGRAPHIC TRENDS

Population Growth

In the 1950s population grew by over 28 million, 97 percent of which was in urban and suburban areas. The average life expectancy increased from 66 in 1955 to 71 in 1970. Dr. Benjamin Spock's *The Commonsense Book of Baby and Child Care* sold an average of 1 million copies a year between 1946 and 1960.

The Sun Belt

Aided by use of air conditioning, Florida, the Southwest, and California grew rapidly, with California becoming the most populous state by 1963. The Northeast, however, remained the most densely populated area.

Suburbs

The suburbs grew six times faster than the cities in the 1950s. William Levitt pioneered the mass-produced housing development when he built 10,600 houses (Levittown) on Long Island in 1947, a pattern followed widely elsewhere in the country. The Federal Housing Administration helped builders by insuring up to 95 percent of a loan and buyers by insuring their mortgages. Thanks in part to the development of the interstate highway system during the Eisenhower administration, auto production increased from 2 million in 1946 to 8 million in 1955, which further encouraged the development of suburbia. As increasing numbers of African Americans moved into the Northern and Midwestern cities, whites moved to the suburbs, a process dubbed "white flight." About 20 percent of the population moved their residence each year.

Middle Class

The number of American families that were classified as middle class changed from 5.7 million in 1947 to more than 12 million by the early 1960s.

Jobs

The number of farm workers dropped from 9 million to 5.2 million between 1940 and 1960. By 1960 more Americans held white-collar than blue-collar jobs.

CONFORMITY AND SECURITY

Corporate Employment

Employees tended to work for larger organizations. By 1960, 38 percent of the workforce was employed by organizations with over 500 employees. Such environments encouraged the managerial personality and corporate cooperation rather than individualism.

Homogeneity

Observers found the expansion of the middle class an explanation for emphasis on conformity. David Riesman argued in *The Lonely Crowd* (1950) that American were moving from an inner-directed to an outer-directed orientation. William Whyte's *The Organization Man* (1956) saw corporate culture as emphasizing the group rather than the individual. Sloan Wilson's *The Man in the Grey Flannel Suit* (1955) expressed similar concerns in fictional form.

Leisure

The standard work week shrank from six to five days. Television became the dominant cultural medium, with over 530 stations by 1961. Sales of books, especially paperbacks, increased annually.

Women

A cult of feminine domesticity re-emerged after World War II. Marynia Farnham and Ferdinand Lundberg published *Modern Woman: The Lost Sex* in

1947; Farnham suggested that science supported the idea that women could find fulfillment only in domesticity. Countless magazine articles also promoted the notion that a woman's place was in the home.

Religion

From 1940, when less than half the population belonged to a church, membership rose to more than 65 percent by 1960. Catholic Bishop Fulton J. Sheen had a popular weekly television show, "Life Worth Living," while Baptist evangelist Billy Graham held huge crusades. Norman Vincent Peale best represented the tendency of religion to emphasize reassurance with his best-seller *The Power of Positive Thinking* (1952). Critics noted the shallowness of this religion. Will Herberg in *Protestant-Catholic-Jew* (1955) said that popular religiosity lacked conviction and commitment. Reinhold Niebuhr, the leading neo-orthodox theologian, criticized the self-centeredness of popular religion and its failure to recognize the reality of sin.

SEEDS OF REBELLION

Intellectuals

Intellectuals became increasingly critical of American life. John Kenneth Galbraith in *The Affluent Society* (1958) argued that the public sector was underfunded. John Keats's *The Crack in the Picture Window* (1956) criticized the homogeneity of suburban life in the new mass-produced communities. The adequacy of American education was questioned by James B. Conant in *The American High School Today* (1959).

Theatre and Fiction

Arthur Miller's *Death of a Salesman* (1949) explored the theme of the loneliness of the other-directed person. Novels also took up the conflict between the individual and mass society. Notable works included J.D. Salinger's *The Catcher in the Rye* (1951), James Jones's *From Here to Eternity* (1951), Joseph Heller's *Catch-22* (1955), Saul Bellow's *The Adventures of Augie March* (1953), and John Updike's *Rabbit, Run* (1960).

Art

Painter Edward Hopper portrayed isolated, anonymous individuals. Jackson Pollock, Robert Motherwell, Willem de Kooning, Arshile Gorky, and Mark Rothko were among the leaders in abstract expressionism, in which they attempted spontaneous expression of their subjectivity.

The Beats

The Beats were a group of young men alienated by twentieth-century life. Their movement began in Greenwich Village, New York, with the friendship of Allen Ginsburg, Jack Kerouac, William Burroughs, and Neal Cassady. They emphasized alcohol, drugs, sex, jazz, Buddhism, and a restless vagabond life, all of which were vehicles for their subjectivity. Ginsberg's long poem *Howl* (1956) and Kerouac's novel *On the Road* (1957) were among the more important literary works to emerge from the Beat movement.

◄——— HISTORICAL TIMELINE ———►
World War II and the Postwar Era (1941–1960)

1941	Axis Powers declare war on the U.S. three days after Pearl Harbor
1942	Japan captures Philippine Islands as Bataan and Corregidor fall War Production Board established U.S. begins interning Japanese-American citizens Germany sinks 400 American ships Battle of Coral Sea Battle of Midway U.S. attacks Vichy forces and Germans in North Africa Manhattan Project begins
1943	Casablanca Conference Americans seize Guadalcanal Island Soviets defeat Germans at Stalingrad Allies invade Italy Teheran Conference
1944	Allies invade France at Normandy (D-Day) June 6 Battle of Leyte Gulf Roosevelt elected president for fourth term Island-hopping campaign retakes Guam Island Battle of the Bulge
1945	Yalta Conference U.S. bombing raids destroy 250,000 buildings in Tokyo 50 nations approve United Nations Charter in San Francisco Conference Hitler commits suicide in Berlin bunker V-E Day Americans recapture the Philippine Islands Potsdam Conference Bomb dropped on Hiroshima Soviets declare war on Japan Bomb dropped on Nagasaki V-J Day
1946	Churchill gives "Iron Curtain" speech George Kennan proposes containment policy
1947	Truman Doctrine aids nations resisting communism Marshall Plan provides economic aid to Europe House Un-American Activities Committee investigates Hollywood Jackie Robinson breaks color line in baseball Taft-Hartley Act slows growth of labor unions

1948	Soviets block access to West Berlin in Berlin Airlift Alger Hiss case begins Truman signs armed forces desegregation order Israel becomes a nation Truman defeats Dewey in presidential election
1949	NATO formed Soviet Union explodes atomic bomb Mao leads communist takeover in China
1950	Korean War begins U.S. troops invade North Korea Chinese troops enter war Rosenberg spy trial begins McCarthy begins anti-communist campaign U.S. begins hydrogen bomb program
1951	Gen. MacArthur relieved of command in Korea Peace negotiations begin in Panmunjon, Korea
1952	U.S. ends Japan occupation Eisenhower elected president
1953	Korean War ends with truce and demilitarized zone Stalin dies
1954	*Brown v. Topeka Board of Education* Army-McCarthy hearings French surrender at Dienbienphu in Vietnam Sen. McCarthy censured by Senate
1955	Martin Luther King Jr. begins Montgomery Bus Boycott
1956	Suez crisis Soviets crush Hungarian revolt
1957	Soviets launch Sputnik Eisenhower Doctrine commits economic aid to Middle East Little Rock school desegregation crisis
1959	Castro takes over in Cuba Soviet Premier Khrushchev visits U.S.

Chapter 14

THE NEW FRONTIER, VIETNAM, AND SOCIAL UPHEAVAL (1960–1972)

KENNEDY'S "NEW FRONTIER" AND THE LIBERAL REVIVAL

Legislative Failures

Kennedy was unable to get much of his program through Congress because of an alliance of Republicans and southern Democrats. He proposed plans for federal aid to education, urban renewal, medical care for the aged, reductions in personal and corporate income taxes, and the creation of a Department of Urban Affairs. None of these proposals passed.

Kennedy did gain congressional approval for raising the minimum wage from $1.00 to $1.25 an hour and extending it to 3 million more workers.

Housing Act

The 1961 Housing Act provided nearly $5 billion over four years for the preservation of open urban spaces, development of mass transit, and the construction of middle-class housing.

CIVIL RIGHTS

Freedom Riders

In May 1961, blacks and whites, sponsored by the Congress on Racial Equality, boarded buses in Washington, D.C., and traveled across the South to New Orleans to test federal enforcement of regulations prohibiting discrimination. They met violence in Alabama but continued to New Orleans. Others came into the South to test the segregation laws.

Justice Department

The Justice Department, under Attorney General Robert F. Kennedy (1925–1968), the president's brother, began to push for civil rights, including desegregation of interstate transportation in the South, integration of schools, and supervision of elections.

Mississippi

In the fall of 1962, President Kennedy called the Mississippi National Guard to federal duty to enable an African American, James Meredith, to enroll at the University of Mississippi.

Dr. Martin Luther King Jr. and Rev. Ralph Abernathy leave Birmingham, Alabama, prison April 19, 1963, after having been arrested eight days earlier, during a Good Friday pilgrimage to City Hall. AP Photo.

March on Washington

Kennedy presented a comprehensive civil rights bill to Congress in 1963. It banned racial discrimination in public accommodations, gave the attorney general power to bring suits on behalf of individuals for school integration, and withheld federal funds from state-administered programs that practiced discrimination. While the bill was held up in Congress, 200,000 people marched on August 28, 1963, in Washington, D.C. During their demonstration, Martin Luther King Jr. gave his seminal "I Have a Dream" speech.

THE COLD WAR CONTINUES

Bay of Pigs

Under Eisenhower, the Central Intelligence Agency had begun training some 2,000 men for an invasion of Cuba to overthrow Fidel Castro, the left-leaning revolutionary who had taken power in 1959. On April 19, 1961, this force invaded at the Bay of Pigs, but was pinned down and forced to surrender. Some 1,200 men were captured.

Berlin Wall

After a confrontation between Kennedy and Khrushchev in Berlin, Kennedy called up reserve and National Guard units and asked for an increase in defense funds. In August 1961, Khrushchev responded by closing the border between East and West Berlin and ordering the erection of the Berlin Wall.

Nuclear Testing

The Soviet Union began the testing of nuclear weapons in September 1961. Kennedy then authorized resumption of underground testing by the United States.

Cuban Missile Crisis

On October 14, 1962, a U-2 reconnaissance plane brought photographic evidence that missile sites were being built in Cuba. Kennedy, on October 22, announced a blockade of Cuba and called on Khrushchev to dismantle the missile bases and remove from Cuba all weapons capable of attacking the United States. Six days later, Khrushchev backed down, withdrew the missiles, and Kennedy lifted the blockade. The United States promised not to invade Cuba, and removed missiles from bases in Turkey, claiming they had planned to do so anyway.

Afterwards, a "hot line" telephone connection was established between the White House and the Kremlin to effect quick communication in threatening situations.

Nuclear Test Ban

In July 1963, a treaty banning the atmospheric testing of nuclear weapons was signed by all the major powers except France and China.

Alliance for Progress

In 1961, Kennedy announced the Alliance for Progress, which would provide $20 million in aid to Latin America.

Peace Corps

The Peace Corps, established in 1961, sent young volunteers to third-world countries to contribute their skills in locally sponsored projects.

JOHNSON AND THE GREAT SOCIETY

Kennedy Assassination

On November 22, 1963, Kennedy was assassinated by Lee Harvey Oswald in Dallas, Texas. Jack Ruby, a nightclub owner, killed Oswald two days later. Conspiracy theories emerged. Chief Justice Earl Warren led an investigation of the murder and concluded that Oswald had acted alone, but questions remain.

Lyndon Johnson

Succeeding Kennedy, Johnson had extensive experience in both the House and Senate, and as a Texan, was the first southerner to serve as president since

Following President Kennedy's assassination, Lyndon Johnson takes the oath of office aboard Air Force One at Love Field, Dallas, Texas. Photo by Cecil Stoughton, New York World-Telegram and the Sun Newspaper Photograph Collection. U.S. Library of Congress.

**Apollo 11's Buzz Aldrin walks on the lunar surface July 20, 1969.
Photo by Neil Armstrong, NASA.**

Woodrow Wilson. He pushed hard for Kennedy's programs, which were languishing in Congress.

A tax cut of more than $10 billion passed Congress in 1964, and an economic boom resulted.

Civil Rights Act

The 1964 Civil Rights Act outlawed racial discrimination by employers and unions, created the Equal Employment Opportunity Commission to enforce the law, and eliminated the remaining restrictions on African-American voting.

Election of 1964

Lyndon Johnson was nominated for president by the Democrats, with Senator Hubert H. Humphrey of Minnesota for vice-president. The Republicans nominated Senator Barry Goldwater, a conservative from Arizona. Johnson won more than 61 percent of the popular vote and could now launch his own "Great Society" program.

Health Care

The Medicare Act of 1965 combined hospital insurance for retired people with a voluntary plan to cover physician's bills. Medicaid provided grants to states to help the poor below retirement age.

Education

In 1965, the Elementary and Secondary Education Act provided $1.5 billion to school districts to improve the education of poor people. Head Start prepared educationally disadvantaged children for elementary school.

Immigration

The Immigration Act of 1965 discontinued the national origin system, basing immigration instead on such things as skills and the need for political asylum.

Cities

The 1965 Housing and Urban Development Act provided 240,000 housing units and $2.9 billion for urban renewal. The Department of Housing and Urban Affairs was established in 1966, and rent supplements for low-income families also became available.

Space

Fulfilling a goal established by Kennedy, Neil Armstrong and Edwin "Buzz" Aldrin became the first humans to walk on the moon, on July 20, 1969.

EMERGENCE OF BLACK POWER

Voting Rights

In 1965, Martin Luther King Jr. announced a voter registration drive. With help from the federal courts, he dramatized his effort by leading a march from Selma to Montgomery, Alabama, between March 21 and 25. The Voting Rights Act of 1965 authorized the attorney general to appoint officials to register voters.

Racial Riots

Seventy percent of African-Americans lived in city ghettos across the country. It did not appear that the tactics used in the South would help them. Frustration built up. In August 1965, Watts, an area of Los Angeles, erupted in riot. More than 15,000 National Guardsmen were brought in; 34 people were killed, 850 wounded, and 3,100 arrested. Property damage reached nearly $200 million. In 1966, New York and Chicago experienced riots, and the following year there were riots in Newark and Detroit. The Kerner Commission, appointed to investigate the riots, concluded that they were directed at a social system that prevented African Americans from getting good jobs and crowded them into ghettos.

Black Power

Stokely Carmichael, chairman of SNCC, was by 1964 unwilling to work with white civil-rights activists. In 1966, he called for the civil rights movements to be "black-staffed, black-controlled, and black-financed." Later, he moved on to the Black Panthers, self-styled urban revolutionaries based in Oakland, California. Other leaders such as H. Rap Brown also called for Black Power.

King Assassination

On April 4, 1968, Martin Luther King Jr. was assassinated in Memphis. James Earl Ray pleaded guilty and was convicted of the murder. Riots in more than 100 cities followed. Ray died in prison in 1998.

Civil rights march from Selma to Montgomery, Alabama, March 23, 1965. AP Photo.

Black Officials

Despite the rising tide of violence, the number of African-Americans achieving elected and appointed office increased. Among the more prominent were Associate Justice of the Supreme Court Thurgood Marshall, Secretary of Housing and Urban Affairs Robert Weaver, and Senator Edward W. Brooke.

ETHNIC ACTIVISM

United Farm Workers

Cesar Chavez founded the United Farm Workers' Organizing Committee to unionize Mexican-American farm laborers. He turned a grape pickers strike in Delano, California, into a national campaign by attacking the structure of the migrant labor system through a boycott of grapes.

Native Americans

The American Indian Movement (AIM) was founded in 1968. At first it staged sit-ins to bring attention to Native American demands. By the early 1970s, it was turning to the courts.

THE NEW LEFT

Demographic Origins

By the mid-1960s, the majority of Americans were under age 30. College enrollments increased fourfold between 1945 and 1970.

Students for a Democratic Society

Students for a Democratic Society was organized by Tom Hayden and Al Haber of the University of Michigan in 1960. Hayden's Port Huron Statement (1962) called for "participatory democracy." SDS drew much of its ideology from the writings of C. Wright Mills, Paul Goodman, and Herbert Marcuse.

Free-Speech Movement

Students at the University of California, Berkeley, staged sit-ins in 1964 to protest the prohibition of political canvassing on campus. Led by Mario Savio, the movement changed from emphasizing student rights to criticizing the bureaucracy of American society. In December, police broke up a sit-in; protests spread to other campuses around the nation.

Vietnam

Student protests began focusing on the Vietnam War. In the spring of 1967, 500,000 gathered in Central Park in New York City to protest the war, many burning their draft cards. SDS became more militant and willing to use violence. It turned to Lenin for its ideology.

1968

More than 200 large campus demonstrations took place in the spring, culminating in the occupation of buildings at Columbia University to protest the university's involvement in military research and its poor relations with minority groups. Police wielding clubs eventually broke up the demonstration. In August, thousands gathered in Chicago to protest the war during the Democratic convention. Although police violence against the demonstrators aroused anger, the antiwar movement began to split between those favoring violence and those opposed to it.

Decline

Beginning in 1968, SDS began breaking up into rival factions. After the more radical factions began using bombs, Tom Hayden left the group. By the early 1970s, the New Left had lost political influence, having abandoned its original commitment to democracy and nonviolence.

THE COUNTERCULTURE

Origins

Like the New Left, the founders of the counterculture were alienated by bureaucracy, materialism, and the Vietnam War, but they turned away from politics in favor of an alternative society. In many respects, they were heirs of the Beats.

Counterculture Expression

Many young people formed communes in such places as San Francisco's Haight-Ashbury district or in rural areas. "Hippies," as they were called, experimented with Eastern religions, drugs, and sex, but most were unable to establish a self-sustaining lifestyle. Leading spokesmen included Timothy Leary, Theodore Roszak, and Charles Reich.

WOMEN'S LIBERATION

Betty Friedan

In *The Feminine Mystique* (1963), Betty Friedan argued that middle-class society stifled women and did not allow them to use their individual talents. She attacked the cult of domesticity.

National Organization for Women

Friedan and other feminists founded the National Organization for Women (NOW) in 1966, calling for equal employment opportunities and equal pay.

Problems

The women's movement was largely limited to the middle class. The Equal Rights Amendment failed to pass. Abortion rights stirred up a counter "right-to-life" movement.

VIETNAM

Background

After the French defeat in 1954, the United States sent military advisors to South Vietnam to aid the government of Ngo Dinh Diem. The pro-Communist Vietcong forces gradually grew in strength, partly because Diem failed to follow through on promised reforms. They received support from North Vietnam, the Soviet Union, and China. The U.S. government supported a successful military coup against Diem in the fall of 1963.

Escalation

In August 1964—after claiming that North Vietnamese gunboats had fired on American destroyers in the Gulf of Tonkin—Lyndon Johnson pushed the Gulf of Tonkin resolution through Congress, authorizing him to use military force in Vietnam. After a February 1965 attack by the Vietcong on Pleiku, Johnson ordered operation "Rolling Thunder," the first sustained bombing of North Vietnam. Johnson then sent combat troops to South Vietnam; under the leadership of General William C. Westmoreland, they conducted search and destroy operations. The number of troops increased to 184,000 in 1965, 385,000 in 1966, 485,000 in 1967, and 538,000 in 1968.

Defense of American Policy

"Hawks" defended the president's policy and, drawing on containment theory, said that the nation had the responsibility to resist aggression. Secretary of State Dean Rusk became a major spokesman for the domino theory, which justified government policy by analogy with England's and France's failure to stop Hitler prior to 1939. If Vietnam should fall, it was said, all Southeast Asia would eventually go. The administration stressed its willingness to negotiate the withdrawal of all "foreign" forces from the war.

Tet Offensive

On January 31, 1968, the first day of the Vietnamese new year (Tet), the Vietcong attacked numerous cities and towns, American bases, and even Saigon. Although they suffered large losses, the Vietcong won a psychological victory, as American opinion began turning against the war.

ELECTION OF 1968

Eugene McCarthy

In November 1967, Senator Eugene McCarthy of Minnesota announced his candidacy for the 1968 Democratic presidential nomination, running on the issue of opposition to the war.

New Hampshire

In February, McCarthy won 42 percent of the Democratic vote in the New Hampshire primary, compared with Johnson's 48 percent. Robert F. Kennedy then announced his candidacy for the Democratic presidential nomination.

Johnson's Withdrawal

Lyndon Johnson withdrew his candidacy on March 31, 1968, and Vice-President Hubert H. Humphrey took his place as a candidate for the Democratic nomination.

Kennedy Assassination

After winning the California primary over McCarthy, Robert Kennedy was assassinated by Sirhan Sirhan, a young Palestinian. This event assured Humphrey's nomination.

The Nominees

The Republicans nominated Richard M. Nixon, who chose Spiro T. Agnew, governor of Maryland, as his running mate in order to appeal to southern voters. Governor George C. Wallace of Alabama ran for the presidency under the banner of the American Independent party, appealing to fears generated by left-wing protestors and big government.

Nixon's Victory

Johnson suspended air attacks on North Vietnam shortly before the election. Nonetheless, Nixon, who emphasized stability and order, defeated Humphrey by a margin of 1 percent. Wallace's 13.5 percent was the best showing by a third-party candidate since 1924.

THE NIXON CONSERVATIVE REACTION

Civil Rights

The Nixon administration sought to block renewal of the Voting Rights Act and delay implementation of court-ordered school desegregation in Mississippi. After the Supreme Court ordered busing of students in 1971 to achieve school desegregation, the administration proposed an antibusing bill, which was blocked in Congress.

Supreme Court

In 1969, Nixon appointed Warren E. Burger, a conservative, as chief justice, but ran into opposition with the nomination of southerners Clement F. Haynesworth, Jr., and G. Harrold Carswell. After these nominations were defeated, he nominated Harry A. Blackmun, who received Senate approval. He later appointed Lewis F. Powell Jr. and William Rehnquist as associate justices. Although more conservative than the Warren court, the Burger court did declare the death penalty, as used at the time, unconstitutional in 1972, and struck down state anti-abortion legislation in 1973.

Revenue Sharing

The heart of Nixon's "New Federalism," passed by Congress in 1972, was a five-year plan to distribute $30 billion of federal revenues to the states.

Congressional Legislation

Congress passed bills giving 18-year-olds the right to vote (1970), increasing Social Security benefits and funding for food stamps (1970), as well as establishing the Occupational Safety and Health Act (1970), the Clean Air Act (1970), laws to control water pollution (1970, 1972), and the Federal Election Campaign Act (1972). None was supported by the Nixon administration.

Economic Problems and Policy

Unemployment climbed to 6 percent in 1970, real gross national product declined in 1970, and in 1971 the United States experienced a trade deficit. Inflation reached 12 percent by 1974. These problems resulted from federal deficits in the 1960s, growing international competition, and rising energy costs.

In 1969, Nixon cut spending and raised taxes. He encouraged the Federal Reserve Board to raise interest rates. The economy worsened. In 1970, Congress gave the president the power to regulate prices and wages. Nixon used this power in August 1971 by declaring a 90-day price and wage freeze and taking the United States off the gold standard. At the end of the 90 days he established mandatory guidelines for wage and price increases. Finally, in 1973, he turned to voluntary wage and price controls, except on health care, food, and construction. When inflation increased rapidly, Nixon cut back on government expenditures, impounding funds already appropriated by Congress.

VIETNAMIZATION

Nixon proposed that all non-South Vietnamese troops be withdrawn in phases, and that an internationally supervised election be held in South Vietnam. The North Vietnamese rejected this plan.

The president then turned to "Vietnamization," the effort to build up South Vietnamese forces while withdrawing American troops. In 1969, Nixon reduced American troop strength by 60,000, but at the same time ordered the bombing of Cambodia, a neutral country, in the interests of flushing out Vietcong.

Protests

Two Moratorium Days in 1969 brought out several hundred thousand protesters, and reports of an American massacre of Vietnamese at My Lai reignited controversy over the nature of the war, but Nixon continued to defend his policy. Troop withdrawals continued, and a lottery system was instituted in 1970 to make the draft more equitable. In 1973, Nixon abolished the draft and established an all-volunteer army.

Cambodia

In April 1970, Nixon announced that Vietnamization was succeeding and that another 150,000 American troops would be out of Vietnam by the end of the year. A few days later, he sent troops into Cambodia to clear out Vietcong sanctuaries and resumed bombing of North Vietnam.

Kent State

Protests against escalation of the war were especially strong on college campuses. During a May 1970 demonstration at Kent State University in Ohio, National Guardsmen opened fire on protestors, killing four students. Soon after, two black students were killed by a Mississippi state policeman at Jackson State University. Several hundred colleges were soon closed down by student strikes, as moderates joined the radicals. Congress repealed the Gulf of Tonkin Resolution.

Pentagon Papers

The publication in 1971 of "the Pentagon Papers," classified Defense Department documents that were leaked to the press, revealed that the government had misled the Congress and the American people about its intentions in Vietnam during the mid-1960s.

End of U.S. Involvement

In the summer of 1972, negotiations between the United States and North Vietnam began in Paris. By October, a draft agreement was developed which included provisions for a cease-fire, the return of American prisoners of war, and the withdrawal of U.S. forces from Vietnam. A few days before the 1972 presidential election, Henry Kissinger, the president's national security advisor, declared that "peace was at hand."

Resumption of Bombing

Nixon resumed bombing of North Vietnam in December 1972, claiming that the North Vietnamese were not bargaining in good faith. In January 1973, the opponents reached a settlement in which the North Vietnamese retained control over large areas of the South and agreed to release American prisoners of war within 60 days. After the prisoners were released, the United States would withdraw its remaining troops. On March 29, 1973, the last American combat troops left South Vietnam. Nearly 60,000 Americans had been killed and 300,000 more wounded; the war's financial cost to the United States was $109 billion.

War Powers Act

Later in 1973, the War Powers Act was passed. It required congressional approval of any commitment of combat troops beyond 90 days.

FOREIGN POLICY

China

With his national security advisor, Henry Kissinger, Nixon took some bold diplomatic initiatives. Kissinger traveled to China and the Soviet Union for secret sessions to plan summit meetings with the Communists. In February 1972, Nixon and Kissinger went to China to meet with Mao Tse-tung and his associates. The United States agreed to support China's admission to the United Nations and to pursue economic and cultural exchanges.

Soviet Union

At a May 1972 meeting with the Soviets, the Strategic Arms Limitation Treaty (SALT) was signed. The signatories agreed to stop making nuclear ballistic missiles and to reduce the number of antiballistic missiles to 200 for each power.

Middle East

Following the Arab-Israeli war of 1973, Arab states staged an oil boycott to push the Western nations into forcing Israel to withdraw from lands controlled since the Six-Day War of 1967. Kissinger, now secretary of state, negotiated the withdrawal of Israel from some of the lands and the Arabs lifted their boycott. The five-member Organization of Petroleum Exporting Countries (OPEC)—composed of Venezuela, Saudi Arabia, Kuwait, Iraq, and Iran—then raised the price of oil from about $3.00 to $11.65 a barrel. U.S. gas prices doubled and inflation shot above 10 percent.

ELECTION OF 1972

George McGovern

The Democrats nominated Senator George McGovern of South Dakota for president and Senator Thomas Eagleton for vice president. After the press revealed that Eagleton had been treated for psychological problems, McGovern eventually forced him off the ticket, replacing him with Sargent Shriver.

George Wallace

George Wallace, a longtime segregationist, ran once again as the American Independent party candidate. While campaigning at a Maryland shopping center on May 15, 1972, he became the victim of an assassination attempt that left him paralyzed below the waist. Arthur Bremer, 21, was sentenced to 63 years for shooting Wallace and three others.

Richard M. Nixon

Richard M. Nixon and Spiro T. Agnew, who had been renominated by the Republicans, won a landslide victory, receiving 521 electoral votes to McGovern's 17.

◄─── HISTORICAL TIMELINE ───►

The New Frontier, Vietnam, and Social Upheaval (1960–1972)

1960	Kennedy and Nixon participate in first televised presidential debates Greensboro sit-in protests Kennedy defeats Nixon
1961	Bay of Pigs invasion fails Freedom rides Berlin Wall built Peace Corps established Alliance for Progress established
1962	Cuban Missile Crisis Students for a Democratic Society formed
1963	Rev. King begins Birmingham desegregation efforts University of Alabama admits first black student Civil Rights March on Washington Premier Diem of South Vietnam toppled by U.S.-approved coup President Kennedy assassinated
1964	President Johnson announces war on poverty Freedom summer vote registration campaign in Mississippi Civil Rights Act passed VISTA established Berkeley Free Speech Movement Gulf of Tonkin Resolution passed U.S. begins bombing of North Vietnam Johnson elected president
1965	Medicare funding begins Race riots in Watts Malcolm X assassinated American combat troops sent to Vietnam
1966	National Organization for Women (NOW) formed Stokely Carmichael leads black power movement
1967	Race riots in Detroit and Newark Massive antiwar protest in Washington, D.C. Israel, Arab neighbors fight Six-Day War

1968	Viet Cong launch Tet Offensive Johnson withdraws from presidential race Dr. Martin Luther King Jr. assassinated Robert Kennedy assassinated Protests at Chicago Democratic Convention Nixon elected president
1969	Woodstock festival Apollo 11 crew lands on moon Stonewall Riots launch gay liberation movement
1970	U.S. invades Cambodia Kent State Massacre
1972	Nixon visits People's Republic of China Détente begins with Soviet Union SALT I Treaty signed with Soviet Union

Chapter 15

WATERGATE, CONSERVATISM'S RISE, AND POST–COLD WAR CHALLENGES (1972–2005)

THE WATERGATE SCANDAL

The Break-In

What became known as the Watergate crisis began during the 1972 presidential campaign. Early on the morning of June 17, James McCord, a security officer for the Committee for the Re-election of the President, and four other men broke into Democratic headquarters at the Watergate apartment complex in Washington, D.C., and were caught while going through files and installing electronic eavesdropping devices. On June 22, Nixon announced that the administration was in no way involved in the burglary attempt.

James McCord

The trial of the burglars began in early 1973, with all but McCord (who was convicted) pleading guilty. Before sentencing, McCord wrote a letter to U.S. District Court Judge John J. Sirica arguing that high Republican officials had known in advance about the burglary and that perjury had been committed at the trial.

Further Revelations

Soon Jeb Stuart Magruder, head of the Nixon re-election committee, and John W. Dean, Nixon's attorney, revealed that they had been involved. Dean testified before a Senate Watergate committee that Nixon had been involved in covering up the incident. Over the next several months, extensive involvement of the White House administration, including payment of "hush" money to the burglars, destruction of

FBI records, forgery of documents, and wiretapping, was revealed. Dean was fired and H. R. Haldeman and John Ehrlichman, who headed the White House staff, and Attorney General Richard Kleindienst, resigned. Nixon claimed that he had not personally been involved in the cover-up but refused, on the grounds of executive privilege, to allow investigation of White House documents.

White House Tapes

Under considerable pressure, Nixon agreed to the appointment of a special prosecutor, Archibald Cox of Harvard Law School. When Cox obtained a sub-poena for tape recordings of White House conversations (whose existence had been revealed in testimony during the Senate hearings)—and the administra-tion lost an appeal in the appellate court—Nixon ordered Elliot Richardson, the attorney general, to fire Cox. Both Richardson and his subordinate, William Ruckelshaus, resigned, leaving Robert Bork, the solicitor general, to carry out the order. This "Saturday Night Massacre," which took place on October 20, 1973, caused a storm of controversy. The House Judiciary Committee, headed by Peter Rodino of New Jersey, began looking into the possibility of impeach-ment. Nixon agreed to turn the tapes over to Judge Sirica and named Leon Jaworski as the new special prosecutor. But it soon became known that some of the tapes were missing and that a portion of another had been erased.

The Vice-Presidency

Vice-President Spiro Agnew was accused of income tax fraud and having ac-cepted bribes while a local official in Maryland. He resigned the vice-presidency in October 1973 and was replaced by Congressman Gerald R. Ford of Michigan under provisions of the new 25th Amendment.

Nixon's Taxes

Nixon was accused of paying almost no income taxes between 1969 and 1972, and of using public funds for improvements to his private residences in California and Florida. The IRS reviewed the president's tax return and assessed him nearly $500,000 in back taxes and interest.

Indictments

In March 1974 a grand jury indicted Haldeman, Ehrlichman, former Attor-ney General John Mitchell, and four other White House aides, and named Nixon as an unindicted coconspirator.

Calls for Resignation

In April, Nixon released edited transcripts of the White House tapes, the contents of which led to further calls for his resignation. Jaworski subpoenaed 64 additional tapes, which Nixon refused to turn over, and the case went to the Supreme Court.

President Nixon departing from the White House following his resignation on Aug. 9, 1974. Richard Nixon Presidential Materials Project.

Impeachment Debate

Meanwhile, the House Judiciary Committee televised its debate over impeachment, adopting three articles of impeachment. It charged the president with obstructing justice, misusing presidential power, and failing to obey the committee's subpoenas.

Resignation

Before the House began to debate impeachment, the Supreme Court ordered the president to release the subpoenaed tapes to the special prosecutor. On August 5, Nixon, under pressure from his advisors, made public the tape of June 23, 1972. This tape, recorded less than a week after the break-in, revealed that Nixon had used the CIA to keep the FBI from investigating the case. Nixon announced his resignation on August 8, 1974, to take effect at noon the following day. Gerald Ford then became president.

Legislative Response

Congress responded to the Vietnam War and Watergate by enacting legislation intended to prevent such situations. In 1974 Congress limited the amounts of contributions and expenditures in presidential campaigns. It also strengthened the 1966 Freedom of Information Act by requiring the government to act promptly when asked for information and to prove its case for classification when attempting to withhold information on grounds of national security.

THE FORD PRESIDENCY

Gerald Ford

Gerald Ford was in many respects the opposite of Nixon. Although a partisan Republican, he was well liked and free from any hint of scandal. Ford almost immediately encountered controversy when, in September 1974, he offered to pardon Nixon. Nixon accepted the offer, although he admitted no wrongdoing and had not yet been charged with a crime.

The Economy

Ford also faced major economic problems, which he approached somewhat inconsistently. Saying that inflation was the major problem, he called for voluntary restraints and asked citizens to wear "Whip Inflation Now," or WIN, buttons. The economy went into decline. Ford asked for tax cuts to stimulate business and argued against spending for social programs.

When New York City teetered on the verge of bankruptcy in 1975, Ford at first opposed federal aid but changed his mind when the Senate and House Banking Committees guaranteed the loans.

Vietnam

As North Vietnamese forces pushed back the South Vietnamese, Ford asked Congress to provide more arms for the South. Congress rejected the request, and in April 1975 Saigon fell to the North Vietnamese.

Election of 1976

Ronald Reagan, formerly a movie actor and governor of California, opposed Ford for the Republican nomination, but Ford won by a slim margin. The Democrats nominated James Earl Carter, formerly governor of Georgia, who ran on the basis of his integrity and lack of Washington connections. Carter, with Senator Walter Mondale of Minnesota as his vice-presidential candidate, narrowly defeated Ford.

CARTER'S MODERATE LIBERALISM

Policy Orientation in the Carter Administration

Carter sought to conduct the presidency on democratic and moral principles. The former peanut farmer, however, often misread political sentiment on Capitol Hill: the administration typically proposed complex programs but failed to support them through the legislative process.

The Economy

Carter approached economic problems inconsistently. In 1978, he proposed voluntary wage and price guidelines. Although somewhat successful, the guidelines did not apply to oil, housing, and food. Carter then named Paul A. Volcker as chairman of the Federal Reserve Board. Volcker tightened the money supply in order to reduce inflation, but this action caused interest rates to go even higher. High interest rates depressed sales of automobiles and houses, which in turn increased unemployment. By 1980, unemployment stood at 7.5 percent, interest at 20 percent, and inflation at 12 percent.

Domestic Achievements

Carter offered amnesty to Americans who had fled the draft and gone to other countries during the Vietnam War. He established the Departments of Energy and Education and placed the civil service on a merit basis. He created a "superfund" for cleanup of chemical waste dumps, established controls over strip mining, and protected 100 million acres of Alaskan wilderness from development.

CARTER'S FOREIGN POLICY

Human Rights

Carter sought to base foreign policy on human rights, but was criticized for inconsistency and lack of attention to American interests.

Panama Canal

Carter negotiated a controversial treaty with Panama, affirmed by the Senate in 1978, that provided for the transfer of ownership of the canal to Panama in 1999 and guaranteed its neutrality.

China

Carter ended official recognition of Taiwan and in 1979 recognized the People's Republic of China. Conservatives called the decision a "sell-out."

SALT II

In 1979, Carter signed the Strategic Arms Limitation Treaty II with the Soviet Union. The treaty set a ceiling of 2,250 bombers and missiles for each side, and set limits on warheads and new weapons systems. It never reached the Senate floor.

Camp David Accords

In 1978 Carter negotiated the Camp David Accords between Israel and Egypt. Bringing Anwar Sadat, president of Egypt, and Menachem Begin, prime minister of Israel, to Camp David, Maryland, for two weeks in September 1978, Carter sought to end the state of war that existed between the two countries. Israel promised to return occupied land in the Sinai to Egypt in exchange for Egyptian recognition, a process completed in 1982. An agreement to negotiate the Palestinian refugee problem proved ineffective.

Afghanistan

The policy of detente went into decline. Carter criticized Soviet restrictions on political freedom and reluctance to allow dissidents and Jews to emigrate. In December 1979 the Soviet Union invaded Afghanistan. In response, Carter stopped shipments of grain and technology to the Soviets, withdrew his support for SALT II, and barred Americans from competing in the 1980 Moscow Summer Olympics.

THE IRANIAN CRISIS

The Iranian Revolution

In 1978 a revolution forced the shah of Iran to flee the country, replacing him with a religious leader, Ayatollah Ruhollah Khomeini. Because the United States had supported the shah with arms and money, the revolutionaries were strongly anti-American, calling the United States the "Great Satan."

Hostages

After Carter allowed the exiled shah to come to the United States for medical treatment in October 1979, some 400 Iranians broke into the American embassy in Teheran on November 4, taking the occupants captive. They demanded that the shah be returned to Iran for trial and that his wealth be confiscated and given to Iran. Carter rejected these demands; instead, he froze Iranian assets in the United States and established a trade embargo against Iran. He also appealed to the United Nations and the World Court. The Iranians eventually freed the African-American and women hostages, but kept 52 others.

In April 1980 Carter ordered a marine rescue attempt, but it collapsed after several helicopters broke down and another crashed, killing eight men. Secretary of State Cyrus Vance resigned in protest before the raid began, and Carter was widely criticized for its failure.

THE ELECTION OF 1980

The Democrats

Carter, whose approval rating in public opinion polls had dropped to about 25 percent in 1979, successfully withstood a challenge from Senator Edward M. Kennedy of Massachusetts for the Democratic presidential nomination.

The Republicans

The Republicans nominated Ronald Reagan of California, who had narrowly lost the 1976 nomination and was the leading spokesman for American conservatism. Reagan chose George Bush, a New Englander transplanted to Texas and former CIA director, as his vice-presidential candidate. One of Reagan's opponents, Congressman John Anderson of Illinois, continued his presidential campaign on a third-party ticket.

The Campaign

While Carter defended his record, Reagan heavily favored increased defense spending, but also called for reductions in government spending and taxes. Reagan talked of granting more power to the states. He advocated what were coming to be called traditional values—family, religion, hard work, and patriotism.

Reagan's Victory

Reagan won by a large electoral majority, and the Republicans gained control of the Senate and increased their representation in the House.

American Hostages

After extensive negotiations with Iran, in which Algeria acted as an intermediary, Carter released Iranian assets and the hostages were freed on January 20, 1981—the day of Reagan's inaugural. It had been 444 days since they had been taken captive.

THE REAGAN PRESIDENCY: ATTACKING BIG GOVERNMENT

Tax Policy

An ideological though pragmatic conservative, Ronald Reagan acted quickly and forcefully to change the direction of government policy. He placed priority on cutting taxes. His approach was based on "supply-side" economics, the idea that if government left more money in the hands of the people, they would invest rather than spend the excess on consumer goods. The results would be greater production, more jobs, and greater prosperity, and thus more income for the government despite lower tax rates.

Economic Recovery Tax Act

Reagan asked for a 30 percent tax cut, and despite fears of inflation on the part of Congress, in August 1983 obtained a 25 percent cut, spread over three years. The percentage was the same for everyone; hence high-income people received greater savings than middle- and low-income individuals. To encourage investment, capital gains, gift, and inheritance taxes were reduced and business taxes liberalized. Anyone with earned income was also allowed to invest up to $2,000 a year in an Individual Retirement Account (IRA), deferring all taxes on both the principal and its earnings until retirement.

Government Spending

Congress passed the Budget Reconciliation Act in 1981, cutting $39 billion from domestic programs, including education, food stamps, public housing, and the National Endowments for the Arts and Humanities. While cutting domestic programs, Reagan increased the defense budget by $12 billion.

SDI

Reagan concentrated on obtaining funding for the development of a computer-controlled Strategic Defense Initiative (SDI) system, dubbed by the press "Star Wars" after the movie of that name. SDI would destroy incoming enemy missiles from outer space. Skeptical about its technological feasibility and fearful of enormous costs, Congress balked and scaled back the proposal during Reagan's second term.

Increasing Revenue

Because of rising deficits, Reagan and Congress increased taxes in various ways. The 1982 Tax Equity and Fiscal Responsibility Act reversed some concessions made to business in 1981. Social Security benefits became taxable income in 1983. In 1984, the Deficit Reduction Act increased taxes by another $50 billion. But the deficit continued to increase.

Assassination Attempt

John W. Hinckley shot Reagan in the chest on March 30, 1981. The president was wounded but made a swift recovery. His popularity increased, possibly helping his legislative program.

Antitrust

Reagan ended ongoing antitrust suits against IBM and AT&T, thereby fulfilling his promise to reduce government interference with business.

Women and Minorities

Although Reagan appointed Sandra Day O'Connor to the Supreme Court, his administration gave fewer of its appointments to women and minorities than had the Carter administration. The Reagan administration also opposed "equal pay for equal work" and renewal of the Voting Rights Act of 1965.

Problems with Appointed Officials

A number of Reagan appointees were accused of conflict of interest, including Anne Gorsuch Burford and Rita Lavelle of the Environmental Protection Agency, Edwin Meese, presidential advisor and later attorney general, and Michael Deaver, the deputy chief of staff. Ray Donovan, secretary of labor, was indicted but later acquitted of charges that he had made payoffs to government officials while he was in private business. By the end of Reagan's term, more than 100 of his officials had been accused of questionable activities.

ASSERTING AMERICAN POWER

Soviet Union

Reagan took a hard line against the Soviet Union, calling it an "evil empire." He placed new cruise missiles in Europe, despite considerable opposition from Europeans.

ELECTION OF 1984

The Democrats

Walter Mondale, a former senator from Minnesota and vice president under Carter, won the Democratic nomination over Senator Gary Hart and Jesse Jackson, an African American civil-rights leader. Mondale chose Geraldine Ferraro, a congresswoman from New York, as his running mate. Mondale criticized Reagan for his budget deficits, high unemployment and interest rates, and reduction of spending on social services.

The Reagan Victory

The Republicans renominated Ronald Reagan and George Bush. Reagan drew support from groups such as the Moral Majority, founded by Fundamentalist evangelist Jerry Falwell. (The Fundamentalists had become a major political presence, voicing opposition to abortion, advocating an amendment to allow prayer in public schools, and identifying with the cause of Israel and a strong military defense budget.) Reagan's appeal also derived from an in-your-face anti-Soviet stance and decreased inflation, interest rates, and unemployment during his watch. He defeated Mondale handily, gaining nearly 60 percent of the vote by breaking apart the Democratic coalition of industrial workers, farmers, and the poor that had existed since FDR's time. Yet his coattails proved short: the GOP lost two seats in the Senate and gained little in the House.

SECOND-TERM FOREIGN CONCERNS

Libya

Reagan challenged Muammar al-Qadhafi, the anti-American leader of Libya, by sending Sixth Fleet ships within the Gulf of Sidra, which Qadhafi claimed. When Libyan gunboats challenged the American ships, American planes destroyed the gunboats and bombed installations on the Libyan shoreline. Soon after, a West German night club popular among American servicemen was bombed, killing a soldier and a civilian. Reagan, believing the bombing was ordered directly by Qadhafi, launched an air strike from Great Britain against Libyan bases in April 1986.

Soviet Union

After Mikhail S. Gorbachev became the premier of the Soviet Union in March 1985 and took a more flexible approach toward both domestic and foreign affairs, Reagan softened his anti-Soviet stance. But despite the Soviets' assurances that they would honor the unratified SALT II agreement, Reagan argued that they in fact had not adhered to the pact; as a result, he sought to expand and modernize the American defense system.

Arms Control

Reagan and Gorbachev had difficulty in reaching an agreement on arms limitations at summit talks in 1985 and 1986. Finally, in December 1987, they signed an agreement eliminating medium-range missiles from Europe.

Iran-Contra

Near the end of 1986, a scandal arose involving William Casey, head of the CIA, Lieutenant Colonel Oliver North of the National Security Council, Admiral John Poindexter, national security advisor, and Robert McFarlane, former national security advisor. In 1985 and 1986, they had sold arms to the Iranians in hopes of encouraging them to use their influence in getting American hostages in Lebanon released. The profits from these sales were then diverted to the Nicaraguan *Contras* in an attempt to get around congressional restrictions on funding the *Contras*. The president was forced to appoint a special prosecutor, and Congress held hearings on the affair in May 1987.

Nicaragua

The Reagan administration did not support a peace plan signed by five Central American nations in 1987, but the following year the *Sandinistas* and the *Contras* agreed on a cease-fire.

SECOND-TERM DOMESTIC AFFAIRS

Tax Reform

The Tax Reform Act of 1986 lowered tax rates, changing the highest rate on personal income from 50 percent to 28 percent and on corporate taxes from 46 percent to 34 percent. At the same time, it removed many tax shelters and tax credits. The law did away with the concept of progressive taxation, the requirement that the percentage of income taxed increased as income increased. Instead, over a two-year period it established two rates, 15 percent on incomes below $17,850 for individuals and $29,750 for families and 28 percent on incomes above these amounts. The tax system would no longer be used as an instrument of social policy.

Economic Patterns

Unemployment declined, reaching 6.6 percent in 1986, while inflation fell as low as 2.2 percent during the first quarter of that year. The stock market was bullish through mid-1987.

Agriculture

With the general slowing of inflation, and the decline of world agricultural prices, many American farmers began to descend into bankruptcy in the mid-1980s, often dragging the rural banks that had made them the loans into bankruptcy as well.

Although it lifted the ban on wheat exports to the Soviet Union, the Reagan administration reduced price supports and opposed debt relief passed by Congress.

Deficits

The federal deficit reached $179 billion in 1985. At about the same time, the United States experienced trade deficits of more than $100 billion annually, partly because management and engineering skills had fallen behind Japan and Germany, and partly because the United States provided an open market to foreign businesses. In the mid-1980s, the United States became a debtor nation for the first time since World War I. Consumer debt also rose from $300 billion in 1980 to $500 billion in 1986.

Black Monday

On October 19, 1987, labeled "Black Monday" on Wall Street, the Dow Jones Industrial Average dropped more than 500 points, or over 20 percent. Between August 25 and October 20, the market lost over a trillion dollars in paper value. Fearing a recession, Congress in November 1987 reduced 1988 taxes by $30 billion.

NASA Tragedy

The explosion of the space shuttle *Challenger* soon after liftoff on January 28, 1986, damaged NASA's credibility and reinforced doubts about the complex technology required to implement the Strategic Defense Initiative. All aboard perished, including a New Hampshire teacher who was the first private citizen to go into space.

Supreme Court

Reagan reshaped the Court. In 1986, he replaced Chief Justice Warren C. Burger with Associate Justice William H. Rehnquist, probably the most conservative member of the Court. Although failing in his nomination of Robert Bork for associate justice, Reagan successfully appointed other conservatives to the Court: Sandra Day O'Connor, Antonin Scalia, and Anthony Kennedy.

ELECTION OF 1988

The Candidates

After a sex scandal eliminated Senator Gary Hart from the race for the Democratic presidential nomination, Governor Michael Dukakis of Massachusetts emerged as the victor over his major challenger, Jesse Jackson (see sidebar). He chose Senator Lloyd Bentsen of Texas as his vice-presidential running mate. Vice President George Bush, after a slow start in the primaries, won the Republican nomination. He chose Senator Dan Quayle of Indiana as his running mate. Bush easily defeated Dukakis, but the Republicans were unable to make any inroads in Congress.

BUSH ABANDONS REAGANOMICS

Budget Deficit

Soon after George H. W. Bush took office as president on January 20, 1989, the budget deficit for 1990 was estimated at $143 billion. With deficit estimates continuing to grow, Bush held a "budget summit" with congressional leaders in May 1990, and his administration continued talks throughout the summer. In September, the administration and Congress agreed to increase taxes on gasoline, tobacco, and alcohol, establish an excise tax on luxury items, and raise Medicare taxes. Cuts were also to be made in Medicare and other domestic programs. The 1991 deficit was now estimated to be over $290 billion. The following month, Congress approved the plan, hoping to cut a cumulative amount of $500 billion from the deficit over the next five years. In a straight party vote—Republicans voting against and Democrats voting in favor— Congress in December gave the power to decide whether new tax and spending proposals violated the deficit-cutting agreement to the

For African-Americans in Politics, Progress Comes Slowly but Surely

Shirley Chisholm, the first African-American woman to be elected to the United States Congress.

Reuters

Civil-rights leader, Baptist minister, and politician, Jesse Jackson was the first black man to make a serious bid for the U.S. presidency—in the Democratic Party's nomination races in 1983–84 and 1987–88. Before him, Shirley Chisholm, who in 1968 had become the first black woman elected to the U.S. Congress, made a bid for the Democratic nomination for U.S. president in 1972, winning 152 delegates before withdrawing from the race. After taking up residency in Washington, D.C., Jackson attained elective office when, in 1990, the Washington City Council created two unpaid offices of "statehood senator"—better known as "shadow senator"—to lobby Congress for statehood for the District of Columbia. Fusing the church pulpit with the bully pulpit, he has been effective not just in articulating the needs of blacks but of the underprivileged class in general. An associate of Rev. Dr. Martin Luther King Jr., Jackson went on to found Operation PUSH (People United to Save Humanity), a Chicago-based organization that advocated black self-help and gave him a platform for his liberal views. A Jackson-led voter-registration drive was key to the election of Harold Washington as Chicago's first black mayor in April 1983. New York, Los Angeles, Cleveland, Baltimore, Atlanta, and Washington, D.C.,

cont'd on next page

Congressional Budget office. This power had been in the hands of the White House Office of Management and Budget.

Savings and Loan Debacle

With the savings and loan industry in financial trouble in February 1989, largely because of bad real-estate loans, Bush proposed to close or sell 350 institutions, to be paid for by the sale of government bonds. In July he signed a bill that created the Resolution Trust Corporation to oversee the closure and merging of savings and loans, and which provided $166 billion over 10 years to cover the bad debts. Estimates of the total cost of the debacle ran to upward of $300 billion.

Scandals In the Financial Markets

also elected black mayors in the last two decades of the twentieth century. Overall, as the century wound down, more blacks were gaining local office, but seldom were they winning statewide elections. According to the Joint Center for Political and Economic Studies, a Washington, D.C., think tank that researches the political and economic conditions of black Americans, the U.S. had 8,868 black elected officials (including Jackson's own son, Rep. Jesse L. Jackson Jr., of Illinois) in 1998, up 212 from the year before. That number, however, accounted for only 1.7 percent of all officials holding elective office in the U.S. Some states, such as Colorado, Georgia, Illinois, and Ohio, have elected black lieutenant governors and state attorneys general, but in Massachusetts on Jan. 4, 2007, Deval Laurdine Patrick became only the second African American elected governor in the nation's history. The first was L. Douglas Wilder, the grandson of slaves, who served one term, from 1989 to 1994. The distinction of being the first black governor belongs to P.B.S. Pinchback, who was acting governor of Louisiana during impeachment proceedings against Henry Clay Warmoth from December 9, 1872, to January 13, 1873.

Charges of insider trading, stock manipulation, and falsification of records resulted in Drexel Burnham Lambert, a major securities firm, pleading guilty in December 1988 to six violations of federal law. The company filed for bankruptcy and Michael Milken, its "junk bond king" (junk bonds are bonds below an investment grade of BB or Bb, which because of their risk carry a two- to three-point interest advantage), pleaded guilty to conspiracy, among other charges, in 1990. Meanwhile, in July 1989, 46 futures traders at the Chicago Mercantile Exchange were charged with racketeering.

Economic Slowdown

The gross national product slowed from 4.4 percent in 1988 to 2.9 percent in 1989. Unemployment gradually began to increase, reaching 6.8 percent in March 1991, a three-year high. Every sector of the economy except for medical services and all geographical areas experienced the slowdown. The "Big Three" automakers posted record losses and Pan American World Airways and Eastern Airlines entered bankruptcy proceedings. In September 1991, the Federal Reserve lowered the interest rate.

OTHER DOMESTIC ISSUES UNDER BUSH

Exxon Valdez Accident

After the *Exxon Valdez* spilled more than 240,000 barrels of oil into Alaska's Prince William Sound in March 1989, the federal government ordered Exxon Corporation to develop a clean-up plan, which it carried out until the weather prevented it from continuing in September. The *Valdez* captain, Joseph Hazelwood, was found guilty of negligence the following year. Exxon, the state of Alaska, and the U.S. Justice Department reached a settlement in October 1991 requiring Exxon to pay $1.025 billion in fines and restitution through 2001.

Congressional Ethics Violations

After the House Ethics Committee released a report charging that Speaker Jim Wright had violated rules regulating acceptance of gifts and outside income, Wright resigned in May 1989. A short time later, the Democratic whip Tony Coelho resigned because of alleged improper use of campaign funds.

Pollution

The Clean Air Act, passed in October 1990 and updating the 1970 law, mandated that the level of emissions was to be reduced 50 percent by the year 2000. Cleaner gasolines were to be developed, cities were to reduce ozone (an ingredient in photo-chemical smog), and nitrogen oxide emissions were to be cut by one-third.

Civil Rights

The Americans with Disabilities Act, passed in July 1990, barred discrimination against people with physical or mental disabilities. In October 1990, Bush vetoed the Civil Rights Act on the grounds that it established quotas, but a year later he accepted a slightly revised version that, among other things, required that employers in discrimination suits prove that their hiring practices are not discriminatory.

Supreme Court Appointments

Bush continued to reshape the Supreme Court in a conservative direction when, upon the retirement of Justice William J. Brennan, he successfully nominated Judge David Souter of the U.S. Court of Appeals in 1989. Two years later, Bush nominated a conservative African American, Judge Clarence Thomas, also of the U.S. Court of Appeals, upon the retirement of Justice Thurgood Marshall. Thomas's nomination stirred up opposition from the NAACP and other liberal groups, which supported affirmative action and abortion rights. Dramatic charges of sexual harassment against Thomas from Anita Hill, a University of Oklahoma law professor, were revealed only days before the nomination was to go to the Senate. The charges provoked a reopening of Judiciary Committee hearings, which were nationally televised. Nonetheless, Thomas narrowly won confirmation in October 1991.

BUSH'S ACTIVIST FOREIGN POLICY

Panama

Since coming to office, the Bush administration had been concerned with Panamanian dictator Manuel Noriega because he allegedly provided an important link in the drug traffic between South America and the United States. After economic sanctions, diplomatic efforts, and an October 1989 coup failed to oust Noriega, Bush ordered 12,000 troops into Panama on December 20. The Americans installed a new government headed by Guillermo Endara, who had earlier apparently won a presidential election which was then nullified by Noriega. On January 3, 1990, Noriega surrendered to the Americans and was taken to the United States to stand trial on drug-trafficking charges, a trial that began in September 1991. Found guilty in 1992, he was sentenced to 40 years' imprisonment. Twenty-three United States soldiers and three American civilians were killed in the Panamanian operation. The Panamanians lost nearly 300 soldiers and more than 500 civilians.

China

After the death in April 1989 of reformer Hu Yaobang, formerly general secretary and chairman of the Chinese Communist party, students began pro-democracy marches in Beijing. By the middle of May, more than one million people were gathering in Beijing's Tiananmen Square and elsewhere in China, calling for political reform. Martial law was imposed and in early June the army fired on the demonstrators. Estimates of the death toll in the wake of the nationwide crackdown on demonstrators ranged between 500 and 7,000. In July 1989 U.S. National Security Advisor Brent Scowcroft and Deputy Secretary of State Lawrence Eagleburger secretly met with Chinese leaders. When they again met the Chinese in December and revealed their earlier meeting, the Bush administration faced a storm of criticism for its policy of "constructive engagement" from opponents arguing that sanctions were needed. Although establishing sanctions on China in 1991 on high-technology satellite-part exports, Bush continued to support renewal of China's Most Favored Nation trading status.

COLLAPSE OF EAST EUROPEAN COMMUNISM

Bush-Gorbachev Summits

Amid the collapse of communism in Eastern Europe, Bush met with Mikhail Gorbachev in Malta from December 1 through 3, 1989; the two leaders appeared to agree that the Cold War was over. On May 30 and 31, 1990, Bush and Gorbachev met in Washington to discuss the possible reunification of Germany, and signed a trade treaty between the United States and the Soviet Union. The meeting of the two leaders in Helsinki on September 9 addressed strategies for the developing Persian Gulf crisis. At the meeting of the "Group of 7" nations (Canada, France, Germany, Italy, Japan, the United Kingdom, and the United States) in July 1991, Gorbachev requested economic aid from the West. A short time later, on July 30 and 31, Bush met Gorbachev in Moscow, where they signed the Strategic Arms Reduction Treaty (START), which cut United States and Soviet nuclear arsenals by 30 percent, and pushed for Middle Eastern talks.

PERSIAN GULF CRISIS

July 1990: Saddam Hussein of Iraq charged that Kuwait had conspired with the United States to keep oil prices low and began massing troops at the Iraq-Kuwait border.

August 1990: On August 2 Iraq invaded Kuwait, an act that Bush denounced as "naked aggression." One day later, 100,000 Iraqi soldiers were poised south of Kuwait City, near the Saudi Arabian border. The United States quickly banned most trade with Iraq, froze Iraq's and Kuwait's assets in the United States, and sent aircraft carriers to the Persian Gulf. After the U.N. Security Council condemned the invasion, Bush on August 6 ordered the deployment of air, sea, and land forces to Saudi Arabia, dubbing the operation "Desert Shield." At the end of August there were 100,000 American soldiers in Saudi Arabia.

September 1990: Bush encouraged Egypt to support American policy by forgiving Egypt its debt to the United States. He also obtained pledges of financial support from Saudi Arabia, Kuwait, and Japan, among other nations, to help pay for the operation.

October 1990: On October 29 the Security Council warned Hussein that further actions might be taken if he did not withdraw from Kuwait.

November 1990: In November, Bush ordered that U.S. forces be increased to more than 400,000. On November 29 the United Nations set January 15, 1991, as the deadline for Iraqi withdrawal from Kuwait.

January 1991: On January 9 Iraq's foreign minister, Tariq Aziz, rejected a letter written by Bush to Hussein. Three days later, after an extensive debate, Congress authorized the use of force in the gulf. On January 17 an international force that included the U.S., Great Britain, France, Italy, Saudi Arabia, and Kuwait launched an air and missile attack on Iraq and occupied Kuwait. The United States called the effort "Operation Desert Storm." Under the overall command of the army's General H. Norman Schwarzkopf, the military effort emphasized high-technology weapons, including F-15E fighter bombers, F-117A stealth fighters, Tomahawk cruise missiles, and Patriot antimissile missiles. Beginning on January 17, Iraq sent SCUD missiles into Israel in an effort to draw that country into the war and hopefully break up the U.S.-Arabian coalition. On January 22 and 23, Hussein's forces set Kuwaiti oil fields on fire and spilled oil into the gulf.

February 1991: On February 23 the allied ground assault began. Four days later, Bush announced that Kuwait was liberated and ordered offensive operations to cease. The United Nations established the terms for the cease-fire: Iraqi annexation of Kuwait to be rescinded, Iraq to accept liability for damages and return Kuwaiti property, Iraq to end all military actions and identify mines and booby traps, and Iraq to release captives.

April 1991: On April 3 the Security Council approved a resolution to establish a permanent cease-fire; Iraq accepted U.N. terms on April 6. The next day the United States began airlifting food to Kurdish refugees on the Iraq-Turkey border who were fleeing the Kurdish rebellion against Hussein, a rebellion that was seemingly encouraged by Bush, who nonetheless refused to become militarily involved. The United States estimated that 100,000 Iraqis had been killed during the war, while the Americans had lost about 115 lives.

Toward a Middle East Conference

On February 6, 1991, the United States had set out its postwar goals for the Middle East. These included regional arms control and security arrangements, international aid for reconstruction of Iraq and Kuwait, and resolution of the Israeli-Palestinian conflict. Immediately after cessation of the conflict, Secretary of State James Baker toured the Middle East attempting to promote a conference to address the problems of the region. After several more negotiating sessions, Saudi Arabia, Syria, Jordan, and Lebanon had accepted the United States proposal for an Arab-Israeli peace conference by the middle of July; Israel conditionally accepted in early August. Despite continuing conflict with Iraq, including U.N. inspections of its nuclear capabilities, and new Israeli settlements in disputed territory which kept the conference agreement tenuous, the nations met in Madrid, Spain, at the end of October. Bilateral talks in early November between Israel and the Arabs concentrated on procedural issues.

BREAKUP OF THE SOVIET UNION

Collapse of Soviet Communism and the End of the Cold War

The Soviet Union began to break up in 1990, when Lithuania declared its independence. In the aftermath of an attemped coup by hard-line Communists later that year, other Soviet republics followed suit. For the United States, the collapse of the U.S.S.R. meant that the Cold War, which had begun in 1945, was finally over. The United States was now the world's only superpower. In September 1991 President Bush announced that the U.S. would carry out the unilateral removal and destruction of ground-based tactical nuclear weapons in Europe and Asia, removal of nuclear-armed Tomahawk cruise missiles from surface ships and submarines, immediate destruction of intercontinental ballistic missiles covered by the START treaty, and an end to the 24-hour alert for strategic bombers which the United States had maintained for decades. Gorbachev responded the next month by announcing the immediate deactivation of intercontinental ballistic missiles covered by START, removal of all short-range missiles from Soviet ships, submarines, and aircraft, and destruction of all ground-based tactical nuclear weapons. He also said that the Soviet Union would reduce its forces by 700,000 troops, and he placed all long-range nuclear missiles under a single command.

New foreign policy challenges emerged, however. Yugoslavia broke up into several different nations, and the region was plunged into a brutal war. Conflict threatened other parts of the world as well. The disintegration of the Soviet Union meant more nations had nuclear weapons, as several of the former Soviet republics had access to them.

THE ELECTION OF 1992

William Jefferson Clinton, governor of Arkansas, overcame several rivals and won the Democratic presidential nomination, choosing Senator Al Gore of Tennessee as his candidate for vice-president. Clinton and Reform Party candidate H. Ross Perot, emphasized jobs and the economy, as well as the debt. Bush stressed traditional values and his foreign policy accomplishments. In the general election Clinton won 43 percent of the popular vote and 370 electoral votes, thereby defeating George Bush, who received 38 percent of the vote, and independent candidate Ross Perot, who took 19 percent of the vote but no electoral votes.

THE CLINTON PRESIDENCY

Rocky Start Upon taking office, Clinton created a storm of protest when he proposed lifting the ban on homosexuals in the military. In July 1993 a compromise "Don't ask, don't tell" policy was struck, requiring gays and lesbians to be discreet about their sexual orientation and not to engage in homosexual acts. On the legislative front, Clinton was strongly rebuffed in a first-term attempt, led by the First Lady, to comprehensively reform the nation's healthcare system. In the 1994 mid-term elections, in what Clinton himself considered a repudiation of his administration, the Republicans took both houses of Congress from the Democrats and voted in Newt Gingrich of Georgia as Speaker of the House. Gingrich had helped craft the Republican congressional campaign strategy to dramatically shrink the federal government and give more power to the states.

Clinton, however, was not without his successes, both on the legislative and diplomatic fronts. He signed a bill establishing a five-day waiting period for handgun purchases, and he signed an anti-crime bill emphasizing community policing. He signed the Family and Medical Leave Act, which required large companies to provide up to 12 weeks' unpaid leave to workers for family and medical emergencies. He also championed welfare reform (a central theme of his campaign), but made it clear that the legislation he signed into law in August 1996 radically overhauling FDR's welfare system disturbed him on two counts—its exclusion of legal immigrants from getting most federal benefits and its deep cut in federal outlays for food stamps; Clinton said these flaws could be repaired with further legislation. In foreign affairs, Clinton signed the North American Free Trade Agreement (NAFTA), which, as of January 1994, lifted most trade barriers with Mexico and Canada. Clinton sought to ease tensions between Israelis and Palestinians, and he helped bring together Itzhak Rabin, prime minister of Israel, and Yasir Arafat, chairman of the Palestine Liberation Organization, for a White House summit. Ultimately, the two Middle East leaders signed a 1994 accord establishing Palestinian self-rule in the Gaza Strip and Jericho. In October 1994 Israel and Jordan signed a treaty to begin the process of establishing full diplomatic relations. Rabin was assassinated a year later by

President Clinton plays the saxophone he received as a gift from a beaming Russian President Yeltsin at a dinner party in 1994. White House photo by Bob McNeely.

a radical, right-wing Israeli. The Clinton administration also played a key role in hammering out a peace agreement in 1995 in war-torn former Yugoslavia—where armed conflict had broken out in 1991 between Serbs, Croats, Bosnian Muslims, and other factions and groups.

Controversy Swirls Around the President The president came to be dogged by a number of controversies, including his and his wife's role in a complex Arkansas real estate deal called Whitewater, the removal of employees from the White House travel office, the suicide of Deputy White House Counsel Vince Foster, and a sexual harassment suit (later settled out of court) brought against the president by Paula Jones, a former Arkansas state employee. Whitewater spawned the Justice Department's appointment of an independent counsel, Robert B. Fiske, to look into it. Fiske's successor, Kenneth W. Starr, would expand the scope of the investigation. (Congress ultimately soured on the independent counsel law—enacted as a kind of coda to Watergate—and allowed it to expire in mid-1999.)

THE ELECTION OF 1996

Clinton recaptured the Democratic nomination without a serious challenge, while longtime GOP Senator Robert Dole of Kansas, the Senate majority leader, had to overcome several opponents but orchestrated a harmonious nominating convention with running mate Jack Kemp, a former New York congressman and Cabinet member during the Bush administration. In November 1996, with most voters citing a healthy economy and the lack of an enticing alternative in Dole or the Reform Party's Perot, Clinton received 49 percent of the vote (47 million popular votes and 379 electoral votes), becoming the first Democrat to be returned to the White House since FDR, in 1936. Dole won 41 percent (39 million popular votes, 159 electoral votes) and Perot polled eight percent of the total (8 million popular votes). The GOP retained control of both houses of Congress.

The Election of 1998 In the congressional elections of 1998, the Democrats gained seats in both the House and the Senate. Seldom does the president's party gain seats in a mid-term election, so it was widely believed that this—in part—might have been backlash to the continued Republican-led prosecution of Clinton for alleged perjury and obstruction of justice.

Domestic Policy Clinton sought a legacy as a preservationist by signing executive orders that set aside vast expanses of public lands, especially in the West.

Foreign Policy During his second term, Clinton faced continued political unrest and civil war in the Balkans. In 1999 the Serbian government attacked ethnic Albanians in Kosovo, a province of Serbia. In response, NATO forces, led by the United States, bombed Serbia. Several weeks of bombing forced Serbian forces to withdraw from Kosovo. Meanwhile, Clinton was instrumental in bringing about a historic peace agreement in Northern Ireland, while the land-for-peace accord he tried to broker between the Palestinians and Israel proved elusive. Clinton also continued to seek a policy of expanding international trade by relaxing or eliminating trade barriers.

Campaign Finance Reform Fails to Pass Though the issue of the influence of money on politics was not new, increasingly high levels of campaign spending and the contributions necessary to make such spending possible began to receive significant attention. Several bills were proposed in Congress, and Clinton pledged to support reform; by the end of his presidency in January 2001, however, no bill had passed.

Historic Economic Boom Falters As of February 1, 2000, the U.S. economy had enjoyed its longest stretch of uninterrupted growth in the nation's history. Much of this growth, which had begun in March 1991, was fueled by a new industry, electronic commerce on the Internet. Stock prices generally rose, but share prices for Internet companies rose especially fast, soaring to extraordinary heights. In 2000, investors came to see e-businesses' and high-tech stock prices as unreasonably high. A number of such stocks tumbled, with some losing as much as 90 percent of their value. Soon many formerly high-flying Internet companies were folding and by the close of 2000 the future of the surviving e-businesses, as well as the economy as whole, was uncertain.

Impeachment and Acquittal In December 1998 Clinton was impeached by the House and in January and February 1999 he was tried and acquitted by the Senate on charges that he had lied about an adulterous affair with a White House intern. The affair had been uncovered by Starr.

THE ELECTION OF 2000

The Democrats nominated Vice-President Al Gore for president and Senator Joseph Lieberman for vice president. The Republican Party nominated Texas Governor George W. Bush (son of President George H. W. Bush). After some conflict, the Reform party nominated Patrick Buchanan. The Green Party ran Ralph Nader. After one of the tightest presidential elections ever, highlighted by a withdrawn initial concession by Gore, a recount in Florida, and several court challenges, Bush was declared the winner.

AMERICAN SOCIETY AT THE DAWN OF THE TWENTY-FIRST CENTURY

Terrorism Hits Home Major symbols of U.S. economic and military might—the World Trade Center in New York and the Pentagon just outside Washington,

D.C.—were attacked on September 11, 2001, when hijackers deliberately crashed commercial jetliners into the buildings, toppling the trade center's 110-story twin towers. Thousands died in the worst act of terrorism in American history. The prime suspect, said President Bush, was Saudi exile Osama bin Laden, the alleged mastermind of previous attacks on U.S. interests overseas. Terrorist attacks had continued to be a grim reality overseas through the 1980s and early 1990s, with Americans frequently targeted. Yet such incidents had

President George W. Bush and First Lady Laura Bush observe a moment of silence for the victims of the Sept. 11, 2001, terror attacks. White House photo by Eric Draper.

come to be viewed as something the United States wouldn't have to face on its own soil—until February 26, 1993, when a terrorist bomb ripped through the underground parking garage of the World Trade Center in New York City, killing six people and injuring more than 1,000. Convicted and sentenced to 240 years each were four Islamic militants. On April 19, 1995, the Oklahoma City federal building was bombed, killing 168 people and injuring 500. Timothy James McVeigh, a member of the American militia movement who had expressed hatred toward the U.S. government and was aggrieved over its assault two years earlier on a self-proclaimed prophet's compound in Waco, Texas, was put to death for the crime in May 2001. A second defendant, Terry Nichols, was convicted on federal charges of conspiracy and involuntary manslaughter and sentenced to life in prison.

A Modern Plague Descends on America In 1981 scientists announced the discovery of Acquired Immune Deficiency Syndrome, or AIDS, which was especially prevalent among—but not confined to—homosexual males and intravenous drug users. Widespread fear resulted, with an upsurge in homophobia. The revelation that a Florida dentist, who died in 1990, had transmitted human immunodeficiency virus, or HIV, to six patients led to calls for mandatory testing of healthcare workers. There were calls as well for fast-tracking drug approvals. In 1998 the federal Centers for Disease Control and Prevention estimated that between 400,000 and 650,000 Americans were HIV-positive,

Patriot Act: Controversial Response to 9/11 Attacks

Following the terror attacks on the World Trade Center and the Pentagon on September 11, 2001, both houses of Congress passed and President Bush signed the USA Patriot Act, which strengthened the authority of U.S. law enforcement agencies to fight terrorist acts both in the United States and in foreign nations.

The Patriot Act has come under criticism by some individuals and groups who believe that portions of it are unnecessary and infringe upon American freedoms, including speech, press, and the right to privacy. The most controversial element is Section 215, which allows government agents to look into phone and Internet records on the basis of "an ongoing investigation concerning international terrorism or clandestine intelligence activities." In addition, this section allows FBI agents to obtain secret warrants from a federal court to review library or bookstore records of an individual connected with an international terrorism or spying investigation. Prior to the Patriot Act, such orders were granted only on the grounds of probable cause as detailed in the Fourth Amendment to the United States Constitution.

Public support for the Patriot Act, which was quite high in the period immediately after the September 11th attacks, began dropping in 2003. According to the Gallup Poll, in January 2002 47 percent of Americans wanted the U.S. government to stop terrorism even if it reduced civil liberties. By November 2003, this number had dropped to 31 percent. By 2005, the public was divided almost evenly for and against the Patriot Act.

cont'd on next page

meaning that they had the virus that causes AIDS.

Urban America Rebounds America's cities showed renewed promise at the dawn of the new century—though much remained to be done to attack a host of social and economic ills. *The Economist* reported in January 1998 that unemployment in the 50 biggest cities had fallen by a third over the prior four years, to about 6 percent. Rates for serious crime fell to their lowest in a generation. Cities such as New York—which two decades before had nearly gone bankrupt—and Los Angeles, victim of race riots and an earthquake during the early and mid-'90s, were "growing in both population and confidence." There were also comebacks like that of New Brunswick, N.J. Moribund in the 1970s, it forged a public–private partnership that resulted in more than $1 billion in investments over 25 years. In 1999 this city of 42,000 boasted a vibrant downtown (with small-business loans awarded to city-based businesses topping $1.2 million), a jobless rate of 6.6 percent (down from as high as 11.8 percent in 1993), a 34 percent drop in crime since 1991 for which so-called community policing got much of the credit, and the U.S. Department of Education's coveted Blue Ribbon Award for one of its elementary schools.

Writers Explore the Kaleidoscope of U.S. Life The 1980s and 1990s saw the emergence of writers who threw light on various, sometimes hidden facets of national life—from the immigrant experience as told by Amy Tan in *The Joy-Luck Club* (1989) and Oscar Hijuelos in *The Mambo Kings Play Songs of Love* (1990) to Tom Wolfe's satirical take on greed and class and racial tensions in New York City in *The Bonfire of the*

One of the main arguments against the Patriot Act is that while significantly expanding federal investigative authority, it did not provide checks and balances protecting civil liberties that was normally included in legislation. The Act did, however, include "sunset," or temporary, provisions that were set to expire on December 31, 2005. After that date, the authority was to remain in effect only for investigations previously begun. The temporary provisions deal with wiretapping in terrorism and computer cases, sharing wiretap and foreign intelligence information, nationwide search warrants for electronic evidence, and several other areas.

The Patriot Act comprises a controversial aspect of post–9/11 American life, as it created a new crime category of "domestic terrorism." It amended immigration, banking and money laundering, and foreign intelligence laws in its attempt to enhance federal law enforcement capabilities. Hailed by many as an important and necessary reaction to terrorism, the Patriot Act also inspired serious concern among others who fear restrictions on civil liberties. The American Civil Liberties Union, for example, filed challenges to a number of Patriot Act provisions and ran an ad campaign beginning in August 2004, claiming, "So the government can search your house…My house…Our house…Without notifying us. Treating us all like suspects. It's part of the Patriot Act."

Vanities (1987) and, later, his look behind the patina of Deep South gentility in *A Man in Full* (1998). Toni Morrison's *Beloved* (1987) dramatized the African-American slave experience.

The U.S. Counts Its People The 2000 decennial census counted 281,421,906 Americans, a 13.2 percent increase since 1990. The most populous state was California (33,871,648), the least populous, Wyoming (493,782).

◀——— HISTORICAL TIMELINE ———▶

Watergate, Conservatism's Rise, and Post–Cold War Challenges (1972–2005)

1972	Watergate break-in occurs at Democratic Headquarters Nixon defeats McGovern for presidency Haiphong Harbor in North Vietnam mined by U.S.
1973	U.S., North Vietnam sign Paris Peace Accords *Roe v. Wade* expands abortion rights Yom Kippur War in Israel Vice-President Agnew resigns in disgrace
1974	Impeachment proceedings begin against Pres. Nixon *U.S. v. Richard Nixon* rules that tapes must be turned over Nixon resigns; Vice-President Ford succeeds him Ford pardons Nixon
1975	U.S. abandons South Vietnam as it falls to North Vietnam
1978	Bakke vs. University of California Regents affirmative action case Camp David Accords between Israel and Egypt
1979	U.S. and China establish diplomatic relations Iran deposes shah Iran militants capture U.S. embassy and take hostages Soviet Union invades Afghanistan Three-Mile Island nuclear accident Sandinistas overthrow Somoza in Nicaragua
1980	U.S. boycotts Moscow Olympics Reagan elected president
1981	Iran releases hostages Reagan breaks air traffic controller strike Sandra Day O'Connor named first female Supreme Court justice AIDS epidemic reaches U.S.
1982	241 Marines killed in Lebanon U.S. invades Grenada
1985	Gorbachev takes power in Soviet Union
1986	Iran-Contra affair *Challenger* space shuttle explodes after takeoff
1989	*Exxon Valdez* runs aground in Alaska Students begin pro-democracy demonstrations in China Berlin Wall falls

1990	Saddam Hussein of Iraq invades Kuwait
1991	Operation Desert Storm ends Iraq's occupation of Kuwait Soviet Union breaks up as Cold War ends
1992	Los Angeles riots follow Rodney King verdict Clinton elected president
1993	North American Free Trade Agreement approved
1995	U.S., NATO forces enforce peace in Bosnia
1999	Clinton acquitted following House impeachment
2000	George W. Bush defeats Gore in disputed election
2001	Hijackers crash planes into World Trade Center towers and Pentagon U.S. invades Afghanistan to overthrow Taliban government Patriot Act gives U.S. broad powers to investigate terrorism
2004	George W. Bush re-elected president
2006	President Bush urges Congress to reauthorize the USA Patriot Act

PRACTICE TEST 1
AP United States History

AP United States History

PRACTICE TEST 1

SECTION I

TIME: 55 Minutes
      80 Questions

DIRECTIONS: Each of the questions or incomplete statements below is followed by five suggested answers or completions. Select the one that is best in each case.

1. The aging of the American population at the end of the 20th century was primarily due to

   (A) fertility and mortality rates below their long-term averages

   (B) a record number of births after World War II

   (C) new methods of contraception and abortion

   (D) decreased immigration rates

   (E) the deterioration of the family unit

2. Which tribe was a member of the Five Nations of Iroquois?

   (A) Aztecs

   (B) Mohawks

   (C) Anasazi

   (D) Incas

   (E) Mayas

3. At the time President George H. W. Bush spoke of building "a new world order," the most significant event confronting him was

   (A) the outbreak of civil war throughout the Balkans and the Caucasus

   (B) the threat of massive destruction from nuclear war

   (C) the rapid democratization of the Soviet bloc

   (D) Henry Kissinger's shuttle diplomacy in the Middle East

   (E) global concern regarding Acquired Immune Deficiency Syndrome

4. Which of the following is true of the Stamp Act Congress?

   (A) It was the first unified government for all the American colonies.

   (B) It provided an important opportunity for colonial stamp agents to discuss methods of enforcing the act.

   (C) It was attended only by Georgia, Virginia, and the Carolinas.

   (D) It provided an important opportunity for colonial leaders to meet and establish ties with one another.

   (E) It rejected the assertion that the colonies ought to protest acts of Parliament deemed to be unconstitutional.

5. The map below depicts the United States immediately after which of the following events?

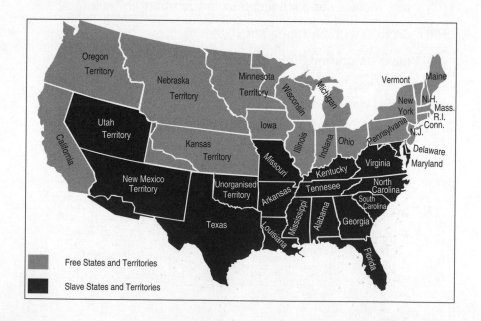

(A)   Passage of the Compromise of 1850

(B)   Negotiation of the Webster-Ashburton Treaty

(C)   Passage of the Northwest Ordinance

(D)   Settlement of the Mexican War

(E)   Passage of the Missouri Compromise

6.   The principle of "popular sovereignty" was

(A)   first conceived by Senator Stephen A. Douglas

(B)   applied as part of the Missouri Compromise

(C)   a central feature of the Kansas-Nebraska Act

(D)   a policy favored by the Whig party during the late 1840s and early 1850s

(E)   successful in solving the impasse over the status of slavery in the territories

7.   In issuing the Emancipation Proclamation, one of Lincoln's goals was to

(A)   gain the active aid of Britain and France in restoring the Union

(B)   stir up enthusiasm for the war in such border states as Maryland and Kentucky

(C)   please the Radicals in the North by abolishing slavery in areas of the South already under the control of Union armies

(D)   please Russia, one of the Union's few overseas friends, where the serfs had been emancipated the previous year

(E)   keep Britain and France from intervening on the side of the Confederacy

8.   All of the following statements are true about Herbert Hoover's responses to the Great Depression EXCEPT:

(A)   He at first stressed the desirability of localism and private initiative rather than government intervention.

(B)   He saw the Depression as akin to an act of nature, about which nothing could be done except to ride it out.

(C)   He urged the nation's business leaders to maintain wages and full employment.

(D) His strategy for ending the Depression was a failure.

(E) He was not able to avoid increasing unpopularity.

9. Which of the following statements is correct about the case of Whitaker Chambers and Alger Hiss?

(A) Hiss accused Chambers, an important mid-ranking government official, of being a Communist spy.

(B) The case gained national attention through the involvement of Senator Joseph R. McCarthy.

(C) Hiss was convicted of perjury for denying under oath that he had been a Communist agent.

(D) The case marked the beginning of American concern about Communist subversion.

(E) Chambers denied ever having had any involvement with the Communist party.

10. Which of the following best characterizes the methods of Martin Luther King Jr.?

(A) Nonviolent defiance of segregation

(B) Armed violence against police and troops

(C) Patience while developing the skills that would make Blacks economically successful and gain them the respect of Whites

(D) A series of petitions to Congress calling for correction of racial abuses

(E) A series of speaking engagements in Northern cities in hopes of pressuring Congress to take action

11. Which of the following best describes the agreement that ended the 1962 Cuban Missile Crisis?

(A) The Soviet Union agreed not to station troops in Cuba, and the United States agreed not to invade Cuba.

(B) The Soviet Union agreed to withdraw its missiles from Cuba, and the United States agreed not to invade Cuba.

(C) The Soviet Union agreed not to invade Turkey, and the United States agreed not to invade Cuba.

(D) The Soviet Union agreed to withdraw its missiles from Cuba, and the United States agreed not to invade Turkey.

(E) The Soviet Union agreed to withdraw its missiles from Cuba, and the United States agreed to withdraw its missiles from Western Europe.

12. The most common form of resistance on the part of black American slaves prior to the Civil War was

(A) violent uprisings in which many persons were killed

(B) attempts to escape and reach Canada by means of the "Underground Railroad"

(C) passive resistance, including breaking tools and slightly slowing the pace of work

(D) arson of plantation buildings and cotton gins

(E) poisoning of the food consumed by their white masters

13. Which of the following best describes the attitudes of Southern Whites toward slavery during the mid-nineteenth century (ca. 1835–1865)?

(A) Slavery was a necessary evil.

(B) Slavery should be immediately abolished.

(C) Slavery was a benefit to both Whites and Blacks.

(D) Slavery should gradually be phased out and the freed slaves colonized to some place outside the United States.

(E) Slavery was a national sin.

14. For farmers and planters in the South, the 1850s was a period of

(A) low prices for agricultural products

(B) rapid and violent fluctuations in crop prices

(C) high crop prices due to repeated crop failures

(D) high crop prices and sustained prosperity

(E) desperate poverty culminating in the Panic of 1857

15. Immigrants coming to America from Eastern and Southern Europe during the late nineteenth century were most likely to

(A) settle in large cities in the Northeast or Midwest

(B) settle on farms in the upper Midwest

(C) seek to file on homesteads on the Great Plains

(D) migrate to the South and Southwest

(E) return to their homelands after only a brief stay in the U.S.

16. Which of the following had the greatest effect in moving the United States toward participation in the First World War?

(A) The German disregard of treaty obligations in violating Belgian neutrality

(B) Germany's declaration of its intent to wage unrestricted submarine warfare

(C) A German offer to reward Mexico with U.S. territory should it join Germany in a war against the United States

(D) The beginning of the Russian Revolution

(E) The rapidly deteriorating situation for the Allies

17. The Berlin Airlift was America's response to

(A) the Soviet blockade of West Berlin from land communication with the rest of the western zone

(B) the acute war-time destruction of roads and railroads, making land transport almost impossible

(C) the unusually severe winter of 1947

(D) a widespread work stoppage by German transportation workers in protest of the allied occupation of Germany

(E) the increased need for flu vaccine in the midst of a serious epidemic

18. The economic theory of mercantilism would be consistent with which of the following statements?

(A) Economies will prosper most when trade is restricted as little as possible.

(B) A government should seek to direct the economy so as to maximize exports.

(C) Colonies are of little economic importance to the mother country.

(D) It is vital that a country imports more than it exports.

(E) Tariff barriers should be avoided as much as possible.

19. The primary American objection to the Stamp Act was that

(A) it was an internal tax, whereas Americans were prepared to accept only external taxes

(B) it was the first tax of any kind ever imposed by Britain on the colonies

(C) its proposed tax rates were so high that they would have crippled the colonial economy

(D) it was a measure for raising revenue from the colonies but it had not been approved by the colonists through their representatives

(E) it constituted an unwarranted interference with the colonial economy in a manner that would have greatly restrained free trade

20. In seeking diplomatic recognition from foreign powers during the War for Independence, the American government found it necessary to

(A) make large financial payments to the governments of France, Spain, and Holland

(B) promise to cede large tracts of American territory to France upon a victorious conclusion of the war

(C) demonstrate its financial stability and self-sufficiency

(D) demonstrate a determination and potential to win independence

(E) agree to grant France a specially favored trading status

21. William Lloyd Garrison, in his publication *The Liberator*, was outspoken in calling for

(A) the gradual and compensated emancipation of slaves

(B)   colonization of slaves to some place outside the boundaries of the United States

(C)   repeal of the congressional "gag rule"

(D)   immediate and uncompensated emancipation of slaves

(E)   the strict maintenance of the constitutional doctrine of states' rights

22.   The Congressional "gag rule" stipulated that

    (A)   no law could be passed prohibiting slavery in the territories

    (B)   no member of Congress could make statements or speeches outside of Congress pertaining to slavery

    (C)   no antislavery materials could be sent through the mail to addresses in Southern states

    (D)   no antislavery petitions would be formally received by Congress

    (E)   no bills pertaining to slavery would be considered

23.   The main idea of Theodore Roosevelt's proposed "New Nationalism" was to

    (A)   make the federal government an instrument of domestic reform

    (B)   undertake an aggressive new foreign policy

    (C)   increase economic competition by breaking up all trusts and large business combinations

    (D)   seek to establish a large overseas empire

    (E)   take an isolationist position in foreign policy while maintaining the status quo domestically

24.   Franklin D. Roosevelt's New Deal program attempted or achieved all of the following EXCEPT

    (A)   raised farm prices by paying farmers not to plant

    (B)   encouraged cooperation within industries so as to raise prices generally

    (C)   supported the creation of the Reconstruction Finance Corporation

    (D)   invigorated the economy by lowering tariff barriers

    (E)   restored confidence in the banking system

25. The Haymarket Incident involved

    (A) a riot between striking workers and police

    (B) a scandal involving corruption within the Grant administration

    (C) allegations of corruption on the part of Republican presidential candidate James G. Blaine

    (D) a disastrous fire that pointed out the hazardous working conditions in some factories

    (E) an early challenge to the authority of states to regulate the railroad industry

26. Which of the following conclusions can be drawn from this chart displaying the relative cost of transporting goods in 1858?

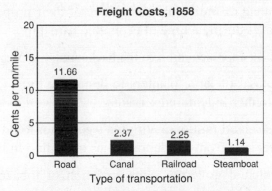

Source: Carl Degler, *Out of Our Past*. New York: Harper, 1984.

    (A) Steamboats were unsafe and thus unpopular.

    (B) Roads provided the cheapest means of transporting freight.

    (C) The building of canals was essentially over in 1858.

    (D) Railroads were extremely cost-efficient in transporting freight when compared to roads.

    (E) Most American cities were linked by canals or railroads.

27. As a result of the Spanish-American War, the United States gained possession of Puerto Rico, Guam, and

    (A) the Philippines

    (B) Cuba

    (C) Bermuda

    (D) the Panama Canal Zone

    (E) Hawaii

28. In what is now Mexico, the Mayas and Aztecs

    (A) successfully resisted the Spanish invasion

    (B) existed without any form of written language

    (C) developed advanced cultures prior to European contact

    (D) lived exclusively in small agricultural villages

    (E) built earthen mounds

29. The immediate issue in dispute in Bacon's Rebellion was

    (A) the jailing of individuals or seizure of their property for failure to pay taxes during a time of economic hardship

    (B) the under-representation of the backcountry in Virginia's legislature

    (C) the refusal of large planters to honor the terms of their contracts with former indentured servants

    (D) the perceived failure of Virginia's governor to protect the colony's frontier area from the depredations of raiding Indians

    (E) the colonial governor's manipulation of tobacco prices for the benefit of himself and a small clique of his friends

30. The Newburgh Conspiracy was concerned with

    (A) betrayal of the plans for the vital fort at West Point, New York

    (B) the use of the Continental Army to create a more centralized Union of the states

    (C) resistance to the collection of federal excise taxes in western Pennsylvania

    (D) New England's threat to secede should the War of 1812 continue

    (E) Aaron Burr's plot to detach the western United States as an empire for himself

31. The Wilmot Proviso stipulated that

    (A) slavery should be prohibited in the lands acquired as a result of the Mexican War

    (B) no lands should be annexed to the United States as a result of the Mexican War

    (C) California should be a free state while the rest of the Mexican Cession should be reserved for the formation of slave states

    (D) the status of slavery in the Mexican Cession should be decided on the basis of "Popular Sovereignty"

    (E) the Missouri Compromise line should be extended through the Mexican Cession to the Pacific, lands north of it being closed to slavery

32. Which of the following was a goal of the Populist movement?

    (A) Free coinage of silver

    (B) Reform of child labor laws

    (C) Using modern science to solve social problems

    (D) Eliminating the electoral college as a method of choosing the nation's president

    (E) National legislation outlawing racial discrimination

33. The settlement-house movement drew its workers primarily from which of the following groups?

    (A) Young, affluent, college-educated women

    (B) Poor Eastern European immigrants

    (C) Disabled veterans of the Spanish-American War

    (D) Idealistic young men who came to the city largely from rural areas

    (E) Often illiterate members of the urban working class

34. In its decision in the case of *Dred Scott v. Sanford*, the Supreme Court held that

    (A) separate facilities for different races were inherently unequal and therefore unconstitutional

    (B) no black slave could be a citizen of the United States

(C)   separate but equal facilities for different races were constitutional

(D)   affirmative action programs were acceptable only when it could be proven that specific previous cases of discrimination had occurred within the institution or business in question

(E)   imposition of a literacy test imposed an unconstitutional barrier to the right to vote

35.   The Whig party turned against President John Tyler because

(A)   he was felt to be ineffective in pushing the Whig agenda through Congress

(B)   he spoke out in favor of the annexation of Texas

(C)   he opposed the entire Whig legislative program

(D)   he criticized Henry Clay's handling of the Nullification Crisis

(E)   he aggressively favored the expansion of slavery

36.   In coining the phrase "Manifest Destiny," journalist John L. O'Sullivan meant that

(A)   the struggle for racial equality was the ultimate goal of America's existence

(B)   America was certain to become an independent country sooner or later

(C)   it was the destiny of America to overspread the continent

(D)   America must eventually become either all slave or all free

(E)   America should seek to acquire an overseas empire

37.   All of the following were causes of the Mexican War EXCEPT

(A)   American desire for California

(B)   Mexican failure to pay debts and damages owed to the U.S.

(C)   U.S. annexation of the formerly Mexican-held Republic of Texas

(D)   Mexican desire to annex Louisiana

(E)   the disputed southern boundary of Texas

38.   The primary motive of those who founded the British colony in Virginia during the seventeenth century was the

(A)   desire for economic gain

(B)   desire for religious freedom

(C)   desire to create a perfect religious commonwealth as an example to the rest of the world

(D)   desire to recreate in the New World the story of feudalistic society that was fading in the Old

(E)   desire to increase the power and glory of Great Britain

39.   Which of the following is true of the Gulf of Tonkin incident?

(A)   It involved a clash of U.S. and Soviet warships.

(B)   In it, two North Vietnamese fighter-bombers were shot down as they neared U.S. Navy ships.

(C)   It involved the seizure, by North Vietnam, of a U.S. Navy intelligence ship in international waters.

(D)   It led to major U.S. involvement in the Vietnam War.

(E)   In it, a U.S. Navy destroyer was damaged by a guided missile fired by a North Vietnamese plane.

40.   Which of the following statements is true of the SALT I treaty?

(A)   It brought sharp reductions in the number of ballistic missiles in both the U.S. and Soviet arsenals.

(B)   It was intended to encourage the deployment of defensive rather than offensive strategic weapons.

(C)   It indicated U.S. acceptance of the concept of Mutual Assured Destruction.

(D)   It was never ratified by the U.S. Senate.

(E)   It created basic equality in the number of ballistic missiles on each side.

41.   Which of the following statements is true of Lincoln's Ten Percent Plan?

(A)   It stipulated that at least ten percent of former slaves must be accorded the right to vote within a given Southern state before that state could be readmitted to the Union.

(B)   It allowed the rights of citizenship only to those Southerners who could take an oath that they had never been disloyal to the Union.

(C)   It allowed high-ranking rebel officials to regain the right to vote and hold office by simply promising future good behavior.

(D)   It was silent on the issue of slavery.

(E)   It provided for the restoration of loyal governments for the erstwhile Confederate states now under Union control.

42.   All of the following were parts of Andrew Johnson's plan for Reconstruction EXCEPT

(A)   recommending to the Southern states that the vote be extended to the recently freed slaves

(B)   requiring ratification of the Thirteenth Amendment

(C)   requiring payment of monetary reparations for the damage caused by the war

(D)   requiring renunciation of secession

(E)   requiring repudiation of the Confederate debt

43.   By "normalcy" President Warren G. Harding meant not only peace after the recent war but also

(A)   a renewal of the Progressivist reform movement

(B)   a return to an emphasis on domestic reform in place of Wilson's foreign adventures

(C)   an end to idealistic crusades and efforts at large-scale reform

(D)   the establishment of new norms of international behavior

(E)   U.S. membership in the newly formed League of Nations

44.   Which of the following words best describes the spirit of American intellectuals in the 1920s?

(A)   Alienation

(B)   Complacency

(C)   Romanticism

(D)   Patriotism

(E)   Pietism

45. Warren G. Harding may best be characterized as

    (A) a personally corrupt and dishonest man

    (B) unsuccessful in foreign policy but highly successful in domestic affairs

    (C) having made a number of misjudgments in the men he appointed and with whom he associated

    (D) probably more dedicated to Progressive reform than either Wilson or Roosevelt had been

    (E) quiet and taciturn

46. The "yellow journalism" of the late nineteenth century might best be described as

    (A) focusing on the influx of Chinese immigrants to the West Coast and calling for restrictions on such immigration

    (B) attempting to alarm the public about the supposed "Yellow Peril" of Japan's growing naval and industrial might

    (C) focusing exclusively on corruptions and abuses in government and big business

    (D) reporting the news in an exaggerated, distorted, and sensationalized manner

    (E) dominated by the funding of large corporations so as to take a stance consistently favorable to big business

47. Which of the following statements best summarizes Theodore Roosevelt's position on trusts?

    (A) Trusts are an economic evil and should be destroyed in every case.

    (B) Only trusts in the railroad and oil industries are acceptable.

    (C) Good trusts should be tolerated while bad trusts are prevented from manipulating markets.

    (D) Only trusts in the meatpacking industry should be broken up.

    (E) Anything that stands in the way of complete and unrestricted economic competition is evil and should be removed.

48. During the 1760s and 1770s the most effective American tactic in gaining the repeal of the Stamp and Townshend Acts was

    (A) tarring and feathering British tax agents

    (B) sending petitions to the king and Parliament

    (C) boycotting British goods

    (D) destroying private property, such as tea, on which a tax was to be levied

    (E) using death threats to intimidate British tax agents

49. In order to deal with the crisis in banking at the time of his inauguration, Franklin Roosevelt

    (A) drastically curtailed government spending and cut taxes

    (B) declared a four-day "banking holiday" and prohibited the export of money

    (C) urged Congress to pass legislation banning fractional reserve banking and holding bank trustees responsible for all deposits

    (D) announced a multibillion-dollar federal bailout package

    (E) announced the nationalization of all banks with over $100 million in total assets

50. The Sherman Silver Purchase Act of 1890

    (A) required the federal government to purchase silver

    (B) forbade the federal government to purchase silver

    (C) made it illegal for private citizens to purchase silver

    (D) made it illegal for private citizens to purchase federal lands with anything but silver

    (E) allowed the federal government to buy silver at the discretion of the president

51. In reaction to a perceived insult to the U.S. flag and in order to hasten the downfall of Mexican leader Victoriano Huerta, President Woodrow Wilson

    (A) ordered General John J. Pershing to take U.S. troops across the border into northern Mexico

    (B) withdrew previously granted U.S. diplomatic recognition of Huerta's regime

(C) ordered the occupation of Mexico City by U.S. troops

(D) ordered U.S. forces to occupy the Mexican port city of Vera Cruz

(E) sent a strong diplomatic protest

52. All of the following were part of Woodrow Wilson's Fourteen Points EXCEPT

(A) self-determination

(B) open diplomacy

(C) freedom of the seas

(D) a League of Nations

(E) a restoration of the balance of power

53. Which of the following was among the objectives of Booker T. Washington?

(A) To keep up a constant agitation of questions of racial equality

(B) To encourage Blacks to be more militant in demanding their rights

(C) To encourage Blacks to work hard, acquire property, and prove they were worthy of their rights

(D) To urge Blacks not to accept separate but equal facilities

(E) To form an organization to advance the rights of Blacks

54. The term "Seward's Folly" referred to Secretary of State William Seward's

(A) advocacy of a lenient policy toward the defeated Southern states

(B) break with the majority radical faction of the Republican party in order to back President Andrew Johnson

(C) belief that the Civil War could be avoided and the Union restored by provoking a war with Britain and France

(D) negotiation of the purchase of Alaska from Russia

(E) ill-fated attempt to gain the presidency in 1860

55. In response to Southern intransigence in the face of President Andrew Johnson's mild reconstruction plan, Congress did all of the following EXCEPT

(A) exclude Southern representatives and senators from participating in Congress

(B)   pass the Civil Rights Act of 1866

(C)   order the arrest and imprisonment of former Confederate leaders

(D)   approve and send on to the states the Fourteenth Amendment

(E)   divide the South into five districts to be ruled by military governors with almost dictatorial powers

56.   When President Andrew Johnson removed Secretary of War Edwin M. Stanton without the approval of the Senate, contrary to the terms of the recently passed Tenure of Office Act, he

(A)   was impeached and removed from office

(B)   came within one vote of being impeached

(C)   was impeached and came within one vote of being removed from office

(D)   resigned to avoid impeachment and was subsequently pardoned by his successor

(E)   was impeached, refused to resign, and his term ended before a vote could be taken on his removal from office

57.   In speaking of "scalawags," white Southerners of the Reconstruction era made reference to

(A)   former slaves who had risen to high positions within the Reconstruction governments of the Southern states

(B)   Northerners who had come south to take high positions within the Reconstruction governments of the Southern states

(C)   the U.S. Army generals who served as military governors in the South

(D)   the Radical Republicans in Congress who imposed the Reconstruction regimes on the South

(E)   Southerners who supported or participated in the Reconstruction regimes

58.   At the time the Second World War began in Europe, the general mood in the United States with regard to the war was

(A)   determination not to become involved

(B)   eagerness to aid Great Britain by all means short of war

(C)   dissatisfaction with Roosevelt for failing to take the U.S. into the war immediately

(D)   mildly favorable to Germany

(E)   relief that the uncertainty of waiting was finally over

59.   The Bay of Pigs incident involved

(A)   the presence of Soviet nuclear missiles in Cuba

(B)   a CIA plot to overthrow Chilean leader Salvador Allende

(C)   a confrontation between U.S. and Soviet troops in Europe

(D)   a clash between a U.S. Navy destroyer and North Vietnamese patrol boats

(E)   a U.S.-sponsored attempt by free Cubans to overthrow Communist dictator Fidel Castro

60.   The purpose of the Treaty of Tordesillas was

(A)   to divide the non-European world between Spain and Portugal

(B)   to specify which parts of North America should be French and which parts Spanish

(C)   to create an alliance of France, Holland, and England against Spanish designs in the New World

(D)   to divide the New World between France and Spain

(E)   to exclude any Portuguese colonization from the Western Hemisphere

61.   In his inaugural address, Franklin D. Roosevelt said that if Congress did not pass the laws he believed it should, he would

(A)   accept this decision as the will of the people

(B)   allow the nation to suffer the consequences of congressional stubbornness

(C)   seek wartime emergency powers to carry out the measures himself

(D)   hold an unprecedented national referendum

(E)   call on the American people to place pressure on their representatives in Congress

62.   One of the purposes of the 1773 Tea Act was to

(A)   prevent overconsumption of tea in America

(B) lower the price of tea in Great Britain by decreasing the demand for it in America

(C) save the British East India Company from financial ruin

(D) create a long-term shift in wealth from Britain's North American colonies to its colony in India

(E) calm labor unrest in India

63. During the American War of Independence, the battle of Saratoga was most significant because it

(A) left the British with inadequate resources to carry on the war

(B) prevented the British from ever mounting another successful invasion of American territory

(C) allowed American forces to seize large portions of Canada

(D) persuaded France to begin supporting the Americans openly

(E) caused Holland to delay its decision to enter the war on the side of the British

64. Besides mass production through the use of interchangeable parts, Eli Whitney also influenced American history by his invention of the

(A) practical river steamboat

(B) cotton gin

(C) incandescent light bulb

(D) telegraph

(E) steam locomotive

65. The Republican response to the 1798 Alien and Sedition Acts included

(A) South Carolina's nullification of the acts

(B) the Virginia and Kentucky Resolutions

(C) the Hartford Convention

(D) the Ostend Manifesto

(E) the Mulligan Letters

66. The Puritans who settled the Massachusetts Bay Colony wanted their settlement to be primarily

    (A) a place where they could get away from persecution

    (B) an example to the rest of the world

    (C) a place where they would have the opportunity to prosper free from government regulation

    (D) a society that practiced complete separation of church and state

    (E) a pluralistic society in which all would be free to practice and teach their beliefs

67. Factors promoting the beginnings of American industrialization during the early nineteenth century included all of the following EXCEPT

    (A) high protective tariffs

    (B) improvements in transportation

    (C) large-scale immigration

    (D) the absence of craft organizations that tied artisans to a single trade

    (E) close and friendly relations with already industrialized Great Britain

68. President Andrew Jackson's Specie Circular stipulated that

    (A) inefficient employees of the federal government should be immediately dismissed regardless of their political affiliation

    (B) federal government deposits should be withdrawn from the Second Bank of the United States

    (C) no federal funds should be spent on internal improvements

    (D) paper money should not be accepted in payment for federal government lands sold

    (E) the government would use force if necessary to collect the tariff in South Carolina

69. The greatest significance of the Supreme Court's decision in *Marbury v. Madison* was that it

    (A) claimed for the first time that the Supreme Court could issue directives to the president

(B) claimed that the Supreme Court alone was empowered to say what the Constitution meant

(C) claimed for the first time that the Supreme Court could declare an act of Congress to be unconstitutional

(D) was openly defied by President Thomas Jefferson

(E) resulted in a major realignment of the first American party system

70. The Missouri Compromise provided that Missouri be admitted as a slave state, Maine be admitted as a free state, and

(A) all of the Louisiana Territory north of the northern boundary of Missouri be closed to slavery

(B) all of the Louisiana Territory north of 36° 30' be closed to slavery

(C) the entire Louisiana Territory be open to slavery

(D) the lands south of 36° 30' be guaranteed to slavery and the lands north of it negotiable

(E) all of the Louisiana Territory north of the southern boundary of Missouri be closed to slavery for 30 years

71. The term "Trail of Tears" refers to

(A) the Mormon migration from Nauvoo, Illinois, to what is now Utah

(B) the forced migration of the Cherokee tribe from the southern Appalachians to what is now Oklahoma

(C) the westward migration along the Oregon Trail

(D) the migration into Kentucky along the Wilderness Road

(E) the migration of German settlers southward from Pennsylvania into the Shenandoah Valley of Virginia

72. The most forceful Southern protest against high protective tariffs during the first half of the nineteenth century was the

(A) Hayne-Webster Debate

(B) Virginia and Kentucky Resolutions

(C) Nullification Controversy

(D) resignation of Vice President John C. Calhoun

(E) imposition of the congressional "gag rule"

73. The Morrill Land Grant Act provided

    (A) 160 acres of free land within the public domain to any head of household who would settle on it and improve it over a period of five years

    (B) large amounts of federal government land to states that would establish agricultural and mechanical colleges

    (C) 40 acres of land to former slaves

    (D) that the land of former Confederates should not be confiscated

    (E) large reservations for the Indians of the Great Plains

74. President Franklin Roosevelt's "court-packing plan" called for

    (A) the addition of up to six new justices if present justices over the age of 70 did not retire

    (B) the immediate and mandatory removal of all Supreme Court justices over the age of 70

    (C) the immediate and mandatory removal of all Supreme Court justices who voted against New Deal legislation

    (D) the addition of up to 15 new justices if present justices over the age of 70 did not retire

    (E) the mandatory retirement of justices over the age of 70 combined with the subsequent expansion of the Court to 15 members

75. All of the following statements are true of Henry George EXCEPT:

    (A) He argued that increasing prosperity was causing increasing poverty.

    (B) He believed government should take a laissez-faire philosophy.

    (C) He asserted that economic inequality was the result of private ownership of land.

    (D) He favored a single tax on the "unearned increment" of land.

    (E) He desired large-scale public works.

76. Edward Bellamy's book *Looking Backward* was

    (A) a fictional exposé of the meatpacking industry

    (B) a detailed program for social reform

(C) the catalyst of the social gospel movement

(D) a denunciation of machine politics in big-city government

(E) a futuristic utopian fantasy

77. Which of the following was passed into law during the presidency of Woodrow Wilson?

(A) The Pure Food and Drug Act

(B) A progressive income tax

(C) A high protective tariff

(D) A national old-age pension

(E) The Sherman Antitrust Act

78. By the Compromise of 1877 the Democrats agreed to allow the Republican candidate to become president in exchange for

(A) a promise that they would be allowed to win the next two presidential elections

(B) an end to Reconstruction

(C) large personal bribes to leading Democrats

(D) a substantial lowering of protective tariffs

(E) retroactive compensation for freed slaves

79. At the time of the Japanese attack on Pearl Harbor, the United States found itself

(A) partially prepared by over a year, in light of the fact that the nation's first peacetime draft had been in place for more than a year

(B) fully prepared through complete mobilization and training beginning at the outbreak of the war in Europe

(C) almost completely unprepared, with one of the smallest armies in the world

(D) with a large and modern navy but an army of under 100,000 men

(E) with a large but untrained army of conscripts called up within the past six weeks

80. What does this chart of America's labor force from 1860 to 2000 illustrate?

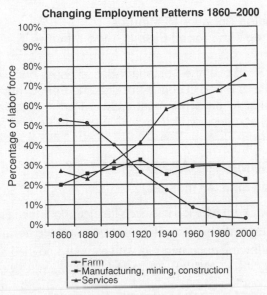

Changing Employment Patterns 1860–2000

**Source: Historical Statistics of the United States: Colonial Times to 1970 (1975);
Statistical Abstract of the United States, 1998, table 675.**

(A) There was a drop in services jobs between World Wars I and II.

(B) Manufacturing, mining, and construction have been steadily declining as the percentage of total jobs since 1900.

(C) The percentage of farm workers dropped significantly between the beginning and the end of the twentieth century.

(D) Increasing tariffs have greatly increased manufacturing jobs since 1920.

(E) Farming jobs doubled from 1900 to 1960.

STOP
This is the end of Section I.
If time still remains, you may check your work only in this section.
Do not begin Section II until instructed to do so.

SECTION II

TIME: **Reading Period – 15 Minutes**
            Writing Time for all Essays – 115 Minutes

DIRECTIONS: Read over the Document-Based Essay question in Part A and the choices in Parts B and C during the Reading Period, and use the time to organize answers. All students must answer Part A (the Document-Based Essay question) and answer ONE question in both Parts B and C.

PART A – DOCUMENT-BASED ESSAY
(Suggested writing time: 45 minutes)

1.   America's war with Mexico has been labeled, both then and since, an unprovoked and unjustifiable war of aggression and territorial aggrandizement. Using the following documents as well as your knowledge of the diplomatic history of the years from 1836 to 1846, evaluate this assertion.

Document A

Source: Joint Congressional Resolution Offering Annexation to Texas (March 1, 1845)

Resolved by the Senate and House of Representatives of the United States of America in Congress assembled: That Congress doth consent that the territory properly included within and rightfully belonging to the Republic of Texas may be erected into a new state, to be called the State of Texas, with a republican form of government to be adopted by the people of said republic by deputies in convention assembled, with the consent of the existing government, in order that the same may be admitted as one of the states of this Union....

Document B

Source: Letter from President James K. Polk to U.S. Senator William H. Haywood (August 1845)

Care has been taken — that all our military and naval movements shall be strictly defensive. — We will not be the aggressor upon Mexico; — but if her army shall cross the [Rio Grande] del Norte and invade Texas, we will if we can drive her army — to her own territory. Less than this — in good faith to Texas, I think this government could not have done. We invite Texas to unite her destinies with our own. She has accepted the invitation, upon the terms proposed,...and if because she has done so, she is invaded by the Mexican Army — surely we are bound to give her our aid in her own defense.

Document C

Source: Memoirs of John Charles Frémont

As affairs resolved themselves, California stood out as the chief subject in the impending war; and with Mr. [Thomas Hart] Benton and other governing men at Washington it became a firm resolve to hold it for the United States. To them it seemed reasonably sure that California would eventually fall to England or to the United States and that the eventuality was near. This was talked over fully during the time of preparation for the third expedition and the contingencies anticipated and weighed. The relations between the three countries made a chief subject of interest about which our thoughts settled as the probability of war grew into certainty. For me, no distinct course or definite instruction could be laid down, but the probabilities were made known to me as well as what to do when they became facts. The distance was too great for timely communication; but failing this I was given discretion to act.

Document D

Source: Diary of President James K. Polk (September–October 1845)

The President, in consultation with the Cabinet, agreed that the Hon. John Slidell of New Orleans, who spoke the Spanish language and was otherwise well qualified, should be tendered the mission.... One great object of the mission, as stated by the President, would be to adjust a permanent boundary between Mexico and the United States, and that in doing this the Minister would be instructed to purchase for a pecuniary consideration Upper California and New Mexico. He said that a better boundary would be the Rio [Grande] del Norte from its mouth to the Passo, in latitude about 32° north, and thence west to the Pacific Ocean, Mexico ceding to the United States all the country east and north of these lines. The President said that for such a boundary the amount of pecuniary consideration to be paid would be of small importance. He supposed it might be had for fifteen or twenty million, but he was ready to pay forty million for it, if it could not be had for less. In these views the Cabinet agreed with the President unanimously.

(October 1845).

The conversation then turned on California, on which I remarked that Great Britain had her eye on that country and intended to possess it if she could but that the people of the United States would not willingly permit California to pass into the possession of any new colony planted by Great Britain or any foreign monarchy and that in reasserting Mr. Monroe's doctrine I had California and the fine bay of San Francisco as much in view as Oregon. Col. Benton agreed that no foreign power ought to be permitted to colonize California, any more than they would be to colonize Cuba. As long as Cuba remained in the possession of the present government we would not object, but if a powerful foreign power was about to possess it, we would not permit it. On the same footing we would place California....

Document E

Source: Order from Secretary of War William L. Marcy to General Zachary Taylor, U.S. Army (January 13, 1846)

Sir: I am directed by the President to instruct you to advance and occupy, with the troops under your command, positions on or near the east bank of the Rio [Grande] del Norte, as soon as it can be conveniently done with reference to the season and the routes by which your movements must be made....

In the positions you may take in carrying out these instructions and other movements that may be made, the use of the Rio [Grande] del Norte may be very convenient, if not necessary. Should you attempt to exercise the right which the United States [has] in common with Mexico to the free navigation of this river, it is probable that Mexico would interpose resistance. You will not attempt to enforce this right without further instructions....

It is not designed, in our present relations with Mexico that you should treat her as an enemy; but, should she assume that character by a declaration of war, or any open act of hostility towards us, you will not act merely on the defensive, if your relative means enable you to do otherwise....

Document F

Source: Proclamation of President Don Mariano Paredes y Arrillaga (April 23, 1846)

...At the time Mr. Slidell presented himself, the troops of the United States occupied our territory, their squadrons threatened our ports, and they prepared to occupy the peninsula of the Californias, of which the question of the Oregon with England is only a preliminary. Mr. Slidell was not received, because the dignity of the nation repelled this new insult. Meanwhile, the army of the United States encamped at Corpus Christi, and occupied the Isla del Padre; following this, they then moved to the point Santo Isabel, and their standard of the stars and stripes waved on the right bank of the Rio Bravo del Norte, opposite the city of Matamoros, blockading that river with their vessels of war. The village of Laredo was surprised by a part of their troops, and a small party of our men, reconnoitering there, were disarmed. Hostilities, then, have been commenced, by the United States of North America, beginning new conquests upon the frontier territories of the departments of Tamaulipas and New Leon, and progressing at such a rate that troops of the same United States threaten Monterey in Upper California. No one can doubt which of the two republics is responsible for this war: a war which any sense of equity and justice, and respect for the rights and laws of civilized nations, might have avoided....

Document G

Source: Diary of James K. Polk (May 8, 1846)

Saw company until twelve o'clock today. Among others the Hon. John Slidell, late United States Minister to Mexico, called in company with the Secretary of State. Mr. Buchanan retired after a few minutes, and Mr. Slidell remained about an hour in conversation concerning his mission and the state of our relation with Mexico. Mr. Slidell's opinion was that but one course towards Mexico was left to the United States, and that was to take the redress of the wrongs and injuries which we had so long borne from Mexico into our own hands, and to act with promptness and energy. In this I agreed with him, and told him it was only a matter of time when I would make a communication to Congress on the subject, and that I had made up my mind to do so very soon.

Document H

Source: Polk's War Message to Congress (May 11, 1846)

The strong desire to establish peace with Mexico on liberal and honorable terms, and the readiness of this Government to regulate and adjust our boundary and other causes of difference with that power on such fair and equitable principles as would lead to permanent relations of the most friendly nature, induced me in September last to seek the reopening of diplomatic relations between the two countries. Every measure adopted on our part had for its object the furtherance of these desired results in communicating to Congress a succinct statement of the injuries which we had suffered from Mexico, and which have been accumulating during a period of more than twenty years, every expression that could tend to inflame the people of Mexico or defeat or delay a pacific result was carefully avoided. An envoy of the United States repaired to Mexico with full powers to adjust every existing difference. But though present on the Mexican soil by agreement between the two Governments, invested with full powers, and bearing evidence of the most friendly dispositions, his mission has been unavailing. The Mexican Government not only refused to receive him or listen to his propositions, but after a long-continued series of menaces have at last invaded our territory and shed the blood of our fellow-citizens on our own soil....

PARTS B AND C – STANDARD ESSAY QUESTIONS
(70 minutes)

> **DIRECTIONS:** Choose ONE question each from Part B and Part C. It is recommended that you spend 5 minutes planning and 30 minutes writing. Support your thesis with germane historical evidence and present your case logically and clearly.

PART B

2. "The Civil War had started to preserve the Union, but for the majority in the North it had become a war to create a more perfect Union."

    Assess the validity of this statement.

3. "The Revolution was effected before the war commenced. The Revolution was in the minds and hearts of the people…. This radical change in the principles, opinions, sentiments, and affections of the people was the real American Revolution."

    Explain the meaning of this 1818 statement by John Adams and assess its validity.

PART C

4. After its startling successes of the late 1880s and early 1890s, why did the Populist Party quickly fade into oblivion after 1896?

5. "After the death of Franklin Roosevelt and the end of the Second World War, the United States deliberately abandoned the wartime policy of collaboration and, exhilarated by the possession of the atomic bomb, undertook a course of aggression of its own designed to expel all Russian influence from Eastern Europe…[leaving] Moscow no alternative but to take measures in defense of its own borders. The result was the Cold War."

    Assess the validity of this statement.

AP UNITED STATES HISTORY

PRACTICE TEST 1

ANSWER KEY

1. (A)	21. (D)	41. (E)	61. (C)
2. (B)	22. (D)	42. (C)	62. (C)
3. (C)	23. (A)	43. (C)	63. (D)
4. (D)	24. (C)	44. (A)	64. (B)
5. (A)	25. (A)	45. (C)	65. (B)
6. (C)	26. (D)	46. (D)	66. (B)
7. (E)	27. (A)	47. (C)	67. (E)
8. (B)	28. (C)	48. (C)	68. (D)
9. (C)	29. (D)	49. (B)	69. (C)
10. (A)	30. (B)	50. (A)	70. (B)
11. (B)	31. (A)	51. (D)	71. (B)
12. (C)	32. (A)	52. (E)	72. (C)
13. (C)	33. (A)	53. (C)	73. (B)
14. (D)	34. (B)	54. (D)	74. (A)
15. (A)	35. (C)	55. (C)	75. (B)
16. (B)	36. (C)	56. (C)	76. (E)
17. (A)	37. (D)	57. (E)	77. (B)
18. (B)	38. (A)	58. (A)	78. (B)
19. (D)	39. (D)	59. (E)	79. (A)
20. (D)	40. (C)	60. (A)	80. (C)

DETAILED EXPLANATIONS
OF ANSWERS

TEST 1

SECTION I

1. **(A)**

Fertility and mortality rates are below their long-term averages. The record number of births after World War II (B) could have been replicated by subsequent generations, but were not. The fertility level in the U.S. has been less than the replacement level of 2.1 children per female since 1972. Work opportunities and better contraception (C) will cause this to continue despite the baby "boomlet." Immigration rates (D), legal and illegal, increase the non-aging population. The definition of family today (E) includes unmarried women with children. In 1994, 33 percent of children were born to unmarried women. Although immigration increases, life expectancy of the aging population (A) has been aided by proper health care and likely will be increased because of the influence of the medical research institutions, and developments in bioengineering and gene therapy.

2. **(B)**

The Mohawks, along with the Cayuga, Oneida, Onondaga, and Seneca, were members of the Five Nations of the Iroquois, a confederation of tribes in the eastern woodland section of what is now the United States. These tribes characterized themselves as "the people of the longhouse." The confederation was probably formed between 1570 and 1600 and is often credited to Dekanawidah, a Huron who persuaded Hiawatha, an Onondaga, to abandon warlike practices and cannibalism. The tribes united in a shared council formed of clan chiefs, with each tribe holding one vote. The Five Nations (later six, when the Tuscarora joined in 1722) used elaborate ceremonies and rituals in the choice of leaders and other important decisions. The nations did not always act in unison, but they did stay united in their opposition to the French and in the eighteenth century became dependent on the British for goods. All of the other choices lived far from the Iroquois: the Aztecs lived in central Mexico, the Anasazi in the American Southwest, the Incas in South America, and the Mayas in the Yucatán and in Central America.

3.   **(C)**

The rapid democratization of the Soviet bloc would cause an avalanche of change. The Union of Soviet Socialist Republics would break up into separate nations and a Russia pressured by threats of further disintegration. Later, (A) the rise of nationalism in areas of repression would cause the outbreak of civil wars and independent attitudes. The communist party in many countries would be repudiated. Although (B) there was concern about nuclear weapons, it was not as great as concern during the "cold war." Henry Kissinger (D) worked during the Nixon administration. President Bush made no concerted effort to combat AIDS (E).

4.   **(D)**

One of the most important aspects of the Stamp Act Congress was the opportunity it provided for colonial leaders to meet and establish acquaintances with one another. Nine colonies — not merely Georgia, Virginia, and the Carolinas (C)   were represented at it, but far from being a unified government for all the American colonies (A), it simply passed mild resolutions protesting the Stamp Act. It was not, therefore, either a vehicle for enforcing the act (B) or opposed to American protests against the act (E).

5.   **(A)**

The map depicts the United States after the Compromise of 1850. The states of Texas and California as well as the Utah and New Mexico Territories were not part of the United States at the time of the 1842 Webster-Ashburton Treaty (B), dealing with the Maine-New Brunswick boundary; the 1787 Northwest Ordinance (C), organizing what was to become the states of Ohio, Indiana, Illinois, Michigan, and Wisconsin; and the 1820 Missouri Compromise (E), regulating the status of slavery in the territory gained by the Louisiana Purchase. California and the two territories were gained as a result of the Mexican War (D), but California statehood, as well as territorial status for Utah and New Mexico, had to await the Compromise of 1850.

6.   **(C)**

The principle of popular sovereignty was a central feature of the Kansas-Nebraska Act. Though championed by Senator Stephen A. Douglas (A) it had previously been put forward by 1848 Democratic presidential candidate Lewis Cass. A favorite policy of Democrats — not Whigs (D) — during the late 1840s and early 1850s, it proved a failure in solving the impasse over the status of slavery in the territories (E). It differed from the system of congressionally specified free and slave areas used in the Missouri Compromise (B).

7.   **(E)**

One of Lincoln's reasons for issuing the Emancipation Proclamation was to keep Britain and France from intervening on the side of the Confederacy. Lincoln neither needed, wanted, nor could have obtained the active aid of these countries in restoring the Union (A), and Russia, which had indeed freed its serfs the previous year, would have been a U.S. ally regardless (D). The Radicals in the North would indeed have been pleased had Lincoln freed the slaves in areas of the South already under the control of Union armies (C), but it was precisely that which the Emancipation Proclamation did not do, largely out of concern for the more-or-less loyal slaveholding border states such as Maryland and Kentucky, who were not at all enthused about Lincoln's action even as it was (B).

8.   **(B)**

Hoover did *not* see the Depression as akin to an act of nature, about which nothing could be done. He did stress the desirability of localism and private initiative (A) and urged the nation's business leaders to maintain wages and full employment (C), but his efforts ended in failure (D), and he was the target of growing unpopularity (E).

9.   **(C)**

Hiss, a mid-ranking government official, was convicted of perjury for denying under oath that he had been a Communist agent, after being accused as such by admitted former Communist (E) Whitaker Chambers, not the other way around (A). The case gained national attention through the involvement of young Congressman Richard Nixon, not Senator Joseph R. McCarthy (B), and while it did increase American concern about Communist subversion, it was by no means the beginning of such concern (D).

10.   **(A)**

Martin Luther King's methods were characterized by nonviolent defiance of segregation. While King and/or his supporters might make speeches (E) or send petitions (D), civil disobedience gave his movement its urgency. Patience while developing the skills that would make blacks economically successful and gain them the respect of whites was the advice of late nineteenth century black leader Booker T. Washington, while armed violence was called for by King's more radical contemporaries of the 1960s.

11.   **(B)**

The agreement ending the Cuban Missile Crisis called for the Soviet Union to withdraw its missiles from Cuba while the United States agreed not to overthrow

Castro's regime there. Turkey pertained to the matter involving the Soviet's objection to U.S. missiles there, but it was not included in the agreement (C) and (D). The agreement also said nothing with regard to Soviet troops in Cuba (A) or U.S. missiles in Europe (E).

12.   **(C)**

Blacks most commonly resisted slavery passively, if at all. The Underground Railroad (B), though celebrated in popular history, involved a relatively minute number of slaves. Arson (D), poisoning (E), and violent uprising (A), though they did sometimes occur and were the subject of much fear on the part of white Southerners, were also relatively rare.

13.   **(C)**

During the period from 1835–1865 Southerners generally defended slavery as a positive benefit to society and even to the slaves themselves. That slavery was a necessary evil (A) and should be gradually phased out as the slaves were colonized outside the United States (D) was the attitude of an earlier generation of white Southerners, including Thomas Jefferson. That slavery was a national sin (E) and should be immediately abolished (B) was the view of the Abolitionists, a minority even in the North during this period.

14.   **(D)**

Farmers and planters in the South enjoyed high crop prices and sustained prosperity during the 1850s. Crops were large (C) and prices were high and steady (A) and (B). Southerners saw this as a sign of the superiority of their slave economy over that of the North, hard hit as it was by the Panic of 1857 (E).

15.   **(A)**

For whatever reasons, immigrants of the "New Immigration" tended to settle in the large cities of the Northeast and Midwest. Very few of them settled on farms (B), filed on homesteads (C), or migrated to the South and Southwest (D). While some eventually returned to their countries of origin, the majority did not (E).

16.   **(B)**

Germany's 1917 declaration of its intent to wage unrestricted submarine warfare was the most important factor in bringing the United States into World War I. German violation of Belgian neutrality in 1914 (A) did nothing to aid Germany's cause in America, and revelation of Germany's suggestions to Mexico (C) was even more damaging, but neither of these had the impact of the U-boats. The fall of the Tsar and beginning of the Russian Revolution (D) may or may not have had an influence on President Woodrow Wilson, and the deteriorating situation for the Allies (E) was not fully known.

17.   **(A)**

The Berlin Airlift was Truman's response to the Soviet blockade of Berlin. Neither wartime destruction (B) nor a severe winter (C) would have necessitated such a measure and no such work stoppage (D) or flu epidemic (E) occurred.

18.   **(B)**

Mercantilists believed the government should seek to direct the economy so as to maximize exports. Mercantilists *did*, however, believe in government interference in the economy (A), high tariff barriers (E), and the possession of colonies (C). Exports, they asserted, must exceed imports, not the other way around (D).

19.   **(D)**

Americans' primary objection to the Stamp Act was its purpose of raising revenue from the Americans without the consent of their representatives. A few Americans and a future British prime minister mistook this for opposition to internal taxes only (A). The proposed tax rate was not ruinously high (C), and the British had previously imposed taxes on America (B). However, these had been taxes for the regulation of trade, which the colonists accepted (E), rather than the collection of revenue.

20.   **(D)**

In order to gain foreign recognition during the War for Independence, it was necessary for the United States to demonstrate a determination and potential to win independence. The U.S. could not have demonstrated financial stability (C) at this time, nor could it have made financial payments (A). It did not prove necessary to make either territorial (B) or trade (E) concessions to France.

21.   **(D)**

Garrison called for the immediate and uncompensated emancipation of all slaves. He was not particularly in favor of states' rights (E), and he definitely opposed either gradualism or compensation (A). He also opposed colonization (B). Though he opposed the congressional gag rule, its repeal was not his main issue of concern.

22.　　**(D)**

The congressional "gag rule" held that no antislavery petitions would be formally received by Congress. It did not directly govern the laws that could be considered (A) and (E) nor did it limit what a member could say outside of Congress (B). Anti-slavery materials sent through the mail would not be delivered to Southern addresses (C), but this was a separate matter.

23.　　**(A)**

Roosevelt's New Nationalism pertained to domestic reform. Unrelated was the fact that Roosevelt always favored an aggressive foreign policy (B) including the establishment of an overseas empire (D). He would, of course, have opposed either isolationism or the holding of the status quo (E). Though he gained a reputation as a trust-buster, Roosevelt was by no means in favor of breaking up all trusts and large business combinations (C).

24.　　**(C)**

It was FDR's predecessor, Herbert Hoover, who in 1932 established the Reconstruction Finance Corporation. In doing so, he broke with many leaders in the Republican party, including Secretary of the Treasury Andrew Mellon, who believed the government had no choice but to let the business cycle run its course. Roosevelt's New Deal contained every other element listed.

25.　　**(A)**

The Haymarket Incident involved the throwing of a bomb at Chicago police and a subsequent riot involving police and striking workers. There were plenty of scandals within the Grant administration (B), but this was not one of them. Allegations of corruption on the part of Republican presidential candidate James G. Blaine (C) were contained in the Mulligan Letters. The disastrous fire that called attention to the hazardous working conditions in some factories (D) was New York's Triangle Shirtwaist Company fire in 1909, in which 146 people, mostly young immigrant women, died. An early challenge to the authority of states to regulate the railroad industry (E) was contained in the Supreme Court case of *Munn v. Illinois*.

26.　　**(D)**

The comparative cost of moving a ton of goods was 2.25 cents per mile for the railroad and 11.86 cents per mile for roads. As railroads spread across the

United States in the nineteenth century, they connected urban and rural areas in a way that dramatically lowered the cost of transporting goods. Railroads covered great distances, were not limited to suppliers or markets located on rivers or canals, and could operate in all types of weather. Compared to roads, railroads were much more cost-efficient in moving goods. All of the other options are either incorrect or cannot be concluded from the information provided in the graph.

27.   **(A)**

The U.S. gained possession of the Philippines through the Spanish-American War. Cuba (B), though originally the primary issue of contention between Spain and the United States, was not annexed but rather granted its independence under the terms of the Platte Amendment. Hawaii (E) and the Panama Canal Zone (D) were acquired within a few years of the Spanish-American War but in unrelated incidents and not from Spain. Bermuda (C) has never been acquired by the United States.

28.   **(C)**

The Mayas and Aztecs developed advanced cultures prior to European contact. The Mayas built stone temples and huge monuments, or steles, carved with images of gods and sacred animals, frequently displaying the date in their unique numbering system. The priests created a calendar and wrote books in the glyph writing system, making paper from the bark of fig trees. The Mayas were among the world's most advanced cultures in their development of mathematics and astronomy. In mathematics, the Mayas utilized the zero, while in astronomy they determined an accurate solar year with 18 months of 20 days. Aztecs developed accurate calendars with a solar year of 365 days and a sacred year of 260 days and built massive pyramids and temples long before their contact with the Spanish conquistadores in the 1500s. The pyramid at Cholula held 15 percent more volume than the tallest Egyptian pyramid and was the largest structure in the Americas. The Aztecs also successfully developed agricultural methods, including intensive cultivation, irrigation, and the reclamation of wetlands. The productivity resulting from these methods resulted in a wealthy and populous nation-state.

29.   **(D)**

Bacon's followers were disgruntled at what they saw as the governor's refusal to protect their frontier area from Indian raids. The jailing of individuals or seizure of their property for failure to pay taxes during a time of economic hardship (A) was the source of Massachusetts' 1786 Shays' Rebellion. The under-representation of the backcountry areas in colonial legislatures (B) was an ongoing source of irritation in the colonial South. The mistreatment of former indentured servants by large planters (C) and the favoritism of Virginia's governor Berkeley to his clique of friends — though he almost certainly could not have manipulated tobacco prices himself (E) — may have been underlying causes but were not the immediate issue in dispute in Bacon's Rebellion.

30.   **(B)**

The Newburgh Conspiracy was composed of army officers disgusted with a central government too weak to collect taxes to pay them and their troops. Betrayal of the plans for the fort at West Point (A) was Benedict Arnold's treason. Resistance to the collection of federal excise taxes in western Pennsylvania (C) took the form of the Whiskey Rebellion of 1791. New England's threat to secede should the War of 1812 continue (D) was made at the 1814 Hartford Convention. Burr's strange plot (E) came to nothing.

31.   **(A)**

The Wilmot Proviso was intended to prohibit slavery in the area acquired through the Mexican War. Congress generally agreed that the United States would acquire some territory from the war (B). That California should be a free state while the rest of the Mexican Cession was reserved for slavery (C), that the status of slavery in the Mexican Cession should be decided on the basis of "Popular Sovereignty" (D), and that the Missouri Compromise line should be extended to the Pacific (E) were all suggestions for a compromise that might calm the furor aroused by the Wilmot Proviso.

32.   **(A)**

The Populists desired free coinage of silver. They also desired direct election of U.S. Senators, not necessarily an end to the electoral college (D). The Progressive movement, which followed Populism, favored the reform of child labor laws (B) and the use of modern science to solve social problems (C). In general, Populists were more likely to favor racial discrimination than to oppose it (E).

33.   **(A)**

The settlement-house workers were often young, affluent, college-educated women such as Jane Addams. Poor immigrants (B), disabled veterans (C), and illiterate workers (E) would have had less opportunity for such things. Idealistic young men (D) were apparently drawn to such enterprises in smaller numbers.

34.   **(B)**

In the 1857 case *Dred Scott v. Sanford* the Supreme Court held that no black slave could be a citizen of the United States. It was in the 1954 case *Brown v.*

Topeka Board of Education that the court held separate facilities for the races to be unconstitutional (A). The reverse (C) was the court's holding in the 1896 case *Plessy v. Ferguson*. Literacy tests were overturned (E) in the 1960s, and Affirmative Action was limited (D) in the 1970s and '80s.

35.   **(C)**

The Whigs turned on Tyler because he opposed their entire legislative program. He did speak out in favor of Texas annexation (B) and he seemed to favor expansion of slavery (E); but these offenses would have been relatively minor in Whig eyes by comparison.

36.   **(C)**

O'Sullivan spoke of America's "manifest destiny to overspread the continent." The idea that America must eventually become either all slave or all free (D) was expressed by Lincoln in his "House Divided" speech and was called by William H. Seward the "Irrepressible Conflict." Racial equality (A) was still not a popular idea when O'Sullivan wrote in the first half of the nineteenth century. By that time, of course, America was already an independent country (B), but the desire for overseas possessions (E) was still half a century off.

37.   **(D)**

Mexico did expect to win the war, invade the U.S., and dictate a peace in Washington, but whatever desire, if any, the Mexicans may have had for the state of Louisiana was not a factor in the coming of the war. The U.S. did, however, desire to annex California (A) and did annex Texas (C); Mexico did refuse to pay its debts (B) and did claim Texas (C); and the southern boundary of Texas was in dispute (E). All of these contributed to the coming of the war.

38.   **(A)**

The colony at Jamestown was founded primarily for economic gain, though a secondary motive was desire to increase the power and glory of Great Britain (E). Desire for religious freedom in some form (B) was the motivation of the settlers of Plymouth and some of those who settled Maryland and Pennsylvania. Desire to create a perfect religious commonwealth as an example to the rest of the world (C) was the motive for the Massachusetts Bay colony; and desire to recreate in the New World the sort of feudalistic society that was fading in the Old (D) was probably a motive of some of the colonial proprietors such as those of the Carolinas.

39.   **(D)**

The Gulf of Tonkin Incident led to major U.S. involvement in the Vietnam War. In the Gulf of Sidra during the 1980s two clashes occurred involving the shooting down of Libyan, not Vietnamese, jets approaching U.S. ships (B). Off the coast of North Korea in 1968, Korean, not Vietnamese, forces seized the U.S. Navy intelligence ship *Pueblo* (C). In an incident in the Persian Gulf in 1987 the U.S. Navy frigate, not destroyer, *Stark*, was struck by a guided missile fired by an Iraqi, not North Vietnamese, plane (E).

40.   **(C)**

The SALT I Treaty indicated U.S. acceptance of the concept of Mutual Assured Destruction. It was ratified by the U.S. Senate (D) — unlike the SALT II Treaty — but did not bring substantial reductions in the number of missiles on either side (A), nor did it require the Soviet Union to reduce the number of its missiles to a level of equality with the United States (E). It discouraged the deployment of defensive weapons (B).

41.   **(E)**

Lincoln's Ten Percent Plan provided for the restoration of loyal government in states formerly in rebellion. It did not require that any of the former slaves be given the right to vote (A). It allowed Southerners to participate in the political process provided they would take an oath of future, not past (B), loyalty to the Union and acceptance of the abolition of slavery (D). High-ranking Confederates were excepted from this provision (C) and had to apply separately to the president for pardon.

42.   **(C)**

Johnson did not require former Confederate states to pay reparations. He did, however, recommend they extend the franchise to Blacks (A), and he did require them to ratify the Thirteenth Amendment (B), renounce secession (D), and repudiate the Confederate debt (E).

43.   **(C)**

"Normalcy" meant an end to idealist crusades and reformist agitation, definitely not a renewal of the Progressivist reform movement (A), a return to domestic reform (B), the establishment of new norms of international behavior (D) as Woodrow Wilson had tried to do, or U.S. membership in the League of Nations (E).

44.   **(A)**

Many American intellectuals of the 1920s expressed a sense of alienation for a country whose manners and direction they found distasteful. They tended to be more cynical than either romantic (C) or complacent (B), and many became expatriates while few if any could be called patriotic (D) or pietistic (E).

45.   **(C)**

Harding made misjudgments about the men around him. He was definitely not a Progressive (D). His administration's greatest accomplishments were in the field of foreign policy (B). He was sociable and talkative (E), unlike his quiet and taciturn vice president Calvin Coolidge, and he was apparently a personally honest man (A).

46.   **(D)**

"Yellow journalism" is the reporting of the news in an exaggerated, distorted, and sensationalized manner. The Muckrakers focused on corruptions and abuses in government and big business (C). While popular concern in one part of the country or another might from time to time focus on the supposed dangers of Chinese immigration (A) or Japanese power (B), and while a large corporation might occasionally have a paper as its mouthpiece (E), none of these characterized a school of journalism in itself.

47.   **(C)**

Roosevelt felt the good trusts should be tolerated and the bad controlled. Despite his reputation as the trust-buster, Roosevelt was by no means in favor of eliminating all trusts (A) and (E). Trusts of which he tended to take a particularly dim view were those in the railroad, oil, and meatpacking industries (B) and (D).

48.   **(C)**

Boycotting British goods, known as non-importation, was the most effective American method of gaining repeal of undesirable acts of Parliament. Tarring and feathering tax agents (A), sending petitions to the king and Parliament (B), and even a certain amount of destruction of private property (D), and intimidation by threats (E) were tried, with more-or-less unsatisfactory results.

49.   **(B)**

Roosevelt declared a banking holiday, closing all banks to prevent anxious depositors from demanding their money and causing the banks to default.

Curtailing government spending and taxes (A) was the last thing Roosevelt wanted to do and would probably have had little effect on the immediate banking crisis at the time of Roosevelt's inauguration. Nationalizing banks (E) on the other hand would have been rather extreme and was probably seen by Roosevelt as politically inadvisable. Banning fractional reserve banking (C) would at least have addressed the root problem but was as extreme in another direction and was not suggested by anyone in government at that time. A multibillion-dollar federal bailout (D) has been the federal government's response to the savings and loan crisis of the late 1980s and early 1990s.

50.   **(A)**

The Sherman Silver Purchase Act required the federal government to purchase a certain specified amount of silver each month (B). The president had no discretion in the matter (E). Private citizens were not directly affected by the Act (C) and (D).

51.   **(D)**

In response to a perceived insult to the U.S. flag and in order to hasten the downfall of Mexican leader Victoriano Huerta, Wilson ordered U.S. forces to occupy the port of Vera Cruz where the original incident had occurred. Anxious to be rid of Huerta, Wilson would probably not have considered a diplomatic protest (E) strong enough, though he did respond with such protests to German U-boat activities in the First World War. Wilson ordered Pershing into Mexico (A) two years later after Mexican bandit Pancho Villa had raided across the border into the United States. Wilson had never granted diplomatic recognition to Huerta's regime (B), and U.S. troops have not occupied Mexico City (C) since the end of the Mexican War in 1848.

52.   **(E)**

Restoration of the balance of power was not a part of Wilson's Fourteen Points. Instead Wilson favored collective security. Self-determination (A), open diplomacy (B), freedom of the seas (C), and a League of Nations (D) were all advocated in the Fourteen Points.

53.   **(C)**

Booker T. Washington encouraged his fellow Blacks to work hard, acquire property, and prove they were worthy of their rights. Washington's contemporary and critic W. E. B. du Bois urged his fellow Blacks to agitate questions of racial equality (A), be more militant in demanding their rights (B), not to accept separate but equal facilities (D), and to form an organization to advance the rights of Blacks (E).

54.   **(D)**

"Seward's Folly" was the name given to the purchase of Alaska. Seward had indeed believed that the Civil War could be avoided and the Union restored by provoking a war with Britain and France (C) — a foolish belief but not well known enough to gain a label. He had attempted to gain the presidency in 1860 and failed (E), though no one would have labeled his campaign a folly. Seward also favored a lenient policy toward the defeated South (A) and broke with the majority wing of his party to support President Andrew Johnson (B), though whether that was folly or courage remains debatable.

55.   **(C)**

Congress did not order the arrest and imprisonment of former Confederate leaders, often because many of them were protected by presidential pardons or the terms of their surrenders. It did, however, exclude Southern representatives (A), pass the Civil Rights Act (B), approve and send on to the states the Fourteenth Amendment (D), and put the South under army occupation and military rule (E).

56.   **(C)**

Johnson was impeached but was never removed from office (A) and (B). He did not resign, was not pardoned, and was never charged with a criminal offense (D). The vote on his removal from office was in fact taken (E) but fell short by one vote.

57.   **(E)**

Scalawags were Southerners who supported or participated in the Reconstruction regimes. Northerners who came south to take up positions with the Reconstruction governments (B) were called carpetbaggers. Blacks in high positions in the Reconstruction governments (A) were simply referred to by the common vulgar racial expression. There is no record of what Southerners called the Reconstruction military governors (C) or the Radical Republicans (D), but there was probably a variety of expressions.

58.   **(A)**

At the beginning of the Second World War in Europe, Americans were generally determined not to become involved. The public was by no means relieved (E), nor desirous that Roosevelt should take the U.S. into the war (C), but at no time was the public favorable to Germany (D). Desire to aid Britain came only later (B).

59.   **(E)**

The Bay of Pigs incident involved a U.S.-sponsored attempt by free Cubans to overthrow Communist dictator Fidel Castro. The presence of Soviet nuclear missiles in Cuba was at issue in the Cuban Missile Crisis. The CIA did, apparently, play a role in the 1973 overthrow of Chilean leader Salvador Allende (B) though this had no direct connection to the Bay of Pigs. The clash between a U.S. Navy destroyer and North Vietnamese patrol boats (D) was the Tonkin Gulf incident and related to the Vietnam War.

60.   **(A)**

The Treaty of Tordesillas (1494) was intended to divide the non-European world between Spain and Portugal. The French, English, and Dutch were left entirely out in the cold (B) and (D). As a result (though certainly not an intent!) of the treaty between Spain and Portugal, they did sometimes form common cause against the Spanish who dominated the New World (C). The Portuguese half of the world was mainly in the Eastern Hemisphere, but Portugal also received Brazil in the Western Hemisphere (E).

61.   **(C)**

There was a tendency to see the Depression as an emergency akin to war, and Roosevelt spoke of seeking such not constitutionally specified emergency powers as the president might be considered by some to have in wartime. None of the other possibilities listed were mentioned by Roosevelt, though calling on the American people to place pressure on their representatives in Congress (E) was used at times by President Ronald Reagan and, in effect, was undoubtedly also used by Roosevelt.

62.   **(C)**

One purpose of the Tea Act was to save the financially troubled East India Company, not so much for the sake of India (D) and (E) as for the sake of wealthy East India Company stockholders who also happened to be members of Parliament. Of course, with this purpose in mind, the British were anxious to increase the demand for and consumption of tea in America as much as possible (A) and (B).

63.   **(D)**

The greatest significance of the battle of Saratoga was that it persuaded France to give its open backing to the United States. Naturally, the British were still quite capable of carrying on the war (A) and mounting further invasions (B), and the Americans were still quite incapable of taking any part of Canada (C). Holland would never have considered entering the war on the side of the British in any case (E).

64.   **(B)**

Eli Whitney had an enormous influence on American history through his invention of the cotton gin. The steamboat (A) was invented by Whitney's contemporary Robert Fulton, the steam locomotive (E) and the telegraph (D) somewhat later in the nineteenth century, and the incandescent light bulb (C), by Thomas Edison, near the end of the century.

65.   **(B)**

The Virginia and Kentucky Resolutions were the centerpiece of the Republican response to the Alien and Sedition Acts. The 1814 Hartford Convention (C), on the other hand, was a Federalist response to Republican policies. South Carolina's nullification (A) was aimed at the highly protective Tariff of 1828. The 1854 Ostend Manifesto (D) dealt with U.S. desires to acquire Cuba from Spain, and the Mulligan Letters (E) incriminated 1884 Republican presidential candidate James G. Blaine in an unsavory stock scheme.

66.   **(B)**

The Puritans wanted to make Massachusetts an example to the rest of the world of what a true Bible commonwealth could be. Escaping persecution (A) was at most a secondary motivation, and desire for prosperity (C) would have come some place behind that. The Puritans, had they thought of such things, would have rejected the idea of separation of church and state (D) or the pluralistic society (E).

67.   **(E)**

The *absence* of anything like close or friendly relations with Great Britain did, in fact, help promote industrialization in America by spurring desire for protective tariffs (A) to make America economically independent of Great Britain. Industrialization was also boosted by improvements in transportation (B), which allowed goods to reach a larger market; large-scale immigration (C), which brought both workers and consumers; and the absence of craft organizations that would have tied artisans to a single trade and smothered economic creativity (D).

68.   **(D)**

The Specie Circular forbade the purchase of federal lands with anything but "specie" — hard money. Jackson's determination to rid the federal bureaucracy of inefficient and corrupt workers (A) is generally associated with his so-called "spoils system." His determination to collect the tariff in South Carolina (E) is associated with the Nullification Controversy. He also withdrew federal funds from the Bank of the United States (B) and opposed the spending of federal funds for internal improvements (C).

69.   **(C)**

Marbury v. Madison asserted for the first time the Supreme Court's right to declare an act of Congress unconstitutional. It did not, however, go so far as to claim that the Supreme Court alone was empowered to say what the Constitution meant (B). In the decision of this case, Chief Justice John Marshall wisely avoided issuing a directive (A) that President Thomas Jefferson would have defied (D) had it been issued. The case did not bring any major political realignment (E).

70.   **(B)**

As part of the 1820 Missouri Compromise, all of the Louisiana Territory north of 36° 30'— that is, the southern (A) boundary of most of Missouri — was closed (C) to slavery. According to the compromise this was to be permanent, though subsequent behavior on the part of some politicians — the 1854 Kansas-Nebraska Act — might lead one to believe the free areas had been left negotiable (D) or closed to slavery only for 30 years (E) — but such was not the case.

71.   **(B)**

The term "Trail of Tears" is used to describe the relocation of the Cherokee tribe from the southern Appalachians to what is now Oklahoma. The migration of Mormons from Nauvoo, Illinois, to the Great Salt Lake in Utah (A), the westward movements along the Oregon Trail (C) and, much earlier, the Wilderness Road (D), and the migration of German settlers into the Shenandoah Valley (E) — earlier still — all took place and could at times be as unpleasant as the Cherokees' trek. They were, however, voluntary and therefore did not earn such sad titles as the "Trail of Tears."

72.   **(C)**

The most forceful Southern protest against the high protective tariffs of the first half of the nineteenth century came in 1832 when South Carolina claimed that it had nullified — suspended the operation of — the tariff laws within its boundaries. The Hayne-Webster Debate (A) dealt with this and related issues, and the resignation of Vice President John C. Calhoun (D) may have been at least in part influenced by disagreements over tariffs. The Virginia and Kentucky Resolutions (B) were a protest against the Alien and Sedition Acts of the late 1790s, not the tariff, and the "gag rule" (E) dealt with slavery.

73.   **(B)**

The Morrill Land Grant Act provided large amounts of federal government land to states that would establish agricultural and mechanical colleges. It was the Homestead Act that granted 160-acre farms free to those who would settle on them (A). After the Civil War there was some talk of providing former slaves with "40 acres and a mule," but nothing came of it (C). Even without a special act of Congress to prevent it, in fact very little land of former Confederates was confiscated (D). Various acts of Congress and decisions of presidents throughout the 1800s dealt with the disposition of the Great Plains Indians (E).

74.   **(A)**

Roosevelt's court-packing plan called for the addition of up to six new justices if present justices over the age of 70 did not retire. While this would raise the *total* number of justices to 15, it is not to be confused with *adding* 15 new justices (D). Also, if those justices currently over 70 years of age did retire, no new justices would be added and the Supreme Court would continue to have nine, not 15 (E), members. Retirement of the justices was to be voluntary rather than mandatory (B), and while the general purpose was to remove or decrease the influence of justices who opposed the New Deal, political considerations, of course, prevented its being stated in those terms (C).

75.   **(B)**

Henry George definitely did not believe in laissez-faire government. He did, however, assert that increasing prosperity was causing increasing poverty (A), that economic inequality was the result of private land ownership (C), and that the government should wipe out this unfair advantage by a single tax on the "unearned" profits of land ownership (D), the money being used for various public works (E).

76.   **(E)**

Bellamy's book was a futuristic utopian fantasy, which, while it may have implied the desirability of certain social reforms, was not a detailed program for such reforms (B). The fictional exposé of the meatpacking industry (A) was Upton Sinclair's *The Jungle*. The best known denunciation of big-city machine politics (D) was Lincoln Steffens' The *Shame of the Cities*, both written, like Bellamy's book, in the late 1800s. During the same period, a number of books were written advancing the social gospel idea (C).

77.　　**(B)**

The income tax became law under Wilson. The Pure Food and Drug Act (A) was passed under Taft, and the Sherman Antitrust Act (E) under Benjamin Harrison. The old-age pension (D) had to wait for Franklin Roosevelt. High protective tariffs (C) have existed at a number of times throughout U.S. history. The Underwood Tariff passed under Wilson represented a lowering of tariff rates.

78.　　**(B)**

The Democrats were promised an end to Reconstruction as part of the Compromise of 1877. Protective tariffs remained high (D), compensation was not paid for freed slaves (E), bribes were neither sought nor given (C), and, of course, no promise was made concerning future elections (A).

79.　　**(A)**

At the time of Pearl Harbor, the U.S. was partially prepared after more than a year of the nation's first peacetime draft (C) and (E) and had an army of some 1.6 million men (D). Much, however, remained to be done (B).

80.　　**(C)**

The percentage of farm workers dropped from about 40 percent in 1900 to less than 5 percent in 2000. As the United States became a more industrialized and urban nation in the twentieth century, the need for farm laborers decreased. While the United States was mainly an agricultural nation throughout the eighteenth and nineteenth centuries, by the beginning of the twenty-first century, farming was not a major sector of the American workforce. All of the other options are either incorrect or cannot be concluded from the evidence of the graph.

SECTION II

Sample Answer to Document-based Question

1.   In assessing guilt for the Mexican War, one must examine the factors that led to it, some of which, as President James K. Polk observed in his war message to Congress, predated it by 20 years. Chronic instability in Mexico had, in those years, resulted in a number of claims by American citizens for reimbursement by the Mexican government for debts owed and damages suffered during the country's frequent upheavals. These claims, amounting to several million dollars, Mexico declined to pay despite the finding of an international arbitrator. This was the first U.S. grievance against Mexico.

Mexico was not without grievances against the U.S., foremost of them the well-known expansionist tendencies that led Americans to desire increasing amounts of Mexican territory. U.S. Army expeditions had explored the territory of what was to become Mexico as early as the first decade of the nineteenth century, and more recently "Pathfinder" John C. Frémont had traveled Mexican lands on two Far West exploring trips. Of special interest to the Americans was California. Though gold had not yet been discovered, the region's other assets had aroused hopes of annexation in the U.S., and this desire was no secret.

Mexicans had therefore been prepared to see the 1836 revolt of the largely American settlers of their northern province of Texas as a Yankee plot to grab more Mexican land, and they believed their suspicions were confirmed when in 1845 Congress by joint resolution agreed to accept Texas' long-standing request to join the Union. Mexico, which had for 20 years threatened war in such an event, broke diplomatic relations with the United States and began making warlike preparations.

Newly inaugurated U.S. President James K. Polk had three concerns with regard to Mexico: 1) As indicated by Frémont's memoirs and Polk's own diary, he and his cabinet feared lest California, only weakly held by Mexico, should fall into the hands of Great Britain; 2) he was concerned that the legitimate claims of U.S. citizens against Mexico be satisfied; and 3) he was concerned about the disputed southern boundary of Texas. There Mexico claimed the land to the Nueces River, the old boundary of the province of Texas. This conflicted with what Congress had claimed in its resolution: "the territory…belonging to the Republic of Texas," which had for a decade claimed and maintained the Rio Grande as its southern and western boundary. To deal with these concerns Polk dispatched 1) Frémont on another western expedition with orders to help take California should war break out, 2) General Zachary Taylor with a military force to protect Texas against possible Mexican invasion, and 3) John Slidell on a mission to Mexico City to deal with all matters of disagreement between the two countries. Polk's diary reveals that Slidell was authorized to purchase California and New Mexico for a price of $10 million to $40 million.

Meanwhile, in Mexico, the government had changed again by yet another military coup. Anxious to gain popularity at home by hostility toward the U.S., the new president refused to receive Slidell, referring to his mission as "this new insult." On his return Slidell recommended to Polk that there was no alternative but to "take the redress of the wrongs and injuries which we have so long borne from Mexico into our own hands." Polk was inclined to agree, and when shortly thereafter news reached Washington of a clash between Taylor's troops and Mexicans in the disputed territory south of the Nueces, Polk presented to Congress his war message claiming that American blood had been shed on American soil.

A careful consideration of this evidence demonstrates that the allocation of guilt for the coming of the Mexican War is by no means as simple as those who complain of U.S. aggression would claim. Causes of the war can be traced to both sides — land-hunger on the U.S. side, belligerence and refusal to negotiate or pay legitimate claims on the Mexican. For all the American guilt, equal or greater Mexican guilt can be found. Therefore, the assertion that the Mexican War was an unprovoked and unjustifiable war of aggression and territorial aggrandizement cannot be maintained.

Sample Answers to Essay Questions

2.   At the outset of the Civil War, the overwhelming majority of Northerners saw the conflict as one to preserve the Union — nothing more. Congress went so far as to pass a resolution to this effect during the first year of the war. Yet as the war went on and sacrifices, both human and financial, continued to mount, its nature began to change — from limited to total — and as it did, so too did the goals of many of those in the North. Several reasons can be cited for this important shift of direction, and understanding them will also aid in understanding just what was the shift in attitudes they created.

More important than any other single man as a catalyst for this change was President Abraham Lincoln. His great political skills, his ability to sense what the public needed and what it would accept, and his knack for putting into words what his fellow countrymen felt but could not express, made his influence enormous during his lifetime and, in one sense, at least, even after it. It was Lincoln who first widened the conflict from a fight to save the Union to a war for a much further-reaching purpose. In September 1862 he issued his preliminary Emancipation Proclamation, declaring free all slaves in areas still in rebellion against the U.S. government as of January 1, 1863. Prior to issuing the proclamation, Lincoln had declared that his purpose in doing something of this sort would be purely for saving the Union, and that was at least part of his motive, since the proclamation was designed to keep Britain and France out of the war. Yet whether for diplomatic purposes or because his own ideas had altered, Lincoln had changed the very nature and goal of the war — from a limited war for the Union to a total war to end slavery, and, necessarily re-shape Southern society.

In doing so Lincoln was a little ahead of the Northern public, and in the congressional elections that fall, his party took losses. Yet the people gradually seemed to come around to the president's point of view. It may be the war itself that changed them. The huge sacrifices — the Civil War cost more American lives than all the rest of the country's wars put together — required some great purpose to make them meaningful. It was in expressing just such a purpose — giving meaning to the deaths of several thousand Northern soldiers interred at a military cemetery at Gettysburg, Pennsylvania, just over a year after the issuing of the preliminary Emancipation Proclamation, that Lincoln put into words what was coming more and more to be the view of Northerners. In his short but famous address he maintained that what was at stake was not just the Union, or even an end to slavery, but the future of representative government itself. He also expressed the hope that, the war won, the nation would experience a "new birth of freedom." That is, it would not simply be restored as it had been, but in a better, freer form. That the majority of Lincoln's fellow Northerners had come to think in these terms was demonstrated in the elections of 1864, when both Lincoln and a solidly Republican Congress were returned to office to press the war to its final conclusion and total Northern victory — with all that these things now entailed.

The final step in the evolving Northern outlook on the Civil War also involved Lincoln, though tragically, only by means of his assassination. Lincoln would have used a mild hand in reconstructing the South, but there were others, many of them in Congress, whose ideas for reconstruction were anything but mild. Lincoln's assassination, as it was at the hour of victory, convinced many in the North that severe and thoroughgoing measures were needed to change the nature of Southern society and even of the federal system itself in order to make such upheavals impossible and to extend freedom more fully to every American. Thus, the war to save the Union, did indeed become, in the minds of many Northerners, a war to create a more perfect Union.

3. In 1763 the inhabitants of the British colonies in North America were happy subjects of His Majesty King George III — proud to be Americans, but proud to be British too. Yet 13 years later the representatives of these colonists could produce a document denouncing this king for an entire list of grievous wrongs and stating the fact that their colonies were completely independent of king and mother country. And even this Declaration of Independence was, by the time it was issued, so commonplace to Americans that most of them took relatively little notice of it. Most of the War of Independence lay before them, and Yorktown was still five years off, yet a revolution of enormous proportions had taken place in the hearts and minds of Americans.

Ironically, this change was in response to a change in British colonial policy. With the end of the French and Indian War in 1763, the British government found itself in possession of a vast empire and determined to make something out of it. It was decided not only to tax the colonies — that had been done before — but to assert the right of Parliament to levy taxes on them without reference to the colonial legislatures, as had previously been the rule. The first such attempt was the 1765 Stamp Act. It drew violent protests from outraged Americans who saw in this a blow at the traditional wellspring of English liberty, the right to be taxed only by the consent of one's representatives — and the Americans were represented in the colonial legislatures and nowhere else. Non-importation, a boycott of all British goods, brought enough economic pressure to bear to obtain Parliament's repeal of the act. Yet significantly, Parliament at the same time passed the Declaratory Act, claiming a right to legislate for and, presumably, tax the Americans at will.

As the British government continued in measures intended to demonstrate this right — the 1768 Townshend Acts and the 1773 Tea Act — the colonists, under the persistent urging of such agitators as Samuel Adams of Massachusetts, came increasingly to believe that they were the targets of a conspiracy. The British would first establish the right to tax the colonists at will, and then gradually strip them of all the rights Englishmen had gained over the centuries through the use of the traditional right of no taxation without representation. This was all the easier to believe because there was at least some grain of truth in it. Through all this — the belief that the British prime minister, cabinet, and a majority of Parliament were conspiring to reduce them to slavery — Americans nevertheless maintained their confidence in the king. They believed him their true friend among the knaves and scoundrels of Parliament.

By the mid-1770s they had lost this illusion, and with it what remained of their loyalty to Great Britain. Heavy-handed efforts to enforce the Tea Act led to the 1773 Boston Tea Party. Parliament retaliated with the Coercive Acts (1774), closing the port of Boston and suspending self-government in Massachusetts. Considering the acts unconstitutional, Americans defied them as best they could and spent the winter of 1774–75 drilling their colonial militias, minutemen, for the expected confrontation with the British occupation forces the next spring. It came in April at Lexington and Concord, followed by Bunker Hill in June. In Philadelphia the Continental Congress adopted as its own the army that had fought these battles. It also adopted the last in a long line of petitions to the king. Respectfully, the Olive Branch petition, like its predecessors, pleaded with the king to intercede on behalf of his loyal subjects in America and put a stop to Parliament's designs on their liberties. As the winter of 1775–76 began, the Continental Army waited outside Boston to see what the British troops would do, and Americans all over the continent waited for the king's answer. It came indirectly. The king ignored the Olive Branch petition and instead gave his approval to the Prohibitory Act, declaring the colonists to be in rebellion, out of his protection, and liable to be made war on not only by British forces but by such foreign mercenaries as they might hire. Their illusions of the king's benevolence shattered, Americans were a receptive audience for Thomas Paine's *Common Sense* (January 1776) and its references to "the royal brute of Britain." By the following summer they had almost come to take their independence for granted before it was declared.

Thus, a revolution did occur in the hearts and minds of Americans, and if it was not completed before the war began, as Adams stated 42 years later, it was certainly so before the war ended or official independence was declared.

4.   The Populist Party's period of prominence represents a unique epoch in American history. From humble beginnings among the sharecroppers of the Farmers' Alliances in the South and the Plains states in the 1880s, it rocketed to a position of national prominence before plunging even more rapidly back into obscurity and, shortly thereafter, disintegration. Yet it left its mark on American politics, and ironically the speed of its demise was directly related to the impact it had.

It had its beginning as the political vehicle of the Farmers' Alliances, groups of poor farmers who felt themselves hopelessly mired in the system of share-cropping, crop-liens, and low farm-commodity prices. They tended to feel that the deck was stacked against them economically, and they desired government intervention in their favor. The Populist Party was to be their means of gaining this. Many of the farmers were in debt, and in order to make it easier for them to get out, they wanted the government to create inflation. Some toyed with the idea of achieving this with paper money, but the party eventually hit on the more politically acceptable scheme of getting the government to monetize silver and increase the money supply in that manner. The idea had the added bonus of bringing with it the support of Western silver-mining interests. So "free-coinage of silver" became the mainstay of the Populist program. The rest of the party's program was also designed to appeal to "the plain people" and included a graduated income tax, public ownership of railroads, and direct election of senators. In 1892 the party's presidential nominee, James B. Weaver, gained over a million votes, and the party made impressive showings in some state races.

However, in 1896 William Jennings Bryan and the free-silver wing of the Democrats captured that party's presidential nomination. The Populists were faced with the choice of campaigning against a proponent of their chief issue or throwing their support behind Bryan. They chose the latter course, and this was the key to their hasty demise: a major party had successfully incorporated their main issue. Bryan lost the election of 1896, but the Populist Party could not be resurrected. In a sense it was a victim of the flexibility and responsiveness of the American two-party system. Its adherents eventually drifted into one of the two major parties, mainly the Democratic party. How completely the Populists' drive was assimilated into the political system is demonstrated by the fact that both a graduated income tax and direct election of senators were established in 1913.

Thus, the Populist Party made a remarkable impact in the course of American politics, but as a party it failed and rapidly disappeared because one of the already existing parties was able to absorb its ideological thrust and most of its support.

5. At the end of the Second World War the coalition that had won it quickly broke apart and formed two hostile power systems. Numerous accusations have been made concerning the guilt for this polarization. The statement above represents the extreme pro-Soviet viewpoint in this debate. In order

to assess its validity, it is necessary to examine the facts surrounding the beginning of the Cold War.

As the Second World War in Europe ended, both the United States and the Soviet Union had large numbers of troops in Europe. In the years immediately following, the great majority of the U.S. troops were withdrawn as America hurried to get back to a peacetime economy and to the more pleasant pursuits of making money and enjoying leisure. The Soviet Union, on the other hand, maintained a large army in Eastern Europe and used it to carve out a Communist empire. Having already absorbed — and gained U.S. and British acceptance of — its conquests of Latvia, Lithuania, Estonia, one-third of Poland, and part of Finland while allied with Hitler, the Soviet Union then proceeded under the guns of the massive Red Army to erect puppet governments in Poland, Hungary, Czechoslovakia, Rumania, and Bulgaria, and more-or-less sympathetic governments in Yugoslavia and Albania. It refused to cooperate with the Allies in the reconstruction of Germany and instead turned its sector into the Communist state of East Germany. In 1949 it attempted to coerce an Allied surrender of Berlin through its Berlin Blockade. Meanwhile in Asia, the Soviet Union supported Mao Tse-Tung and his Communists in the conquest of China, annexed territory at the expense of Japan (with whom it had been at war for only a matter of weeks), and trained and equipped the North Korean army with offensive weapons for its 1950 war of aggression against South Korea.

On the other hand, the United States, far from taking an aggressive course toward the Soviet Union, actually showed itself to be remarkably tolerant. Except for a few stern words, no resistance whatsoever was offered by the United States to the systematic Soviet program of conquest until 1947, when President Harry S. Truman announced his "Truman Doctrine" of aid to states threatened with Communist takeover and extended such aid to Greece and Turkey. In the face of the highly provocative Berlin Blockade, Truman responded not with military action, though treaty obligations would have justified him in doing so, but with the Berlin Airlift, designed to avoid — rather than create or win — confrontation. The Soviet-sponsored North Korean war against South Korea was so successful in its early days largely because the

United States, unlike the Soviet Union in North Korea, had allowed South Korea to have only a small and lightly equipped army.

In view of these facts, it seems much more accurate to say that the Soviet Union, rather than the United States, was responsible for creating the Cold War through its aggessive policies. The above statement must therefore be rejected as not compatible with historical fact.

PRACTICE TEST 2
AP United States States History

AP United States History

PRACTICE TEST 2

SECTION I

TIME: 55 Minutes
80 Questions

> **DIRECTIONS:** Each of the questions or incomplete statements below is followed by five suggested answers or completions. Select the one that is best in each case.

1. The Farmers' Alliances of the 1880s appealed primarily to

    (A) small farmers in the Northeast who found themselves unable to compete with large Western farms

    (B) Southern and Great Plains farmers frustrated with low crop prices and mired in the sharecrop and crop lien systems

    (C) established and well-to-do farmers who desired to limit production in order to sustain high prices

    (D) owners of the giant "bonanza" farms of the northern plains states who sought special advantages from the government

    (E) Chinese immigrants serving as agricultural workers with low pay and poor working conditions, primarily in the Eastern states

2. All of the following were among President Andrew Jackson's objections to the First Bank of the United States EXCEPT

    (A) it allowed the economic power of the government to be controlled by private individuals

    (B) it threatened the integrity of the democratic system

(C)   it was preventing the government from achieving its policy of creating inflation

(D)   it could be used irresponsibly to create financial hardship for the nation

(E)   it benefited a small group of wealthy and privileged persons at the expense of the rest of the country

3.   After 45 years of conflict, a series of developments in the 1990s showed improvement in relations between Israel and the Palestine Liberation Organization. Which of the following did not occur in the 1990s?

(A)   An agreement on Palestinian autonomy

(B)   Washington, D.C., ceremony signing an agreement to expand Palestinian West Bank self-rule

(C)   Israel and Jordan formally end the state of war between them

(D)   Egypt and Israel sign the Camp David Accords

(E)   In Cairo, leaders Yasir Arafat, Hosni Mubarek and Yitzhak Rabin condemn violence

4.   During the Congressional campaigns in 1994, a year in which Republicans would take control of both houses of Congress, Newt Gingrich and 300 other Republican House candidates dramatically pledged to pass

(A)   health care reform

(B)   a Contract with America

(C)   social welfare legislation

(D)   increased funding for education

(E)   new civil rights measures

5.   One mound-building culture, Cahokia, supported perhaps 40,000 people near what modern-day city?

(A)   New York City

(B)   Mexico City

(C)   St. Louis

(D)   Seattle

(E)   Miami

6.   Which of the following factors came closest to giving the Confederacy what could have been a decisive foreign policy success during the Civil War?

(A)   The U.S. Navy's seizure of Confederate emissaries James M. Mason and John Slidell from the British mail steamer *Trent*

(B)   French objections to the Union blockade

(C)   The acute economic dislocation in Britain and France caused by the cut-off of cotton imports from the South

(D)   The concerns of French financial interests that had loaned large amounts of money to the Confederacy

(E)   The skillful negotiating of Confederate diplomats in Europe

7.   The following map depicts the United States as it was immediately after which of the following events?

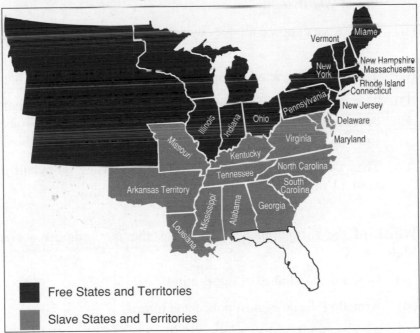

(A)   Passage of the Compromise of 1850

(B)   Passage of the Missouri Compromise

(C)   Passage of the Northwest Ordinance

(D)   Settlement of the Mexican War

(E)   Negotiation of the Webster-Ashburton Treaty

8. The 1932 demonstration known as the "Bonus March" involved

    (A) farmers disgruntled about low prices for meat, grain, and dairy products

    (B) homeless persons building shantytowns near Washington, D.C.

    (C) Japanese-Americans protesting forced relocation from the West Coast

    (D) World War I veterans demanding financial aid from the federal government

    (E) migrant farm workers seeking employment in California

9. Which of the following statements is true about the case of Julius and Ethel Rosenberg?

    (A) They were accused of giving atomic secrets to Germany during World War II.

    (B) They were exposed as spies by former Communist agent Whitaker Chambers.

    (C) They were convicted of espionage, condemned, and electrocuted.

    (D) They were convicted but were later pardoned by President Eisenhower because public opinion did not favor harsh treatment of accused Communist spies.

    (E) They confessed to having carried out espionage on behalf of the Soviet Union.

10. Which of the following best describes the methods advocated by Malcolm X?

    (A) Nonviolent defiance of segregation

    (B) Armed violence against police and troops

    (C) Patience while developing the skills that would make Blacks economically successful and gain them the respect of Whites

    (D) Gradual assimilation of the two races until they became indistinguishable

    (E) Meek acceptance of "Jim Crowism" until increasingly enlightened Southern Whites were prepared to change it

11. In 1960 which of the following contributed most directly to Soviet leader Nikita Khrushchev's cancellation of a scheduled summit meeting with President Dwight Eisenhower?

(A) The rise to power of Fidel Castro in Cuba

(B) The failure, at the Bay of Pigs, of a U.S.-sponsored attempt to oust Castro

(C) The sending of U.S. troops to Lebanon

(D) The downing of an American U-2 spy plane over the Soviet Union

(E) The success of the Soviet space program in launching the Sputnik satellite

12. Which of the the following was most responsible for the change shown between 1815 and 1830?

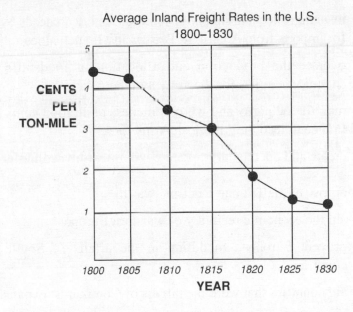

Average Inland Freight Rates in the U.S.
1800–1830

CENTS PER TON-MILE

YEAR

(A) The development of practical steam-powered railroad trains

(B) The development of a network of canals linking important cities and waterways

(C) The growth in the nation's mileage of improved roads and turnpikes

(D) Improvements in the design of keelboats and flatboats

(E) The development of steamboats

13. During the period of Reconstruction, most of the states of the former Confederacy, in order to regain admission to the Union, were required to

    (A) grant Blacks all the civil rights that Northern states had granted them before the war

    (B) ratify the Fourteenth Amendment

    (C) provide integrated public schools

    (D) ratify the Sixteenth Amendment

    (E) provide free land and farming utensils for the recently freed slaves

14. The primary function of the Food Administration during the First World War was to

    (A) keep farm prices high by limiting the amount of food produced on American farms

    (B) insure an adequate supply of food for American needs by arranging for imports from America's British and French allies

    (C) oversee the production and allocation of foodstuffs to assure adequate supplies for the army and the Allies

    (D) monitor the purity and wholesomeness of all food items shipped to France to feed the American Army there

    (E) create and operate large-scale government-owned farms

15. The purpose of the Truman Doctrine was to

    (A) aid the economic recovery of war-torn Europe

    (B) prevent European meddling in the affairs of South American countries

    (C) aid countries that were the targets of Communist expansionism

    (D) reduce the dependence of the European economy on overseas empires

    (E) expand the Monroe Doctrine to include Eastern Asia

16. The Molasses Act was intended to enforce England's mercantilist policies by

    (A) forcing the colonists to export solely to Great Britain

    (B) forcing the colonists to buy sugar from other British colonies rather than from foreign producers

(C) forbidding the colonists to engage in manufacturing activity in competition with British industries

(D) providing a favorable market for the products of the British East India Company

(E) creating an economic situation in which gold tended to flow from the colonies to the mother country

17. The British government imposed the Townshend Acts on the American colonies in the belief that

(A) the American position regarding British taxation had changed

(B) it was necessary to provoke a military confrontation in order to teach the colonists a lesson

(C) its provisions were designed solely to enforce mercantilism

(D) it had been approved by the colonial legislatures

(E) the Americans would accept it as external rather than internal taxation

18. In his famous "Freeport Doctrine" set forth in his debate with Abraham Lincoln at Freeport, Illinois, Stephen A. Douglas stated that

(A) any territory desiring to exclude slavery could do so simply by declining to pass laws protecting it

(B) any state wishing to secede from the Union could do so simply by the vote of a special state constitutional convention

(C) no state had the right to obstruct the operation of the Fugitive Slave Act by the passage of "personal liberty laws"

(D) the Dred Scott decision prohibited any territorial legislature from excluding slavery until a state constitution was drawn up for approval by Congress

(E) any slaveholder was free to take his slaves anywhere within the United States without hindrance by state, federal, or territorial governments

19. Government subsidies for the building of transcontinental railroads during the nineteenth century mainly took the form of

(A) large cash payments based on the mileage of track built

(B) a one-time blanket appropriation for the building of each separate transcontinental line

(C) generous land grants along the railroad's right-of-way

(D) the option of drawing supplies and materials from government depots

(E) the provision of large amounts of convict labor at no charge to the railroad company

20. During William H. Taft's administration, the federal government moved to strengthen its regulatory control over the railroad industry by

(A) passage of the Mann-Elkins Act

(B) creation of the Federal Trade Commission

(C) passage of the "Granger Laws"

(D) taking over and operating the railroads

(E) removal of former legal obstacles to consolidation of the railroads into giant corporations

21. Which of the following regions was most heavily represented among immigrants to the United States during the years from 1865 to 1890?

(A) Northern and Western Europe

(B) Southern and Eastern Europe

(C) Asia

(D) Africa

(E) Central and South America

22. The slogan "Fifty-four forty or fight" had to do with

(A) the so-called "Aroostook War," involving a boundary dispute between Maine and New Brunswick

(B) the demand for the annexation of all of the Oregon country

(C) the demand for the readjustment of the boundary with Mexico

(D) the demand by free-soil Northerners that some limit be placed on the spread of slavery in the territories

(E) the demand by Southerners that the Missouri Compromise line be extended through the Mexican Cession

23. All of the following statements are true of William H. Taft EXCEPT:

(A) He was an able and efficient administrator.

(B)   He was little inclined to making rousing speeches or engage in po-litical conflict.

(C)   He reversed Theodore Roosevelt's conservationist policies.

(D)   He disliked publicity.

(E)   His administration was more active in prosecuting trusts than Roosevelt's had been.

24.   The primary issue in dispute in Shays' Rebellion was

(A)   the jailing of individuals or seizure of their property for failure to pay taxes during a time of economic hardship

(B)   the underrepresentation of western Massachusetts in the state legis-lature leading to accusations of "taxation without representation"

(C)   the failure of Massachusetts to pay a promised postwar bonus to soldiers who had served in its forces during the Revolution

(D)   the failure of Massachusetts authorities to take adequate steps to protect the western part of the state from the depredations of raiding Indians

(E)   economic oppression practiced by the banking interests of eastern Massachusetts

25.   All of the following were weaknesses of the Articles of Confederation government EXCEPT:

(A)   It lacked the power to levy taxes.

(B)   It lacked the power to regulate commerce.

(C)   It lacked the power to borrow money.

(D)   It could not compel the states to abide by the terms of international treaties it had made.

(E)   It lacked a strong executive.

26.   Congress's most successful and effective method of financing the War of Independence was

(A)   printing large amounts of paper money

(B)   obtaining grants and loans from France and the Netherlands

(C)   levying heavy direct taxes

(D) issuing paper securities backed by the promise of western land grants

(E) appealing to the states for voluntary contributions

27. All of the following are true statements of the Compromise of 1850 EXCEPT:

(A) It provided for the admission of California to the Union as a free state.

(B) It included a tougher fugitive slave law.

(C) It prohibited slavery in the lands acquired as a result of the Mexican War.

(D) It stipulated that land in dispute between the state of Texas and the territory of New Mexico should be ceded to New Mexico.

(E) It ended the slave trade in the District of Columbia.

28. A member of the Social Gospel movement would probably

(A) consider such social sins as alcohol abuse and sexual permissiveness as society's most serious problems

(B) assert that the poor were themselves at fault for their circumstances

(C) maintain that abuses and social degradation resulted solely from a lack of willpower on the part of those who committed them

(D) hold that religion is an entirely individualistic matter

(E) argue that Christians should work to reorganize the industrial system and bring about international peace

29. In its decision in the case of *Plessy v. Ferguson*, the Supreme Court held that

(A) separate facilities for different races were inherently unequal and therefore unconstitutional

(B) no black slave could be a citizen of the United States

(C) separate but equal facilities for different races were constitutional

(D) affirmative action programs were acceptable only when it could be proven that specific previous cases of discrimination had occurred within the institution or business in question

(E) imposition of a literacy test imposed an unconstitutional barrier to the right to vote

30. Henry Clay's "American System" advocated all of the following EXCEPT

    (A) federal funding for the building of roads

    (B) a national bank

    (C) high protective tariffs

    (D) an independent treasury

    (E) federal funding for the building of canals

31. Which of the following groups was the first target of congressional legislation restricting immigration expressly on the basis of national origin?

    (A) Northern and Western Europeans

    (B) Chinese

    (C) Italians

    (D) Africans

    (E) Latin Americans

32. The main issue of the 1850s Free-Soil party was that

    (A) the federal government should permit no further spread of slavery in the territories

    (B) a homestead act should be passed, granting 160 acres of government land in the West free to anyone who would settle on it and improve it for five years

    (C) the federal government should oversee immediate and uncompensated abolition of slavery

    (D) freed slaves should be provided with 40 acres and two mules to provide them the economic means of independent self-support

    (E) the United States should annex Cuba

33. The most controversial portion of Alexander Hamilton's economic program was

    (A) federal assumption of state debts

    (B) assessment of direct taxes on the states

(C) creation of the Bank of the United States

(D) imposition of high protective tariffs

(E) establishment of a bimetallic system

34. In the Nullification Controversy, some Southerners took the position that

(A) the federal government had the right to nullify state laws that interfered with the right to hold property in slaves

(B) the federal courts had the right to nullify acts of Congress that restricted the spread of slavery in the territories

(C) the states had the right to nullify acts of the federal government they deemed to be unconstitutional

(D) Southern states had the right to nullify statutes of Northern states interfering with the recapture of escaped slaves

(E) Congress should refuse to receive any petitions against slavery

35. The Mayflower Compact could best be described as

(A) a detailed frame of government

(B) a complete constitution

(C) a business contract

(D) a foundation for self-government

(E) an enumeration of the causes for leaving England and coming to the New World

36. All of the following statements about the Taft-Hartley Act are true EXCEPT:

(A) It had long been the goal of a number of large labor unions.

(B) It allowed the president to call an eight-day cooling-off period to delay any strike that might endanger national safety or health.

(C) It outlawed the closed shop.

(D) It was backed by congressional Republicans.

(E) It was vetoed by President Truman.

37. Which of the following statements is true of the Wade-Davis Bill?

    (A) It allowed restoration of a loyal government when as few as ten percent of a state's prewar registered voters swore future loyalty to the Union and acceptance of emancipation.

    (B) It explicitly required that the vote be accorded to the recently freed slaves.

    (C) It allowed high-ranking rebel officials to regain the right to vote and hold office by simply promising future good behavior.

    (D) It was pocket-vetoed by Lincoln.

    (E) It provided substantially more lenient terms of reconstruction than those favored by Lincoln.

38. Sinclair Lewis generally depicted small-town America as

    (A) an island of sincerity amid the cynicism of American life

    (B) the home of such traditional virtues as honesty, hard work, and wholesomeness

    (C) merely a smaller-scale version of big-city life

    (D) dreary, prejudiced, and vulgar

    (E) open and accepting but naive and easily taken in

39. As president, Calvin Coolidge generally

    (A) favored large government building projects

    (B) urged Congress to raise taxes

    (C) kept government spending low and encouraged private business

    (D) took an active role in pushing legislation through Congress

    (E) argued that the protective tariff should be lowered in order to provide a more healthy economic environment

40. A people who dominated a large kingdom in the Andes Mountains of Peru when the first Europeans arrived were the

    (A) Incas

    (B) Mayas

    (C)   Aztecs

    (D)   Mohecans

    (E)   Pueblos

41.   The Spanish-American War spurred building of the Panama Canal by

    (A)   demonstrating the need to shift naval forces quickly from the Atlantic to the Pacific

    (B)   demonstrating the ease with which Latin American countries could be overcome by U.S. military force

    (C)   discrediting congressional opponents of the project

    (D)   removing the threat that any possible canal could be blockaded by Spanish forces based in Cuba and Puerto Rico

    (E)   demonstrating that such tropical diseases as malaria and yellow fever could be controlled

42.   "We have nothing to fear but fear itself" is a statement from

    (A)   Woodrow Wilson's 1917 message to Congress asking for a declaration of war against Germany

    (B)   a speech by President Herbert Hoover two weeks after the October 1929 stock market crash

    (C)   Franklin D. Roosevelt's first inaugural address

    (D)   Franklin D. Roosevelt's message to Congress asking for a declaration of war against Japan, December 8, 1941

    (E)   Harry S. Truman's announcement of the dropping of the atomic bomb on Hiroshima

43.   All of the following statements about the Civilian Conservation Corps are true EXCEPT:

    (A)   Its members lived in camps, wore uniforms, and were under semi-military discipline.

    (B)   It engaged in such projects as preventing soil erosion and impounding lakes.

(C) It eventually came to employ over one-third of the American work force.

(D) It provided that some of the workers' pay should be sent home to their families.

(E) It was part of President Franklin D. Roosevelt's New Deal.

44. In personally taking over the task of setting the dollar amount the government would pay for gold, Franklin Roosevelt's announced purpose was to

(A) maintain the value of the dollar at a constant level

(B) prevent inflation

(C) prevent a run on the banks, which would be likely to deplete the nation's gold supply dangerously

(D) manipulate the price of gold so as to raise prices

(E) revise the value of the dollar so as to force prices down to affordable levels in America's depressed economy

45. The underlying issue that led to the outbreak of war between the United States and Japan in 1941 was

(A) Japanese aid to the Germans in their war against Britain

(B) U.S. desire to annex various Pacific islands held by Japan

(C) Japanese desire to annex the Aleutian Islands

(D) Japanese desire to annex large portions of China

(E) American resentment of Japanese trading policies and trade surpluses

46. In the *Arabic* Pledge of 1916 Germany promised not to

(A) aid Mexico in any war against the United States

(B) attempt to buy war materials in the United States

(C) use submarines for any purpose but reconnaissance

(D) attempt to break the British blockade

(E) sink passenger ships without warning

47. In the negotiations leading to the Treaty of Versailles, Woodrow Wilson was willing to sacrifice other portions of his Fourteen Points in order to gain Allied approval of

   (A) a ban on secret diplomacy

   (B) a strengthening of the Austrian Empire in order to restore the balance of power

   (C) a union of Germany and Austria in accordance with the right of self-determination of peoples

   (D) new rules of blockade that would provide more complete freedom of the seas

   (E) a League of Nations

48. Which of the following is true of W. E. B. Du Bois?

   (A) He founded the National Association for the Advancement of Colored People.

   (B) He was the chief author of the Atlanta Compromise.

   (C) He was an outspoken critic of the Niagara Movement.

   (D) He believed that Blacks should temporarily accommodate themselves to Whites.

   (E) He worked closely with Booker T. Washington.

49. In response to President Andrew Johnson's relatively mild reconstruction program, the Southern states did all of the following EXCEPT

   (A) refuse to repudiate the Confederate debt

   (B) elect many former high-ranking Confederates to Congress and other top positions

   (C) refuse to grant Blacks the right to vote

   (D) attempt to reinstitute slavery

   (E) pass special "Black codes" restricting the legal rights of Blacks

50. Andrew Johnson was impeached and nearly removed from office on the grounds of his

   (A) refusal to carry out the provisions of the Military Reconstruction Act

   (B) alleged involvement in a corrupt stock-manipulating scheme carried out by one of his associates

(C) refusal to carry out the provisions of the Civil Rights Act of 1866

(D) violation of the Tenure of Office Act in removing Secretary of War Edwin M. Stanton

(E) general failure to cooperate with the Radical Republicans in their efforts to carry out Reconstruction

51. In speaking of "redemption" in a political sense, white Southerners of the Reconstruction era made reference to

(A) ridding the South of the Reconstruction governments

(B) atoning for their society's sin of slavery by granting full legal and social equality to Blacks

(C) atoning for the Southern states' secession by displaying extreme patriotism to the restored United States

(D) regaining personal rights of citizenship by taking an oath of allegiance to the Union

(E) buying back from the federal government plantations confiscated during the war

52. The primary underlying reason that Reconstruction ended in 1877 was that

(A) Southerners had succeeded in electing anti-Reconstruction governments in all the former Confederate states

(B) all the goals set by the Radical Republicans at the end of the Civil War had been accomplished

(C) leading Radicals in the North had become convinced that Reconstruction had been unconstitutional

(D) Northern voters had grown weary of the effort to Reconstruct the South and generally lost interest

(E) Republican political managers had come to see further agitation of North-South differences arising from the Civil War as a political liability

53. In the Second World War the Allied strategy, agreed upon by the U.S. and Great Britain, was to

(A) concentrate on defeating Japan first before turning on Germany

(B) divide all resources equally between the war against Japan and that against Germany

(C)   fight only against Japan, leaving the Russians to fight Germany alone

(D)   take a passive role and limit operations to reacting to Axis moves

(E)   concentrate on defeating Germany first before turning on Japan

54.   The Marshall Plan was

(A)   a strategy for defeating Germany

(B)   a strategy for defeating Japan

(C)   an American economic aid program for Europe

(D)   an American commitment to give military and economic aid to any nation resisting Communist aggression

(E)   a civil-defense plan for surviving a Soviet nuclear strike

55.   Which of the following was the most important factor in John F. Kennedy's 1960 presidential election victory over Richard Nixon?

(A)   Americans' deep and growing dissatisfaction with the Eisenhower Administration

(B)   Revelations of corrupt activities on the part of Nixon

(C)   Kennedy's better showing in nationally televised debates

(D)   Kennedy's long record of administrative experience as governor of Massachusetts

(E)   Nixon's failure to serve in the armed forces during the Second World War

56.   After concluding its investigation of the assassination of President John F. Kennedy, the Warren Commission announced its finding that

(A)   Lee Harvey Oswald acted alone in assassinating the president

(B)   Oswald was assisted by two other marksmen on the "grassy knoll" in front of the presidential motorcade

(C)   Oswald had been the only gunman but was part of a widespread conspiracy

(D)   Oswald in fact had nothing to do with the assassination

(E) the true facts of the assassination and any possible conspiracy involved with it will probably never be known

57. The chief significance of French explorer Samuel de Champlain's alienation of the Iroquois Indians was

(A) to prevent the French from establishing a profitable fur trade in Canada

(B) to prevent Champlain from founding any permanent settlement along the St. Lawrence River

(C) to prevent Champlain from making it back to France alive

(D) to prevent New France from expanding southward into what is now the United States

(E) the creation of an alliance of British and French colonists against the Iroquois

58. In founding the colony of Pennsylvania, William Penn's primary purpose was to

(A) provide a refuge for persecuted English Quakers

(B) provide a refuge for persecuted Christians of all sects from all parts of Europe

(C) demonstrate the possibility and practicality of establishing truly friendly relations with the Indians

(D) make a financial profit

(E) provide a refuge for English debtors

59. During the first two decades under the United States Constitution, the main factor that separated Federalists from Republicans was

(A) whether they accepted the Constitution or opposed it

(B) whether they favored the French Revolution or opposed it

(C) whether they leaned more toward states' rights or national sovereignty

(D) their personal like or dislike for the personalities of Thomas Jefferson and Alexander Hamilton

(E)   whether they had been patriots or loyalists during the American War of Independence

60.   When colonial Massachusetts' Governor Thomas Hutchinson attempted to force the sale of taxed tea in Boston in 1773, Bostonians reacted with the

(A)   Boston Massacre

(B)   Boston Tea Party

(C)   Declaration of Independence

(D)   Articles of Confederation

(E)   Massachusetts Circular Letter

61.   The international incident known as the XYZ Affair involved

(A)   a French foreign minister's demand for a bribe before he would meet with American envoys

(B)   the British refusal to evacuate their forts on American territory

(C)   General Andrew Jackson's incursion into Spanish-held Florida

(D)   the British seizure of American crewmen from a U.S. Navy warship in Chesapeake Bay

(E)   Aaron Burr's secret plot to detach the western United States in order to create a new nation of which he would be ruler

62.   The most unusual feature of the charter of the Massachusetts Bay Colony was that it

(A)   provided that the colony should be run as a religious common-wealth

(B)   made the colony completely independent of all English authority

(C)   assured the colonists all the rights they would have had if they had been born and living in England

(D)   did not specify where the company's headquarters should be

(E)   specified that only Parliament, not the king, was to have authority over the colony

63. During the first two decades of the seventeenth century all of the following aided in the establishment and growth of the colony at Jamestown, Virginia, EXCEPT

    (A) the establishment of the Virginia House of Burgesses

    (B) the establishment of the ownership of private property

    (C) the beginning of tobacco cultivation

    (D) good relations with the local Indians

    (E) large influxes of supplies and colonists from England

64. The first religious development to have an impact throughout colonial America was

    (A) the establishment of religious toleration in Maryland

    (B) the spread of Quaker ideas from Pennsylvania

    (C) the Halfway Covenant

    (D) the Parsons' Cause

    (E) the Great Awakening

65. President Andrew Jackson's Maysville Road veto dealt with

    (A) federally financed internal improvements

    (B) foreign policy

    (C) the power of the Second Bank of the United States relative to that of other financial institutions

    (D) the efficiency and honesty of government employees

    (E) the purchase of government land with paper money

66. All of the following contributed to the coming of the War of 1812 EXCEPT

    (A) the *Chesapeake-Leopard* Incident

    (B) British impressment of American seamen from American ships on the high seas

    (C) the concerns of Western Americans that the Indian raids they suffered were being carried out with British encouragement

(D) the Congressional "War Hawks" desire to annex Canada

(E) the armed confrontation between U.S. and British forces along the Maine-Canada border

67. The Monroe Doctrine stated that the United States

(A) was not concerned with the type of government other countries might have

(B) was concerned only with the type of government that the countries of the Western Hemisphere might have

(C) would not tolerate any new European colonization in the New World

(D) claimed the Western Hemisphere as its exclusive zone of influence

(E) was prepared to drive out by force any European power that did not give up its colonies in the Western Hemisphere

68. The most divisive and controversial aspect of the slavery issue during the first half of the nineteenth century was

(A) the status of slavery in the District of Columbia

(B) the right of abolitionists to send their literature through the U.S. mail

(C) the enforcement of the draconian Fugitive Slave Law

(D) the status of slavery in the territories

(E) the prohibition of the international slave trade

69. When President Andrew Jackson's enemies spoke of the "Kitchen Cabinet" they were referring to

(A) a group of old friends and unofficial advisors of the president

(B) a number of persons of low social standing, including a former cook, who were appointed by Jackson to high cabinet positions

(C) a suggestion as to where Jackson might keep the federal government's money if he removed it from the Bank of the United States

(D) a coterie of Jackson supporters in the U.S. Senate

(E) several state governors who supported Jackson

70. The 1840s Pre-emption Act, signed by President John Tyler, provided that

    (A) the status of slavery in a territory was to be decided by the settlers there

    (B) slave law pre-empted free law in disputes involving escaped slaves

    (C) settlers who had squatted on government land would have first chance to buy it

    (D) the vice president automatically became president upon the death of the president

    (E) federal law pre-empted state law in matters pertaining to slavery

71. The Homestead Act provided

    (A) that Indians should henceforth own their lands as individuals rather than collectively as tribes

    (B) 160 acres of free land within the public domain to any head of household who would settle on it and improve it over a period of five years

    (C) large amounts of federal government land to Great Plains cattle ranchers who would contract to provide beef for the Union army

    (D) 40 acres of land to each former slave above the age of 21

    (E) that the land of former Confederates should not be confiscated

72. Henry George's most famous book was

    (A) *Looking Backward*   (D) *The Shame of the Cities*

    (B) *Progress and Poverty*   (E) *Sister Carrie*

    (C) *The Jungle*

73. All of the following statements are true of John Dewey EXCEPT:

    (A) He strove to alter radically both the content and purpose of schooling.

    (B) He strove to strengthen the child's respect for parental and other traditional authority.

    (C) He substituted the authority of the peer group for that of the teacher so that the child would be socialized and schooling would be made relevant to him.

(D) He was much inflamed by William James.

(E) He has been called the father of Progressive Education.

74. "Waving the bloody shirt" was the name given to the practice of

(A) scaring black potential voters into staying away from the polls

(B) voting large appropriations of federal funds for unnecessary projects in a powerful congressman's district

(C) using animosities stirred up by the Civil War to gain election in the postwar North

(D) inciting the country to go to war with Spain

(E) machine politics as practiced in many major cities during the late nineteenth century

75. Which of the following expresses the first policy taken by the federal government toward the Indians of the Great Plains?

(A) The Indians should be confined to two large reservations, one north of the Platte River and the other south of it.

(B) Since the Great Plains are a desert anyway, the Indians may be allowed to keep the entire area.

(C) Indians should be given individual parcels of land by the government rather than holding land communally as tribes.

(D) Indians are subhuman and ought to be exterminated.

(E) The Indians should be induced to accept permanent residence on a number of small reservations.

76. One of the goals of the Populist movement was to induce the government to introduce

(A) free coinage of silver

(B) prohibition of all immigration from China and Japan

(C) the building of a transcontinental railroad at government expense

(D) a "single tax" on land

(E)   more stringent regulations for the health and safety of factory workers

77.   Georgia O'Keeffe, Thomas Hart Benton, and Edward Hopper were all

(A)   American painters of the 1920s

(B)   pioneers in the field of a distinctly American music

(C)   known for their abstract paintings of flowers and other objects

(D)   pioneers in the building of skyscrapers

(E)   American literary figures of the first decade of the twentieth century

78.   The 1944 Dumbarton Oaks Conference involved primarily

(A)   the trial and punishment of Nazi war criminals

(B)   the decision on whether or not to use the atomic bomb

(C)   startling revelations of the Nazi atrocities against Jews

(D)   American plans for redrawing the map of Eastern Europe

(E)   the formation of the United Nations

79.   Which of the following statements is true of the Bland-Allison Act?

(A)   It gave the president discretion to purchase up to 1 million ounces of silver per year.

(B)   It required the government to purchase from $2 million to $4 million worth of gold per month.

(C)   It was intended to raise the market price of gold and thus create a slight inflationary effect.

(D)   It provided for a floating rate of exchange between silver and gold.

(E)   It was vetoed by President Rutherford B. Hayes.

80.   In the 1790s political conflict between Thomas Jefferson and Alexander Hamilton, Jefferson would have been more likely to

(A)   take a narrow view of the Constitution

(B)   favor Britain over France in the European wars

(C)   favor the establishment of a national bank

(D)   win the cooperation of presidents George Washington and John Adams

(E)   oppose the efforts of Citizen Genet in America

STOP

This is the end of Section I.
If time still remains, you may check your work only in this section.
Do not begin Section II until instructed to do so.

SECTION II

TIME: **Reading Period – 15 Minutes**
                 Writing Time for all Essays – 115 Minutes

DIRECTIONS: Read over the Document-Based Essay question in Part A and the choices in Parts B and C during the Reading Period, and use the time to organize answers. All students must answer Part A (the Document-Based Essay question) and answer ONE question in both Parts B and C.

PART A – DOCUMENT-BASED ESSAY
(Suggested writing time: 45 minutes)

1.   Using the following documents as well as your knowledge of the events surrounding the outbreak of the Civil War, assess the wisdom of Abraham Lincoln's decision to hold Fort Sumter and Jefferson Davis's decision to take it.

Document A
Source: Lincoln's first inaugural address (March 4, 1861)

It is safe to assert that no government proper ever had a provision in its organic law for its own termination....No state upon its own mere motion can lawfully get out of the Union. I shall take care, as the Constitution itself expressly enjoins upon me, that the laws of the Union be faithfully executed in all the states. Doing this I deem to be only a simple duty on my part; and I shall perform it, so far as practicable, unless my rightful masters, the American people, shall withhold the requisite means, or in some authoritative manner direct the contrary....The power confided in me will be used to hold, occupy and possess the property and places belonging to the government, and to collect the duties and imposts....In your hands, my dissatisfied fellow countrymen, and not in mine, is the momentous issue of civil war. The government will not assail you. You can have no conflict without being yourselves the aggressors. You have no oath registered in heaven to destroy the government, while I shall have the most solemn one to "preserve, protect and defend" it.

Document B
Source: Memorandum from Secretary of State William H. Seward to Lincoln (April 1, 1861)

....The occupation or evacuation of Fort Sumter, although not in fact a slavery or a party question, is so regarded. Witness the temper manifested by the Republicans in the free States, and even by the Union men in the South.

I would therefore terminate it as a safe means for changing the issue. I deem it [un]fortunate that the last administration created the necessity.

Document C

Source: Charleston Mercury (January 24, 1861)

Border southern States will never join us until we have indicated our power to free ourselves — until we have proven that a garrison of seventy men cannot hold the portal of our commerce. Let us be ready for war.... The fate of the Southern Confederacy hangs by the ensign halliards of Fort Sumter.

Document D

Source: A Mobile, Alabama, newspaper (January 1861)

The spirit and even the patriotism of the people is oozing out under the do-nothing policy. If something is not done pretty soon...the whole country will become so disgusted with the sham of southern independence that the first chance the people get at a popular election they will turn the whole movement topsy-turvy.

Document E

Source: The diary of Edmund Ruffin (early 1861)

The shedding of blood will serve to change many voters in the hesitating states, from the submission or procrastinating ranks, to the zealous for immediate secession.

Document F

Source: Statement of Confederate Secretary of State Robert Toombs to Davis at cabinet meeting (April 9, 1861)

The firing on that fort will inaugurate a civil war greater than any the world has yet seen, and I do not feel competent to advise you. Mr. President, at this time it is suicide, murder, and you will lose us every friend at the North. You will wantonly strike a hornets' nest which extends from mountains to ocean. Legions now quiet will swarm out and sting us to death. It is unnecessary. It puts us in the wrong. It is fatal.

Document G

Source: Note from U.S. State Department official R.S. Chew to South Carolina Governor F.W. Pickens (April 8, 1861)

I am directed by the President of the United States to notify you to expect an attempt will be made to supply Fort Sumter with provisions only, and that if such an attempt be not resisted, no effort to throw in men, arms, or ammunition will be made without further notice, or in case of an attack upon the fort.

Document H

Source: Order from Davis to General Pierre G.T. Beauregard (April 10, 1861)

If you have no doubt as to the authorized character of the agent who communicated to you the intention of the Washington government to supply Fort Sumter by force, you will at once demand its evacuation, and, if this is refused, proceed in such manner as you may determine to reduce it.

PARTS B AND C – STANDARD ESSAY QUESTIONS
(70 minutes)

> **DIRECTIONS:** Choose ONE question each from Part B and Part C. It is recommended that you spend 5 minutes planning and 30 minutes writing. Support your thesis with germane historical evidence and present your case logically and clearly.

PART B

2. The sectional compromises of the first half of the nineteenth century were not in fact compromises but rather "sectional sellouts" in which the North gave in to the insistent demands of the slaveholding South.

    Assess the validity of this statement.

3. Analyze the appeal of Dwight D. Eisenhower to voters in the 1950s.

PART C

4. The Spanish-American War was the result of shrewd maneuvering on the part of a number of Washington imperialists, such as Theodore Roosevelt, who pressured the weak and vacillating McKinley into war in order to gain a colonial empire in the Caribbean and the Western Pacific.

    Evaluate this statement.

5. The Civil War was doubly tragic because it was completely unnecessary. Slavery had been ended in other nations by the stroke of a pen, and so it could have been in the United States.

    Assess the validity of this statement.

AP UNITED STATES HISTORY

PRACTICE TEST 2

ANSWER KEY

1. (B)	21. (A)	41. (A)	61. (A)
2. (C)	22. (B)	42. (C)	62. (D)
3. (D)	23. (C)	43. (C)	63. (D)
4. (B)	24. (A)	44. (D)	64. (E)
5. (C)	25. (C)	45. (D)	65. (A)
6. (A)	26. (B)	46. (E)	66. (E)
7. (B)	27. (C)	47. (L)	67. (C)
8. (D)	28. (F)	48 (A)	68. (D)
9. (C)	29. (C)	49. (D)	69. (A)
10. (B)	30. (D)	50. (D)	70. (C)
11. (D)	31. (B)	51. (A)	71. (B)
12. (E)	32. (A)	52. (D)	72. (B)
13. (B)	33. (C)	53. (E)	73. (B)
14. (C)	34. (C)	54. (C)	74. (C)
15. (C)	35. (D)	55. (C)	75. (B)
16. (B)	36. (A)	56. (A)	76. (A)
17. (E)	37. (D)	57. (D)	77. (A)
18. (A)	38. (D)	58. (A)	78. (E)
19. (C)	39. (C)	59. (B)	79. (E)
20. (A)	40. (A)	60. (B)	80. (A)

DETAILED EXPLANATIONS
OF ANSWERS

TEST 2

SECTION I

1.   **(B)**

Farmers of the Great Plains and the South often saw the Alliance movement as the only way to get out of the seemingly endless cycle of debt (crop liens), sharecropping, and/or low commodity prices. Small farmers in the Northeast could not, in fact, compete with Western farms, but they had no need to since they could concentrate on production of perishable items for nearby metropolitan areas (A). This was also the age of the giant "bonanza" farms of the northern Plains, but neither the owners of such farms (D) nor established, well-to-do farmers (C) had any need for the kind of government help the Farmers' Alliances sought. There were also a number of Chinese immigrants in the Western states at this time, not, however, in the Farmers' Alliances.

2.   **(C)**

Jackson did *not* object to the bank's preventing inflation, though some of his followers may have. Jackson, on the other hand, desired a gold standard. He believed the bank allowed the economic power of the government to be wielded by private individuals (A), the bank's directors. He believed it benefited this small and wealthy group, and their friends, at the expense of the rest of the country (E). He believed it could create economic hardship for the nation (D) and had in 1819; and he believed it threatened the integrity of the democratic system by using its influence in elections (B).

3.   **(D)**

All events listed except the Camp David Accords (1979) occurred in the 1990s. The Camp David Accords saw the first comprehensive peace agreement between an Arab and an Israeli leader. In September of 1993 Israel and the Palestine Liberation Organization exchanged letters recognizing (A) each other. They also signed an agreement including Palestinian autonomy in Israeli-held territories. In 1994, Palestinian autonomy, to a limited extent, began in the Gaza Strip and the West Bank. Also in 1994, Israel and Jordan signed a peace treaty formally ending their 46 years of war (C). In February of 1995 leaders in the Middle East condemned violence (E). On September 28, 1995, during a White House ceremony (B), the Israelis and the Palestinians agreed to expand Palestinian West Bank self-rule.

4.　　**(B)**

On September 27, 1994, at the Capitol Building, Newt Gingrich and Republican House candidates pledged to pass a Contract with America, which called for legislation to lower taxes, increase defense spending and pass a balanced budget amendment to the Constitution. Concern regarding the return of Reaganomics and an increased budget deficit did not influence the majority of the voters. Health care reform (A) had failed to materialize in 1994 and had little chance in 1995, when the interest on Capitol Hill shifted to a balanced budget. The welfare legislation (C) taken up was welfare reform. The Republican House sought decreases in education funding (D). Opposition to unfunded mandates and affirmative action did not lead to new civil rights measures (E).

5.　　**(C)**

The largest of the mound-building centers, Cahokia, was located near the present city of St. Louis. This Mississippi Valley culture built massive earthen mounds of varying size and function. The Cahokia inhabitants built flat-top mounds for buildings and other types of mound structures for cemeteries. The largest Cahokian mound, Monks Mound, featured a massive base measuring over 700,000 square feet and two terraces and was 25 percent larger than the Great Pyramid of Giza. Cahokia's population was greater than any European city of its day, and the first European-American city that matched it in population was eighteenth-century Philadelphia. The other four cities (New York City, Mexico City, Seattle, and Miami) were settled by other Indian groups.

6.　　**(A)**

The U.S. Navy's seizure of Confederate emissaries James M. Mason and John Slidell from the British mail steamer *Trent* came closest to giving the Confederacy the foreign help it needed by nearly bringing on a war between Great Britain and the United States. Confederate diplomats were not, on the whole, very skillful negotiatiors (E). There was some objection in Europe to the Union blockade (B), but Britain, the only country that could have done anything about it, favored permissive rules for blockading. Large prewar stocks of cotton in Britain and France, along with the discovery of alternate sources of cotton, prevented the economic dislocation in those countries that Confederate leaders had hoped would bring their aid (C). Some French financiers did float a bond issue for the Confederacy, but they slyly made sure they got their money first, assuring that if anyone got bilked it would be the small, uninfluential investors.

7.   **(B)**

This map depicts the United States as it was after the Missouri Compromise in 1820. Maine and Missouri have become states, and the territory remaining from the Louisiana Purchase has been divided between slave and free areas along the line of 36° 30'. Arkansas and Michigan have not yet become states as would have been the case before the Webster-Ashburton Treaty (E). The Mexican Cession has not yet been added as would have been the case after the settlement of the Mexican War (D) or the Compromise of 1850 (A). However, at the time of the Northwest Ordinance (C), the Louisiana Purchase area would not yet have been added.

8.   **(D)**

The "Bonus March" involved World War I veterans demanding financial aid from the federal government during the Depression. A few of the Bonus Marchers did build shacks near Washington, D.C. (B). Many farmers — and others — were disgruntled in 1932 (A), but the means of expressing it was generally by voting for Franklin D. Roosevelt for president. There were also during this time a number of farm workers seeking employment in California (E). Later, during the Second World War, Japanese-Americans were relocated (C), but they could hardly have protested by marching on Washington.

9.   **(C)**

Julius and Ethel Rosenberg were convicted of espionage, condemned, and electrocuted. They were accused of giving atomic secrets to the Soviet Union, not Germany (A), but they refused to confess (E). Public opinion was very much in favor of harsh treatment of Communists, and Eisenhower did not pardon the Rosenbergs (D). It was not the Rosenbergs but Alger Hiss who was exposed as a spy by Whitaker Chambers (B).

10.   **(B)**

Malcolm X advocated armed violence against police and troops. Nonviolent defiance of segregation (A) was the policy of Martin Luther King Jr. Patience while developing the skills that would make Blacks economically successful and gain them the respect of Whites (C) and (E) was the policy of Booker T. Washington. Gradual assimilation of the two races (D) was exactly the opposite of what Malcolm X taught.

11.   **(D)**

Khrushchev used the Soviet downing of the U-2 spy plane as a pretense to cancel the summit, thereby embarrassing Eisenhower. Castro had recently risen to power in Cuba (A), but the Bay of Pigs fiasco (B) was yet to come. Several years earlier, in unrelated incidents, the U.S. had sent troops into Lebanon (C) and the Soviet Union had launched Sputnik (E).

12.   **(E)**

The largest impact on the reduction of inland freight rates during this period was created by the introduction of steamboats. Railroads (A) came somewhat later. Keelboats, flatboats (D), turnpikes (C), and canals (B) were of less importance.

13.   **(B)**

Southern states were required to ratify the Fourteenth Amendment. Actually, Blacks had not always been granted full civil rights even in Northern states before the Civil War and after (A). Integrated public schools were more than a century off (C). The Sixteenth Amendment (D), allowing a federal income tax, was ratified in 1913. Some radicals talked of providing land to the freed slaves (E) but nothing ever came of it.

14.   **(C)**

The primary function of the World War I Food Administration was to oversee the production and allocation of foodstuffs to assure adequate supplies for the army and the Allies. It did not become involved in operating farms (E) nor did it, as a general rule, specially monitor the food produced (D). Farm prices were considered to be high enough already (A), and the U.S. would hardly have imported food from its somewhat undernourished Allies (B).

15.   **(C)**

The purpose of the Truman Doctrine was to aid countries that were the targets of Communist expansionism. Preventing European meddling in the affairs of South American countries (B) was the essence of the Monroe Doctrine, which was not directly related to the Truman Doctrine (E). It was the Marshall

Plan, also instituted during Truman's presidency, that aided the economic recovery of Europe from the Second World War (A).

16.   **(B)**

The Molasses Act was intended to force the colonists to buy sugar from more expensive British colonial sources rather than from foreign producers. Forcing the colonists to export solely to Great Britain (A), forbidding them to engage in manufacturing activity in competition with British industries (C), and creating an economic situation in which gold tended to flow from the colonies to the mother country (E) were also goals of mercantilism. Providing a favorable market for the products of the British East India Company (D) was the purpose of the Tea Act.

17.   **(E)**

The British government mistakenly thought the colonists would accept the Townshend Act as an external tax after having rejected the previous Stamp Act, an internal tax. They were under no illusions about the American position on taxation having changed (A), and they had not yet decided to provoke a military confrontation to teach the colonists a lesson (B). The act was designed to collect revenue, not merely enforce mercantilism (C), and it had not been approved by the colonial legislatures (D), though in either case the Americans would probably have accepted it.

18.   **(A)**

Douglas' Freeport Doctrine was that any territory desiring to exclude slavery could do so simply by declining to pass laws protecting it, notwithstanding the Dred Scott decision (D). That decision had also asserted that any slaveholder was free to take his slaves anywhere within the United States without hindrance by state, federal, or territorial governments (E). Many Northern states were, by this time, attempting to block the operation of the Fugitive Slave Law through their own "personal liberty laws" (C). Douglas did not believe that a state had the right to secede (B).

19.   **(C)**

Subsidies to transcontinental railroads generally took the form of land grants along the railroad's right-of-way. Occasionally, loans, rather than cash payments (A), were granted on a per-mile basis. Blanket appropriations (B) and provision of supplies and materials (D) were generally not used. In the Southeastern U.S., convict labor was sometimes rented to railroads (E), but not for the trans-continental railroads, much of whose track lay, of necessity, far from centers of population.

20.   **(A)**

The Mann-Elkins Act strengthened government regulation of the railroads during Taft's administration. The Federal Trade Commission (B) did not apply primarily to the railroads. The Granger Laws (C) did, but came long before Taft's administration. The government was still opposed to large business combinations (E), as Taft broke up more trusts than famed "trust-buster" Theodore Roosevelt. The government did not, however, take over and run the railroads (D) until during the First World War, under Wilson.

21.   **(A)**

Surprisingly, the Old Immigration, made up of those from Northern and Western Europe, still predominated after the Civil War until about 1890. Thereafter, the New Immigration, composed primarily of those from Southern and Eastern Europe (B), was most prevalent.

22.   **(B)**

The 1844 campaign slogan of the supporters of James K. Polk called for annexation of all of the Oregon country. After being elected Polk settled for a compromise deal. During Polk's presidency the readjustment of the nation's border with Mexico (C) and the demand by Northern free-soilers that limits be placed on the spread of slavery (D) were both significant issues. In response to the latter, Southerners suggested that the Missouri Compromise line be extended through the Mexican Cession (E). The "Aroostook War" (A) was settled by the Webster-Ashburton Treaty during the presidency of Polk's predecessor, John Tyler.

23.   **(C)**

Taft did not reverse Theodore Roosevelt's conservationist policies but in fact advanced them more than Roosevelt had. He did this, however, in a quiet way, since he disliked publicity (D) and was little inclined to make rousing speeches or engage in political conflict (B). In much the same way, he went about prosecuting trusts to a greater degree than Roosevelt had done (E). He was also an able administrator (A).

24.   **(A)**

The primary issue in Shays' Rebellion was the jailing of individuals or seizure of their property for failure to pay taxes during a time of economic hardship. Economic oppression by eastern Massachusetts bankers (E) and underrepresentation of the western part of the state (B) may have been contributing factors. Indians were by this time not a serious problem in Massachusetts (D), and there was no unpaid bonus (C).

25.   **(C)**

The Articles of Confederation government did have the power to borrow money and that is how it financed most of what it did. It did not, however, have the power to levy taxes (A), regulate commerce (B), or compel the states to abide by treaties (D), and it lacked a strong executive (E).

26.   **(B)**

The most successful method of financing the War of Independence was by obtaining grants from foreign countries. Printing large amounts of paper money (A), issuing paper securities backed by the promise of Western land grants (D), and appealing to the states for voluntary contributions (E) were tried with very little success. Congress did not have the power to levy direct taxes (C).

27.   **(C)**

It did not prohibit slavery in the lands acquired as a result of the Mexi-can War. Although California was admitted as a free state (A), the Utah and New Mexico Territories were left open on the subject of slavery. The Compromise also included a tougher fugitive slave law (B), stipulated that land in dispute between Texas and New Mexico should go to New Mexico (D), and ended the slave trade — but not slavery — in the District of Columbia (E).

28.   **(E)**

A member of the Social Gospel movement would probably argue that Christians should work to reorganize the industrial system and bring about international peace. He would probably not be very concerned about such "ordinary" sins as alcohol abuse and sexual permissiveness (A), nor would he hold the poor at fault for their plight (B) or suggest that those who committed abuses simply lacked will-power (C) — all this was society's fault. He did not see religion as individualistic (D) but rather as a social matter.

29.   **(C)**

In *Plessy v. Ferguson* (1896), the Supreme Court upheld separate but equal facilities. It overturned this ruling with *Brown v. Topeka Board of Education* in 1954 (A). The ruling that no black slave could be a citizen of the United States was the 1857 case *Dred Scott v. Sanford*. Various Supreme Court decisions in the 1950s, '60s, and '70s dealt with literacy tests (E) and affirmative action (D).

30.   **(D)**

Henry Clay's "American System" did not call for an independent treasury, which actually became a goal of Clay's opponents, the Democrats. Instead,

Clay favored a national bank (B). His system also called for federal funding for the building of roads (A), high protective tariffs (C), and federal funding for the construction of canals (E).

31.   **(B)**

The first national group upon whom Congress placed immigration restrictions was the Chinese. The Chinese Exclusion Act of 1882 was the vehicle for doing do. The first quantitative U.S. immigration law was adopted in 1921. It set temporary annual quotas according to nationality; quotas were made permanent in 1924. In 1952, the United States' many immigration and naturalization laws then on the books were brought under one comprehensive statute that limited immigration from the Eastern Hemisphere while leaving immigration from within the Western Hemisphere unrestricted. It wasn't until 1978 that the separate caps for Eastern and Western hemispheric immigration were combined into one global limit of 290,000.

32.   **(A)**

The Free-Soil party's main issue was a federal ban on the spread of slavery in the territories. Later in the decade the Free-Soil party was swallowed up by the Republican party, which also espoused its chief issue as well as calling for a homestead act (B). Only the radical abolitionists during the 1850s called for the immediate and uncompensated abolition of slavery (C), just as after the Civil War it was only the most radical of the Republicans who called for providing the freed slaves with "forty acres and a mule" (D). During the 1850s it was Southerners who desired to annex Cuba (E), hoping it would become a slave state.

33.   **(C)**

Creation of the Bank of the United States was more controversial than federal assumption of state debts (A) or the imposition of protective tariffs (D), though these, too, were controversial to a degree. Neither direct taxes (B) nor establishment of a bimetallic system (E) were part of Hamilton's program, though a century later the bimetallic issue did become very controversial.

34.   **(C)**

The position of the Nullifiers was that the states could nullify acts of the federal government they held to be unconstitutional. That the federal courts had the right to nullify acts of Congress that restricted the spread of slavery in the territories (B) was expressed in the Supreme Court's 1857 Dred Scott decision. The idea that Southern states had the right to nullify statutes of Northern states interfering with the recapture of escaped slaves (D) is similar to the idea behind the Fugitive Slave Act except in that case it was the federal government that was overriding free-state law. That Congress should refuse to receive any petitions against slavery (E) was the "gag rule." Free states, of course, still had the right to prohibit the ownership of property in slaves, but only for their own citizens, not for Southerners passing through.

35.   **(D)**

The Mayflower Compact could best be described as a foundation for self-government. It was not a detailed frame of government (A) or a complete constitution (B), and it was certainly not a business contract (C). It did not deal with the causes for leaving England and coming to the New World (E).

36.   **(A)**

The Taft-Hartley Act was definitely not sought but rather vehemently opposed by the labor unions. It did allow the president to call a cooling-off period (B), and it outlawed the closed shop (C). It was backed by Congressional Republicans (D), vetoed by President Truman (E), and passed over his veto.

37.   **(D)**

The Wade-Davis Bill was pocket-vetoed by Lincoln. Allowing restoration of a loyal government when as few as ten percent of the state's total prewar registered voters would take the oath of allegiance (A) was part of Lincoln's Ten Percent Plan, which the Wade-Davis Bill was meant to supersede with far harsher terms (E). It did not explicitly demand the vote for Blacks (B), but under its terms no Southern state could have established a government without doing so unless it waited for a whole new generation to rise to voting age. Its terms toward former high-ranking rebels were not at all lenient (C).

38.   **(D)**

Sinclair Lewis depicted small-town America as dreary, prejudiced, and vulgar, rather than in any of the more traditional and positive ways reflected in the other answer choices.

39.   **(C)**

Coolidge kept government spending low and encouraged private business. He kept taxes low (B), except for the tariff (E), and opposed government involvement in major projects (A). As was still traditional for presidents at that time, he did not take an active role in pushing legislation through Congress (D).

40.   **(A)**

The Incas built the most advanced culture in South America in the Andes Mountains region of Peru. At their height, in the sixteenth century, they may have controlled a population of about 12 million people. Inca society was strictly stratified and the emperor ruled with the assistance of an aristocratic bureaucracy. The Incas developed an elaborate irrigation system to support their agricultural economy, which grew maize, potatoes, squash, tomatoes, cassava, and cotton. They built an extensive network of roads, one of which was about 2,250 miles long. They also constructed suspension bridges made of vines and dug rock tunnels through the mountains. A message system based on relay runners was able to deliver news as fast as 150 miles per day. The other tribes did not live in South America.

41.   **(A)**

The Spanish-American War showed the need of shifting naval forces rapidly between the Atlantic and the Pacific. There had never been much doubt about overcoming Latin American countries if that were necessary, or of dealing with any (highly unlikely) threat from Spain (D). The war did nothing to discredit opponents of the project (C), and such tropical diseases as malaria and yellow fever were not dealt with successfully (E) until during the actual building of the canal.

42.   **(C)**

Though one can easily imagine it being said by any of the other persons on any of the other occasions, this statement was part of Franklin Roosevelt's first inaugural address.

43.   **(C)**

The Civilian Conservation Corps never employed anywhere near one-third of the U.S. work force, but it was part of FDR's New Deal (E). Its workers did live in camps under semi-military discipline (A) and work on such projects as preventing soil erosion (B), and it did provide that some of the workers' pay be sent home to help their families.

44.   **(D)**

Roosevelt wanted to manipulate the dollar amount the government would pay for gold in order to raise prices, since it was believed this would relieve the Depression. Since Roosevelt had already made it impossible for Americans to own gold, there could be no run on the banks by people wanting to get it (C).

Maintaining the dollar's value at a constant level (A), preventing inflation (B), or lowering prices (E) were all just the opposite of what Roosevelt hoped to accomplish.

45.   **(D)**

The basic issue in the coming of war between the U.S. and Japan in 1941 was Japan's desire to annex large portions of China. The Japanese were not yet aiding the Germans in their war against Britain (A) and did not desire to annex the Aleutians (C) — although during the course of the war they did attack and occupy a couple of them. The U.S. did not desire the Japanese-held islands in the Pacific (B) — though during the war it wound up taking a great many of them. American resentment of Japanese trading policies (E) characterizes more the last quarter of the twentieth century.

46.   **(E)**

The *Arabic* Pledge, named after a torpedoed British liner, was a German promise not to sink passenger ships without warning. German submarines could still be used to attack warships without warning or passenger ships after giving warning (C). The Germans, of course, made no promise not to try to break the British blockade (D) but had little hope of doing so, and unless they did could not hope to buy war supplies in the U.S. (B). The following year, 1917, the Germans did offer to aid Mexico in a war against the United States (A), an offer contained in the famous Zimmermann Telegram.

47.   **(E)**

Woodrow Wilson's most prized part of his Fourteen Points was the League of Nations. The Fourteen Points also included freedom of the seas (D), open diplomacy (A), and the right of self-determination — though not of a union of Germany and Austria in accord with such a right (C). Wilson would definitely have opposed either strengthening the Austrian Empire or restoring the balance of power (B).

48.   **(A)**

W. E. B. Du Bois founded the National Association for the Advancement of Colored People. He was a leader of the Niagara Movement (C) and an outspoken critic of the Atlanta Compromise (B), which was the work of Booker T. Washington (E) whose teaching was that Blacks should temporarily accommodate themselves to Whites (D).

49. **(D)**

The Southern states did not attempt to reinstitute slavery, but some or all of them did refuse to repudiate the Confederate debt (A), elect former Confederates to high positions (B), refuse to grant Blacks the right to vote (C), and pass special "black codes" restricting the legal rights of Blacks (E), resulting in the imposition of harsh congressional Reconstruction despite Johnson's efforts to prevent it.

50. **(D)**

It was for violation of the Tenure of Office Act in removing Secretary of War Stanton that Johnson was impeached and almost removed from office. His refusal to cooperate with the Radical Republicans (E) or to carry out the spirit, if not the letter, of the Military Reconstruction Act (A) and the Civil Rights Act (C) were the reasons the heavily radical Congress was anxious to be rid of him, but even they could not bring themselves to impeach him without some actual breach of a law — thus, the Tenure of Office Act. It was Grant, rather than Johnson, whose associates were involved in not one but a number of highly questionable schemes (B).

51. **(A)**

When white Southerners during the era of Reconstruction spoke of "redemption" in political terms they meant ridding their states of the Reconstruction governments. They would hardly have thought it necessary to atone for slavery or secession (B) and (C), and regaining personal rights (D) was relatively easy for the great majority of Southerners who had not held high positions in the Confederacy or in the U.S. government before joining the Confederacy. Very few, if any, plantations were confiscated as a result of the war (E).

52. **(D)**

Northern voters simply lost interest and grew tired of Reconstruction. Leading Radicals in the North had never cared much whether Reconstruction was constitutional or not (C), but many of them were dead by 1877. Agitating wartime animosities was still a useful electoral tactic (E), but it did not necessarily need to be linked to reconstructing the South. The goals of the Radical Republicans had not been accomplished (B), but neither had the Southerners regained all the state governments (A).

53. **(E)**

Allied strategy was to beat Germany first rather than the other way around (A) or an even division of resources (B).

54.   **(C)**

The Marshall Plan was an American economic aid program for Europe. The Truman Doctrine was the American commitment to help countries threatened by Communism (C).

55.   **(C)**

Kennedy came off looking better in the televised debates. Americans were perhaps somewhat bored with Eisenhower, though not deeply dissatisfied (A). There were no revelations of corruption on Nixon's part during this election (B), though there were during his 1952 run for vice president and his 1972 run for re-election as president. Kennedy had never been governor of Massachusetts and was short of administrative experience (D). Nixon, like Kennedy, had served in the Navy during World War II (E), though without achieving the fame Kennedy had gained on the PT-109.

56.   **(A)**

The Warren Commission held that Oswald acted alone. Many since then, however, have suggested that Oswald was part of a large conspiracy (C) and that he was aided by marksmen on a "grassy knoll" (B). Some have indeed gone so far as to suggest that Oswald had nothing to do with the assassination (D). In fact, there are very few allegations, however bizarre, that have not been made about the Kennedy assassination, and, not surprisingly, many Americans seem to believe that the true facts of the matter will probably never be known (E).

57.   **(D)**

The hostility of the fierce Iroquois helped keep the French out of what is now the United States. The French did establish a profitable fur trade in Canada (A), and Champlain did found a permanent settlement, Quebec, along the St. Lawrence (B) and did make it back to France alive (C). Instead of a British-French alliance against the Iroquois (E), what developed was an alliance system that pitted the British and Iroquois against the French and Algonquins.

58.   **(A)**

Penn's purpose was to create a refuge for Quakers, but other persecuted sects also found a haven there (B). Penn was also able to establish friendly relations with the Indians (C), and while he had hoped to make a financial profit out of the colony while he was at it (D), in this he was disappointed. The colony founded as a refuge for debtors was Georgia.

59.   **(B)**

Though many factors might contribute to an individual's choice of party, including, perhaps, the character of the party's leader (D), and the party's stand on such issues as states' rights (C), the chief factor during this period was acceptance or rejection of the French Revolution — Jefferson and his supporters saw it as good, Hamilton and the Federalists did not. By this time the Constitution had virtually universal acceptance in the U.S. (A). Though during the days of the fight over ratification, those favoring the Constitution were known as Federalists; they are not to be confused with the political party bearing the same name that gradually took form AFTER the Constitution was in effect. Patriot and Loyalist divisions came to mean increasingly less (E).

60.   **(B)**

The Bostonians reacted by throwing the tea into the harbor rather than allow the tax to be paid on it. The Boston Massacre (A) was a bloody clash between British troops and American colonists during the unrest growing out of the Townshend Acts. The Massachusetts Circular Letter (E) was also part of the colonial reaction to the Townshend Acts. The Declaration of Independence (C) did not come for another three years after the Boston Tea Party, and the Articles of Confederation (D), the nation's first frame of national government, came after that.

61.   **(A)**

The XYZ Affair involved the demand of French foreign minister Talleyrand that he receive a bribe before he would meet with American envoys. Immediately following the War of Independence, the British did refuse to evacuate their forts on American territory, particularly on the northwestern frontier (B). In 1818 Andrew Jackson did lead an incursion into Spanish-held Florida (C) in pursuit of raiding Indians. The 1807 British seizure of American crewmen from a U.S. Navy warship in Chesapeake Bay (D) was the *Chesapeake-Leopard* Incident. Finally, Aaron Burr did indeed seem to have some sort of bizarre plot in mind during the first decade of the 1800s though nothing came of it (E).

62.   **(D)**

The most unusual feature of the charter of the Massachusetts Bay Colony was that it did not specify where the company's headquarters should be. It did not specify that the colony should be run as a religious commonwealth (A) or make the colony completely independent of all English authority (B), but by allowing the headquarters to be moved to America, it allowed the former and virtually insured the latter for the time being. It did not specify that Parliament rather than the king should have authority of the colony (E), and it did assure that the colonists were to enjoy all the rights they would have had if they had been born and living in England (C), but so did the rest of the colonial charters.

63.   **(D)**

Relations with the Indians in colonial Virginia were not especially good. The colonists lived in constant fear of them and for good reason. The colony was kept alive by large influxes of supplies and recruits (E), drawn by promises of political rights represented by the House of Burgesses (A), and the hope of becoming rich through the cultivation of tobacco (C) on their own private property (B).

64.   **(E)**

The Great Awakening was the first religious development to have an impact throughout colonial America. Toleration in Maryland (A) and Quakerism in Pennsylvania (B) showed little tendency to spread to the other colonies. The Half-Way Covenant (C) was a late-seventeenth-century religious compromise involving only colonial New England. The Parsons' Cause (D) involved Anglican Church establishment in eighteenth-century Virginia.

65.   **(A)**

Jackson's veto of the Maysville Road dealt with the matter of federally financed internal improvements. The power of the Second Bank of the United States (C) was the issue in Jackson's "Bank War," and the efficiency and honesty of government employees (D) was the issue in Jackson's so-called "Spoils System." Jackson's Specie Circular forbade the purchase of government land with paper money (E).

66.   **(E)**

The armed confrontation — brief and bloodless — along the Maine-Canada border was the "Aroostook War" and took place in 1842, 30 years after the outbreak of the War of 1812. The other items, the *Chesapeake-Leopard* Incident (A), the British impressment of American seamen from American ships on the high seas (B), the concerns of Western Americans that the British were inciting the Indians (C), and the "War Hawks'" desire to annex Canada (D) were all real and all contributed to the coming of the war.

67.   **(C)**

The Monroe Doctrine stated that the United States would not tolerate any new European colonization in the New World. The U.S. did desire to see republican governments instituted in countries all over the world (A) and (B), it stated, but would intervene only to prevent new, not to remove existing (D) and (E) European colonization in the New World.

68.   **(D)**

The status of slavery in the territories proved the most divisive aspect of the slavery issue. Relatively little controversy surrounded the international slave trade (E), and Congress prohibited it in 1808, as soon as it was constitutionally empowered to do so. The status of slavery in the District of Columbia (A), the right to send antislavery literature through the mail (B), and the enforcement of the Fugitive Slave Law (C) were all highly controversial and divisive issues though ultimately not to the degree of the territorial issue that eventually led to civil war.

69.   **(A)**

The "Kitchen Cabinet" was a group of old friends and unofficial advisors to Andrew Jackson, so called by his political enemies from the derisive suggestion that they entered the White House through the kitchen, or servants' entrance. Jackson's cabinet may not have been socially acceptable among some of Jackson's aristocratic critics, but it certainly included no former cooks (B). It was not suggested that government funds be kept on the premises of the White House (C).

70.   **(C)**

The Pre-emption Act provided that those who settled on government land would have first chance to buy it. Tyler did set a precedent for the vice president's becoming a full-fledged (rather than merely acting) president when the incumbent dies (D). The idea that the status of slavery in a territory should be decided by the settlers there (A) was popular sovereignty. Slave law pre-empted free law in disputes involving escaped slaves (B) by means of the Fugitive Slave Law, and that was the only case in which federal law pre-empted state law in matters pertaining to slavery (E).

71.   **(B)**

The Homestead Act granted 160 acres to anyone who would settle on it and improve it. It was the Dawes Severalty Act of 1887 that provided for Indians to own their land individually (A). The Homestead Act was sometimes abused by Great Plains ranchers to obtain control of large amounts of land (C), though not in exchange for supplying beef to the Army. Talk of giving land to former slaves during the Reconstruction (D) era came to nothing, and, once again, there were virtually no confiscations as a result of the Civil War (E).

72.   **(B)**

Progress and Poverty was Henry George's most famous book. The other books listed were all written by George's contemporaries and, like George, all intended to make social statements: *Looking Backward* (A) by Edward Bellamy, *The Jungle* (C) by Upton Sinclair, *The Shame of the Cities* (D) by Lincoln Steffens, and *Sister Carrie* (E) by Theodore Dreiser.

73.   **(B)**

Dewey was not concerned with strengthening a child's respect for parental or other traditional authority. He has been called the father of Progressive Education (E); he was influenced by the ideas of "Pragmatist" philosopher William James (D); he strove to alter the content and purpose of schooling (A) and to socialize the child through his peer group (C).

74.   **(C)**

"Waving the bloody shirt" was the practice of using wartime animosities to gain election in the North. Machine politics were practiced in many cities during the late nineteenth century (E), though there is no special name for this other than "corruption." The voting of large appropriations of federal funds for unnecessary projects in a powerful congressman's district (B) might also be called corruption but is more often referred to as a "pork barrel scheme," a general term for a politician's buying of votes with government appropriations. Inciting the country to go to war with Spain (D) was one of the things accomplished just before the turn of the century by "Yellow Journalism."

75.   **(B)**

The first policy toward the Plains Indians was simply to let them have the entire area, which was actually believed to be a desert. Later the policy changed to dividing the Indians between two large reservations (A), then to confining them to a number of small reservations (E), then to giving them their land in individual parcels (C), and then back to reservations again. The idea that Indians should be exterminated (D) was never a policy of the government but, unfortunately, was held by some individuals.

76.   **(A)**

The main goal of the Populist movement was free coinage of silver. Prohibition of immigration from China and Japan (B) was a popular idea on the West Coast during that era. The transcontinental railroad (C) had been completed

20 years before the Populist movement got under way. A "single tax" on land (D) was Henry George's idea. And stringent regulations for the workplace (E) was one of the reforms sought by the Progressive movement.

77.   **(A)**

Georgia O'Keeffe, Thomas Hart Benton, and Edward Hopper were all American painters of the 1920s (E). This was the age of jazz (B) and of skyscrapers (D). Georgia O'Keeffe was known for her abstract paintings of flowers and animal skulls against the background of the New Mexico desert (C).

78.   **(E)**

The Dumbarton Oaks Conference was one of the important meetings that led to the formation of the United Nations. Punishment of Nazi war criminals (A) was dealt with at the Nuremberg Trials. The map of Eastern Europe (D) was discussed at the Yalta Conference. The decision to drop the atomic bomb (B) was made by President Truman.

79.   **(E)**

The Bland Allison Act, requiring the government to purchase silver, not gold (B) and (C), was vetoed by President Hayes but subsequently passed over his veto. It did not give the president discretion as to whether or not silver should be bought (A), and it did not provide for a floating rate of exchange between gold and silver (D), probably one of its greatest weaknesses.

80.   **(A)**

Jefferson would have been more likely to take a narrow view of the Constitution, Hamilton a broad and permissive one. Hamilton, rather than Jefferson, also favored Britain over France in the European war (B), favored the establishment of a national bank (C), won the cooperation of presidents George Washington and John Adams most of the time (D), and opposed the efforts of Citizen Genet in America (E).

SECTION II

Sample Answer to Document-based Question

1.   Few leaders have faced decisions as difficult as those confronting Abraham Lincoln and Jefferson Davis in April 1861. At stake was the allegiance of the northern tier of slaves states, wavering between the Union and their sister slave states. Beyond that, Lincoln had to find some way to get all the states back into the Union, and Davis to prevent it. All this now focused on Fort Sumter.

Located on an island inside the harbor of Charleston, South Carolina, and garrisoned by less then 100 U.S. soldiers, Fort Sumter was to both North and South a symbol of national authority in the states claiming to have seceded. At his inaugural Lincoln promised not to initiate hostilities against the South but nevertheless to "hold, occupy and possess the property and places belonging to the government." This wise policy avoided alienating the border states, for the time being, but also maintained the federal government's claim to sovereignty in South Carolina. Some disagreed. Secretary of State William H. Seward was foremost in urging that the fort be abandoned in order to mollify the South and keep the issue from being seen as one of slavery versus abolitionism or Democratic versus Republican party. Against all such urgings, Lincoln remained firm.

Davis was faced with the problem of whether to await the hoped-for Northern evacuation of the fort or to order a Southern attack. It was an unpleasant dilemma. To allow a garrison of "foreign" troops to remain in a fort in the harbor of one of its chief cities would appear to indicate the Confederacy was neither independent nor in earnest about becoming so. On the other hand, to attack the fort would be to take upon the South the onus of firing the first shot and initiating a civil war, making the South appear the aggressor, rather than the victim of aggression, as Davis and most other Southerners believed it to be. Meanwhile, the South clamored for Davis to take some sort of action. "The border states will never join us," complained the Charleston Mercury, "until we have indicated our power to free ourselves" by taking Fort Sumter.

An Alabama newspaper even suggested that at the present rate the people would soon consider Southern independence mere hollow words and give up and go back to the Union. From elsewhere came assertions that all that was needed to rally every slave state around the cause of the Confederacy was "the shedding of blood."

Davis's hope in all of this was Lincoln's dilemma: the fort was running out of food. Unless supplies could be gotten to it soon, its commander, Major Robert Anderson, would have to evacuate. Davis waited to see if this would spare him the necessity of choosing one unpleasant alternative or the other. Lincoln was determined to do something about it. An expedition was sent to re-supply the fort, and notice duly given the South Carolina governor. No effort was to be made "to throw in men, arms, or ammunition…without further notice" unless Sumter was attacked. With that Lincoln had checkmated his Confederate counterpart, who would now have to acquiesce in the permanent presence of a federal garrison in Charleston harbor or else take the responsibility of firing the first shot and firing it to keep food from hungry men. Lincoln probably hoped Davis would not choose war, but he was willing to risk the result if he did.

The Confederacy's own secretary of state, Robert Toombs, pleaded with Davis not to attack. "You will want only strike a hornets' nest…," he warned. "Legions now quiet will swarm out and sting us to death. It is unnecessary. It puts us in the wrong. It is fatal." Davis did not take Toombs' advice, but it was eventually proved at least partially correct. The Confederate firing on Fort Sumter and Lincoln's response in calling for 75,000 volunteers to put down the rebellion did have the effect of galvanizing the South. Arkansas, Tennessee, North Carolina, and crucial Virginia seceded and joined the Confederacy. Yet it also rallied the loyal states in a way that probably nothing else could have. The flag had been fired on; war had been initiated by Southern aggression. A wave of martial enthusiasm swept over the North.

Ultimately, Lincoln's course must appear the wiser. Davis, by initiating the conflict had given the North a strength and unity without which it probably could not have won the war that followed. Yet in fairness it must be said that for the Confederate president there were no easy alternatives.

Sample Answers to Essay Questions

2. Two major compromises marked the sectional relations of the first half of the nineteenth century, the 1820 Missouri Compromise and the Compromise of 1850. The Missouri Compromise settled a controversy arising from the petition of Missouri, a part of the Louisiana Purchase, to be admitted to the Union as a slave state. The slave state of Louisiana had already been formed out of the Louisiana Purchase, but slavery had existed there before U.S. ownership. Missouri represented an area settled largely by Americans, and Northerners were loath to see slavery following the flag to areas where it was previously unknown. Anxious to see some limit placed on the spread of slavery, they moved to admit Missouri on the condition that it emancipate its slaves within a generation.

   Southerners were outraged at this not only because it would have assured their section the minority status in the Senate that it already had in the House, but also because they considered it an insult. The compromise that resolved this crisis stipulated that Missouri be admitted as a slave state but that the remaining Louisiana Territory be divided along latitude 36° 30', the area south of the line reserved for slavery, north of it, forever free.

   Here the charge of "sectional sellout" is partially true. Southerners obtained Missouri as a slave state, and though the division of the remaining territory seemed favorable to the North, it actually gave the South at least half and probably two-thirds of the area suitable for the establishment of slavery in the first place. Yet the North did at least win the principle that slavery could be excluded in some of the territories, and a small area of land that might have been suitable for slavery was reserved for freedom.

   The Compromise of 1850 quieted the uproar over the status of slavery in the lands acquired through the Mexican War. Sectional tempers had heated over the past quarter century, and many Northerners were prepared to see the war as a plot to add new slave states to the Union. Their feeling that the war should be fought, if at all, for national, rather than slave, expansion, was expressed in the Wilmot Proviso, stipulating that slavery be prohibited throughout the Mexican Cession. Introduced several times in Congress during the late 1840s, it was never passed.

Southerners were again outraged. Since the majority of the nation's unorganized land holdings had previously lain in the North and been closed to slavery, they felt the new lands added in the South should naturally be open to slavery. The matter was brought to a head when California petitioned for admission to the Union as a free state. The resulting compromise must again be considered at least in part a sectional sellout. Though the North got California and at least a chance at the rest of the Mexican Cession, it is doubtful if slavery could have prospered in that arid region anyway. The South got Congress to profess its lack of power to do two things the Constitution and laws clearly gave it power to do: abolish slavery in the District of Columbia and ban the interstate slave trade. In the odious Fugitive Slave Law, another part of the compromise, the federal government was made the instrument of some of the ugliest abuses of the system of slavery.

In short, it can be concluded that though "sectional sellout" may be too strong a word for agreements from which the North clearly received some gains, it is also clear that the compromises did to a large extent sacrifice justice and the national interest to the aggressive demands of the militant slaveholding South.

3.   Dwight D. Eisenhower had enormous appeal with voters in the 1950s because he was a war hero, because he had the common touch, because he was reassuring, and because he was seen as moderate and non-partisan.

During the Second World War Eisenhower had been a supreme allied commander in Europe, where he had gained a reputation as a skillful manager and conciliator. One of the most distinguished generals of the war, he was seen by the public as the man who beat Hitler, and this was a major source of his popularity.

Yet at the same time he had the appeal of the common man, having been born in a small town in Texas and grown up in a poor but hard-working family in Abilene, Kansas. He expressed issues in simple terms and had the air of an ordinary, honest man.

Eisenhower was also reassuring. The country had just come through more than two decades of constant upheaval: stock market crash, Depression, government reforms on a magnitude previously unheard of, a World War, the Korean War, and the threat of Soviet Communism. Eisenhower, without doing very much — or perhaps because he did not do very much — was a reassuring influence to the American people. He was a president who would not "rock the boat" with drastic reforms or overseas emergencies.

He was also seen as moderate and non-partisan. Not having been a professional politician before coming to the presidency, he could project the image of being above partisan bickering. His moderation consisted of steering a middle course between the bureaucratic welfare state and the traditional laissez-faire republic of pre-New Deal days. Americans, still somewhat enamored of some of the New Deal programs but uncomfortable with this radical departure from their traditions of government, appreciated Eisenhower's moderate mixing of the two.

Taken together, these factors made Eisenhower one of the most popular presidents of the post-World War II era.

4.   While the influence of Theodore Roosevelt and other influential and empire-minded persons may have helped to persuade McKinley to enter the Spanish-American War, the weight of public opinion must be considered as a major factor in the president's decision.

The 1890s were the heyday of "Yellow Journalism." Named for "the Yellow Kid," a cartoon character regularly appearing in the mass circulation papers of the time, Yellow Journalism grew out of the competition for circulation between the mass-market papers of William Randolph Hearst and Joseph Pulitzer. In order to boost their circulation, the papers were not above sensationalizing, distorting, falsifying, or even creating news.

This had its most striking effect in helping to bring on the Spanish-American War. Newspapers gave sensationalized reports of Spanish attempts to suppress a rebellion in Cuba, making it appear that the Spaniards were guilty of extreme human rights violations. As public outrage grew, so too did pressure on the McKinley administration to take a hard line with Spain. Spain was conciliatory, but McKinley felt compelled to send the battleship U.S.S. *Maine* to the harbor of Havanna, Cuba, to show the flag and generally uphold American interests. While there the *Maine* was torn by an explosion and sank with heavy loss of life. The yellow press immediately roared its opinion that this was the doing of Spain, though the cause of the explosion was and remains unknown.

The public outcry raised by such reporting, coupled with the public's sincere but in part mislead humanitarian desire to free the Cubans from Spanish tyranny and bestow on it the benefits of a free government, finally drove McKinley to decide for war with Spain. Though imperialists in high places in Washington may have helped him toward such a decision for reasons of their own, the primary reason must be viewed as the pressure of public opinion, artificially created by an irresponsible press, on an astute politician like William McKinley.

5. While it is true that other countries did away with slavery without the resort to civil war, this could have happened in the United States only had the South been willing to part with slavery under some other circumstances. Unfortunately, that was not the case.

Attempts to deal with the issue of slavery in the United States go back to the period of the Articles of Confederation. The Northwest Ordinance, drafted in 1787 by Virginia slaveholder Thomas Jefferson, prohibited slavery in what was to become the states of Ohio, Indiana, Illinois, Michigan, and Wisconsin. Jefferson believed slavery was evil and inconsistent with American ideals but that it could not be abolished suddenly in the areas where it already existed. He did not, however, desire its spread — an attitude reflected in the Northwest Ordinance and shared by most Southerners throughout the United States' first half-century of independence. The slave trade was abolished in 1808 without controversy, and various schemes were discussed for the gradual and compensated emancipation of the slaves, usually coupled with plans to repatriate them to Africa. In these, Northerners and Northern state legislatures offered their financial help, but little came of them as most slaveholders seemed more willing to confess the evil of slavery in principle than to part with their own valuable investments in human chattels.

As the 1830s began both anti-slavery rhetoric on the part of Northern opponents of the institution as well as the attitudes of the slaveholders themselves began to become more extreme. It is hard to say which phenomenon was caused by the other. They were mutually aggravating. Abolitionists denounced slavery as a national sin, and slaveholders began to defend it not as an unavoidable evil but now as a positive good for both white man and black.

The issue that finally led to civil war was that of slavery in the territories. Northerners, or at least the vast majority of them, freely conceded that the federal government had no right to prohibit slavery in the states were it existed, and repeatedly assured the South that they had no intention of doing so. They did, however, believe the federal government had the right to keep slavery from spreading into new territories and felt it their duty to achieve this. As expressed by Abraham Lincoln, their goal in this was to "place slavery where the public may rest assured that it is in the course of ultimate extinction." This was much the same attitude Thomas Jefferson had held with regard to the Northwest Ordinance, but by the mid-nineteenth century Southern attitudes had changed. Southerners too saw the limitation of slavery expansion as an indication that slavery would some day in the distant future cease to exist in their states as well, and as such they rejected it, determined to have slavery not only for the present but for the indefinite future as well.

Several attempts were made to limit the spread of slavery — the Missouri dispute of 1819-20 and the struggle over the Wilmott Proviso (1846-50) — but each ended in a compromise that gave more land to slavery. When in 1861 the Republican party came to power on a platform calling for no further spread of slavery and then refused to compromise away the results of the election, Southerners responded by seceding and setting up their own republic where slavery might never be threatened.

Thus, while it is possible to say that slavery could have been ended in the United States without a civil war — if the South would have agreed to give up its slaves on any other terms — Southern determination to preserve the institution at all costs made such a course impossible and war was the only means to rid the country of slavery.

PRACTICE TEST 3
AP United States History

AP United States History

PRACTICE TEST 3

SECTION I

TIME: 55 Minutes
80 Questions

> **DIRECTIONS:** Each of the questions or incomplete statements below is followed by five suggested answers or completions. Select the one that is best in each case.

1. In 1804, Aaron Burr killed Alexander Hamilton in a duel that was fought because

    (A) Hamilton had formally accused Burr of treason and Burr felt he had to defend his honor.

    (B) Burr blamed his loss of the 1804 election for governor of New York on Hamilton's charges that Burr was dangerous and untrustworthy.

    (C) Hamilton had uncovered Burr's plan to form an independent republic comprised of American territories west of the Appalachians.

    (D) Burr had caught his wife in a sexual liaison with Hamilton and felt that he had to defend his honor.

    (E) Burr believed that Hamilton had financially destroyed him in a real estate deal in which Burr lost nearly all of his wealth.

2. The following cartoon refers to the results of which war?

President McKinley (the tailor) measures Uncle Sam for a new suit to fit the fattening results of his imperial appetite.

(A)   War of 1812   (D)   World War I

(B)   Civil War   (E)   World War II

(C)   Spanish-American War

3.   All of the following are true of the Confederate war effort during the Civil War EXCEPT:

(A)   Confederate industry was never able to adequately supply Confederate soldiers with the armaments they needed to successfully fight the war.

(B)   Confederate agriculture was never able to adequately supply the people of the South with the food they needed.

(C)   Inflation became a major problem in the South as the Confederate government was forced to print more paper currency than it could support with gold or other tangible assets.

(D)   The inadequate railroad system of the South hindered movement of soldiers, supplies, and food from the places where they were stationed (or produced) to the places where they were most needed.

(E)   Tremendous resentment at the military draft developed among poor and middle class Southerners because wealthy Southern males could pay to have a substitute take their place in the army.

4.   What was the *overall* U.S. unemployment rate during the worst periods of the depression?

(A)   10%   (D)   60%

(B)   25%   (E)   90%

(C)   40%

5.   All of the following were main principles of the Navigation Acts EXCEPT:

(A)   Trade in the colonies was limited to only British or colonial merchants.

(B)   It prohibited the colonies from issuing their own paper currencies, greatly limiting their trading capabilities.

(C)   All foreign goods bound for the colonies had to be shipped through England where they were taxed with British import duties.

(D) The colonists could not build or export products that directly competed with British export products.

(E) Colonial enumerated goods could only be sold in England.

6. Which of the following statements explains why slavery flourished in the Southern English colonies and not in New England?

(A) Most New England farms were too small for slaves to be economically necessary or viable, whereas in the South the cultivation of staple crops such as rice and tobacco on large plantations necessitated the use of large numbers of indentured servants or slaves.

(B) Blacks from the tropical climate of Africa could not adapt to the harsh New England winters. Their high death rates made their use as slave laborers unprofitable.

(C) A shortage of females in the Southern English colonies led to many female black Africans being imported as slaves and as potential wives for white planters in the region.

(D) Whereas New England religious groups such as the Puritans forbade slavery on moral grounds, the Anglican church, which dominated the Southern English colonies, encouraged the belief that Blacks were inferior, thus, not deserving of equal status.

(E) The Stono uprising in 1739 convinced New Englanders that the cost of controlling slaves was not worth their marginal economic benefits.

7. Which battle was the turning point in the Pacific war between Japan and the U.S.?

(A) Leyte Gulf   (D) Midway

(B) Pearl Harbor   (E) Guadalcanal

(C) Coral Sea

8. The United States Supreme Court Case of *Brown v. Board of Education of Topeka* was significant because it

(A) prohibited prayer in public schools on the grounds of separation of church and state

(B) legally upheld the doctrine of "separate but equal" educational facilities for Blacks and Whites

    (C)   clarified the constitutional rights of minors and restricted the rights of school administrators to set dress codes or otherwise infringe on students' rights

    (D)   upheld school districts' rights to use aptitude and psychological tests to "track" students and segregate them into "college prep" and "vocational" programs

    (E)   ordered the desegregation of public schools, prohibiting the practice of segregation via "separate but equal" schools for Blacks and Whites

9.   The Great Awakening of the mid-eighteenth century refers to

    (A)   a series of religious revivals that swept through the English colonies spreading evangelistic fervor and challenging the control of traditional clerics over their congregations

    (B)   the intellectual revolution that served as a precursor to the Enlightenment and challenged orthodox religion's claims to knowledge of humankind and the universe

    (C)   the beginnings of the Industrial Revolution in England and its New World colonies

    (D)   the growing realization among English colonists that independence from England was only a matter of time and was the key to their future success

    (E)   the sudden awareness among North American Indians that their only chance for survival against the rapidly growing number of European colonists was to fight them before the Europeans grew any stronger

10.   One of the major effects of the Industrial Revolution of the late nineteenth century in the United States was

    (A)   an increased emphasis on worker health and safety issues

    (B)   an increased emphasis on speed rather than quality of work

    (C)   an increased emphasis on high-quality, error-free work

    (D)   an increase in the number of small industrial facilities, which could operate more efficiently than larger, more costly industrial plants

    (E)   a decrease in worker productivity as a result of continuous clashes between unions and management

11. The key event that guaranteed Lincoln's reelection in 1864 was

    (A) the fall of Vicksburg to General Grant

    (B) the capture of New Orleans by Admiral Farragut

    (C) the defeat of Lee's army by General Meade at Gettysburg

    (D) the fall of Atlanta to General Sherman

    (E) the successful defense of Nashville by General Thomas against repeated Confederate counterattacks

12. The American Hostage Crisis in Iran was precipitated by

    (A) the American government allowing the deposed Shah of Iran to come to the United States for cancer treatment

    (B) Jimmy Carter's involvement in arranging the Camp David accords between the Egyptians and the Israelis

    (C) American air strikes against Iran's ally, Libya

    (D) American support for Israel's 1980 invasion of southern Lebanon

    (E) American attempts to overthrow the newly emplaced government of Ayatollah Khomeini

13. The Compromise of 1877 resulted in

    (A) the ascension of Republican Rutherford B. Hayes to the presidency in return for assurances that what was left of Reconstruction in the South would be ended

    (B) the division of the Dakota Territory into North Dakota and South Dakota

    (C) government financing for a Southern transcontinental railroad route in return for financial grants allowing the completion of the Great Northern Railroad from Minnesota to the Pacific Northwest

    (D) the ascension of Republican Rutherford B. Hayes to the presidency in return for the passage of an Amnesty Act which would pardon former Confederate soldiers, allowing them to regain their voting rights

    (E) the formal separation of Virginia and West Virginia and the official acceptance of statehood for West Virginia

14. Actions taken by the United States in response to Iraq's invasion of Kuwait in August 1990 included all of the following EXCEPT

    (A) U.N. coordination

    (B) protection of Saudi Arabia

    (C) imposing economic sanctions

    (D) Operation Desert Shield

    (E) immediate military response

15. All of the following were New World crops that enhanced European diets EXCEPT

    (A) tomatoes

    (B) potatoes

    (C) coffee

    (D) maize (corn)

    (E) chocolate

16. When Bill Clinton defeated President George Bush and Independent Ross Perot in 1992, the issue that most influenced the voters was

    (A) eruptions of violence and racial tension in Los Angeles

    (B) reports of ethnic cleansing in the former Yugoslavia

    (C) U.N. relief efforts in Somalia and elsewhere

    (D) the condition of the U.S. economy

    (E) the breakup of the Soviet Union into 15 new nations

17. The thrust of Roosevelt's "Good Neighbor" policy was to

    (A) retreat from the military interventionism and blatant economic domination which had characterized previous American policy toward Latin America

    (B) guarantee the protection of Latin America and South America from European aggression by permanently stationing U.S. forces in the region

    (C) promote "Good Samaritanism" in the United States by encouraging people who still owned their own homes to provide temporary housing for their neighbors who had become homeless because of the Great Depression

(D)   force Latin American countries to cooperate peacefully with each other and end their petty border disputes or face United States military intervention

(E)   supply Britain with the food and nonmilitary essentials they needed to maintain their struggle against Nazi Germany

18.   Which of the following was NOT true of the Northwest Ordinance of 1787?

(A)   It recognized the territorial claims of the various Indian tribes within the Northwest Territory.

(B)   It guaranteed freedom of religion to settlers in the Northwest Territory.

(C)   It guaranteed the right to a jury trial to settlers in the Northwest Territory.

(D)   It prohibited slavery within the Northwest Territory.

(E)   It specified procedures through which settlers could organize state governments and eventually apply for full statehood.

19.   Reaganomics is most closely associated with

(A)   the "trickle-down" theory

(B)   the "controlled growth" theory

(C)   the "bubble up" theory

(D)   New Deal reform economics

(E)   Fair Deal progressivist economics

20.   The "White Man's Burden" referred to

(A)   the financial cost of running the huge European colonial empires

(B)   the cost in human lives of diseases, such as smallpox, to which only white people were susceptible

(C)   the duty of white laborers to rise up and overthrow the wealthy industrialists who were abusing their power and their workers

(D)   the cost of the wars that resulted from nineteenth-century militarism

(E)   the belief that it was the duty of Whites to "civilize" non-white people through colonization or economic dominance of non-white lands

21. The paternalistic view of slavery held that

   (A) slavery was a necessary evil that should be phased out as soon as it was economically possible

   (B) slavery was a totally unjustifiable abuse of humanity demanding immediate abolition

   (C) slavery was an artifact of a more primitive past that would eventually fade out on its own

   (D) slavery was necessary to protect Blacks from the mistreatment and abuse they would receive if they were freed

   (E) slavery was necessary to keep Blacks from developing their superior potential and eventually dominating the white race

22. Mark Twain's classic stories, such as *Tom Sawyer* and *Huckleberry Finn*, typified a trend toward which of the following themes in turn-of-the-century American literature?

   (A) Romantic   (D) Realistic

   (B) Gothic   (E) Heroic

   (C) Fantasy

23. What proposal did President Woodrow Wilson make in 1918 that convinced the Germans they would be treated fairly if they surrendered?

   (A) The Twenty-One demands

   (B) The Fourteen Points

   (C) The Versailles Proposals

   (D) The Balfour Declaration

   (E) The "New Freedom" policy

24. This engraving of the Nat Turner revolt takes what point of view?

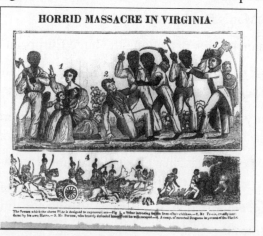

(A) The revolt of the slaves was justified.

(B) Northern abolitionists were responsible for the revolt.

(C) The revolt was an attack upon innocent victims.

(D) The slaves were ineffective revolutionists.

(E) The slave revolt was successful.

25. The main reason that President Grant's administration is considered a failure is

(A) his failure to retreat from the radical Reconstruction policies of his predecessors

(B) his failure to effectively quell the Indian uprisings in the Western territories

(C) his failure to control the corruption permeating his administration

(D) his attempts to destroy the Democratic party and return the country to a one-party system

(E) his failure to be reelected after serving his first term in office

26. "If your neighbor's house was on fire, and he didn't have a garden hose, wouldn't it make sense to let him use your hose to fight the fire so the fire could be put out before it spread to your house?" This question was raised by Franklin Roosevelt to justify

(A) the Neutrality Acts   (D) the Good Neighbor policy

(B) the Atlantic Charter   (E) the Selective Service Act

(C) the Lend-Lease Act

27. The most significant aspect of the Mexican-American War on the United States during the 20 years following the war was that it

(A) led to the development of the idea of "passive resistance" among those who opposed the war

(B) ended years of hostility between the United States and Mexico

(C) reignited the slavery conflict in regards to all the territories newly acquired from Mexico

(D) gave America undisputed control over Mexican foreign policy for the next 20 years

(E)   revealed the shocking ineptitude of American military forces, leading to massive reforms in military training and procedures throughout the 1850s

28.   U.S. presidents between 1876 and 1900 were considered among the weakest in American history. A major reason for this was that

(A)   none of them served more than one term in office

(B)   they considered themselves caretakers, not dynamic initiators of new legislation

(C)   Congress enacted several new laws restricting presidential power during this period

(D)   they were the products of machine politics, political followers who were typically incompetent leaders

(E)   they were limited in their actions by the overwhelming Populist sentiment of their time

29.   The most active people in the religious revivals of the mid-nineteenth century were

(A)   Roman Catholics   (D)   Quakers

(B)   Jews   (E)   Evangelical Christians

(C)   mainstream Protestants

30.   The Bay of Pigs affair had what effect on John Kennedy's presidency?

(A)   It made Kennedy a national hero for his tough, uncompromising stand against Castro and Communist Cuba.

(B)   It forced Soviet Premier Khrushchev to schedule an early summit meeting with Kennedy to avoid future American-Soviet confrontations.

(C)   It had virtually no effect on Kennedy's presidency, as it was kept secret until after Kennedy's assassination.

(D)   It forced Kennedy to allow Soviet occupation of military bases in Cuba.

(E)   It was a major embarrassment to Kennedy's administration and led to further crises in American-Cuban relations.

31. In what way did the muckrakers contribute to the rise of Progressivism in the early years of the twentieth century?

   (A) Their lurid stories of European abuses led directly to American isolationism until World War I.

   (B) Their stories glorifying the rich and famous led to the supremacy of laissez-faire economic theories during this period.

   (C) Their horror stories of Marxist infiltration into workers' unions led to public support for crackdowns against reform-minded unions and alliances.

   (D) Their exposés of government and business corruption, abuse, and mismanagement led to widely supported public demands for effective reform.

   (E) They created a repugnance for the national press that generalized into a distrust for all government and business institutions.

32. In the mid-eighteenth century, the first wave of non-English-speaking immigrants (other than African slaves) arrived in the English colonies. They were ethnic

   (A) Poles   (D) Italians

   (B) Scandinavians   (E) Russians

   (C) Germans

33. All of the following were characteristic of the 1920s EXCEPT

   (A) voting rights for women

   (B) prohibition and bootlegging

   (C) consumerism and easy credit

   (D) Progressivist reform and union growth

   (E) Ku Klux Klan power and popularity

34. Lincoln won the 1860 presidential election primarily because

   (A) there was overwhelming support throughout the country for the Republicans' antislavery platform

   (B) he was seen as a moderate, by both Northerners and Southerners, who could possibly negotiate a compromise between abolitionists and slaveholders

(C)   he gathered overwhelming support in the highly populated Northern states while his three opponents divided the anti-Lincoln vote in the North, West, and South

(D)   the Know-Nothing party gave Lincoln its endorsement, and combined with Republican support, the two parties were able to outpoll the politically isolated Democrats

(E)   he was able to discredit his chief opponent, Stephen Douglas, as a "closet abolitionist"

35.   Senator Joseph McCarthy was known for

(A)   leading a "witch hunt" to expose communists in the U.S.

(B)   recommending large-scale American intervention in Vietnam

(C)   helping to formulate a major economic aid plan for Western Europe in the late 1940s

(D)   leading the peace faction of the Democratic party in the 1968 presidential campaign

(E)   being the first American Senator convicted of spying for the Soviet Union (in 1956)

36.   Which of the following is true of the Mayas?

(A)   They created a writing system that used both syllables and written characters.

(B)   Their city-states remained at peace throughout their history.

(C)   They had no known religion.

(D)   They had no knowledge of astronomy.

(E)   Their cultures survived and even thrived after Spanish contact.

37.   All of the following "New Deal" agencies were created during the Great Depression to provide jobs for the unemployed EXCEPT

(A)   Farm Security Administration (FSA)

(B)   Civil Works Administration (CWA)

(C)   Civilian Conservation Corps (CCC)

(D)   Works Progress Administration (WPA)

(E)   National Youth Administration (NYA)

38. The most important factor in the destruction of the Plains Indians' societies by Whites in the late nineteenth century was

(A) the use of modern weapons by white soldiers and cavalrymen

(B) the destruction of the Buffalo herds by Whites

(C) the introduction of alcohol by Whites to Indian society

(D) the encroachment of railroads onto Indian lands

(E) the use of reservations by Whites to limit the movements of Indians

39. The first successful English colony in North America was located in

(A) Roanoke, Virginia

(B) Plymouth, Massachusetts

(C) Jamestown, Virginia

(D) Salem, Massachusetts

(E) Manhattan, New York

40. The sharecropping system in the South following Reconstruction had the effect of

(A) allowing many former slaves and poor white tenant farmers, who could have never otherwise owned land, to buy their own farms

(B) moving many former slaves and poor white tenant farmers into the middle class

(C) pushing tenant farmers and poor independent farmers into deep levels of debt to large landowners and merchants

(D) helping to limit the power of former plantation owners and Northern business interests

(E) changing the basic attitudes of Whites and Blacks who were now forced to work side by side farming the same land

41. The Interstate Commerce Act of 1887 was aimed primarily at

(A) increasing interstate trade by forbidding states from levying tariffs on goods transported from other states

(B) curbing abusive pricing and hauling policies by the nation's railroads

    (C)   increasing interstate trade through government assistance in efforts to build new canals, roads, and railroads

    (D)   curbing abusive pricing and hauling policies by the nation's ocean-going, river-going, and canal-going shipping companies

    (E)   increasing interstate commerce by offering financial incentives to companies that operated offices or manufacturing plants in more than one state

42.   The only dominant, broad-based labor union in the United States from 1870–1890 was the

    (A)   National Labor Union

    (B)   Industrial Workers of the World (IWW)

    (C)   American Federation of Labor (AFL)

    (D)   Congress of Industrial Organization (CIO)

    (E)   Knights of Labor

43.   Andrew Jackson's election in 1828 is seen by many historians to represent

    (A)   the end of the Federalist party in America

    (B)   the rise of individualism and popular democracy in America

    (C)   the first true consolidation of federal power over the states since the drafting of the Constitution

    (D)   the beginnings of a genuine American aristocracy in government

    (E)   the low point of power for the executive branch of government in the 1800s

44.   The political machines such as Tammany Hall which ran American cities at the turn of the century derived their strongest support from

    (A)   industrial leaders and business elites

    (B)   organized religion

    (C)   wealthy landowners living in rural areas outside the cities

    (D)   the middle class

    (E)   poor immigrants and ethnic communities in the inner city

45. The "black codes" of many Southern states in the 1830s were intended to

   (A) force Northern states to return runaway slaves to their Southern masters

   (B) prevent slave rebellions by allowing the execution of any slave found guilty of attempting to gain his or her freedom

   (C) limit the rights of freed Blacks and force them to migrate to Northern states where they couldn't serve as models for slaves to idolize or emulate

   (D) keep all Blacks in servitude by refusing to recognize any Black as free and allowing so-called "free Blacks" to be rounded up and enslaved whenever a shortage of slave labor developed

   (E) deal with the increased number of people of mixed race (due to white slaveholders impregnating black slaves) by setting up strict standards as to who was genetically white and who was genetically black

46. The combination of European musical influences with African musical influences came together in 1890s New Orleans to form a new distinctly American musical style called

   (A) gospel   (D) country

   (B) jazz   (E) blues

   (C) folk

47. The Louisiana Purchase resulted primarily from

   (A) efforts to prevent Spain from closing off westward expansion by the United States

   (B) glowing reports of the vast beauty and potential of the region as reported by Lewis and Clark on their return from their famous exploration of the region

   (C) American efforts to prevent war with France over control of the Louisiana Territory and secure American commerce rights in New Orleans and along the Mississippi River

   (D) Federalist desires to establish a strong confederation of antislavery states west of the Mississippi River and further limit the power of the Southern Republicans

   (E) Republican desires to further dilute the Federalist power base in New England by expanding the country and reducing Federalist influence

48. How did the U.S. government initially react toward movements to establish trade unions in businesses and factories in the latter half of the nineteenth century?

   (A) It strongly supported the trade union movement and forced businesses to allow the development of unions

   (B) It mildly supported the development of trade unions but took no active measures to help establish unions until business abuses of workers became undeniable

   (C) It stayed out of business affairs, supporting neither businesses nor unions, unless one side or the other broke the law

   (D) It supported the establishment of unions in all businesses except defense industries and jobs which had civil service organizations

   (E) It actively supported business efforts to destroy unions before they could effectively establish themselves

49. In 1968, Viet Cong guerrillas and North Vietnamese regulars launched a massive series of attacks which failed militarily, but succeeded in ending U.S. fantasies about an early end to the Vietnam War. This episode of the war became known as the

   (A) Pleiku Offensive   (D) Battle of Khe Sahn

   (B) NLF Offensive   (E) Tet Offensive

   (C) Gulf of Tonkin affair

50. Which of the following was not a provision of the Paris Peace Treaty ending the American Revolution?

   (A) Louisiana was returned to French control.

   (B) Florida was returned to Spanish control.

   (C) The United States was recognized as an independent nation.

   (D) The lands between the Mississippi and the Appalachians were given to the U.S. in disregard for the rights of Indian tribes living in those regions.

   (E) The British granted the American fishing rights off the coast of Newfoundland.

51. What event triggered President Truman to announce the "Truman Doctrine"?

    (A) The overthrow of the Czechoslovakian government by Soviet Communists

    (B) Russian actions in Iran

    (C) The Greek Civil War

    (D) The Hungarian Revolution

    (E) The Korean War

52. The primary cause of the Spanish-American War was

    (A) Spanish occupation of the Panama Canal

    (B) American expansionism and support for Cuban nationalism

    (C) the murder of two U.S. diplomats in Spain on a peaceful diplomatic mission

    (D) Spanish attacks on U.S. commercial ships off the coast of Cuba

    (E) the sinking of the battleship *Maine* in Havana Harbor by Spanish military agents

53. Which of the following is NOT true of English colonial families in mid-eighteenth-century America?

    (A) Physical punishment was the normal method of enforcing unquestioned obedience from children.

    (B) Women lost virtually all of their legal rights as individuals once they married.

    (C) Most families bore children who lived long enough to bear children of their own.

    (D) Women, while subservient to their husbands, set the moral standards by which children were raised and decided how the children would be educated and trained.

    (E) More than 90 percent of families lived in rural areas at about this time.

54. What was the reaction of most Filipinos when they were liberated from Spanish control and occupied by American forces following the Spanish-American War?

(A) They applied for statehood, but their application was rejected by Congress which feared that the Philippines were too far away to effectively govern.

(B) They welcomed the Americans as heroes and were thrilled when the United States government announced that the Philippines would eventually be granted its independence when the people had been educated and trained in running their own government.

(C) Their reaction was relatively neutral. They had known nothing but colonial status for hundreds of years and had become resigned to their fate.

(D) While there was some resentment at the American refusal to grant them immediate independence, there was little violence. Most Philippine hostility was expressed in a few scattered peaceful protests.

(E) Filipinos, angered at American actions, declared themselves independent and launched a violent rebellion that killed thousands and took two years to quell.

55. Henry David Thoreau, Nathaniel Hawthorne, Ralph Waldo Emerson, James Fenimore Cooper, Herman Melville, Margaret Fuller, and Theodore Parker were all involved in developing the transcendentalist philosophy of the

(A) Shaker community in New Lebanon, New York

(B) Mormon community in Palmyra, New York

(C) New Harmony community in Indiana

(D) Oneida community in upstate New York

(E) Brooke Farm community in Roxbury, Massachusetts

56. The War of 1812 had all of the following effects EXCEPT:

(A) It strengthened American industrial and manufacturing production.

(B) It virtually destroyed the Federalist party as a credible opposition to the Republican party.

(C) It restored a sense of pride in most Americans and led to a wave of nationalism throughout the country after the conclusion of the war.

(D) It destroyed the power of the Indian tribes in the Northwest Territory.

(E) It led to an increased and more active American role in world politics.

57. What was the reaction in the U.S. Senate to the terms of the 1918 Treaty of Versailles?

(A) The Senate overwhelmingly supported the major provisions of the treaty and only demanded a few minor adjustments before ratifying it.

(B) The Senate felt that in many ways the treaty was too harsh on Germany, but that overall it was a good plan for postwar peace.

(C) The Senate was angry at Wilson for the way he handled the negotiations, but felt that the treaty was too important to be destroyed by partisan politics. As a result, the Senate narrowly passed the ratification measure making the treaty official.

(D) The Senate was angry at Wilson for the way he handled the negotiations and had problems with several treaty articles. As a result, the Senate didn't ratify the treaty until the second time Wilson sent it to them. Even then, the Senate refused to ratify the provisions calling for U.S. membership in a League of Nations.

(E) The Senate was angry at Wilson for the way he handled the negotiations and for the treaty that the peace conference produced. Wilson refused to compromise on various treaty provisions and the Senate rejected the treaty both times it was sent to them.

58. Which of the following best describes the administrations of Warren Harding and Calvin Coolidge?

(A) "The trusts must be broken!"

(B) "The only thing we have to fear is fear itself!"

(C) "The business of government is business!"

(D) "The taste of empire is in the mouths of the people!"

(E) "The world must be made safe for democracy!"

59. In the 1830s and 1840s, the primary difference between the Whigs and the Democrats was that

(A) the Whigs favored economic expansion while the Democrats favored a stable but retracted economy

(B)   the Democrats favored the abolition of slavery while the Whigs favored retaining the current system of slavery being allowed in the Southern states that desired it, but no further expansion of slavery north of the Mason-Dixon line

(C)   the Whigs favored an expanded, activist federal government while the Democrats favored a limited non-interventionist federal government

(D)   the Democrats were strongly supported by Evangelical Christians and supported a wide range of moral reforms while the Whigs were supported by Westerners who favored individual choice over morally based restrictions on behavior

(E)   the Whigs favored limitations on westward expansion while the Democrats favored the concept of "manifest destiny" and expansion to the Pacific Ocean

60.   The "Lost Generation" refers to

(A)   those young adults whose lives and families were devastated by the Great Depression of the 1930s

(B)   the millions of young men killed in the senseless trench warfare of World War I

(C)   young writers disillusioned by the materialism, decadence, and conformity dominating 1920s America

(D)   the thousands of workers killed or injured in efforts to form and promote worker safety in turn-of-the-century America

(E)   the generation of young Americans caught up in the turmoil of war protests and moral collapse during the 1960s

61.   In the cartoon shown below Thomas Nast presents Boss Tweed as

THE "BRAINS"

THAT ACHIEVED THE TAMMANY VICTORY AT THE ROCHESTER DEMOCRATIC CONVENTION.

(A)   a politician ruled by greed

(B)   a benefactor of the public

(C)   a political reformer

(D)   a politician corruptly influenced by business

(E)   a politician who rejected business influence

62.   All of the following contributed to the Great Depression EXCEPT

(A)   excessive stocks and securities speculation

(B)   protectionist trade measures

(C)   huge farm debts resulting from collapsed crop prices

(D)   lack of credit to help consumers sustain economic growth

(E)   an imbalance of distribution of wealth in which the rich controlled far too much of the available income

63.   After the collapse of the Reconstruction governments, the men who came to power in the "New South" were called

(A)   carpetbaggers   (D)   freedmen

(B)   scalawags   (E)   redeemers

(C)   copperheads

64.   The Nullification Crisis of 1832 revolved around

(A)   states' rights to overrule or disallow any federal legislation they found unacceptable

(B)   the federal government's right to nullify any antislavery legislation passed by the territories west of the Mississippi

(C)   the Supreme Court's right to nullify Congressional legislation deemed unconstitutional

(D)   the refusal of state militias to submit themselves to federal control in time of war

(E)   the right of Congress to override a presidential veto on matters of foreign policy

65.   The Indian Reorganization Act of 1934 sought to

(A)   end federal subsidies to landless Indian tribes and force them to support themselves

(B)   prohibit the division of tribal lands into allotments and allow Indians to resume using their own tribal languages and rituals on their lands

(C) requisition desirable land from Indian tribes and force those tribes to relocate on smaller jointly occupied reservations, in which several tribes would reside, intermingle, and share the same land

(D) break up tribal reservations into individual allotments of land that could be occupied by Indians or purchased by whites

(E) prohibit Indians from using tribal languages or practicing ancient tribal religions on government reservations

66. Parliament claimed the right to tax and legislate England's American colonies whenever it desired, without direct American representation in Parliament, through passage of

(A) the Declaratory Act   (D) the Intolerable Acts

(B) the Proclamation of 1763   (E) the Currency Act

(C) the Townshend Acts

67. A major impact of the French and Indian War on the attitudes of Americans was

(A) it led many Americans to question the superiority of English colonial rule and to support French colonial rule

(B) it convinced most Americans to avoid further exploration and settlement of the Ohio and Mississippi valleys until after the American Revolution

(C) it bound the American colonists more tightly to England than ever before and made most of them realize they needed English protection from foreign powers such as the French

(D) it led many colonists who had previously supported independence from England to call for moderation because they feared that the huge British military presence in the colonies (brought over from England to fight the French) could now be turned on rebellious colonists

(E) with the threat of the French now gone from their borders, many colonists now felt that English protection was unnecessary and they felt free to take a more independent stand toward Britain than they had taken previously

68. The battle that is considered to be the "turning point" of the Civil War and the last chance at a military victory by the Confederacy is

(A) Antietam   (D) Chattanooga

(B) Shiloh   (E) Chickamaugua

(C) Gettysburg

69. During the campaign to ratify the Constitution, the Federalists argued

    (A) for a return to the Articles of Confederation as the framework of federal government

    (B) that a bill of rights, to correct flaws in the Constitution, must be in place before the Constitution could be ratified

    (C) for rejection of the Constitution and the convening of a new Constitutional Convention to come up with a better framework for government

    (D) for ratification of the Constitution, with a possible bill of rights to be discussed after ratification

    (E) against a strong national government of any kind and an increase in the powers of states to govern themselves

70. The biggest failure of Reconstruction governments was that they

    (A) failed to reestablish an effective plantation system to rejuvenate the South's devastated economy

    (B) were dominated by Blacks, which aroused white hostility that, combined with the inexperience of black legislators, doomed Reconstruction governments to failure

    (C) failed to reestablish an effective public education system in the occupied South

    (D) failed to effectively industrialize the South

    (E) failed to change basic white attitudes in the South and they were unable to effectively reorganize the South's social structure

71. All of the following contributed to the success and stability of the New England colonies, and the bare survival of the Chesapeake Bay colonies EXCEPT

    (A) New England colonists tended to arrive in family units while the vast majority of Chesapeake Bay colonists were young single males who arrived as indentured servants.

    (B) The Chesapeake Bay region had a much higher death rate among its colonists than did the New England region.

    (C) Women were treated more as equals in the New England colonies than they were in the Chesapeake Bay region, making it more difficult to attract women to Chesapeake Bay.

(D) The ratio of males to females in Chesapeake Bay was much more imbalanced than in New England, making it more difficult for males in Chesapeake Bay to find wives and start families.

(E) The population increased faster in New England, allowing for the development of stable communities, than it did in the Chesapeake Bay region.

72. The Treaty of Ghent signaled the end of the

(A) Revolutionary War

(B) Spanish-American War

(C) War of 1812

(D) Mexican-American War

(E) quasi-war with France

73. The American system of manufacturing which emerged in the early 1800s was successful because of its use of

(A) slave labor

(B) handmade, individually crafted, high-quality items

(C) the "putting out" system — distributing raw materials and collecting finished products for distribution

(D) early electric power to provide cheap energy for new factories

(E) interchangable parts to allow for mass production of high-quality items

74. Which of the following was used as "scientific evidence" by wealthy American industrialists in the latter half of the nineteenth century to prove that they deserved the wealth they had accumulated?

(A) Broca's research into the functioning of various centers of the human brain

(B) Darwin's theory of natural selection

(C) Freud's theories of human psychology

(D) The research of Louis Pasteur on biological processes

(E) Karl Marx's research on the economic development of societies

75. What was the name of the U.S.-sponsored economic aid plan designed to rebuild Europe after WW II had ended?

    (A) The Marshall Plan   (D) The Eisenhower Doctrine

    (B) The Atlantic Charter   (E) The Truman Doctrine

    (C) The Schleiffen Plan

76. In announcing the Emancipation Proclamation, Lincoln's immediate purpose was to

    (A) free black slaves in all of the slave states

    (B) free black slaves in only the border slave states which had remained loyal to the Union

    (C) let the Southern states know that whether or not they chose to secede from the Union, slavery would not be tolerated by his administration once he took office

    (D) rally Northern morale by giving the war a higher moral purpose than just preserving the Union

    (E) recruit freed Blacks into the Union army and overcome the shortage of white soldiers in the army at that time

77. Which Revolutionary War battle is considered the "turning point" in the war because it led to direct French assistance for the Americans?

    (A) Trenton   (D) Yorktown

    (B) Bunker Hill   (E) Saratoga

    (C) Princeton

78. What event, in 1957, caused a near panic among U.S. leaders and led to a massive increase in spending for science programs, etc. in U.S. schools and research institutions?

    (A) The revelation of huge Soviet stockpiles of deadly chemical weapons to be used in any future confrontation with the United States

    (B) The launching of *Sputnik* by the Soviet Union

    (C) The detonation of a hydrogen bomb by the Soviet Union

    (D) The development of the microprocessor by the Soviet Union

    (E) Soviet Premier Nikita Khrushchev's promise to "bury" the West

79. The Wilmot Proviso was most likely to be supported by

   (A) Jacksonian Democrats

   (B) advocates of nullification

   (C) secessionists

   (D) free-soilers

   (E) advocates of popular sovereignty

80. Lyndon Johnson's Great Society program was aimed primarily at

   (A) spurring advances in American science and technical education and increasing funding to high-tech research facilities

   (B) sending American volunteers to impoverished foreign nations to help educate their people and build their economic base

   (C) securing civil rights for all Americans and eliminating poverty

   (D) providing minimum-wage jobs for all unemployed Americans and shifting tax dollars from the military to the civilian sector of the economy

   (E) retraining adults who had dropped out of school and increasing the number of Americans who attended college

STOP
This is the end of Section I.
If time still remains, you may check your work only in this section.
Do not begin Section II until instructed to do so.

SECTION II

TIME: Reading Period – 15 Minutes
Writing Time for All Essays – 115 Minutes

DIRECTIONS: Read over the Document-Based Essay question in Part A and the choices in Parts B and C during the Reading Period, and use the time to organize answers. All students must answer Part A (the Document-Based Essay question) and answer ONE question in both Parts B and C.

PART A – DOCUMENT-BASED ESSAY
(Suggested writing time: 45 minutes)

1.   On December 7, 1941, the Japanese attacked the United States naval station and its associated air defense bases at Pearl Harbor in Hawaii. The attack killed more than 2,400 Americans, knocked out eight American battleships, and destroyed nearly 400 American warplanes on the ground. It was the worst single defeat ever inflicted on the United States Navy. Using the following documents and your knowledge of the military and diplomatic history of this time, evaluate how this disaster could have happened and who was primarily responsible for the disaster — government officials in Washington or local commanders at Pearl Harbor.

Document A

Source: Message of November 27, 1941, from the Navy Department in Washington, D.C., to Admiral Kimmel, Commander in Chief, Pacific Fleet, in command of United States naval forces at Pearl Harbor

"This dispatch is to be considered a war warning. Negotiations with Japan... have ceased and an aggressive move by Japan is expected within the next few days. The number and equipment of Japanese troops and the organization of the naval task forces indicate an amphibious expedition against either the Philippines, Thai, or Kra Peninsula, or possibly Borneo. Execute an appropriate defensive deployment."

Document B

Source: Rear Admiral Richard Turner, Chief of War Plans, United States Navy in the Joint Committee on the Investigation of the Pearl Harbor Attack

"We expected all war scouting measures to be undertaken, submarines to be sent out to protect our fleet and territory. The carriers with their protective vessels to put out to sea and stand in readiness for war...a high degree of readiness on board ships against attack of any form; and on shore...a high degree of readiness of defensive troops, including antiaircraft. The [war warning] dispatch was prepared jointly with the Army. We expected a deployment of the Army on shore appropriate with a defensive state of readiness, such as manning the coastal guns and moving troops out to their deployment positions."

Document C

Source: Henry L. Stimson, United States Secretary of War, in the Joint Committee on the Investigation of the Pearl Harbor Attack

"We had spent several hundred million [dollars] in defense of Hawaii. We had our greatest fleet out there. That Hawaii could be attacked if Japan went to war was obvious to everyone…. Of course we had had information for a great many years which had been considered in all our war plans in Hawaii that there was a certain part of the Pacific Ocean that we called the 'Vacant Sea' in which there were practically no ships and in which large movements of ships could occur without anybody seeing them…. It would have been almost a military intelligence miracle had we been able to spot a task force in forming and have known before it sailed where it was going.

"Under these circumstances…[for General Short] to cluster his planes in such groups and positions that in an emergency they could not take off for several hours, and to keep his antiaircraft ammunition so stored that it could not be promptly and immediately available, and to use his best reconnaissance system, the radar, only for a very small fraction of the day and night, in my opinion betrayed a misconception of his real duty which was almost beyond belief.

"I had no idea that [General Short's response to the 'war warning' dispatch] of being 'alerted to prevent sabotage' was an…implied denial of being alert against attack from Japan's armed forces. The very purpose of a fortress such as Hawaii is to repel such an attack and Short was the commander of that fortress. Furthermore, Short's statement [responding to the war warning dispatch]…gave the impression that the various reconnaissance and other defensive measures in which the cooperation of the Army and Navy is necessary were under way and a proper alert was in effect."

Document D

Source: Japanese Intelligence Report from Tokyo to Pearl Harbor attack force on December 6, 1941

"No [air defense] balloons, no torpedo-defense nets deployed around battleships in Pearl Harbor. All battleships are in. No indications from radio activity that ocean-patrol [reconnaissance] flights being made in Hawaiian area."

Document E

Source: General Walter Short, Commander of the Department of Hawaii, and of all United States Army and Army Air Corps forces stationed at Pearl Harbor in December, 1941, in the Joint Committee on the Investigation of the Pearl Harbor Attack

"There was...an abundance of information which was vital to me but which was not furnished to me. This information was absolutely essential to a correct estimate of the situation and correct decision.... Had this information been available to me, I am sure that I would have gone on all-out alert.... The War Department had nine days in which to tell me my [preparations against sabotage only and not against enemy air attack] was not what they wanted. I accepted their silence as full agreement with the action taken.... I was singled out [by the War Department] as...the scapegoat for the disaster."

Document F

Source: Admiral Huband E. Kimmel, Commander in Chief, United States Pacific Fleet at the time of the Pearl Harbor attack, in the Joint Committee on the Investigation of the Pearl Harbor Attack

"The Pacific fleet was deprived of a fighting chance to avert the disaster of December 7, 1941, because the Navy Department withheld information which indicated the probability of an attack at Pearl Harbor at the time it came.... The so-called 'war warning' dispatch of November 27 did not warn the Pacific Fleet of an attack on the Hawaiian area. The phrase 'war warning' cannot be made a catch-all for the contingencies hindsight may suggest.... I was entitled to know of the intercepted dispatches between Tokyo and Honolulu on and after September 24, 1941, which indicated that a Japanese move against Pearl Harbor was planned in Tokyo."

Document G

Source: Coded messages from the Japanese government to its embassy in Washington on the night of December 6th, 1941 (These messages were decoded by American intelligence analysts by 1 A.M., December 7 Eastern time but were sent to Pearl Harbor by commercial telegram rather than military priority cable. They were received at Pearl Harbor and decoded AFTER the Japanese attack.)

"The Japanese government regrets to have to notify hereby the American government that in view of the attitude of the American government it cannot but consider that it is impossible to reach an agreement through further negotiations."

"Will the [Japanese] Ambassador please submit to the United States government (if possible to the Secretary of State) our reply [above] to the United States at 1:00 P.M. on the 7th, your time [Eastern time – 7:30 A.M. Pearl Harbor time]."

Document H

Source: Colonel Rufus Bratton, Chief of Army Intelligence, Far Eastern Section in the Joint Committee on the Investigation of the Pearl Harbor Attack

"Nobody in the Office of Naval Intelligence [in Washington]...knew that any major element of the fleet was in Pearl Harbor on Sunday morning the 7th of December. We all thought they had gone to sea.... Because that was part of the war plan and they had been given a war warning."

Document I

Source: Report of the Joint Committee on the Investigation of the Pearl Harbor Attack

"It was Washington's responsibility to give Admiral Kimmel its best estimate of where the major strategic enemy effort would come. It was Admiral Kimmel's responsibility as commander in chief of the Pacific Fleet to be prepared for the worst contingency, and when he was warned of war and ordered to execute a defensive deployment it was necessarily in contemplation that such action would be against all possible dangers with which the Hawaiian situation was fraught."

PARTS B AND C – STANDARD ESSAY QUESTIONS
(70 minutes)

DIRECTIONS: Choose ONE question each from Part B and Part C. It is recommended that you spend 5 minutes planning and 30 minutes writing. Support your thesis with germane historical evidence and present your case logically and clearly.

PART B

2. Discuss the significance of the election of Andrew Jackson to the presidency in 1828.

3. "With the end of Reconstruction, we in the South can now return to our normal lives." Examine the significance of this statement for both whites and blacks in the post-Reconstruction American South.

PART C

4. "The taste of empire is in the mouths of the people!" Assess the validity of this statement made at the conclusion of the Spanish-American War.

5. Compare and contrast the fundamental differences between Herbert Hoover's and Franklin Roosevelt's approach to the Great Depression. Summarize the effectiveness of each approach.

AP UNITED STATES HISTORY

PRACTICE TEST 3

ANSWER KEY

1. (B)	21. (D)	41. (B)	61. (A)
2. (C)	22. (D)	42. (E)	62. (D)
3. (A)	23. (B)	43. (B)	63. (E)
4. (B)	24. (C)	44. (E)	64. (A)
5. (B)	25. (C)	45. (C)	65. (B)
6. (A)	26. (C)	46. (B)	66. (A)
7. (D)	27. (C)	47. (C)	67. (E)
8. (E)	28. (B)	48. (E)	68. (C)
9. (A)	29. (E)	49. (E)	69. (D)
10. (B)	30. (E)	50. (A)	70. (E)
11. (D)	31. (D)	51. (C)	71. (C)
12. (A)	32. (C)	52. (B)	72. (C)
13. (A)	33. (D)	53. (D)	73. (E)
14. (E)	34. (C)	54. (E)	74. (B)
15. (C)	35. (A)	55. (E)	75. (A)
16. (D)	36. (A)	56. (E)	76. (D)
17. (A)	37. (A)	57. (E)	77. (E)
18. (A)	38. (B)	58. (C)	78. (B)
19. (A)	39. (C)	59. (C)	79. (D)
20. (E)	40. (C)	60. (C)	80. (C)

DETAILED EXPLANATIONS
OF ANSWERS

TEST 3

SECTION I

1. **(B)**

Burr and Hamilton had never been close friends, and Hamilton made no secret of the fact that he did not trust Burr. During the congressional voting to resolve the outcome of the presidential election of 1800, when Burr might have become the third president of the United States, Hamilton had made attacks against Burr's personal character. In 1804, as Burr ran for governor of New York, Hamilton repeated and expanded those charges. When Burr lost the election, he blamed Hamilton, although there is no clear evidence that Hamilton's charges led to Burr's defeat. Burr demanded "satisfaction" through a duel and Hamilton accepted. Hamilton's death not only deprived the young nation of one of its premiere thinkers and statesmen, but it ruined Burr's political career. He was charged with murder and forced to flee to avoid arrest. It was after this disaster that he began formulating his plan for an independent Western empire. Thus, choice (C) is incorrect.

2. **(C)**

The question deals with the growth of the United States during President McKinley's tenure. President Madison was in office during the War of 1812. President Lincoln headed the government during the Civil War. President Wilson led the country in World War I. President F. D. Roosevelt was the leader in World War II. Thus, the correct answer is (C).

3. **(A)**

Contrary to myth, Confederate industry did a masterful job in producing weapons and ammunition for the Confederate military during the war. While it is true that the Confederates never had the abundance of weapons possessed by Union forces, particularly in artillery, it was only near the end of the war, when Union forces had overrun many production centers and totally destroyed the South's transportation network, that severe shortages of ammunition and weapons developed. It is also true that in the beginning of the war Confederate industry could not arm everyone who volunteered for military service; the Union had that same problem. Most Southerners had their own weapons so that despite the lack of government-produced weapons, there was no shortage of available weapons for soldiers. The biggest problem faced by the Confederate armies in regard to weapons and ammunition was a lack of uniformity for the vast array of "home grown" weapons and ammunition used by their soldiers, not a shortage of weapons themselves.

4.   **(B)**

The national unemployment rate soared to approximately 25 percent of the work force in early 1933. This meant that approximately 13 million workers were unemployed. While 25 percent was the national unemployment rate, in some cities the number of unemployed approached 90 percent. This was at a time when there were no welfare benefits or unemployment funds in most areas of the country. What made things worse was the sheer amount of time workers remained unemployed. By early 1937, unemployment had fallen to 14.3 percent, still representing 8 million unemployed workers. Then the recession of 1937 put an additional 2 million workers out of work again. The suffering of being unemployed as long as many of these workers is beyond description. Hobo camps and "Hoovervilles" popped up in virtually every American city.

Worse, even for those who kept their jobs, poverty became widespread. Crop prices for farmers dropped by 60 percent. Wages, for workers who still had jobs, dropped 40 percent. Banks continued to collapse, taking the personal savings of depositors down with them, leaving depositors with no savings to help them through this period. So, while 25 percent may not sound catastrophic at first, combined with the collapse of wages and crop prices, as well as the collapse of banks and the sheer amount of time many people were out of work, the nation's economy was close to total collapse.

5.   **(B)**

The Navigation Acts were designed to force the colonies to trade exclusively with England and to give the British government extensive regulatory control over all colonial trade. All of the choices except choice (B) were major principles of these acts. The prohibition of the colonies from issuing paper currencies, while also having a major impact on colonial trade, was the focal point of the Currency Act of 1764 (approximately 100 years later than the Navigation Acts).

6.   **(A)**

Slavery never effectively established itself in New England, in large part because the economic system of the New England colonies and the large population of New England, which provided a large pool of workers, rendered the need for large numbers of slaves unnecessary. Most New England farms were relatively small, self-sufficient farms, and the members of farming communities depended on each other to keep their communities economically viable. In the Southern English colonies, there was less community cohesion among the colonists, there were fewer people, and there was a constant demand for laborers to cultivate the cash crops necessary to keep the colonies economically afloat. At first this demand was met by the use of indentured servants, but after the 1660s the supply of potential servants dwindled and the only immediate replacement labor pool was imported slave labor.

7.   **(D)**

In early 1942, the Japanese high command, angered at air raids from American aircraft carriers, decided to force what was left of the American Pacific fleet into a decisive battle in which the American Navy and its carriers would be destroyed. They decided on an invasion of the American-held island of Midway. Midway was a logical choice. It was 1,100 miles northwest of Hawaii. More importantly, it had a seaplane base and an airstrip. In American hands it provided the United States with an observation post to monitor Japanese actions throughout the central Pacific. In Japanese hands, it would provide them with an airbase from which they could launch continuous air attacks on Pearl Harbor, making it unusable as an American base. If Japan invaded Midway, the Americans would have to send their fleet to defend it or face the loss of Pearl Harbor and Hawaii.

On paper, the plan seemed ideal. The Japanese could throw up to 10 aircraft carriers into the operation. They believed the Americans had only two available aircraft carriers (actually, the Americans had three usable carriers because the U.S.S. *Yorktown*, which the Japanese thought they had sunk at the Battle of Coral Sea, had survived and was repaired in time to fight at Midway). The Japanese had dozens of battleships and heavy cruisers. The Americans had only two battleships available, which they chose not to use, and only eight heavy cruisers. On paper, there seemed to be no way the Americans could win.

Unfortunately for the Japanese, the battle was not fought on paper. American cryptographers deciphered enough Japanese messages to uncover the plan. In addition, the overconfident Japanese, expecting to surprise a scattered American fleet, didn't concentrate their forces into an overwhelming single attack force. Instead they divided their fleet into four separate attack forces, each of which was vulnerable to American attack if caught off guard. When the Japanese arrived at Midway, a well-prepared, tightly concentrated American fleet was waiting. Despite a series of nearly catastrophic errors, the Americans caught the Japanese by surprise, sinking four of their largest aircraft carriers and killing 600 of Japan's best pilots. Without adequate air protection, the invasion was cancelled and the Japanese fleet returned to base. Midway was saved. At the time, American analysts thought they had just bought the United States some additional time until the Japanese regrouped and attacked again. In reality, the Japanese were so stunned by the defeat that they readjusted their war plans, switching to defensive operations. They never returned to Midway. With the Japanese now on the defensive, the United States was able to seize the initiative at Guadalcanal, beginning an island-hopping campaign that took America to Japan's outer islands. Midway was undoubtedly the turning point as it marked the first significant American victory over the Japanese and the end of major Japanese offensive operations in the central Pacific.

8.   **(E)**

Brown v. Board of Education of Topeka was the first legal shot in the war to desegregate America's public schools. Up to this time, many school districts, particularly in the South, had segregated schools for black and white schoolchildren under the doctrine of "separate but equal" education. Sadly, most education facilities for black children were anything but equal. Blacks usually got dilapidated facilities, the worst teachers, and an inferior education. Frustrated black parents challenged the "separate but equal" doctrine in several states and those challenges were consolidated into one case to be presented before the United States Supreme Court in 1954. Up until this case, previous civil rights cases had been heard before conservative Supreme Courts which had upheld the "separate but equal" doctrine. However, by 1954, the Court was a more liberal court, more sensitive to constitutional protections for all people.

9.   **(A)**

The Great Awakening was a series of religious awakenings, or rebirths, centered primarily in New England but spread throughout the colonies which changed the lives of English colonists. It challenged the old hierarchical religious order in which ordained clergy were deferred to and were believed to have knowledge based on extensive formal learning that the average member of a congregation lacked. It brought a much broader sense of community to colonists making them aware of others with similar questions and beliefs who lived outside their village or town. In many ways, it was the first of a series of events that helped to forge distinctively American regional identities, separate from their European heritage, among the North American colonists.

10.   **(B)**

There were many major changes resulting from the rapid industrial development in the United States from 1860 through 1900. First, there was a shift to building larger and larger industrial facilities to accommodate the new machine technologies coming into existence. Small factories could not absorb the cost of much of the machinery and did not produce enough to make the machinery profitable. So contrary to choice (D), there was an increase in large industrial plants and a relative decline in small factories.

11.   **(D)**

In the autumn of 1864, a war-weary North faced a presidential election that offered them a clear choice. Abraham Lincoln ran on a platform of continuing the Civil War until the South was totally defeated. His opponent, former general George McClellan, ran on a platform calling for an armistice and recognition of the South as a separate nation. Early in the campaign, Lincoln looked to be in trouble. Although the Union had made deep penetrations into the western half of the Confederacy and had complete control of the Mississippi River, the Confederate armies in the East still fought valiantly on. It looked as if the Union armies could never destroy them and many people were questioning if it was worth the cost to try. The war had now been raging for three-and-one-half years. The cost in human lives, time, and money had far surpassed everyone's worst fears. Many Northerners just wanted it to be over. Both Lincoln and Confederate President Jefferson Davis realized this. Accordingly, the Confederate strategy was to just hold on and deny the North any major victories before the election. Lincoln realized he needed a decisive victory before the election, pointing to a a rapid defeat of the Confederacy, if he was to win. That victory occurred in September 1864 when Union forces under the command of William T. Sherman occupied Atlanta and followed up on this victory with his infamous "march to the sea." This victory pointed to the imminent destruction of the Confederacy. Finally, people could see a "light at the end of the tunnel" and desire to completely defeat the Confederates rose again in the North. The capture of Atlanta guaranteed Lincoln's reelection and sealed the fate of the Confederate States of America.

12.   **(A)**

After he was overthrown by revolutionary forces in 1978, the Shah of Iran, then residing in Mexico, asked for permission to enter the United States to receive cancer treatment. President Carter was warned that admitting the Shah to the United States, for any reason, would look to the Iranians like America still supported the Shah's regime and would lead to trouble. However, other advisors told Carter that the United States owed the Shah a large debt of gratitude for the favors he had done for America and also for the lack of decisive support from the U.S. when his government was overthrown. Carter had previously refused to grant the Shah exile in the United States, but when he was told of the Shah's need for cancer treatment, he decided to allow the Shah to enter the U.S. on humanitarian grounds. As predicted, the Iranians were infuriated by this. On November 4, 1979, young Iranian males, backed by their government and claiming to be students, seized the American embassy compound and took 76 hostages, 62 of whom were held for more than a year. It was the beginning of one of the worst nightmares in American foreign policy, and it helped ruin Carter's presidency.

13.   **(A)**

In the presidential election of 1876, Samuel Tilden defeated his Republican opponent, Rutherford B. Hayes, in the popular vote by 250,000 votes. However, there were 20 contested votes in the electoral college. If Hayes received all the contested electoral votes, he would win the election by one vote in the Electoral College and he would gain the presidency. The matter was turned over to Congress, where a Republican-dominated commission awarded the disputed electoral votes to Hayes. The Senate ratified the commission's decision, but the Democrats in the House threatened to use political means to gain Tilden's victory through a House vote. Republicans negotiated the issue and the Compromise of 1877 was the result. Hayes got the presidency. Democrats received assurances that federal soldiers would be withdrawn from Southern states (effectively ending Reconstruction) and that blanket federal government support for Republicans in the South would end. This opened the door for Democrats to regain control in all the Southern states (they had already effectively regained control in all but three). None of the other choices listed in the question were in any way involved in the Compromise of 1877.

14.   **(E)**

Operation Desert Shield became Operation Desert Storm on January 16, 1991, when President George Bush announced, "The world could wait no longer...." U.S. air and sea forces together with U.N. coalition allies utilized the high-tech weapons of the U.S. Allied forces to free Kuwait and appeared to have crushed the Iraqi army in a 100-hour ground offensive. Immediate steps were taken to coordinate efforts with the U.N. (A), protect Saudi Arabia (B), impose economic sanctions (C), and designate these efforts Operation Desert Shield (D).

15.   **(C)**

Tomatoes, potatoes, maize (corn), and chocolate were all New World crops. Coffee was first cultivated in Africa. Tomatoes, which grow wild in the Andes

Mountains, were cultivated by the Incas in 700 C.E. The Incas also first grew potatoes as an agricultural crop, with archaeological evidence suggesting its cultivation as early as 200 B.C.E. Maize first appeared in southern Mexico as early as 5000 B.C.E. Chocolate was first consumed by the Aztecs and Mayas. By 1000 C.E. cocoa beans were used as currency.

16.   **(D)**

The federal budget deficit, which was driven up by the high costs of Social Security, defense, and payments on the national debt, was not seriously challenged by the Congress or the President. A recession was further influenced by a drop in military spending. Unemployment reached 7.8 percent, an eight-year high, and the GNP declined. Bush's promise, "Read my lips, no new taxes," was believed broken. The average growth rate while Bush was in office was less than 0.5 percent. Although inflation was low, the recurring theme of the Clinton campaign was, "It's the economy, stupid!" Domestic (A) and foreign (B, C, E) division and strife did not capture the attention of the American voter.

17.   **(A)**

The "Good Neighbor" policy sought to smooth over relations between the United States and Latin America by retreating from the blatant interventionism which dominated U.S. policy into the 1930s. The effects of interventionism had become increasingly costly to the point that the benefits derived were not worth the expense. In 1933, Franklin Roosevelt officially consolidated many changes already under way in U.S. policy toward Latin America under the heading of the "Good Neighbor" policy. Under this plan, the United States would pull back from the nearly constant use of military intervention to control Latin American nations. The United States government would cease acting unilaterally in Latin American affairs and would attempt to consult with and seek the approval of Latin American governments before intervening in the region. In addition, the United States would support Latin American governments headed by strong, independent leaders and would help train Latin American military forces so they could defend themselves. United States banks would also provide loans and other economic assistance to help stabilize fragile Latin American economies.

While the United States still dominated many aspects of Latin American life, with the enactment of the "Good Neighbor" policy that domination was handled more diplomatically, with somewhat more respect for local authorities. Many of the leaders who emerged at this time were military dictators who were trained by American military personnel as part of the effort to train Latin American military forces. These dictators owed their power to the United States and often stayed in power only as a result of U.S. backing. So, while the days of the "Big Stick" effectively ended with the "Good Neighbor" policy, U.S. domination of the region continued, albeit at a somewhat reduced level of visibility.

18.   **(A)**

The Northwest Ordinance of 1787, like the previous ordinances of 1784 and 1785, ignored the Indian tribes' claims to the land contained within the Northwest Territory. The Shawnee, Delaware, and Miami, armed with weapons supplied by the British, attacked whites who settled north and west of the Ohio River and prevented settlement of the region for nearly 10 years. While the Northwest

Ordinance was a progressive document for its time, it was meaningless until the Indian problem was resolved and settlement of the area was achieved. Contained within the Northwest Ordinance were the provisions listed in choices (B) through (E). The antislavery prohibition is particularly notable because it reflected a growing concern, particularly in the North, about the institution of slavery. It marked the first regional limitation of slavery in the U.S. beyond individual state boundaries.

19.   **(A)**

"Reaganomics" was the term coined for President Ronald Reagan's supply-side economic policies. Reagan believed that the way to repair the shattered economy he inherited from the Carter administration was to cut federal spending on domestic programs while at the same time cutting taxes for the wealthy and for corporations. The "supply-side" theory advocated by Reagan asserted that by cutting taxes to businesses and to the rich, money would be freed up for future investments and the creation of new jobs. This investment income would offset the initial loss of tax revenue caused by the tax cuts. Eventually, through the creation of new jobs and investments, the money freed up by tax cuts to the rich would "trickle down" to the middle-classes and the poor. While this sounded good on paper, it never worked out quite as well in real life. Yes, the tax cuts did spur investment, but the investments often didn't translate into jobs that paid well. The "trickle-down" was uneven and often quite limited. Many wealthy people pocketed the money rather than investing it. Still, new jobs were created and the nation began an economic expansion that has lasted into the 1990s.

20.   **(E)**

Nineteenth-century Europeans and Americans fully believed in the superiority of their cultures, of the white race, and of Christianity. In their minds, it was perfectly acceptable to go into undeveloped non-white lands and do what they pleased with the lands and the natives. Since the natives of these lands were overwhelmingly non-white, non-Christian, and technologically undeveloped, Americans and Europeans rationalized their domination of these lands and the subjugation of the natives. They viewed their actions as a noble mission to "civilize" the "savages" and give them the benefits of Western culture. This "mission" was called the "white man's burden" because it was characterized as a burden that only the shoulders of the Western white male were big enough to handle.

21.   **(D)**

The paternalistic view of slavery, held by most Southern plantation owners, held that blacks were inferior, mentally weak and ignorant, requiring "protection" from the evils that could befall them if they were left on their own. In this view, slaveowners were benevolent protectors who took care of their black slaves almost as parents take care of children. This was a comforting myth that most slaveholders really appear to have believed. It was comforting in that if they were really protectors of their poor black "children," then holding slaves wasn't sinful at all. It was, rather, a social service providing a good for everybody involved. Unfortunately, this twisted rationalization denied the fact that slaves were horribly mistreated and often abused or killed for little or no provocation. If they were ignorant or childlike, it is only because they were denied educational opportunities and many slaves learned that acting with childlike deference to their "master" often got them better treatment. In other words, their childishness was often an act based on a powerful instinct to survive rather than any limitations of mental capacity.

22.   **(D)**

Mark Twain's writings pioneered a trend toward realism in American literature at the turn of the century. This trend portrayed the lives of real, flawed, and often quite colorful human beings. There was no effort to make the characters in these stories "larger than life" or pillars of virtue to be admired for their flawless character. These people struggled with the everyday issues of life as well as the bigger social and moral questions of the day, sometimes reaching successful resolutions to their quests, more often than not finding only partial answers to their problems. The focus of these stories was often on the temptations of sin, sexuality, and other of life's evils. The hero or heroine often faced difficult tests or questions regarding what was right or wrong in their particular situation. The realistic school of writing was in many ways a coming of age for American literature and bore its own unique stamp as a uniquely American contribution to the world of written fiction.

23.　　**(B)**

In January 1918, Woodrow Wilson proposed Fourteen Points which enunciated his goals for the peace that would follow World War I. These were idealistic goals based on notions of open diplomacy, the elimination of secret treaties, self-determination, arms reduction, open trade, and a League of Nations to serve as an international forum to prevent future wars. The thrust of the Fourteen Points emphasized fairness and openness in international relationships. By November 1918, the Germans faced military and political collapse, but they approached an armistice with the Allies convinced that the postwar treaty would be a fair one based upon Wilson's Fourteen Points. They reasoned that since the United States had turned the tide and saved France and Britain from almost certain defeat, the United States would dominate the peace negotiations. Unfortunately, they reasoned incorrectly and the Treaty of Versailles reflected British and French desires for vengeance more than it reflected the Wilsonian principles elucidated in his Fourteen Points.

24.　　**(C)**

This engraving emphasizes the innocence and helplessness of the victims.

25.　　**(C)**

Grant was an intensely loyal man who was, sadly, not the best judge of character in choosing his administrative appointees. During his first term in office, his administration was beset with financial scandals involving the vice president, Grant's brother-in-law, and a well-known financial entrepreneur named Jay Gould. In his second term, the "whiskey ring" scandal implicated Grant's private secretary. His secretary of war was implicated in a bribery scandal. While few believed Grant to be corrupt, Grant's loyalty to his corrupt associates tarnished his image in virtually everyone's eyes. It also crippled the effectiveness of his administration.

26.　　**(C)**

While the United States was technically neutral in World War II until the Japanese attack on Pearl Harbor, Franklin Roosevelt made no secret of his distaste for Nazi Germany, Fascist Italy, and militaristic Japan. He openly sought repeal of the neutrality laws so the United States could sell weapons and supplies to Britain and France to help them stop Hitler in Europe. Congress finally agreed, in November 1939, to allow cash sales of goods to European belligerents, meaning France and Britain. When France fell to the Nazi *blitzkrieg*, England stood alone and quickly used up its cash reserves trying to replace its war losses and brace for the expected German invasion. Churchill told Roosevelt of the desperate British situation and predicted that without some means of obtaining American weapons Britain would quickly fall. Realizing that the British needed the help but could not pay for the weapons, Roosevelt proposed Lend-Lease, a policy through which Britain would be allowed to borrow the weapons it needed and would be expected to return the weapons when the war was over. Realizing that there was nothing subtle about this circumvention of the cash-and-carry law, Roosevelt used the analogy of the neighbor's burning house to justify Lend-Lease. Although critics attacked the proposal, it was passed by Congress and was critical in the eventual success of the Allied war effort.

27.   **(C)**

While the slavery issue had never died out, a series of compromises had smoothed over many of the underlying issues left unresolved throughout the 1830s and 1840s. With the acquisition of California, Texas, and the New Mexico Territory from Mexico, combined with the treaty giving the United States complete control of southern Oregon Territory, the whole slavery issue resurfaced like an open wound. Fierce debates would dominate the political scene over which states should be "slave states" or "free states." Some people desired popular sovereignty in which residents of a territory could decide for themselves if they wanted to allow slavery. Others, primarily Southerners, argued that such popular sovereignty was unconstitutional. The debates often turned violent, as was notably true in Kansas in the 1850s. Eventually, the slavery debate, reopened by the Mexican-American War, would lead to the separationism and secessionism in the South that sparked the Civil War.

28.   **(B)**

The years between 1876 and 1900 were years of relative political equality between the Republicans and Democrats. It was also a time when most Americans were rejecting or resisting the cries for reform by political activists. Most people wanted the federal government to remain inactive and uninvolved as much as possible. The concept of laissez-faire leadership was flourishing. This resulted in little significant reform legislation from the Congress. It also led to the election of presidents who saw themselves as political caretakers of the office of the presidency, rather than advocates of social or political reform. The equality between the two parties at this time also made it difficult for any president to push for major changes, because the political base of support was too evenly divided to provide the necessary votes in Congress for effective action. While none of these presidents were incompetent (as asserted by choice (D)), they just didn't see the presidency as an office appropriate for taking strong initiatives. They believed their major job was to insure Congressional legislation was effectively carried out and to veto any legislation in which they felt Congress had exceeded its powers. Such an attitude does not tend to lead to inspirational, dynamic leadership. Their style was such that they believed the *less* they were noticed, the better they were doing their job. This has left the long-term impression of them being "weak" presidents.

29.   **(E)**

Soured by the liberalism and intellectualism of the mainstream churches, as well as the government's increasing separation from religion at both the federal and state levels, and the growing emphasis on secular, rather than religious education in state-funded schools, many people turned to religion to resolve their alienation. Their religious fervor led them to blame most of the country's problems on the decline of "living by the Good Book." They demanded reforms and believed that the reforms had better come quickly, for they fervently believed that the second coming of Christ was at hand. They pushed for political and economic reforms, as well as temperance, abolitionism, educational reform, and some even supported women's rights. Many of the utopian communities of this time period were radical outgrowths of this religious upwelling. Most of the major reform movements of the mid-nineteenth century were related to the religious revivals sparked by Evangelical Christians.

30.   **(E)**

When John Kennedy became president in January 1961, he inherited a program from President Eisenhower guaranteed to cause him headaches. Eisenhower had begun a CIA-backed program to train Cuban exiles to return to Cuba and militarily overthrow Fidel Castro and his Communist regime. The program was ready to begin operations when Kennedy assumed office. When Kennedy asked the CIA about the feasibility of an invasion by Cuban exiles and their chances of success, he was told that Castro was hated by the Cuban people; that most Cubans were waiting for the chance to rise up and overthrow Castro; and that the CIA-trained Cuban exiles would have an easy time swarming to victory if the United States just provided them with the transportation to Cuba to launch the invasion.

Kennedy, just two months into his first term of office (April 1960), put too much trust in the glowing CIA reports and decided to go ahead with the project. The Cuban exiles were ferried ashore at the Bay of Pigs in Cuba with American support and equipment, but once they got there the entire plan broke down. The Cuban people, most of whom in reality supported Castro, did not rise up in revolt. The Cuban military responded quickly and pinned the invaders to the beaches. For two days they remained trapped there. The CIA and some members of the military pushed Kennedy to launch air strikes to support the operation, but Kennedy refused, fearing active American involvement could lead to a full-scale and costly war, and could also lead to Soviet retaliation in Turkey or Europe. Besides, without the support of the Cuban people, no amount of American military intervention could change the long-term result. After the second day, the survivors, comprising only 20 percent of the original invasion force, were rescued from the beaches and returned to the United States.

The Bay of Pigs affair was a humiliating embarrassment to the new president. It also set the stage for further problems with Cuba. Partly because of the Bay of Pigs affair and other American attempts to overthrow or destabilize the Cuban government, the Cubans and the Soviets secretly conspired to install intermediate-range nuclear missiles in Cuba. Such missiles, if successfully installed, would provide a powerful deterrent to further American intervention in Cuban affairs. American discovery of the construction of missile launching sites in Cuba led to the Cuban Missile Crisis of 1962, perhaps the most difficult crisis in Kennedy's presidency.

31.   **(D)**

Muckrakers got their name from Theodore Roosevelt who compared the sensationalistic exposés of high-level corruption to "raking muck." Their stories tended to focus on the very worst behaviors of industrial leaders and politicians. The stories were designed to arouse the public and play to their "baser instincts." They explored all of the flaws in American society and provided a method of airing the nation's "dirty laundry." While political and industrial leaders were horrified by the tone and focus of the stories, the general public couldn't get enough. The stories confirmed in many people's minds what they had long suspected: rather than protecting the public interest, many public and private leaders were using their positions to further their own self-interest at the expense of everyone else. The stories led to an outcry for reform and provided Progressivists with just the ammunition and public support they needed to insure passage of legal reforms.

32.   **(C)**

The first wave of immigration to the English colonies by non-English-speaking people was dominated by ethnic Germans fleeing from the Rhine region of what is now Germany. Most were farmers fleeing from war and starvation in their homeland. Some were seeking a respite from religious persecution. Many of them settled in western Pennsylvania and began successful farming communities where they were inaccurately labeled "the Pennsylvania Dutch." While the ethnic groups listed in the remaining choices were all involved in waves of immigration to the New World, they all came at later dates, mostly after the mid-nineteenth century.

33.   **(D)**

The 1920s were a mixture of both conservative and liberal trends. On the liberal side, women were granted the right to vote with ratification in 1920 of the Ninteenth Amendment to the Constitution. With new forms of credit and advertising, combined with increases in wages and productivity, consumerism became the new American ethic.

On the conservative side, prohibition was enacted with the passage of the Eighteenth Amendment to the Constitution in 1919. Its enforcement began on a large scale in 1920, opening the door for bootlegging and the rise of organized crime in America. The Ku Klux Klan, using new advertising techniques to market itself, reached a peak membership of 5 million people in 1925, before sex scandals, corruption, poor leadership, and public revulsion at Klan activities broke its power base and discredited it as a major political force. Throughout the mid-1920s, however, the Klan was a force to be feared and accommodated, and Klan activities had a very intimidating effect on local and regional politics in the South, Midwest, and mid-Atlantic regions of the country.

The only choice not characteristic of the 1920s is choice (D). The Progressive movement, so forceful before World War I, was eclipsed by the pro-business economic growth philosophies of Harding, Coolidge, Hoover, and the Republicans. Progressivist reforms were rolled back throughout the 1920s, negating many gains previously made in regulating businesses and securing labor rights. These gains were sacrificed on the altars of economic growth and laissez-faire capitalism. Progressivism would not return to the fore until the enactment of Franklin Roosevelt's "New Deal" in the 1930s, where Progressivist principles were carried far beyond anything hoped for at the turn of the century.

34.   **(C)**

In the election of 1860, Abraham Lincoln only received 40 percent of the national vote. But his three opponents divided the anti-Lincoln vote in such a way that Lincoln still received the largest vote total of any single candidate. Lincoln's closest opponent was Stephen Douglas, who received about 30 percent of the popular vote. Furthermore, Lincoln's popular support was concentrated in the North, the most populous region of the country where most of the Electoral College votes were. He did not even appear on the ballot of some Southern states. By concentrating on the North and winning decisively there, he gathered so many electoral votes that even had his opponents combined their popular votes, which would have totaled 60 percent of the national vote, they would have lost the election in the Electoral College.

35.   **(A)**

Joseph McCarthy, the junior senator from Wisconsin, set the tone for the early 1950s in America with his relentless attacks on the "Communist menace" in America. McCarthy used American fears of Communist subversion to catapult himself out of obscurity in the United States Senate and into national prominence. He made his initial charges in a Lincoln's Birthday speech in Wheeling, West Virginia, claiming that the U.S. State Department was infested with Communists. Although he was lying, his charges struck a chord in the national psyche and within days people were clamoring for the ouster of the alleged Communists. He used these charges to build a political base of support from which he went on to blame virtually all of America's failures since World War II on wealthy intellectuals supposedly selling out the country to the Communists. His attacks played upon latent bigotry, racism, and anti-Semitism, but the Korean War and the arrest of alleged spies such as the Rosenbergs, convinced enough people that he was probably correct in his allegations, that few attempted to stop him. President Eisenhower tried to ignore McCarthy and hoped he would undercut himself with his reckless allegations and unfounded charges.

Eventually, McCarthy did ruin his own career. His charges became more and more spectacular and more and more unprovable. Finally, when he charged that the Army officer corps was a hotbed of Communist activity, Eisenhower decided enough was enough. Senate hearings were called in 1954 to investigate McCarthy's charges, and they were nationally televised. McCarthy was as bullying and overbearing as ever, attempting to ruin the reputation of virtually anyone who stood up to him. In the end, these tactics disgusted the American public and fellow senators. McCarthy's popularity plummeted and the Senate condemned him. He remained a senator but finished his career a broken man. He died of alcohol-related causes in 1957.

36.   **(A)**

The Mayas had a sophisticated writing system, which utilized glyphs, symbols composed of both syllables and written characters. Over 800 individual glyphs were used and were paired in columns that read together from both left to right and top to bottom. These glyphs then could be combined to form any word or idea, including the names of gods, buildings, numbers, dynastic events, places, and food. Glyphic inscriptions were carved in wood or stone on Maya monuments and architecture, or sometimes painted on paper and pottery. The Maya writing system unit is the glyphic cartouche, which is equivalent to the words and sentences of a modern language. Maya cartouches could contain as few as three or as many as fifty glyphs. Many Maya glyphs can have multiple meanings, and many Maya concepts were written in more than one way. Numbers can be represented with numerical symbols or with a picture of a god, or a combination of the two symbols. Some glyphs signify more than one sound, while also representing an idea. This means that a single concept can be presented in glyphs in a variety of ways. There is no Maya alphabet.

37.   **(A)**

The Farm Security Administration was created to help restore faith in America by sending photojournalists around the country to photograph Americans and American life. The focus of the resulting publications was on how people had survived, rather than succumbed to, the Great Depression. This program was designed as a public relations program, not as a jobs creation program.

38.   **(B)**

The Plains Indians depended upon buffalo for almost every aspect of their survival. When they killed a buffalo, they used virtually every part of it, from the hide to the bones. In 1850, over 13 million Buffalo meandered along their migration routes in the Great Plains. By 1890, fewer than 1,000 remained. Without the buffalo, the Plains Indians could not live according to their traditional ways. They were forced to either adapt to white rules (usually on reservations) or fight for their survival, as the Sioux and Cheyenne did in the 1870s. Fighting the whites was hopeless, but to many Indians, it was more honorable than dying in subjugation. While they managed a few victories such as at Little Big Horn, they were too badly outmanned and outgunned to have a long-term chance at victory. Without the buffalo, the entire Indian way of life was undermined and it led directly to the destruction of the Plains Indians' societies in a much broader way than any of the other choices listed in the question.

39.   **(C)**

While the Roanoke colony (1587) actually preceded the Jamestown colony (1607), the Roanoke colony was not successful. A supply ship sent to Roanoke in 1590 could find no survivors at the colony. The word "croatoan," which referred to a nearby island, carved into a tree was the only clue left behind. No other sign of the colonists was ever found.

40.   **(C)**

The sharecropping system allowed poor tenant farmers and poor independent farmers to borrow seed, equipment, and supplies for planting and harvesting a crop. In return, sharecroppers had to pledge their crop, or a portion of their crop, as collateral. While this arrangement allowed sharecroppers to continue to farm the land and squeeze out a minimal survival, the costs charged to farmers for supplies and equipment as well as the exorbitant interest rates charged for loaning those supplies effectively kept sharecroppers in permanent debt. Interest rates ranged as high as 200 percent. Most sharecroppers never accumulated enough cash to work their way out from under the tremendous debt load they incurred trying to work their small plots of lands. The only ones who got wealthy from this system were the landowners and the merchants who controlled the sharecroppers. This system did nothing to bring poor farmers into the middle class. Neither did it expand the number of independently owned farms in the South. It had no restrictive effect on the power of former plantation owners or Northern business interests. Finally, it did nothing to enhance the relationship between Blacks and Whites as it did not force them to work side by side. In fact, in many ways it was used by Southern ruling elites to maintain the old social and racial order.

41.   **(B)**

During the 1880s and 1890s, America's railroads had a stranglehold on the transportation of goods, particularly agricultural goods, to the marketplace. In major markets where there were several competing rail lines, shipping costs were low. However, many farmers and manufacturers lived in areas served by only one major rail line or a "short line." On these noncompetitive lines, railroads charged exorbitantly high rates, often so high that the producers of goods could not make a profit on their goods. After bitter struggles in Congress and several Supreme Court challenges, the Interstate Commerce Act of 1887 was passed to curb pricing and other abuses by the railroad industry. In the related court cases, the Supreme Court ruled that only Congress had the right to regulate interstate commerce. This act created the Interstate Commerce Commission, whose major purpose was to keep an eye on railroad policies and to prevent further abuses.

42.   **(E)**

The Knights of Labor were founded in 1869 by workers in Philadelphia's garment district. They were the only broad-based union to survive the economic depression of 1873. They were also the only major union of their time to extend membership to blacks, women, and unskilled workers. They preached a long-term philosophy of achieving a society where employees and managers would work together cooperatively for all society's benefit. They reached the peak of their success in the mid-1880s, but following a series of failed strikes culminating in the disastrous Haymarket Square riot in 1886, the Knights began to splinter into smaller crafts unions and various other more radical workers groups. They never regained their dominance and were eventually supplanted and replaced by the AFL in the 1890s as America's major labor union.

43.   **(B)**

Andrew Jackson's election marked the culmination of a movement whose roots lay in the philosophy of Thomas Jefferson that the country was best governed when people were allowed to govern themselves and the federal government interfered as little as possible. Following the activist presidency of John Quincy Adams in which he tried to expand federal power, Andrew Jackson swung the pendulum in the reverse direction. He was a frontiersman, the first truly common man elected to the presidency. He was a self-made man. He was a rugged individualist who was committed to reducing the concentration of political and economic power in Washington, D.C., and returning that power to the states and to the people where (in his opinion) it was less likely to be abused. His election was symbolic of the rise of the notion of "popular sovereignty" which asserted that the people could do no wrong and didn't need an elite aristocratic class to lead them.

44.   **(E)**

Political machines and the politics of political bosses dominated the workings of city governments at the turn of the century. Many of these organizations stayed in power through bribery, graft, and other corrupt practices. In return, however, the machines took care of the interests of many of their most influential constituents. They provided many services which helped the poor survive in return for support at the polls. Many reformers, mostly from the middle and upper classes, demanding changes to end the corruption, found themselves stymied at the polls by large blocks of poor and immigrant voters who supported the political machines. The machines were often successfully able to portray themselves as protectors of the poor who fought against upper-class reformers interested only in themselves.

While the political machines were able to enlist the support of some industrial leaders, and sometimes got indirect support from organized religion, they got little support from the middle class and virtually no support from wealthy landowners living outside the city.

45.   **(C)**

The "black codes" were designed to limit the rights of free Blacks in the South so they would move north where they couldn't threaten the slave system in the South. These codes ranged from bans on assembly to laws forbidding Blacks from learning to read or write. By driving out freed Blacks, of whom there were a steadily growing number throughout the early to mid-1800s, Southern Whites hoped to remove role models to whom enslaved Blacks could look up to. There was also the fear that freed Blacks would use their freedom to help foment slave uprisings. The codes were quite effective in that they drove large numbers of Blacks northward, but the number of slaves freed for one reason or another continually outnumbered the number of Blacks who emigrated to the North, so the codes were never completely successful. They just stirred up more resentment regarding slavery and its dehumanization of a whole race of people.

46.   **(B)**

New Orleans in the 1890s provided the perfect opportunity for the European musical influences followed by wealthy Creoles (half white, half black) to intermingle with African musical influences dominating the culture of poor Blacks. The result was a distinctly American musical form called jazz. Jazz players of turn-of-the-century New Orleans were among the highest-paid "workers" in the South. The almost exclusively black performers were wealthier than virtually any other Blacks in the country at the time. They also enjoyed a certain amount of respect and recognition denied to most other Blacks at the time. Eventually, these New Orleans jazz musicians took their music with them to other parts of the country. But it was in New Orleans that black musicians gave America its first truly original music form, jazz.

Blues was a somewhat similar music form that also developed in New Orleans. Its development preceded jazz somewhat and was dominated by African musical influences. It never integrated the influences of European music with African musical traditions in the way jazz did.

47.   **(C)**

Up until 1801, Spain had controlled the Louisiana Territory. While Spanish control theoretically threatened U.S. Mississippi River commerce and blocked westward U.S. expansion, in reality the Spanish kept the Mississippi open to American commerce. Also, Spain was a weak power whose future looked bleak. It was commonly believed that Louisiana could be "obtained" from Spain one way or another whenever it suited American purposes. However, in 1801 Spain secretly turned over control of Louisiana to Napoleon and the French. Napoleon had openly discussed a French empire in North America, and in 1802 the Port of New Orleans was closed to American shipping. This precipitated a crisis for Jefferson. A French empire blocking U.S. westward expansion was unacceptable as was French blocking of U.S. trade along the Mississippi. Jefferson considered joining with England in an effort to drive out the French militarily, but decided to try negotiations first. Due to a variety of factors, Napoleon decided the vast Louisiana territory was not worth the cost of possession and maintenance. He thereby stunned American negotiators by offering the entire Louisiana Territory to the U.S. for approximately four cents an acre ($15 million). The purchase secured U.S. trading rights along the Mississippi and opened up the trans-Mississippi West to American exploration and expansion.

48.   **(E)**

In the late nineteenth century, as unions began to emerge as major forces in the American workplace, the United States government tended to support management in its efforts to crush unions or at least severely limit their effectiveness. In many smaller disputes, the government did not get involved. However, in larger disputes like the Pullman strike of 1894, the government actively supported management, with President Grover Cleveland sending in federal soldiers to help break up the strike. In addition, strikers often found their rights limited by Supreme Court decisions which interpreted the Constitution on narrow grounds and either repealed or restricted progressive labor legislation. Many unions in this period preached goals involving radical social change that went well beyond the workplace. With unions such as the International Workers of the World (IWW) openly preaching workers' revolution, many government leaders saw unions as not just an attempt to protect workers' rights, but an attempt to bring down America's capitalist system. With those fears in mind, they did whatever they could to hinder or derail the weak, but growing union movement.

49.   **(E)**

The Tet Offensive marked a turning point in the Vietnamese War. Up until Tet, press coverage of the war, while raising some questions and more graphic than anything Americans had ever seen before, was mostly positive. American military leaders were talking about seeing "light at the end of the tunnel." Many Americans still believed a military victory was possible. With the Tet Offensive, all illusions of a military victory ended.

What is ironic is that Tet was a military disaster for the North Vietnamese. Up until Tet, the Viet Cong had stalled the American war effort by engaging in partisan warfare which accented their advantages in the villages and jungle terrain and neutralized American superiority in conventional arms and equipment. They avoided the kind of massive pitched battles in which American technical superiority could be focused to destroy them. The repeated midnight raids and "hit and run" raids on villages, convoys, and military bases kept the South Vietnamese and the Americans constantly off-balance and unable to use their forces effectively.

With Tet, the North Vietnamese scrapped this policy in favor of an all-out military assault on key bases and provincial capitals in South Vietnam. At first, caught by surprise, American and South Vietnamese forces reeled back at the ferocity of the North Vietnamese assaults. But soon, the Americans recovered and the North Vietnamese found themselves tied down in the very pitched battles that they could not hope to win. When it was over, the North Vietnamese had suffered over 400,000 casualties which would take them more than four years to replace. It was the biggest American/South Vietnamese military victory of the war. But it was also the biggest American political disaster of the war.

Tet came just as Lyndon Johnson was preparing to run for reelection in the 1968 political campaign. It called into question all the assurances by the government that the North Vietnamese were beaten and would collapse in the near future. People asked, "If they're beaten, how could they mount an offensive as large as this?" The fact that the offensive had failed was irrelevant. What Americans focused on was that it had taken place at all. Now many Americans began to see Vietnam as a tunnel with no way out, and press coverage became increasingly negative. Talk shifted from winning to just getting out. Johnson withdrew from the presidential campaign. The North Vietnamese, seeing the political effect, dug in their heels and were determined to outlast faltering American support for the war. After Tet, it was just a matter of how long it would be until America pulled out of Vietnam, and under what circumstances that pullout would take place.

50.   (A)

The Paris Peace Treaty was very generous to the United States. Britain was war weary, particularly in light of the potential cost to its empire of continued war with France and Spain (both of whom were now fighting the British at sea). Spain and France had suffered some serious naval setbacks and were also anxious for peace. All of the provisions listed were included in the treaty except the return of Louisiana to France. Louisiana wouldn't return to French control until 1800 when the Spanish ceded the territory to France.

51.   (C)

In 1947, the British government told the American government that it could no longer afford the expense of economic and military aid to Greece and Turkey. At the time, both countries were locked in struggles against Communist insurgents. Greece was in virtual civil war and could not have won against Communist rebels without Western help. President Truman was determined that Greece should not be allowed to fall under Communist control. In response, he delivered a speech to Congress committing the United States to aid free people anywhere in the world in their struggle to preserve their freedom from foreign intervention or armed insurgents. This policy quickly became known as the

Truman Doctrine. Congress approved aid to both Greece and Turkey, which both survived their respective Communist insurrections.

The aid to Greece and Turkey was just a first step in what became a massive aid program to non-communist governments all over the world. Regrettably, many of the non-communist governments receiving U.S. aid were led by brutal dictators every bit as evil as the Communist insurgents Truman wanted to suppress. American policy was so focused around Truman's effort to contain Communist expansion, however, even brutal dictators were seen as preferable to Communists.

52.   **(B)**

Spanish occupation of Cuba had been a sore point in Spanish-American relations for some time before the war. In 1894, the U.S. enacted a tariff on Cuban sugar, greatly disrupting the Cuban economy. Shortly thereafter, Cuban rebels operating from American soil began a revolution resulting in bloody reprisals by both the Spanish and the revolutionaries. Yellow journalism, fed by lurid stories of Spanish atrocities, sensationalized the revolution and whipped up powerful emotional support among Americans for the Cuban nationalists. Many Americans saw the Spanish as evil incarnate and believed that the U.S. had a God-given duty to intervene on behalf of the rebels, whom many compared to the American revolutionaries of 1776. Added to this were desires by American businessmen for new markets and an independent Cuba would be "ripe for the picking." Many other Americans just wanted Spain out of the Caribbean and wanted expanded American control in the region.

All of this came to a head with the sinking of the battleship *Maine* in Havana harbor in February 1898. Americans blamed the Spanish, despite evidence indicating that an explosion of coal dust in the ship's coal bunkers was the real culprit. While the sinking of the *Maine* was the excuse that many people used to justify the war, the primary motives were support for Cuban nationalism and American expansionist desires in the region.

53.   **(D)**

All of the other choices are true. Physical punishment was the norm for disciplining children, as most religions preached the "spare the rod, spoil the child" philosophy. Children were treated as miniature adults and were expected to conform to adult standards of behavior. Behavioral standards were strict and punishments were severe, for both adults and children, when those standards were broken.

Women were limited in their legal rights to own property and engage in commerce even when single. Once they married they lost whatever legal rights they had. They could no longer own property, earn their own income, or enact contracts. They were legally under the complete dominion of their husbands.

Most families during this period did bear children who survived until adulthood and bore their own children. Life expectancies, particularly in the South, increased during this period as did the population in the colonies. Women, however, did *not* set the moral standards for their children, nor did they decide how the children were to be educated or trained. Those duties were considered the husband's responsibilities, although it was the wife's duty to enforce her husband's decisions where children were concerned.

Finally, the vast majority of families did live in rural areas. Most colonial cities were in reality small towns. Even the largest, such as Boston, New York, and Philadelphia, had fewer than 20,000 inhabitants. While the cities expanded greatly during this period, over 90 percent of the colonies' inhabitants lived in small, rural villages and towns.

54.   (E)

Philippine nationalists believed that when the United States drove out the Spanish, the Philippines would be given independence. Comments by the commander of the U.S. naval forces in the region, Commodore Dewey, were interpreted as promises of independence. When the U.S. began formal occupation of the islands and it became clear that independence was not forthcoming, the nationalists began agitating against U.S. rule. In addition, Americans treated the Filipinos with contempt. Much of this was in large part due to latent racism against the nonwhite Filipinos. Racial slurs were commonly used, and they were treated in much the same manner as Southerners treated ex-slaves after the Civil War.

Frustration soon reached a boiling point and in 1899 the leader of the nationalists, Emilo Aguinaldo, declared Philippine independence and launched an insurrection against American control. The rebellion took over two years to control and it resulted in countless atrocities by both Filipinos and Americans. The ensuing bloodbath resulted in over 500,000 Filipinos killed and approximately 5,000 American dead.

While the Filipinos lost the revolution, it did lead to reforms in U.S. policy. In 1916, the Filipinos were promised that they would be granted their independence (when the United States felt they were capable of successfully governing themselves).

55.   (E)

All of the choices are utopian communities which evolved as part of the religious revivals, or the Second Great Awakening, of the 1820s, 1830s, and 1840s. But only one of those communities, Brooke Farm, was the source of the transcendentalist philosophy espoused by Thoreau, Melville, and others who lived and worked there. Brooke Farm focused on the importance of spiritualism over materialism. Members of the community lived a communal life-style and all shared in the upkeep of the community. The writers who lived there explored the workings of nature and the individual and became some of the most prominent American writers of the nineteenth century. During their prime they were a part of what is now called the American Renaissance.

56. **(E)**

The psychological reaction of most Americans to the Napoleonic Wars that drew America into the War of 1812 was one of withdrawal. Most people remembered Washington's words of being wary of European entanglements, and the war confirmed in their minds that Washington had been correct. Rather than seeking a more active and dominant role in European "intrigues," most Americans sought isolationism and avoidance of European commitments. Others wished to further reduce U.S. involvement with Europe by keeping Europe out of the Americas. This wish was expressed nine years after the conclusion of the 1812 war in the Monroe Doctrine.

57. **(E)**

When Woodrow Wilson left Washington for the Paris Peace Conference, he had already taken steps to insure Senate opposition to whatever treaty emerged from the negotiations. The Senate was dominated by Republicans and Wilson, a Democrat, neglected to ask any senators to accompany him to the negotiations. He also neglected to ask any Republicans to accompany him. These errors of omission guaranteed anger and resentment among Republicans in general and senators in particular. When the Treaty of Versailles was presented to the Senate, Senators found plenty of grist to grind in opposing the treaty. Contrary to Wilson's pre-negotiation pledges, the treaty was punitive and failed to come close to approaching the principles of humanitarianism and self-determination that Wilson had so nobly espoused before and during the Paris Peace Conference. One senator prophetically called the treaty a "blueprint for another war."

Wilson made matters worse by refusing to compromise with the Senate on provisions senators found objectionable. Instead, he lectured them like a teacher would lecture some errant schoolchildren. Then, he embarked on a cross-country speaking tour by train to try to go "over the heads" of the senators and sell the treaty directly to the American people. During this trip he engaged in name-calling and direct attacks on the intelligence of the Senate. To a body of people as proud as those in the Senate, this was both insulting and infuriating, and their reaction was predictable. In addition, on his return to Washington, Wilson suffered a stroke which incapacitated him and he refused to negotiate further with treaty critics. Not surprisingly, when the treaty came up for ratification in November 1919, it was voted down. It came up for a vote again in March 1920, but Wilson still refused to compromise and the treaty was again voted down. The treaty was never ratified in its original form. The United States later signed a separate peace treaty with Germany.

58.   (C)

Both Harding and Coolidge promoted policies favorable to business. They firmly believed in an association between business and government that would help the nation prosper. Their policies reflected a repudiation of Progressivism and a philosophy that what is good for business is good for the country. In that sense, they truly felt that "The business of government IS business." They believed strong business growth would provide jobs and would improve the entire economy. Their policies helped spur the tremendous economic growth that drove the nation forward from 1922 through 1929. Unfortunately, these same anti-regulatory, laissez-faire business policies permitted greed and abuses leading directly to the stock market crash of 1929 and the Great Depression that followed.

59.   (C)

In the 1830s and 1840s, the Democrats supported the Jeffersonian principles of limited power to the federal government. They felt that what power the government wielded should be exercised at the state and local level. Democrats distrusted a strong, centralized government and opposed policies which would give the federal government too much control, such as a national bank, protective tariffs, or government support for private industry.

Their opponents, the Whigs, favored all of these policies. The Whigs believed in using the power of the federal government to help build the country and expand the nation's economy. The Whigs supported policies favored by business owners, the middle class and the wealthy.

60.   (C)

Most Americans welcomed the economic growth and prosperity of the mid-1920s. However, some found the collapse of Progressivism, the subsequent dominance of materialistic consumerism, laissez-faire capitalism with its greed, corruption, and conspicuous consumption, as well as the emphasis on social conformity and dearth of spirituality, to be morally repugnant. This repugnance and cynicism regarding America's social framework were captured most poignantly in the works of several young American authors. F. Scott Fitzgerald, H. L. Mencken, Ernest Hemingway, and Sinclair Lewis wrote stories of heroes as flawed as the villains they sought to conquer. Their works raised questions about traditional assumptions of right and wrong and often left those questions unanswered. They painted unsettling pictures of American society, frequently with a sharply critical, sometimes satirical portrayal of American hypocrisy and decadence.

Their unsettling works, with the inherent crying out at the loss of ideals, values, and purpose as well as the interwoven criticism of the current dominance of materialism, led critics and historians to label them the "Lost Generation." A whole generation of young writers faced what they believed to be a spiritually lost America desperately needing to find new and meaningful goals and values. These writers' works attempted to point out the folly of 1920s America and rekindle the idealism and sense of deeper purpose they felt necessary for America to live up to its potential for all its citizens.

61.   **(A)**

This cartoon presents Tweed as ruled by greed. Ths source of his money is not indicated.

62.   **(D)**

Of the choices listed, a lack of available credit was the only choice that did not contribute to the Great Depression. In fact, just the opposite was true. Throughout the 1920s, to help spread the new ethic of consumerism, banks and industries made several new forms of credit and installment loans available to the public. This credit was essential because while industry was pushing people to consume, it was refusing to pay workers the wages they needed to buy the whole range of new consumer goods being made available. Credit was also essential to farmers who could not earn enough from their crops, because of depressed crop prices, to break even. Without the new forms of credit being offered, consumers and farmers could not have sustained the economy as long as they did. Even with the new credit extensions, without wage increases and increases in crop prices workers and farmers could not continue to purchase new goods and equipment indefinitely. Eventually, they reached their credit limits and often found they couldn't pay off   their loans. The resulting foreclosures and bankruptcies weakened the entire banking system, making banks particularly vulnerable when the stock market crash began the final collapse of the economic boom of the 1920s. So, if anything, it was the easy availability of too much credit with too little screening to make sure those who borrowed could pay back the loans that contributed to the Great Depression.

63.   **(E)**

During the waning years of Reconstruction, when Southern voters voted Reconstructionist Republicans out of office and replaced them with Democrats,

Southerners said that the state had been "redeemed." In other words, the state was said to have been saved from the "clutches" of Yankee Reconstructionism. Thus, the leaders of these new post-Reconstruction, Democratic administrations were called "redeemers." Since many of these "redeemers" came from the former ruling elites, to others wishing to return the South to "the good old days," the presence of these "old school" leaders must have seemed like political redemption for the South.

64.   **(A)**

The doctrine of nullification was developed in South Carolina as a means of protecting residents from what they saw as the "tyranny of the majority." This doctrine claimed that individual states could choose to ignore federal mandates or laws if they found those laws offensive or unfair to their interests. This issue became a crisis in 1832 when South Carolina invoked nullification in regard to an unpopular federal tariff. Andrew Jackson forced the tariff to be collected and some South Carolinians began discussing secession. The crisis was resolved through the passage of a compromise tariff leading to the repeal of the nullification law by South Carolina. While a more serious crisis had been averted, this incident set the stage for further talk of secessionism as the slavery issue escalated tensions throughout the 1840s and 1850s.

65.   **(B)**

The Indian Reorganization Act represented a reversal of previous government policy which had worked against Indian control of their lands and preservation of Indian traditions. Under the new law, Indian lands could not be divided up and parcelled off in allotments that effectively broke up tribal reservations and allowed whites to move in and exploit Indian lands. Further allotments were prohibited and Indians were provided funds with which they could purchase new land and regain control of land previously lost to allotments. Indians were also given the right to draw up their own tribal constitutions, as separate tribal "nations," and establish their own tribal governments. Federal funds were offered to help Indian tribes construct schools, hospitals, and welfare agencies. Finally, the Act ended restrictions on the rights of Indians to practice tribal religions, rituals, and use tribal languages.

66.   **(A)**

The Declaratory Act, whose passage was coupled with the defeat of the detested Stamp Act, stated that Parliament had the right to tax any English colony when it chose and as it chose. The fact that the colonists had no representatives to Parliament was denied by Parliament's belief that IT represented all English citizens whether they lived in England itself or in England's overseas colonies. Therefore, Parliament believed that it alone had the right to tax England's colonies and could do so at will. Coupling the passage of this act with the repeal of the Stamp Act blunted the American reaction because Americans were so busy celebrating the repeal of the Stamp Act, most ignored the implications of the Declaratory Act.

67.   **(E)**

The French and Indian War was an overwhelming victory for the English and the American colonies. It resulted in the French being totally driven from the North American continent. It ended the American Indian tactic of playing one European power against another. It also led to Spain, a French ally, ceding Florida to England. The net result was that the American colonists no longer had to fear direct threats by a major foreign power. Colonists fighting side by side with the English had learned much about America, the English, and themselves. They learned that the British were not invincible. They learned to resent the arrogant attitudes of the British toward the colonists. They also gained confidence in themselves and gained a corps of well-trained officers who honed their skills fighting for the British. This led to a more independent, knowledgeable, and assertive attitude by Americans who now felt more free in their ability to challenge the British and resist British efforts to restrict their activities.

68.   **(C)**

Gettysburg marked the "high tide" of Robert E. Lee's Army of Northern Virginia. In June of 1863, the Confederacy was still hoping for recognition by France and England. Confederate leaders believed a major military victory on Northern territory would give the Europeans the proof they needed that the Union could never defeat the South militarily. On that basis, Lee who had just defeated Union forces at Chancellorsville, pushed his Army into Maryland and Pennsylvania. He hoped to force a battle on his terms in Northern territory that would demoralize the numerically superior Army of the Potomac and perhaps even allow Confederate forces to isolate or capture Washington, D.C. Such a success would have relieved Union pressure on the South and almost assuredly obtained formal European recognition for the Confederacy. Unfortunately for Lee, the two forces met unexpectedly at the little Pennsylvania town of Gettysburg. Outnumbered Union forces held on throughout the first day and were reinforced that night by the remainder of the Army of the Potomac. From that point on, the battle was basically fought on Union terms, despite Lee pressing the initiative. After futile efforts to break the superior Union lines for two days, and inflicting only 28,000 casualties (out of 67,000 soldiers at the start of the battle), Lee was forced to retreat. Followed by news of Union victory at Vicksburg at the same time Lee was being defeated at Gettysburg, the South never regained the initiative. There were no further major incursions into Northern territory, and while Lee fought doggedly on the defensive, no European recognition was ever announced. Now it was only a matter of time until the superior manpower and industrial capacity of the North wore down and finished the South. While all of the remaining Civil War battles influenced the course of the war, none of them had the decisive impact of Gettysburg.

69.   **(D)**

The Federalists' name implied that they did not support a strong national government. However, the leaders of the Federalist movement believed strongly in the necessity of a relatively strong central government. They strongly supported ratification of the Constitution and believed that discussion of a bill of rights should be delayed until after the Constitution was ratified. Alexander Hamilton, James Madison, and John Jay wrote a series of essays contained within *The Federalist* which brilliantly argued the Federalist position and captured support of all the nation's major newspapers. This campaign made the difference in the battles for ratification in several key states.

The chief opponents of ratification, the Antifederalists, argued against ratification primarily on the basis of choice (B), that a bill of rights needed to be in place before ratification of the Constitution. Many Antifederalists opposed the Constitution entirely based on the belief in choice (E), that no strong national government could or should ever exist. They believed that a strong national government would become corrupt and lose touch with the needs of the local people. They believed that the best path was for the states to govern themselves within the framework of an extremely limited national government. Few people wanted either choice (A), a return to Articles of Confederation which had clearly not worked, or (C), a new constitutional convention.

70.   **(E)**

The biggest failure of Reconstruction in the South was its failure to effectively change Southern social structure and eliminate the racism inherent within. When Reconstruction ended, the Republican governments which had run the South during Reconstruction were universally voted out of office. When they were gone, the South was in many ways little different than it had been before the war. Most of the wealth was still concentrated in the hands of a few white landowners. While Blacks were no longer technically slaves, they owned no land. Various restrictions and lack of capital effectively prevented them from acquiring land. Without land and money, Blacks remained targets of white exploitation. New "black codes" limited their voting rights, education rights, property rights, and their rights to use public facilities. The passage of these new codes symbolized how little attitudes had changed. Blacks were still economic slaves, if not legal slaves, and lived in terror of white oppression. Whites still felt that Blacks were inferior and, in many cases, blamed Blacks (and Yankees) for the Civil War as well as every other problem experienced since the war. As a result, while the Civil War held the Union together and ended legalized slavery, it would be another 80 years after the end of Reconstruction before types of social changes hoped for at the start of Reconstruction could begin.

71.   **(C)**

All of the other choices were true. Most New England immigrants arrived as family units. This provided the New England colonies with a relatively stable social structure from their inception. In Chesapeake Bay, most colonists were single young males, many of whom were indentured servants. The ratio of men to women was 6 to 1 before 1640. This made it exceedingly difficult to find eligible mates and start families. In addition, the climate in the Chesapeake Bay region was an unhealthy climate. Men and women died between 10 to 20 years earlier on average than they did in New England, leaving them little time to start families when they did find mates. This severely limited population growth in Chesapeake Bay, where the population increases were entirely due to continued immigration rather than indigenous colonists. A population whose growth depends on a continuous flood of newcomers is not nearly as stable as a population whose growth is based on established couples having children and raising them in stable family environments as occurred in New England.

The only choice that was untrue was choice (C). There were basically no differences in the way women were viewed (in terms of their social role or their rights) in New England or Chesapeake Bay. In fact, some historians argue that because women were so rare and in such demand in the Chesapeake region, they were more likely to be treated more as equals than women in New England, who were plentiful and more likely to be locked into the traditional wifely role. A woman in Chesapeake Bay might succeed in rebelling against social norms simply because she was so badly needed, males couldn't afford to reject her. A woman in New England who rebelled against social expectations had no chance of being accepted by males who could find plenty of other women who were willing to "accept their place" in society.

72.   **(C)**

The War of 1812 officially ended with the Treaty of Ghent, signed in the Belgian city of Ghent on December 24, 1814. The treaty gave neither side what it initially demanded and effectively returned matters to their prewar standing.

73.   **(E)**

Innovations by Eli Whitney and Simeon North in the use of inter-changable parts to produce small arms for the military pioneered the beginnings of the machine tool industry. The use of precision engineered, high-quality interchangeable parts led to the mass production of a wide variety of high-quality products not previously available to consumers. This brought the United States slowly but steadily into the Industrial Revolution and laid the groundwork for the American manufacturing colossus which emerged by the end of the nineteenth century.

74.   **(B)**

Charles Darwin published his theories of natural selection, or evolution, at about the time many American industrialists were beginning to make their fortunes. A British utilitarian writer, Herbert Spencer, wrote several articles championing a social application of Darwin's theories called "Social Darwinism." According to this principle, just as only the fittest animals survive in nature, only the fittest people survive and succeed in human society. Therefore, wealthy people obtained their wealth because they were biologically superior to those around them. Poor people were poor because they were somehow inferior and therefore didn't deserve any success. This ruthless perversion of Darwin's ideas provoked heated debate among social scientists of the day. But it was very well received among the wealthy industrialists of America, as well as the political leaders of the major European powers, who used it to excuse their treatment of the peoples they had subjugated in building their huge colonial empires.

75.   **(A)**

The "Marshall Plan" was conceived by Truman's secretary of state, General George Marshall. After World War II, Europe was socially and economically devastated. Industries were destroyed. Farmers' fields were often too torn up from the war to cultivate. People were homeless and starving. The governments of Western Europe no longer had the resources to rebuild the cities and restore the economies to reasonable working order. There was a very real possibility that unless the economic situation in Western Europe was turned around, Communists would win control of several governments in free elections.

In addition, there was growing anti-American sentiment in Western Europe. America was viewed as big, fat, selfish, and lazy by many Europeans. They believed that America had the power to ease the poverty and pain being suffered by Europeans, but was too preoccupied with itself to do the job.

In response, in 1947 George Marshall conceived a massive economic aid plan to help Europe rebuild. The plan eventually resulted in more than $12.5 billion being given to Europe to finance reconstruction of the battered European infrastructure. With that money, the starvation problem eased, people were put back to work as new industries were built, and Communist opposition to the plan led to the collapse of Communist party support in many Western European countries. While the plan was not universally successful, it was one of the most innovative and well received policies ever conceived by the United States.

76.   **(D)**

Lincoln's immediate purpose in announcing the Emancipation Proclamation was to rally flagging Northern morale. Lincoln waited until after a major Union victory, at Antietam in 1862, so he couldn't be charged with making the announcement as an act of desperation. He recognized that the costs of the war had reached a point where preserving the Union would not be a powerful enough reason to motivate many Northerners to continue the war. Framing the war as a war against slavery would mobilize powerful abolitionist forces in the North and perhaps create an atmosphere of a "holy crusade" rather than one of using war to resolve a political conflict.

While the Emancipation Proclamation had the announced purpose of freeing the slaves, Lincoln himself indirectly stated that freeing the slaves was a means to a greater end, preserving the Union. In a statement released before the Emancipation Proclamation, Lincoln asserted, "If I could save the Union without freeing any slave I would do it, and if I could save it by freeing all the slaves I would do it…What I do about slavery, and the colored race I do because I believe it helps to save the Union."

77.   **(E)**

Saratoga marked the doomed ending to a British three-pronged campaign to split New England from the other colonies. With the surrender of Burgoyne's army, the Americans had won a major victory and captured an entire British army. This victory gave the French the evidence they needed that the Americans could actually win the war, and gave them a chance to avenge their loss to the British in the Seven Years' War. The French now recognized the American government and declared war on England. The entrance of France into the war steadily turned the tide in favor of the Americans. England now found itself fighting not only its American colonists, but a global struggle against its chief European rival. Of the remaining battles, only Yorktown rivals Saratoga in significance because it marked the end of active large-scale hostilities in the war and led the British Parliament to request peace negotiations.

78.   **(B)**

The launching of *Sputnik* reverberated across the United States like nothing had since Pearl Harbor. After World War II Americans were taught to fear the Soviet Union through the glasses of the Cold War. However, one area of American-Soviet relations in which nearly all Americans felt more than secure was the superiority of American technology and American scientific know-how. Sure, the Russians had developed an atomic bomb and later a hydrogen bomb, but only after their spies had managed to steal plans from America. The inferiority of Soviet weapons was well known and widely joked about. Then came *Sputnik*, a little metal sphere which, when placed in orbit around the earth making it the world's first man-made orbital satellite, shook the world.

Suddenly Soviet technological ineptitude was no longer a laughing matter. It became increasingly unhumorous when repeated American attempts to duplicate *Sputnik* failed miserably. American self-confidence was badly shaken. The quality of American science education was questioned, as was the moral fiber of the country. For the military, a new term suddenly blossomed into existence: Intercontinental Ballistic Missile (ICBM). If the Soviets could put a satellite into orbit, then it was no great leap for them to place a nuclear warhead on top of a missile and drop it right down Washington's collective throat. American Cold War fears intensified.

Using *Sputnik* as an excuse, Washington demanded and got increased funding for the military, particularly funding for missile research, as well as increased funding for education. Most of the education money was directed at colleges and universities and focused on mathematics and science education. It roused America from its complacency and led to a new wave of technical advances related to the influx of science-related funding.

79.   **(D)**

The Wilmot Proviso, an unsuccessful attempt to forbid slavery in any territories acquired as a result of the Mexican-American War, became the slogan for many abolitionist groups who wanted a total end to slavery. It also became a rallying cry for a group known as free-soilers. Free-soilers did not necessarily want to abolish slavery. However, they wanted to stop its spread into the Western territories. They feared that the expansion of slavery into the West would prevent free whites from obtaining land and jobs which would be open to them without slavery. While their motives were somewhat selfish rather than altruistic, the Wilmot Proviso would have achieved their purpose. They added another voice to the growing chorus of people calling for the restriction or abolition of slavery.

Of the other choices listed, all supported restricted federal power and some form of states' rights. As such, all of the groups listed in the remaining choices would have opposed the Wilmot Proviso.

80.　　**(C)**

Lyndon Johnson's "Great Society" was the collective name for several separate programs aimed at ending civil rights abuses and combatting poverty. In the area of civil rights, the Civil Rights Act of 1964 was a piece of landmark legislation. It forbade discrimination based on racial, ethnic, or sexual origin or religious beliefs in job hiring, promotion, and firing. It also forbade such discrimination in access to public accommodations and gave the federal government powers to cut funding to federally aided industries or agencies found guilty of discrimination. It also actively involved the United States government in attacking segregated school systems and forcing them to desegregate.

Related to this, the Voting Rights Act of 1965 gave the government the power to intervene and supervise voter registration in areas where minorities had been illegally restricted or discouraged from registering to vote in significant numbers.

Economically, Johnson declared a war on poverty, backing several bills to combat poverty and its causes in the United States. Medicare, followed by Medicaid, was aimed at providing quality medical care to the elderly. Several programs were initiated to increase the quality of teachers and education in poverty-stricken areas. Most notably, Project Headstart, which attempted to provide quality preschool training for impoverished preschoolers, involved the government in attacking the failure to succeed in school which marked the lives of so many of the nation's poor.

Johnson also initiated the Neighborhood Youth Corps, and the Job Corps to provide job training and experience for inner-city youths. There were also tax cuts and economic aid programs to provide increased welfare benefits, especially to mothers with young children.

While the programs showed some initial success, and some programs such as Project Headstart were undeniably successful, many of the programs were tied to qualifications which helped lead to the destruction of the family unit among those seeking aid. Some economists argue that there is more poverty now than there was before the "Great Society" programs began. Many programs led to long-term dependence on government aid rather than fostering the independence needed to get off government support. While the civil rights aspects of the "Great Society" were quite successful in ending legal abuses to civil rights, many abuses continue today, albeit at a more subtle, insidious level. So, the intentions of Johnson's "Great Society" programs were inarguably good, but the results have been a mixed success at best.

SECTION II

Sample Answer to Document-Based Question

1.   In the 1930s Japanese militarists, in an effort to restore a Japanese economy devastated by the world depression, and to establish a Japanese hegemony over Eastern Asia and the Western Pacific, embarked on an expansionist campaign, primarily in China, designed to emplace Japan as the dominant power in Asia and the Pacific. This began with the Manchurian campaign in 1931, the seizure of five Northern Chinese provinces a few years later, and the full-scale invasion of China in 1937. The major roadblocks to Japanese expansion were the British, who were well established in Southeast Asia and the Southwest Pacific, and the Americans who were entrenched in the Central Pacific and determined to get Japan out of China.

Tension built steadily between the Japanese and the Americans following the "rape of Nanking" and other Japanese atrocities against the Chinese. The two nations approached war in 1938 when the Japanese sunk the American gunboat Panay while it was on a mission to transport some diplomats from China. While the Japanese apologized and payed reparations for the incident, it was symbolic of growing Japanese-American tensions.

In 1940, with the Japanese joining the Rome-Berlin Axis as a third ally, Roosevelt ordered the United States Pacific fleet to Pearl Harbor in Hawaii. From here the fleet would be able to intervene more quickly and effectively against Japanese aggression in the Pacific. Roosevelt's concern here was primarily Japanese aggression against British possessions in the Pacific while the British were tied down fighting Hitler. Japanese occupation of French Indochina, bordering British controlled Burma and Malaysia, confirmed these fears.

Throughout 1941, the Japanese and the Americans attempted to negotiate a way out of the developing conflict. Many Japanese wanted a way out of the morass they had gotten into in China. But they wanted a way out that would allow them to save face and keep much of the territory they had already occupied. American negotiators were insensitive to Japanese codes of honor and need to "save face." The Americans demanded unconditional withdrawal of Japanese forces from China and restoration of Chinese sovereignty. This was unacceptable to the Japanese. When Roosevelt ordered an embargo of scrap metal and fuel oil to Japan, the Japanese government began planning a strike against the United States.

The Japanese had stockpiled oil and metal in case of an American embargo, but these supplies wouldn't last forever. Seizure of British and Dutch possessions in Southeast Asia would provide access to the raw materials and oil they needed to keep their war machine and their economy running. However, the Japanese were convinced that any move against the British would result in American intervention. The only way to prevent that intervention was to neutralize the American Navy now stationed at Pearl Harbor. While the Japanese did not desire war with the United States, and did not envision conquering the Americans, they hoped to neutralize the American Navy long enough to take control of the lands they desired in Southeast Asia and the Western Pacific, dig in, and make the cost of retaking the lands too great for the Americans to bother with it.

While the restationing of the fleet did put it in a position to more effectively intervene against Japanese aggression, it also left the fleet more vulnerable to Japanese surprise attack. American attitudes toward the Japanese increased this risk. Every American naval war game exercise in the 1930s planned on a confrontation with the Japanese. In virtually every one of those exercises the Japanese attacked Pearl Harbor if they attacked first. American commanders knew the Japanese could attack Pearl Harbor, as expressed in Document C. The problem was, virtually every American in command at Pearl Harbor and many of those in charge in Washington assumed that because Pearl Harbor had been equipped for defense against such an assault, the Japanese would never dare to assault it. Americans talked of such a Japanese assault as too risky, or even suicidal. Through such talk, the Americans in charge effectively convinced themselves that they didn't need to prepare for a Japanese air or naval assault because it couldn't happen. In other words, they focused on what they believed the Japanese *would do* rather than what the Japanese *could do*.

In accordance with those beliefs, the war warning message of November 27, 1941 (Document A) was not interpreted as an immediate threat of attack against Pearl Harbor. While military officials in Washington expected that the war warning message would result in full mobilization at Pearl Harbor and the fleet going out to sea (Documents C and H), Admiral Kimmel failed to send out the fleet and General Short failed to prepare the airfields and antiaircraft batteries for immediate action. Both were convinced that the only real threat to Hawaii was from local saboteurs and prepared their defenses accordingly. General Short was convinced that since Washington hadn't questioned his response to the war warning dispatch, in which he stated he was prepared to defend against sabotage (Document E), that his failure to prepare for conventional attack was acceptable. Washington did not understand that his response meant he was *only* prepared for sabotage. Officials assumed he was prepared for both sabotage and conventional attack (Document C).

Obviously, there were some major misunderstandings between Washington officials and Pearl Harbor commanders. The various assumptions they made resulted in a nearly total breakdown in communications. This breakdown was climaxed by the failure of Washington intelligence officials to send the decoded Japanese war declaration (Document G) to Pearl Harbor in time to warn them about the break in American-Japanese negotiations and the 7:30 A.M. (Pearl Harbor time) deadline for delivering the message to the secretary of state. It was this failure, as well as the failure to notify Pearl Harbor of other intercepted Japanese messages that led to Kimmel's charges (Document F) and Short's charges (Document E) that they weren't given enough information to prepare for the attack.

Their argument begs the case. As documents B, C, and I indicate, a war warning was sent to Pearl Harbor more than a week before the attack. With a war warning, no matter what their biases and assumptions, it was the duty of both Kimmel and Short to prepare for the worst possible situation: a surprise attack against the fleet in the harbor. This was not done. As documents C and D indicate, not even the most basic preparations such as torpedo nets around the battleships or dispersion of the aircraft were made. There is no way a lack of specific advanced warning of an attack can excuse this. There is no proof, that given their biases, further warning or deciphered documents would have significantly changed the actions of Kimmel and Short. They were so convinced it couldn't happen that without specific warning of a direct attack on the base, it appears unlikely they would have made adequate preparations.

In conclusion, the prime responsibility of the debacle has to lie with Kimmel and Short, who failed to make adequate preparations to repel any type of assault, even after a war warning was sent to them. But officials in Washington must also share some blame for not checking to make sure that the defensive preparations they *assumed* were being made, were *actually* being conducted. Washington also didn't give serious thought to a Japanese attack on Pearl Harbor and didn't pay close attention to Pearl Harbor's situation. Washington could have been more clear in its messages to Pearl Harbor as to exactly what was expected of the local commanders. Finally, Washington could have provided Pearl Harbor with several intercepted messages (including Document G). While this probably would not have made a difference, there is always the possibility that it might have changed their behavior. Overall, American arrogance toward the Japanese led to assumptions that even if the Japanese could attack they wouldn't dare try or wouldn't be able to "pull it off." It was this arrogance as well as the resulting communications breakdown which contributed the most to the disaster.

Sample Answers to Essay Questions

2. At the time of Andrew Jackson's election to the presidency, the United States was just beginning to evolve a true, two-party system. When the United States was formed, there were no political parties. However, during George Washington's presidency two competing philosophies emerged, each represented by its own political party — the Federalist party, dominant in New England and supporting the Hamiltonian philosophy of a strong federal government with national monetary policy, and the Republican party, strongest outside of New England and supporting the Jeffersonian position of limited federal power.

With the War of 1812, the Federalists discredited themselves as secessionists at the Hartford Convention of 1814. This left the Republican party as the sole major political party in the nation. For the next several years the United States was basically a one-party political system. Even in the election of 1824, by which time major differences had erupted between the opposing candidates, the candidates did not run under separate party affiliations.

There were too many differing views about the power of the federal government, states' rights, government taxation and monetary policies, slavery, and class differences for a one-party system to last forever. The election of 1824, in which Andrew Jackson won a plurality in the popular vote but lost the election when it was sent to Congress, highlighted those differences and helped to shape the new second party, the Democrats, which would oppose the Republicans. By 1828, Andrew Jackson was running again as a Democrat with a clear agenda to change Republican-dominated government policies. With his election, he established the Democrats as a second major political force and ushered in 12 consecutive years of Democrat rule in the White House.

John Quincy Adams, the Republican president who preceded Jackson and who opposed Jackson in the 1828 election, represented the essence of what Jackson stood against. He was well educated, a Harvard professor. He represented the traditional model of the landed aristocrat who had typically led the United States. He supported high federal tariffs and a strong federal government to enforce collection of the tariff, despite state or local opposition. He also supported a broader role for the federal government in building roads, supporting education, and supporting the arts. Adams' vision of government was based on an expanded federal government reigning supreme over states' rights and enacting national programs for the good of the majority even if some states opposed the measures because they would be adversely affected.

These ideas ran counter to the basic Jeffersonian principles under which the Republican party was founded. Many Republicans wanted another option. Andrew Jackson gave them that option. Jackson portrayed himself as a common man; a man of the people. He was not well educated, but he was a war hero. Since most other Americans weren't well educated and distrusted people with "too much" education, Jackson was able to use his lack of education against the well-educated Adams and turn it to his own advantage.

He was also a master politician who knew how to rally people to his cause. He promoted the philosophy of "sovereignty of the people," which emphasized that the common people knew what was best for themselves and didn't need educated elites telling them what to do.

It was this philosophy of "rule of the common people" which made Jackson so popular and won the Democratic party immediate support. The time was right and people, frustrated with government policies believed to be helping only the rich, were ready for a change. Jackson won a landslide election in 1828 and his followers nearly destroyed the White House in the process of celebrating his victory. Historians mark Jackson's rise to power as a turning point in American politics for it was the first time that a presidential election became the centerpiece of American politics, and it brought thousands of people into the political system who had previously been ignored. It marked the beginning of true democracy in the American political system.

Once in power, Jackson expanded the powers of the presidency. Many saw him as a tyrant. Others praised him for standing up to what they saw as congressional abuse of power. He lowered tariffs and worked to eliminate laws which favored the wealthy and restricted opportunity for workers and "common people." He attempted to eliminate the national bank, and he cut back or eliminated federal programs aimed at road building, education, and the arts. Jackson worked toward a smaller federal government so that people at the state and local level could decide their own fate, rather than be dictated to by a federal bureaucracy in Washington. While he believed in limited government at the federal level, he did not support states' rights. He believed that the federal government had to reign supreme over the states or the Union could not survive. He also believed that states had no right to secede or disobey federal mandates.

Jackson's presidency was also known for its reliance on the "spoils system" of appointing officials to federal office. Jackson was not subtle about this and made no apologies for it, although it was one area where even the "common people" didn't always support him or his appointees.

Overall, Jackson's presidency of the "common man" firmly changed the course of American politics. It reestablished the two-party system and reopened political debate on many crucial issues. It also actively involved many people in the political system who had never before actively participated in politics. He truly did involve the "common person," often for the first time, in governing the United States. This set a precedent to which all Americans owe a debt of gratitude.

3. Reconstruction refers to that period of time following the Civil War in which Southern states were placed under military rule by the Congress. This period is generally considered to include the years from 1867 to 1876. With the passage of the Reconstruction Acts in 1867, the South was divided into five military districts. New state constitutions were to be drawn up at constitutional conventions. The delegates to these conventions were to be elected by "eligible" voters, which included Blacks and excluded many Whites such as former Confederate officials. These elections resulted in control of the the conventions by Republican delegates.

For Southern states to be readmitted to the Union, they had to ratify the Thirteenth, Fourteenth, and Fifteenth Amendments to the Constitution. These amendments, respectively, prohibited slavery, endowed citizenship on all persons born in the United States, reduced Congressional representation of states which restricted the right to vote, prohibited former Confederates from holding political office, and prohibited the denial of franchise because of race, color, or past enslavement.

Reconstruction governments in the South were dominated by Whites, despite Southern propaganda that the governments were led by illiterate Blacks and corrupt Northerners. While there certainly was corruption in these governments, there is no evidence that the level of corruption was significantly greater than the corruption in the governments preceding Reconstruction. Whatever corruption existed was certainly no greater than the corruption in post-Reconstruction state governments in the South. Blacks never controlled the governorship of any Southern state and held a majority in both houses of only one state legislature, South Carolina's, and then for only a two-year period. Blacks who held office in Southern legislatures were, for the most part, well-educated and concerned about improving living conditions in their state. Northern Whites who came South and participated in state legislatures or organizations like the Freedmen's bureau, usually came to help build a better land and make a better life for themselves in that land, not to "rape" the South and run off with Southern riches at the expense of Southerners. Newly enfranchised black voters were at least as qualified to vote as the scores of illiterate rural white farmers who had voted for years.

Reconstruction governments, in general, were more democratic than any preceding governments and far more democratic than subsequent nineteenth-century Southern state governments. They passed laws dropping voting restrictions, supporting effective public education for all Southerners, expanding the number of elective offices, and generally opening up the government to Blacks and poor rural Whites who had previously been excluded from Southern politics. Unfortunately, they also raised taxes to pay for many of the new measures, and it was the raising of taxes that led to most of the charges of corruption.

The main problem with Reconstruction was the rigid, inflexible attitudes of white Southerners. Congress had passed the Reconstruction Acts precisely because after the end of the Civil War Southern Whites returned to their old practices of subjugating Blacks. While Blacks were technically free, former Confederates were returned to office and led the passage of legislation restricting black rights to the point that Blacks were still effectively, if not legally, enslaved. In effect, Southern Whites were going to gain back through legal manipulation what they had lost on the battlefield. Outraged by Southerners' conduct, Northerners supported congressional radicals' attempts to "lower the boom" on Southern states. Reconstruction was the result.

Southern Whites reacted with fury to Reconstruction. Northerners who came South were called "carpetbaggers." Southern Republicans who voted in support of Reconstruction governments were called "scalawags." Every effort was made to circumvent Reconstruction provisions granting Blacks equal rights. When laws could not be evaded, terror from groups such as the "Ku Klux Klan" was often used to intimidate Blacks from using their newly won civil rights. The problem Reconstruction never solved was that it could force some change in Southerners' behaviors through legal mandate, but it could not change the underlying attitudes which drove white Southerners' behaviors. Whenever the opportunity arose, the old attitudes and behaviors would resurface. Without a change in underlying Southern attitudes toward Blacks and toward Northern efforts at reform, it was only a matter of time before the reform efforts collapsed.

By the mid-1870s, Northerners were exhausted from continuously battling Southern resistance to Reconstruction. Other political issues had arisen which needed attention, particularly in the economy, and Northerners were "fed up" with constant Southern hostility. The Republican party had refocused its goals toward maintaining power and protecting the wealthy rather than protecting the vulnerable and reforming the system. Most Southern states had been re-admitted to the Union but were still being closely watched. The election of 1876 and the subsequent Compromise of 1877 put Rutherford B. Hayes, another Republican, in office. The cost of this compromise was the end of Union military rule in the South and the final death knell for Reconstruction.

With Northern military rule eliminated, and full voting rights restored to Southern Whites, it did not take long for the reforms of Reconstruction to disappear. Because Southern white attitudes had not changed, the attitude typically was "Now we can return to business as usual." Reconstructionist leaders were replaced by "Redeemers," Southern Whites still loyal to the ide-ologies of the Old South and determined to return things to their "proper" order. These redeemers were dedicated to returning power to the privileged white elites who had previously dominated Southern life. They formed political machines, or "rings," to coordinate their activities. They also supported white supremacy and used racist arguments to discredit their opponents and used poll taxes, literacy tests, and other restrictive measures to deny Blacks their right to vote.

While Reconstruction offered a glimmer of hope to newly freed Blacks, and poor, rural Southern Whites, it so enraged most Southern Whites that unless attitudes could be changed it was guaranteed to create a severe backlash. Northern white reformers let themselves get discouraged by Southern in-transigence and distracted by economic and political problems in the North. Subsequently, they rescinded Reconstruction before it could really affect long-term changes in attitude. With Reconstruction over, the white backlash which had been building was released in a fury on Blacks who were blamed for nearly all the South's post–Civil War problems. The window opened by Reconstruction was quickly slammed shut, and Blacks would have to wait another 90 years before seeing that window cracked open again.

4. Following the Spanish-American War, the United States found itself in command of an overseas empire. As a result of the war, the United States controlled Cuba, the Philippines, Guam, and Puerto Rico. These possessions were in addition to American control of Alaska, Hawaii, the Canal Zone in Panama, and American dominance in several Central American countries. This new empire caused deep divisions in the American psyche.

Most Americans were philosophically opposed to European-style colonialism. Having been a colony once, Americans preached a philosophy of self-determination. Despite American meddling in the Caribbean via "Dollar Diplomacy" and the "Big Stick" policies, most Americans rejected the notion of formal American colonization of Central American nations.

When America went to war against Spain, most Americans supported the war effort in the belief that it was for the just cause of liberating Cuba from ruthless Spanish control. They did not go into war looking for an empire. The victory over Spain and subsequent American control over former Spanish territories left these Americans uncomfortable because it violated the very principles of self-determination for which they thought the war had been fought.

Other Americans were not so altruistic. Having acquired these territories, many Americans, particularly industrialists and conservative political disciples of Manifest Destiny, saw the opportunity to exploit and develop these lands to the advantage of American business and American military security. They were hesitant to let them go with the distinct possibility that some other nation might economically or politically dominate them. These two radically different philosophies stirred a major debate in the United States over U.S. policy in regard to empire building.

The Philippines were a classic case. Filipinos wanted their independence. For the United States to annex them against their will violated American ideals of self-determination. However, Manila harbor was one of the most desirable sites for a naval base in the Pacific. The Philippines would also provide an ideal stopping point for American vessels travelling between Asia and the American West Coast. A debate raged in Congress over a proposed amendment to the Treaty of Paris which would have promised the Philippines independence as soon as they were able to establish a legitimate, stable, government. The debate ended in a tie vote in the Senate, so deep was the philosophical division, which was broken by the vice president, who voted against the Philippines independence amendment. The pro-empire forces won a narrow victory.

America also chose to annex Guam. This added to our previous annexations of Wake Island, Hawaii, Johnston Island, and Samoa. Cuba was not annexed despite the desires of some business leaders, primarily because the Teller Amendment, which led to the war, declared Cuba a free and independent nation and justified American use of force only to rid Cuba of its Spanish occupiers. To annex Cuba would have been the peak of hypocrisy. Even without formal annexation, Cuba was occupied by American troops for 14 of the 24 years between 1898 and 1922. Its government was tightly controlled by American policies and America maintained, as it still maintains, a naval base at Guantanamo. Cuba was a de facto colony even though it was formally independent.

Despite the revulsion felt by many Americans over the acquisition of new territory following the Spanish-American War, the majority of those in power accepted and welcomed the economic and political benefits to be derived from control of these new lands. And this really wasn't a new trend. This phase of American expansionism was just an extension of the "Manifest Destiny" which had led to the westward American push during the nineteenth century. This new phase, called by expansionist supporters "the large policy," called for expanded American control into the Caribbean and Central America. Therefore, the statement that the "taste of empire is in the mouths of the people" was to a large degree valid. While certainly it left a bitter taste in many people's mouths, to the majority of those in political and industrial leadership, the taste was sweet and they used every economic, military, and political argument and rationalization available to support their beliefs. The fact that retaining these possessions violated American principles of self-determination was conveniently overlooked for the moment. The Philippines were not promised independence until passage of the Jones Amendment in 1916. The remaining territories either became states or remain as American territories today.

5.   Herbert Hoover was elected to the presidency in 1928, following eight consecutive years of Republican rule. Under Harding and Coolidge, the nation had seen an unprecedented period of economic growth, particularly in the stock market. Hoover saw his election as a mandate to continue the pro-business, anti-regulation policies of his Republican predecessors. Hoover was philosophically committed to a small federal government, operating on a balanced budget, helping American business prosper, and taking a laissez-faire approach to other problems whenever possible. He was also committed to the idea that people needed to help themselves out of poverty. He fully believed that any individual could, through hard work, improve himself or herself without government assistance.

When the stock market crashed in October of 1929, and the economy began its slow but steady decline into depression, Hoover was not particularly worried. Economic theorists of the time asserted that depressions occurred regularly as part of the business cycle. Some even argued that periodic recessions or depressions were good for the economy because they "weeded out" poorly run, inefficient, and obsolete businesses, providing healthy businesses with new opportunities for further growth. Hoover fully expected business to lead the nation to recovery from this depression. He realized that he would have to take action to help in that recovery, but his philosophical ideals severely limited how far he would go to lead that recovery.

At first, he tried to talk, or "jawbone" the economy into recovery with a series of "pep talks" with business leaders, encouraging them to keep workers employed and to wait out the business slump. He also made a series of public speeches which tried to reassure the public that the economy was "fundamentally sound" and that recovery was "right around the corner." What Hoover failed to realize was that business had been too severely injured by the stock market crash and the following economic collapse to pull the economy out of the Depression without a massive influx of federal money. Hoover was unwilling to commit to such federal intervention because it would result in massive deficit spending, to which he was firmly opposed, and because he believed it would make people dependent on federal help to the point that they would lose their self-respect and become permanently wedded to federal aid to survive.

By 1932, even Hoover realized that some government intervention was needed. He requested the formation of the Reconstruction Finance Corporation which was supposed to provide credit to banks, railroads, and insurance companies to help them offer loans to workers, businessmen, and farmers. He also backed creation of the Federal Home Loan Bank System which provided money to the home construction industry. The problem with these programs was that they were not funded enough to make a significant difference and they were enacted too late to have a significant impact on the Depression. In addition, people didn't need credit, they needed jobs.

In the midst of this, Hoover signed the Smoot-Hawley tariffs, which Europeans termed an "economic declaration of war." He also signed bills raising personal and corporate income taxes and he supported an increase in the sales tax. At the very time people needed more income, Hoover, to maintain a balanced federal budget, was taking income out of their pockets and lowering their buying power. This made the Depression even worse.

While Hoover did enact some public works programs, they were so limited in their funding that they were equivalent to a drop of water in the Sahara. Unless Hoover was willing to abandon the balanced budget, support massive government intervention through public works and relief programs, and enact strict business regulations, the economy could not recover. Hoover, trapped by his traditionalist ideals, could not bring himself to do this and the economy wallowed near total collapse as a result.

Franklin Roosevelt brought to the government an entirely different perspective. Perhaps his major difference from Hoover was his ability to communicate effectively with the common person. With his "fireside chats" Roosevelt used the radio as a means of calming the fears of Americans. He emerged as a benevolent "father figure" to many people. Whereas Hoover, despite his inner pain at the suffering caused by the Depression, seemed distant and uncaring,

Roosevelt seemed concerned and involved. Hoover's lack of effective action left him vulnerable to the charge of doing nothing and being insensitive to the poor. Roosevelt, from the very beginning, made sure people saw him doing *something*. With his "New Deal" he promised an active, involved government which would make things better for the average American. He was not very specific at first about what those changes would be (because he was not yet sure what they would be), but by 1932, so many people had been suffering for so long they did not care what the changes were as long as there were changes.

Once in power, Roosevelt used his "brains trust," his circle of advisors drawn from the greatest universities and "think tanks" in the nation, to draw up a series of significant reforms. These reforms were enacted in a flurry of legislative activity known as the "first hundred days." Despite his determination to make changes, at first Roosevelt attempted to follow Hoover's policy of maintaining a balanced budget. He soon realized that this was impossible. Pragmatically, he dropped the balanced budget effort and enacted a series of relief and public works programs to get people back to work. He devalued the dollar, abandoned the gold standard, and changed monetary policies to make credit more available. Roosevelt realized that government had to "prime the pump" and get more money into the economy or it would never reignite itself. While Roosevelt was willing to run a deficit at first, he never gave up on the principle of balancing the budget. In 1937, he tightened monetary policy in an effort to rebalance the federal budget. He felt that the basic problems causing the Depression had been solved and there was no further need for "excessive" government spending. His cutbacks quickly resulted in a new economic collapse and Roosevelt found himself opening the budget deficit again to restore the economy. The biggest complaint about Roosevelt's New Deal policies before World War II was that he didn't run a big enough deficit to really restore the economy to full health. Given the mood of the times, he ran about as large a deficit as he could afford to, but it wasn't until the military buildup for World War II that the Congress would support deficits big enough to spark full employment.

Roosevelt greatly expanded the size and power of the federal government. Through Social Security, minimum wage, banking regulation, anti-monopoly regulation, farm support, and support for public works, Roosevelt redefined the relationship between the government and the people. The government was now involved in every aspect of people's lives, and more and more people would turn to the federal government for help. While the "New Deal" was certainly not universally effective, as it took World War II to really restore the economy to health, it restored people's faith in themselves and in the United States government. It bought time for the nation and even some conservatives have said that Roosevelt saved capitalism from the capitalists.

Neither Roosevelt nor Hoover liked the idea of deficit spending or making people dependent on relief, or "the dole." Many of Roosevelt's early relief agencies were created for only short periods of time to prevent long-term public dependency. The major difference between the two men, beyond their ability to communicate with the public, was that Hoover remained to the end inflexible, rigid, unwilling to bend on his idealistic principles, and unable to see the real needs of the nation. Roosevelt was more practical. While he understood Hoover's principles and agreed with most of them, he realized that those principles needed to be bent to deal with the immediate economic crisis. Roosevelt was willing to be flexible, to compromise, and to experiment with whatever was necessary to restore the economic health of the country. Where Hoover was closed-minded and pessimistic, Roosevelt was openminded, confident, and optimistic. Both men were honest, caring, decent men. Roosevelt was just more active, creative, and imaginative in his efforts to resolve the economic crisis created by the Great Depression.

PRACTICE TEST 4
AP United States History

AP United States History

PRACTICE TEST 4

SECTION I

TIME: 55 Minutes
80 Questions

DIRECTIONS: Each of the questions or incomplete statements below is followed by five suggested answers or completions. Select the one that is best in each case.

1. The "Zimmerman Papers" were infamous because they

   (A) exposed German atrocities against Jews and other prisoners of war and contributed directly to the U.S. entry into World War I

   (B) exposed a German plot to enlist Mexico into an alliance with Germany in a war against the United States

   (C) exposed corruption in the U.S. Justice Department leading to a total reorganization of the department and the formation of the FBI

   (D) exposed a British plot to disguise their warships as American merchant ships, encouraging German submarines to attack any ship flying the American flag, hopefully luring the United States into World War I

   (E) revealed the existence of Communist spies in the highest levels of American government, following World War I, and led to the "Red Scare" in which hundreds of innocent people were victimized in witch hunts trying to weed out Communists

2. The term "robber baron" refers to

   (A) wealthy landowners in the antebellum South

   (B) late-nineteenth-century industrialists

    (C)   early-nineteenth-century Federalists

    (D)   early-twentieth-century Populists

    (E)   late-eighteenth-century British mercantilists

3.   The establishment of penitentiaries during the 1840s reflected

    (A)   a public desire to completely remove criminals from public view and permanently separate them from society so women and children would not be offended by having to look at them

    (B)   a new attitude by the public that criminals were sinners who were beyond redemption; therefore, they should be forced into isolation to protect society from their depradations

    (C)   a new attitude that emphasized more intense corporal punishment for criminals rather than the old religious-based efforts which had emphasized forgiveness

    (D)   the shortage of space to house criminals during the massive crime waves that surged through East Coast cities beginning in 1842

    (E)   a new attitude that looked upon criminals as misguided, in need of help, and penitentiaries were designed to help these misguided souls reform

4.   The Trent Affair was important because

    (A)   it discredited the revolutionary government in France in the eyes of most Americans

    (B)   it prevented the Confederacy from being able to purchase several warships from Britain and France for use against Union shipping

    (C)   it was the first clear case of treason by a United States official and it badly embarrassed the administration of John Adams

    (D)   it resulted in the sinking of the Confederate raider, the *Alabama*

    (E)   it nearly led to British recognition of the Confederacy and war between Britain and the Union

5.   "Jim Crow" laws were laws that

    (A)   effectively prohibited Blacks from voting in state and local elections

    (B)   restricted American Indians to U.S. government reservations

    (C)   restricted open-range ranching in the Great Plains

    (D)   established separate segregated facilities for Blacks and Whites

    (E)   restricted the consumption and distribution of alcohol within the limits of pro-temperance communities

6.   The Smoot-Hawley Tariffs and other protectionist trade measures had the long-term effect of

    (A)   improving the competitiveness of U.S. industry in foreign markets

    (B)   improving U.S. economic strength in the long-term, although short-term economic performance was weakened

    (C)   making little difference in the economies of Europe and the U.S.

    (D)   sparking retaliatory measures from Europe which weakened both their economies and ours

    (E)   providing European leaders with the incentive to finally put their differences aside and form an economic confederation, which would eventually evolve into the European Common Market

7.   The Iran-Contra affair upset most Americans because it involved

    (A)   illegal support for the Contra rebels in Nicaragua

    (B)   illegal support for government backed "death squads" in El Salvador

    (C)   a presidential coverup similar to, and to some extent worse than, the Watergate affair

    (D)   trading arms to Iran for release of American hostages

    (E)   providing funding for Contra rebels to be trained by Iranians in terrorist tactics to be used against the Nicaraguan government

8.   Colonies such as the Carolinas were known as "restoration colonies" because

    (A)   their creation was mainly due to the restoration of the Stuarts to the English throne

    (B)   they were created as places to send criminals to restore them to civilized behavior and give them a chance to lead decent, honest lives

    (C)   their creation was mainly due to an effort by the English government to restore a balance of power in the New World between the thriving

English colonies in New England and the less successful English colonies in the South

(D) their creation was mainly due to the restoration of the power of English Parliament over the king

(E) their creation was an attempt to restore the supremacy of the Anglican church in the colonies

9. The phrase "Eight hours for work, eight hours for rest, and eight hours for what we will" emphasizes a turn-of-the-century trend toward

(A) more daily devotion to religious activities

(B) a greater emphasis on volunteerism and civic activities among the wealthy industrialists and landowners

(C) a greater emphasis on the Protestant work ethic by the middle and upper classes

(D) a greater availability of leisure time for working Americans

(E) the deterioration of moral standards among the middle class at this time

10. The Morgan Affair of 1826 was responsible for

(A) the revolt by Texans to obtain their independence from Mexico

(B) the collapse of John Quincy Adams' presidency and his loss of the 1828 election to Andrew Jackson

(C) the collapse of efforts to revive a national bank

(D) the establishment of the anti-Masonic movement

(E) the founding of the modern temperance movement

11. By 1760, the biggest problem with the economy of the English colonies was

(A) smuggling

(B) a trade surplus so large that England was threatening to confiscate American assets to help balance the English economy

(C) a lack of demand for the vast quantities of high-quality American manufactured goods now being produced, leading to high unemployment in the American colonies

(D)　a huge balance-of-trade deficit that threatened the solvency of the colonial economy

(E)　a lack of adequate deep-water ports to provide loading and unloading facilities for the large number of ships now trying to bring goods to or carry goods from the colonies

12.　The Hartford Convention of 1814 focused on

(A)　revising military strategy against the British in the stalemated War of 1812

(B)　the creation of a national bank to stabilize U.S. currency and establish U.S. credit overseas

(C)　Federalist desires for a massive rewriting of the Constitution to neutralize the power of Southern Republicans

(D)　Republican desires for lessened federal control and increased states' rights in matters of international trade critical to New England's survival

(E)　devising plans to convince Canada to join the United States in its war against England (the War of 1812) in return for Canadian independence after the war

13.　Between 1860 and 1910, the area of the United States which underwent the largest *percentage* increase of population was

(A)　the Northeast　　　　(D)　the Far West

(B)　the Old South　　　　(E)　the Great Plains

(C)　the Mid-Atlantic

14.　The key issue that prevented the American colonists from resolving their problems with England without open rebellion was

(A)　the sovereignty of King George III over the colonies

(B)　the sovereignty of Parliament's edicts over the colonies

(C)　the stationing of British soldiers on American soil

(D)　American desire for total independence from Britain

(E)　the use of boycotts by American colonists to resist taxes passed by Parliament

15. Andrew Johnson was impeached primarily because

(A) he was an alcoholic and made several major speeches while totally drunk

(B) angry Northern Congressmen resented the fact that Johnson, a Southerner (from Tennessee), had become president following Lincoln's death and was administering Southern Reconstruction

(C) members of Congress felt that Johnson's Reconstruction policies were too harsh and unfairly penalized former Confederate leaders trying to rebuild their homeland

(D) he demanded suffrage for Blacks in addition to the abolition of slavery

(E) he obstructed the enforcement of congressional Reconstruction policies that he felt were too harsh

16. The canal building period of the 1820s resulted primarily from

(A) the need for a more effective public transportation system between major Northeastern cities and towns

(B) speculators trying to find a quick and cheap method of moving European immigrants to unexplored frontiers in the West

(C) the need to move U.S. naval forces quickly from the Atlantic to the Great Lakes and the Mississippi River

(D) a shortage of usable fresh water in the trans-Appalachian states

(E) the need for an economical method of shipping farm goods from the Western states and territories directly to Eastern markets

17. The Fourteenth Amendment to the Constitution was important because it

(A) prohibited slavery within the United States

(B) guaranteed equal protection under the law for every American citizen

(C) prohibited any state from denying an American citizen the right to vote based on race/ethnic background, color, or having previously been a slave

(D) prohibited any state from denying women the right to vote

(E) provided Congress with the power to establish and collect income taxes

18. The recession of 1937 was primarily caused by

    (A) overextension of easy credit and high inflation

    (B) excess business speculation in the rebounding stock market

    (C) failure of New Deal programs to effectively lower unemployment and restore faith in the economy

    (D) overregulation of key national industries, resulting in massive lay-offs

    (E) premature tightening of credit and cutbacks in spending for New Deal programs

19. A leader of the Nationalist movement in the United States in the 1780s was

    (A) Alexander Hamilton   (D) Richard Henry Lee

    (B) Thomas Jefferson   (E) Thomas Payne

    (C) Samuel Adams

20. The overall strategic policy of the Union to destroy the Confederacy through a combination of constant pressure and slowly wearing down the South's ability to wage war was called

    (A) the Nutcracker Plan   (D) the Attrition Plan

    (B) the Anaconda Plan   (E) the Sausalito Plan

    (C) the Squeeze Plan

21. The growth of most American cities in 1880 was determined primarily by

    (A) urban planning by local officials

    (B) public needs

    (C) federal regulations

    (D) British models of ideal urban growth patterns

    (E) profit motives

22. The XYZ Affair was important in that it

    (A) underlined the importance of a strong, impartial federal judiciary in resolving Constitutional disputes between the state and federal governments

(B) led to U.S. abrogation of the 1778 peace treaty and brought the U.S. into a quasi-war with France

(C) nearly brought Britain into the Civil War on the side of the Confederacy

(D) discredited Aaron Burr and forced his removal from the 1800 presidential election ticket as Thomas Jefferson's running mate

(E) led the U.S. to seek a declaration of war against Britain in 1812 for impressing American seamen onto British ships

23. What event made Kennedy a national hero in 1962 due to the way in which people believed he successfully stood up to the Russians?

(A) The Berlin Blockade

(B) The Berlin Wall Crisis

(C) The Pueblo Incident

(D) The Cuban Missile Crisis

(E) The Gulf of Tonkin Incident

24. The *Marbury v. Madison* case was important because it

(A) firmly established the principle of one man, one vote

(B) affirmed the Supreme Court's power to judge the constitutionality of laws passed by Congress

(C) limited the power of the individual states to interfere with legal business contracts or commercial activity

(D) found that Congress had the constitutional power to issue bank charters, thus opening the door for a strong national bank

(E) ruled that slavery could not be prohibited from U.S. territories, increasing tensions which would eventually explode into the Civil War

25. The first textile workers in America were primarily

(A) farmers' daughters from New England

(B) freed slaves who moved North from the repressive labor markets in the South

(C) Irish immigrants

(D)   ex-soldiers and war veterans who often could find work nowhere else

(E)   uneducated males from the working class who comprised America's first generation of "blue collar" workers

26.   What view of the relationship of Congress and business is Thomas Nast presenting in this cartoon?

From the collection of MacCulloch Hall Historical Museum, Morristown, N. J.

Pan-Ic in Session.
Death to us (the people) and fun for them ("Statesmen").

(A)   Congress has established too much regulatory power over business.

(B)   Business is the benefactor of the American people.

(C)   Congress is the upholder of the national interest.

(D)   Congress is subject to the corrupt influence of business.

(E)   Business has little influence in national affairs.

27. The Watergate scandal led to Richard Nixon's downfall primarily because

   (A) of his role in planning and coordinating the Watergate break-in and other illegal campaign activity

   (B) the press, the Democrats, and some liberal Republicans united to rid themselves of Nixon and his conservative philosophy

   (C) he was already so unpopular because of his Vietnam War policies that virtually anything he did wrong would have been used as an excuse to remove him from office

   (D) of his role in directing the cover-up of the Watergate Affair

   (E) of his involvement with organized crime in carrying out political "dirty tricks" against his Democratic opponent, George McGovern

28. The invention of the cotton gin by Eli Whitney was important because it

   (A) reduced the need for large numbers of slaves to pick Southern cotton, providing abolitionists with one more argument for the elimination of slavery

   (B) allowed cotton to be grown in areas that had previously been unsuitable for cotton production

   (C) led to the development of the South's first large textile factories and the beginnings of a strong Southern manufacturing base

   (D) allowed cotton to be picked and processed much more quickly, thus vastly increasing the profitability of cotton and the need for more slaves to pick it

   (E) required skilled workers to operate it leading to the development of the South's most prominent educational and training institutions which provided workers with the necessary education and skills

29. The Dominion of New England was established by the English government in 1686 to

   (A) increase the power of the Puritans

   (B) end the Glorious Revolution and restore James II to the English throne

   (C) stimulate trade among the fledgling New England colonies

   (D) increase the effectiveness of the various New England legislatures

   (E) increase the authority of the English government over the New England colonies

30. Woodrow Wilson's "New Freedom" and Theodore Roosevelt's "New Nationalism" were similar in that both

    (A) removed restrictions on the rights of women and minorities

    (B) removed restrictions on the rights of unions to organize within the workplace

    (C) expanded the rights of states to regulate business operations within state borders

    (D) expanded the government's role in regulating businesses and business monopolies

    (E) expanded the notion of individualism inherent in their laissez-faire economic policies

31. The Atlantic Charter

    (A) set collective war strategy and long-term war goals for Britain and the United States

    (B) guaranteed American neutrality in World War II as long as American warships stayed out of British territorial waters

    (C) pledged South and Central American neutrality after Germany and Japan declared war on the United States

    (D) provided Britain with 50 World War I vintage American destroyers in return for American control of British military bases in the Caribbean and the Mid-Atlantic

    (E) repealed the American arms embargo and allowed Britain and France to buy American war materials on a cash-and-carry basis

32. The prominent issue in national politics in the 1840s was

    (A) the abolition of slavery

    (B) the temperance movement

    (C) the westward expansion of U.S. territory

    (D) the creation of a new national bank

    (E) women's rights

33. John Foster Dulles is most closely associated with the

    (A) policy of mutually assured destruction

    (B) flexible response policy

(C)   zero option policy

(D)   Strategic Defense Initiative

(E)   policy of massive retaliation

34.   In the English colonies in the mid-eighteenth century, formal education beyond minimal reading and writing skills was considered

(A)   essential for both males and females

(B)   essential for males but not for females

(C)   essential for the children of poor colonists so the children would have a better chance of obtaining wealth

(D)   something every colonial government should provide for its colonists

(E)   nonessential for both males and females, except as a status symbol for those who could afford to pay for it

35.   The Compromise of 1850 had the effect of

(A)   providing a compromise that offered only limited expansion of slavery into territories west of the Mississippi, satisfying both pro-slavery Southerners and abolitionist Northerners, and resolving the issue of slavery west of the Mississippi

(B)   postponing and evading, rather than resolving, the problems related to slavery in American territories west of the Mississippi

(C)   ending Southern demands for the expansion of slavery into American territories west of the Mississippi

(D)   ending Northern demands for the prohibition of slavery in American territories west of the Mississippi

(E)   providing a compromise that allowed all American territories west of the Mississippi to decide the slavery issue for themselves

36.   Theodore Roosevelt's policy toward business trusts was to

(A)   support deregulation of business trusts so they could consolidate and better compete with international competition

(B)   quash reform efforts aimed at regulating business trusts because he believed the reformers were led by socialists and Marxists

(C)   seek regulation of only those trusts that used their powers to unfairly manipulate their markets and the economy

(D)   seek to bust, or destroy, all business trusts as antidemocratic and harmful to free competition

(E)   let the individual states deal with trusts as they chose. He did not believe that the federal government had the power to intervene

37.   What specific disagreement took a full year to rectify before peace negotiations actually began to end the Vietnam War?

(A)   The city in which the negotiations would be held

(B)   The governments which would be allowed to attend the negotiations

(C)   The shape of the negotiating table

(D)   The actual border between North and South Vietnam

(E)   The participation of representatives from the People's Republic of China as moderators of the negotiations

38.   The battles of Lexington and Concord were significant because

(A)   they convinced the British that the colonists could not be defeated militarily and led to the British abandonment of the port of Boston

(B)   they proved the superiority of European military tactics as well as the superiority of British regulars to the ragtag American militias

(C)   they marked the first organized battles between British regulars and colonial militiamen and ended any hopes for a peaceful resolution to the disagreement between England and its colonies

(D)   they marked the turning point of the American Revolution. After Concord, the British were never again able to regain the offensive against the Americans

(E)   they led to Benedict Arnold's betrayal of the American cause when he felt he wasn't given enough recognition for his role in leading the Americans to victory

39.   Abraham Lincoln took the Union into war against the Confederate States of America with the stated purpose of

(A)   protecting federal installations in Confederate territories

(B)   freeing the slaves and abolishing slavery from American soil

(C) preserving the Union

(D) punishing the South for its arrogance, rebelliousness, and the enslavement of Blacks by Southern slaveholders

(E) protecting the Union from Southern attacks on Union territories in the border states remaining loyal to the Union

40. The Japanese surprise attack on Pearl Harbor succeeded for all of the following reasons EXCEPT

(A) a conspiracy by the United States government to let the Japanese attack Pearl Harbor by surprise so America would have a legitimate excuse to enter World War II

(B) commanders at Pearl Harbor were convinced that the only real threat to the base was from local saboteurs, not a Japanese naval attack

(C) a message ordering the base on maximum war alert was sent via commercial telegraph rather than military cable and did not arrive until the day after the attack

(D) Americans did not believe the Japanese would dare attempt such a risky attack and did not believe the Japanese *could* pull it off if they tried

(E) interservice rivalry effectively kept the military intelligence services from sharing and coordinating the information they had collected which could have allowed them to anticipate the Pearl Harbor attack

41. President Carter's administration had its greatest difficulties with its

(A) Central American policy

(B) energy conservation policy

(C) land conservation policy

(D) Middle East policy

(E) economic policy

42. The establishment of transcontinental rail lines and the construction of America's massive rail network had all of the following effects EXCEPT:

(A) They led to the rapid industrialization of the Old South following the Civil War.

(B)   They allowed for rapid distribution of goods throughout the country.

(C)   Their building spurred a series of important technical advances.

(D)   They made the country smaller in the sense that they dramatically reduced the time needed to traverse the continent.

(E)   They resulted in the establishment of standardized time zones throughout the country.

43.   Thomas Paine's pamphlet *Common Sense* was significant in that it

(A)   emotionally aroused thousands of colonists to the abuses of British rule, the oppressiveness of the monarchy, and the advantages of colonial independence

(B)   rallied American spirits during the bleak winter of 1776, when it appeared that Washington's forces, freezing and starving at Valley Forge, had no hope of surviving the winter, much less defeating the British

(C)   called for a strong central government to rule the newly independent American states and foresaw the difficulties inherent within the Articles of Confederation

(D)   asserted to its British readers that they could not beat the American colonists militarily unless they could isolate New England from the rest of the American colonies

(E)   explained the urgent need for a "bill of rights" to expressly guarantee certain freedoms not specifically laid out in the newly adopted United States Constitution

44.   The decline of "open range" ranching in the West resulted primarily from

(A)   low beef prices, which made "open range" ranching unprofitable

(B)   government policies giving priority use of the range to sheepherders, thus denying cattlemen equal access to the open range

(C)   overgrazing and intense competition for use of the land between ranchers and farmers

(D)   the increased use of sharecropping techniques by cattle ranchers, which lessened their need for open-range policies

(E)   the high cost of replacing cattle, which constantly wandered off in the open range

45. William Howard Taft's approach to American Imperialism was known as

   (A) "Dollar Diplomacy"   (D) the "Good Neighbor" policy

   (B) the "Big Stick" policy   (E) "appeasement"

   (C) the "Open Door" policy

46. The use of alternating current to allow transmission of electric power over long distances was perfected by

   (A) Thomas Edison   (D) John G. Rockefeller

   (B) George Westinghouse   (E) Andrew Carnegie

   (C) J. P. Morgan

47. The "Gospel of Wealth" referred to the idea that

   (A) excess wealth would prevent those who possessed it from going to heaven. Therefore, the only way they could get to heaven was to give away their wealth to charities and philanthropic causes

   (B) real wealth comes from the love of those around you, not from money

   (C) money talks

   (D) being wealthy wasn't sinful so long as you didn't hurt other people in the process of gathering that wealth

   (E) rich people obtained their wealth because God gave it to them

48. What was the main goal of the Truman Doctrine?

   (A) Enforcement of the "Domino Theory"

   (B) Containment of communism

   (C) Ending nationalistic revolts in American territories and colonies

   (D) Elimination of communism

   (E) Rebuilding Western Europe after World War II

49. Joseph Pulitzer was a pioneer in the development of

   (A) news journals aimed exclusively at the upper class and social elites in America

   (B) weekly journals focusing exclusively on economic news

(C)   yellow journalism

(D)   ethics in journalism laws to prevent slanderous news stories which often ruined innocent people's lives

(E)   the nation's first national wire service, UPI

50.   In the 1880s, the issue of tariffs on imported goods became a major controversy because

(A)   the free-trade policies in effect at that time were allowing under-priced foreign goods to destroy fledgling American industries and virtually eliminate American crop exports to Europe

(B)   individual states refused to give up their right to enact tariffs on goods brought across state lines from neighboring states

(C)   high tariffs were resulting in unnecessarily high prices on manufactured goods, hurting both farmers and consumers while protecting several wealthy manufacturers

(D)   Democrats forced the enactment of free trade legislation in the U.S. but European countries responded by raising their tariffs on U.S. manufactured goods, throwing the U.S. economy into a depression

(E)   Democrats allowed tariffs to be enacted only on imported farm goods, which protected American farmers but left U.S. manufacturers vulnerable to European tariffs

51.   Jacob Coxey is most well known for

(A)   leading an army of unemployed workers on a march from Ohio to Washington, D.C., in 1894 to rally for a federal jobs program

(B)   leading an army of World War I veterans on a march from New York City to Washington, D.C., in 1932 to demand payment of military pensions to veterans promised by Congress back in 1918

(C)   leading the Populist movement in its campaign for free coinage of silver in the 1896 presidential election campaign

(D)   organizing the first national movement for national public health legislation to curb the spread of communicable diseases

(E)   his work in the Social Gospel movement in which he organized the first settlement houses

52. What incident led to Lyndon Johnson escalating American involvement in Vietnam by sending more than 550,000 American soldiers to actively fight the Viet Cong and the North Vietnamese?

(A) The Mayaguez Affair   (D) The attack on Khe Sahn

(B) The Pueblo Incident   (E) The Tet Offensive

(C) The Gulf of Tonkin Incident

53. The Sugar Act and the Townshend Acts differed from the previously passed Navigation Acts in that

(A) the Navigation Acts taxed goods imported to the colonies directly from Britain, whereas the Sugar Act and the Townshend Acts taxed only goods imported to the colonies from outside of Britain

(B) the Navigation Acts taxed only the ships on which goods were transported to the colonies, not the merchandise carried by those ships. The Sugar Act and the Townshend Acts taxed specific merchandise carried by ships to the colonies

(C) the Navigation Acts taxed goods based on the distance the goods travelled to reach America, whereas the Sugar Act and the Townshend Acts taxed the goods themselves, regardless of how far they travelled to reach America

(D) the Navigation Acts taxed only goods imported to the colonies from outside of Britain, whereas the Sugar Act and the Townshend Acts taxed goods imported to the colonies directly from Britain

(E) the Sugar Act and the Townshend Acts put specific limits on which goods imported to the colonies could be taxed, whereas the Navigation Acts had taxed virtually everything transported by ship from Britain to the colonies

54. Secretary of State William Seward's purchase of Alaska from the Russians in 1867 was based primarily on

(A) his realization that fishing rights in Alaskan waters would be a boon to American fishermen

(B) his desire to secure the vast oil reserves rumored to be hidden deep within Alaska's forbidding interior

(C) fears of Russian attempts to expand their control into western Canada and possibly the northwestern United States

(D)   his desires to help the Russians, who desperately needed the money they would get for dumping this "wasteland" on the Americans

(E)   his dream of an American empire that would subsume all of North America, including Canada, Mexico, and Greenland

55.   The picture below reflects the architectural style favored by which of the following?

(A)   Thomas Jefferson   (D)   Dr. William Thornton

(B)   Benjamin Latrobe   (E)   William Jenney

(C)   Charles Bullfinch

56.   Industrial committees which helped mobilize the country's war efforts during World War I were

(A)   instrumental in preventing corruption and labor dissension from crippling the mobilization campaign

(B)   so dominated by greedy businessmen cashing in on the war they were disbanded and replaced by the War Industries Board

(C)   the key to an efficient war effort following the collapse of the War Industries Board

(D)   ruled unconstitutional by the conservative Supreme Court and were forced to reorganize as unfunded private consulting groups

(E)   not formed until so late in the war effort that they had little impact other than to streamline the process for the transfer of men and equipment from the United States to France

57. The rejection of the Versailles Treaty by the United States Senate signaled what future for American foreign policy?

   (A) The United States retreated into isolationism and backed away from a world leadership role.

   (B) The United States rejected playing a secondary role to the European powers and took a more aggressive role in dominating world politics.

   (C) The United States began taking an active part in promoting internationalism through its leadership in the League of Nations.

   (D) The United States formed a defensive alliance with Britain and France to protect against any further abuses by the Germans.

   (E) The United States launched an aggressive campaign to force all the European powers to relinquish their colonial holdings to American control and eventual independence.

58. Which of the following is true of women in the Iroquois society?

   (A) The elder women selected the male chief.

   (B) They sometimes became chiefs.

   (C) They were largely responsible for hunting and fishing activities.

   (D) They served as the religious priests.

   (E) They controlled all aspects of tribal life.

59. The Scopes Trial had the effect of

   (A) eliminating state restrictions on the teaching of evolution in schools

   (B) highlighting the intolerance of religious fundamentalism and its conflict with contemporary science and secularism

   (C) emphasizing the importance of the First Amendment when a person's ideas are not popular among the majority of Americans

   (D) pointing out the necessity of preventing the state from interfering in religious matters

   (E) reestablishing the predominance of fundamentalist religious ideas over secular scientific pronouncements which had dominated American thought throughout the early 1920s

60. In 1948, what city did the U.S., Britain, and France have to keep supplied for over 300 days in a massive airlift due to the Soviets cutting off all land-based supply routes in an effort to drive the Westerners out of the city?

    (A) Helsinki

    (B) Warsaw

    (C) Bonn

    (D) Berlin

    (E) Prague

61. The philosophy behind the New Deal was primarily to

    (A) restore the laissez-faire capitalism which had worked so well in the early 1920s

    (B) eliminate the massive federal deficit which had led to the Great Depression by mandating a balanced federal budget

    (C) establish a socialist system in which government would take over private industry, set all prices, and guarantee employment for workers

    (D) cut down the size of government, which had become a massive drain on the nation's economy, and return more power to the states so they could each deal with their specific economic problems in their own way

    (E) expand the role of federal government in providing jobs, relief for the unemployed, better wages, and regulation of industry to control the abuses of the past which had led to the current depression

62. The Kansas-Nebraska Act of 1854 created a firestorm of opposition because it

    (A) prohibited slavery in Kansas and Nebraska as well as confirming the rights of New Mexico and Arizona settlers to prohibit slavery

    (B) extended the northernmost boundary for slavery, as defined in the Missouri Compromise, from the southern border of Missouri and the western border of the Louisiana territory to the Pacific Ocean

    (C) allowed slavery north of the line agreed upon in the Missouri Compromise, effectively repealing it

    (D) mandated the extension of slavery in all Western territories except California in return for the creation of the Nebraska and Kansas territories

    (E) legally repealed the doctrine of popular sovereignty in the Western territories

63. Fearing the U.S. Supreme Court would find much of his second term New Deal legislation unconstitutional, as it had done for much of the New Deal legislation passed during his first term, Franklin Roosevelt responded by

    (A) withdrawing the proposed legislation

    (B) ignoring the court's rulings

    (C) stripping the court of its power

    (D) threatening to increase the number of justices

    (E) offering bribes to seven of the nine justices

64. The "Panic of 1837" was in large part precipitated by

    (A) unrestricted land speculation in the new territories west of the Mississippi River

    (B) fears of a war with Britain over disputed territory along the border between Canada and Maine

    (C) fears of a war with Mexico over disputed territory in Texas

    (D) tight monetary policies by Jacksonian Democrats culminating in the issuance of the Specie Circular

    (E) uncontrolled inflation following actions by Jacksonian Democrats to take the U.S. dollar off the "gold standard"

65. Which of the following was the *major* reason Truman used to justify his decision to drop the atomic bomb on Hiroshima in August 1945?

    (A) He believed it would shorten the war and eliminate the need for an invasion of Japan.

    (B) He believed it would end up saving Japanese civilian lives, when compared to the casualties expected from an invasion of Japan.

    (C) He wanted to send a strong warning message to the Russians to watch their step in the Pacific after Japan was defeated.

    (D) He believed it would be an appropriate revenge for the Japanese attack on Pearl Harbor.

    (E) Once the bomb was completed, Truman felt he had to use it in order to justify the huge investments in time, resources, scientific expertise, and expense involved in developing it.

66. The Mexican War of 1846 was fought primarily to

    (A) avenge the slaughter of 186 Texans at the Alamo by Santa Anna's Mexican forces

    (B) drive the Spanish from Mexico and establish Mexican freedom once and for all

    (C) stop raids by Mexican "bandits" into U.S. territory in Texas and Arkansas

    (D) acquire California, New Mexico, and disputed territory along Texas' southern and western borders from Mexico

    (E) depose the Mexican dictator Santa Anna and replace his regime with a democratically elected government friendly to the United States

67. The United States declared war on Britain in June of 1812 for all of the following reasons EXCEPT

    (A) British occupation of the Mississippi River delta south of New Orleans

    (B) desires by some Americans to occupy Canada and annex it to the U.S.

    (C) the British navy's impressment of American sailors from American ships at sea

    (D) British seizure of American merchant ships

    (E) British collusion with Indian tribes in the Northwest Territory, aiding Indian efforts to prevent American settlement of this region

68. The Taft-Hartley Labor Act of 1947 had the effect of

    (A) prohibiting strikes by government employees

    (B) granting railroad workers the right to strike and to organize unions

    (C) extending the right to strike and to organize unions, previously allowed to railroad workers only, to all workers

    (D) allowing unions to force management into binding arbitration when contract negotiations broke down

    (E) forbidding unions from closing shops to nonunion employees

69. Turn-of-the-century American artists of the realist school tended to make wich of the following the subject of most of their paintings?

    (A) Urban scenes

    (B) American frontier life

    (C) Rural family life

    (D) Wild natural landscapes

    (E) Pastoral scenes

70. The Coercive Acts were passed in reaction to

    (A) the Seven Years' War

    (B) the Boston Massacre

    (C) the Declaration of Independence

    (D) the formation of the Sons of Liberty

    (E) the Boston Tea Party

71. John Brown's raid on the federal arsenal at Harper's Ferry and his subsequent trial and execution had the effect of

    (A) making a martyr of John Brown and convincing many Southerners that secession from the Union was the only way they could prevent the increasingly abolitionist North from interfering with slavery in the South

    (B) discrediting the abolitionist movement in the eyes of most people and convincing most Southerners that the North would not support forceful efforts to end slavery, despite verbal attacks on slavery by Northern abolitionists

    (C) inciting a series of slave revolts that resulted in the deaths of thousands of Southern slaves, further enraging both Northern abolitionists and Southern slaveholders

    (D) sparking a virtual civil war in the state of Nebraska over the issue of slavery

    (E) exposing a pro-slavery plot to assassinate the leaders of several abolitionist groups and discrediting the prosecution despite Brown being found guilty

72. The veto of the Maysville Road Bill of 1830 was sparked by

    (A) Andrew Jackson's belief that it was unconstitutional for the federal government to provide funds for a road built within the borders of a single state

(B)   Andrew Jackson's belief that it was unconstitutional for the federal government to provide funds for a road built across the borders of two or more states

(C)   Andrew Jackson's resentment that the Maysville Road would be built in Kentucky, a state he had failed to carry in the 1828 election

(D)   Andrew Jackson's realization that the Maysville Road would be built by unpaid black slaves rather than paid workers

(E)   Andrew Jackson's belief that it was unconstitutional for the federal government to provide funds for any type of road building or road improvement project, whether or not it crossed state borders

73.   The battle between the *Monitor* and the *Merrimack* was important because

(A)   it was the first successful effort by the Confederate navy to break the Union naval blockade

(B)   it signified the last major effort by the Confederate navy to break the Union naval blockade

(C)   it broke the Union stranglehold on Hampton Roads, Virginia, and opened the door for General Lee's offensive into Maryland

(D)   it signaled the end of the wooden warship as the ultimate naval vessel and marked the beginning of the age of iron/steel warships

(E)   the *Merrimack*'s failure to break the Union naval blockade cost the Confederacy its last hope of achieving official recognition by France or Britain

74.   Jane Addams was a turn-of-the-century activist most well-known for her work in

(A)   settlement houses

(B)   the temperance movement

(C)   nursing home care for war veterans

(D)   the suffrage movement

(E)   children's literature

75.   The U.N. coalition's main objective in Operation Desert Storm was to

(A)   establish Democracy in Iraq

(B)   expel Iraq from Kuwait

(C)   take over the Iraqi oil supply

(D)   establish an area for new Muslim settlements

(E)   punish Saddam Hussein

76.   Which of the following is a feature of all Indian religions?

(A)   Women can hold no leadership positions in the culture.

(B)   A belief in many gods (polytheism).

(C)   A belief in just one god (monotheism).

(D)   Human sacrifice.

(E)   Worship of the sun and moon.

77.   The rotation system of government espoused by Andrew Jackson refers to

(A)   the practice of government officials periodically switching, or rotating, their job duties with other officials so they could learn a wider variety of administrative skills

(B)   the "spoils system" in which an elected official replaced appointed officeholders with new appointees who were political friends and supporters

(C)   the practice of rotating, or replacing, members of the president's cabinet every two years to provide his administration with new ideas and prevent it from growing "stale"

(D)   the mandatory rotation, or switching, of national power from one political party to the other at least once every eight years

(E)   a fluid, back and forth flow of power between the states and the federal government in which they would act as equal partners in governing the country

78.   In general, state governments in the South during Reconstruction

(A)   were ineffective because they were dominated by freed slaves and others who were incompetent to hold office

(B)   were totally ineffective because of the restrictive rule of the Union military bureaucracy, which kept a tight reign on state governments

(C)   accomplished some notable items, but basically squandered their opportunity to effectively rebuild the South because of the greed and corruption of "scalawags" and Yankee "carpetbaggers"

(D) were much more successful than the pre–Civil War governments that preceded them

(E) accomplished some notable achievements and were comparable in their effectiveness to the pre–Civil War governments that preceded them

79. The internment of Japanese-Americans by the United States during World War II was primarily because

(A) of evidence and suspicions that they were involved in treasonous activity

(B) they were Japanese

(C) of desires by business leaders to grab valuable Japanese-owned properties in California

(D) many of them openly supported Japanese government policies, even after Pearl Harbor, although none of them actually engaged in treasonous behavior

(E) most of them refused to take oaths of loyalty to the United States even though they also publicly denounced Japanese government actions and condemned the Pearl Harbor attack

80. Which of the answer choices best expresses the point of view of the cartoon on the following page?

(A)   Southern Whites and Blacks can never be reconciled.

(B)   Southern Whites would willingly be reconciled with Blacks.

(C)   Blacks have no interest in reconciliation with Southern Whites.

(D)   The president must take a forceful role in reconciling Southern Whites and Blacks.

(E)   Reconciliation of Southern Whites and Blacks is simply a matter of recognizing the new realities.

STOP
This is the end of Section I.
If time still remains, you may check your work only in this section.
Do not begin Section II until instructed to do so.

Section II

Part A – Document-Based Essay

TIME: **Reading Period – 15 Minutes**
Writing Time for all Essays – 115 Minutes

DIRECTIONS: Read over the Document-Based Essay question in Part A and the choices in Parts B and C during the Reading Period, and use the time to organize answers. All students must answer Part A (the Document-Based Essay question) and answer ONE question in both Parts B and C.

PART A – DOCUMENT-BASED ESSAY
(Suggested writing time: 45 minutes)

1.   "The removal of General McClellan represents a loss for the army of the Potomac and a victory for the interfering politicians in Washington."

Evaluate this statement based upon the following documents and your knowledge of the political and military history of the period from 1860 through 1862.

Document A
Source: General McClellan's Account of the Peninsular Campaign of 1862
"The more serious difficulties of my position began with Mr. Stanton's accession to the War Office. It at once became very difficult to approach him, even for the transaction of ordinary and current business.... The impatience of the executive [Lincoln] immediately became extreme, and I can attribute it only to the influence of the new Secretary.... The government soon manifested a great impatience in regard to the opening of the Baltimore and Ohio Railroad and the destruction of the Confederate batteries on the Potomac."

Document B
Source: Letter from Abraham Lincoln to General McClellan in 1862
"Your dispatches complaining that you are not properly sustained, while they do not offend me, pain me very much.... I think it is the precise time to strike a blow. By delay, the enemy will gain steadily on you — that is, he will gain faster by fortifications and reenforcements than you can by reenforcements alone."

"I beg to assure you that I have never written or spoken to you in greater kindness of feeling than now, nor with a fuller purpose to sustain you, so far as in my most anxious judgment I consistently can. But you MUST ACT."

Document C

Source: Telegram from General George McClellan to Secretary of War Stanton following the Union defeat at the Battle of Gaines Mills during the Peninsular Campaign of 1862

"Our men did all that men could do…but they were overwhelmed by vastly superior numbers, even after I brought my last reserves into action. I have lost this battle because my force is too small…. The government must not and cannot hold me responsible for this result…. I have seen too many dead and wounded comrades to feel otherwise than that the government has not sustained this army…. If I save this army now, I tell you plainly that I owe no thanks to you or any other persons in Washington. You have done your best to sacrifice this army."

Document D

Source: Confederate Army Lieutenant-General James Longstreet's account of the Peninsular Campaign

"He [General McClellan] had 100,000 men and insisted to the authorities in Washington that Lee had 200,000. In fact, Lee had only 90,000. General McClellan's plan to take Richmond by siege was wise enough, and it would have been a success if the Confederates had consented to such a programme. In spite of McClellan's excellent plans, General Lee, with a force inferior in numbers, completely routed him, and while suffering less than McClellan, captured over ten thousand of his men. General Lee's plans in the Seven Days' Fight were excellent, but were poorly executed. General McClellan was a very accomplished soldier and a very able engineer, but hardly equal to the position of field-marshal as a military chieftain. He organized the Army of the Potomac cleverly but did not handle it skillfully when in actual battle."

Document E

Source: Union Major-General Jacob Cox in his account of the Battle of Antietam

"McClellan estimated Lee's at nearly double their actual number and… what was taken for proof of Lee's superiority in force on the field was a series of reverses which resulted directly from the piecemeal and disjointed way in which McClellan's morning attacks had been made."

Document F

Source: George McClellan's memoirs in "McClellan's Own Story," in this passage referring to his meeting with Lincoln following the Confederate retreat from Antietam and McClellan's failure to follow them

"The President more than once assured me that he was fully satisfied with my whole course from the beginning; that the only fault he could possibly find was that I was too prone to be sure that everything was ready before acting, but that my actions were all right when I started. I said to him that I thought a few experiments with those who acted before they were ready would probably convince him that in the end I consumed less than they did."

Document G

Source: Letter from George McClellan to his wife, following the Battle of Antietam, regarding Lincoln's visit to see him

"His ostensible purpose is to see the troops and the battlefield; I incline to think that the real purpose of his visit is to push me into a premature advance into Virginia.... The real truth is my army is unfit to advance."

Document H

Source: Former Illinois Secretary of State, Ozias Hatch, personal notes regarding a conversation with Lincoln during Lincoln's visit to the Antietam battlefield a few days after the battle

Lincoln: "Hatch, Hatch, what is all this?"

Hatch: "Why Mr. Lincoln, this is the Army of the Potomac."

Lincoln: "No, Hatch, no. This is General McClellan's bodyguard."

Document I

Source: Letter from President Lincoln to General McClellan, three weeks after the Battle of Antietam, with McClellan still in Maryland, having failed to pursue the Confederate Army

"My Dear Sir, — You remember my speaking to you of what I called your over-cautiousness. Are you not overcautious when you assume that you cannot do what the enemy is constantly doing? Should you not claim to be at least his equal in prowess, and act upon that claim? Change positions with the enemy, and think you not he would break your communication with Richmond within the next twenty-four hours? You dread his going into Pennsylvania; but if he does so in full force, he gives up his communication to you absolutely, and you have nothing to do but follow him and ruin him.... Exclusive of the water-line, you are now nearer Richmond than the enemy is, by the route that you CAN and MUST take.... It is all easy if our troops march as well as the enemy, and it is unmanly to say they cannot do it. This letter is in no sense an order."

PARTS B AND C – STANDARD ESSAY QUESTIONS
(70 Minutes)

DIRECTIONS: Choose ONE question each from Part B and Part C. It is recommended that you spend 5 minutes planning and 30 minutes writing. Support your thesis with germane historical evidence and present your case logically and clearly.

PART B

2.   Discuss the United States as it existed under the Articles of Confederation. What were the strengths and weaknesses of the Confederation government, and how did the Constitution attempt to correct those flaws?

3.   "A house divided against itself cannot stand. I believe this government cannot endure permanently half slave and half free." Examine the significance of this statement by Abraham Lincoln in light of the growing sectionalism in the pre–Civil War United States.

PART C

4.   Describe the relationship between the United States and Europe at the turn of this century in terms of their attitudes toward and involvement with each other. Given this relationship, explain the U.S. entry into World War I.

5.   "The business of government *is* business!" Explain the significance of this statement in terms of United States government policies in the 1920s and the long-term impact of those policies.

AP UNITED STATES HISTORY

PRACTICE TEST 4

ANSWER KEY

1.	(B)	21.	(E)	41.	(E)	61.	(E)
2.	(B)	22.	(B)	42.	(A)	62.	(C)
3.	(E)	23.	(D)	43.	(A)	63.	(D)
4.	(E)	24.	(B)	44.	(C)	64.	(D)
5.	(D)	25.	(A)	45.	(A)	65.	(A)
6.	(D)	26.	(D)	46.	(B)	66.	(D)
7.	(D)	27.	(D)	47.	(E)	67.	(A)
8.	(A)	28.	(D)	48.	(B)	68.	(E)
9.	(D)	29.	(E)	49.	(C)	69.	(A)
10.	(D)	30.	(D)	50.	(C)	70.	(E)
11.	(D)	31.	(A)	51.	(A)	71.	(A)
12.	(C)	32.	(C)	52.	(C)	72.	(A)
13.	(E)	33.	(E)	53.	(D)	73.	(D)
14.	(B)	34.	(E)	54.	(E)	74.	(A)
15.	(E)	35.	(B)	55.	(A)	75.	(B)
16.	(E)	36.	(C)	56.	(B)	76.	(B)
17.	(B)	37.	(C)	57.	(A)	77.	(B)
18.	(E)	38.	(C)	58.	(A)	78.	(E)
19.	(A)	39.	(C)	59.	(B)	79.	(B)
20.	(B)	40.	(A)	60.	(D)	80.	(E)

DETAILED EXPLANATIONS
OF ANSWERS

TEST 4

SECTION I

1.   **(B)**

In 1917, with the war going badly, Germany resumed its campaign of un-restricted submarine warfare against all ships entering British coastal waters. Since many of these ships were American and the United States had previously denounced unrestricted submarine warfare, the Germans anticipated that the policy would bring the United States into the war. Their main hope of victory was in disrupting British shipping so badly that the British could be driven out of the war before the Americans could effectively mobilize.

The Germans were aware that relations between the United States and Mexico were very tense at this time. Someone in the German government decided to take advantage of this in a manner that would hopefully delay meaningful U.S. intervention in the war. German Foreign Secretary Arthur Zimmerman sent a letter to the German ambassador to Mexico outlining a proposal. In return for a military alliance with Germany in which Mexico would attack the United States (if the U.S. entered World War I), the Mexicans would recover all the land they had previously lost to the Americans after the Mexican-American War once the U.S. was defeated.

The ploy backfired when the British intercepted the telegram in which the plan was outlined and released it to the United States. It was the combination of the release of this telegram with the resumption of unrestricted submarine warfare by the Germans that led to the U.S. entry into World War I.

2.   **(B)**

The term "robber baron" was used primarily to describe wealthy industrial-ists of the late nineteenth century. These men made their fortunes on the backs of factory workers and, for the most part, had little sympathy for the needs or problems of those workers. They ran their factories like the absolute monarchs of Europe ran their kingdoms. They saw the factory and its workers as their personal property to do with as they chose, and had little patience for workers' efforts to organize unions or improve working conditions. While immensely wealthy, these leaders often gave precious little back to the workers or the community. They used their economic power to warp the political system and effectively diffuse any major efforts to disrupt their control or restrict their power. These actions led to tremendous resentment by workers toward the "robber barons" and the political system which let them operate unimpeded. Unfortunately for the workers, their efforts to counter the power of these industrialists through unionization met with only limited success.

3.   **(E)**

The establishment of penitentiaries in the 1840s reflected a dramatic shift in public opinion toward criminals. Up until this time, criminals tended to be seen as sinners. Punishments were usually public and corporal. Jails were seen as temporary holding facilities to house criminals until they could be tried and appropriately punished. The belief was that public punishment, or the fear of it, would prevent most people from criminal behavior and would deter criminals from repeating their offenses. There was no thought to rehabilitation beyond punishment. By the 1840s, many people had concluded that crime was a social disease that should be treated with education and rehabilitation. Penitentiaries were viewed as places where criminals could spend time in isolation, reflecting about their crimes and exploring how they could improve themselves for a better future life. While penitentiaries were not a perfect solution, they represented a marked improvement over the public punishments that preceded them and a true shift toward a rehabilitation approach to crime. This shift came at about the same time people were reforming efforts to treat insanity. Again this shift was one that moved people away from an "isolate them and treat them like animals" approach to an approach of providing a caring, quiet environment where they hopefully could be treated and recover. The first sanitariums were intended to rehabilitate the insane, just as the first penal institutions were intended to rehabilitate criminals.

4.   **(E)**

The Trent Affair resulted from the overaggressive pursuit of two Confederate ambassadors to England by an American naval officer. The two Confederates, John Mason and James Slidell, were on their way to Europe aboard a British packet ship to become permanent envoys to England and France. The captain of the Union vessel, the *San Jacinto*, found out that the Confederate envoys were on the British vessel. He intercepted the British ship in international waters, stopping and boarding the vessel and removing the two Confederate envoys, who were returned as prisoners to the United States. The British vehemently protested the seizure as a violation of their maritime rights. They threatened war with the United States, which would have included recognition of the Confederacy, if the two diplomats were not returned. Many in the North were determined to keep the diplomats whether it meant war with Britain or not. Fortunately, Lincoln had a more realistic assessment of the situation. He realized that the Union could not afford a war with England while simultaneously trying to subdue the Confederacy. He also realized that turning the diplomats over to England immediately would cause a firestorm of protest at home. So he stalled for time, posturing to the British to make it sound like the U.S. would never back down. After a few weeks, when tensions had subsided at home and people's attention had shifted to other matters, he quietly arranged the release of the two diplomats to the British. While the incident was a dangerous gaffe by the Union, and was a major short-term embarrassment, in the long-term, Lincoln's handling of the matter earned him much respect in Britain and laid the groundwork for better future relations between the two powers. It did not, however, prevent the Confederacy from purchasing several warships such as the Alabama from the British before the war was over.

5.   **(D)**

In the 1880s and 1890s, the U.S. Supreme Court struck down desegregation laws and upheld the doctrine of segregated "separate but equal" facilities for Blacks and Whites. These laws became known as "Jim Crow" laws. Their impact was to allow racist governments in the South to set up "separate but unequal" facilities in which Blacks were forced to sit in the rear of streetcars and buses, in the back rooms of restaurants, or were excluded completely from white businesses, and had to use separate and usually inferior public restroom facilities. These laws allowed white supremacists to "put Blacks in their place" and effectively kept Blacks from achieving anything near equal status. It wasn't until the 1950s and 1960s that new Supreme Court decisions finally forced the repeal of these laws.

6.   **(D)**

The Smoot-Hawley Tariffs were enacted in 1930, a time when the world economy had already been badly weakened and was still collapsing. These protectionist measures protected a few powerful industries but at high cost. Europeans called the measures an "economic declaration of war" and responded with their own retaliatory tariffs. What few jobs the Smoot-Hawley Tariffs initially saved were far outnumbered by the other jobs lost when European tariffs took effect. Additionally, Europeans now could not sell their goods to Americans, because of the high tariffs, and thus could not earn the money they needed to buy American products. At a time when trading doors needed to be opened wide and international trade needed to be expanded, Smoot-Hawley had the effect of closing those doors and stifling what little was left of international trade between Europe and the United States.

7.   **(D)**

Most Americans were angered about the Iran-Contra affair not because of the illegal funding of the Contra rebels in Nicaragua, but because of the shipment of arms to Iran for Iranian help in releasing American hostages in Lebanon. Despite the fact that the support for the Contra rebels involved direct violations of Congressional restrictions, which was a more serious legal concern than shipping arms to Iran, Congress had changed its rules several times regarding aid to the Contras and many Americans felt they should be supported, regardless of what Congress said.

This is not to say that Americans were not upset by the illegal aid to the Contras. Many Americans opposed any aid to the Contras and to find out it had been done illegally by members of the government outraged many. But the level of rage and the numbers of people outraged did not come close to matching the anger felt over the "arms for hostages" aspects of the affair.

8.   **(A)**

The Carolinas were granted to supporters of the Stuarts as a reward for their loyalty during the Stuarts' exile during the English civil war. With the Stuarts' restoration to the throne, eight courtiers loyal to the Stuarts were granted proprietorship of the land extending from Virginia to Florida.

9.   **(D)**

During the latter half of the nineteenth century, the invention of numerous mechanized tools and devices allowed workers to accomplish their tasks in shorter times. Combined with changing attitudes about work and leisure, these devices led to reductions in the workday for large numbers of American workers. This reduced workday for urban workers gave them more leisure time than any generation of Americans had ever previously acquired. Now the question became what to do with all the free time. Sports became a primary means of spending free time, and this period of American history was marked by the emergence of professional college leagues for football, basketball, and baseball. Cycling, croquet, and swimming became common sporting activities for the middle classes. In addition, popular entertainment activities included vaudeville, which was peaking in popularity at this time, stage plays, circuses, carnivals and amusement parks, and later on, silent movies. All competed to separate the American worker and his family from their entertainment dollar.

10.   **(D)**

William Morgan, an ex-Freemason, planned to write a book detailing problems with and unfavorable activities involving members of the Masonic movement. Before the book could be published, Morgan was kidnapped and never seen nor heard from again. People commonly assumed that the Freemasons had killed him to prevent him from exposing their activities. Since the Masons tended to be secretive, they never publicly refuted the charges, convincing even more people of their guilt in the affair. Since the secrecy of Freemasonry was seen by many as un-American and undemocratic, the Morgan Affair confirmed people's suspicions and led to an anti-Masonic movement that pitted the poor (mostly anti-Masons) against the rich (mostly Masons). It bred distrust of political leaders (mostly Masons) by common citizens who now believed that their political leaders and the wealthy in general were involved in some type of elaborate Freemason plot to subvert the government from within and take over the country. Anti-Masons were very active politically, being the first political group to use political conventions to nominate their candidates. They achieved only limited support as an independent political party and they eventually supported the reform-minded platform of the Whigs, whose views were similar to the views of most anti-Masons.

11.   **(D)**

While smuggling (A) was a problem, most smuggling was designed to obtain goods without paying stiff English tariffs. As such, smuggling was a problem for the English, but in many ways helped the colonial economy in America.

The colonies had no trade surplus (B) at this time. In fact, the situation was just the opposite. By 1760, the English colonies had amassed a trade deficit of over 2 million British pounds (sterling), a huge debt for that time. Although the colonial economy was exporting nearly all the excess agricultural goods it could produce, the colonies had developed a huge appetite for fine quality British manufactured goods. This appetite was leading to such massive imports of English goods to the colonies that the fledgling, mostly agricultural, colonial economy could not keep pace. This imbalance led to a shortage of "hard" cash to pay for the imported goods, creating severe problems keeping the economy solvent. Thus, answer (D) describes the biggest problem with the colonial economy.

12.   **(C)**

The Hartford Convention signaled the death knell for the Federalist party. Originally, the delegates to the convention sought only to revise the Constitution in a way that would reduce what they saw as the disproportionate power wielded by the Republican-dominated Southern states. Some extremists may have called for secession, but no resolution threatening secession was passed. Unfortunately for the Federalists, their proposals reached Washington shortly after news of Jackson's victory at New Orleans. In the wave of nationalistic celebration that followed the New Orleans victory, the Federalists' Hartford proposals seemed the product of a bunch of fanatics and they were accused of treason by many people, and totally discredited by others. The Federalist party as a whole never recovered from the aftershocks of this debacle.

13.   **(E)**

The Midwestern Great Plains saw the largest percentage of population growth during this period. Immigrants from Europe and migrants from the East Coast and eastern Midwest were drawn to rich farmlands of the Great Plains by measures such as the Homestead Act, which granted them 160 acres of land in return for promises to stay and farm the land. Railroad developers gave settlers tracts of land in return for developing the land adjacent to railroad rights of way. Finally, state and territorial governments, hungry for more residents to help develop local economies and help broaden and stabilize the economic structure of the state or territory, set up land grants and programs to encourage settlement. While virtually every area of the country experienced some population growth during this period, it was the Great Plains region with its vast tracts of undeveloped farmlands that experienced the greatest percentage of growth.

14.   **(B)**

The whole "taxation without representation" issue revolved around Parliament's belief that its laws were sovereign (unchallengeable) in all parts of the empire, including the colonies. This sovereignty of parliamentary rule meant that Parliament could pass any taxes or laws in regard to the colonies and the colonies could not legally resist the enactment of these taxes or laws. The colonists, however, believed that without direct representation in Parliament, their rights as English citizens were being violated. In their view, the Parliament had no right to tax them or regulate them unless they were given direct parliamentary representation. Neither side was willing to compromise on the issue and without compromise, no solution to the problems related to this conflict could be developed.

15.   **(E)**

Under Johnson's Reconstruction policies, many Southern states attempted to reenter the Union led by former Confederates, pardoned by Johnson. Once in office, these ex-Confederates helped legislate a new wave of "black codes" that limited the rights of Blacks. They also did little or nothing to ensure that the rights of freed slaves were protected. Johnson was willing to let the old Southern ruling elites take power again as long as they understood that they could not reinstitute slavery, nor could they secede. Since Johnson, himself, did not see Blacks as equals, he was not willing to demand any further guarantees that black rights be protected. Northern congressmen saw the new "black codes" as a new type of economic and political slavery. They felt that the old ruling elites of the South should be punished for their actions and should be forbidden from holding public office.

Efforts by Southern leaders to restrict black rights convinced many congressional leaders that Southern leaders had failed to learn from their military defeat. When Congress implemented its own, tougher reconstruction policy, Johnson fought it by replacing appointed officials who attempted to enforce congressional Reconstruction policy. When Johnson attempted to replace a member of his cabinet, Edward Stanton, in disregard of congressional legislation requiring Senate approval of the removal of any cabinet member by the president, the House of Representatives voted for impeachment. The impeachment trial was close but Johnson survived it by one vote. Despite his close victory in the trial, Johnson enforced congressional Reconstruction policies for the remainder of his term.

16.   **(E)**

Canals were built for the primary purpose of providing economical transportation for bulk goods from Western farms to Northeastern markets and for manufactured goods to travel from Eastern factories to the rapidly developing communities along the Great Lakes and the Ohio River Valley. They opened up these regions to more rapid growth and development by making them accessible to otherwise inaccessible markets and supply sources. The period of canal building was short-lived, however, because most canals were unprofitable, financial woes limited government's ability to keep building them, and the development of inland railroads in the 1840s made many of them too expensive to be economically competitive.

17.   **(B)**

Many legal scholars consider the Fourteenth Amendment to the Constitution the most important amendment. It mandates that the federal government must provide equal protection under the law for every American citizen. This amendment was drawn up by Congress during Andrew Johnson's administration in an attempt to guarantee that civil rights legislation would be enforced. At the time, Johnson was accused, accurately, of not enforcing laws designed to protect the rights of freed blacks and former slaves. By passing this amendment, Congress hoped to guarantee enforcement of these laws. To ensure that the returning Southern states would not block overall ratification of the amendment, Congress mandated that states seeking readmission must ratify the amendment as a precondition for readmission.

18.   **(E)**

The recession of 1937 stemmed primarily from changes in government policy based upon Roosevelt's mistaken belief that the Depression had been overcome. Although employment, wage, and production figures had shown steady improvement since the enactment of New Deal legislation in 1933, none of those statistics had yet reached 1929 levels, an indication that despite improvements the economy had still not reached former levels of prosperity. Roosevelt became convinced that the trends started by the New Deal could now sustain themselves, and began cutbacks in New Deal spending which would allow him to restore a balanced federal budget. At the same time, the Federal Reserve Board tightened the money supply to curb rising inflation. The double-hit was too much for the nation's still-fragile economy and it began a new collapse. Unemployment rose by another 5 percent, to over 19 percent. Businesses and banks again began to feel the pressure and industrial activity diminished across the nation. Alarmed by the drastic downturn, Roosevelt reversed himself and requested that Congress restore spending cuts in New Deal programs and resume running a federal budget deficit to restore health to the national economy.

19.   **(A)**

The Nationalist movement in the United States believed that the Articles of Confederation left the federal government too weak to function effectively. They sought a strong national government to which the states would be subservient. They believed that only through a strong national government could the country grow and advance as a cohesive unit. Without centralized power, they believed that the states would bicker and argue amongst themselves to the point that the United States would dissolve into paralysis and separationism. Alexander Hamilton was a prominent spokesperson for the Nationalist cause. His expertise in monetary matters led him to believe that without workable taxation authority at the national level, the United States would never be able to raise the revenues it needed to develop its economy effectively. The only way to obtain such taxation authority was to completely amend or rewrite the

Articles of Confederation to allow for a stronger federal role and weaker state control in government.

The remaining choices were all prominent men of Hamilton's time. But they all opposed the Nationalist movement and a strong central government. They all feared that such a government would eventually abuse its power and, as such, carry the risk of turning into another monarchy or military dictatorship.

20.   **(B)**

The Anaconda Plan envisioned the Union wrapping itself around the Confederacy like a giant boa constrictor, or anaconda, and slowly squeezing the life out of the Confederacy. The plan emphasized the Union's greatest area of superiority over the Confederacy, its large, well-equipped navy. The plan called for the Union navy to blockade Confederate ports along the Atlantic and Gulf coasts and to seize those ports whenever the opportunity arose. This would deny the Confederates the ability to import desperately needed goods or export cotton for badly needed cash. It would also open the door for potential Union land invasions anywhere along the thousands of miles of Confederate coastline, forcing the Confederates to spread out their forces wastefully. Secondly, the plan called for combined land and naval operations along the Mississippi River. Control of the Mississippi would effectively cut off Texas, Arkansas, and Louisiana from the rest of the Confederacy. It would also open the door for Union advances anywhere along the Mississippi River. Finally, the plan called for continuous pressure against the Confederate armies by Union land forces. The theory was that this combination of naval and land pressure would force the Confederacy to stretch its forces too thin, leaving weak spots in the defenses which Union forces could exploit. The blockade would isolate the South from international aid and cause its economy to collapse on itself. The plan did work; however, the South proved much more resilient than Northern planners had expected. As a result it took four years for the South to finally collapse, rather than the one to two years envisioned by Union planners when the Anaconda Plan was adopted.

21.   **(E)**

The tremendous growth in most late-nineteenth-century American cities was not the result of long-term or even short-term planning. It was not based on British growth models (D) or affected by federal regulations (C) or by the needs of the public (B), especially the poverty stricken members of the public. It was determined almost entirely by the desire of entrepreneurs to turn a profit. Nearly all of the major housing projects, skyscrapers, and transportation systems built in the cities at this time were financed by private businessmen who believed their investments could make them rich. While this led to the development of grandiose and spectacular projects, many of them quite practical, it also led to uncoordinated growth with little thought to the needs of the people living nearby. There was tremendous waste resulting from needless competition because city governments failed to coordinate projects. Basic public needs such as garbage disposal and water and sewage treatment often went unmet because no one saw a way to make a big profit from providing those services. Economically depressed areas of a city, needing the most help, often got the least because profits could be better made in middle- and upper-class neighborhoods. This led to cities that were a hodgepodge of inefficient, uncoordinated, inconsistent, and often inadequate city facilities and services, making most American cities dirty, foul smelling, overcrowded, disease ridden, and ugly monuments to greed over public need.

22.   **(B)**

The XYZ Affair involved three French agents who demanded a $250,000 bribe as a precondition for negotiations between French and American diplomats over French seizure of American vessels in international waters. The seizures occurred in the context of a British-French war and French beliefs that the Americans had sold out to the British. An American negotiating team was sent to France to try to peacefully resolve the situation and keep America neutral. The demands for a bribe effectively ended the mission before it started. When the French demands became public knowledge, American support for France (which had been substantial in some quarters) dissolved into cries for war. While President Adams refused to declare war, an undeclared war was fought at sea between French and American vessels. It also led to passage of the Alien and Sedition Acts, designed to prevent immigration to the U.S. of people with French/Republican sympathies. The XYZ Affair was unrelated to the events described in the remaining choices.

23.   **(D)**

The Cuban Missile Crisis was the ultimate test of John Kennedy's administration. It brought the two superpowers closer to nuclear war than they had ever been before, or have ever been since. Until the Cuban Missile Crisis, Kennedy's attempts to confront Soviet moves had been largely ineffectual. He had been badly humiliated in the Bay of Pigs debacle. This was followed by a failed summit in which Soviet Premier Khrushchev totally dominated the proceedings. Then there was the building of the Berlin Wall, which occurred while Kennedy and his family were vacationing in Massachusetts. By the time Kennedy returned to Washington, the wall was already being installed and the

White House found itself with no options but verbal protestations. Again, the president looked weak and unprepared.

With the discovery of construction of nuclear missile bases in Cuba, Kennedy knew he had to act decisively or face total loss of credibility in dealing with the Soviets. The Soviets and Cubans had been emboldened to attempt constructing these bases precisely because of Kennedy's previous, and ineffectual, efforts to oust Castro from Cuba, and Khrushchev's belief that Kennedy was a weak and inexperienced foe. Kennedy's challenge was to eliminate the bases without sparking a full- scale nuclear war.

The majority of Kennedy's advisors recommended military strikes against Cuba. Kennedy feared this would spark Soviet retaliation against American allies in Europe or against Turkey. Other advisors recommended direct talks with the Soviets. Kennedy feared that such talks would be used by the Soviets to stall for time until the missile bases were completed. Then it would be impossible to remove the missiles. Finally, Kennedy settled on a naval blockade to prevent Cuba from receiving the materials they needed to complete the missile sites. While technically, a naval blockade is an act of war, it is still a nonviolent act that in this case forced the Soviets to make the next move. New evidence indicates that the Soviets came much closer to going to war than was previously thought. They sent their ships right up to the blockade, and they had submarines in position to attack American ships enforcing the blockade. Kennedy held firm. The Soviet ships were turned back, without violence. Faced with the decision of starting a full-scale war or backing down, and faced with a five to one American superiority in nuclear warheads, Khrushchev backed down. Kennedy was hailed as a hero and many historians view this crisis as the high point of Kennedy's presidency. What was not publicized is that while the press was focusing on the success of the naval blockade, behind the scenes Kennedy made promises to stay out of Cuba and to remove American nuclear missiles from Turkey. It was these pledges more than the highly publicized blockade that led to the Russian withdrawal of their missiles from Cuba.

24.   **(B)**

Marbury v. Madison was a landmark case in which Justice John Marshall steered the court through a minefield of potentially disastrous constitutional confrontations to a stronger and more respected position than ever before. The case was used by Marshall to affirm the court's right to judge the constitutionality of congressional legislation by declaring part of the Judiciary Act (previously passed by Congress) to be unconstitutional. In the case the court restricted some of its own rights to issue legal writs, making it difficult for opponents of the decision to launch any broad-based attacks upon the court itself. The case served to elevate the court to equal standing with the other two branches of government.

25.   **(A)**

The textile industry was one of the few nineteenth-century industries to employ females on a large scale. This was because when the first textile mills opened up there was a shortage of labor in their locations. Since there were not enough males to fill the positions, companies recruited young, single females. While most Americans still believed females should ultimately strive for marriage and raise children, widows and young unmarried women were accepted as workers because of their circumstances. Since most textile mills were located in southern New England, most of the workers were recruited from the farms and cities in that region.

Females had traditionally hand-spun most fabrics and clothing in America. So it was natural to recruit them into the new textile mills as workers, since they already understood fabrics and principles of weaving cloth. Factory work was not a socially acceptable choice for married women, so choosing widows and young single women was the best available option. People were still worried about protecting their daughters as they went to work in the mills, so a paternalistic system, called the Lowell System, was set up to guide and protect them. Women lived in company-sponsored boarding houses. They were chaperoned and provided with a good salary and education.

Working at the mills was not seen as a permanent option for women. It was, rather, a temporary stop on the way to their true goal of marriage and family. Eventually, the use of young women cloistered in these company dormitories was phased out as an influx of cheaper labor from repeated waves of immigration provided companies with an adequate supply a cheaply paid male workers.

26.   **(D)**

In this cartoon, Thomas Nast presents a Congress that is ready and willing to be bought.

27.   **(D)**

What got Nixon into trouble was his involvement in covering up White House involvement with the entire Watergate Affair. What began as a second-rate burglary by a group of unknowns became a national scandal when the burglars' connections with the White House became public. Nixon actively involved himself in trying to prevent White House involvement in Watergate from reaching the public and it was this effort that ruined his presidency.

Had Nixon admitted White House involvement from the beginning, firing those involved, and making a public apology for the "excesses" of his underlings, he probably would have completed a successful second term. However, he and his advisors felt that the damage from Watergate could be contained if White House involvement was kept secret. Documents were shredded, records were changed, people were paid off, and Nixon was involved every step of the way. When the press finally began unravelling the mystery, Nixon continued to deny involvement and continued the coverup. When it was revealed that the White House had a taping system which had recorded Nixon's conversations during the period in question, Nixon refused to release the tapes. Eventually, in April 1974, under increasing pressure and surrounded by growing stacks of incriminating evidence, Nixon released edited versions of the tapes. This move sparked even more controversy because the edited portions of the tapes included suspicious gaps where crucial conversations should have been.

Finally, under Supreme Court order, Nixon handed over unedited tapes which, combined with the other evidence, confirmed Nixon's involvement in a massive, illegal coverup of the Watergate Affair. Nixon, facing impeachment, was forced to resign in disgrace. Later, he was pardoned before being brought to trial, by new President Gerald Ford.

28.   **(D)**

One of the biggest drawbacks to cotton production prior to the cotton gin was that the sticky and useless cotton seeds were very difficult to separate from the valuable cotton fibers. The time and effort required made cotton only minimally profitable, even with slave labor. Most cotton farms were small and used only a few slaves. With the introduction of the cotton gin, the seeds could be separated from the fibers quickly and cheaply and the profitability of cotton soared. Combined with dramatically increased demand for cotton in Europe, this led to large cotton farms and plantations with vast numbers of slaves to harvest and process the cotton. Where slavery had been dying out in some areas of the South and only marginally useful in others, now slavery was mandatory to supply the demand for labor to keep the large cotton plantations operating.

29.   **(E)**

James II detested legislative bodies and the English government felt that the New England legislatures were already too powerful and too independent. Perhaps the major reason for the restructuring of the New England colonial governments into a single autocratically controlled Dominion was to limit the power of the colonial legislatures and increase their subservience to Parliament and the throne.

30.   **(D)**

While Wilson's rhetoric was more idealistic than Roosevelt's, their actual policies were quite similar. Both men pushed for expanded federal government regulatory power in controlling the activities of business trusts. Neither man wanted total government control of business, but both wanted to curb business abuses and felt that strong, decisive leadership from Washington was the only way this could be accomplished. Both men felt that business monopolies had concentrated so much power that true competition was nonexistent. They believed that government regulation was the only way to curb this power and restore any hope of free competition. Both Roosevelt's "New Nationalism" policy and Wilson's less sweeping "New Freedom" policy emphasized this need for more effective government regulation of business abuses.

31.   **(A)**

The Atlantic Charter was the end product of a meeting between Winston Churchill and Franklin Roosevelt in August 1941 aboard the American Augusta off the coast of Newfoundland, Canada. The document pledged Britain and the United States to mutual cooperation in working for the defeat of Hitler. This was significant because America was still officially neutral, but Roosevelt's signature of the Atlantic Charter made the United States and Britain de facto allies. Roosevelt was convinced that it was now just a matter of time before the United States would have to fight Hitler's Germany, and he was determined not to let the British fall before the United States could become fully engaged. The Atlantic Charter cemented these beliefs and laid out long-term military and political goals in a combined Anglo-American war effort. The Charter was the foundation of the extremely successful coordination of operations between the two countries for the remainder of the war.

It did not exchange American destroyers for British bases. Nor did it repeal the Neutrality Acts and allow cash-and-carry sales of arms to Britain. The destroyers for bases exchange had taken place in 1940. Cash-and-carry had been supplanted by Lend-Lease five months previously.

32.   **(C)**

While all of the choices were national issues in the 1840s, the limits of U.S. westward expansion was by far the dominant issue. During this period Texas was admitted to the Union and a war with Mexico resulted. California was acquired, as well as present-day Arizona and New Mexico. The border of the Oregon territory was finally established and by the end of the decade, the United States stretched from coast to coast. With the gold strikes in California in 1849, a mad rush to the West Coast ensued and with it a whole new array of problems with the Plains Indians.

33.   **(E)**

John Foster Dulles was secretary of state under President Eisenhower. During Dulles' tenure in office, the United States found itself inferior to the Soviet Union and the People's Republic of China (Communist China) in conventional land forces. The United States enjoyed overwhelming superiority, however, in nuclear weapons and their delivery systems. This imbalance was based in large part on the fact that conventional forces were very costly to build and maintain. Since the Chinese had no nuclear weapons yet, and the Soviets had far fewer nuclear weapons than the United States, they felt they had no choice but to maintain large conventional forces. The United States did not want to shoulder the massive expense of a huge buildup of conventional military forces. Nuclear weapons, by comparison, were much cheaper to build and maintain. Military planners of the day emphasized that nuclear weapons provided "more bang for the buck." Based on this thinking, American defense policy focused on American technological advantages emphasizing long-range airpower and nuclear weapons.

The policy of massive retaliation was enacted in the Eisenhower/Dulles era to take advantage of these American advantages and to keep both the Soviets and Chinese off balance. The policy threatened retaliation for any Soviet or Chinese aggression with all of America's nuclear arsenal. It was hoped that this threat would deter Soviet and Chinese aggression. The policy turned out to be all bluff, for Americans were not willing to risk nuclear war except under the most dire circumstances and it soon became clear that America's nuclear arsenal was, for the most part, unusable.

This policy was replaced in the 1960s when it became clear that the Soviet Union had enough nuclear warheads to destroy the United States in a nuclear exchange. The policy replacing it was known as "Mutually Assured Destruction." This policy emphasized, but did not promise, that American nuclear weapons would be used only to respond to a nuclear first strike by the Soviets. It focused on the need to maintain enough nuclear weapons to survive a Soviet first strike and still deliver enough retaliatory fire to annihilate Soviet Russia.

34.   **(E)**

The colonies at this time were overwhelmingly rural and children were most valuable as laborers to help run the family farms that dominated the communities. Males helped with the fieldwork and females helped with childrearing and household chores. Formal education did not provide children with any additional skills usable on the farm and deprived the farm of the child's labor while he or she was being educated. For most families, this was not a sensible trade-off. As a result, most children were taught basics so they could read the Bible, which was seen as the greatest teacher of the day, and write legibly. Anything beyond that was considered superfluous, and the only people who provided their children with extensive formal educations were those who were rich enough to afford it, as were many wealthy plantation owners in the South, or those who were using it as a status symbol.

There was no publicly funded education at the time, and the idea of publicly funded education was still years away. While education was seen as more essential for males than for females, because there was nothing, career wise, a female could do with a formal education, it was still seen as a luxurious extra even for males.

35.   **(B)**

The Compromise of 1850 resolved virtually none of the major issues regarding slavery west of the Mississippi. Basically it just bought the United States some time to hopefully resolve the slavery issue in the future. For the most part, it evaded the major issue of slavery itself and just postponed the inevitable conflict developing between the pro-slavery South and the increasingly abolitionist North. The Compromise allowed California to enter the Union as a "free state." In return, New Mexico and Arizona were allowed to become U.S. territories and were allowed to decide the slavery question for themselves "within the limits delineated in the Constitution." This is where the "catch" appeared. Northerners argued that the Constitution allowed territories to prohibit slavery if they desired. Southerners argued that it was unconstitutional for territories to try to prohibit slavery. So the Compromise used wording that inevitably led to further conflict. Northerners were convinced that the Compromise gave New Mexico and Arizona the right to prohibit slavery. Southerners were convinced that the compromise could not give slavery prohibition rights to territories. In other words, Southerners believed they had gained two more potential slave states in return for allowing California to enter the Union as a free state.

The Compromise of 1850 also provided for a much stricter fugitive slave act, allowing slaveowners to legally pursue escaped slaves into free states and force them to return. While many antislavery people in Congress were willing to make this concession (in the short term) for getting California into the Union, once Southern slaveowners actually began enforcing the law through the courts, it stirred up even more passionate arguments from the abolitionists and created more intense disputes about the slavery issue.

So, rather than solving any problems, the Compromise of 1850 bought a little time for the United States, but in the long term created even more difficulties. It didn't end either Northern or Southern demands regarding slavery west of the Mississippi. It was a compromise that left neither side satisfied with its results. Finally, it did not effectively allow territories west of the Mississippi the right to decide for themselves despite that intent, because the constitutionality of this type of self-determination was effectively challenged by the Southern states.

36.   **(C)**

Although Theodore Roosevelt developed a reputation as a "trustbuster," he actually was very selective in which trusts he pursued. Roosevelt believed that some business trusts helped the economy, and he did not wish to interfere with them. However, he was a firm believer in fair treatment of workers and was outraged at the abuses of many business trusts. His policy was to selectively pursue strong regulation of only those trusts which had abused their powers or acted unfairly to workers or the nation's interests. He specifically singled out the railroads, the oil companies, and the meatpacking monopolies because they were by far the most flagrant abusers. He never sought to destroy all business trusts or monopolies. His approach was to use a scalpel rather than a meat cleaver to solve the problem.

37.   **(C)**

When peace negotiations began in 1969 in Paris between the United States and the North Vietnamese, it was already clear in the minds of the Vietnamese that America wanted to get out of Vietnam. Thus, their strategy was to stall the talks as long as possible, giving as little as possible, and hoping that further American discouragement would result in the United States withdrawing on North Vietnamese terms.

On the other side, American negotiators were determined to insure that the peace talks did not leave an image of North Vietnamese domination and American impotence. The result was that neither side was willing to compromise on even the most simple issues in the first years of the talks. The most blatant example of this was the dispute about the shape of the table at which all sides would sit to negotiate the peace. The North Vietnamese demanded a round table, the Americans demanded a rectangular table. Neither side would compromise and the peace talks could not seriously begin until a compromise was reached. It took a year of haggling before both sides finally agreed to an oval shaped table. While this issue was certainly not the most important issue discussed at the peace talks, it is symbolic of the attitude both sides brought to the talks and helps explain why it took until 1973 to finally reach an agreement.

38.   **(C)**

The shots fired at Lexington have been labelled "the shots heard round the world." Up until this time, many colonists and English rulers still believed some type of compromise short of violence could be worked out. Many Englishmen believed just a strong "show of force" by the British military would send rebellious colonists scurrying back to their farms. The British rout at Concord proved that however ragtag the colonial forces looked, they were willing to fight and die for their cause and could even beat the British in the right circumstances. While the British at this point considered the debacle at Concord to be a fluke, the violence marked the end of any hope of a nonviolent settlement to the British-American conflict. Britain would now have to attempt to militarily crush the colonies, and the colonists were committed to open rebellion from the motherland.

39.   **(C)**

Lincoln firmly believed that the Southern states did not have the constitutional right to secede from the Union. He only went to war when Southerners attacked Fort Sumter, and then he mobilized Union forces to put down "a state of insurrection" in the Southern states. Throughout the war Lincoln repeatedly emphasized that his purpose in warring with the South was to preserve the Union of which he felt the Southern states were an integral part.

40.   **(A)**

Pearl Harbor was the worst defeat ever suffered by the American Navy. To be caught as unprepared as the commanders at Pearl Harbor were was unbelievable to most Americans. American racism against the Japanese led many people to believe that the Japanese could never have pulled off their stunning raid without "inside help" of some sort. Suspicions immediately turned to Washington where Roosevelt's desire to bring America into World War II were well known. To these people, a conspiracy by Washington to let the Japanese get away with the attack, stirring up American anger and bringing America into the war, answered so many questions about the Japanese success that many felt it had to be the real reason Pearl Harbor had succeeded for the Japanese.

Evidence indicates that there was no plot. While American intelligence analysts knew the Japanese were about to attack somewhere, they did not know where. Since Japanese ships had been spotted sailing south it was natural to assume that they were going to attack Southeast Asia or the Philippines, where British and American naval strength were too weak to effectively deter them. Military leaders sold themselves on this idea to the point that they ignored evidence indicating Pearl Harbor was also a target.

In addition, prejudice against the Japanese played a large role in the base being unprepared. Commanders at the base refused to focus on what the Japanese were capable of doing and instead focused on what seemed to make sense for them to do. To these commanders, a Japanese attack on Pearl Harbor was senseless. The odds against their fleet approaching Hawaii without being detected were slim. The risks involved with attacking the bulk of the American Pacific

Fleet, in its home harbor with the hundreds of defensive aircraft and antiair-craft guns, were so high that to Americans it seemed suicidal for the Japanese to attempt an attack. Americans felt that the Japanese wouldn't dare try it and ignored the fact that they had the capability to pull it off if they got lucky. Based on these assumptions, base commanders prepared only for the immediate threat of sabotage from local Japanese-Americans on Hawaii. They never seriously considered preparation for a full-scale Japanese assault, in spite of repeated war warnings from Washington, until the bombs actually began to fall.

While a message warning Pearl Harbor was sent before the attack, it was sent over commercial telegraph services rather than priority military lines. It did not arrive until after the attack, too late to make a difference. Some histori-ans question if the telegram would have changed the result even if it had arrived on time, so convinced were Pearl's commanders that the Japanese wouldn't dare attack.

Finally, one of the major contributors to the belief in a government conspiracy was the amount of intelligence gathered before the attack which clearly indicated Pearl Harbor was at risk. In hindsight, the failure to effectively use this intelligence was shocking. Unfortunately, the intelligence was gathered in bits and pieces by several different intelligence agencies within the Army and Navy. At the time the two services didn't share their intelligence with each other, due to interservice rivalry and other logistical factors. As a result each intelligence service had only some of the necessary "bits" of information needed to piece the entire picture together. It was only *after* the attack that all the intelligence was put together and the obviousness of Pearl Harbor as a target became clear.

41.   **(E)**

While many people would argue, because of the highly publicized hostage crisis, that Carter's greatest difficulties were with his Middle East policy, the Camp David Accords, which many consider Carter's greatest success, were a cen-tral part of those policies. Carter's Central American policies, while somewhat criticized at home, were considered successful by most Central American experts. The Panama Canal Treaty and other Carter policies focused on human rights, earning him tremendous respect among Central and South American leaders.

Domestically, Carter's greatest successes were in the areas of energy and land conservation. Carter was determined to develop new alternative sources of energy to free the United States from dependence on foreign oil. He was also a naturalist determined to protect the environment. His funding of alternative fu-els research and of the Environmental Protection Agency were positive moves of which most Americans approved.

Carter's biggest failure was in economic policy. While it can be argued that many of the economic calamities which befell Carter were not entirely his fault, as many of the country's economic difficulties can be traced back to Nixon's and Johnson's policies, Carter still failed to effectively deal with them. Carter was determined to cut federal spending and reduce the federal deficit in an effort to control rising inflation. Unfortunately, his policies resulted in increasing unemployment, higher interest rates, and continued inflation. By 1979, the prime lending rate reached a historic high of 20 percent. Home mortgage rates reached 16 percent in many areas, putting many people out of the home buying market and sending the housing industry into a tailspin. Unemployment rose to over 7.5 percent and inflation was approaching 14 percent annually.

Carter's political opponents created a new measuring standard called the "misery index" to rate how poorly the nation's economy was doing. None of Carter's efforts seemed to effect the downwardly spiraling economy. When the Iran hostage crisis hit, Carter's presidency was already in ruins. Carter's failure to free the Iran hostages simply added to the public perception of his ineptitude and was symbolic of the collapse of his leadership. While people remember the hostage crisis, had the nation's economy been relatively healthy, Carter's image would have probably been much different. People might have been more willing to see the hostage crisis as not being his fault. With the economy in shambles, it was easy to add the hostage crisis as one more thing to blame on Carter's incompetence.

42.   **(A)**

The completion of America's rail network was a feat of monumental proportions. It led to dramatic changes in the lives of most Americans. Goods could now be shipped from the most distant corners of the land to virtually anywhere else in the country within just a few days. This allowed farmers access to markets which would otherwise have been denied them. It allowed for more efficient distribution of goods throughout the country. It also made the country smaller in that one could now travel from coast to coast in just six to ten days, whereas the trip could take weeks or months by stagecoach or horse and wagon.

Before the railroads, time was kept by individual communities according to the position of the sun overhead in that community. This led to a confusing mix of varying times as a traveller went from one community to the next. It made it almost impossible for the railroads to draw up workable timetables for running their trains. In response, the railroads drew up plans for a national system of "time zones" in which every community within a specific zone would share the same local time. Eventually, this system was universally adapted and evolved into the four time zones with which we are familiar today.

Finally, railroad construction and development led to some important technical improvements in things like boiler construction, air brakes, automatic coupling devices, steel construction techniques, and bridge building. Choice (A), the industrialization of the Old South, is the only listed effect that was not a direct result of the railroad building in the last half of the nineteenth century. First, most railroad construction linked factories and consumers in the Northeast with Midwest farmers and Far West miners and farmers. Railroad construction lagged in the South by comparison. Secondly, the South continued to remain primarily a rural agricultural region well into the twentieth century. Industrialization would not flourish in the South until the rail industry had passed its peak and was beginning its mid-twentieth century decline.

43.   **(A)**

Thomas Paine wrote several pamphlets before and during the American Revolution. *Common Sense* was the most significant because it carefully documented abuses of the British parliamentary system of government, particularly in its treatment of the American colonies. Paine portrayed a brutish monarchy interested only in itself and pointedly argued how independence would improve the colonies' long-term situation. His argument was directed at the common man, and it struck a chord unlike anything previously written in the colonies. Its publication in 1774 was perfect in reaching the public at just the moment that their questions and concerns regarding British rule were peaking. The answers provided in Paine's essays were pivotal in the subsequent behavior of many colonists who, until that time, had been unsure of what they believed regarding independence and British rule.

Answer (B) is incorrect. Paine wrote another essay called *American Crisis* during the winter of 1776. THIS essay, not *Common Sense*, helped rally American spirits during that long, demoralizing winter.

Answers (C) through (E) are incorrect. Paine wrote to an American, not a British audience. He also wrote *Common Sense* well before American independence was achieved and constitutional issues became relevant.

44.   **(C)**

Open-range ranching was a technique in which a rancher would purchase a relatively small plot of land, usually located near a stream. This land also bordered on public domain land which was open to public use. The ranchers along this land would then let their cattle graze in the vast open ranges of public domain land bordering their property. Since no one else was using the land, this was at first a very cost-effective method of raising cattle. However, as development of the Western states continued, more and more people crowded into the territories and competed to use this open range land. Sheepherders, "sodbusters" or crop farmers, and others all took their share of the land at the expense of the cattle ranchers. This process did not always occur peacefully. Several "range wars" broke out between cattle ranchers and farmers, leading to many injuries and deaths. Farmers started fencing in their lands to deny access to the cattle. Cattle ranchers, in turn, began fencing in large tracts of public domain land to protect land they needed for their herd to graze. Eventually, the pressures of overgrazing and competition eliminated or greatly curtailed the practice of open-range ranching. Ranching became more industrialized and large cattle companies dominated the cattle industry. By the mid-1890s, the age of open-range ranching was over.

The other choices are incorrect. Low beef prices did not affect open-range ranching (A), as it was one of the most cost-effective ways to raise cattle, if the open range was available for grazing. While cattle did occasionally wander off (E), use of branding limited ranchers' losses and the losses rarely reached unacceptable levels. The government never enacted laws giving sheepherders priority use of the land (B). Finally, cattle ranchers never, on a wide scale, adopted sharecropping techniques (D), which would have been inappropriate for most cattle-raising operations.

45.   **(A)**

President William Howard Taft (1909–1913) believed that the best way to improve Latin American stability and promote American interests in the region was to use American dollars, bolster Latin American regimes, and spur investment in those regions. Taft felt that in the long run, this would be more cost-effective than Roosevelt's "Big Stick" approach and would drive European economic influence out of the region. This approach of spending American money to economically dominate the Caribbean became known as "Dollar Diplomacy."

46.   **(B)**

While Thomas Edison (A), founder of the Edison Electric Company, developed the incandescent light bulb and founded the country's first electric power plant, Edison's power transmission system had one major flaw: it used direct current. Direct current could only transmit electric power effectively for short distances. George Westinghouse overcame this problem by applying Nikola Tesla's concept of alternating current which allowed electric power to be effectively transmitted long distances at lower voltages. Edison always believed that eventually there would be a way to send direct current over long distances, but thus far Westinghouse's system is the one that has prevailed.

While J.P. Morgan (C) didn't invent alternating current, he helped spread Westinghouse's power transmission system by helping to organize General Electric Company. John G. Rockefeller (D) was not involved in the development of alternating current; he made his fortune in the oil industry by pioneering new methods of refining oil. Andrew Carnegie (E) made his fortune using new techniques to produce steel.

47.   **(E)**

In the late nineteenth and early twentieth centuries, many Americans such as Carnegie, Morgan, and Rockefeller amassed fortunes unlike anything previously seen in American history. They often gathered their fortunes on the backs of poor and middle-income workers. Many Americans looked at money as "the root of all evil," forcing these rich magnates to defend their accumulated wealth. One way some of these wealthy leaders of industry defended themselves was through the "Gospel of Wealth." This "gospel" stated that the rich got rich because it was "God's will" that they be rich. In other words, they were rich because they had received God's blessing in the form of fabulous wealth. From this frame of reference, God approved of their riches and must have approved of how they obtained it. So, to be this wealthy, they must be good people or God wouldn't have let them accumulate their wealth. Andrew Carnegie, who espoused this theory quite vocally, also added that this meant the rich had a social responsibility to use the wealth wisely to help society. Unfortunately, most others who preached the "Gospel of Wealth" did not feel the social obligations Carnegie felt. So, while giving some of your money to charity, etc., was a social obligation to some, it was not a central part of the "Gospel of Wealth."

48.   **(B)**

The main goal of the Truman Doctrine was the containment of Communist expansion beyond those areas already under Communist control. The Truman Doctrine was the result of requests for American aid to the Turkish and Greek governments, both of which were fighting Communist insurgencies. Truman, instead of just requesting aid for Turkey and Greece, responded with a general policy statement declaring American intent to aid free people everywhere in their efforts to protect themselves from internal Communist uprisings or external pressure from Communist countries. Truman's "doctrine" did not extend to attempting to eliminate Communist governments where they already held power. It just promised to help countries resist Communist expansion to non-Communist countries. It committed the United States to an expensive long-term policy of propping up non-Communist governments even when those governments were more brutal than the Communists attempting to oust them. It placed the United States in the position of leader of the "free world" but guaranteed greater future tensions with the Soviet Union.

The Truman Doctrine also did not seek to enforce the Domino Theory. The Domino Theory did not exist in the 1940s. It came into existence as a rationale for American involvement in Vietnam. According to the Domino Theory, the war in Vietnam was the beginning of a massive Communist effort to expand control into Southeast Asia. If Vietnam fell, according to this theory, then Cambodia, Laos, Burma, and Thailand would all fall shortly afterwards, like a row of dominoes. Current evidence provides little support for this theory.

49.　　(C)

Pulitzer believed that newspapers should be targeted at the masses. In this vein, his newspaper, *New York World*, used a collection of sensationalist stories, muckraking, and a publishing style designed to make the news read like a soap opera, to popularize newspapers among the middle class and the poor. His tactics worked. Using banner headlines, emphasizing the most scandalous or gory aspects of a story, exaggerating stories or making up details designed to arouse the reader, all served to catch people's attention and bring them back for more. Since his paper used a cheap yellow ink in printing a popular comic strip of the time, the term "yellow journalism" came to symbolize this early form of "tabloid" style news reporting. Pulitzer's techniques were so effective in increasing his newspaper's readership that soon newspaper publishers throughout the nation were copying his style and "yellow journals" were springing up in nearly every major U.S. city.

50.　　(C)

In 1885, the federal government had enacted tariffs on more than 4,000 separate manufactured items. While this protected the manufacturers of these items, it also needlessly raised prices paid by consumers. Democrats began a major push at this time to enact "free trade" legislation, charging that most tariffs benefitted rich industrialists while hurting poor and middle-class consumers. They also charged that since nearly all the tariffs protected manufactured goods and few tariffs protected agricultural products, that farmers were being hurt by tariffs. Farmers had to pay the inflated prices for imported manufactured goods (or inflated prices for domestic goods because many American manufacturers raised their prices to levels near the artificially high import prices, making a huge profit) but could not get inflated prices for their unprotected agricultural products. Despite their efforts, high tariffs remained in effect throughout the period. Republican claims that the tariffs were necessary to protect American industries were strongly supported by the business leaders of the country, and Democratic reforms were defeated or so watered down as to be useless.

51.   **(A)**

Jacob Coxey was a businessman from Massillon, Ohio. In 1894, he led an "army" of approximately 500 unemployed workers on a march from Ohio to the steps of the Capitol building in Washington, D.C. There he hoped to protest current government inaction toward poverty and the unemployed and demand the creation of a massive, federally financed jobs program. He also hoped that his "army" would be joined by hundreds of thousands of other unemployed workers resulting in a protest so large that the government could not ignore it. While his "army" reached the Capitol grounds, the thousands of others Coxey hoped would join them failed to materialize. Coxey was arrested before he could speak and his followers were brutally dispersed by the police, resulting in the collapse of his movement and his dream. The phrase "They looked like Coxey's army!" quickly came into widespread use as an indictment of the appearance of people who were poorly dressed or who wore "rags" because they were impoverished.

52.   **(C)**

In the summer of 1964, the war between North and South Vietnam was not going well for the American-backed South. Corrupt government leaders, poorly trained and motivated soldiers, and a lack of support from the people left the South Vietnamese government in precarious straits. While the United States publicly admitted to having advisors in Vietnam, in reality these "advisors" had been actively engaged in combat missions for almost three years. American intelligence estimates indicated that South Vietnam would not survive without increased American involvement in the war. The United States either had to pull out of Vietnam or expand the war. President Johnson reluctantly decided to expand American involvement in the war.

This expansion was dramatically increased following an incident in which an American warship, operating in international waters off the coast of North Vietnam, in the Gulf of Tonkin, was attacked by North Vietnamese patrol boats. A second, but never confirmed, attack was reported soon after. Based on these attacks, President Johnson went to Congress to request authority to take whatever measures necessary to repel attacks against American forces. The Tonkin Gulf Resolution, as it was called, passed unanimously in the House and nearly unanimously in the Senate. Johnson used this resolution as a "carte blanche" to do whatever he felt was necessary to defeat the North Vietnamese. This led to increased bombing of North Vietnam and increased numbers of American soldiers fighting in South Vietnam. By 1968, the number of Americans stationed in South Vietnam approached 550,000. All of this expansion can be traced back to the Gulf of Tonkin Incident and the Tonkin Gulf Resolution that followed. While the war probably would have been expanded anyway, this incident provided the excuse and the congressional backing Johnson needed to expand the war in 1964.

53.   **(D)**

The Navigation Acts were passed in the mid-eighteenth century to coerce the colonies into trading directly with their mother country, England. These acts were not designed to raise money for England. However, the Sugar Act and the Townshend Acts represented a shifting of English policy toward the colonies. These acts were designed to raise money from the colonies by taxing goods imported directly from England. The purpose of taxing the colonies this way was to raise money to cover the costs to Britain for defending and administering the American colonies.

54.   **(E)**

William Seward was a fervent believer in the concept of Manifest Destiny. He was an extremist in this regard who firmly believed that one day the United States would govern all of North and Central America, including the Caribbean, Greenland, and even Iceland. Obtaining Alaska from the Russians not only removed one more European influence from American shores, but it also brought the U.S. one step closer to Seward's expansionist dreams. While Seward's dream has yet to be realized — and probably never will be — it was the driving force behind his support of the Alaska purchase.

55.   **(A)**

The architectural style depicted is known as the Romanesque style, and it was favored by America's most renowned architect of the early nineteenth century, Thomas Jefferson. The building shown is the old state capitol building in Richmond, Virginia, which was designed by Jefferson and still stands. Its soaring front columns and undecorated facades, its narrow but deep floor plan, and its solid, simple, classical lines are typical of the Romanesque style. This style was quite popular during Jefferson's time, largely because Jefferson favored it. It was supplanted by the similar, but more elegant, Greek Revival style which was favored by Benjamin Latrobe (B) and Dr. William Thornton (D). Charles Bullfinch (C) of Boston, another prominent early American architect, was known for his Georgian designs. William Jenney (E) was an American architect who lived in the second half of the nineteenth century and was responsible for using cast iron and steel to design and construct America's first skyscrapers.

56.   **(B)**

When the United States declared war on Germany and entered World War I, a massive mobilization effort was needed to prepare the nation for wartime requirements. Procedures for drafting, training, and transporting soldiers had to be quickly organized. Industrial production had to be regeared for wartime production needs. At first, this mobilization effort was headed by a number of industrial committees that advised the government on selection and cost of equipment. However, it soon became apparent that many of the businessmen running these committees had more than the nation's interests at heart. Many were using the committees as vehicles to quick wartime riches. Press reports of the corruption quickly led to public demands for reform. Wilson responded by disbanding the various committees and replacing them in July 1917 with the War Industries Board (WIB). The WIB coordinated war production for the remainder of the war.

57.   **(A)**

The rejection of the Versailles Treaty by the United States Senate signaled not only anger and frustration at Woodrow Wilson, but a generalized rejection of his whole effort to make America an international leader. Many Americans, examining the provisions of the Versailles Treaty, felt betrayed by the European "Allies" whom we had saved from German domination. Many accurately feared that the harsh, punitive provisions against Germany would inevitably lead to another European war and we would again be called upon to save the Europeans from themselves. Many felt that Wilson had allowed the United States to be "used" by the Europeans for their own purposes and these people were determined never to let it happen again.

The result was not only the rejection of the Versailles Treaty, but a rejection of internationalism and a determination to return America to George Washington's principles of "avoiding European entanglements." American leaders sought a return to isolationism in the belief that the Atlantic Ocean provided a big buffer between the United States and Europe and from now on it was better that the Europeans stay on their side of it and we would stay on ours. The refusal of the United States Senate to allow U.S. entry into the League of Nations, for fear that League membership would allow Europe to draw American forces into future wars, epitomized American feelings at this time.

The election of Warren G. Harding in 1920, with his emphasis on domestic politics and economic prosperity, reflected the desires of most Americans to take care of the "home front" and let Europe take care of itself. During the 1920s, when weak European leadership might have been positively swayed by active American involvement in world affairs, the United States withdrew, letting the Europeans flounder. This would pose tremendous difficulties for Franklin Roosevelt in the late 1930s when he realized that Hitler and Nazi expansionism would have to be dealt with by American military force. Yet he could not convince the powerful forces of isolationism that America needed to prepare for war until it was nearly too late.

58.　　(A)

In the matrilineal system of Iroquois government, women played an important role in the political and social life of the tribe. Clan mothers selected the representatives to speak at tribal meetings. Property passed from mother to daughter, and women had the responsibility of nominating the male chiefs and also removing them if duties were not correctly performed. Women participated in tribal discussions and were consulted in all matters of importance to the community and the Iroquois Confederacy.

59.　　(B)

The Scopes "Monkey Trial" was instigated when in 1925 a Dayton, Tennessee, biology teacher, John Scopes, challenged a state law prohibiting the teaching of evolution. His trial that summer became a national news story as the state brought in former Secretary of State William Jennings Bryan as an expert witness. The defense was led by well-known trial lawyer Clarence Darrow. The case took on a circus atmosphere with vendors and crowds of reporters milling about the courtroom and the surrounding environs.

Bryan's unswerving defense of the literal truth of the Bible was attacked as foolish and ignorant. He was made a laughingstock in the national press. Despite the fact that Scopes admitted breaking the law and was found guilty, defense attorneys claimed victory in that they had pointed out the intolerance of religious fundamentalism and showed it to be out of place in modern society.

Observers of the trial saw it to be a clash between reactionary social elements trying to resist the onslaught of changing values, life-styles, and technology by desperately clinging to antiquated belief systems, and modernists trying to replace traditional thought with newer secular ideas based on individualism and supported by scientific evidence. While the fundamentalists won the verdict, it was a Pyrrhic victory in that the trial painted them in such a bad light that they lost ground in their efforts to sway society from becoming increasingly secular.

60.　　(D)

In post–World War II Europe, Berlin was a headache for both the United States and the Soviet Union. The city was jointly occupied by the French, British, Americans, and the Soviets. It was situated about 100 miles inside the

Soviet zone of occupation in eastern Germany. For the Western Allies, Berlin was a headache because in the event of Soviet aggression the city was virtually indefensible. It was also vulnerable to supply cutoffs because all its supplies had to be transported through Russian-controlled East Germany. At the same time, a Western pullout from the city was politically unacceptable in the super-charged Cold War atmosphere of the time.

Berlin was a headache for the Russians because it sat right in the middle of their occupation zone in eastern Germany. It provided the Americans with an ideal observation post from which to monitor Soviet troop movements. It also sat on one of the main supply routes needed by Soviet forces if they were forced to fight the Western Allies. Soviet leaders called it a "bone in the throat" of Russia.

In June 1948, Stalin decided to drive the Westerners permanently out of Berlin. Rather than force the issue by starting a war, Stalin decided to block-ade the city, cutting off its land supply routes. In this way, if a war started, the undermanned forces of the Western Allies would have to start it. Stalin knew the Allies' conventional military forces were not capable of winning a war at this time against Soviet forces in Germany. He also doubted that Truman would initiate a nuclear war over Berlin. Without resorting to war, there seemed to be no way for the West to maintain its forces in western Ber-lin. Stalin also hoped to pressure the West Germans and the Americans into ceasing their efforts to create a separate sovereign state of West Germany. If nothing else, cutting off Berlin might force a compromise which would pre-vent a new West German state.

While Stalin's blockade was capable of closing the highways and rail-roads into the city, the World War II agreements regarding the occupation of Berlin had given the Allies use of air space on several approaches to Berlin. Stalin could not blockade this air space without himself resorting to war, which he did not want to do. With this loophole in mind, President Truman initiated a massive airlift to keep the city supplied. For 11 months the planes flew back and forth supplying the beleaguered Berliners. While the Berlin-ers did not live well, they survived. When it became apparent that Truman would maintain the airlift no matter how long it took, Stalin decided the cost to the Soviets' international image wasn't worth it and he ordered the blockade lifted.

The blockade backfired on Stalin in an additional manner. Rather than forc-ing a compromise on the issue of a West German state, the blockade unified West Germans more than ever and convinced the Americans even further of the need for a strong, independent West Germany. The Federal Republic of Ger-many was the result. It was founded in May 1949 within two weeks of Stalin lifting the Berlin blockade.

61.   **(E)**

During the 1932 election campaign, Franklin Roosevelt promised the American people a "New Deal." This "New Deal" pledged to replace the detached, inactive, and seemingly insensitive government of Herbert Hoover and the Republicans with an expanded government that would take an activist role in changing the conditions which had led to the Great Depression. Roosevelt promised massive federal public works programs and relief programs, modeled on those he had pioneered as governor of New York State. While Roosevelt was often vague on the specifics of how this "New Deal" would be paid for, people were so desperate for the government to do *something*, not many people were concerned about the payment issue. While Hoover emphasized what the government couldn't do, because of the need to keep the budget balanced, Roosevelt gave lip service to the balanced budget and hammered away at all the things a caring, involved government could do and would do if he was elected. Roosevelt understood that his programs would require running large federal deficits for a long time, as well as expanding the size of the federal government. He also knew that people didn't want or need to hear about the cost of his programs; they needed to have hope that the government was going to do something to help them get back on their feet.

While some people accused Roosevelt of planning to destroy capitalism and replace it with a socialist system in which the government ran the entire economy, he never intended to go that far with his reforms. His plan was to restore confidence in America, put people back to work no matter what it took to get them there, then work to reform the abuses by banks, business, and industry which had caused the depression. He didn't want to replace capitalism with socialism, he just wanted reforms forcing capitalism to "clean up its act" and protect the weaker members of American society.

62.   **(C)**

While the Kansas-Nebraska Act did not mandate slavery in the Western territories, nor did it prohibit slavery in those territories, it gave settlers the right to decide for themselves whether they wanted to prohibit slavery. This extended the notion of "popular sovereignty" into the Kansas and Nebraska territories. Unfortunately, this left open the possibility of both territories allowing slavery. Since both territories were north of Missouri's southern border, and both were comprised of land from the original Louisiana Purchase, this arrangement violated the Missouri Compromise which forbade slavery in this part of the Louisiana territory. Abolitionist forces were enraged and saw the new policy as a "sellout" to the "slave power" and a betrayal of principle. The outrage led to increased debate between North and South and left many Northerners convinced that no compromise on slavery could now be trusted. Extremists argued that the Kansas-Nebraska Act was part of a larger plot to spread slavery across the entire West, and eventually the entire country. This legislation politically split the country more than any other legal act in American history. From this point on there would be no further compromises between North and South regarding slavery.

63.   **(D)**

Roosevelt repeatedly found himself stymied in his efforts to pass progressive "New Deal" legislation by a Supreme Court loaded with aging, conservative, strict constructionist justices who consistently found "New Deal" laws to be unconstitutional. Desperate to avoid this from happening again in his second term of office, Roosevelt proposed expanding the Court by up to six more justices. This would allow him to "outflank" the conservative justices by appointing enough liberals to outvote them and guarantee the constitutionality of the "New Deal" proposals. The Senate, the court, and much of the public responded with outrage at Roosevelt's "tampering with the Court." But two justices, who represented "swing votes," got the message and where they had consistently voted against Roosevelt's proposals before, they now began consistently voting for "New Deal" laws. These two votes were enough to get Roosevelt the majority he needed to protect "New Deal" legislation from Court interference.

In addition, proposed new pensions for retiring court justices resulted in seven justices retiring in the next four years. This allowed Roosevelt to "pack the court" with liberal, loose constructionist justices who would dominate the court for the next four decades.

64.   **(D)**

While the Panic of 1837 had many root causes, several of them international in scope, one of the main sources of blame for the economic collapse were the tight monetary policies of Andrew Jackson and the Democratic party. One of Jackson's chief goals as president had been to destroy the Second Bank of the United States and strengthen state banks. Although he succeeded in destroying the Bank of the United States, it is debatable how much he actually strengthened the state banks. His tight money policies culminated in the issuance of the Specie Circular in 1836 which allowed banks to accept only gold or silver for public land purchases. This quickly ended a land purchasing boom, cut available credit, and created a shortage of specie (gold or silver). When Martin Van Buren took over as president in 1837, he attempted to restore some of the damage done by the destruction of the National Bank, but he still followed a basic tight money policy and refused to effectively expand the economy or the banking system. As a result, the country wallowed in an economic depression that began in 1837 as Van Buren took over, and lasted, with one brief respite in 1838, his entire term. Van Buren's inaction cost him the 1840 presidential election.

65. **(A)**

While each of the choices was a factor in Truman's decision to drop the atomic bomb, the major factor was Truman's belief that it would shorten the war and save lives. Germany had already surrendered, and Americans wanted the war to end. Thus far, the Japanese had been fighting fanatically, usually to the last man, to defend the islands approaching Japan itself. Casualties had been heavy for both sides. It looked as if the only way the Japanese would surrender was through an all-out invasion of the Japanese home islands. Given the ferocity of Japanese defenses of the outlying islands, predictions of casualties ranged up to 2 million Americans dead and 10 million Japanese dead in an all-out invasion. Given that the United States had lost only 300,000 servicemen throughout the entire war thus far, 2 million dead American servicemen was a politically unacceptable cost to Truman if it could possibly be avoided. The atomic bomb gave him a tool to avoid that cost. Predictions also emphasized that the invasion could take from one to four more years to eliminate major centers of Japanese resistance, and the United States could face a protracted struggle against Japanese partisans. A Japanese surrender before a full-scale invasion could prevent this. Again, the atomic bomb gave Truman a tool to avoid an invasion. Therefore, if it worked it would shorten the war and save American lives.

66. **(D)**

When the independent Republic of Texas asked to be admitted to the United States, the government of Mexico threatened war if Texas was admitted. When the U.S. admitted Texas, a confrontation between the U.S. and Mexico rapidly developed over the southwestern border of Texas. President Polk sent American forces to guard the disputed lands claimed by Texas. Mexican forces attacked a small contingent of those forces. America retaliated by declaring war.

67. **(A)**

The War of 1812 was really an outgrowth of the Napoleonic Wars in Europe. The U.S. attempted to remain neutral and trade with both Britain and France. This eventually led to both Britain and France retaliating against American ships, seizing those they accused of trading with their enemy. In addition, the British, desperately short of sailors to man the ships of their huge navy, began stopping American ships at sea to impress sailors (mostly accused of being

British navy deserters) to meet their manpower needs. These actions were insulting to most Americans, all the more so because under Jefferson's rule (1800–1808) the military had been so reduced that the United States could effectively do nothing to stop it. Economic embargoes against Britain and France hurt U.S. exporters as much or more than it hurt France or Britain. Increasing frustration at home led to charges of British backing of Indian tribes whose attacks in the Northwest Territory effectively blocked settlement north and west of the Ohio River. While there was some truth to these charges, they were greatly overblown. Also, many Americans believed that eventually Canada was destined to be a part of the United States. These people saw British actions as a wonderful excuse to declare war and grab Canada from Britain, while the bulk of British forces were occupied with Napoleon.

The only choice listed that did not lead to the American declaration of war is choice (A). The British did not formally occupy any U.S. territory, outside of some outposts they illegally maintained in the Northwest Territory, before the war began. British soldiers didn't land in Louisiana until December 1815, as the war was approaching its conclusion.

68.   **(E)**

The Taft-Hartley Labor Act of 1947 reflected the culmination of increasing public and government disaffection with labor unions. A series of strikes in the steel industries, coal mines, automobile factories, and the railroads had left Truman and many others feeling that unions were acting beyond the legitimate interests of workers and were engaging in actions which could endanger the nation. Truman led the attack with calls for laws giving the government greater authority to control striking unions and punish their members.

In the 1946 election, conservative Republicans gained control of Congress. They were even more anti-union than Truman. Led by Republican Robert Taft, conservatives passed the Taft-Hartley Act over the veto of President Truman, who felt that it went too far in controlling unions. The law prohibited unions from running "closed shops" in which workers had to join the union to keep their jobs. It also gave the president the power to call for a "cooling off" period in strikes which threatened the national security. It forced union leaders to sign affidavits certifying they were not Communists. Finally, it reduced the ability of unions to actively participate in elections by restricting union contributions to election campaigns.

69.   **(A)**

Throughout the nineteenth century, most American artists celebrated the American frontier, pastoral landscapes, or the wild natural landscapes of the as yet unconquered American frontier. Very few works commemorated city life. But as American cities revolutionized in both their size and nature by the end of the nineteenth century, American artists began to take notice. This new "realistic school" of American art dramatically portrayed the hustle-bustle, the dynamism, and often the urban squalor of American cities. The construction of skyscrapers, elevated railways, trolley cars, and the advent of electric lighting gave artists a whole new range of subjects to portray. Often the contrast between the glamorous new technological advances of the city with the pallor of the adjacent city ghettos made for poignant artistic themes and statements. While many criticized this movement as "ash can" art, it had a dramatic impact on the American art world of its time and left us with some remarkable images of turn-of-the-century city life.

70.   **(E)**

The Coercive Acts, or Intolerable Acts, were punitive measures aimed at Massachusetts in particular, and the colonies in general, for resistance to the Tea Act of 1773. This resistance had culminated in the Boston Tea Party. The Coercive Acts closed the port of Boston until the tea dumped into Boston Harbor by Bostonians was paid for. The acts also reorganized the Massachusetts government, allowed officials accused of crimes while enforcing the law to be tried in Canada or England, and required colonists to let their houses be used for troops quarters when local military commanders requested it.

The incorrect choices all list events that were related to the growing split between Britain and America, but did not directly lead to the passage of the Coercive Acts. The Seven Years' War (A) (called the French and Indian War in America) had ended in 1763, ten years before the Coercive Acts, and had no connection with their passage. The Boston Massacre (B) occurred in 1770, and while it signaled the depth of antagonism between Britain and Bostonians, it was followed by three years of calm. As such, it was not a direct cause of the passage of the Coercive Acts, although it was certainly indirectly related. The Declaration of Independence (C) would not be written for another three years. Finally, the formation of the Sons of Liberty took place in 1765. While they were involved in the Tea Party, their formation was not related to the passage of the Coercive Acts.

71.   **(A)**

John Brown's raid climaxed the growing hostility between pro-slavery Southerners and antislavery Northerners. His execution made him a martyr in many people's eyes. Despite the condemnations of Brown's tactics issued by several Northern leaders, such as Abraham Lincoln, most Southerners were convinced that Northerners agreed with Brown's goals and were upset only because he had failed. After John Brown's raid, both sides' views polarized further and many Southerners became convinced that the North would not rest until slavery had been abolished. Therefore, the only way they could preserve their "peculiar institution" was to secede from the Union and establish their own confederacy where slavery could continue unimpeded.

72.   (A)

Andrew Jackson was convinced that the government should follow a strict interpretation of the Constitution. Under this view, the federal government could not constitutionally provide funds for any improvement project that involved only internal improvements for one state. A project must involve improvements across state lines. In other words, the project must benefit two or more states before Jackson believed it was constitutional for the federal government to provide aid. Since the Maysville Road project involved a road connecting two cities in Kentucky, in Jackson's view it was unconstitutional and he vetoed it. Slaves may or may not have been used in the construction of the road. However, their use was not relevant to Jackson's decision. So choice (D) is incorrect. As for choice (C), it is also incorrect. Jackson carried Kentucky in the 1828 election so there was no vendetta against Kentucky in his veto of the road bill.

73.   (D)

The battle between the *Monitor* and the *Merrimack* ushered in a whole new age of warship construction. The ease with which the *Merrimack* had destroyed the Union's wooden warships the day before it met the *Monitor*, proved that the old wooden ships were obsolete in comparison to this new iron monster. While wooden warships would still be a major part of the naval forces of both sides for the remainder of the war, increasingly the new warships were made with metal plating on their sides and many of the old ones were retrofitted with metal plating. The day of the wooden warship was clearly over.

74.   (A)

Jane Addams was a leading Progressivist who was most well-known for her work in settlement houses. Her work was part of the whole social reform movement of this time in which religious activists sought to apply their religious principles by helping the poor. These people believed that Christian principles dictated that those who were well off had a Christian duty to help those less fortunate. This "Social Gospel" movement led many middle- and upper-class adults to build churches and settlement houses in the inner city slums. These settlement houses were places where middle-class social workers could live and hopefully provide the poverty stricken around them with an example of how to improve their lives. From these settlements, workers could make direct contact with the poor and work with them to improve their education, their cultural knowledge, their religious faith, and their ability to get themselves "on their feet" economically. They also provided child-care to allow parents to work and helped people learn job skills. Finally, they provided temporary shelter for some and helped others find better long-term housing arrangements. Our modern social work system essentially evolved from the goals established by these early settlement houses and workers like Jane Addams.

75.   **(B)**

After forcing Iraq out of Kuwait and seeing the multinational force advance into Iraq itself, all within a mere four days into the ground war, George Bush ordered the end of offensive actions in the Gulf, stating that liberating Kuwait was the single objective of the United Nations resolution. Some criticized Bush for this, noting that he could have continued into Baghdad and removed Hussein from power. But Bush remained firm in his conviction that the goals had been accomplished and that they weren't to remove Hussein from power (E) or alter Iraq's government (A) or interfere with Iraq's economic (C) or class structure (D).

76.   **(B)**

While Indian tribal religions differed in a number of ways, all worshipped many gods, a feature of polytheistic religions. Option (A) is incorrect as some tribes, such as those of the Iroquois Confederacy, conferred large responsibility on women, including the choice of male chiefs. Option (C) is incorrect, as all Indian tribes were polytheistic, not monotheistic. Only a few Indian tribes practiced human sacrifice, so Option (D) is incorrect. Option (E) is incorrect for the same reason.

77.   **(B)**

Andrew Jackson was the first president to openly support the spoils system, and he did not try to hide his use of it to staff government jobs with political favorites. He believed that most federal jobs were so easy that virtually anyone with any intelligence at all could perform the job duties, so why not make sure that the jobs were filled with people who owed their allegiance to him? This practice had nothing to do with widening people's job skills (A), states' rights

(E), rotating cabinet members (C), or reversing party control of federal power (D). It dealt exclusively with political appointments to government positions based on political loyalty and returning favors for past political support.

78.   **(E)**

The state governments in the South during Reconstruction actually did a remarkable job, given the conditions under which they labored. The office holders were at least as qualified as those who preceded them. The legions of freed slaves were mostly illiterate, but no more so than the poor white rural farmers who had the right to vote before the Civil War. While greed and corruption certainly existed in Reconstruction governments, there is no evidence that it was much worse than the corruption that existed in Southern state governments before or during the Civil War. Reconstruction governments did a surprisingly effective job beginning the Herculean task of rebuilding the South's infrastructure. Housing, roads, railroads, and industry all needed to be rebuilt almost from scratch. The plantation system was in ruins, as was the entire Southern economy. Any government would have had difficulties operating in this environment. Despite this, Reconstruction governments founded the South's first adequate public education systems and helped establish a whole range of public services such as facilities to care for the poor or the mentally ill. Voting rights were expanded and for the first time, the poor and middle class could elect representatives from their own economic class. While these governments were not demonstrably superior to the governments which preceded them, they were certainly comparable. Many of the problems keeping Reconstruction governments from doing a better job were related to inexperience and, in many cases, corruption. However, more often than not, problems stemmed from active resistance to needed reforms by Southern whites who resented reforms and particularly resented being represented by "Yankees" or Blacks. Unfortunately, many of the notable reforms enacted by these governments were wiped out by conservative white Democrats who regained power after Reconstruction ended.

79.   **(B)**

The primary reason for the internment of Japanese-American citizens by the United States was that they were Japanese. There was tremendous anger at Japan because of the Pearl Harbor attack. The Japanese were also victims of
unabashed racism. American attitudes toward Japan were much different than they same. Thus, hostility at anyone of Japanese descent was much greater than that aimed at German- or Italian-Americans.

Japanese-Americans were never found to be involved in treasonous activities. Most were appalled at the Japanese government's attack on Pearl Harbor and very few openly supported Japanese government policy. Many were insulted that they would be expected to take an oath of loyalty to the United States, but there is no evidence that they would have refused to do so. In fact, many Japanese-Americans joined the American military where, organized into an independent infantry unit, they fought extremely well in Italy against the Germans. While there were many businessmen who took advantage of the Japanese internment to buy up valuable property for almost nothing from the internees, this was not the primary motive for interning them. The major motive was based on prejudice, anger, and to a minor degree, a desire to protect them from attacks by angry, racist Americans who had already attacked some Japanese-Americans several times.

80.   **(E)**

This cartoon portrays a rather passive role for President Grant suggesting that Southerners need only heed his advice to accept the new social reality and all will be well. There is no hint that the federal government might need to bring its weight to bear upon the situation (D). Though the road to reconciliation will be difficult, there is no guarantee that it will not occur or that Blacks do not want to be reconciled with Southern Whites (A), (B), and (C).

SECTION II

Sample Answer to Document-Based Question

1.   Following the defeat of the Army of the Potomac at the first Battle of Bull Run, the Union government searched for a new leader for the army, which was the largest Union army facing the Confederates. The political situation in Washington was thorny. People expected a quick end to the war. Bull Run had eliminated that possibility. Lincoln was under immense pressure to act quickly against the Confederacy. While the North enjoyed numerical and industrial superiority over the South, no one was sure how long support for the war could be maintained. European recognition of the South was possible, and the longer the South survived, the more likely that possibility became. Washington needed a general who could quickly turn the Army of the Potomac into a decisive instrument for destroying the Confederate Army of Northern Virginia and capturing the Confederate capital of Richmond while support for the war was still strong and before any European powers gave full diplomatic recognition to the Confederacy.

   Lincoln and his advisors settled on General George McClellan, a confident young officer who was notable for leading Union forces to victory in some relatively minor engagements in western Virginia, securing that region for the Union. Despite the fact that the engagements were small, they were virtually the only Union victories in the East worth noting at that time. McClellan, whose greatest skills were as an army engineer, boasted "I can do it all."

   He took hold of the Army of the Potomac and rapidly turned it from a bedraggled collection of militiamen into a first rate, well-drilled fighting machine. His skills as a trainer of soldiers are unchallenged, and his men loved him like they would love no other commander during the war. Unfortunately, once he had built this machine, as evidenced by Confederate General Longstreet's opinion of him (Document D), he didn't know what to do with it.

   Part of this may have resulted from McClellan's extreme perfectionism. As he admits himself (Document F), he was hesitant to move until everything was just the way he wanted it. Unfortunately, in war, the enemy rarely does exactly what one wants it to, so McClellan spent a lot of time waiting and training. In fact, before the Peninsular Campaign, McClellan spent more than three months waiting when the army was clearly ready to fight. Despite Lincoln's entreaties (Document B) for McClellan to attack, he didn't feel the situation was right. He also overestimated the size of the Confederate forces arrayed against him. This was something he did consistently, and it paralyzed him (Documents C, D, and E). This made his problems worse because he convinced all his subordinates that Washington was asking him to attack a superior force without enough men and equipment. In most cases, he had a numerical superiority over his Confederate counterpart of 2- or 3- to -1, but he refused to move, convinced that he was outnumbered. This led to Lincoln's often repeated comment, "He has the slows." It also forced Lincoln to order McClellan to attack.

Another aspect of McClellan's problem may have been that he fully felt the weight of the responsibilities upon him. He realized that if the Army of the Potomac was destroyed, it would cost the Union the war. This undoubtedly made him more cautious than he should have been as he was hesitant to make any move which might risk losing the army. Unfortunately, it meant that he also could not take any risk which might win him the war. He was so anxious to outmaneuver his enemy and save his soldiers' lives, that he refused to confront and demolish his enemy head-on even when he had overwhelming superiority. This resulted in his enemy outmaneuvering him and in the long run, cost many more lives than he would have lost if he had attacked.

In the Peninsular Campaign, McClellan had Confederate forces outnumbered and pinned against the outskirts of Richmond. Had he acted decisively he could have ended the war in 1862. Instead, he scattered his forces and let Robert E. Lee outmaneuver him. When Lee attacked McClellan's right flank, he risked everything because it left Richmond defenseless. But Lee, unlike McClellan, understood that taking calculated risks was the only way to win. Lee also understood the cautious McClellan and he knew if he threw McClellan off balance, McClellan would probably retreat. Lee was correct. Instead of attacking a virtually undefended Richmond and forcing Lee to retreat to save the city, McClellan retreated his army from the gates of Richmond. While the Confederates lost more men than McClellan, giving him room to claim victory, they saved their capital and prolonged the war.

At Antietam, McClellan not only had Lee pinned down with his back to the Potomac, but Lee's army was divided. Lee had sent Stonewall Jackson's corps to Harper's Ferry to capture the Union garrison there. McClellan had more than a 2-to-1 advantage against Lee, and McClellan knew Lee's army was split. Had he acted swiftly he could have crushed Lee and then turned to crush Jackson. Again, he waited. When he finally attacked, he attacked piecemeal and Lee's army was able to beat back the uncoordinated assaults (Document E). When McClellan's forces finally began to coordinate their assaults, Jackson's corps arrived and beat back the federal forces.

Then McClellan made matters worse by failing to pursue Lee's battered forces across the Potomac into Virginia. For more than three weeks Lee's men straggled southward while McClellan rested his men in Maryland. Again, Mc-Clellan was convinced his army wasn't capable of offensive action (Document G), and he stalled until Lincoln ordered him to pursue Lee.

The tragedy here was that McClellan did not see how he was failing (Document F). He was convinced that 1) he was right in moving cautiously, 2) Washington officials were not supporting him adequately or were pressuring him to attack prematurely (Documents A, C, F, and G), and 3) he was facing vastly superior forces to his own (Documents C, D, and E). With McClellan's failure to aggressively pursue Lee, Lincoln had seen enough. Documents H and I attest to Lincoln's frustration with McClellan after Antietam. Lincoln finally realized that as brilliant an organizer as McClellan was, he did not have the ability to take the risks necessary to win decisively in battle, and he would never be a match for Robert E. Lee.

Lincoln knew McClellan's removal would cause an uproar, for he was loved by his men and had built a substantial political base of support in Washington. But had Lincoln left McClellan in charge, the Army of the Potomac would never have carried the war to the Confederacy the way they finally did under General Grant. The Union could not have won the war with McClellan in command. McClellan had done his job in organizing the Army of the Potomac, now Lincoln needed to find someone who knew how to lead it into combat. Eventually he would settle on U.S. Grant. Grant wasn't a sophisticated strategist. In fact many called him a butcher. But Grant knew how to fight and he knew what had to be done to defeat Lee. What Grant instinctively understood was miles beyond McClellan's grasp.

Sample Answers to Essay Questions

2.   The Articles of Confederation established a federal government consisting of one branch of government: Congress. There was no federal judiciary, nor was there an executive branch. Under the Articles of Confederation, the power of the individual states reigned supreme. The federal government's only role was to coordinate the activities of the various states, and then only if they agreed with federal desires. The states retained sovereignty, as independent nations, and were granted all legal control over commerce and legislation within their boundaries, except those not "expressly delegated to the United States" government. The Articles granted very few powers expressly to that government.

In addition, ratification of the Articles or amendment of those Articles required unanimous consent of the states. This proved to be quite difficult to achieve. As it was, it took three years to get the Articles themselves adapted, because one state, Maryland, refused to ratify them until some concerns over land acquisition were resolved. This provided a glimpse of the types of difficulties to be experienced under the provisions of the Articles of Confederation.

Most people considered the strength of the Confederation to be its focus on local self-government. By limiting the federal government, people could rule themselves as they felt best at the state and local level. No one need worry about some distant tyrant, ignorant of local needs, dictating over them. There was a real fear of a strong central government deteriorating into a European-style monarchy, and few wanted to renew that experience. While the Articles guaranteed there could be no autocracy in America, this very strength was the weakness which undid the Articles. For under the rule of the Articles, there could be no effective central government at all. States could do virtually whatever they wanted, resulting in no cohesive national policies on anything.

Under the Articles of Confederation, the federal government could not collect taxes to fund the government properly. The Congress had to request the various states to send funding, but it could not demand such payment. Individual states could refuse to appropriate funds if they so desired. This alone made it difficult for the government to operate effectively.

Since individual states could "veto" most federal mandates, the United States government, to its embarrassment, found that it could not even enforce its international treaties! For example, the Treaty of Paris ending the American Revolution called for repayment of prewar debts owed to British merchants and return of lands confiscated from Tories (British loyalists) during the war. Many states opposed these provisions and passed laws to prevent their enforcement. This proved to be a national embarrassment because it revealed the inherent weaknesses in the Confederation government. The Congress had no power to prevent individual states from blocking enforcement of the treaty provisions.

Shays' Rebellion also exemplified the weakness of the Confederation government in that it carried the basic beliefs about local sovereignty to their extreme. It raised the possibility of rebellions of a much greater scale unless a philosophy cementing the states together in a permanent union subservient to a strong federal government was established. In a country as geographically large as the United States, with priorities which varied so greatly from one section of the nation to the other, there was no hope of survival unless the sovereignty of the individual states was sublimated under a centrally controlled federal government.

Under the Constitution, the sovereignty of the federal government replaced the sovereignty of the individual states. While states retained certain rights, state laws were subservient to federal laws. States could no longer refuse to enforce federal treaties and laws. Congress was given the power to raise taxes and states could not refuse to pay them. An executive branch was created with an elected president who controlled foreign policy. A federal judiciary was set up to resolve legal disputes regarding the Constitution and the actions of Congress, the executive branch, and the various states. This "checks and balances" structure prevented any one branch of government from totally dominating the system. While it protected many of the rights of states, it placed enough power in the hands of the federal government to ensure that the government could carry out effective foreign policy, could regulate interstate commerce, and collect taxes.

While many issues regarding states' rights and individuals' rights remained to be worked out, and it would take a civil war to resolve some of those issues, the Constitution and the accompanying Bill of Rights struck a working balance which proved to be much more effective than the balance struck under the Articles of Confederation. Only a majority was required to pass most Congressional legislation. The bicameral legislature protected the rights of both large and small states. The executive branch provided a focus for policy and enforcement of policy previously lacking. The Bill of Rights protected individuals from unreasonable government activity. It is not surprising, in hindsight, that the United States Constitution is today the oldest working constitution in the world.

3. Lincoln's statement reflects his realization that the United States could not continue to carry on its internal feud regarding slavery. Either the slavery issue would be resolved with the entire nation adopting slavery or the entire nation abolishing slavery. Anything less than this would tear the country apart.

Lincoln made this statement reflecting on more than 40 years of efforts to "dance" around the slavery issue and reach some sort of compromise pleasing to both slaveowners and abolitionists. Like the abortion issue today, the issue of slavery was a powerful, passionately emotional issue in which sides tended to polarize, and people tended to take extreme positions leaving little room for compromise. It involved moral issues in which each side believed it had the moral "high ground," and thus, were even more resistant to compromise.

The slavery issue was mostly ignored in the first years of United States history, as it was considered too divisive to negotiate. States were allowed to make their own decisions regarding slavery. As time went on, particularly in the North and in New England, opposition to the principle of enslavement steadily grew. Importation of slaves from abroad was prohibited in 1808. This prohibition was not seriously challenged by Southern slaveholding states, because it did not interfere with slaveowners' rights to continue owning slaves, it just stopped the importation of new slaves. By now there were enough slaves in the country to continue slavery by enslaving the children of the slaves already here.

The first major efforts at compromise date back to the Missouri Compromise of 1820. By now, many Northern Whites saw slavery as immoral and were determined to prevent its spread north of the northern boundaries of the current slave states. When Missouri sought entrance to the Union as a slave state, the issue came to a head. Slavery in Missouri would extend slavery far north of its current borders. Abolitionists refused to accept this. A compromise was worked out where Missouri was accepted into the Union as a slave state in return for the admission of Maine as a "free" state. This helped preserve the balance of political power between slave states and free states. In addition, slavery was prohibited from the remainder of the Louisiana territory north of Missouri's southern border. This compromise did not solve the slavery problem, but it did buy time to hopefully work out a better solution in the future.

America's westward expansion soon raised new questions about slavery and eventually undid the Missouri Compromise. In the North, abolitionism continued to grow. Southerners responded with fear of Northern intentions to completely abolish slavery and enacted rules such as the "Gag Rule" of 1836 which automatically kept abolitionist legal proposals off the congressional agenda. This just inflamed the passions of abolitionists even more, seeing a Southern plot backed by a mythical force they called "the slave power" to force slavery on every state.

The second major Compromise was reached in 1850. California was allowed to enter the Union as a free state, while the Fugitive Slave Law was strengthened and Utah and New Mexico territories were allowed to decide the slavery question on their own under the concept of popular sovereignty. Unfortunately, nobody agreed on the exact limits of popular sovereignty and the addition of new Western lands required a new compromise four years later.

The Kansas-Nebraska Act of 1854 repealed the Missouri Compromise by allowing, under popular sovereignty, the people of Kansas and Nebraska territories to decide for themselves whether or not they would be slave states. Since both territories were north of Missouri's southern border, the Kansas-Nebraska Act re-opened the possibility of slavery north to the Canadian border. Abolitionists believed this was proof of "the slave power" attempting to spread slavery throughout the land despite earlier compromises. Southerners charged that Northerners were interfering with popular sovereignty. The Kansas-Nebraska Act ended any realistic hopes of a peaceful compromise between slave states and free states. Both sides polarized after this, and the major political parties broke down along regional and sectional lines.

The Dred Scott Case of 1857 was the final blow. With the Dred Scott Case, the Supreme Court ruled that black slaves were not citizens and had no legal rights as citizens even if they lived in free states. The court also ruled Congress had no power to prohibit slavery from American territories. In other words, virtually all new territories could be developed as slave territories and could eventually join the Union as slave states. This would tip the political balance of power decisively in favor of slave states. Abolitionists were infuriated. This, for them, was the ultimate proof of the slave power. Lincoln himself said that the next court ruling would prohibit states from barring slavery.

It was against this background that Lincoln made his statement about "a divided house." Lincoln understood that passions had reached too great a level for the nation to remain unified unless the slavery issue was resolved once and for all. He also realized that there was no room for further compromise on slavery. While Lincoln did not believe individual states had the right to secede from the Union, and it was upon this principle that he used the military to force them to return to the Union during the Civil War, he believed the nation had to reach a unified policy to survive. It was Lincoln's belief that slave states were attempting to make that unified policy a pro-slavery policy, and that unless abolitionist forces acted to stop it, slavery would soon be the law of the land.

By the time Lincoln made his speech, both abolitionists and slaveholders were convinced that the opposing side had to be eliminated. Abolitionists would never again compromise with Southerners on the slavery issue. Southerners were convinced that they had to defend their "rights." With neither side willing nor able to compromise, conflict was inevitable. The conflict would begin over states' rights, but the issue driving it continued to be slavery.

4.   At the turn of the century, Americans were focused mainly on domestic issues. While Roosevelt talked of a "big stick" in Central America and we were willing to engage in blatant imperialism in the region, we were largely resistant to involvement in European affairs. The Monroe Doctrine still governed American attitudes toward European involvement in the Americas. While for years that Doctrine had been more bluff than threat, by 1900, the United States was powerful enough to be able to back it up with effective military force.

Washington had warned the United States about "avoiding European entanglements," and for the most part, people still agreed with him. Europe and its labyrinthian politics was still looked at suspiciously by most Americans. While Americans admired much about French fashion or British culture, Americans tended to see European political leaders as corrupt, sneaky, and basically amoral. While we were willing to trade with the Europeans, we did not want any deep level commitments to Europe and were determined to keep the Europeans out of the Americas.

Americans still viewed themselves as the "New Israel" and believed that it was our duty to spread the American version of democracy wherever we could. Europe was not seen as open to the American vision and so it was best left alone. As a result, our main international involvements were tied to the little countries of the Caribbean and Central America where we could easily dominate them and show them the "glories of American democracy."

The Europeans, observing all of this, developed a wide range of reactions. Many Europeans immigrated to the United States because they saw it as the land of opportunity. Even America's critics in Europe admired American drive, creativity, energy, and mechanical ingenuity. However, they looked at American preachings of self-determination and compared it to American actions in Central America and the Philippines and saw us as a nation of hypocrites. Many Europeans saw America as socially primitive, culturally backward, hopelessly idealistic, substantially naive, and overwhelmingly arrogant. Many still pictured America as a land of "cowboys and Indians."

Given these attitudes, it is somewhat surprising that America got embroiled in World War I. The major reason for this involvement was American international trade. When World War I began, President Woodrow Wilson declared American neutrality. In 1916, Wilson ran for reelection on a peace platform symbolized by the slogan "He kept us out of war." But staying out of the European war would not be that simple.

The United States was trading with both the Germans and the British at the outset of the war. Virtually all of this trade was necessarily conducted via merchant shipping. Wilson was pledged to protect the principle of "freedom of the sea." In other words, America believed that since we were not at war, our ships should be allowed to sail into ports of any of the belligerent countries without interference. The British and the Germans did not see things quite this way. Within a few months of the war's outbreak, Britain declared a naval blockade against shipment of possible war material to Germany. Later this blockade was expanded to include any shipments to Germany. American vessels were stopped and cargoes were seized.

The Germans responded with a submarine blockade of British waters. The German policy of unconditional submarine warfare meant that any ship entering the German-declared war zone in the waters around Britain could be sunk without warning. Since the British used warships disguised as merchant ships (sometimes flying American flags) to trap and sink German submarines, the Germans quickly learned to shoot first and ask questions later. Inevitably, tragedies would occur. The sinking of the Lusitania off the coast of Ireland with the resultant deaths of over 100 Americans led to strong American protests and nearly brought the United States into the war.

Wilson protested British actions, but demanded that Germany stop the submarine campaign against civilian vessels. The Germans argued that the submarine was their most effective weapon in forcing Britain out of the war and that in light of British abuses, Wilson was being unfair. Wilson did not want war and the Germans did not want America in the war, so Wilson backed down when the Germans agreed to cease their unconditional warfare. Despite German pledges, civilian vessels continued to be sunk, albeit at a much reduced rate. Based on the continued sinkings, and British propaganda outlining gruesome German atrocities (most of which were fabricated), American outrage grew to the point that most Americans saw the Germans as the evil ones and the French and British as "good guys" in the war.

By 1917, the Germans, desperate to end the war, announced a return to unconditional submarine warfare. Immediately, American vessels were among those attacked. Combined with the release of the Zimmerman papers outlining a German scheme to enlist Mexico in a war against the United States, Americans felt the Germans had gone too far and Wilson asked for a declaration of war against Germany.

Even in this war, America's sense of duty in spreading democracy was a driving motivation. Wilson now called World War I "the war to make the world safe for democracy." His Fourteen Points, announced in January 1918, were an idealistic American vision of what the world should be. While the Germans welcomed the Fourteen Points as the basis for what they hoped would be a fair settlement (when it became obvious that they could not win the war), and the French and British grudgingly gave "lip service" to them, the Fourteen Points confirmed their belief in American naivety and arrogance.

In conclusion, America's involvement in World War I was a sharp departure from traditional American isolationism. It was based on Wilson's desire to protect freedom of the seas and rising moral outrage at German behavior. Even during the war, America maintained many of its traditional attitudes about the superiority of American democracy and ideals. European rejection of those ideals after the war led to a renewed isolationist movement in the United States in the 1920s and 1930s.

5.   Following World War I, the United States experienced a profound shift in national attitudes and priorities. Basking in newfound confidence at our emergence as a world power, while at the same time leery of further European involvements, America turned inward, becoming more isolationist in its foreign policy and focusing on domestic economic concerns. Wilson's internationalism, and unfortunately his Progressivism, were swept away in the 1920 elections which carried Warren Harding and the Republicans into power.

While Wilson had preached traditional moralism, traditional values and America's responsibilities to a new global society, Harding and the Republicans repudiated Wilson's internationalism and called for a return to domestic economic growth. Where Wilson preached Progressive reform and regulation of business, Harding refused to preach and called for government support of business expansion. Where Wilson saw big business as a source of oppression and corruption, Harding saw big business as the source of economic growth and increased wealth for the entire nation.

Harding's election reflected an upwelling of optimism about America and its future. America had emerged from World War I an economic giant. And while the country struggled with a postwar recession in 1920 and 1921, a solid and prolonged recovery began in 1922. Harding's administration was firmly in support of helping business expand. Many Progressivist measures helping labor at the expense of business were repealed. Union membership declined as business began offering pensions and other benefits designed to keep unions out of their shops. Corporate taxes were reduced and import tariffs were increased to help business expansion. Government regulation of businesses was relaxed and regulation agencies often worked hand in hand with business leaders to help in the business expansion.

Business responded with one of the most dramatic expansions in modern history. Between 1922 and 1929 industrial output doubled, productivity increased dramatically, and profits and wages also increased. New products such as electric appliances and automobiles flooded the marketplace and new mass advertising techniques convinced Americans that they needed these products. Higher wages allowed Americans to buy more than they had previously been able to buy and what they couldn't afford to pay for they could buy through one of the dozens of new credit plans being offered to finance the new consumer ethic.

Along with the new consumer ethic came a change in traditional values. While prohibition limited the drinking habits of many for a while, within a few years organized crime was supplying plenty of alcohol to those who wanted it. Sexual permissiveness increased. People had more free time and the entertainment business became a major growth industry. Movies, sports, and eventually, radio all exposed Americans to whole new worlds of excitement and to new ways of dressing, acting and thinking. While traditional morality still held firm in the rural hinterlands, in the rapidly growing cities, consumerism was the new ethic and Harding's administration fit that ethic perfectly.

With Harding's death in 1923, Calvin Coolidge became president. Coolidge was basically a "do-nothing" president who continued Harding's pro-business policies, while eliminating the notorious corruption of Harding's regime. Under Coolidge's control, the economic expansion continued unabated. Taxes were reduced, the budget was balanced, and people spoke glowingly of "Coolidge prosperity."

The long-term impact of Republican pro-business policies in the 1920s was not nearly so glowing as people initially thought they would be. Business monopolies took advantage of their power and gouged consumers with overpriced poor-quality goods. Wages did not keep up with price increases and soon workers could not afford to buy the products necessary to sustain healthy economic growth. As wealth increasingly gravitated to the top of the economic ladder, business sales declined. Protectionist trade measures designed to help business resulted in retaliation from foreign governments that hurt American businesses. As sales declined and inventories piled up, businesses laid off workers or cut wages, making it even more difficult to sustain the economy. Easy credit led to many people overextending themselves and toward the end of the 1920s, bankruptcies and foreclosures began to rise. Poor farm policies led to a collapse of farm prices which stripped farmers of their abilities to buy new equipment. Finally, unregulated speculation on the stock market led to hyperinflated stock prices which attracted many people looking for a quick profit, and guaranteed a major economic disaster when it finally collapsed in 1929.

In many ways, the Great Depression of the 1930s had its roots planted directly in the excesses of Republican policies in the 1920s. So, while the party was enjoyable while it lasted, its excesses left the nation with an economic hangover which nearly destroyed it in the 1930s.

PRACTICE TEST 5
AP United States History

AP United States History

PRACTICE TEST 5

SECTION I

TIME: 55 Minutes
80 Questions

> **DIRECTIONS:** Each of the questions or incomplete statements below is followed by five suggested answers or completions. Select the one that is best in each case.

1. The first humans to inhabit North America came

   (A) by migrating from Asia across the Bering Strait

   (B) on rafts from Polynesia

   (C) in giant canoes from Africa

   (D) in sailing vessels from Scandinavia

   (E) with advanced Iron Age skills and written languages

2. The agreement that ended most trade barriers among the United States, Canada, and Mexico was

   (A) SALT

   (B) START

   (C) NAFTA

   (D) the Gulf of Tonkin Resolution

   (E) SDI

3. The first female justice named to the Supreme Court was

   (A) Ann Richards

   (B) Ruth Bader Ginsberg

    (C)   Madeleine Albright

    (D)   Sandra Day O'Connor

    (E)   Dee Dee Meyers

4.   The doctrine of nullification put forth by John C. Calhoun in *The South Carolina Exposition and Protest*, published anonymously in 1828, held that

    (A)   federal laws could be nullified only by amending the Constitution

    (B)   the Supreme Court had the sole power to nullify state and federal laws through the process of judicial review

    (C)   state and federal laws could be nullified only by the legislative bodies passing them

    (D)   the citizens of a state in a called convention could nullify state laws if these laws contradicted federal policies

    (E)   if a state judged a federal law to violate the Constitution, the state could declare the law null and void within its borders

5.   Which of the following authors is correctly paired with the work that he wrote?

    (A)   Herman Melville: *The Sketch Book*

    (B)   James Fenimore Cooper: *Conspiracy of Pontiac*

    (C)   Nathaniel Hawthorne: *The Scarlet Letter*

    (D)   Washington Irving: "The Raven"

    (E)   Edgar Allan Poe: *The House of the Seven Gables*

6.   The statement that "all men and women are created equal" and that "the history of mankind is a history of repeated injuries and usurpations on the part of man toward woman, having in direct object the establishment of an absolute tyranny over her...." was issued by the

    (A)   organizers of the National Organization of Women (NOW)

    (B)   United Nations Educational, Scientific, and Cultural Organization (UNESCO) in support of women's suffrage

    (C)   Seneca Falls women's rights convention in its "Declaration of Sentiments and Resolution"

    (D)   supporters of the Equal Rights Amendment (ERA)

    (E)   National Women's Suffrage Association and the American Women's Suffrage Association in a joint unity resolution

7. Gabriel Prosser, Denmark Vesey, and Nat Turner were leaders of

    (A) the post-Revolutionary movement to establish separate and independent churches for the nation's free Blacks

    (B) unsuccessful slave revolts in the Southern states

    (C) the efforts to provide educational opportunities for free Blacks during the antebellum period

    (D) the movement to return freed slaves to Africa

    (E) the American Anti-Slavery Society, the American Colonization Society, and the Knights of Liberty, respectively

8. In general, most Europeans considered the American Indians to be

    (A) descendants of one of the lost tribes of Israel

    (B) survivors of the ancient civilization of Atlantis

    (C) heathens who were inferior beings

    (D) equal to the Europeans

    (E) innocent "children" who should not be contaminated by European civilization

9. In the cartoon shown below, Ulysses Grant is presented as

(A)   adequately prepared for a third term

(B)   honest and competent

(C)   caught up in several types of corruption

(D)   weeding out corruption

(E)   a powerful president

10.   The completion of the Erie Canal in 1825 resulted in all of the following EXCEPT

    (A)   increased profitableness of farming in the Old Northwest

    (B)   encouraging the emigration of European immigrants and New England farmers to the Old Northwest

    (C)   forcing many New Englanders either to abandon their farms or to switch to dairy, fruit, and vegetable farming

    (D)   a weakened political alliance between the farmers of the Old Northwest and the planters of the South

    (E)   strengthening the dependency of farmers in the Old Northwest on the Mississippi River system for access to markets

11.   Black Americans during World War I, for the most part,

    (A)   were treated with dignity in Europe

    (B)   suffered little discrimination at home

    (C)   believed integration was becoming a reality in American society

    (D)   refused to participate in the war effort

    (E)   endorsed the policy of nonviolent resistance

12.   Following World War I, Senator Henry Cabot Lodge led the fight against the

    (A)   establishment of the new nations of Europe

    (B)   harsh treatment of Germany

    (C)   United States occupation of Germany

    (D)   discrimination of Blacks and women

    (E)   League of Nations

13. President Warren G. Harding's administration could best be compared to that of

(A) Abraham Lincoln   (D) James Buchanan

(B) James Madison   (E) John Tyler

(C) Ulysses Grant

14. Droughts, high tariffs, bankruptcies, and low prices during the late 1920s had the greatest impact on

(A) urban America

(B) the United States Stock Market

(C) rural America

(D) maritime ventures

(E) Northern manufacturers

15. Louis Sullivan's pupil who opposed the construction of skyscrapers and favored a form of architecture in harmony with natural surroundings was

(A) George Gray Barnard   (D) Lorado Taft

(B) Virgil Thomson   (E) Frank Lloyd Wright

(C) Victor Herbert

16. Pocahontas

I.   was taken captive by an English trader and held as a hostage at Jamestown

II. was converted to Christianity at her own request

III. married John Rolfe

IV. died in England

(A) I only   (D) II and IV only

(B) II only   (E) I, II, III, and IV

(C) I and III only

17. The trial of John Peter Zenger in 1735 for seditious libel

(A) established the government's right to censor the press

(B) encouraged editors to be more critical of public officials

(C)   resulted in a "hung jury" and a dismissal of the charges.

(D)   determined that government censorship of the press was unconstitutional.

(E)   found Zenger guilty

18.   William M. Tweed of New York City

(A)   headed a "ring" of politicians that cheated New York City of $100 million through fraudulent city contracts and extortion

(B)   was an outspoken supporter of fiscal integrity in municipal government

(C)   pioneered the regulation of tenement house construction and sanitation

(D)   urged the New York state legislature to adopt the governmental reforms advocated by the Progressives

(E)   served as Secretary of Interior in President Ulysses Grant's administrations

19.   Thomas Paine's pamphlet *Common Sense* introduced a new element into the debate with Britain by

(A)   calling for complete independence of the colonies and attacking not only King George III but also the idea of monarchy

(B)   emphasizing that both internal and external taxes could be levied on the colonies by the Parliament in London

(C)   rejecting John Locke's contract theory of government

(D)   arguing that taxation for the purpose of paying the government debt contracted during the French and Indian War was acceptable

(E)   suggesting that the colonies reconcile their difference with the government in London

20.   New York was an English colony because the

(A)   English conquered the area from the Dutch

(B)   English settlers in the area gradually overwhelmed the French and Swedes

(C)   England laid claim to the area by right of colonization

(D) Dutch and Swedes of the area petitioned the English to annex the colony

(E) Treaty of Tordesillas gave the area to the English

21. The Scotch-Irish immigrants to the English colonies in North America

I. felt little loyalty to either the English government or the Anglican church

II. came in large numbers in the century due to deteriorating conditions in the Irish woolens industry

III. generally settled on the frontier where they demonstrated a remarkable degree of resourcefulness, rugged individuality, and self-reliance

IV. were predominantly Roman Catholics

(A) I only

(B) II only

(C) I, II, and III only

(D) II, III, and IV only

(E) I, II, III, and IV

22. Most of the slaves who came to the 13 mainland colonies in British North America

(A) were from the southern part of Africa in what is today South Africa

(B) were granted their freedom after a specified period of service

(C) never made up more than 5 percent of the population of any colony

(D) were considered to be property and as such could be used as collateral for loans

(E) were protected from physical harm by the Roman Catholic Church's *Canon Law*

23. The Battle of Saratoga resulted in

(A) Spain entering into a military alliance with the British in order to protect the Spanish colonies in the Americas

(B) the French formally recognizing American independence and making an open treaty of alliance with the Americans

(C) convincing the Indians to join the Americans in their struggle against the British

    (D)   isolating New England from the other colonies

    (E)   the Americans accepting British offers of reconciliation

24.   The new state constitutions adopted during the American Revolution

    (A)   eliminated all property qualifications for voting

    (B)   generally did not contain a bill of rights

    (C)   abolished the office of governor

    (D)   provided for unicameral legislatures

    (E)   generally protected the people's civil liberties with a bill of rights

25.   The Connecticut Compromise advocated by Roger Sherman proposed settling the issue of representation in Congress by

    (A)   giving each state two senators with the vote in the Senate to be by individuals and not states

    (B)   having the members of both houses of Congress chosen by the state legislatures

    (C)   providing for the popular election of both houses of Congress

    (D)   apportioning representation in the House of Representatives according to population

    (E)   both (A) and (D)

26.   In *An Economic Interpretation of the Constitution*, which of the following argued that the men who wrote the Constitution primarily held their wealth in property, government securities, and other kinds of paper wealth?

    (A)   Charles A. Beard   (D)   Arthur Schlesinger Jr.

    (B)   Forrest McDonald   (E)   Bruce Catton

    (C)   Will Durant in collaboration with Ariel Durant

27.   While Chief Justice John Marshall presided over the Supreme Court, its decisions

    (A)   were generally protective of states' rights

    (B)   showed no clear leaning toward either a "broad" or "strict" interpretation of the Constitution

(C)   laid the groundwork for a "broad" interpretation of the Constitution

(D)   reflected the impact of Thomas Jefferson's Kentucky Resolutions

(E)   were hostile to the development of business

28.   The Treaty of Ghent ending the War of 1812

(A)   created an Indian buffer state between the United States and Canada

(B)   provided for a restoration of the *status quo ante bellum*

(C)   settled the issue of the impressment of American seamen

(D)   indemnified American shipowners for any ships seized by the British during the war

(E)   required the British to denounce the right of search and seizure

29.   George Washington responded to the Whiskey Rebellion in the western counties of Pennsylvania by

(A)   ignoring it until it died out

(B)   dispatching Alexander Hamilton, Secretary of the Treasury, to negotiate a reduced tax with the protesters

(C)   calling a special session of Congress to deal with the problem

(D)   sending an army larger than any he had ever commanded in the Revolution to put down the revolt

(E)   requesting an advisory opinion from the Supreme Court on the constitutionality of the excise tax

30.   These words are attributed to which of the following?

"The great rule of conduct for us, in regard to foreign nations is…to have with them as little political connection as possible…It is our true policy to steer clear of permanent alliances with any portion of the foreign world.…"

(A)   James Monroe, annual message to Congress (December 1823)

(B)   George Washington, "Farewell Address" (September 1796)

(C)   Thomas Jefferson, first inaugural address (March 1801)

(D)   George Washington, "Proclamation of Neutrality" (April 1793)

(E)   Theodore Roosevelt, annual message to Congress (December 1904)

31. The purchase of the Louisiana territory

    I.   doubled the size of the United States

    II.   guaranteed Western farmers access to the Mississippi River as an avenue of trade

    III. presented Jefferson with a constitutional dilemma since he was a "strict" constructionist

    IV. gave the United States control of the port of New Orleans

(A)   I and II only   (D)   I, II, and IV only

(B)   I and III only   (E)   I, II, III, and IV

(C)   I, II, and III only

32. The Webster-Ashburton Treaty of 1842

(A)   forced the United States to give up the Mesabi iron range

(B)   was concerned in part with joint Anglo-American efforts to suppress the African slave trade

(C)   settled the dispute over the Oregon boundary

(D)   was not ratified by the Senate

(E)   led to Daniel Webster's resignation as secretary of state

33. The Kansas-Nebraska Act (1854)

(A)   repeated the basic ideas of the Missouri Compromise

(B)   ended the controversy over slavery in Kansas

(C)   did not allow the use of popular sovereignty in either Kansas or Nebraska

(D)   reopened the intense sectional controversy over the question of slavery in the territories

(E)   was supported by Abraham Lincoln

34. The most valuable export from the United States in 1860 was

(A)   wheat   (D)   iron ore

(B)   corn   (E)   cotton

(C)   hemp

35. The ultimate goal of Andrew Jackson's policy toward the Indians during his presidency was

(A) to advocate their complete assimilation into white society

(B) to extend citizenship and the franchise to adult Indian male property owners

(C) to remove them to lands in the trans-Mississippi West

(D) to preserve their culture as a vital part of American civilization

(E) to encourage the peaceful coexistence of Indians and whites in an atmosphere of trust

36. The shaded area of the map below shows the land claims of which of the following in the wake of the Treaty of Paris in 1763?

(A) The French   (D) The British

(B) The Spanish   (E) Native Americans

(C) The Portuguese

37. Andrew Jackson defended his policy of "rotation in office" which became known as the "spoils system" by asserting that

    I.   a man should serve a term in office then return to the status of private citizen

    II. men who held office too long became corrupted by a sense of power

    III. the duties of government were too complex for the average citizen

    IV. political appointments by newly elected officials promoted democracy

    (A) I and II only   (D) I, II, and IV only

    (B) II and III only   (E) I, II, III, and IV

    (C) III and IV only

38. During World War II, labor unrest was kept to a minimum with the exception of John L. Lewis's

    (A) United Mine Workers   (D) American Federation of Labor

    (B) United Auto Workers   (E) Teamsters

    (C) United Farm Workers

39. The "War on Poverty" was an attempt by

    (A) President Richard Nixon to aid Latin American nations

    (B) President Lyndon Johnson to end hunger and economic despair in America

    (C) President John F. Kennedy to organize the Peace Corps

    (D) George Marshall to feed the people of Europe after World War II

    (E) President Dwight Eisenhower to reduce the number of people on public assistance

40. William Lloyd Garrison persuaded the American Anti-Slavery Society to endorse the concept of

    (A) compensated emancipation

    (B) gradual emancipation

    (C) immediate emancipation

(D)   colonization

(E)   violent revolution

41. All of the following characterize the Church of Jesus Christ of Latter-day Saints (Mormons) EXCEPT:

(A)   Was founded by Joseph Smith Jr. in the "Burned-Over District" of upstate New York

(B)   Believed that the Indians were descendants of the lost tribes of Israel

(C)   Established a close-knit communitarian social pattern

(D)   Stressed the work ethic

(E)   Held the Anasazi in especially high esteem

42. In the presidential election of 1860,

I.   the Democratic party factionalized and nominated two candidates

II.   the election evolved into a contest between Abraham Lincoln and Stephen A. Douglas in the North and John C. Breckinridge and John Bell in the South

III. Abraham Lincoln won less than 50 percent of the popular vote

IV.   no candidate received a majority of the popular vote

(A) I and II only   (D)   II, III, and IV only

(B) II and III only   (E)   I, II, III, and IV

(C) III and IV only

43. The presidential election in 1876 between Samuel J. Tilden and Rutherford B. Hayes

I.   resulted in contested electoral votes being submitted from three Southern states

II.   forced Congress to appoint an Electoral Commission to decide the issue of the contested electoral votes

III. was decided by the House of Representatives when neither the Democratic nor Republican candidate received a majority of the electoral vote

IV.   spurred violent protests that led to a declaration of martial law

(A) I only

(B) I and III only

(C) II and III only

(D) I and II only

(E) IV only

44. When the Civil War started, Abraham Lincoln's primary objective was

(A) to abolish slavery

(B) to promote the growth of industry in the North

(C) to preserve the Union

(D) to expand presidential powers

(E) to punish the South

45. As established in 1945, the Security Council of the United Nations was to

(A) make recommendations for the peaceful settlement of disputes

(B) decide legal questions referred to it by disputing nations

(C) look after the welfare of people in colonial areas

(D) make recommendations regarding world economic, social, cultural, and health problems

(E) be the police authority, responsible for preventing war

46. The radical abolitionists who appeared in the early 1830s viewed slavery as

(A) a great moral evil

(B) an economic problem

(C) a problem with no solution

(D) a dying institution

(E) a problem whose solution should be left to the slave states

47. Both President Andrew Johnson's plan for Reconstruction and that of Congress required the former Confederate states to

(A) enfranchise the freed slaves

(B) extend civil and political equality to the freed slaves

(C) ratify the Thirteenth, Fourteenth, and Fifteenth amendments

(D) draft new state constitutions

(E) compensate the slaveowners for the loss of their slaves

48. The Progressives attacked a number of social, political, and economic evils in the American system EXCEPT

(A) child labor

(B) the rights of African-Americans

(C) low wages for women

(D) unequal wealth

(E) gigantic corporations

49. The Teller Amendment of 1898 guaranteed the sovereignty of

(A) Puerto Rico   (D) Panama

(B) the Philippines   (E) Cuba

(C) the Virgin Islands

50. Most of the decimation of the Indian population in the Americas during the sixteenth century resulted from

(A) tribal warfare

(B) famine

(C) European diseases

(D) enslavement by the Europeans

(E) wars with the Europeans

51. All of the following were responsible for the development of Western European expansion in the fifteenth century EXCEPT

(A) the desire to break the monopoly of the Italian states on trade with Asia

(B) advances in navigational knowledge and ship design

(C) the emergence of nation-states

(D) an ideology that claimed superiority for the Europeans and inferiority for other peoples

(E) Thomas Malthus' theory that the population of Western Europe would eventually outstrip its food supply.

52. Woodrow Wilson's career included all of the following except

    (A) serving as governor of New Jersey

    (B) teaching political science

    (C) serving as governor of Virginia

    (D) serving as president of Princeton University

    (E) writing the Fourteen Points

53. The scandal in 1919 that affected the integrity of major league baseball was

    (A) "The Red Sox Scam"

    (B) "The Yankee Giveaway"

    (C) "The Philadelphia Folly"

    (D) "The Red Stockings Cash Deal"

    (E) "The Black Sox Scandal"

54. Marcus Garvey, leader of the Universal Negro Improvement Association, argued for

    (A) equal rights

    (B) a return to Africa

    (C) racial desegregation

    (D) violence in the cities

    (E) more representation in Congress for Washington, D.C.

55. "The business of our nation is business" were the words of

    (A) Calvin Coolidge   (D) Franklin Roosevelt

    (B) Herbert Hoover   (E) Charles Evans Hughes

    (C) Warren G. Harding

56. When the United States Supreme Court failed to rule favorably on New Deal legislation, President Franklin Roosevelt

    (A) introduced a judiciary reorganization bill that would increase the number of Supreme Court justices

    (B) attempted to circumvent the Court by having cases involving New Deal legislation appealed to state supreme courts

    (C) called for the election of federal judges

(D)   used his emergency powers and appointed three new justices to the Supreme Court

(E)   threatened to have Congress reduce the justices' salaries

57.   The first woman to serve in a Cabinet-level position was

(A)   Frances Perkins

(B)   Barbara Jordan

(C)   Shirley Chisholm

(D)   Lucy C. Stanton

(E)   Susan B. Anthony

58.   The Roosevelt Corollary to the Monroe Doctrine, enunciated by President Theodore Roosevelt in his annual message to Congress in May 1904, did all of the following EXCEPT

(A)   asserted that the United States would take action to guarantee that Latin American nations paid their debts

(B)   stated that the United States could intervene in the affairs of Western Hemisphere nations to forestall the intervention of other powers

(C)   was preceded by Roosevelt's assertion that the Monroe Doctrine prohibited Europeans from using force in the Americas

(D)   led to protracted intervention in Santo Domingo and, subsequently, to intervention in Haiti, Nicaragua, and Cuba

(E)   proposed a massive foreign aid program to stabilize the governments of Latin America

59.   The first permanent English colony in North America was

(A)   on Roanoke Island in North Carolina, developed by Sir Walter Raleigh

(B)   the Massachusetts Bay colony, developed by the Puritans

(C)   the Jamestown colony, developed by the Virginia Company

(D)   the Avalon colony in Newfoundland, developed by Lord Baltimore

(E)   the Plymouth colony on Cape Cod Bay, developed by the settlers from the *Mayflower*

60.   The Maryland Toleration Act of 1649 provided for

(A)   the tolerance of most Christian churches

(B)   freedom of conscience for those not accepting the Trinity

(C)   an end to tax support for any church

(D)   a complete separation of church and state

(E)   the extension of the vote to Jews and non-Christians

61. The colony founded as a haven for Quakers was

(A) New Jersey   (D) Pennsylvania

(B) Maryland   (E) Virginia

(C) Rhode Island

62. The French and Indian War resulted in all of the following EXCEPT:

(A) New lands in the trans-Mississippi West were opened to the colonists

(B) Colonists began thinking of themselves as Americans rather than English or British

(C) Spain gained control of Louisiana

(D) The treaty ending the war eliminated the French from the American colonial frontier

(E) The myth of British invincibility was shattered

63. The important staple for export in colonial Virginia was

(A) tobacco   (D) indigo

(B) cotton   (E) sugar cane

(C) hemp

64. The colony established by James Oglethorpe as a refuge for honest people imprisoned for debt was

(A) South Carolina   (D) North Carolina

(B) Georgia   (E) Delaware

(C) Pennsylvania

65. The fundamental goal of mercantilism in the seventeenth and eighteenth centuries was

(A) to eliminate the obstacles to free trade among the countries of Europe

(B) to have "mother" countries serve as a source of raw materials and the colonies as a source of manufactured goods

(C) to limit foreign imports and to encourage a favorable balance of trade

(D) to encourage wealthy nations to provide economic assistance to the developing areas of the world

(E) to discourage the growth of economic nationalism

66. To most Americans in the 1840s and 1850s, the idea of Manifest Destiny meant all of the following EXCEPT

    (A) the Americans would irresistibly spread their democratic institutions over North America and possibly South America

    (B) God had "manifestly" destined the American people for a hemi-spheric career

    (C) American civilization and "Anglo-American stock" were supe-rior to the non-white and Hispanic peoples and cultures of North America

    (D) justification for the annexation of Texas

    (E) the extension of civil and political equality to Indians and free Blacks

67. The doctrine advocated by Lewis Cass and Stephen A. Douglas that the people of a territory, under the principles of the Constitution, should themselves determine the status of slavery in the territory was known as

    (A) universal manhood suffrage

    (B) nullification

    (C) abolitionism

    (D) territoriality

    (E) popular sovereignty

68. The principle of actual representation put forth by the American colonists in their resistance to the Stamp Act meant that

    (A) all laws passed by the colonial legislatures without the consent of Parliament were unconstitutional

    (B) representatives must be residents of the geographic districts they represented

    (C) any revenue raised by the stamp tax must be spent for the defense of the colonies

    (D) sovereignty was indivisible and ultimately rested with Parliament

    (E) each member of Parliament represented the interests of the whole empire

69. On March 5, 1782, the House of Commons authorized King George III to make peace with the American colonies as a result of General Charles Cornwallis' defeat at

    (A) Saratoga   (D) King's Mountain

    (B) Guilford Courthouse   (E) Charleston

    (C) Yorktown

70. The Northwest Ordinance

    I. provided for the admission of new states to the Union on an equal footing with the original 13

    II. prohibited slavery in the Western territory above the Ohio River

    III. stipulated that the land and property of the Indians "shall never be taken from them without their permission"

    (A) I only   (D) I and III only

    (B) II only   (E) I, II, and III

    (C) I and II only

71. The Constitutional Convention of 1787

    I. was dominated by Thomas Jefferson, Patrick Henry, John Adams, and George Washington

    II. published daily summaries of its debates in the Philadelphia newspapers

    III. was called by the Confederation Congress for the sole purpose of revising/amending the Articles of Confederation

    IV. outlawed the foreign slave trade

    (A) I only   (D) I, II, and IV only

    (B) II only   (E) I, II, III, and IV

    (C) III only

72. All of the following statements apply to the Bill of Rights EXCEPT:

    (A) Comprises the first ten amendments to the Constitution

    (B) Limited the powers of the federal government to those specifically named in the Constitution

    (C) Gave citizens freedom of religion, assembly, speech and press, and the right of petition

(D) Guaranteed the rights of persons accused of a crime

(E) Granted

73. *The Federalist Papers*

(A) were written anonymously by Alexander Hamilton, John Jay, and James Madison

(B) argued that under the Constitution the states would relinquish too much sovereignty

(C) opposed ratification of the Constitution without the addition of a bill of rights

(D) convinced Patrick Henry to support the Constitution

(E) stressed that the Constitutional Convention was instructed to revise the Articles of Confederation, not to write a new constitution

74. The point of view expressed in the anti-Whig editorial shown below would have pleased which of the following?

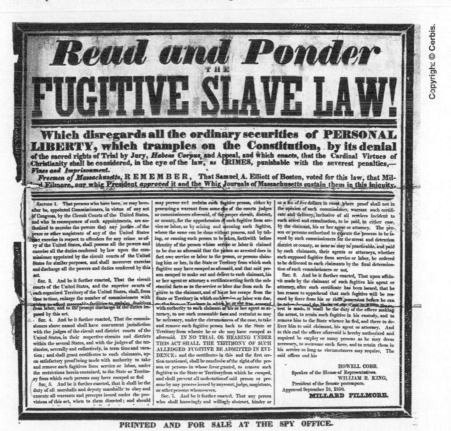

(A)   Daniel Webster   (D)   John C. Calhoun

(B)   Henry Clay   (E)   George Fitzhugh

(C)   William Lloyd Garrison

75.   The Federalist party headed by Alexander Hamilton

I.   advocated a pro-British foreign policy

II.   supported a "loose" or "broad" interpretation of the Constitution

III. favored a government run by yeomen farmers and mechanics

IV.   championed the concept of a strong central government

(A)   I and II only   (D)   I, II, and III only

(B)   II and III only   (E)   I, II, and IV only

(C)   III and IV only

76.   Which of the following groups is not matched to its correct geographical region?

(A)   Anasazi—American Southwest

(B)   Aztecs—Mexico City region

(C)   Natchez—California and the Pacific Northwest

(D)   Maya—Yucatán peninsula

(E)   Mohawk—Eastern Woodland

77.   Slavery was declared illegal throughout the United States by the

(A)   Emancipation Proclamation

(B)   Thirteenth Amendment

(C)   Force Acts

(D)   Freedmen's Bureau

(E)   Wade-Davis Bill

78.   Harriet Beecher Stowe wrote *Uncle Tom's Cabin*, a novel about slavery, in response to the

(A)   Nat Turner Insurrection (1831) in Southampton County, Virginia

(B)   trial and execution of John Brown

    (C)   passage of the Fugitive Slave Law in 1850

    (D)   admission of Missouri into the Union as a slave state

    (E)   annexation of Texas

79.   The Indian Removal Act of 1830 which sought to continue the Jeffersonian policies toward the Eastern tribes

    (A)   was vetoed by Andrew Jackson

    (B)   proposed moving the Eastern tribes to the trans-Mississippi West

    (C)   conferred citizenship and the franchise on Indian adult male property owners

    (D)   did not apply to either the Cherokees or the Seminoles

    (E)   declared the Eastern tribal lands to be independent nations

80.   The Cuban Missile Crisis of 1962

    (A)   displayed Soviet nuclear superiority

    (B)   forced President Kennedy to quarantine military equipment shipped to Cuba

    (C)   boosted Nikita Krushchev's position in the international community

    (D)   enabled the Cubans to deploy nuclear warheads

    (E)   helped the United States prepare for the Bay of Pigs invasion

STOP

This is the end of Section I.
If time still remains, you may check your work only in this section.
Do not begin Section II until instructed to do so.

Section II

TIME: Reading Period – 15 Minutes
Writing Time for all Essays – 115 Minutes

DIRECTIONS: Read over the Document-Based Essay question in Part A and the choices in Parts B and C during the Reading Period, and use the time to organize answers. All students must answer Part A (the Document-Based Essay question) and answer ONE question in both Parts B and C.

PART A – DOCUMENT-BASED ESSAY
(Suggested writing time: 45 minutes)

1. *The debate over the relationship between the states and the federal government and over the principles of interposition and nullification began with the struggle to ratify the Constitution and continued to the end of the Civil War.*

Evaluate this statement using the documents and your knowledge of constitutional history from 1789 to 1865.

Document A
Source: "The Constitution of the United States"

PREAMBLE
WE THE PEOPLE of the United States, in Order to form a more perfect Union, establish Justice, insure domestic Tranquility, provide for the common defence, promote the general Welfare, and secure the Blessings of Liberty to ourselves and our Posterity, do ordain and establish this Constitution for the United States of America.

ARTICLE I, Section 8
To make all Laws which shall be necessary and proper for carrying into Execution the foregoing Powers, and all other Powers vested by this Constitution in the Government of the United States, or in any Department or Officer thereof.

ARTICLE VI
This Constitution, and the Laws of the United States which shall be made in Pursuance thereof; and all Treaties made, or which shall be made, under the Authority of the United States, shall be the supreme Law of the

Land; and the Judges in every State shall be bound thereby, any Thing in the Constitution or Laws of any State to the Contrary notwithstanding.

AMENDMENT X

The powers not delegated to the United States by the Constitution, nor prohibited by it to the States, are reserved to the States respectively, or to the people.

Document B

Source: "Virginia Resolutions" (December 24, 1798)

That this Assembly doth explicitly and peremptorily declare that it views the powers of the Federal Government as resulting from the compact to which the states are parties, as limited by the plain sense and intention of the instrument constituting that compact; as no further valid than they are authorized by the grants enumerated in that compact; and that, in case of a deliberate, palpable, and dangerous exercise of other powers not granted by the said compact, the states, who are parties thereto, have the right and are in duty bound to interpose for arresting the progress of the evil, and for maintaining within their respective limits the authorities, rights, and liberties appertaining to them.

Document C

Source: "Kentucky Resolutions" (November 16, 1798)

I.   Resolved, that the several States composing the United States of America, are not united on the principle of unlimited submission to their general government; but that by compact under the style and title of a Constitution for the United States and of amendments thereto, they constitute a general government for special purposes, delegated to that government certain definite powers, reserving each State to itself, the residuary mass of right to their own self-government; and that whensoever the general government assumes undelegated powers, its acts are unauthoritative, void, and of no force: That to this compact each State acceded as a State, and is an integral party, its co-States forming, as to itself, the other party: That the government created by this compact was not made the exclusive or final judge of the extent of the powers delegated to itself; since that would have made its discretion, and not the Constitution, the measure of its powers; but that as in all other cases of compact among parties having no common Judge, each party has an equal right to judge for itself, as well of infractions as of the mode and measure of redress.

Document D

Source: "Report and Resolutions of the Hartford Convention" (January 4, 1815)

That it be and hereby is recommended to the legislatures of the several states represented in the Convention, to adopt all such measures as may be necessary effectually to protect the citizens of said states from the operation and effects of all acts which have been or may be passed by the Congress of the United States, which shall contain provisions, subjecting the militia or other citizens to forcible drafts, conscriptions, or impressments, not authorized by the institution of the United States.

Document E

Source: "South Carolina Ordinance of Nullification" (November 24, 1832)

We, therefore, the people of the State of South Carolina in Convention assembled, do declare and ordain,... That the several acts and parts of acts of the Congress of the United States, purporting to be laws for the imposing of duties and imposts on the importation of foreign commodities,...and, more especially, ...[the tariff acts of 1828 and 1832]..., are unauthorized by the Constitution of the United States, and violate the true meaning and intent thereof, and are null, void, and no law, nor binding upon this State, its officers or citizens; and all promises, contracts, and obligations.

Document F

Source: Marbury v. Madison (1803)

It is emphatically the province and duty of the judicial department to say what the law is. Those who apply the rule to particular cases must of necessity expound and interpret that rule. If two laws conflict with each other, the courts must decide on the operation of each.

Thus, the particular phraseology of the Constitution of the United States confirms and strengthens the principle, supposed to be essential to all written constitutions, that a law repugnant to the Constitution is void, and that courts, as well as other departments, are bound by that instrument.

Document G

Source: McCulloch v. Maryland (1819)

The government of the United States, then, though limited in its powers, is supreme; and its laws, when made in pursuance of the constitution, form the supreme law of the land, "anything in the constitution or laws of any State, to the contrary, notwithstanding."

Document H

Source: "Mississippi Resolution on Secession" (November 30, 1860)

Whereas, The Constitutional Union was formed by the several States in their separate sovereign capacity for the purpose of mutual advantage and protection.

That the several States are distinct sovereignties, whose supremacy is limited so far only as the same has been delegated by voluntary compact to a Federal Government, and when it fails to accomplish the ends for which it was established, the parties to the compact have the right to resume, each State for itself, such delegated powers;....

Document I

Source: "The Constitution of the Confederate States of America" (March 11, 1861)

We the people of the Confederate States, each State acting in its sovereign and independent character, in order to form a permanent federal government, establish justice, insure domestic tranquility, and secure the blessings of liberty to ourselves and our posterity — invoking the favor and guidance of Almighty God — do ordain and establish this Constitution for the Confederate States of America.

PARTS B AND C – STANDARD ESSAY QUESTIONS
(70 minutes)

> **DIRECTIONS:** Choose ONE question each from Part B and Part C. It is recommended that you spend 5 minutes planning and 30 minutes writing. Support your thesis with germane historical evidence and present your case logically and clearly.

PART B

2. During the presidential election in 1920, the Republican candidate, Warren G. Harding, called for a "return to normalcy" after the activism of the Progressive era. How did Harding and his successor, Calvin Coolidge, respond to the public clamor for a "return to normalcy"?

3. During the Civil War, the federal government increased its power. Give at least five examples of the central government expanding its power in the North during the Civil War.

PART C

4. Compare the work of the Progressives at the local and state levels.

5. What was the Great Awakening? What impact did it have on the colonies?

AP UNITED STATES HISTORY

PRACTICE TEST 5

ANSWER KEY

1. (A)	21. (C)	41. (E)	61. (D)
2. (C)	22. (D)	42. (E)	62. (A)
3. (D)	23. (B)	43. (D)	63. (A)
4. (E)	24. (E)	44. (C)	64. (B)
5. (C)	25. (E)	45. (E)	65. (C)
6. (C)	26. (A)	46. (A)	66. (E)
7. (B)	27. (C)	47. (D)	67. (E)
8. (C)	28. (B)	48. (B)	68. (B)
9. (C)	29. (D)	49. (E)	69. (C)
10. (E)	30. (B)	50. (C)	70. (E)
11. (A)	31. (E)	51. (E)	71. (C)
12. (E)	32. (B)	52. (C)	72. (E)
13. (C)	33. (D)	53. (E)	73. (A)
14. (B)	34. (E)	54. (D)	74. (C)
15. (E)	35. (C)	55. (A)	75. (E)
16. (E)	36. (D)	56. (A)	76. (C)
17. (B)	37. (D)	57. (A)	77. (B)
18. (A)	38. (A)	58. (E)	78. (C)
19. (A)	39. (B)	59. (C)	79. (B)
20. (A)	40. (C)	60. (A)	80. (B)

DETAILED EXPLANATIONS
OF ANSWERS

TEST 5

SECTION I

1.   **(A)**

Historians and archaeologists believe that the first humans came to North America in several waves over a land bridge between Siberia and Alaska in what is now the Bering Strait. This is one of the world's oldest known migrations. These Indian ancestors then spread out over North and South America over a period of thousands of years. It is believed that the first wave of immigrants were hunters of big game, such as bison and mammoths, and were the ancestors of the Indians of South America and most North Americans. The second wave may have occurred at the same time along the southernmost coast of the Bering land mass and were the ancestors of Eskimos and Aleuts. The third group of migrants probably came several thousand years later than the first two and were nomadic hunter-gatherers.

2.   **(C)**

From the protests of organized labor and former presidential candidates Pat Buchanan and Ross Perot to the cheers of Republicans and business interests, the North American Free Trade Agrement was a widely debated measure. Originally negotiated by the Bush administration, NAFTA loosened trade restrictions between Canada, Mexico, and the United States. SALT (A) and START (B) dealt with limiting arms production, while the Gulf of Tonkin Resolution (D) dealt with Vietnam. SDI (E) was a plan to implement a space-based missile defense system.

3.   **(D)**

President Reagan chose the conservative jurist Sandra Day O'Connor to be the first woman to sit on the Supreme Court. Ruth Bader Ginsberg (B) was the second woman to sit on the court. Madeleine Albright (C) became the first female Secretary of State, Ann Richards (A) was governor of Texas, and Dee Dee Meyers (E) was at one time the press secretary to Clinton.

4.   **(E)**

The doctrine of nullification was based on the contention that the Constitution was a compact among the sovereign states. When the states entered into the compact, they retained their essential sovereignty and delegated limited and clearly specified powers to the federal government. If a state judged a federal law to violate the compact, it could nullify the law within its borders.

According to the doctrine of nullification/interposition, each state could be the judge of the legality or constitutionality of national action and could "interpose" its sovereignty to nullify invalid federal action. Southern leaders reactivated the theory in opposition to the desegregation rulings of the Supreme Court. The federal courts have rejected the doctrine as contrary to the national supremacy clause of Article VI of the Constitution.

5.   **(C)**

The Scarlet Letter (1850) and *The House of the Seven Gables* (1851) were Nathaniel Hawthorne's two greatest novels. *The Scarlet Letter* was a grim yet sympathetic analysis of adultery. In this novel, Hawthorne did not condemn the woman, Hester Prynne, but the people who judged her.

6.   **(C)**

In 1848, the Seneca Falls women's rights convention, organized by Lucretia Mott and Elizabeth Cady Stanton, adopted a "Declaration of Sentiments and Resolutions." This document was modeled after the Declaration of Independence in form and language.

7.   **(B)**

Gabriel Prosser organized and led a rebellion of slaves in Henrico County, Virginia, in 1800. Denmark Vesey, a free Black, inspired a group of slaves in Charleston, South Carolina, with the idea of seizing their freedom in 1822. Nat Turner planned and led a slave uprising in 1831 in Southampton County, Virginia. These slave rebellions failed and Prosser, Vesey, and Turner were executed.

8.   **(C)**

Most Europeans assumed that since the Indians were non-European they were inferior beings. Likewise, the Europeans dismissed the Indians as being heathens, since they were not Christian. The colonists also considered the Indians to be the epitome of savagery and barbarism.

9. **(C)**

This cartoon shows Ulysses Grant caught within several strands of corruption, including the Whiskey Ring and corruption in the Navy Department.

10. **(E)**

Prior to the completion of the Erie Canal, farmers in the Old Northwest depended on the Mississippi River system to get their produce to market. The completion of the Erie Canal resulted in the shifting of the commerce of the Old Northwest from the Mississippi River system to the Great Lakes and the Erie Canal.

11. **(A)**

Black Americans, both military and civilian, were better treated in Europe than in the United States. Generally, they were not subjected to the discrimination and segregation they experienced in the United States.

12. **(E)**

Henry Cabot Lodge, United States Senator from Massachusetts from 1893 to 1924, was a conservative Republican. Lodge was a bitter foe of Woodrow Wilson's Fourteen Points; and as the chairman of the Senate Foreign Relations Committee, he led the attack on the Treaty of Versailles and the League of Nations.

13. **(C)**

Warren Harding's administration, like that of Ulysses Grant, was plagued by graft and corruption. Both Harding and Grant were betrayed and humiliated by men they appointed to office.

14. **(B)**

Droughts, high tariffs, bankruptcies, and low prices had either a direct or indirect impact on all segments of society. Nevertheless, their greatest and most direct impact was on the stock market.

15. **(E)**

Frank Lloyd Wright served a seven-year apprenticeship in the Chicago office of Louis Sullivan. Wright established himself at Oak Park, Illinois, where he practiced radical innovations and introduced methods of building that stressed a harmony with natural surroundings.

16.   **(E)**

Pocahontas was the daughter of the powerful Indian chieftan Powhatan. While being held as a hostage at Jamestown, she converted to Christianity and was baptized Rebecca. In 1614, she married John Rolfe and accompanied him to England. As Pocahontas was preparing to return to Virginia, she died suddenly.

17.   **(B)**

John Peter Zenger was accused of seditious libel for publishing criticisms of New York's governor. Zenger was imprisoned for ten months and brought to trial in 1735. Ignoring the established rule in English common law that one might be punished for criticism which fostered "an ill opinion of the government," the jury considered the attack on the governor to be true and found Zenger innocent. Although the libel law remained the same, the jury's verdict emboldened editors to criticize officials more freely.

18.   **(A)**

William Marcy Tweed, or "Boss Tweed," led the powerful Democratic political machine that was able to control or crush the opposition. In two years (1869–1871), Tweed milked the City of New York of approximately $100 million. Tweed eventually was sent to prison in 1872, where he died four years later.

19.   **(A)**

Thomas Paine published his pamphlet *Common Sense* in January 1776. Written at a time when others were debating the issue of home rule, *Common Sense* called on the American colonies to declare their independence from Great Britain. Paine refocused the hostility previously vented on Parliament and directly attacked allegiance to the king.

20.   **(A)**

The Dutch founded the colony of New Netherlands on the Hudson River. Despite this, Charles II bestowed a large tract of land south of the Massachusetts Bay Colony upon his brother in 1664. Although it took three Anglo-Dutch wars to secure it, New Netherlands was under British control by the end of 1664.

21. **(C)**

Although the Scotch-Irish spoke English, they felt little loyalty to either the English government or the Anglican church. Most of the Scotch-Irish were Presbyterian and had been treated badly by the English government. They came to America because of the deteriorating economic conditions in the Irish woolens industry and generally settled on the frontier.

22. **(D)**

Slavery was recognized in the laws of all the colonies, but it flourished in the Tidewater South. South Carolina had a black majority through most of the eighteenth century. About half the slaves imported into the mainland colonies came from Congo-Angola and the Bight of Biafra. Nearly all the rest of the slaves came from the Atlantic coast of Africa up to Senegambia. Although the slave codes varied from colony to colony, they were essentially the same. These codes legally transformed the slaves into property.

23. **(B)**

After being defeated at the Battle of Brandywine Creek, the American patriots, led by Horatio Gates and Benedict Arnold, forced General John Burgoyne to surrender his entire army at Saratoga in October 1777. This was one of the most significant military victories of the war for the Americans. The victory at Saratoga prevented the isolation of the New England states and convinced the French that the Americans might well make good their claim to independence. In December 1777, the French recognized the United States as an independent country.

24. **(E)**

The first state constitutions varied mainly in detail. These constitutions formed governments much like the colonial governments, with elected governors and senates instead of appointed governors and councils. The first state constitution generally embodied a separation of powers and included a bill of rights protecting the rights of petition, freedom of speech, trial by jury, etc.

25. **(E)**

The Connecticut Compromise, advanced by Oliver Ellsworth and Roger Sherman, was submitted to the Constitutional Convention to break the deadlock created by the rejection of the Randolph Plan and Paterson Plan. The compromise provided for a bicameral legislature. One chamber of the legislature was to have equal representation from each state, and the other chamber was to be based on proportional representation.

26.   **(A)**

In 1913, Charles A. Beard advanced the thesis that the delegates to the Constitutional Convention were not true patriots but selfish men out to protect their own interests. According to Beard, the delegates held large amounts of depreciated government securities and stood to gain financially from a strong national government. Forrest McDonald announced in his book, *We the People: The Economic Origins of the Constitution*, published in 1958 that Beard's economic interpretation of the Constitution does not work.

27.   **(C)**

Chief Justice John Marshall viewed the Constitution as an instrument of national unity, a document that created its own sanctions by its implied powers. Marshall's decisions affirmed the constitutional power of the Court to engage in judicial review of federal and state legislation, gave judicial sanction to the doctrine of centralization of powers at the expense of the states, and erected barriers against attacks upon property rights.

28.   **(B)**

The Treaty of Ghent ending the War of 1812 was signed in December 1814 and ratified by the Senate on February 15, 1815. The treaty provided for each belligerent to restore places and territory it had taken from the other in the war — the restoration of the *status quo ante bellum*. The treaty said nothing about impressment, ignored neutral rights and Indian issues, and left the United States-Canadian boundary where it had been.

29.   **(D)**

Alexander Hamilton's revenue proposals included an excise tax on whiskey. The backcountry farmers resisted this tax, and this resistance culminated when the farmers of western Pennsylvania took up arms to prevent the collection of the tax. Washington responded to this challenge by sending a force of 13,000 militiamen to put down the Whiskey Rebellion.

30.   **(B)**

Washington decided to step down after his second term of office. To make his wishes clear to the American people, Washington composed his "Farewell Address," which was published in a Philadelphia newspaper. In this address, he warned against "permanent alliances" with any portion of the foreign world.

31.   **(E)**

While the Louisiana Purchase more than doubled the size of the United States, it also guaranteed Western farmers access to the Mississippi River as an avenue of trade. Importantly, the purchase of this territory gave the United States control of the port of New Orleans. Jefferson was troubled by the fact that according to his oft-repeated "strict" interpretation of the Constitution, the United States technically lacked the constitutional power to purchase the Louisiana territory. Nevertheless, Jefferson approved its purchase.

32.   **(B)**

The Webster-Ashburton Treaty (1842) fixed the present northeastern Maine-Canada border and provided for a joint Anglo-American effort to suppress the African slave trade.

33.   **(D)**

After the discovery of gold in California in 1848 and the admission of California to the Union in 1850, the West began to fill up rapidly. Consequently, there arose a demand for a transcontinental railroad to connect the East with the Pacific Coast. The bone of contention was the location of the eastern terminus. Should it be in the North or the South? The favored section would reap rich rewards in wealth, population and influence.

Those supporting a southern route argued that (a) it would be easier to build because the mountains were less high; (b) unlike the proposed northern lines, it would not pass through unorganized territory. Texas was already a state. New Mexico, with the Gadsden Purchase added, was an organized territory with federal troops available to give protection against the Indians; and (c) any northern or central line would have to be built through the unorganized territory of Nebraska. The advocates of a northern route countered with the argument that if organized territory was the test, then Nebraska should be given organized status. Thousands of land hungry pioneers were already poised on the Nebraska border; and if the area were given territorial status, it would rapidly fill up.

At this point in 1854, Stephen A. Douglas, Senator from Illinois, entered the fray. Douglas had invested heavily in Chicago real estate and railway stock; and he was anxious to have Chicago become the eastern terminus of the proposed Pacific Railroad. Douglas would thus (a) endear himself to the voters of Illinois, (b) benefit his own section, and (c) enhance the value of his private holdings. He knew that the South would never favor the creation of a new territory without some concession to slavery. In order to secure Southern votes for the northern route, he pushed through Congress the Kansas-Nebraska bill. This legislation provided that

  i.   instead of one territory, two would be organized. Kansas, to the west of Missouri, would presumably be slave, and Nebraska, to the west of Iowa, would presumably be free;

ii.   the Missouri Compromise would be repealed; and

iii. the status of slavery in the two territories would be settled by "popular sovereignty."

The Southern members of Congress, who at first had not thought of Kansas as slave soil, rose to the bait. Here was a chance to get one more desperately needed slave state. They voted almost unanimously for the bill. Most of the Northern members of Congress voted against it. They regarded the repeal of the Missouri Compromise, which prohibited slavery in all the Nebraska Territory that lay north of the 36° 30' line, as a breach of faith.

34.   **(E)**

From 1856 to 1860, cotton accounted for over 50 percent of the total exports of the United States. In contrast, domestic manufactures during this period accounted for only 12 percent of the total exports. In 1860, the total value of goods exported from the United States was $333,576,000 and the value of the cotton exported was $191,806,555.

35.   **(C)**

Andrew Jackson believed that Indians were better off out of the way. By the time of his election as president in 1828, he was fully in agreement with the view that the Indians should be moved onto the plains west of the Mississippi. In response to Jackson's request, Congress approved the Indian Removal Act.

36.   **(D)**

The map shows the gains made by Britain stemming from the Treaty of Paris. The British extended their dominion, at the expense of the French, westward to the Mississippi River. France lost nearly all its North American possessions. Spain gained land from Mexico to the Mississippi, including the strategic port of New Orleans. The Portuguese had no land holdings in North America. As for the Native Americans, their disposition in the wake of the treaty would depend on whether they were allied with the British or the French. No treaty was signed between the British and the Indians, and animosity remained between the two groups.

37.   **(D)**

Andrew Jackson advanced the principle of rotation in office. He held that "no man has any more intrinsic right to official station than another." According to Jackson's reasoning, "those holding government jobs for a long time are apt to acquire a habit of looking with indifference upon the public interests and of tolerating conduct from which an unpracticed man would revolt." To Jackson, rotation in office meant that more citizens could participate in running the government; and in a democracy, this was an advantage since it made government more responsive to the electorate.

38.   **(A)**

Shortly after Pearl Harbor, the unions responded to an appeal from President Franklin Roosevelt by giving a no-strike pledge. In 1943, however, a major coal strike occurred involving 450,000 soft coal miners and 80,000 hard coal miners. Under heavy pressure from President Roosevelt, John L. Lewis, head of the United Mine Workers, agreed to end the strike.

39.   **(B)**

In his 1964 State of the Union message, President Lyndon Johnson called for a "War on Poverty." The Economic Opportunity Act of 1964 established the Office of Economic Opportunity to carry out antipoverty programs.

40.   **(C)**

William Lloyd Garrison was the most vehement of the Massachusetts abolitionists. From 1831 to 1865, he advocated the immediate and complete emancipation of slaves. Garrison edited a militantly abolitionist weekly paper, the *Liberator*. In its pages, he attacked moderate abolitionists, advocated Northern secession, and castigated slaveholders. On July 4, 1854, Garrison publicly burned a copy of the Constitution and informed the holiday gathering: "So perish all compromises with tyranny."

41.   **(E)**

The Church of Jesus Christ of Latter-day Saints (Mormons) was founded in 1830 by Joseph Smith in upstate New York. The dedication and economic efficiency of the Mormons attracted a large number of converts, but this close-knit body of poor farmers and artisans was regarded with suspicion by nonbelievers. Smith was eventually murdered by a mob. The Mormons did not single out the Anasazi for any special recognition among Native Americans.

42.   **(E)**

In April 1860, at their nominating convention in Charleston, South Carolina, the Democrats failed to nominate a candidate. Eventually, at a convention in Baltimore, the Northern Democrats nominated Stephen A. Douglas. The

Southern Democrats held a separate convention at Richmond and nominated John C. Breckinridge. When the Republicans met in Chicago, they nominated Abraham Lincoln on the third ballot. A fourth party, the Constitutional Union party, entered the presidential contest and nominated John Bell. In the election, Lincoln garnered only 39 percent of the popular vote, but he received a clear majority in the electoral college. Lincoln carried every free state except New Jersey. Although Douglas received the second highest popular vote, he gained only 12 electoral votes.

43.   **(D)**

In the presidential election of 1876, the Democrats nominated Samuel J. Tilden, governor of New York and a symbol of honest government. The Republicans nominated Rutherford B. Hayes, governor of Ohio and also a symbol of honest government. Tilden carried states with 184 votes in the Electoral College, one short of the necessary majority, and received 51 percent of the popular vote. Hayes received 165 undisputed electoral votes, but the votes of South Carolina, Florida, and Louisiana were in dispute. To avert any possibility of violence, Congress created a special commission of 15 Congressmen and Supreme Court justices to pass judgment upon the disputed electoral votes. After a series of maneuvers and compromises, the commission voted to award the disputed electoral votes to Hayes. Therefore, Hayes won the election by one electoral vote and with 48 percent of the popular vote.

44.   **(C)**

When the Civil War broke out, Abraham Lincoln made it clear that his primary objective was to preserve the Union. In calling for volunteers, Lincoln made no mention of abolishing slavery.

45.   **(E)**

The Security Council was to be the police authority of the world, responsible for preventing war. The General Assembly was to make recommendations for the peaceful settlement of disputes. The International Court of Justice was to decide legal questions referred to it by disputing nations. The Trusteeship Council was to look after colonial areas. The Economic and Social Council was to make recommendations regarding world economic, social, cultural, and health problems.

46.   **(A)**

The radical abolitionists viewed slavery as a moral issue not a political issue. Accordingly, they debated slavery in terms of morality and not political expediency. The radical abolitionists wanted the immediate emancipation of the slaves.

47.   **(D)**

Andrew Johnson's plan for Reconstruction called for the loyal white citizens in the former Confederate states to draft and ratify new constitutions and to elect state legislatures, which were to repeal the ordinance of secession, repudiate the Confederate state debts, and ratify the Thirteenth Amendment. The Congressional plan for Reconstruction called for new lists of registered voters, including former slaves, to be compiled. In each of the states, the newly registered voters would elect a constitutional convention. The new state constitutions were required to provide guarantees of universal manhood suffrage. When a state had adopted a constitution acceptable to Congress and had ratified the Fourteenth Amendment, its senators and representatives would be admitted to Congress.

48.   **(B)**

The Progressive movement advocated programs that included attacks against big business, child labor, unequal wealth, industrial accidents, low wages for women, prohibition, and city and state reform. The worst failure of the Progressives was their inability and unwillingness to deal with the problems of African-Americans. "Jim Crow" laws in the South had a legal basis with the *Plessy v. Ferguson* decision of 1896 that promoted segregation. The Fourteenth and Fifteenth Amendments were virtually ignored.

49.   **(E)**

The Teller Amendment guaranteed Cuban sovereignty once the island was liberated from Spanish rule. The amendment did not forbid annexation of other former Spanish colonies in the Caribbean.

50.   **(C)**

European diseases, smallpox and measles, to which the Indians had no resistance decimated the Indian population of the Americas. When Cortez invaded Mexico, its Indian population numbered at least 20 million. A century later it had declined to 2 million.

51.   **(E)**

Thomas Malthus published his *Essay on Population* in 1789. In it, he contended that, since population increased by a geometric ratio and food supply increased only by an arithmetic ratio, it was basic natural law that population would outstrip food supply. Malthus did not have an impact on fifteenth century Western Europe.

52.   **(C)**

[Thomas] Woodrow Wilson was born in Staunton, Virginia, the son of a Presbyterian minister. Upon graduation from Princeton, he studied law at the University of Virginia. Wilson opened a law office in Atlanta, but he soon abandoned the practice of law to study government and history at Johns Hopkins University where he earned his Ph.D. After receiving his degree, he taught jurisprudence and political economy. In 1902, he was elected president of Princeton University, the first nonclerical head of the institution. Wilson was elected governor of New Jersey in 1910. As governor, he established a record which brought him to the forefront of national politics. In 1912, he received the Democratic presidential nomination and won the election. Wilson was reelected in 1916. Upon the outbreak of World War I, he was determined to keep the United States neutral. After the United States entered the war, Wilson proposed his Fourteen Points as a basis for peace (January 1918).

53.   **(E)**

The Chicago White Sox team was accused of intentionally losing the 1919 World Series.

54.   **(B)**

Marcus Garvey, a West Indian, was the leading force in the Universal Negro Improvement Association. In the early 1920s the association attracted hundreds of thousands of followers. Garvey had nothing but contempt for Whites, for light-skinned Negroes, and for the National Association for the Advancement of Colored People (NAACP) that sought to bring Whites and Blacks together to fight segregation and other forms of prejudice. He preached that the black man must "work out his salvation in his motherland," Africa.

55.   **(A)**

Calvin Coolidge made this comment in a presidential speech. His advocacy of tax cuts, economy in government, and a strong laissez-faire policy toward business coincided with an era of general prosperity. Coolidge's comment reflected his philosophy and that of the nation.

56.   **(A)**

During his second term, Franklin Roosevelt decided to ask Congress to shift the balance on the Supreme Court to pro-New Deal justices. He thinly disguised his plan by making it part of a general reorganization of the judiciary. Roosevelt's plan provided for the retirement of Supreme Court justices at the age of 70 with full pay. If a justice chose not to retire, the president was to appoint an additional justice, up to a maximum of six, to ease the work load for the aged justices who remained on the court. Congress failed to pass Roosevelt's plan.

57.   **(A)**

Franklin Roosevelt appointed Frances Perkins to his cabinet as Secretary of Labor. She was the first woman cabinet member and held her post for 12 years (1933–1945).

58.   **(E)**

Early in his presidency, Theodore Roosevelt faced the Venezuelan debt crisis. Venezuela owed sizable debts to European and American creditors. Germany and Great Britain attempted to collect their debts in December 1902 by force. Roosevelt joined the Venezuelan president in urging arbitration, and the British and Germans agreed. In this crisis, Roosevelt made it clear that he would not permit European powers to intervene in Western Hemisphere affairs in any way that might endanger American interests.

After the settlement of the crisis, Roosevelt continued to be concerned about the intervention of European powers in Latin America. He believed that such intervention could be prevented only if the U.S. assumed responsibility for maintaining political and economic stability in the region. Therefore, in his annual message to Congress in May 1904, Roosevelt asserted that not only did the U.S. have the right to oppose European intervention in the Western Hemisphere, but it also had the right to intervene in the domestic affairs of the Western Hemisphere states to maintain order and to prevent intervention of others.

59.   **(C)**

After several unsuccessful efforts, the English established a permanent settlement in North America in 1607. This settlement, Jamestown, was located on a peninsula near the mouth of the James River in Virginia.

60.   **(A)**

Although Maryland was founded as a haven for Roman Catholics, there existed from the beginning a large Protestant majority. Lord Baltimore solved this problem by accepting a Toleration Act (1649) that gave freedom of religion to anyone "professing to believe in Jesus Christ."

61.   **(D)**

William Penn secured proprietary rights in 1681 to the region north of Maryland and west of the Delaware River. He was a devout Quaker who viewed his colony as a holy experiment. In 1682, Penn constructed a "Frame of Government" that guaranteed complete religious freedom to the colonists.

62.   (A)

The Peace of Paris (1763) gave Britain all French North American possessions east of the Mississippi River and all of Spanish Florida. France ceded Louisiana to Spain in compensation for Spain's loss of the Floridas. Therefore, the trans-Mississippi West was not open to the colonists.

63.   (A)

Although the settlers of Virginia tried to produce things that were needed in England, it was tobacco that became the staple crop. Tobacco plants could be set on semi-cleared land and cultivated with a hoe.

64.   (B)

Georgia was the last colony to be founded. It was established to provide a new start in life for Englishmen imprisoned for debt and to erect a military barrier against the Spaniards on the southern border of English America.

65.   (C)

Mercantilism, the pursuit of economic power through national self-sufficiency, was the dominant economic doctrine in Western Europe by 1660. This doctrine encouraged the state to encourage manufacturers, to develop and protect its own shipping, and to make use of colonies as sources of raw materials and markets for its manufactured goods.

66.   (E)

Manifest Destiny was a term that gained currency in the 1840s. It implied the inevitability of the continued territorial expansion of the United States into the undeveloped continental areas to the West and South. It was cited as a reason for the annexation of Texas. Many Americans believed that all North America was to be theirs to make into one mighty nation — a showcase to display the virtues of democracy. Manifest Destiny served at times to justify selfish national interest and often sanctioned the brutal disregard of the rights of others because it contained a large degree of cultural and racial chauvinism.

67.   (E)

Senator Lewis Cass first enunciated the principle of popular sovereignty. Cass contended that the people of a territory had the right to determine whether slavery would exist in their territory. In drafting the Compromise of 1850, Stephen A. Douglas included the principle of popular sovereignty. He coined the phrase in the Kansas-Nebraska Act (1854).

68.   **(B)**

When the colonists protested the Stamp Tax, George Grenville, first lord of the treasury, had one of his subordinates prepare an answer to the protest. This answer developed the theory of virtual representation. This theory contended that each member of Parliament represented the interests of the whole country and empire. The colonists responded with the theory of actual representation which held that representatives must be residents of the geographic districts they represent.

69.   **(C)**

Weakened by a series of battles, Lord Charles Cornwallis fled to Yorktown on the peninsula between the York and the James Rivers in Virginia in hopes of being evacuated by the British fleet. With fortunate timing and French assistance, Washington marched his force of French and American troops down from the north at just the time the French fleet appeared off the coast of Virginia. Caught between a hostile army and navy, Cornwallis surrendered. This defeat convinced the British that it would be too difficult and too expensive to attempt to put down the rebellion.

70.   **(E)**

The Northwest Ordinance was a major accomplishment of the Confederation Congress. By excluding slavery from the Northwest, it ensured that the entire North would be free territory. By establishing the precedent that new states would enter the Union on an equal footing with the original 13, it ensured the continued settlement of the West. The ordinance also stipulated that the land and property of the Indians "shall never be taken from them without their permission."

71.   **(C)**

The Confederation Congress endorsed the calling of a convention as "expedient" but stipulated that the convention should be called "for the sole and express purpose of revising the Articles of Confederation." Conspicuous by their absence from the convention were Thomas Jefferson, John Adams, Patrick Henry, and John Hancock. The delegates to the convention voted to hold their deliberations in secret. During their deliberations, the delegates failed to deal with the emancipation of slaves.

72.   (E)

The Bill of Rights, the first ten amendments to the Constitution, was proposed by Congress (1789) and ratified by the states (1791). The first nine limited Congress by forbidding it to encroach upon certain basic rights — freedom of religion, speech, and press, immunity from arbitrary arrest, and trial by jury. The Tenth Amendment reserved to the states all powers except those specifically withheld from them or delegated to the federal government. It wasn't until the ratification of the Nineteenth Amendment in 1920 that women were enfranchised on an equal footing with men.

73.   (A)

The Federalist Papers, a collection of 85 essays, were written anonymously by Alexander Hamilton, John Jay, and James Madison. Seventy-seven of the essays originally appeared in New York newspapers under the pseudonym "Publius." These essays argued for the ratification of the Constitution by stressing the inadequacies of the Articles of Confederation.

74.   (C)

William Lloyd Garrison was a leading abolitionist who would have approved of this editorial condemning the Fugitive Slave Law of 1850. Daniel Webster and Henry Clay both played roles in bringing about the Compromise of 1850, of which the law is a part. John C. Calhoun and George Fitzhugh were staunch defenders of slavery.

75.   (E)

The Federalist party that developed around Alexander Hamilton stood for the following principles: (a) rule by the "best people," (b) a powerful central government at the expense of the states, (c) a "loose" interpretation of the Constitution, (d) government fostering business, and (e) a pro-British foreign policy.

76.   (C)

The Natchez Indians were part of the Mississippi Valley culture and were not located along the Pacific Ocean. All of the other groups are correctly matched with their region. The Natchez Indians were among the latest Indian groups to reside in what is now the state of Mississippi. The Natchez Indian culture began around 700 c.e. and lasted until the 1730s, when the tribe was dispersed in a war with the French. Their language is related to the Muskogean language family. Natchez Indian society was organized in chiefdoms with two major ranks (nobles and commoners), with membership determined by matrilineal descent. The Natchez chief was called Great Sun and inherited his position of leadership from his mother's family. The Natchez were farmers of squash, beans, and corn and also hunted and fished.

77.   **(B)**

The Emancipation Proclamation issued on January 1, 1863, had a very limited impact. It declared the slaves free only in those parts of the nation where federal law could not be enforced. Slavery was declared illegal in all the nation by the Thirteenth Amendment.

78.   **(C)**

Uncle Tom's Cabin, a novel by Harriet Beecher Stowe, was published in 1852. Dismayed by the passage of the Fugitive Slave Law, Stowe was determined to awaken the North to the wickedness of slavery by portraying its darker side. The success of the book at home and abroad was sensational. It sold 300,000 copies the first year. It was translated into many foreign languages and also put on the stage as "Tom Shows." The South condemned the book as an "unfair" indictment. Stowe had never witnessed slavery in the Deep South, but she had lived for many years in Ohio, a center of Underground Railway activity. The story left a profound impression on the North.

79.   **(B)**

In response to Andrew Jackson's urging, Congress approved the Indian Removal Act in 1830. This act provided for the removal of the Eastern tribes to the trans-Mississippi West. In the South, the Seminoles and Cherokees resisted removal.

80.   **(B)**

During the late summer of 1962, reports began to circulate about Soviet plans to install intermediate-range missiles in Cuba. On October 14, U-2 reconnaissance flights over Cuba provided confirmation that missile sites were being prepared for the installation of Soviet-made missiles. President John F. Kennedy was determined to force the removal of the missiles. Ruling out both an air strike against the missile sites and a full-scale invasion, Kennedy announced an American naval quarantine of Cuba to prevent Soviet ships from bringing additional offensive weapons to Cuba. On October 28, the Cuban missile crisis ended when the Soviets agreed to dismantle the missile launching pads and remove the missiles. In return, Kennedy pledged not to invade Cuba.

SECTION II

Sample Answer to Document-Based Question

1.   Fearing the centralist tendencies of the Constitution, a substantial number of people opposed its ratification. The Antifederalists were alarmed by the final paragraph of Article I, section 8, which delegated legislative powers to Congress. That Congress could pass all laws "necessary and proper" to carry out the functions assigned to it by the Constitution seemed alarmingly inclusive. The Antifederalists feared that the Constitution would destroy the independence of the states, and the document's first sentence, beginning "We the *people* of the United States" rather than "We the states," strengthened this fear. The Antifederalist opposition to the Constitution focused attention on the relationship of the states to the federal government, and the Tenth Amendment was added to the Constitution in response to Antifederalist criticisms. This amendment "reserved to the States respectively, or to the people" all powers not mentioned in the Constitution.

    The Tenth Amendment failed to resolve the debate about the relationship of the states to the federal government, and the passage of the Alien and Sedition Acts by a Federalist Congress revived the debate. To offset the Acts, Thomas Jefferson and James Madison, members of the Republican minority, drafted the Virginia and Kentucky Resolutions. These resolutions denounced the Alien and Sedition Acts as unconstitutional and advanced the state compact theory. Jefferson and Madison contended that the Constitution arose as a compact among the states; therefore, the states should assume the right to say when Congress had exceeded its powers. According to this theory, each state was to be the judge of the legality or constitutionality of national action, and might "interpose" its sovereignty to nullify invalid federal action. The Virginia Resolutions drafted by Madison declared that states "have the right and are in duty bound to interpose for arresting the progress of evil." In the second set of Kentucky Resolutions, Jefferson clearly established the theory of nullification when he wrote: "That a nullification of those sovereignties of all unauthorized acts done under color of that instrument is the rightful remedy."

During the presidency of James Madison, the New England Federalists, now in the minority, revived the arguments put forth by Jefferson and Madison in the Kentucky and Virginia Resolutions. At the Hartford Convention, they approved a statement that was similar to the concept expressed in the Kentucky and Virginia resolves by the Republicans when they were in the minority.

The demise of the Federalist party failed to resolve the issue of nullification and interposition; and South Carolina, in 1832, attempted to nullify the Tariff Acts of 1828 and 1832. John C. Calhoun, in defending South Carolina's position, reactivated the theory of nullification, a logical extension of the theory of interposition. John C. Calhoun contended that the Union was a compact among the sovereign states, and the national government was not the final judge of its own powers. Calhoun reasoned that a state may nullify any national law and even secede from the Union.

Chief Justice John Marshall rejected the theories of nullification and interposition, and he worked to establish judicial supremacy. In *Marbury v. Madison*, Marshall argued that the Constitution was the supreme law and that judges were bound by their oath and the nature of their positions to act as guardians of the Constitution. Marshall reasoned that any law in conflict with the Constitution could not be enforced by the courts. In *Marbury v. Madison*, the Supreme Court, for the first time in American history, struck down an act of Congress as unconstitutional. Speaking for the Supreme Court in *McCulloch v. Maryland*, Marshall weakened the doctrine of interposition and nullification. This decision firmly established the principle of "national supremacy," which denied the states any right to interfere in the constitutional operations of the national government.

Despite Marshall's efforts to establish the principles of judicial supremacy and national supremacy, the South continued to insist that the Union was a compact of states and to embrace the theories of nullification and interposition. Finally, the debate reached a critical juncture. Feeling threatened, 11 Southern slave states seceded from the Union and formed the

Confederacy. The Constitution of the Confederate States stressed that the Confederacy was a compact. The document's preamble stressed that "each State acting in its sovereign and independent character" formed the Confederate States of America. Only with the defeat of the Confederacy was the debate resolved.

Although the defeat of the Confederacy apparently resolved the issue of nullification and interposition, the Southern states resurrected these doctrines in the 1950s and 1960s. Opposing the Supreme Court decision in *Brown v. Board of Education* and subsequent congressional legislation, the advocates of states' rights revived the arguments put forth by Thomas Jefferson, James Madison, John C. Calhoun, and seceding states.

Sample Answers to Essay Questions

2.   After the activism of the Progressive era, the American people craved a period of calm. Therefore, they elected both Warren G. Harding and Calvin Coolidge because the two men promised to be relatively inactive presidents. The voters also clearly wanted the government and business interests to reconcile their differences. Harding, with guidance from Secretary of the Treasury Andrew W. Melton, pushed for less government regulation of business, a high protective tariff, and tax reductions designed to benefit business and the wealthy. Additionally, the Harding administration worked to reduce the federal budget and national debt by cutting expenditures and promoting more efficient administration.

With Harding's unexpected death, Coolidge succeeded to the presidency and preserved the public's faith in the honesty of the executive branch. Coolidge believed in minimal activity by the federal government. His advocacy of tax cuts, economy in government, and his strong laissez-faire policy toward business coincided with an era of general prosperity. Coolidge, cautious in domestic affairs and virtually an isolationist in relation to Europe, typified the Republican philosophy of conservatism endorsed by an overwhelming majority of Americans during the 1920s.

Both Harding and Coolidge were avowed champions of business and financial enterprise. They believed that American prosperity depended upon the prosperity of the upper classes, and they (a) sponsored tariff and tax policies designed to promote special interests, (b) brought federal administrative agencies into close cooperation with the business community, (c) opposed measures that would discourage investment or would carry the government into new areas of regulation, (d) shifted the burden for providing social and economic needs to the states, (e) pursued "do nothing" policies, and (f) were concerned with balancing the budget and reducing the federal debt.

3.   (a) Conscription: In March 1863, Congress acted to draft men aged 20 to 45. The federal government had never before drafted men, and the draft flouted an American tradition of voluntary service. It was held to be arbitrary and unconstitutional and encountered widespread opposition.

(b) Taxation: The federal government imposed excise taxes on manufacturers and the practice of nearly every profession. On top of the excises came an income tax. Additionally, Congress created a Bureau of Internal Revenue.

(c) Borrowing: The federal government borrowed from major institutions and private individuals to finance the war.

(d) Banking: Under the National Banking Acts of 1863 and 1864, the Union created the National Banking System, which lasted without serious modification until 1913. The national banks issued bank notes backed by federal government bonds.

(e) Currency: For the first time, the federal government issued paper money, greenbacks, backed up only by the proviso that it was legal tender for all debts. Beginning with the Legal Tender Act (1862), Congress ultimately authorized $450 million of the notes.

(f) Railroads: The expansion of the Union government's power in financial areas was matched by its intrusion into transportation. The federal government subsidized a transcontinental route (Pacific Railway Act of 1862), controlled and coordinated all existing rail lines, and constructed 650 miles of new track.

(g) Communication: The federal government controlled the telegraph system.

(h) Agriculture: In 1861, the federal government created the Department of Agriculture. This was followed by the passage of the Morrell Land Grant College Act (1862), which set aside several million acres of federal land for the support of agriculture, industrial higher education, and the Homestead Act (1862), which provided free land in the West to any citizen who was the head of a family and over 21.

(i) Civil Rights: Lincoln suspended *habeas corpus*, the traditional protection of accused parties against arbitrary imprisonment, in areas where disloyalty seemed to endanger the war effort. He also endorsed congressional legislation imposing severe penalties on persons guilty of treason or conspiracy to commit treason. Lincoln signed an order in September 1863 making anyone who sought to discourage enlistment, came out against conscription, or engaged in disloyal practices subject to martial law.

(j) Race Relations: Lincoln emancipated the slaves in the rebellious states.

(k) Expansion of the Bureaucracy: In 1861, the Union had 40,000 civil service employees. By 1865, the number had increased to 195,000 to handle the enlarged functions of government.

(l) Economy: As a major purchaser of supplies, the federal government stimulated the Union's economy.

4. The Progressive movement was essentially the ideological and political response to the transformation of the United States from a rural, commercial economy to an urban, industrial one. The Progressives were never a single group seeking a single objective, but they made a concerted effort to provide the basic political, social, and economic reforms necessary for an urban, industrial society.

Although Progressivism sprang from many sources, it grew out of a need for reform. During the nineteenth century, enormous advances had been made in establishing a continental nation. These advances had been achieved at the cost of the concentration of economic power, inequitable taxation, wasteful consumption of the nation's resources, corrupt machine politics, sweatshops, child labor, and crowded slums. The Progressives wanted to end these abuses and to make government at the local, state, and national levels more responsive to the needs of the people.

The first expressions of Progressive discontent were manifested at the local level. A number of Progressives focused their zeal for political reform of municipal government and worked to destroy the political bosses and their machines. In their efforts to destroy the machine politics that dominated many urban centers, the Progressives favored giving the voters more effective control over city government and giving the cities more power to control special interests. State legislatures were encouraged to give cities greater freedom to determine the nature of their governments. The legislatures of 12 states had approved some form of home rule for cities by 1912.

The Progressive reformers promoted two forms of city government: the city manager and the commission. In the city manager form of municipal government, a professional administrator managed the city under the general supervision of an elected mayor and council. In the commission form of municipal government, a group of qualified officials headed the major departments and ran the city with one of the commissioners serving as mayor.

Only so much could be achieved at the local level, and the Progressives turned their attention to state government. They sought to reduce the power of party organizations and state legislatures and to increase the power of the voters. The Progressives pushed for the adoption of the initiative, referendum, recall, and direct primary. Also on the state level, the Progressives worked to restrict the activities of lobbyists, to prohibit political contributions by corporations, and to forbid railroads from giving free passes to legislators and other public officials.

Many state legislatures responded to the Progressives' demands for reform by enacting a wide range of social legislation. While some states passed laws prohibiting child labor and regulating work by women, others established minimum wages and maximum hours and health and safety standards in factories. Workmen's compensation laws were also enacted by several states. State after state also regulated utilities, taxed incomes, and made elected representatives more accountable. Other goals of the Progressives at the state level included the direct election of United States senators, prohibition, and women's suffrage. Importantly, a major thrust of Progressive reformers at the state level was to break the alliances between state governments and business.

Wisconsin became something of a model for Progressivism at the state level. Robert LaFollette, elected governor in 1900, was the key figure in Wisconsin; and he pushed for a broad program of political and economic reforms.

Prior to LaFollette's election to the United States Senate in 1906, Wisconsin had adopted the initiative, referendum, and direct primary. The state also (a) established stricter controls over railroads and public utilities, (b) imposed higher taxes on railroads and corporations, (c) placed restrictions on the activities of lobbyists, (d) provided for a merit system in state employment, (e) enacted legislation regulating standards of health and safety in factories, and (f) passed a workmen's compensation law. As governor, LaFollette also pushed for the passage of a state income tax, and this became a reality after he left the governorship.

5.   The American Great Awakening was a series of religious revivals which swept over the American colonies during the second quarter of the eighteenth century, almost simultaneously in New England, the Middle colonies, and the South. It began in different ways in different places, but much of its activity began among the Presbyterians and the Dutch Reformed churches in the Middle colonies. During the 1730s, emotional and passionate revivalists called people back to God by threatening them with eternal damnation for sin. Noted revivalist preachers, like Jonathan Edwards and George Whitfield, magnified the revival into a religious event spreading throughout the colonies.

The preachers of the Great Awakening were often poorly educated; and their exhortations were emotional, popular, and anti-intellectual, frequently touching off extravagant reactions by their audiences. These revivalists maintained that a heart open to the divine spirit was more important than a highly trained intellect and stirred up much strife by accusing conservative, educated clergymen of spiritual coldness. Importantly, these preachers of the Great Awakening rejected Calvinist predestination and taught that the people could earn their own salvation. This simplified message brought thousands of Americans back to religion, increasing the size of old and new denominations. The more popular Protestant denominations — the Baptists, the revivalistic Presbyterians, and Methodists — grew by leaps and bounds. However, the Great Awakening produced a doctrinal split between those who believed in the emotional new way and those who preferred to follow older doctrines, and this weakened the hold of the established churches. Despite its anti-intellectual character, the Great Awakening prompted the establishment of three colonial colleges designed to train ministers for the revivalist wing of the sponsoring denominations: the Presbyterians' College of New Jersey (Princeton, 1746), the Baptist College of Rhode Island (Brown, 1764), and the Dutch Reformed Church's Queen's College (Rutgers, 1766).

In terms of pure religion, it is impossible to estimate the effects of the Great Awakening; but its social significance was immense. It brought more people into the Protestant churches which it also helped to splinter. By the end of the eighteenth century, America had so many different religions that religious conformity could not be imposed. The Great Awakening also prompted missionary efforts among the Indians and resulted in the establishment of Dartmouth College for the Indians. Also, before the Revolution, it was a factor in creating opposition to royal officials, who generally supported the Anglican church. The Great Awakening created a democratic spirit in religion similar to that which was urging the colonists toward political independence.

PRACTICE TEST 6

AP United States History

AP United States History

PRACTICE TEST 6

SECTION I

TIME: 55 Minutes
80 Questions

DIRECTIONS: Each of the questions or incomplete statements below is followed by five suggested answers or completions. Select the one that is best in each case.

---

1. In the Kentucky and Virginia Resolutions, Thomas Jefferson and James Madison asserted that

    (A) the states, not the Supreme Court, were the final judges of the limits of federal power

    (B) the states were creations of the federal government

    (C) the federal judiciary was the sole arbiter of the constitutionality of federal and state laws

    (D) the "implied powers" of the Constitution gave the president the power to enforce the Alien and Sedition Acts

    (E) a "dual presidency" modelled on ancient Rome's consulship would serve to protect the states from the federal government

2. John C. Calhoun's political theory that the states were the only proper judges of whether the federal government had exceeded the powers delegated to it was known as the doctrine of

    (A) judicial review

    (B) preemption and graduation

    (C) nullification

    (D)   abolitionism

    (E)   checks and balances

3.   Identify the source of the following citation: "…the American continents… are henceforth not to be considered as subjects for future colonization by any European powers…." and the "policy [of the United States] in regard to Europe…is not to interfere in the internal concerns of any of its powers…."

    (A)   Washington's "Farewell Address"

    (B)   Preamble to treaty with France for the purchase of Louisiana

    (C)   Monroe Doctrine

    (D)   Washington's "Proclamation of Neutrality"

    (E)   Treaty of Ghent ending the War of 1812

4.   At the Seneca Falls women's rights convention organized by Lucretia Mott and Elizabeth Cady Stanton in 1848, the delegates

    (A)   organized a political party to nominate candidates for public office

    (B)   unanimously endorsed the ratification of an amendment to the Constitution giving women the right to vote in national elections

    (C)   accepted the prevailing notion that women were endowed with weaker intellectual abilities than men

    (D)   issued the pamphlet *Treatise on Domestic Economy*, instructing women on how to make their homes more efficient and more moral

    (E)   declared that "all men and women are created equal" and that "the history of mankind is a history of repeated injuries and usurpations on the part of man toward woman…"

5.   In 1831, Nat Turner organized and led a slave insurrection in Southhampton County, Virginia, that resulted in

    (A)   the gradual and compensated emancipation of the majority of slaves in Virginia

    (B)   increased miscegenation between the white and slave populations of the slave states

    (C)   the immediate emancipation and eventual transportation of Nat Turner and his followers to Santo Domingo

(D)   Congress passing a stringent fugitive slave law

(E)   the Southern states expanding their militia systems and strengthening the slave codes

6.   At the Hartford Convention which was held from December 15, 1814, to January 5, 1815, the Federalist delegates did all the following EXCEPT

(A)   manifested their discontent with the War of 1812

(B)   asserted the doctrine of states' rights

(C)   recommended a constitutional amendment which would require a two-thirds vote of Congress to declare war and admit new states

(D)   renominated DeWitt Clinton, governor of New York, for president

(E)   attempted to secure financial assistance from Washington because the shores of New England were being blockaded by British squadrons

7.   In 1914, President Woodrow Wilson sent General John J. Pershing into Mexico with the purpose of ending raids on United States soil and capturing

(A)   Pancho Villa   (D)   Venustiano Carranza

(B)   Porfirio Diaz   (E)   Victoriana Huerta

(C)   Francisco Madera

8.   The case of Nicola Sacco and Bartolomeo Vanzetti in the 1920s best illustrated

(A)   America's "Return to Normalcy"

(B)   the lack of compassion toward immigrants

(C)   the treatment of Italians

(D)   the reckless vigilante spirit that existed in the Southern states

(E)   the extent of the "Red Scare"

9.   W. C. Handy, Joe "King" Oliver, and "Jelly Roll" Morton were known for their accomplishments in

(A)   jazz   (D)   boxing

(B)   baseball   (E)   football

(C)   the civil rights movement

10. The Reconstruction Finance Corporation and the Home Loan Bank Act of 1932 were enacted during what United States president's administration to help ease the effects of the Great Depression?

    (A) Herbert Hoover   (D) William H. Taft

    (B) Franklin D. Roosevelt   (E) Harry S. Truman

    (C) Calvin Coolidge

11. Abraham Lincoln's Emancipation Proclamation

    (A) freed the slaves in the border states and the District of Columbia

    (B) freed the slaves only in those areas still in rebellion in the South

    (C) freed the slaves only in those areas of the South occupied by the Union army

    (D) authorized Union officers to free slaves only if the masters were compensated

    (E) provided for the resettlement of freed slaves in Africa

12. McCarthyism in the 1950s was an attempt to reveal

    (A) communist infiltration in the United States government

    (B) corruption in the Truman administration

    (C) the plot to sell weapons to belligerent nations

    (D) misuse of corporate funds for political purposes

    (E) the dangers of nuclear energy

13. The jury in the 1735 trial of John Peter Zenger for the seditious libel of New York's governor

    (A) found Zenger guilty of fostering "an ill opinion of the government"

    (B) declared that the governor could censor the press

    (C) asserted that restrictions on the freedom of the press were unconstitutional

    (D) could not reach a verdict and dismissed the charges against Zenger

    (E) acquitted Zenger of libel because his criticism of the governor had been true

14. The first permanent European settlement in North America was

   (A) Jamestown, in what is now Virginia

   (B) New Orleans, in what is now Louisiana

   (C) Santa Fe, in what is now New Mexico

   (D) St. Augustine, in what is now Florida

   (E) Mobile, in what is now Alabama

15. The headright system adopted in the Virginia colony

   (A) determined the eligibility of a settler for voting and holding office

   (B) toughened the laws applying to indentured servants

   (C) gave 50 acres of land to anyone who would transport himself to the colony

   (D) encouraged the development of urban centers

   (E) prohibited the settlement of single men and women in the colony

16. Roger Williams believed that

   I. religious dissenters should be expelled from any colony

   II. the state should not impose any authority in matters of faith

   III. ministers should assume more authority in governmental matters

   IV. colonists had no right to land until it was purchased from the Indians

   (A) I and II only   (D) I, II, and III only

   (B) II and III only   (E) I, II, III, and IV

   (C) II and IV only

17. By 1730 Blacks were a majority of which mainland English colony's population?

   (A) Virginia   (D) Georgia

   (B) Maryland   (E) North Carolina

   (C) South Carolina

18. Which of the following tribes was the ancestor of the Pueblo Indians?

    (A) Oneida   (D) Anasazi

    (B) Creek   (E) Aztecs

    (C) Choctaw

19. The famous cartoon of 1754 by Benjamin Franklin offered a warning to the 13 colonies if they did which of the following?

U.S. Library of Congress.

    (A) Refused to enter the Seven Years' War

    (B) Continued to follow the British policy of merchantilism

    (C) Did not protest the Stamp Act

    (D) Continued trading with French Canada

    (E) Rejected the Albany Plan

20. During the colonial period, most of the attempts to abolish slavery were led by

    (A) Anglican bishops

    (B) Quakers

    (C) the yeoman farmers of the South

    (D) the free black population of New England

    (E) Methodist ministers

21. At the beginning of the eighteenth century, how did the English colonies differ from the Spanish colonies in the Americas?

    (A) Spain permitted its colonies a greater degree of self-government.

    (B) While private investment was responsible for the development of the Spanish colonies, royal money was primarily responsible for the development of the English colonies.

    (C) The compact pattern of Spanish settlements sharply contrasted with the English pattern of far-flung settlements.

    (D) Unlike the Spanish, the English allowed settlers from a variety of nationalities and dissenting sects.

    (E) The Spanish colonies were more responsive to the new circumstances of the Americas than the English colonies.

22. The new constitutions adopted by the states during the American Revolution vested power in the

    I.   courts
    II. legislatures
    III. governors

    (A) I only   (D) I and II only

    (B) II only   (E) II and III only

    (C) III only

23. The measure passed by the Confederation Congress prohibiting slavery in the Western territories above the Ohio River was the

    (A) Northwest Ordinance   (D) Treaty of Paris, 1783

    (B) Articles of Confederation (E) Homestead Act

    (C) Proclamation of 1763

24. In which of the following areas of America did the French mostly settle?

    (A) Hudson Bay

    (B) Chesapeake Bay

    (C) St. Lawrence River Valley and the West Indies

    (D)   Hudson Valley

    (E)   Delaware Valley

25.   The Connecticut Compromise settled the Constitutional Convention's deadlock over

    (A)   taxation

    (B)   the regulation of foreign trade

    (C)   the requirements for voting in national elections

    (D)   representation in Congress

    (E)   the presidential veto

26.   The Continental Congress adopted the Articles of Confederation in November 1777, but the states did not ratify them until March 1781. This delay was caused by

    (A)   the reluctance of New England merchants to give the central government the power to regulate foreign commerce

    (B)   the opposition of Southern planters to giving the central government the authority to impose tariffs

    (C)   the issue of whether the Congress or the states would administer the lands in the West

    (D)   disputes over the claims to Indian lands within the states

    (E)   the debate over the powers of the judicial branch of the central government

27.   Under the Articles of Confederation,

    I.   the national government did not have the power to impose taxes on the citizens of the states

    II.   the states were to retain their individual sovereignty and each, regardless of population, was to have one vote in the Confederation Congress

    III.   there was to be no single, separate, powerful executive

    IV.   an amendment required the approval of all the states

    (A)   I only   (D)   I, II, and III only

    (B)   II only   (E)   I, II, III, and IV

    (C)   I and II only

28. The Bill of Rights

    I.   delegated to the federal government all the rights not specifically given to the states

    II.   extended the franchise to all white male adult property owners

    III.   guaranteed the right to freedom of speech, press, and religion

    IV.   established a viable two-party political system

    (A) I only   (D) I, III, and IV only

    (B) II only   (E) I, II, III, and IV

    (C) III only

29. Which of the following authors is NOT correctly paired with a novel or short story that he wrote?

    (A) Herman Melville: *Moby Dick*

    (B) James Fenimore Cooper: *Conspiracy of Pontiac*

    (C) Nathaniel Hawthorne: *The Scarlet Letter*

    (D) Washington Irving: "Rip Van Winkle"

    (E) Edgar Allan Poe: "The Fall of the House of Usher"

30. The Supreme Court's decision in *McCulloch v. Maryland*

    I.   weakened the implied powers of the Congress

    II.   asserted the principle of strict and limited construction of the Constitution

    III.   confirmed the Hamiltonian, or "loose," interpretation of the Constitution

    IV.   established the constitutionality of the Bank of the United States

    (A) I only   (D) II, III, and IV only

    (B) I and II only   (E) III and IV only

    (C) I, II, and III only

31. The Republican party that developed around Thomas Jefferson and James Madison in its early stages

    (A) supported legislation for a protective tariff

    (B) favored a strong central government

(C)   was an alliance of local and state groups greatly influenced by parochial issues and personalities

(D)   advocated a broad interpretation of the Constitution

(E)   introduced legislation creating a national bank

32.   In order to secure the support of Thomas Jefferson and James Madison for the federal assumption of state debts, Alexander Hamilton promised

(A)   to resign as Secretary of the Treasury

(B)   to sponsor legislation favoring the expansion of slavery

(C)   to support the locating of a permanent capital for the nation on the Potomac

(D)   to withdraw his proposal for the levying of a protective tariff

(E)   to endorse Jefferson as a presidential candidate

33.   The Whiskey Rebellion among the frontier farmers of western Pennsylvania ended when

(A)   Alexander Hamilton negotiated a reduced tax with the farmers

(B)   Congress agreed to repeal the tax

(C)   the Supreme Court declared the tax unconstitutional

(D)   Washington sent an army to put down the revolt

(E)   Congress levied a high tariff on imported whiskey

34.   Thomas Jefferson hesitated in accepting the Louisiana Purchase because

(A)   it would bring the United States into conflict with the interests of Spain in North America

(B)   Alexander Hamilton and the Federalists opposed expanding the United States west of the Mississippi River

(C)   he believed the Constitution did not give him the authority to acquire new land

(D)   it would involve the United States in an entangling alliance with a European country

(E)   it would open new lands to slavery

35. The United States policy of Lend-Lease in 1940 benefitted what allied nation the most?

    (A) France   (D) Finland

    (B) Great Britain   (E) Sweden

    (C) Denmark

36. According to the following map and table, which state had the greatest degree of urbanization in 1860?

    (A) New York   (D) Massachusetts

    (B) Pennsylvania   (E) Virgina

    (C) Illinois

37. Which of the following represents an 1842 treaty between the United States and Great Britain which was concerned in part with joint Anglo-American efforts to suppress the African slave trade?

    (A) Adams-Onis Treaty

    (B) Webster-Ashburton Treaty

    (C) Clayton-Bulwer Treaty

    (D) Hay-Pauncefote Treaty

    (E) Rush-Bagot Treaty

38. The most persuasive single instrument of antislavery propaganda written in response to the Fugitive Slave Law of 1850 was

   (A) Harriet Beecher Stowe's *Uncle Tom's Cabin*

   (B) Henry David Thoreau's "On Civil Disobedience"

   (C) Hinton Rowan Helper's *Impending Crisis*

   (D) George Fitzhugh's *Cannibals All*

   (E) Frederick Douglass' *My Bondage*

39. Stephen A. Douglas, senator from Illinois, framed the Kansas-Nebraska Act (1854) mainly because he

   (A) wanted Southern support for a transcontinental railroad with a terminus at Chicago

   (B) opposed the doctrine of popular sovereignty

   (C) endorsed the Free-Soil party's creed: "free soil, free speech, free labor and free men"

   (D) wanted Southern support for the presidency

   (E) favored a transcontinental railroad being built through New Mexico

40. The phrase "to the victor belongs the spoils" is closely associated with

   (A) George Washington's "Farewell Address"

   (B) General Cornwallis' surrender at Yorktown

   (C) the Treaty of Ghent ending the War of 1812

   (D) Andrew Jackson's idea concerning patronage and rotation in office

   (E) George Washington's defense of his first cabinet appointments

41. The Church of Jesus Christ of Latter-day Saints (Mormons), Adventists, and Shakers originated

   (A) in Germany during the Protestant Reformation

   (B) in the manufacturing districts of England during the Industrial Revolution

   (C) in the colleges of New England

   (D) in the "Burned-Over District" of upstate New York in the 1830s

   (E) during the American Revolution as a protest to Anglican dogma

42. In response to Andrew Jackson's toast: "Our Union— It must be preserved!," who toasted: "The Union, next to our liberty most dear! May we all remember that it can only be preserved by respecting the rights of the states and distributing equally the benefit and the burden of the Union"?

    (A) Henry Clay   (D) Stephen A. Douglas

    (B) Robert Y. Hayne   (E) John C. Calhoun

    (C) Daniel Webster

43. In the presidential election of 1860, the major issue to Southern slaveowners was the

    (A) passage of a federal slave code

    (B) falling price of cotton and rising cost of slaves

    (C) immediate abolition of slavery

    (D) extension of slavery

    (E) admission of California as a slave state

44. The controversy over the presidential election in 1876 between Samuel J. Tilden and Rutherford B. Hayes arose because

    (A) the Greenback-Labor party's presidential candidate prevented either Tilden or Hayes from winning a majority of the electoral votes

    (B) no candidate received a majority of the popular vote as required by the Constitution

    (C) three Southern states, South Carolina, Louisiana, and Florida, submitted contested electoral votes

    (D) the Democratic party withdrew its nomination of Tilden

    (E) Ulysses S. Grant, the incumbent president, refused to vacate the presidency to either Tilden or Hayes

45. General Winfield Scott's "Anaconda" strategy for securing a Union victory over the Confederate States

    I.   proposed a naval blockade of the European countries shipping the Confederacy military supplies

    II. proposed a naval blockade of the Confederacy's Atlantic and Gulf coastlines

III. proposed to divide and subdivide the Confederacy by gaining control of the Mississippi, Tennessee, and Cumberland rivers

IV. was supported by the press as being prudent and brilliant

(A) I and II only

(D) I, II, and III only

(B) II and III only

(E) II, III, and IV only

(C) III and IV only

46. The "court-packing" scheme proposed by President Franklin D. Roosevelt on February 5, 1937

I. was triggered by Supreme Court decisions that undid much of the first New Deal

II. was withdrawn when a majority of the Supreme Court justices retired

III. became unnecessary when the Supreme Court began reversing previous decisions and upholding New Deal legislation

IV. was replaced by a Judiciary bill that denied the president the power to enlarge the federal courts but conceded badly needed procedural reforms

(A) I and II only

(D) II, III, and IV only

(B) I, II, and IV only

(E) I, II, III, and IV

(C) I, III, and IV only

47. What vice president, charged with accepting bribes and kickbacks while he was a county executive, pleaded *nolo contendere* to tax evasion charges and resigned from office?

(A) Walter Mondale

(D) Nelson Rockefeller

(B) Spiro T. Agnew

(E) Richard Nixon

(C) John C. Calhoun

48. The muckrakers

I. were crusading journalists, novelists, historians, economists, sociologists, and philosophers who exposed corruption in government and business

II.   aroused the public to support consumer protection reforms, direct election of senators, municipal ownership of utilities, and the city-manager system

III.   were partly responsible for the success of the Progressive movement in the period before World War I

(A)   I only   (D)   I and II only

(B)   II only   (E)   I, II, and III

(C)   III only

49.   Helen Hunt Jackson's book entitled *A Century of Dishonor* (1880) recounted

(A)   American imperialism and its effects on the middle class

(B)   discriminatory practices employed by the United States government against African-Americans

(C)   the atrocities of the Spanish-American War

(D)   the long record of broken treaties and injustices against American Indians

(E)   the abuses involving big business trusts in America

50.   The Populist party in the 1890s had a great economic and political impact on the United States mainly due to

(A)   the elimination of the income tax

(B)   its platform that raised the issue of uncontrolled industrial capitalism

(C)   James B. Weaver's advocacy of complete government ownership of all railroads

(D)   the free gold issue

(E)   its fight against the presidential veto

51.   President Woodrow Wilson's idealism led to

(A)   international acceptance of the Fourteen Points

(B)   conflicts with European leaders

(C)   the creation of the United Nations

(D)   the Treaty of Versailles

(E)   conciliation between France, Great Britain, and Germany

52.   The Nineteenth Amendment, added to the United States Constitution in 1920, did which of the following?

(A)   Limited the president to two terms

(B)   Created the federal income tax

(C)   Outlawed the sale and transportation of alcoholic beverages

(D)   Enfranchised women

(E)   Ended prohibition

53.   "All men are created equal...[and] they are endowed by their Creator with certain unalienable rights...among these are life, liberty, and the pursuit of happiness; that to secure these, governments are instituted among men, deriving their just powers from the consent of the governed; that whenever any form of government become destructive of these ends, it is the right of the people to alter or abolish it..."

The above passage from the Declaration of Independence reflects

(A)   the divine right monarchy theory of government

(B)   the principle of anarchism

(C)   John Locke's contract theory of government

(D)   the impact of Thomas Paine's essay *The Rights of Man* on Thomas Jefferson

(E)   Thomas Jefferson's belief in Calvinism

54.   The enclosure movement which had been going on since the sixteenth century in England helped prepare the way for English colonization in North America by

(A)   improving the standard of living of the English factory worker

(B)   displacing farmers and creating a class of unemployed who could migrate to the colonies

(C)   encouraging religious toleration between the Catholics and Protestants

    (D)   increasing the demand for skilled farmers in England

    (E)   forcing Queen Elizabeth to negotiate a treaty with Phillip II of Spain allowing English ships unhindered access to North America

55.   The English colony at Jamestown

    (A)   was developed on a high plateau overlooking the James River

    (B)   was settled mostly by farmers from the rural areas of England

    (C)   nearly collapsed because the colonists refused to cooperate, searched for gold instead of planting crops, and antagonized the Indians

    (D)   survived the "starving time" by forging a temporary alliance with the Spanish

    (E)   was abandoned

56.   The Maryland Act of Toleration (1649)

    I.   was passed in response to the charge that the colony was intolerant toward Protestantism

    II.   was developed when it appeared that Roman Catholics would be outvoted by Protestants in the colony

    III. was repealed when the Puritans gained control of the colony

    IV. provided for the execution of those not accepting the Trinity

    (A)   I and II only   (D)   I, III, and IV only

    (B)   I, II, and III only   (E)   I, II, III and IV

    (C)   I, II, and IV only

57.   During the seventeenth century, French settlements in North America were primarily

    (A)   permanent fishing villages shipping fish to the Catholic countries of Europe

    (B)   shipbuilding centers located near the sources of naval stores

    (C)   places of refuge for French Huguenots wanting to practice their religion

    (D)   commercial agricultural centers depending upon the exporting of wheat and corn

    (E)   forts and trading stations serving the fur traders

58. Which of the following is true of Eastern Woodland tribes?

    (A) No society had much in common with other societies.

    (B) All had strict class systems with nobles and workers.

    (C) All had kinship-based communities.

    (D) All had women in complete religious and political authority.

    (E) All built permanent residential communities.

59. Indentured servants were usually

    (A) slaves who had been emancipated by their masters

    (B) free Blacks forced to sell themselves into slavery by economic conditions

    (C) paroled prisoners bound to a lifetime of service in the colonies

    (D) persons who voluntarily bound themselves to labor for a set number of years in return for transportation to the colonies

    (E) the sons and daughters of slaves

60. General Charles Cornwallis' surrender at Yorktown resulted largely from the

    (A) failure of the British to capture and hold Charleston as a base of operations

    (B) French fleet winning control of the Chesapeake Bay

    (C) mass desertion of Hessians from the British army

    (D) arrival of fresh Spanish soldiers to reinforce Washington's army

    (E) the defection of Benedict Arnold at West Point

61. The French formally recognized American independence and made an open treaty of alliance with the Americans as a result of the

    (A) defection of Benedict Arnold to the British in 1780

    (B) defeat of General Cornwallis at Cowpens and his turn northward

    (C) increasing strength of the Tories in the Southern colonies

    (D) defeat of the Hessians at Trenton

    (E) surrender of Burgoyne at Saratoga

62. As a result of his role as mediator in the Russo-Japanese War peace talks in 1905, Theodore Roosevelt

    (A) received the Nobel Peace Prize in 1906

    (B) won the presidential election of 1912

    (C) antagonized the Chinese government that nearly resulted in war with the United States

    (D) created a cold war atmosphere between the United States and Russia

    (E) signed the Treaty of Sakhalin Island that ended the war

63. The Virginia Plan presented to the Constitutional Convention by Governor Edmund Randolph on behalf of the Virginia delegation

    (A) urged the delegates to scrap their instructions to revise the Articles of Confederation and to submit an entirely new document to the states

    (B) provided for a unicameral national legislature

    (C) proposed the election of a "National Executive" by a direct vote of the people

    (D) eliminated all property requirements for either voting or holding office

    (E) failed to provide for a national judiciary

64. In opposing ratification of the Constitution, Anti-Federalists

    I. contended that the Constitutional Convention had exceeded its instructions and the document was illegal

    II. demanded a bill of rights to protect individuals from the central government

    III. stressed that the Constitution was counterrevolutionary because it undermined the prerogatives of state and local government

    IV. found the ratification process highly irregular and illegal under the Articles of Confederation

    (A) I and II only   (D) II, III, and IV only

    (B) II and III only   (E) I, II, III, and IV

    (C) III and IV only

65. In *An Economic Interpretation of the Constitution*, Charles A. Beard argued

    (A) the continued existence of the United States as a world power depended upon acceptance of the Constitution

    (B) the men who wrote the Constitution were selfish men who wanted to protect their own interests

    (C) the Constitution was sponsored by debtors in an effort to reduce the powers of government over them

    (D) the men who wrote the Constitution were not wealthy but were yeomen farmers, mechanics, and small businessmen

    (E) the opponents of the Constitution held their wealth primarily in property, government securities, and other kinds of paper wealth

66. The Battle of New Orleans in 1815

    I.   resulted in the emergence of Andrew Jackson as a military hero

    II.   ended the possibility of a British Empire on the lower Mississippi River

    III. strengthened the Federalist party's grip on the national government

    IV.   assured the ratification of the treaty ending the war without notable changes by the British

    (A) I and II only   (D) I, II, and III only

    (B) II and III only   (E) I, II, and IV only

    (C) III and IV only

67. The greatest support for the War of 1812 came from

    (A) New England merchants who blamed the decline of foreign trade on Great Britain

    (B) Roman Catholics who wanted to bring the Catholic population of Quebec into the Union

    (C) the agricultural areas of the South and West

    (D) military leaders who wanted to end the Spanish presence in the trans-Mississippi West

    (E) the areas of New England and the Middle States where commerce and international trade were primary occupations

68. In his "Farewell Address" of 1796, George Washington

    (A) indicated his belief that political parties were necessary for the survival of democracy

    (B) urged the nation to avoid permanent alliances of any sort with foreign powers

    (C) denounced American isolationism in world affairs

    (D) endorsed the presidential candidacy of Alexander Hamilton

    (E) condemned Thomas Jefferson's presidential aspirations

69. The United States Supreme Court ruled in *Brown v. Board of Education* (1954) that

    I.   segregation in public schools was unconstitutional

    II.   the schools of Topeka, Kansas, must integrate

    III. the decision in *Plessy v. Ferguson* was unconstitutional

    IV.   separate was not equal

    (A) I and II only   (D) I, II, and III only

    (B) II and III only   (E) I, II, III, and IV

    (C) III and IV only

70. The following 1871 cartoon by Thomas Nast suggests what?

U.S. Library of Congress.

    (A)   Justice prevails in New York

    (B)   Political influence is sold for cash

    (C)   The wealthy control New York politics

    (D)   New York government is inefficient

    (E)   The people are being well-served by New York government

71.   In *Dred Scott v. Sanford*, the Supreme Court ruled that

    (A)   the Missouri Compromise violated the Constitution

    (B)   slaves were federal citizens and therefore could bring suit in federal courts

    (C)   slavery was a nationwide institution and was excluded only where states specifically abolished it

    (D)   Congress had the right to bar slavery from any territory

    (E)   Dred Scott was free

72.   In the 1850s, an economic cause of increasing sectional conflict was the decreasing importance of

    (A)   cotton exports   (D)   New York City as a port

    (B)   wheat exports   (E)   indigo exports

    (C)   the Mississippi River

73.   Before the radicalization of the antislavery movement in the 1830s, most of those who opposed slavery agreed that the best solution to the problem was

    (A)   to declare all slaves to be indentured servants with a term of service of ten years

    (B)   to compensate the slaveowners for the immediate emancipation of their slaves

    (C)   to colonize freed slaves in Africa

    (D)   to impose economic sanctions on slaveowners

    (E)   to provide for the emancipation of the children of slaves

74.   In the presidential campaign of 1860, Abraham Lincoln ran on a platform that

    (A)   reaffirmed the Republican party's support of John Brown

    (B)   proposed the immediate abolition of slavery in the states

(C) supported the passage of a fugitive slave code

(D) promised to protect the rights of each state "to order and control its own domestic institutions"

(E) avoided the issue of slavery in the states and territories

75. In undertaking to reconstruct the defeated Confederate states, it was President Andrew Johnson's view that they

(A) had committed "state suicide" by seceding from the Union

(B) were to be treated as conquered territory

(C) had never actually been out of the Union

(D) should be made to indemnify the government for the cost of the war

(E) should never be readmitted to the Union

76. The main dispute that delayed ratification of the Articles of Confederation by the newly independent states of the United States was

(A) disagreement about the nature and composition of the national legislature

(B) disagreement about the powers and method of selecting a national president

(C) the refusal of some states to give up separate treaties made independently between themselves and foreign countries

(D) the refusal of some states to give up extensive claims to the lands west of the Appalachians

(E) the reluctance of slaveholding states to join in a union with states that considered slavery to be evil

77. "There is no right to strike against the public safety, anywhere, any time," was said by

(A) Rutherford B. Hayes with regard to the Great Railroad Strike of 1877

(B) Grover Cleveland on sending federal troops to help put down the Pullman strike

(C) Calvin Coolidge on calling out the Massachusetts National Guard during the Boston police strike

(D) Senator Robert A. Taft speaking in favor of the Taft-Hartley Act

(E) Ronald Reagan with regard to the air traffic controllers' strike

78. In founding the colony of Georgia, James Oglethorpe's primary purpose was to

(A) provide a refuge for persecuted English Quakers

(B) provide a refuge for persecuted Christians of all sects from all parts of Europe

(C) gain a base for launching English expeditions against Spanish-held Florida

(D) make a financial profit

(E) provide a refuge for English debtors

79. Under the crop lien system, a farmer

(A) borrowed money against his next harvest in order to buy more land

(B) borrowed money against the pervious year's harvest, which was stored in warehouses until the market was favorable for selling

(C) was likely to diversify the crops he planted

(D) mortgaged his next harvest to a merchant in order to buy seed and supplies and support his family

(E) could usually become completely debt-free within seven to 10 years

80. The Truman Doctrine was issued in response to

(A) the threat of Communist expansion in Greece and Turkey

(B) the devastated economic condition of post-war Europe

(C) the threat presented by the Red Army in Central Europe

(D) the Communist North Korean invasion of South Korea

(E) the Communist threat to South Vietnam

STOP
This is the end of Section I.
If time still remains, you may check your work only in this section.
Do not begin Section II until instructed to do so.

SECTION II

TIME: Reading Period – 15 Minutes
       Writing Time for all Essays – 115 Minutes

> **DIRECTIONS:** Read over the Document-Based Essay question in Part A and the choices in Parts B and C during the Reading Period, and use the time to organize answers. All students must answer Part A (the Document-Based Essay question) and answer ONE question in both Parts B and C.

PART A – DOCUMENT-BASED ESSAY
(Suggested writing time: 45 minutes)

1. By 1836, the abolitionists had radicalized the antislavery movement.

    Evaluate this statement using the following documents and your knowledge of United States history from 1776 to 1836.

Document A

Source: Inquiry into the Character and Tendency of the American Colonization and American Anti-Slavery Societies by William Jay (1838)

On the 23d December, 1816, the Legislature of Virginia passed a resolution requesting the Governor to correspond with the President of the United States, "for the purpose of obtaining a territory on the coast of Africa, or at some other place not within any of the States, or territorial governments of the United States, to serve as an asylum for such persons of colour as are now free, and may desire the same, and for those who may thereafter be emancipated within this commonwealth."

Within a few days of the date of this resolution, a meeting was held at Washington to take this subject into consideration. It was composed almost entirely of Southern gentlemen. Judge Washington presided; Mr. Clay, Mr. Randolph and others, took part in the discussions which ensued, and which resulted in the organization of the American Colonization Society. Judge Washington was chosen President, and of the seventeen Vice Presidents, only five were selected from the free States, while the twelve managers were, it is believed, without one exception, slave-holders.

The first two articles of the constitution, are the only ones relating to the object of the Society. They are as follows:

Art. I. This Society shall be called the American Society for colonizing the free people of colour of the United States.

Art. II. The object, to which its attention is to be exclusively directed, is to promote and execute a plan for colonizing (with their consent) the free people of color residing in our country in Africa, or such other place as Congress shall deem most expedient. And the Society shall act to effect this object in co-operation with the general government and such of the States as may adopt regulations on the subject.

It is worthy of remark, that this constitution has no preamble setting forth the motives which led to its adoption, and the sentiments entertained by its authors. There is no single principle of duty or policy recognized in it, and the members may, without inconsistency, be Christians or Infidels: they may be the friends of enemies of slavery, and may be actuated by kindness or by hatred towards "the free people of colour."

Document B

Source: "Fourth of July Oration" delivered by Peter Williams, pastor of St. Phillips Episcopal Church in New York (1830)

We are the NATIVES of this country, we ask only to be treated as well as FOREIGNERS. Not a few of our fathers suffered and bled to purchase its independence; we ask only to be treated as well as those who fought against it. We have toiled to cultivate it, and to raise it to its present prosperous condition; we ask only to share equal privileges with those who come from distant lands, to enjoy the fruits of our labour. Let these moderate requests be granted, and we need not go to Africa nor anywhere else to be improved and happy. We cannot but doubt the purity of the motives of those persons who deny us these requests, and would send us to Africa to gain what they might give us at home.

The African Colonization Society is a numerous and influential body. Would they lay aside their own prejudices, much of the burden would be at once removed; and their example (especially if they were as anxious to have justice done us here as to send us to Africa) would have such an influence upon the community at large as would soon cause prejudice to hide its deformed head.

But, alas! the course which they have pursued has an opposite tendency. By the scandalous misrepresentations which they are continually giving of our character and conduct we have sustained much injury, and have reason to apprehend much more.

Document C

Source: "Walker's Appeal in Four Articles; together with a Preamble, to the Coloured Citizens of the World, but in Particular, and very expressly, to those of the United States of America," by David Walker (1829)

I speak Americans for your good. We must and shall be free I say, in spite of you. You may do your best to keep us in wretchedness and misery, to enrich you and your children, but God will deliver us from under you. And wo, wo, will be to you if we have to obtain our freedom by fighting. Throw away your fears and prejudices then, and enlighten us and treat us like men, as we will like you more than we do now hate you, and tell us now no more about colonization, for America is as much our country, as it is yours. Treat us like men, and there is no danger but we will all live in peace and happiness together. For we are not like you, hard hearted, unmerciful, and unforgiving. What a happy country this will be, if the whites will listen. What nation under heaven will be able to do any thing with us, unless God gives us up into its hand? But Americans, I declare to you, while you keep us and our children in bondage, and treat us like brutes, to make us support you and your families, we cannot be friends. You do not look for it, do you? Treat us then like men, and we will be your friends. And there is not a doubt in my mind, but that the whole of the past will be sunk into oblivion, and we yet, under God, will become a united and happy people. The whites may say it is impossible, but remember that nothing is impossible with God.

Document D

Source: The Liberator (January 1, 1831)

Assenting to the "self evident truth" maintained in the American Declaration of Independence, "that all men are created equal, and endowed by their Creator with certain inalienable rights — among which are life, liberty and the pursuit of happiness," I shall strenuously contend for the immediate enfranchisement of our slave population. In Park-Street Church, on the Fourth of July, 1829, in an address on slavery, I unreflectingly assented to the popular but pernicious doctrine of gradual abolition. I seize this opportunity to make a full and unequivocal recantation, and thus publicly to ask pardon of my God, of my country, and of my brethren the poor slaves, for having uttered a sentiment so full of timidity, injustice and absurdity. A similar recantation, from my pen, was published in the *Genius of Universal Emancipation* at Baltimore, in September, 1829. My conscience is now satisfied.

I am aware that many object to the severity of my language; but is there not cause for severity? I will be as harsh as truth, and as uncompromising as justice. On this subject I do not wish to think, or speak, or write, with moderation. No! No! Tell a man whose house is on fire, to give a moderate alarm; tell him to moderately rescue his wife from the hands of the ravisher; tell the mother to gradually extricate her babe from the fire into which it has fallen; — but urge me not to use moderation in a cause like the present. I am in earnest — I will not equivocate — I will not excuse — I will not retreat a single inch — AND I WILL BE HEARD. The apathy of the people is enough to make every statue leap from its pedestal, and to hasten the resurrection of the dead.

Document E

Source: "The American Anti-Slavery Society: Constitution" (December 4, 1833)

Art. II. The object of this Society is the entire abolition of Slavery in the United States. While it admits that each State, in which Slavery exists, has, by the Constitution of the United States, the exclusive right to legislate in regard to its abolition in said State it shall aim to convince all our fellow-citizens, by arguments addressed to their understandings and consciences, that Slaveholding is a heinous crime in the sight of God, and that the duty, safety, and best interests of all concerned, require its immediate abandonment, without expatriation. The Society will also endeavor, in a constitutional way to influence Congress to put an end to the domestic Slave trade, and to abolish Slavery in all those portions of our common country which come under its control, especially in the District of Columbia, — and likewise to prevent the extension of it to any State that may be hereafter admitted to the Union.

Art. III. This Society shall aim to elevate the character and condition of the people of colour by encouraging their intellectual, moral, and religious improvement, and by removing public prejudice, that thus they may, according to their intellectual and moral worth, share an equality with the whites, of civil and religious privileges; but this Society will never, in any way, countenance the oppressed in vindicating their rights by resorting to physical force.

Document F

Source: The American Anti-Slavery Society's "Particular Instructions" to Theodore Weld (1834)

Our object is the overthrow of American slavery, the most atrocious and oppressive system of bondage that has existed in any country. We expect to accomplish this, mainly by showing to the public its true character and legitimate fruits, its contrariety to the first principles of religion, morals, and humanity, and its special inconsistency with our pretensions, as a free, humane, and enlightened people. In this way, by the force of truth, we expect to correct common errors that prevail respecting slavery, and to produce a just public sentiment, which shall appeal both to the conscience and love of character, of our slave-holding fellow citizens, and convince them that both their duty and their welfare require the immediate abolition of slavery.

You will inculcate everywhere the great fundamental principle of IMMEDIATE ABOLITION, as the duty of all masters, on the ground that slavery is both unjust and unprofitable. Insist principally on the SIN OF SLAVERY, because our main hope is in the consciences of men, and it requires little logic to prove that it is always safe to do right. To question this is to impeach the superintending Providence of God.

PARTS B AND C – STANDARD ESSAY QUESTIONS
(70 minutes)

> **DIRECTIONS:** Choose ONE question each from Part B and Part C. It is recommended that you spend 5 minutes planning and 30 minutes writing. Support your thesis with germane historical evidence and present your case logically and clearly.

PART B

2. How did the problem of slavery in the territories create tensions that contributed to the breakup of the Union in 1860–61?

3. In the late 1800s, the United States embarked on a new wave of expansionism during which it acquired overseas territories. Explain the reasons for this new wave of expansionism.

PART C

4. How did the "Old Immigration" of the 1840s and 1850s differ from the "New Immigration" that began in the 1880s?

5. Who were the muckrakers? Why were they important to Progressivism?

AP UNITED STATES HISTORY

PRACTICE TEST 6

ANSWER KEY

1. (A)	21. (D)	41. (D)	61. (E)
2. (C)	22. (B)	42. (E)	62. (A)
3. (C)	23. (A)	43. (D)	63. (A)
4. (E)	24. (C)	44. (C)	64. (E)
5. (E)	25. (D)	45. (B)	65. (B)
6. (D)	26. (C)	46. (C)	66. (E)
7. (A)	27. (E)	47. (B)	67. (C)
8. (E)	28. (C)	48. (E)	68. (B)
9. (A)	29. (B)	49. (D)	69. (E)
10. (A)	30. (E)	50. (B)	70. (B)
11. (B)	31. (C)	51. (B)	71. (A)
12. (A)	32. (C)	52. (D)	72. (C)
13. (E)	33. (D)	53. (C)	73. (C)
14. (D)	34. (C)	54. (B)	74. (D)
15. (C)	35. (B)	55. (C)	75. (C)
16. (C)	36. (A)	56. (E)	76. (D)
17. (C)	37. (B)	57. (E)	77. (C)
18. (D)	38. (A)	58. (C)	78. (E)
19. (E)	39. (A)	59. (D)	79. (D)
20. (B)	40. (D)	60. (B)	80. (A)

DETAILED EXPLANATIONS
OF ANSWERS

TEST 6

SECTION I

1.   **(A)**

In the Kentucky and Virginia Resolutions, Thomas Jefferson and James Madison evoked the compact theory of the Constitution. They asserted that the federal government had been created by a compact among the states. Since the states had surrendered none of their sovereignty to the federal government, it was an agent of the states. Therefore, the states were the final judges of the limits of federal power.

2.   **(C)**

Nullification was based on the assertion that the Constitution was a compact among the states. Thus, the states were the only proper judges of whether the federal government had exceeded the powers delegated to it by the constitutional compact.

3.   **(C)**

At the urging of Secretary of State John Quincy Adams, President James Monroe decided to address the issue of European colonization in the Americas. On December 23, 1823, in his regular message to Congress, Monroe declared that the era of European colonization in the Americas had ended. Additionally, he pledged that the United States would not intervene in European affairs. These paragraphs in Monroe's annual message to Congress became known as the Monroe Doctrine.

4.   **(E)**

The convention adopted a "Declaration of Sentiments and Resolutions" modelled after the Declaration of Independence in form and language. The ninth resolution of this document demanded that women be given the right to vote, but many delegates believed this demand was too controversial. When the delegates voted on the resolutions, only the ninth resolution was not adopted unanimously.

5.   **(E)**

The ferocity of the Nat Turner insurrection surprised the planters. After the uprising, the slave states reacted by expanding their militia systems, passing new slave codes, strengthening existing slave codes, and severely restricting the activities of slaves.

6.   **(D)**

The Hartford Convention was a manifestation of the discontent of New England Federalists with the War of 1812. Its immediate goal was to secure financial assistance from Washington, because the New England ports were being blockaded by British ships. The convention adopted a series of resolutions, the Hartford Resolutions, that affirmed the doctrine of states' rights and proposed several constitutional amendments. One of the proposed amendments would require a two-thirds vote of Congress to declare war, impose commercial restrictions, and admit new states. The convention did not nominate a presidential candidate.

7.   **(A)**

In August 1914, Venustiano Carranza seized power in Mexico, and Pancho Villa emerged as the leader of an anti-Carranza movement. In January 1916, Villa's forces killed 18 Americans in northern Mexico; and in March, he raided across the border into New Mexico killing 17 Americans. President Wilson secured Carranza's permission and dispatched an American force, commanded by General John Pershing, into northern Mexico in an unsuccessful pursuit of Villa.

8.   **(E)**

Events in Europe as well as this country after World War I convinced many Americans that the Communists and their sympathizers were using the postwar bitterness to secure political power. The apparent success of the Communist revolution in Russia put state and federal law enforcement agencies on their guard against radical uprisings — the Red Scare. In one of the last episodes of the Red Scare, two philosophical anarchists, Nicola Sacco and Bartolomeo Vanzetti, were arrested for a robbery and murder which many believed they did not commit. Despite impassioned agitation for their release, Sacco and Vanzetti were executed in 1927.

9.   **(A)**

Jazz is the result of a 300-year blending of European and West African musical traditions, and it is an art form indigenous to the United States. It originated during the last part of the nineteenth century in New Orleans where pre-dominantly European music patterns drew upon rhythms brought in from the West Indies. W. C. Handy, Joe "King" Oliver, and "Jelly Roll" Morton, black Americans, were known for their accomplishments in jazz.

10.   **(A)**

Although Herbert Hoover opposed direct federal assistance to the needy, he sought to promote the recovery of private business. In January 1932, Congress established, at Hoover's recommendation, a new federal lending agency, the Reconstruction Finance Corporation (RFC). The RFC was authorized to make loans to banks, insurance companies, financial institutions, and railroads. Hoover hoped that these loans would combat deflation in industry and agriculture and contribute to increased employment and purchasing power. He also obtained some reform of the Federal Reserve System and the establishment of home loan banks, together with further capital for existing loan banks, to help prevent mortgage foreclosures.

11.   **(B)**

Prior to the Emancipation Proclamation, the Radicals pushed through Congress legislation abolishing slavery in the territories and the District of Columbia. This legislation was followed by the Second Confiscation Act of 1862 which declared the property of all persons supporting the rebellion to be forfeited and proclaimed escaped or captured slaves to be free. By the time Congress passed the Second Confiscation Act, Lincoln was becoming aware of the value of an emancipation policy in helping to win the war, especially by gaining friends for the Union in Great Britain and France. On January 1, 1863, he issued the Emancipation Proclamation. This proclamation freed only those slaves living in areas in a state of rebellion. Lincoln justified the action on the ground of "military necessity." As the Union armies conquered the areas in rebellion, the freedom proclaimed by the proclamation became meaningful. Not until the Thirteenth Amendment became a part of the Constitution in 1865 was slavery outlawed throughout the country.

12.   **(A)**

In February 1950, shortly after the conviction of Alger Hiss for perjury, Republican Senator Joseph R. McCarthy of Wisconsin claimed that he had a list of Communists and Communist sympathizers in the United States Department of State. He repeated his charge and leveled others about Communist influence in government but never produced any evidence to substantiate them.

13.   **(E)**

John Peter Zenger was accused of seditious libel for publishing criticisms of New York's governor. Zenger was imprisoned for ten months and brought to trial in 1735. Ignoring the established rule in English common law that one might be punished for criticism which fostered "an ill opinion of the government," the jury considered the attack on the governor to be true and found Zenger innocent. Although the libel law remained the same, the jury's verdict emboldened editors to criticize officials more freely.

14.   **(D)**

In 1562, French Huguenots established a short-lived colony at Port Royal, South Carolina, and two years later another at Ft. Caroline, Florida. In response to these attempted French encroachments, the Spanish established an outpost in 1565 in present-day Florida. This Spanish settlement, St. Augustine, became the first European town in the present-day United States. St. Augustine is the oldest urban center in the United States except for the pueblos of New Mexico. In contrast, the first permanent English settlement in North America was Jamestown, founded in 1607.

15.   **(C)**

The colony of Virginia, in desperate need of labor to develop the land, used the headright system to encourage settlement. For each "head" entering the colony, the government issued the "right" to take any 50 acres of unoccupied land. To receive title to the property, the holder of the headright had to plant a crop and construct some sort of habitation. All the southern colonies, Pennsylvania, and New Jersey adopted this system.

16.   **(C)**

Roger Williams was a protégé of Sir Edward Coke and appeared to be destined for a career in law; but after receiving his degree from Pembroke College, Cambridge, he took Anglican orders. Williams soon broke with the Church of England, became a Puritan, and migrated to New England. Soon after arriving in the Massachusetts Bay colony, Williams challenged the legality of its charter, which he condemned for its unfairness to the Indians. He advanced the radical idea that it was wrong for anyone, including the king, to take possession of any land in America without buying it from the Indians. As if this were not enough, Williams denied the authority of civil government to regulate religious behavior. This outspoken opposition to the alliance of church and civil govern-ment turned both the magistrates and ministers of the colony against him. The General Court banished Williams from the colony.

17.   **(C)**

The production of tobacco, rice, and indigo were labor-intensive, and slave labor predominated on the South Carolina rice plantations from the beginning. By 1750, Blacks accounted for nearly half the population of Virginia; and in South Carolina, they outnumbered whites two to one. South Carolina had a black majority through most of the eighteenth century.

18.   **(D)**

The Pueblo tribes, which currently reside in the American Southwest, are de-scendants of the Anasazi people. Beginning in about 1050, the Anasazi began building large apartment-like dwellings under the overhangs of cliffs. These cliff dwellings, located where the current states of Utah, Colorado, Arizona, and New Mexico intersect, were as much as five stories high. Within three hundred years the dwellings were abandoned. A severe drought and internal fighting may have caused the culture's decline. The term anasazi is the Navajo word for "ancient enemies," causing some modern-day descendents to consider it a derogatory name. These modern tribes, which include the Pueblo and Hopi, use the name Hisatsinom, which means "ancient people" in Hopi.

19.   **(E)**

Franklin's famous engraving was intended to muster support for his plan for colonial unity in 1754 known as the Albany Plan. The 13 colonies would not be united under a single plan of government until the American Revolution through the Continental Congress and later the Articles of the Confederation. The Seven Years' War did not begin until 1756, while the Stamp Act was in 1765. The colonies never sought to break from the system of mercantilism and traded with Canada even during the Seven Years' War.

20.   **(B)**

During the colonial period, talk of abolishing slavery was almost nonexis-tent. A few isolated reformers, mostly Quakers, attacked slavery on religious grounds.

21.   **(D)**

The compact pattern of English settlement in North America differed from Spain's far-flung conquests. Geography reinforced England's bent for the concentrated occupation and settlement of its colonies. Although there was a compact pattern of settlement in the English colonies, there was more centralized control in the Spanish colonies. Additionally, the Spanish government tightly controlled immigration to its colonies and generally barred religious and political dissenters. In contrast, the English colonies attracted religious and political dissenters.

22.   **(B)**

The state constitutions adopted during the American Revolution deliberately created governments with weak executive and judicial branches. These state constitutions reflected a deep distrust of despotic royal governors and arbitrary judges. Therefore, the legislatures were invested with sweeping powers. Importantly, the first state constitutions generally included a bill of rights protecting the rights of petition, freedom of speech, trial by jury, etc.

23.   **(A)**

The Northwest Ordinance was a major accomplishment of the Confederation Congress. By excluding slavery from the Northwest, it ensured that the entire North would be free territory. By establishing the precedent that new states would enter the Union on an equal footing with the original 13, it ensured the continued settlement of the West. The ordinance also stipulated that the land and property of the Indians "shall never be taken from them without their permission."

24.   **(C)**

After 1600, the French focused most of their attention in the Americas on the West Indies. Other Frenchmen followed Samuel de Champlain to the St. Lawrence River Valley, where he founded Quebec in 1605. Champlain hoped to establish a profitable fur trade in the area surrounding Quebec.

25.   **(D)**

The Connecticut Compromise, advanced by Oliver Ellsworth and Roger Sherman, was submitted to the Constitutional Convention to break the deadlock created by the rejection of the Randolph Plan and Patterson Plan. The compromise provided for a bicameral legislature. One chamber of the legislature was to have equal representation from each state and the other was to be based on each state's population.

26.   **(C)**

In July 1776, a committee appointed by the Continental Congress reported its "Articles of Confederation and Perpetual Union." Congress debated the articles intermittently for over a year, and in November 1777 adopted the articles and submitted them to the states. Disputes among the 13 states, particularly over the issue of whether Congress or the states would administer the lands in the West, delayed ratification. Six of the states had no holdings beyond the Allegheny Mountains and seven were favored with enormous holdings on the basis of earlier sea-to-sea charters. When it became apparent that the seven states would surrender their western claims to the central government, the Articles of Confederation were ratified.

27.   **(E)**

The Articles of Confederation gave the Confederation Congress the powers of conducting war, maintaining foreign relations, and appropriating, borrowing, and issuing money, but not the powers of regulating trade, levying taxes, or drafting troops. The Confederation Congress would have to petition the states for troops and taxes. The Articles of Confederation did not create a single, separate, powerful executive, but the Confederation Congress was to oversee the execution of the laws through a committee of 13 — one representative from each state. Under the Articles, the states were to retain their individual sovereignty, and each state was to have only one vote in the Confederation Congress. Importantly, *all* 13 states would have to approve any amendment to the Articles.

28.   **(C)**

The Bill of Rights, the first ten amendments to the Constitution, was proposed by Congress (1789) and ratified by the states (1791). The first nine amendments limited Congress by forbidding it to encroach upon certain basic rights — freedom of religion, speech, and press, immunity from arbitrary arrest, and trial by jury. The Tenth Amendment reserved to the states all powers except those specifically withheld from them or delegated to the federal government.

29.   **(B)**

The *Conspiracy of Pontiac* (1851) was written by Francis Parkman, a New England historian. This book is the beginning of Parkman's account of the struggle between France and Great Britain for control of North America. James Fenimore Cooper, a novelist, wrote a series of tales focusing on Indians and settlers. *The Last of the Mohicans* (1826) was one of his most famous novels.

30.   **(E)**

In 1819, the Supreme Court expanded the power of the federal government over the states. Maryland had attacked the Second Bank of the United States by taxing its paper-money issues. The issue in *McCulloch v. Maryland* was: (a) did Congress have the power to charter a federal bank? and (b) could the states tax federal property? Maryland held that since the Constitution did not specifically give the federal government the right to charter a national bank, it could not. In rendering the Supreme Court's opinion, Marshall upheld the constitutionality of the Bank of the United States, using the doctrine of implied powers. As for state taxation of federal agencies, Marshall held the Maryland law unconstitutional.

31.   **(C)**

In the early stages of development neither the Federalists nor the Republicans were a tightly organized political party. There were no structured national party organizations with a party chairman, national committee, national convention, etc., for either party. In large measure, both the Federalists and the Republicans were local and state alliances greatly influenced by parochial issues and the personalities of local leaders.

32.   **(C)**

Alexander Hamilton proposed that the federal government assume over $20 million in unpaid debts that the states had incurred in fighting the Revolution. The proposed assumption of these state debts aroused opposition from states, like Virginia, that had already paid off many of their own debts. James Madison was a leader of the opposition.

The proposed assumption was stalled, until Hamilton adroitly connected it with the simultaneous controversy among New York, Pennsylvania, and the Southern states over the permanent location of the national capital. At a dinner, which Madison and Thomas Jefferson attended, it was agreed that the two Virginians would draw off some of the opposition to assumption and that in turn the national capital would be moved for ten years to Philadelphia and then permanently to a ten-mile-square tract on the Potomac River between Virginia and Maryland. This tract was to be selected by Washington.

33.   **(D)**

Alexander Hamilton's revenue proposal included an excise tax on whiskey. The backcountry farmers resisted this tax, and this resistance culminated when the farmers of western Pennsylvania took up arms to prevent the collection of the tax. Washington responded to this challenge by sending a force of 13,000 militiamen to put down the Whiskey Rebellion.

34.   **(C)**

While the Louisiana Purchase more than doubled the size of the United States, it also guaranteed Western farmers access to the Mississippi River as an avenue of trade. Importantly, the purchase of this territory gave the United States control of the port of New Orleans. Jefferson was troubled by the fact that according to his oft-repeated "strict" interpretation of the Constitution, the United States technically lacked the constitutional power to purchase the Louisiana territory. Nevertheless, Jefferson approved its purchase.

35.   **(B)**

The Lend-Lease Act (1941) gave the president the authority to lend or lease equipment to any nation "whose defense the President deems vital to the defense of the United States." During World War II, the United States provided $50 billion in lend-lease aid to its allies, and the British received over $31 billion of the total.

36.   **(A)**

New York had two cities over 100,000 in population and three with between 35,000 and 100,000.

37.   **(B)**

To resolve the problems with Great Britain, President John Tyler instructed Secretary of State Daniel Webster to negotiate with British minister Lord Ashburton. By terms of the Webster-Ashburton Treaty (1842), the United States and Great Britain agreed on a Canadian-American boundary from the Atlantic Ocean to the Rocky Mountains. It was also agreed that each nation would keep a naval squadron off the African coast and enforce its laws concerning the slave trade on those ships flying its flag.

38.   **(A)**

Uncle Tom's Cabin, published in 1852, was a propaganda novel by Harriet Beecher Stowe. Dismayed by the passage of the Fugitive Slave Law, Stowe was determined to awaken the North to the wickedness of slavery by portraying its darker side. The success of the book at home and abroad was sensational. It sold 300,000 copies the first year. It was translated into many foreign languages and also put on the stage as "Tom Shows." The South condemned the book as an "unfair" indictment of slavery. Stowe had never witnessed slavery in the Deep South, but she had lived for many years in Ohio, a center of Underground Railway activity. The story left a profound impression on the North.

39.   **(A)**

After the discovery of gold in California in 1848 and the admission of California to the Union in 1850, the West began to fill up rapidly and there arose a demand for a transcontinental railroad to connect the East with the Pacific Coast. The bone of contention was the location of the Eastern terminus. Should it be in the North or the South? The favored section would reap rich rewards in wealth, population, and influence.

At this point in 1854, Stephen A. Douglas, senator from Illinois, entered with a plan. He had invested heavily in Chicago real estate and in railway stock and was anxious to have Chicago become the eastern terminus of the proposed Pacific Railroad. He would thus (1) endear himself to the voters of Illinois, (2) benefit his own section, and (3) enhance the value of his private holdings. Douglas knew that the South would never favor the creation of a new territory without some concession to slavery, for this territory would soon be carved into free-soil states. In order to secure southern votes for the northern route, Douglas pushed through Congress the Kansas-Nebraska bill.

40.   **(D)**

Andrew Jackson advanced the principle of rotation in office. He held that "no man has any more intrinsic right to official station than another." According to Jackson's reasoning, those holding government jobs for a long time "are apt to acquire a habit of looking with indifference upon the public interests and of tolerating conduct from which an unpracticed man would revolt." Rotation in office meant that more citizens could participate in running the government. This was an advantage in a democracy in that it made the government more responsive to the people. Jackson contended that since the duties of public officials are "plain and simple," rotation in office would present no problems.

41.   **(D)**

The Church of Jesus Christ of Latter-day Saints (Mormons) was founded in 1830 by Joseph Smith in upstate New York. The dedication and economic efficiency of the Mormons attracted a large number of converts, but this close-knit body of poor farmers and artisans was regarded with suspicion by nonbelievers. Smith was eventually murdered by a mob.

42.   **(E)**

John C. Calhoun outlined the doctrine of nullification in the *South Carolina Expositior and Protest*. Since Calhoun was vice president of the United States, he authored the protest anonymously; and it was issued as a committee report of the South Carolina legislature. Only after the failure of the Jackson administration to push tariff reform did Calhoun's supporters begin a campaign in South Carolina for actual nullification. Soon the president and John C. Calhoun clashed openly over nullification. This clash occurred on April 13, 1830, at the Jefferson Day Dinner held in Washington. Andrew Jackson and his secretary of state, Martin Van Buren, agreed that Jackson should present a toast at the dinner and this toast would clearly indicate his opposition to nullification. When Jackson's turn came to present a toast, he pointedly looked at Calhoun and proclaimed: "Our Union — It must be preserved!" Calhoun, responded with a toast in which he announced: "The Union, next to our liberty most dear! May we all remember that it can only be preserved by respecting the rights of the states and distributing equally the benefit and burthen of the Union!" Thus, the battle lines were drawn between the states' righters and the supporters of a strong national government.

43.   **(D)**

In the 1860 presidential election, the Republican platform demanded the limitation of slavery though it did not specify how it was to be achieved. It also deplored disunion, attacked the fanaticism of John Brown, and endorsed the right of each state to control its local institutions, including slavery. Thus, the issue in the 1860 presidential election was the expansion of slavery into the territories and not the abolition of slavery.

44.   **(C)**

In the presidential election of 1876, the Democrats nominated Samuel Tilden, governor of New York and a symbol of honest government. The Republicans nominated Rutherford B. Hayes, governor of Ohio and also a symbol of honest government. Tilden carried states with 184 votes in the electoral college, one short of the necessary majority. Hayes received 165 undisputed electoral votes; but the votes of South Carolina, Florida, and Louisiana were in dispute. To avert any possibility of violence, Congress created a special commission of 15 to pass judgment upon the disputed electoral votes. After a series of maneuvers and compromises, the commission voted to award the disputed electoral votes to Hayes. Therefore, Hayes won the election by one electoral vote.

45.   **(B)**

When the Civil War broke out, Winfield Scott, 75 years old, was general-in-chief of the nation's army. Although a Southerner by birth, Scott opposed secession and remained loyal to the Union. Believing that the conflict would be a long struggle, Scott formulated the "Anaconda" strategy. This plan would (a) impose a naval blockade on the Confederacy's Atlantic and Gulf coastlines and (b) divide and subdivide the Confederacy by pushing southward along the Mississippi, Tennessee, and Cumberland Rivers. Although the newspapers ridiculed Scott's plan of attrition, it remained the Union policy to the end.

46.   **(C)**

After the Supreme Court overturned several important New Deal measures, President Franklin D. Roosevelt and Congress knew further reform legislation faced additional judicial reprimands. Emboldened by his emphatic victory in the 1936 presidential election, Roosevelt decided to confront the issue. Without consulting with the congressional leaders of his party, the president submitted to Congress a Judiciary Reorganization bill on February 5, 1937. This bill would empower the president to appoint a new federal judge whenever an incumbent failed to retire within six months after reaching the age of 70. The number of additional judges would be limited to 50, and not more than six of them could be named to the Supreme Court.

Roosevelt's "court-packing" scheme encountered unexpected opposition in Congress. He was accused of wanting to destroy the Constitution and to establish a personal dictatorship. Nevertheless, it was not congressional opposition alone that persuaded Roosevelt and his advisors to abandon the fight for the bill. The decisive factor was a change in the opinions being delivered by the Supreme Court. The Court's decisions now validated New Deal legislation. Responding to the opposition and the Supreme Court decisions, Vice President John Garner and Senate Majority Leader Alben Barkley came forward with a new bill that denied the presidential power to enlarge the courts but conceded badly needed procedural reforms. Roosevelt signed the Judicial Procedure Reform Act on August 26, 1937.

47.   **(B)**

Vice President Spiro T. Agnew was accused of income tax fraud and of having accepted bribes while county executive of Baltimore County and governor of Maryland. Agnew admitted that he had been guilty of tax evasion and resigned as vice president.

48.   **(E)**

The muckrakers were members of the progressive movement who were instrumental in stirring up public resentment against the existing evils of the time. Theodore Roosevelt compared them to the character in *Pilgrims Progress* who was so busy digging in the muck that he did not have the time to look up to heaven.

49.   **(D)**

Helen Hunt Jackson's book *A Century of Dishonor* (1880) recounted the long record of broken treaties and gross injustices against the Native Americans. She sent a copy to all the members of Congress.

50.   **(B)**

The Populists (The People's Party) raised questions of social, political, and economic consciousness. By incorporating issues in their platform such as the eight-hour day for government employees, government control of big business, a graduated income tax, and government ownership of communications and the railroad, the party enjoyed an appeal to farmers and blue collar workers in the 1890s. The Free Silver Issue that called for the free and unlimited coinage of silver at a ratio of (with gold) 16 to 1 led to the demise of the party.

51.   **(B)**

The leaders of the victorious European powers sought revenge against Germany and did not agree with Woodrow Wilson's conciliatory philosophy. At the peace conference, a fundamental and bitter clash developed between Premier Georges Clemenceau of France and Wilson. While Clemenceau wanted a hard peace that would mutilate Germany and make her harmless in the future, Wilson wanted a "just" peace free of any kind of vindictiveness.

52.   **(D)**

In 1890, the two major women's groups combined as the National American Women's Suffrage Association (NAWSA). NAWSA made women's suffrage its main objective and concentrated on a state-by-state approach. By 1896, Wyoming, Utah, Colorado, and Idaho had been won over to women's suffrage, and California voted for women's suffrage in 1911. The suffragists then shifted the campaign back to the national level. By 1920, three-quarters of the states had ratified the Nineteenth Amendment.

53.   **(C)**

The contract theory of government was developed by political philosophers during the Middle Ages. It challenged the existing absolutism based on the theory of the divine right of kings. The new doctrine gradually gained adherents, and the absolute power of some monarchs was mildly curtailed. The advocacy of the contract theory by John Locke, Jean Jacques Rousseau, and James Harrington helped to gain the support of the intellectual classes and laid the foundations for the English, American, and French Revolutions. The Declaration of Independence, described by Thomas Jefferson as "pure Locke," based its justification of revolution on the violation of the contract by the English government.

John Locke's *Two Treatises on Government* (1690) deeply influenced the thinking of the Revolutionary generation. Locke maintained that life, liberty, and property were the inalienable rights of every individual, and that man's happiness and security were the ends for which government came into existence. In his *Letters on Toleration*, Locke declared that in some circumstances that revolution is not only right but it is also necessary.

54.　　**(B)**

In the Sixteenth century, the English peasants were being forced off the land by the enclosure movement. The landed nobility taking advantage of the demand for wool were turning their farming lands into pastures for sheep. Thousands of dispossessed peasants roamed the countryside as beggars or drifted to the cities.

55.　　**(C)**

Jamestown was established in a malarial swamp, because to the colonists it appeared easily defensible against Indian attack. The settlers lacked the skills that pioneers need, and more than a third of them were "gentlemen" unused to manual labor. The colonists were soon threatened by the neighboring Indians who resented their encroachment. Importantly, when the men in the settlement should have been growing food, they were hunting for gold and piling up lumber, naval stores, and iron ore for export. By January 1608, when a ship arrived with additional men and supplies, about two-thirds of the first arrivals were dead.

56.　　**(E)**

Although Maryland was established as a haven for Roman Catholics, there existed a large Protestant majority in the colony from its beginning. Lord Baltimore solved this problem by accepting a Toleration Act (1649) that gave freedom of religion to anyone "professing to believe in Jesus Christ." Baltimore's Toleration Act was repealed in 1654 during the Cromwellian period and reenacted in 1657. When the Anglican church was made the established religion of Maryland in 1692, the act was again repealed.

57.　　**(E)**

Permanent French settlement in North America began in 1608, the year after the establishment of the English settlement at Jamestown, with the planting of a colony at Quebec. The charter granted by the king to the Company of a Hundred Associates limited the growth of New France. Although the company had a profitable monopoly of the fur trade, it had to limit the European population of new France to French Catholics. This meant that neither the enterprising Huguenots of coastal France nor foreigners of any faith could settle in New France. Therefore, the colony remained a scattered patchwork of Jesuit missionaries, priests, soldiers, *coureurs de bois*, and a few dependent peasants. The *coureurs de bois* ranged the interior of the continent in quest of furs. Louis de Buade, the governor of New France from 1672 to 1682 and 1689 to 1698, encouraged the fur traders and missionaries and converted their outposts into military stations.

58.   **(C)**

The Eastern Woodland tribes were kinship-based communities with tribal groups often consisting of large groups of related individuals. Option (A) is incorrect, as the Eastern Woodland tribes, particularly those that were part of the Iroquois Confederacy, had much in common. Option (B) is incorrect. While tribes of the Mississippi Valley had a strict class system, this did not exist in Eastern Woodland tribes. Option (D) is incorrect because even though women had extensive responsibility, men still were chiefs and religious leaders. Option (E) is incorrect, as many of the Eastern Woodland Indians were nomadic and moved seasonally.

59.   **(D)**

The English colonies in North America were attractive to a large number of poor peasants and laborers. Since they could not afford the price of the Atlantic passage, the solution to their dilemma lay in contracting their labor or in agreeing to be an "indentured servant." In return for having the cost of their passage paid, the indentured servant agreed to work for a specified period of time at a specified wage. Additionally, the employer also often agreed to "freedom duties" at the end of the indenture period.

60.   **(B)**

Weakened by a series of battles, Lord Charles Cornwallis fled to Yorktown on the peninsula between the York and the James Rivers in Virginia in hopes of being evacuated by the British fleet. With fortunate timing and French assistance, Washington marched his force of French and American troops down from the north at just the time the French fleet appeared off the coast of Virginia. Caught between a hostile army and navy, Cornwallis surrendered. This defeat convinced the British that it would be too difficult and too expensive to attempt to put down the rebellion.

61.   **(E)**

After being defeated at the Battle of Brandywine Creek, the American patriots, led by Horatio Gates and Benedict Arnold, forced General John Burgoyne to surrender his entire army at Saratoga in October 1777. This was one of the most significant military victories of the war for the Americans. The victory at

Saratoga prevented the isolation of the New England states and convinced the French that the Americans might well make good their claim to independence. In December 1777, the French recognized the United States as an independent country.

62.   **(A)**

President Theodore Roosevelt believed that a Japanese victory in the war between Japan and Russia would upset the balance of power in Asia. He therefore took an active role in peace negotiations. The result was the Treaty of Portsmouth, New Hampshire, that was signed by the delegates of Russia and Japan. Roosevelt won the Nobel Peace Prize in 1906 for his role in the peace process.

63.   **(A)**

Edmund Randolph and James Madison made the first proposal to the Constitutional Convention — the Virginia Plan. They encouraged not a revision of the Articles of Confederation but a complete new government with separate legislative, executive, and judicial branches. The Virginia Plan called for a bicameral Congress in which representation in both houses would be based upon population. The lower house would elect the members of the upper house, and the two houses combined would elect an executive and judges for the courts.

64.   **(E)**

When the framing of the Constitution was completed, 39 of the 55 original delegates approved and signed the document. The next step was ratification by the states. Opposition came from the Antifederalists who were generally the radicals of the Revolutionary period. They feared a strong central government and objected to (a) the lack of a federal bill of rights, (b) the enlarged powers of the executive, (c) the lessening of the powers of the states; and (d) the concept of dual taxation, i.e., by both state and federal governments.

65.   **(B)**

In 1913, Charles A. Beard advanced the thesis that the delegates to the Constitutional Convention were not true patriots but selfish men out to protect their own interests. According to Beard, the delegates held large amounts of depreciated government securities and stood to gain financially from a strong national government. Forrest McDonald announced in his book, *We the People: The Economic Origins of the Constitution*, published in 1958 that Beard's economic interpretation of the Constitution did not work.

66.   **(E)**

The Battle of New Orleans was in reality a standoff, but the American public, starved for a victory, viewed it as the battle that won the war. The battle was unique in that it had no military value since it was fought two weeks after the treaty ending the war had been signed. Word of the battle reached Washington almost simultaneously with the news of the Treaty of Ghent. In an euphoric atmosphere, the Senate ratified the treaty unanimously.

The Battle of New Orleans made Andrew Jackson a national hero and started him on a career that led to the presidency. Additionally, Jackson's perceived victory in the battle completed the destruction of the Federalist party. The Federalists had not supported the war effort, and they argued that the British could not be defeated. As long as the war remained in doubt, the Federalist opposition to it won considerable support; but the battle of New Orleans made the party an object of ridicule.

67.   **(C)**

In June 1812, President James Madison recommended that Congress declare war on Great Britain. The vote in both houses of Congress clearly showed that the American people were divided over the issue of war. In the House of Representatives the vote was 79 to 49 for war, and in the Senate it was 19 to 13 for war. The division of public opinion was clearly revealed in the presidential election of 1812. DeWitt Clinton of New York was nominated by a peace faction of the Republican party to oppose Madison, and the Federalists supported him. While most of the electors in the Northeast voted for Clinton and peace, all those in the South and West sustained Madison and war.

68.   **(B)**

Washington decided to step down after his second term of office. To make his wishes known to the American people, Washington composed his "Farewell Address." This address was published in a Philadelphia newspaper. In it, Washington warned the nation against political party factionalism and "permanent alliances" with any part of the world.

69.   **(E)**

In May 1954, the United States Supreme Court delivered its decision in *Brown v. Board of Education of Topeka*. In a unanimous decision drafted by Chief Justice Earl Warren, the Supreme Court rejected the doctrine of "separate but equal" in public education. The court declared that separate facilities "are inherently unequal." This decision marked the beginning of the end of segregation; and in the spring of 1955, the court ordered the implementation of the Brown decision.

70.   **(B)**

Boss Tweed's moneybag and the dollar and cents signs indicate that political influence was up for sale. The cartoon does not say who was buying influence nor does it bring up the issue of efficiency.

71.   **(A)**

Dred Scott, a slave and the property of an army surgeon, had been held in bondage in the slave state of Missouri. Later, the army surgeon, Dr. John Emerson, took Scott with him to Illinois and then to Wisconsin, both free-soil states. They resided for five years in the free-soil states and then returned to Missouri. Sponsored by interested abolitionists, Scott sued for his freedom on the ground that his residence in free territory had set him free.

In order that the case might be carried to the United States Supreme Court, Mrs. Emerson, who owned Scott after her husband's death, sold him to her brother, a resident of New York, in a fictitious sale. The case could now be brought into the United States Supreme Court for it was a case between citizens of different states — Scott of Missouri and Sanford of New York.

The court ruled that Dred Scott was a Negro slave and not a citizen, and hence could not sue in the courts. This should have ended the case, but a majority of the justices decided to go further. A final judgment on the larger issue of slavery in the territories seemed desirable. Therefore, a majority of the justices under the leadership of Chief Justice Roger B. Taney added an *obiter dictum*. This decree held that since slaves were private property, they could be taken into the territories and held there — regardless of what Congress or the territorial legislatures might say. The court went even further. It ruled that the now repealed Missouri Compromise, which had forbidden slavery north of 36° 30', had always been unconstitutional.

The South was delighted with this unexpected victory. Slavery could not henceforth be barred in any of the territories as long as they were territories. On the other hand, foes of slavery's extension, especially the Republicans, were infuriated by the Dred Scott setback. Their chief rallying cry had been the banishing of slavery from the territories. They now insisted that the ruling of the court was merely an opinion and not a decision.

72.   **(C)**

Prior to the completion of the Erie Canal, farmers in the Old Northwest depended on the Mississippi River system to get their produce to market. The completion of the Erie Canal resulted in the shifting of the commerce of the Old Northwest from the Mississippi River system to the Great Lakes and the Erie Canal.

73.   **(C)**

In the 1780s, many opponents of slavery began advocating the colonizing of freed slaves in either the West or in Africa. The colonization idea became popular in Virginia in the 1790s, but nothing was achieved until after the founding of the American Colonizations Society in 1817. The society, supported by James Madison, James Monroe, and John Marshall, purchased land in Africa and established the Republic of Liberia. Despite these efforts, the society accomplished little and rapidly declined after about 1830. The decline of the colonization movement was closely tied to the rise of militant abolitionism.

74.   **(D)**

The Republican party platform adopted in Chicago on May 16, 1860, denied "the authority of Congress, of a territorial legislature, or of any individuals, to give legal existence to Slavery in any Territory of the United States." While demanding the limitation of slavery, the platform did not specify how this was to be achieved. The Republican platform denounced the fanaticism of John Brown, deplored disunion, and endorsed the right of each state to control its local institutions, including slavery.

75.   **(C)**

As the Civil War came to its end, Abraham Lincoln was advocating a policy of moderation towards the Confederate States. The Radical Republicans in Congress, led by Charles Sumner of Massachusetts in the Senate and Thaddeus Stevens of Pennsylvania in the House, rejected Lincoln's moderation. In July 1864, Congress passed the Wade-Davis Bill which stated that the Confederate States were to be treated as conquered territory. Lincoln pocket vetoed the bill. Before Lincoln and the Radical Republicans could reconcile their differences, Lincoln was assassinated by John Wilkes Booth. Andrew Johnson succeeded to the presidency. Like Lincoln, Johnson favored a moderate approach to Reconstruction. He also rejected suggestions that the Southern states should be treated as conquered provinces. Following Lincoln's logic, Johnson contended that secession was unconstitutional. Therefore, in a legal sense, the Confederate states had never left the Union.

76.   **(D)**

The ratification of the Articles of Confederation was delayed while some states, such as Maryland, refused to approve until others, such as Virginia, agreed to give up their extensive Western land claims. Disagreement about the nature and composition of the national legislature (A) was present but was less significant in delaying ratification. There could be no disagreement on the powers of the president under the Articles (B), since they provided for none. State treaties with other countries (C) did not exist, and the slavery issue (E) was not yet heated enough to prevent union.

77.   **(C)**

Calvin Coolidge made this statement. Reagan took a similar attitude in his handling of the 1981 air traffic controllers' strike (E). Hayes and Cleveland also took uncompromising attitudes toward such labor disturbances as the Great Railroad Strike of 1877 (A) and the Pullman Strike (B). Senator Robert A. Taft was co-sponsor of the Taft-Hartley Act (D), aimed at restraining the excesses of labor unions.

78.   **(E)**

Oglethorpe's primary purpose was providing a refuge for English debtors. A secondary purpose was carrying on war against Spain (C). Making a financial profit (D) came relatively far down the list for Oglethorpe and his fellow trustees. Some persecuted Christians from various parts of Europe did come to Georgia (B), but Oglethorpe had distinctly mixed feelings about the presence of such "religious enthusiasts." Fifty years prior to the founding of Georgia, Pennsylvania had been founded as a refuge for Quakers (A).

79.   **(D)**

Under the crop lien system, a farmer mortgaged his next harvest to a merchant in order to buy seed and supplies and support his family through the year. It was a system under which a farmer was likely neither to diversify his crops (C) nor get out of debt anytime soon (E). He would hardly be buying more land (A). Some of those who felt trapped in the system expressed through the Farmers' Alliances of the 1880s their desire that the government should loan them money against the previous year's harvest, which would be stored in warehouses until the market was favorable for selling (B), but nothing came of this.

80.   **(A)**

The Truman Doctrine was issued in response to the threat of Communist expansion in Greece and Turkey. The Marshall Plan was issued in response to the devastated economic condition of post-war Europe (B). The threat posed by the Red Army in Central Europe (C) led to the creation of the North Atlantic Treaty Organization, NATO. The Communist invastion of South Korea (D) began the Korean War, and the Communist threat to South Vietnam (E) led to American involvement in the Vietnam War.

SECTION II

Sample Answer to Document-Based Question

1. From the Revolution to the beginning of the abolitionist crusade, few Southern whites showed much disposition to defend slavery. The scattered antislavery groups and publications that existed prior to the 1830s were found mainly in the upper South. These groups and publications urged the masters to free their slaves voluntarily. Most critics of slavery confined themselves to urging "colonization" or persuading slaveowners to treat their property humanely.

The organization of the American Colonization Society in 1817 gave the emancipation movement a new thrust. The society aimed at colonizing freed slaves in Africa, and its supporters included such prominent figures as James Madison, James Monroe, Henry Clay, John Marshall, and Daniel Webster. Some Southern planters supported the society in the hope that exporting freed slaves would strengthen the institution of slavery. In contrast, Northern philanthropists endorsed colonization with the expectation that it would purify American democracy by ridding the country of slaves. Thus, the American Colonization Society embraced two irreconcilable points of view. Nevertheless, both Northern and Southern colonizationists were agreed on one crucial issue—Blacks were inherently inferior to Whites and had no place in a democratic society.

Rejecting the sweeping assumption that free Blacks were not fit to live in the United States, the pioneer abolitionists' first strategic objective in the early 1830s was the destruction of the American Colonization Society. Articulate free Blacks denounced the American Colonization Society from its beginning. They insisted that America was their native land. Most free Blacks were not prepared to accept the premise that they could never prosper in the United States. Peter Williams, pastor of St. Phillips Episcopal Church in New York, emphasized that "not a few of our fathers suffered and bled to purchase its [the United States] independence." Williams stressed that the American Colonization Society had created tensions between Whites and free Blacks "by the scandalous misrepresentations which they are continually giving of our character and conduct."

In the 1830s the antislavery movement moved from favoring gradualism to demanding the immediate end of slavery. The abolitionists argued that slavery was a sin and a crime—a sin because it denied to Blacks the status of human beings, a crime because it violated the natural rights to life, liberty, and the pursuit of happiness guaranteed in the Declaration of Independence. These two beliefs — in the spiritual equality of all believers and the political equality of all Americans — served as the abolitionists' chief weapon in the attack on slavery. Three dramatic events marked the transition from favoring gradualism to demanding immediate emancipation. In 1829, *Walker's Appeal... to the Colored Citizens of the World* appeared. The author of the pamphlet, David Walker, was a free Black. He preached insurrection and violence as a proper response to the wrong that Blacks suffered.

Two other major events closely followed *Walker's Appeal*. On January 1, 1831, William Lloyd Garrison began publication in Boston of a new antislavery newspaper, *The Liberator*. In the paper's first issue, Garrison renounced "the popular but pernicious doctrines of gradual emancipation" and denounced moderation. He promised: "I will be as harsh as truth and as uncompromising as justice. On this subject, I do not wish to think, or speak, or write with moderation...." Approximately three years after Garrison began publishing *The Liberator*, the American Anti-Slavery Society adopted its constitution. Although the society conceded the right of each state to legislate on its domestic institutions, it attempted to convince the nation's white population "that Slaveholding is a heinous crime in the sight of God, and that the duty, safety, and best interests of all concerned require its immediate abandonment, without expatriation." Going beyond the issue of emancipation, the society argued that Blacks should "share an equality with the Whites, of civil and religious privileges." The American Anti-Slavery Society clearly favored emancipation without colonization. Unlike the American Colonization Society, it did not link emancipation to colonization.

Capitalizing on new mass propaganda techniques and the organizational skills of men like Theodore Wild, the American Anti-Slavery Society appealed to the public by demanding the immediate abolition of slavery and by insisting that slavery was a sin. In commissioning Theodore Weld to serve as the society's agent, organizer, and recruiter in Ohio, the society instructed him to "inculcate everywhere, the great fundamental principle of immediate abolition" and to insist that slavery was a sin. Thus, by 1836, the abolitionists had radicalized the antislavery movement by demanding the immediate abolition of slavery without colonization and by making slavery a moral issue — an issue of good versus evil.

Sample Answers to Essay Questions

2. (a) Slavery defined the South in negative terms and set it apart from the North. In the 1830s, Alexis de Tocqueville found the origins of Southern distinctiveness in the institution of slavery. Nearly a century later, the Southern historian U.B. Phillips argued that the "central theme" of Southern history was "a common resolve" by Whites that they should retain their control. He asserted that this resolve led to a sense of racial unity that muted class conflict among Whites. Slavery involved Southerners in its contradictions, and they could neither deal with it rationally nor long endure the tensions and anxieties it generated. The defense of slavery against attacks from other areas of the country gradually affected the thinking of most white Southerners and led them to seek independence. The most fundamental difference between the North and South was slavery. In fact, slavery lay behind much of the economic, political, and intellectual conflict between the sections.

(b) The Louisiana Purchase and Mexican Cession created the necessity of organizing new territories. Therefore, the question of which areas should be free and which should be slave was constantly being resurrected. The Missouri Compromise, the Compromise of 1850, and the Kansas-Nebraska Act were attempts to settle the issue of slavery in the Louisiana Purchase and Mexican Cession.

(c) The Wilmot Proviso (1846) and the Kansas-Nebraska Act moved the debate over slavery in the territories from practicality to principle. The issue was: did slaveholders have the right to move their slaves wherever they wanted? The quarrel over the extension of slavery erupted on the floor of Congress when Representative David Wilmot from Pennsylvania introduced a proviso stipulating that slavery should never exist in any territory that might be acquired from Mexico. Although the Wilmot Proviso was blocked by the South, it served notice on the slaveholders that the extension of slavery into the Mexican Cession territory would be resisted. The extension of slavery became the most important political issue facing the nation after the Wilmot Proviso of 1846. While Wilmot's efforts to limit slavery's expansion angered the Southern members of Congress, the repeal of the Missouri Compromise by the Kansas-Nebraska Act alienated the Northern members of Congress. Importantly, the bill to organize the Kansas and Nebraska territories changed the problem of slavery in the territories into a symbolic issue.

(d) Political opinion on the extension of slavery into the territories broke into three camps — free-soilers, advocates of popular sovereignty, and anti-free-soilers. The free-soilers thought Congress should keep the territories free. The free-soil forces, consolidated by the struggle over the Wilmot Proviso, organized a political party and adopted the slogan: "Free soil, free speech, free labor and free men." In contrast to the free-soilers, the advocates of popular sovereignty were the anti-free-soilers. They argued that Congress had no power to decide the issue of slavery, only a state could decide it.

(e) The civil war in Kansas — "Bleeding Kansas" discredited popular sovereignty and encouraged Northern free-soilers and Southern anti-free-soilers to become more rigid in their stances.

(f) The issue of slavery in the territories put an enormous strain on the Whig and Democratic parties. The Northern and Southern Whigs were badly divided over the slavery issue, and it had cost them the presidential election of 1852. The Kansas-Nebraska Act destroyed the Whig party everywhere in the South except in the border states. Similarly, the Democratic party split over slavery when the Northern Democrats attacked the Kansas-Nebraska Act. Ultimately, all antislavery and anti-Kansas-Nebraska groups united under the banner of the Republican party. The objective of the Republican party was to prevent the further extension of slavery into new territory.

(g) The issue of slavery in the territories was reopened by the Supreme Court's decision in *Dred Scott v. Sanford* (1857). Although the court ruled that Dred Scott was not a citizen and hence could not sue in the courts, the majority of justices under the leadership of Chief Justice Roger B. Taney added an *obiter dictum*. This decree held that since slaves were private property, they could be taken into the territories and held there regardless of what Congress or the territorial legislatures might say. This meant that slavery could not be banned in any of the territories as long as they were territories. The Supreme Court went even further and ruled that the now-repealed Missouri Compromise had always been unconstitutional.

The recently organized Republican party reacted to the Dred Scott decision by insisting that the court's *obiter dictum* was an opinion not a decision. The Republicans continued to advocate the banishing of slavery from the territories. The South was delighted with the decision and insisted that slavery could no longer be barred from any of the territories.

3. By the beginning of the twentieth century, the United States had completed its transcontinental expansion and had gained first place in manufacturing among the nations of the world. As the country's industrial and agricultural output increased, there was a movement to create a commercial empire for the United States in the Caribbean, Central and South America, and Asia. Acquiring new markets for American agricultural and industrial products would increase the profits of the nation's merchants, industrialists, and farmers.

A belief in the superiority of American values and Christianity combined to create a spirit among Americans which encouraged expansionism. Many of the country's political and religious leaders believed that the Anglo-Saxons (the British and the Americans) represented two great ideas: political liberty and a "pure spiritual Christianity." These men asserted that the Anglo-Saxons had been "divinely commissioned" to spread the blessings of democracy and Protestant Christianity throughout the world.

The quest for national glory also played a role in the new wave of expansionism in the late nineteenth century. Many Americans believed that overseas expansion was the natural way to demonstrate the nation's vitality and greatness. These people also believed that the failure to expand was a sign of weakness and decadence. Theodore Roosevelt expressed this spirit of expansionism in the late 1890s. For people like Roosevelt, the pursuit of "national honor" was far more important than achieving any economic gain. The shapers of the nation's foreign policy believed that the United States must prove its power by an aggressive foreign policy.

Captain Alfred Thayer Mahan and his book, *The Influence of Sea Power Upon History* (1890), had a powerful impact on American expansionists. Mahan rejected internationalism in foreign policy for the realism of the struggle for power and national self-interest. He stressed the importance of navies in determining political history and convincingly argued that the development of sea power was the key to promoting the prosperity and greatness of a nation. Mahan urged the United States to develop a great navy and a large merchant fleet. Likewise, the nation should promote its foreign trade. To achieve the new American empire, the United States should acquire naval bases and colonies in both the Caribbean and the Pacific. Mahan also declared that this new American empire should be united by an American-built and an American-operated canal joining the Caribbean Sea with the Pacific Ocean. He believed that all nations either expanded or died and that all of the great nations throughout history were naval powers.

4.   The flow of immigrants into the United States was slow during the late eighteenth and early nineteenth centuries, and fewer than 300,000 immigrants entered the country between 1775 and 1820. The Irish potato blight and a series of crop failures changed this, and in the 1840s and 1850s the number of immigrants coming from Ireland, Germany, and Scandinavian countries increased dramatically ("Old Immigration"). With the advent of the 1880s, the stream of immigrants to the United States began flowing from another source — Eastern and Southern Europe. Among the new ethnic stocks coming to the country were Austrians, Hungarians, Bohemians, Poles, Serbs, Italians, Russians, and Jews from Poland and Russia ("New Immigration").

The "Old Immigration" differed from the "New Immigration" in several ways:

(a) The "old immigrants" came by the thousands from Northwestern

Europe — England, Ireland, Germany, and the Scandinavian countries. In contrast, the "new immigrants" came by the millions from Southern and Eastern Europe.

(b) Although there had been some friction between the "old immigrants" and "native" Americans, the "old immigrants" in culture and outlook were essentially similar to the "native" Americans. Therefore, they were assimilated without too much difficulty. The "new immigrants" provoked more fear and resentment among the "native" Americans than had the "old immigrants." To the "native" Americans, the "new immigrants" seemed strange. They had different cultural and economic standards and spoke a diversity of languages. Additionally, they were in overwhelming numbers Catholics in a predominantly Protestant country.

(c) "Native" Americans discredited the "new immigrants," alleging that they were "inferior," illiterate, and politically backward. Their influx called into existence a short-lived nativist organization — the American Protective Association which was anti-alien and anti-Catholic.

(d) "Native" Americans blamed the "new immigrants" for the disorder, vice, and violence in the cities.

(e) Racist theories proclaiming the supremacy of "Nordics" over "Mediterraneans" were widely accepted by "native" Americans

(f) Of the "old immigrants" only the Irish had tended to live in the Eastern cities. Most of the Germans went West to become farmers. Those Germans who had a proclivity for urban life settled in Midwestern cities. Nearly all the Scandinavians took up land in the Midwest or the Great Plains. The "old immigrant" urban dwellers were — with the exception of the Irish — businessmen, professional men, or skilled laborers. In contrast, the "new immigrants" flocked to the industrial cities (before 1900, primarily those in the East) and became unskilled laborers.

5. The muckrakers were those editors, novelists, journalists, and essayists who dramatized the need for reform by seeking to expose the evils and ills of American society. Muckraking had been inaugurated as a movement in 1881 by Henry Demarest Lloyd in his *Atlantic Monthly* broadside portraying the

methods of the Standard Oil Company. The movement gained momentum in the period of the agrarian revolt, the 1890s.

McClure's Magazine was one of the most important muckraking publications. In late 1902, *McClure's* published the first of a series of articles by Lincoln Steffens who had studied political corruption in a number of American cities. These articles focused on the need for reform in municipal government. *McClure's* also carried Ida Tarbell's first article on the Standard Oil Company.

Muckrakers began to attract attention toward the end of 1902 and were at their peak of popularity in 1906. Although there had long been a literature of exposure, the greatest outpouring of exposé journalism in American history came from the muckrakers. They probed into every national abuse; and they touched the public's nerves, confirmed the popular uneasiness, aroused public opinion, and created local and national support for reforms — consumer protection, the direct election of United States senators, municipal ownership of utilities, and the city manager system. The scale of the revelations by the muckrakers and the rapid attraction of a wide audience was new.

The muckrakers seldom saw beneath the surface, and they did not offer solutions to the problems that they uncovered. The task of analyzing the nature of unrestrained private property and the vulnerability of the ordinary citizen fell to more sophisticated thinkers. In their efforts to save political and economic democracy, the muckrakers enlisted the support of many brilliant critics of American life.

By making the public aware of the issues, the muckrakers contributed to the success of Progressivism. While the muckrakers focused the nation's attention on the problems, the Progressives made a concerted effort to provide the basic social, political, and economic reforms that would solve the problems. The Progressives, like the muckrakers, were responding to the transformation of the United States from a rural, commercial economy to an urban, industrial one.

While Lincoln Steffens, Ida Tarbell, Thomas W. Lawson, and Ray Stannard Baker made substantial contributions to the muckraking movement with their exposé literature and journalism, Henry George and Thorstein Veblen made lasting contributions to economic thought. The writings of Jacob Riis,

Jane Addams, and John Spargo criticized social conditions and exposed political corruption. Writers of fiction — Edward Bellamy, David Graham Phillips, Stephen Crane, Jack London, Frank Norris, and Upton Sinclair — also joined the muckraking movement and produced works that focused on the period's social problems.

Answer Sheets

AP UNITED STATES HISTORY
PRACTICE TEST 1
SECTION I

ANSWER SHEET

1. Ⓐ Ⓑ Ⓒ Ⓓ Ⓔ
2. Ⓐ Ⓑ Ⓒ Ⓓ Ⓔ
3. Ⓐ Ⓑ Ⓒ Ⓓ Ⓔ
4. Ⓐ Ⓑ Ⓒ Ⓓ Ⓔ
5. Ⓐ Ⓑ Ⓒ Ⓓ Ⓔ
6. Ⓐ Ⓑ Ⓒ Ⓓ Ⓔ
7. Ⓐ Ⓑ Ⓒ Ⓓ Ⓕ
8. Ⓐ Ⓑ Ⓒ Ⓓ Ⓔ
9. Ⓐ Ⓓ Ⓒ Ⓓ Ⓔ
10. Ⓐ Ⓑ Ⓒ Ⓓ Ⓔ
11. Ⓐ Ⓑ Ⓒ Ⓓ Ⓔ
12. Ⓐ Ⓑ Ⓒ Ⓓ Ⓔ
13. Ⓐ Ⓑ Ⓒ Ⓓ Ⓔ
14. Ⓐ Ⓑ Ⓒ Ⓓ Ⓔ
15. Ⓐ Ⓑ Ⓒ Ⓓ Ⓔ
16. Ⓐ Ⓑ Ⓒ Ⓓ Ⓔ
17. Ⓐ Ⓑ Ⓒ Ⓓ Ⓔ
18. Ⓐ Ⓑ Ⓒ Ⓓ Ⓔ
19. Ⓐ Ⓑ Ⓒ Ⓓ Ⓔ
20. Ⓐ Ⓑ Ⓒ Ⓓ Ⓔ
21. Ⓐ Ⓑ Ⓒ Ⓓ Ⓔ
22. Ⓐ Ⓑ Ⓒ Ⓓ Ⓔ
23. Ⓐ Ⓑ Ⓒ Ⓓ Ⓔ
24. Ⓐ Ⓑ Ⓒ Ⓓ Ⓔ
25. Ⓐ Ⓑ Ⓒ Ⓓ Ⓔ
26. Ⓐ Ⓑ Ⓒ Ⓓ Ⓔ
27. Ⓐ Ⓑ Ⓒ Ⓓ Ⓔ

28. Ⓐ Ⓑ Ⓒ Ⓓ Ⓔ
29. Ⓐ Ⓑ Ⓒ Ⓓ Ⓔ
30. Ⓐ Ⓑ Ⓒ Ⓓ Ⓔ
31. Ⓐ Ⓑ Ⓒ Ⓓ Ⓔ
32. Ⓐ Ⓑ Ⓒ Ⓓ Ⓔ
33. Ⓐ Ⓑ Ⓒ Ⓓ Ⓔ
34. Ⓐ Ⓑ Ⓒ Ⓓ Ⓔ
35. Ⓐ Ⓑ Ⓒ Ⓓ Ⓔ
36. Ⓐ Ⓑ Ⓒ Ⓓ Ⓔ
37. Ⓐ Ⓑ Ⓒ Ⓓ Ⓔ
38. Ⓐ Ⓑ Ⓒ Ⓓ Ⓔ
39. Ⓐ Ⓑ Ⓒ Ⓓ Ⓕ
40. Ⓐ Ⓑ Ⓒ Ⓓ Ⓔ
41. Ⓐ Ⓑ Ⓒ Ⓓ Ⓔ
42. Ⓐ Ⓑ Ⓒ Ⓓ Ⓔ
43. Ⓐ Ⓑ Ⓒ Ⓓ Ⓔ
44. Ⓐ Ⓑ Ⓒ Ⓓ Ⓔ
45. Ⓐ Ⓑ Ⓒ Ⓓ Ⓔ
46. Ⓐ Ⓑ Ⓒ Ⓓ Ⓔ
47. Ⓐ Ⓑ Ⓒ Ⓓ Ⓔ
48. Ⓐ Ⓑ Ⓒ Ⓓ Ⓔ
49. Ⓐ Ⓑ Ⓒ Ⓓ Ⓔ
50. Ⓐ Ⓑ Ⓒ Ⓓ Ⓔ
51. Ⓐ Ⓑ Ⓒ Ⓓ Ⓔ
52. Ⓐ Ⓑ Ⓒ Ⓓ Ⓔ
53. Ⓐ Ⓑ Ⓒ Ⓓ Ⓔ
54. Ⓐ Ⓑ Ⓒ Ⓓ Ⓔ

55. Ⓐ Ⓑ Ⓒ Ⓓ Ⓔ
56. Ⓐ Ⓑ Ⓒ Ⓓ Ⓔ
57. Ⓐ Ⓑ Ⓒ Ⓓ Ⓔ
58. Ⓐ Ⓑ Ⓒ Ⓓ Ⓔ
59. Ⓐ Ⓑ Ⓒ Ⓓ Ⓔ
60. Ⓐ Ⓑ Ⓒ Ⓓ Ⓔ
61. Ⓐ Ⓑ Ⓒ Ⓓ Ⓔ
62. Ⓐ Ⓑ Ⓒ Ⓓ Ⓔ
63. Ⓐ Ⓑ Ⓒ Ⓓ Ⓔ
64. Ⓐ Ⓑ Ⓒ Ⓓ Ⓔ
65. Ⓐ Ⓑ Ⓒ Ⓓ Ⓔ
66. Ⓐ Ⓑ Ⓒ Ⓓ Ⓔ
67. Ⓐ Ⓑ Ⓒ Ⓓ Ⓔ
68. Ⓐ Ⓑ Ⓒ Ⓓ Ⓔ
69. Ⓐ Ⓑ Ⓒ Ⓓ Ⓔ
70. Ⓐ Ⓑ Ⓒ Ⓓ Ⓔ
71. Ⓐ Ⓑ Ⓒ Ⓓ Ⓔ
72. Ⓐ Ⓑ Ⓒ Ⓓ Ⓔ
73. Ⓐ Ⓑ Ⓒ Ⓓ Ⓔ
74. Ⓐ Ⓑ Ⓒ Ⓓ Ⓔ
75. Ⓐ Ⓑ Ⓒ Ⓓ Ⓔ
76. Ⓐ Ⓑ Ⓒ Ⓓ Ⓔ
77. Ⓐ Ⓑ Ⓒ Ⓓ Ⓔ
78. Ⓐ Ⓑ Ⓒ Ⓓ Ⓔ
79. Ⓐ Ⓑ Ⓒ Ⓓ Ⓔ
80. Ⓐ Ⓑ Ⓒ Ⓓ Ⓔ

SECTION II

Use the following pages on which to write your essays. If you need more space than is provided here, use your own standard ruled paper on which to complete additional pages.

AP UNITED STATES HISTORY
PRACTICE TEST 2
SECTION I

ANSWER SHEET

1. Ⓐ Ⓑ Ⓒ Ⓓ Ⓔ
2. Ⓐ Ⓑ Ⓒ Ⓓ Ⓔ
3. Ⓐ Ⓑ Ⓒ Ⓓ Ⓔ
4. Ⓐ Ⓑ Ⓒ Ⓓ Ⓔ
5. Ⓐ Ⓑ Ⓒ Ⓓ Ⓔ
6. Ⓐ Ⓑ Ⓒ Ⓓ Ⓔ
7. Ⓐ Ⓑ Ⓒ Ⓓ Ⓔ
8. Ⓐ Ⓑ Ⓒ Ⓓ Ⓔ
9. Ⓐ Ⓑ Ⓒ Ⓓ Ⓔ
10. Ⓐ Ⓑ Ⓒ Ⓓ Ⓔ
11. Ⓐ Ⓑ Ⓒ Ⓓ Ⓔ
12. Ⓐ Ⓑ Ⓒ Ⓓ Ⓔ
13. Ⓐ Ⓑ Ⓒ Ⓓ Ⓔ
14. Ⓐ Ⓑ Ⓒ Ⓓ Ⓔ
15. Ⓐ Ⓑ Ⓒ Ⓓ Ⓔ
16. Ⓐ Ⓑ Ⓒ Ⓓ Ⓔ
17. Ⓐ Ⓑ Ⓒ Ⓓ Ⓔ
18. Ⓐ Ⓑ Ⓒ Ⓓ Ⓔ
19. Ⓐ Ⓑ Ⓒ Ⓓ Ⓔ
20. Ⓐ Ⓑ Ⓒ Ⓓ Ⓔ
21. Ⓐ Ⓑ Ⓒ Ⓓ Ⓔ
22. Ⓐ Ⓑ Ⓒ Ⓓ Ⓔ
23. Ⓐ Ⓑ Ⓒ Ⓓ Ⓔ
24. Ⓐ Ⓑ Ⓒ Ⓓ Ⓔ
25. Ⓐ Ⓑ Ⓒ Ⓓ Ⓔ
26. Ⓐ Ⓑ Ⓒ Ⓓ Ⓔ
27. Ⓐ Ⓑ Ⓒ Ⓓ Ⓔ

28. Ⓐ Ⓑ Ⓒ Ⓓ Ⓔ
29. Ⓐ Ⓑ Ⓒ Ⓓ Ⓔ
30. Ⓐ Ⓑ Ⓒ Ⓓ Ⓔ
31. Ⓐ Ⓑ Ⓒ Ⓓ Ⓔ
32. Ⓐ Ⓑ Ⓒ Ⓓ Ⓔ
33. Ⓐ Ⓑ Ⓒ Ⓓ Ⓔ
34. Ⓐ Ⓑ Ⓒ Ⓓ Ⓔ
35. Ⓐ Ⓑ Ⓒ Ⓓ Ⓔ
36. Ⓐ Ⓑ Ⓒ Ⓓ Ⓔ
37. Ⓐ Ⓑ Ⓒ Ⓓ Ⓔ
38. Ⓐ Ⓑ Ⓒ Ⓓ Ⓔ
39. Ⓐ Ⓑ Ⓒ Ⓓ Ⓔ
40. Ⓐ Ⓑ Ⓒ Ⓓ Ⓔ
41. Ⓐ Ⓑ Ⓒ Ⓓ Ⓔ
42. Ⓐ Ⓑ Ⓒ Ⓓ Ⓔ
43. Ⓐ Ⓑ Ⓒ Ⓓ Ⓔ
44. Ⓐ Ⓑ Ⓒ Ⓓ Ⓔ
45. Ⓐ Ⓑ Ⓒ Ⓓ Ⓔ
46. Ⓐ Ⓑ Ⓒ Ⓓ Ⓔ
47. Ⓐ Ⓑ Ⓒ Ⓓ Ⓔ
48. Ⓐ Ⓑ Ⓒ Ⓓ Ⓔ
49. Ⓐ Ⓑ Ⓒ Ⓓ Ⓔ
50. Ⓐ Ⓑ Ⓒ Ⓓ Ⓔ
51. Ⓐ Ⓑ Ⓒ Ⓓ Ⓔ
52. Ⓐ Ⓑ Ⓒ Ⓓ Ⓔ
53. Ⓐ Ⓑ Ⓒ Ⓓ Ⓔ
54. Ⓐ Ⓑ Ⓒ Ⓓ Ⓔ

55. Ⓐ Ⓑ Ⓒ Ⓓ Ⓔ
56. Ⓐ Ⓑ Ⓒ Ⓓ Ⓔ
57. Ⓐ Ⓑ Ⓒ Ⓓ Ⓔ
58. Ⓐ Ⓑ Ⓒ Ⓓ Ⓔ
59. Ⓐ Ⓑ Ⓒ Ⓓ Ⓔ
60. Ⓐ Ⓑ Ⓒ Ⓓ Ⓔ
61. Ⓐ Ⓑ Ⓒ Ⓓ Ⓔ
62. Ⓐ Ⓑ Ⓒ Ⓓ Ⓔ
63. Ⓐ Ⓑ Ⓒ Ⓓ Ⓔ
64. Ⓐ Ⓑ Ⓒ Ⓓ Ⓔ
65. Ⓐ Ⓑ Ⓒ Ⓓ Ⓔ
66. Ⓐ Ⓑ Ⓒ Ⓓ Ⓔ
67. Ⓐ Ⓑ Ⓒ Ⓓ Ⓔ
68. Ⓐ Ⓑ Ⓒ Ⓓ Ⓔ
69. Ⓐ Ⓑ Ⓒ Ⓓ Ⓔ
70. Ⓐ Ⓑ Ⓒ Ⓓ Ⓔ
71. Ⓐ Ⓑ Ⓒ Ⓓ Ⓔ
72. Ⓐ Ⓑ Ⓒ Ⓓ Ⓔ
73. Ⓐ Ⓑ Ⓒ Ⓓ Ⓔ
74. Ⓐ Ⓑ Ⓒ Ⓓ Ⓔ
75. Ⓐ Ⓑ Ⓒ Ⓓ Ⓔ
76. Ⓐ Ⓑ Ⓒ Ⓓ Ⓔ
77. Ⓐ Ⓑ Ⓒ Ⓓ Ⓔ
78. Ⓐ Ⓑ Ⓒ Ⓓ Ⓔ
79. Ⓐ Ⓑ Ⓒ Ⓓ Ⓔ
80. Ⓐ Ⓑ Ⓒ Ⓓ Ⓔ

SECTION II

Use the following pages on which to write your essays. If you need more space than is provided here, use your own standard ruled paper on which to complete additional pages.

AP UNITED STATES HISTORY
PRACTICE TEST 3
SECTION I

ANSWER SHEET

1. Ⓐ Ⓑ Ⓒ Ⓓ Ⓔ   28. Ⓐ Ⓑ Ⓒ Ⓓ Ⓔ   55. Ⓐ Ⓑ Ⓒ Ⓓ Ⓔ
2. Ⓐ Ⓑ Ⓒ Ⓓ Ⓔ   29. Ⓐ Ⓑ Ⓒ Ⓓ Ⓔ   56. Ⓐ Ⓑ Ⓒ Ⓓ Ⓔ
3. Ⓐ Ⓑ Ⓒ Ⓓ Ⓔ   30. Ⓐ Ⓑ Ⓒ Ⓓ Ⓔ   57. Ⓐ Ⓑ Ⓒ Ⓓ Ⓔ
4. Ⓐ Ⓑ Ⓒ Ⓓ Ⓔ   31. Ⓐ Ⓑ Ⓒ Ⓓ Ⓔ   58. Ⓐ Ⓑ Ⓒ Ⓓ Ⓔ
5. Ⓐ Ⓑ Ⓒ Ⓓ Ⓔ   32. Ⓐ Ⓑ Ⓒ Ⓓ Ⓔ   59. Ⓐ Ⓑ Ⓒ Ⓓ Ⓔ
6. Ⓐ Ⓑ Ⓒ Ⓓ Ⓔ   33. Ⓐ Ⓑ Ⓒ Ⓓ Ⓔ   60. Ⓐ Ⓑ Ⓒ Ⓓ Ⓔ
7. Ⓐ Ⓑ Ⓒ Ⓓ Ⓔ   34. Ⓐ Ⓑ Ⓒ Ⓓ Ⓔ   61. Ⓐ Ⓑ Ⓒ Ⓓ Ⓔ
8. Ⓐ Ⓑ Ⓒ Ⓓ Ⓔ   35. Ⓐ Ⓑ Ⓒ Ⓓ Ⓔ   62. Ⓐ Ⓑ Ⓒ Ⓓ Ⓔ
9. Ⓐ Ⓑ Ⓒ Ⓓ Ⓔ   36. Ⓐ Ⓑ Ⓒ Ⓓ Ⓔ   63. Ⓐ Ⓑ Ⓒ Ⓓ Ⓔ
10. Ⓐ Ⓑ Ⓒ Ⓓ Ⓔ   37. Ⓐ Ⓑ Ⓒ Ⓓ Ⓔ   64. Ⓐ Ⓑ Ⓒ Ⓓ Ⓔ
11. Ⓐ Ⓑ Ⓒ Ⓓ Ⓔ   38. Ⓐ Ⓑ Ⓒ Ⓓ Ⓔ   65. Ⓐ Ⓑ Ⓒ Ⓓ Ⓔ
12. Ⓐ Ⓑ Ⓒ Ⓓ Ⓔ   39. Ⓐ Ⓑ Ⓒ Ⓓ Ⓔ   66. Ⓐ Ⓑ Ⓒ Ⓓ Ⓔ
13. Ⓐ Ⓑ Ⓒ Ⓓ Ⓔ   40. Ⓐ Ⓑ Ⓒ Ⓓ Ⓔ   67. Ⓐ Ⓑ Ⓒ Ⓓ Ⓔ
14. Ⓐ Ⓑ Ⓒ Ⓓ Ⓔ   41. Ⓐ Ⓑ Ⓒ Ⓓ Ⓔ   68. Ⓐ Ⓑ Ⓒ Ⓓ Ⓔ
15. Ⓐ Ⓑ Ⓒ Ⓓ Ⓔ   42. Ⓐ Ⓑ Ⓒ Ⓓ Ⓔ   69. Ⓐ Ⓑ Ⓒ Ⓓ Ⓔ
16. Ⓐ Ⓑ Ⓒ Ⓓ Ⓔ   43. Ⓐ Ⓑ Ⓒ Ⓓ Ⓔ   70. Ⓐ Ⓑ Ⓒ Ⓓ Ⓔ
17. Ⓐ Ⓑ Ⓒ Ⓓ Ⓔ   44. Ⓐ Ⓑ Ⓒ Ⓓ Ⓔ   71. Ⓐ Ⓑ Ⓒ Ⓓ Ⓔ
18. Ⓐ Ⓑ Ⓒ Ⓓ Ⓔ   45. Ⓐ Ⓑ Ⓒ Ⓓ Ⓔ   72. Ⓐ Ⓑ Ⓒ Ⓓ Ⓔ
19. Ⓐ Ⓑ Ⓒ Ⓓ Ⓔ   46. Ⓐ Ⓑ Ⓒ Ⓓ Ⓔ   73. Ⓐ Ⓑ Ⓒ Ⓓ Ⓔ
20. Ⓐ Ⓑ Ⓒ Ⓓ Ⓔ   47. Ⓐ Ⓑ Ⓒ Ⓓ Ⓔ   74. Ⓐ Ⓑ Ⓒ Ⓓ Ⓔ
21. Ⓐ Ⓑ Ⓒ Ⓓ Ⓔ   48. Ⓐ Ⓑ Ⓒ Ⓓ Ⓔ   75. Ⓐ Ⓑ Ⓒ Ⓓ Ⓔ
22. Ⓐ Ⓑ Ⓒ Ⓓ Ⓔ   49. Ⓐ Ⓑ Ⓒ Ⓓ Ⓔ   76. Ⓐ Ⓑ Ⓒ Ⓓ Ⓔ
23. Ⓐ Ⓑ Ⓒ Ⓓ Ⓔ   50. Ⓐ Ⓑ Ⓒ Ⓓ Ⓔ   77. Ⓐ Ⓑ Ⓒ Ⓓ Ⓔ
24. Ⓐ Ⓑ Ⓒ Ⓓ Ⓔ   51. Ⓐ Ⓑ Ⓒ Ⓓ Ⓔ   78. Ⓐ Ⓑ Ⓒ Ⓓ Ⓔ
25. Ⓐ Ⓑ Ⓒ Ⓓ Ⓔ   52. Ⓐ Ⓑ Ⓒ Ⓓ Ⓔ   79. Ⓐ Ⓑ Ⓒ Ⓓ Ⓔ
26. Ⓐ Ⓑ Ⓒ Ⓓ Ⓔ   53. Ⓐ Ⓑ Ⓒ Ⓓ Ⓔ   80. Ⓐ Ⓑ Ⓒ Ⓓ Ⓔ
27. Ⓐ Ⓑ Ⓒ Ⓓ Ⓔ   54. Ⓐ Ⓑ Ⓒ Ⓓ Ⓔ

SECTION II

Use the following pages on which to write your essays. If you need more space than is provided here, use your own standard ruled paper on which to complete additional pages.

AP UNITED STATES HISTORY
PRACTICE TEST 4
SECTION I

ANSWER SHEET

1. Ⓐ Ⓑ Ⓒ Ⓓ Ⓔ
2. Ⓐ Ⓑ Ⓒ Ⓓ Ⓔ
3. Ⓐ Ⓑ Ⓒ Ⓓ Ⓔ
4. Ⓐ Ⓑ Ⓒ Ⓓ Ⓔ
5. Ⓐ Ⓑ Ⓒ Ⓓ Ⓔ
6. Ⓐ Ⓑ Ⓒ Ⓓ Ⓔ
7. Ⓐ Ⓑ Ⓒ Ⓓ Ⓔ
8. Ⓐ Ⓑ Ⓒ Ⓓ Ⓔ
9. Ⓐ Ⓑ Ⓒ Ⓓ Ⓔ
10. Ⓐ Ⓑ Ⓒ Ⓓ Ⓔ
11. Ⓐ Ⓑ Ⓒ Ⓓ Ⓔ
12. Ⓐ Ⓑ Ⓒ Ⓓ Ⓔ
13. Ⓐ Ⓑ Ⓒ Ⓓ Ⓔ
14. Ⓐ Ⓑ Ⓒ Ⓓ Ⓔ
15. Ⓐ Ⓑ Ⓒ Ⓓ Ⓔ
16. Ⓐ Ⓑ Ⓒ Ⓓ Ⓔ
17. Ⓐ Ⓑ Ⓒ Ⓓ Ⓔ
18. Ⓐ Ⓑ Ⓒ Ⓓ Ⓔ
19. Ⓐ Ⓑ Ⓒ Ⓓ Ⓔ
20. Ⓐ Ⓑ Ⓒ Ⓓ Ⓔ
21. Ⓐ Ⓑ Ⓒ Ⓓ Ⓔ
22. Ⓐ Ⓑ Ⓒ Ⓓ Ⓔ
23. Ⓐ Ⓑ Ⓒ Ⓓ Ⓔ
24. Ⓐ Ⓑ Ⓒ Ⓓ Ⓔ
25. Ⓐ Ⓑ Ⓒ Ⓓ Ⓔ
26. Ⓐ Ⓑ Ⓒ Ⓓ Ⓔ
27. Ⓐ Ⓑ Ⓒ Ⓓ Ⓔ

28. Ⓐ Ⓑ Ⓒ Ⓓ Ⓔ
29. Ⓐ Ⓑ Ⓒ Ⓓ Ⓔ
30. Ⓐ Ⓑ Ⓒ Ⓓ Ⓔ
31. Ⓐ Ⓑ Ⓒ Ⓓ Ⓔ
32. Ⓐ Ⓑ Ⓒ Ⓓ Ⓔ
33. Ⓐ Ⓑ Ⓒ Ⓓ Ⓔ
34. Ⓐ Ⓑ Ⓒ Ⓓ Ⓔ
35. Ⓐ Ⓑ Ⓒ Ⓓ Ⓔ
36. Ⓐ Ⓑ Ⓒ Ⓓ Ⓔ
37. Ⓐ Ⓑ Ⓒ Ⓓ Ⓔ
38. Ⓐ Ⓑ Ⓒ Ⓓ Ⓔ
39. Ⓐ Ⓑ Ⓒ Ⓓ Ⓔ
40. Ⓐ Ⓑ Ⓒ Ⓓ Ⓔ
41. Ⓐ Ⓑ Ⓒ Ⓓ Ⓔ
42. Ⓐ Ⓑ Ⓒ Ⓓ Ⓔ
43. Ⓐ Ⓑ Ⓒ Ⓓ Ⓔ
44. Ⓐ Ⓑ Ⓒ Ⓓ Ⓔ
45. Ⓐ Ⓑ Ⓒ Ⓓ Ⓔ
46. Ⓐ Ⓑ Ⓒ Ⓓ Ⓔ
47. Ⓐ Ⓑ Ⓒ Ⓓ Ⓔ
48. Ⓐ Ⓑ Ⓒ Ⓓ Ⓔ
49. Ⓐ Ⓑ Ⓒ Ⓓ Ⓔ
50. Ⓐ Ⓑ Ⓒ Ⓓ Ⓔ
51. Ⓐ Ⓑ Ⓒ Ⓓ Ⓔ
52. Ⓐ Ⓑ Ⓒ Ⓓ Ⓔ
53. Ⓐ Ⓑ Ⓒ Ⓓ Ⓔ
54. Ⓐ Ⓑ Ⓒ Ⓓ Ⓔ

55. Ⓐ Ⓑ Ⓒ Ⓓ Ⓔ
56. Ⓐ Ⓑ Ⓒ Ⓓ Ⓔ
57. Ⓐ Ⓑ Ⓒ Ⓓ Ⓔ
58. Ⓐ Ⓑ Ⓒ Ⓓ Ⓔ
59. Ⓐ Ⓑ Ⓒ Ⓓ Ⓔ
60. Ⓐ Ⓑ Ⓒ Ⓓ Ⓔ
61. Ⓐ Ⓑ Ⓒ Ⓓ Ⓔ
62. Ⓐ Ⓑ Ⓒ Ⓓ Ⓔ
63. Ⓐ Ⓑ Ⓒ Ⓓ Ⓔ
64. Ⓐ Ⓑ Ⓒ Ⓓ Ⓔ
65. Ⓐ Ⓑ Ⓒ Ⓓ Ⓔ
66. Ⓐ Ⓑ Ⓒ Ⓓ Ⓔ
67. Ⓐ Ⓑ Ⓒ Ⓓ Ⓔ
68. Ⓐ Ⓑ Ⓒ Ⓓ Ⓔ
69. Ⓐ Ⓑ Ⓒ Ⓓ Ⓔ
70. Ⓐ Ⓑ Ⓒ Ⓓ Ⓔ
71. Ⓐ Ⓑ Ⓒ Ⓓ Ⓔ
72. Ⓐ Ⓑ Ⓒ Ⓓ Ⓔ
73. Ⓐ Ⓑ Ⓒ Ⓓ Ⓔ
74. Ⓐ Ⓑ Ⓒ Ⓓ Ⓔ
75. Ⓐ Ⓑ Ⓒ Ⓓ Ⓔ
76. Ⓐ Ⓑ Ⓒ Ⓓ Ⓔ
77. Ⓐ Ⓑ Ⓒ Ⓓ Ⓔ
78. Ⓐ Ⓑ Ⓒ Ⓓ Ⓔ
79. Ⓐ Ⓑ Ⓒ Ⓓ Ⓔ
80. Ⓐ Ⓑ Ⓒ Ⓓ Ⓔ

SECTION II

Use the following pages on which to write your essays. If you need more space than is provided here, use your own standard ruled paper on which to complete additional pages.

AP UNITED STATES HISTORY
PRACTICE TEST 5
SECTION I

ANSWER SHEET

1. Ⓐ Ⓑ Ⓒ Ⓓ Ⓔ   28. Ⓐ Ⓑ Ⓒ Ⓓ Ⓔ   55. Ⓐ Ⓑ Ⓒ Ⓓ Ⓔ
2. Ⓐ Ⓑ Ⓒ Ⓓ Ⓔ   29. Ⓐ Ⓑ Ⓒ Ⓓ Ⓔ   56. Ⓐ Ⓑ Ⓒ Ⓓ Ⓔ
3. Ⓐ Ⓑ Ⓒ Ⓓ Ⓔ   30. Ⓐ Ⓑ Ⓒ Ⓓ Ⓔ   57. Ⓐ Ⓑ Ⓒ Ⓓ Ⓔ
4. Ⓐ Ⓑ Ⓒ Ⓓ Ⓔ   31. Ⓐ Ⓑ Ⓒ Ⓓ Ⓔ   58. Ⓐ Ⓑ Ⓒ Ⓓ Ⓔ
5. Ⓐ Ⓑ Ⓒ Ⓓ Ⓔ   32. Ⓐ Ⓑ Ⓒ Ⓓ Ⓔ   59. Ⓐ Ⓑ Ⓒ Ⓓ Ⓔ
6. Ⓐ Ⓑ Ⓒ Ⓓ Ⓔ   33. Ⓐ Ⓑ Ⓒ Ⓓ Ⓔ   60. Ⓐ Ⓑ Ⓒ Ⓓ Ⓕ
7. Ⓐ Ⓑ Ⓒ Ⓓ Ⓔ   34. Ⓐ Ⓑ Ⓒ Ⓓ Ⓔ   61. Ⓐ Ⓑ Ⓒ Ⓓ Ⓔ
8. Ⓐ Ⓑ Ⓒ Ⓓ Ⓔ   35. Ⓐ Ⓑ Ⓒ Ⓓ Ⓔ   62. Ⓐ Ⓑ Ⓒ Ⓓ Ⓔ
9. Ⓐ Ⓑ Ⓒ Ⓓ Ⓔ   36. Ⓐ Ⓑ Ⓒ Ⓓ Ⓔ   63. Ⓐ Ⓑ Ⓒ Ⓓ Ⓔ
10. Ⓐ Ⓑ Ⓒ Ⓓ Ⓔ   37. Ⓐ Ⓑ Ⓒ Ⓓ Ⓔ   64. Ⓐ Ⓑ Ⓒ Ⓓ Ⓔ
11. Ⓐ Ⓑ Ⓒ Ⓓ Ⓔ   38. Ⓐ Ⓑ Ⓒ Ⓓ Ⓔ   65. Ⓐ Ⓑ Ⓒ Ⓓ Ⓔ
12. Ⓐ Ⓑ Ⓒ Ⓓ Ⓔ   39. Ⓐ Ⓑ Ⓒ Ⓓ Ⓔ   66. Ⓐ Ⓑ Ⓒ Ⓓ Ⓔ
13. Ⓐ Ⓑ Ⓒ Ⓓ Ⓔ   40. Ⓐ Ⓑ Ⓒ Ⓓ Ⓔ   67. Ⓐ Ⓑ Ⓒ Ⓓ Ⓔ
14. Ⓐ Ⓑ Ⓒ Ⓓ Ⓔ   41. Ⓐ Ⓑ Ⓒ Ⓓ Ⓔ   68. Ⓐ Ⓑ Ⓒ Ⓓ Ⓔ
15. Ⓐ Ⓑ Ⓒ Ⓓ Ⓔ   42. Ⓐ Ⓑ Ⓒ Ⓓ Ⓔ   69. Ⓐ Ⓑ Ⓒ Ⓓ Ⓔ
16. Ⓐ Ⓑ Ⓒ Ⓓ Ⓔ   43. Ⓐ Ⓑ Ⓒ Ⓓ Ⓔ   70. Ⓐ Ⓑ Ⓒ Ⓓ Ⓔ
17. Ⓐ Ⓑ Ⓒ Ⓓ Ⓔ   44. Ⓐ Ⓑ Ⓒ Ⓓ Ⓔ   71. Ⓐ Ⓑ Ⓒ Ⓓ Ⓔ
18. Ⓐ Ⓑ Ⓒ Ⓓ Ⓔ   45. Ⓐ Ⓑ Ⓒ Ⓓ Ⓔ   72. Ⓐ Ⓑ Ⓒ Ⓓ Ⓔ
19. Ⓐ Ⓑ Ⓒ Ⓓ Ⓔ   46. Ⓐ Ⓑ Ⓒ Ⓓ Ⓔ   73. Ⓐ Ⓑ Ⓒ Ⓓ Ⓔ
20. Ⓐ Ⓑ Ⓒ Ⓓ Ⓔ   47. Ⓐ Ⓑ Ⓒ Ⓓ Ⓔ   74. Ⓐ Ⓑ Ⓒ Ⓓ Ⓔ
21. Ⓐ Ⓑ Ⓒ Ⓓ Ⓔ   48. Ⓐ Ⓑ Ⓒ Ⓓ Ⓔ   75. Ⓐ Ⓑ Ⓒ Ⓓ Ⓔ
22. Ⓐ Ⓑ Ⓒ Ⓓ Ⓔ   49. Ⓐ Ⓑ Ⓒ Ⓓ Ⓔ   76. Ⓐ Ⓑ Ⓒ Ⓓ Ⓔ
23. Ⓐ Ⓑ Ⓒ Ⓓ Ⓔ   50. Ⓐ Ⓑ Ⓒ Ⓓ Ⓔ   77. Ⓐ Ⓑ Ⓒ Ⓓ Ⓔ
24. Ⓐ Ⓑ Ⓒ Ⓓ Ⓔ   51. Ⓐ Ⓑ Ⓒ Ⓓ Ⓔ   78. Ⓐ Ⓑ Ⓒ Ⓓ Ⓔ
25. Ⓐ Ⓑ Ⓒ Ⓓ Ⓔ   52. Ⓐ Ⓑ Ⓒ Ⓓ Ⓔ   79. Ⓐ Ⓑ Ⓒ Ⓓ Ⓔ
26. Ⓐ Ⓑ Ⓒ Ⓓ Ⓔ   53. Ⓐ Ⓑ Ⓒ Ⓓ Ⓔ   80. Ⓐ Ⓑ Ⓒ Ⓓ Ⓔ
27. Ⓐ Ⓑ Ⓒ Ⓓ Ⓔ   54. Ⓐ Ⓑ Ⓒ Ⓓ Ⓔ

SECTION II

Use the following pages on which to write your essays. If you need more space than is provided here, use your own standard ruled paper on which to complete additional pages.

AP UNITED STATES HISTORY
PRACTICE TEST 6
SECTION I

ANSWER SHEET

1. Ⓐ Ⓑ Ⓒ Ⓓ Ⓔ
2. Ⓐ Ⓑ Ⓒ Ⓓ Ⓔ
3. Ⓐ Ⓑ Ⓒ Ⓓ Ⓔ
4. Ⓐ Ⓑ Ⓒ Ⓓ Ⓔ
5. Ⓐ Ⓑ Ⓒ Ⓓ Ⓔ
6. Ⓐ Ⓑ Ⓒ Ⓓ Ⓔ
7. Ⓐ Ⓑ Ⓒ Ⓓ Ⓔ
8. Ⓐ Ⓑ Ⓒ Ⓓ Ⓔ
9. Ⓐ Ⓑ Ⓒ Ⓓ Ⓔ
10. Ⓐ Ⓑ Ⓒ Ⓓ Ⓔ
11. Ⓐ Ⓑ Ⓒ Ⓓ Ⓔ
12. Ⓐ Ⓑ Ⓒ Ⓓ Ⓔ
13. Ⓐ Ⓑ Ⓒ Ⓓ Ⓔ
14. Ⓐ Ⓑ Ⓒ Ⓓ Ⓔ
15. Ⓐ Ⓑ Ⓒ Ⓓ Ⓔ
16. Ⓐ Ⓑ Ⓒ Ⓓ Ⓔ
17. Ⓐ Ⓑ Ⓒ Ⓓ Ⓔ
18. Ⓐ Ⓑ Ⓒ Ⓓ Ⓔ
19. Ⓐ Ⓑ Ⓒ Ⓓ Ⓔ
20. Ⓐ Ⓑ Ⓒ Ⓓ Ⓔ
21. Ⓐ Ⓑ Ⓒ Ⓓ Ⓔ
22. Ⓐ Ⓑ Ⓒ Ⓓ Ⓔ
23. Ⓐ Ⓑ Ⓒ Ⓓ Ⓔ
24. Ⓐ Ⓑ Ⓒ Ⓓ Ⓔ
25. Ⓐ Ⓑ Ⓒ Ⓓ Ⓔ
26. Ⓐ Ⓑ Ⓒ Ⓓ Ⓔ
27. Ⓐ Ⓑ Ⓒ Ⓓ Ⓔ

28. Ⓐ Ⓑ Ⓒ Ⓓ Ⓔ
29. Ⓐ Ⓑ Ⓒ Ⓓ Ⓔ
30. Ⓐ Ⓑ Ⓒ Ⓓ Ⓔ
31. Ⓐ Ⓑ Ⓒ Ⓓ Ⓔ
32. Ⓐ Ⓑ Ⓒ Ⓓ Ⓔ
33. Ⓐ Ⓑ Ⓒ Ⓓ Ⓔ
34. Ⓐ Ⓑ Ⓒ Ⓓ Ⓔ
35. Ⓐ Ⓑ Ⓒ Ⓓ Ⓔ
36. Ⓐ Ⓑ Ⓒ Ⓓ Ⓔ
37. Ⓐ Ⓑ Ⓒ Ⓓ Ⓔ
38. Ⓐ Ⓑ Ⓒ Ⓓ Ⓔ
39. Ⓐ Ⓑ Ⓒ Ⓓ Ⓔ
40. Ⓐ Ⓑ Ⓒ Ⓓ Ⓔ
41. Ⓐ Ⓑ Ⓒ Ⓓ Ⓔ
42. Ⓐ Ⓑ Ⓒ Ⓓ Ⓔ
43. Ⓐ Ⓑ Ⓒ Ⓓ Ⓔ
44. Ⓐ Ⓑ Ⓒ Ⓓ Ⓔ
45. Ⓐ Ⓑ Ⓒ Ⓓ Ⓔ
46. Ⓐ Ⓑ Ⓒ Ⓓ Ⓔ
47. Ⓐ Ⓑ Ⓒ Ⓓ Ⓔ
48. Ⓐ Ⓑ Ⓒ Ⓓ Ⓔ
49. Ⓐ Ⓑ Ⓒ Ⓓ Ⓔ
50. Ⓐ Ⓑ Ⓒ Ⓓ Ⓔ
51. Ⓐ Ⓑ Ⓒ Ⓓ Ⓔ
52. Ⓐ Ⓑ Ⓒ Ⓓ Ⓔ
53. Ⓐ Ⓑ Ⓒ Ⓓ Ⓔ
54. Ⓐ Ⓑ Ⓒ Ⓓ Ⓔ

55. Ⓐ Ⓑ Ⓒ Ⓓ Ⓔ
56. Ⓐ Ⓑ Ⓒ Ⓓ Ⓔ
57. Ⓐ Ⓑ Ⓒ Ⓓ Ⓔ
58. Ⓐ Ⓑ Ⓒ Ⓓ Ⓔ
59. Ⓐ Ⓑ Ⓒ Ⓓ Ⓔ
60. Ⓐ Ⓑ Ⓒ Ⓓ Ⓔ
61. Ⓐ Ⓑ Ⓒ Ⓓ Ⓔ
62. Ⓐ Ⓑ Ⓒ Ⓓ Ⓔ
63. Ⓐ Ⓑ Ⓒ Ⓓ Ⓔ
64. Ⓐ Ⓑ Ⓒ Ⓓ Ⓔ
65. Ⓐ Ⓑ Ⓒ Ⓓ Ⓔ
66. Ⓐ Ⓑ Ⓒ Ⓓ Ⓔ
67. Ⓐ Ⓑ Ⓒ Ⓓ Ⓔ
68. Ⓐ Ⓑ Ⓒ Ⓓ Ⓔ
69. Ⓐ Ⓑ Ⓒ Ⓓ Ⓔ
70. Ⓐ Ⓑ Ⓒ Ⓓ Ⓔ
71. Ⓐ Ⓑ Ⓒ Ⓓ Ⓔ
72. Ⓐ Ⓑ Ⓒ Ⓓ Ⓔ
73. Ⓐ Ⓑ Ⓒ Ⓓ Ⓔ
74. Ⓐ Ⓑ Ⓒ Ⓓ Ⓔ
75. Ⓐ Ⓑ Ⓒ Ⓓ Ⓔ
76. Ⓐ Ⓑ Ⓒ Ⓓ Ⓔ
77. Ⓐ Ⓑ Ⓒ Ⓓ Ⓔ
78. Ⓐ Ⓑ Ⓒ Ⓓ Ⓔ
79. Ⓐ Ⓑ Ⓒ Ⓓ Ⓔ
80. Ⓐ Ⓑ Ⓒ Ⓓ Ⓔ

SECTION II

Use the following pages on which to write your essays. If you need more space than is provided here, use your own standard ruled paper on which to complete additional pages.

INDEX

Index

A

Abolitionist movement, in Age
  of Jackson, 100–101
Abominations, Tariff of, 89
Abortion, 102
Act of Religious Toleration, 17
Ada Lois Sipuel v. Board of Regents, 320
Adams, Brooks, 183
Adams, Charles Francis, 147, 192
Adams, Henry C., 177
Adams, John, 59, 63
  election of 1796, 63
  election of 1800, 64
  Quasi-War (1798–1799), 63
  vice president, 59
  XYZ affair, 63
Adams, John Quincy, 88
  administration of, 88–89
  election of 1824, 87–88
  election of 1828, 89
  John C. Calhoun and nullification, 89
Adams, Samuel, 32, 34, 43, 51
Adamson Act of 1916, 218
Adams-Onis Treaty, 73–74, 113
Addams, Jane, 170, 187, 213
Administration of Justice Act, 36
Advertising, in twenties, 244
Afghanistan, Soviet invasion of, 353
Africa, 249
  in 1887–1892, 179
African Americans.
  See also Civil rights; Slavery
  in army during WW I, 321
  black power, 334–336
  Democratic Party and 1936, 280
  election, 278–280
  emergence of black power, 334–336
  employment during WW I, 231
  Jim Crow laws, 104
  Ku Klux Klan, 252
  leaders in 1877–1882, 167
  Marcus Garvey and UNIA, 249
  during New Deal, 282–283
  political office, 335
  race riots of 1919, 238
  racial riots in 1960s, 335
  role of, in northern states in Age
    of Jackson, 87
  segregation of, in government
    agencies, 220
  during twenties, 252
  voting, 321, 333
Agnew, Spiro T.
  Vice President of United States, 348
  Watergate, 374–375
Agricultural Adjustment Act,
  273, 282, 298
Agricultural Adjustment Administration
  (AAA), 273–275
Agricultural Marketing Act, 266–267, 298
Agriculture
  agricultural militancy in 1877–1882,
    169–170
  under Eisenhower, 331
  expansion of, in 1882–1887, 174
  Farm Holiday Association, 269
  farming in post-Revolution era, 82
  farm policy under Truman, 317
  farm problems during twenties,
    245–246
  food and drug inspection, 178
  food supply during WW I, 228
  Hundred Days programs, 271–273
  low farm prices in 1882–1887, 176
  McNary-Haugen Bill, 260
  Reagan administration and, 358–359

Agriculture *(continued)*
  revolution of, in northern states
    during Age of Jackson, 87
  rural-urban conflict, 251
  during 1850s, 104
  Southern states during Age
    of Jackson, 110
Aguinaldo, Emilio, 195
AIDS, 371–372, 374
Airplanes, 290
Aix-la-Chapelle, Treaty of, 25, 26
Alabama, 171
Alaska
  purchase of, 156
  as state, 320
Aldrich, Nelson, 207, 216
Aldrin, Edwin, 334
Algeciras Conference, 203
Algiers, 73
Alien Act, 64
Allen, Ethan, 37
Allen, Horace, 182
Alliance for Progress, 332
Amana Community, 98
American Civil Liberties Union, 372
American Expeditionary Force, 227
American Federation of Labor,
  176, 204, 213, 237, 245, 259, 283,
  formation of, 213
American Fur Company, 113
American Indian Movement, 336
American Liberty League, 275
American Neutrality Patrol, 293
American Protective League, 230
American Revolution, 31–47
  Articles of Confederation, 44–45
  coming of American Revolution, 31–36
  creation of new government, 43
  war for independence, 36–43
American Society for Promotion
  of Temperance, 98
Americans with Disabilities Act, 362
American Tobacco Trust, 208
Anaconda Plan, 145
Anderson, John, 354
Andros, Edmond, 22
Antietam, Battle of, 150–151
Antifederalists, 59
Anti-Saloon League, 187, 253

Antitrust policy
  Clayton Antitrust Act, 207
  under Reagan, 356
  under Roosevelt, 197
  Sherman Anti-Trust Act, 180, 206
  under Taft, 204–206
Arafat, Yasir, 367
Arbitration treaty, in Latin America, 211
Argentina, 222
Arkwright, Richard, 79
Armistice, WW I, 233
Armstrong, Neil, 333, 334
Army
  African Americans in, during
    WW I, 321
  draft in World War I, 226
  preparedness for WW I, 319
  war with Spain, 190
  women in, during WW I, 226
Army Act, 158
Army of Potomac, 146
Arnold, Benedict, 37–38, 41–42
Arrostook War, 116
Arthur, Chester A., 168
Articles of Confederation, 44–45, 49
Astor, John Jacob, 78, 112
Asylums for mentally ill, 99
Atlantic Charter, 294, 299, 301
Atlee, Clement, 308
Atomic bomb. *See also* Nuclear arms
  Soviet Union and, 306
  test suspension in 1958, 313
  in WW II, 306
Atomic Energy Act, 309
Atomic Energy Commission, 314
Austin, Stephen, 114
Austria, 290
  German occupation, 293
Automobiles, 243
Aztecs civilization, 1–2
  significance, 2–4

B

Bacon, Nathaniel, 21
Badoglio, Pietro, 304
Baekeland, Leo, 210
Baker, Newton, 198
Baker, Ray Stannard, 201

Balboa, Vasco Vúñez de, 8
Balkans, 308, 368
Ballinger, Richard, 205
Ballinger-Pinchot dispute, 205
Bankhead-Jones Farm Tenancy Act, 281
Banking
    crisis of 1933, 271
    Federal Farm Loan Act of
        1916, 218
    Federal Home Loan Bank Act, 267
    Federal Reserve System, 216
    Hundred Days legislation, 298
    Jackson and, 117
    panic of 1837, 92–93
    panic of 1907, 199–200
    Postal Savings Banks, 208
    during twenties, 245
Banking Act
    of 1933, 272
    of 1935, 278
Bao Dai, 312
Barbary Wars, 73
Barker, Wharton, 189
Barnard, Henry, 99
Barnum and Bailey, 181
Barrett, John, 222
Baruch, Bernard M., 228
Batista, Fulgencio, 287, 314
Bay of Pigs, 331
Bear Flag Revolt, 122
Beats, 326, 337
Beauregard, P. G. T., 143, 145, 147
Begin, Menachem, 352
Belknap, W. W., 162
Bell, Alexander Graham, 168
Bell, John, 139
Bellamy, Edward, 186
Bellow, Saul, 325
Bentsen, Lloyd, 360
Berkeley, John Lord, 18
Berkeley, William, 21
Berle, Adolph A., Jr., 270
Berlin Conference, 178
Berlin Wall, 331
Bethlehem Steel Corporation, 208
Beveridge, Albert, 192, 198
Biddle, Nicholas, 92
Big Stick diplomacy, 202
Bill of Rights, 51–53,

ratification of Constitution and, 44
    in state constitutions, 56
Bin Laden, Osama, 370
Birney, James G., 118
Birth control, 102, 239, 248
Black codes, 155–156
Black Friday scandal, 161
Black Monday, 359
Blackmun, Harry A., 340
Black power, 335
Black Tuesday, 263
Blaine, James G., 167
    election of 1884, 174
    Secretary of State, 172, 179,
        182, 185
Blair, Francis P., Jr., 159
Bliss, Tasker, 233
Boer War, 188
Bolivia, 172
Bonus Expeditionary Force, 268–269
Boone, Daniel, 46
Booth, John Wilkes, 154
Borah, William, 288
Bork, Robert, 348, 359
Boston Massacre, 34
Boston Port Act, 36
Boxer Rebellion, 196
Braddock, Edward, 27
Bradford, William, 15
Bradley, Omar, 304
Bragg, Braxton, 151
Brandeis, Louis D., 218
Brandywine Creek, 40
Brannan, Charles F., 317
Brazil, 7
    in 1894, 180
Breckinridge, John C., 139
Bremer, Arthur, 344
Brennan, William J., 319, 362
Bretton Woods, 310
Briand, Aristide, 262
Bridges, Jim, 112
British East India Company, 35
Britton, Nan, 256
Brooke, Edward W., 336
Brook Farm, Massachusetts, 97
Brooks, Preston, 133
Browder, Earl, 293
Brown, John, 137, 138, 140

Brown v. Board of Education of Topeka, 320–321
Bryan, Charles W., 259
Bryan, William Jennings, 215, 254, **255–257**
  creationism and Scopes trial, 254
  election of 1896, 184–185
  election of 1908, 204
  election of 1924, 259–260
  Secretary of State, 211, 223
Bryan-Chamorro Treaty, 221–222
Bryn Mawr, 120, 133–135, 139–140, 177
Buchanan, James, 120
  election of 1856, 133–134
  Lecompton constitution, 135–136
  President of United States, 140
Buchanan, Patrick, 369
Budge Reconciliation Act, 355
Budget and Accounting Act, 258
Buell, Don Carlos, 146
Buenos Aires Convention, 287
Bulganin, Nikolai, 313
Bulge, Battle of, 304
Bull Run
  First Battle of, 145
  Second Battle of, 146, 150
Bunker Hill, 37–38
Burford, Anne Gorsuch, 356
Burger, Warren E., 340, 359
Burgoyne, John, 37, 40–41
Burnside, Ambrose E., 151
Burr, Aaron
  duel with Hamilton, 64
  election of 1800, 64
Burroughs, William, 326
Busch, Adolphus, 210
Bush, George H. W., **371–372**
  abandons Reaganomics, 360–361
  domestic issues, 362–363
  foreign policy, 363–364
  Persian Gulf crisis, 364–365
  President of United States, 360–361
  Vice President of United States, 360
Bush, George W.
  election of 2000, 369
  election of 2004, **372**

Iraq war, 364
President of United States, 360–371
Butler, Andrew, 133

C

Cabinet, 208
Cabot, John, 9
Caldwell, Erskine, 284
Cahokia, 3
Calhoun, John C., 71, 89, 125
  Compromise of 1850, 128
  concurrent majority, 112
  Secretary of State, 117
  Senator for South Carolina, 125
  Vice President of United States, 89
California
  Compromise of 1850, 127–128
  gold rush and statehood, 124
California Trail, 120
Calvert, George, 17
Cambodia, 341–342
Camden, Battle of, 42
Campaign finance reform, 369
Camp David Accords, 352
Canada
  after French and Indian War, 26–27
  reciprocal trade agreement of 1911, 208
  War of 1812, 70–71
Canal era, 79
Cannon, James, Jr., 261
Cannon, Joseph, 205
Cantwell, Robert, 284
Capone, Al, 253–254
Cardenas, Lazaro, 287
Carnegie, Andrew, 168, 175
Carnegie Steel Company, 185–186
Caroline Affair, 116
Carranza, Venustiano, 222
Carswell, G. Harrold, 340
Carter, James Earl
  election of 1976, 351
  President of United States, 351
Carteret, George, 18
Cartier, Jacques, 9, 13
Carver, George Washington, 171

Casablanca Conference, 306
Case, Jerome, 105
Cass, Lewis, 126
Casey, William, 358
Cassady, Neal, 326
Castro, Fidel, 314, 331
Catholics
    anti-Catholic sentiments, 98, 130
    discrimination against, 102–103
    election of Kennedy, 322
    immigration restrictions, 252–253
    Ku Klux Klan, 252
    during twenties, 250
Central Intelligence Agency, 315, 331
Chambers, Whittaker, 317
Champlain, Samuel de, 13
Chancellorsville, Battle of, 151
Charbonneau, Toussaint, **66**
Charles I, King of England, 13, 15
Charles II, King of England, 17–18, 21–23
Charles River Bridge case, 94
Charleston, 42, 91, 109–110, 139, 143
Chase, Salmon P., 149, 158
Chase, Samuel, 66
Chattanooga, Battle of, 152
Chautauqua movement, 187
Chávez, Cesar, 336
Cheney, Richard B., 205
Cherokee Nation, 90
Chesapeake colonies
    life in, 19–20
    Navigation Acts, 20–21
Chesapeake-Leopard affair, 70
Chiang Kai-shek, 306, 311–312
Chicago
    race riots of 1919, 238
    World's Fair, 187
Chickamauga, Battle of, 151
Child Labor Act of 1916, 218
Childrearing, in 1887–1892, 181
Chile, 222
    in 1887–1892, 172
China
    after war with Spain, 188
    Boxer Rebellion, 196
    Carter and, 352
    Chinese revolution of 1911, 212

containment in, 311
George H. W. Bush administration
    and, 363
immigration from, 253
Korean War, 311
Manchurian crisis, 289
Nixon administration and, 340
Open Door policy, 188, 294
Sino-Japanese war, 187–188, 290
Chisholm, Shirley, **360–361**
Christian Science, Church of, 170
Chrysler, 244
Churchill, Winston, 294, 306–310
Church of Jesus Christ of Latter Day
    Saints, 98
Cities. *See also* Urbanization
    growth of, by 1860, 102–103
    growth of, in 1877–1882, 170–171
    renewal of 2000, 369
    in 1960s, 248
City government
    in 1877–1882, 171–172
    commission form of, 197
    progressive reform in 1902–1907, 197
Civilian Conservation Corps, 273
Civil Rights, voting rights, 334
Civil rights
    black power, 334–336, 345
    Brown v. Board of Education of Topeka,
        320–321
    desegregation of schools, 321, 340
    emergence of black power, 334–336
    emergence of nonviolence, 321
    ending massive resistance, 321–322
    Freedom Riders, 329
    under George H. W. Bush, 362–363
    initial Eisenhower action, 320
    March on Washington, 330–331
    Nixon administration, 340
    racial riots, 335
    in 1960s, 321
    sit-ins, 323
    Truman on, 314
Civil Rights Act, 321, 333, 362
Civil Rights Commission, 320–321
Civil War. *See also* Reconstruction
    Anaconda Plan, 145

Civil War *(continued)*
Emancipation Proclamation, 150
Fort Sumter, 143–144
home front, 301–303
Lincoln finds Grant, 151–152
Lincoln tries McClellan, 146
Peninsula Campaign, 146
strengths of North and South
   at outset, 250
success of northern diplomacy, 147–148
turning point in the east, 150–151
Union victories in the west, 146–147
war at sea, 226–227
Civil War, causes of
Bleeding Kansas, 132–133
Compromise of 1850, 127–128
crisis of 1850 and America at
   mid-century, 125–131
Dred Scott case, 134–135
Hinton Rowan Helper's Book, 138
John Brown's raid, 137–138
Kansas-Nebraska Act, 132
Lecompton constitution, 135–136
Lincoln-Douglas debates, 136–137
Republican Party formation, 132
secession crisis, 140
strengthened Fugitive Slave Law, 131
Uncle Tom's Cabin (Stowe), 131
Wilmot Proviso, 125–126
Civil Works Administration, 273
Clark, "Champ, " 226
Clark, Edward Y., 252
Clark, George Rogers, 42
Clark, William, **65–67**
Clay, Henry, 71, 76–77, 88
Compromise of 1850, 127–128
election of 1824, 87–90
election of 1832, 92
election of 1844, 117–118
Clayton Antitrust Act, 217
Clean Air Act, 341, 362
Clemenceau, Georges, 233
Cleveland, Grover, 174–175, 179, 183–188
election of 1888, 179
election of 1892, 183
President of United States, 175, 185,
   188, 192
Clinton, Henry, 37, 41–42
Clinton, William Jefferson

election of 1992, 366–368
election of 1996, 368–369
President of United States, 366–369
Coal, 228
Coal strike, 199
Coelho, Tony, 362
Coercive Acts, 36
Cold War
anticommunism in 1940–1950,
   317–318
Bay of Pigs, 331
Berlin crisis, 309
Berlin Wall, 331
collapse of East European
   communism, 364–365
collapse of Soviet Union and end
   of, 366
containment in Asia, 310–311
Eisenhower-Dulles foreign policy,
   311–314
emergence of cold war and
   containment, 308–310
Korean War, 311
nuclear testing in 1960s, 331
in 1960s, 366
Truman Doctrine, 366
Vietnam war, 337, 350, 352
Collier, John, 282
Colombia, 172
Colonial Period, 7–29
age of exploration, 7–11
beginnings of colonization, 11–18
colonial world, 19–24
eighteenth century, 25–26
Columbia Broadcasting System, 251
Commerce and Labor, Department of,
   199, 208
Commission form of government, 197
Commodity Credit, 274
Communes, 337
Communism
anticommunism in 1940–1950,
   317–318
collapse of East European, 364–365
emergence of cold war and
   containment, 308–310
Red Scare, 237–238
Compact theory, 64
Compromise of 1850, 127–128

Compromise of 1877, 164, 167
Conant, James B., 325
Conciliation treaties, 221
Concord, 36–37
Concurrent majority, 89, 112
Confederate States of America. *See also*
    Civil war formation of, 140
Congress
    Articles of Confederation, 44–45
    First Continental Congress, 36
    Reconstruction acts, 158
    Second Continental Congress, 36, 38
Congress of Industrial Organization,
    36, 38
Conkling, Roscoe, 167
Connecticut
    colonial founders, 16–17
    state constitution, 43–44
Conroy, Jack, 284
Conservation, Ballinger-Pinchot
    dispute, 205
Conservation laws, 199
Constitution, state, 43–44
Constitutional Convention, 50–51
    Great Compromise, 50
    New Jersey Plan, 50
    presidency, 50–51
    slavery, 50
    Three-Fifths Compromise, 50
    Virginia Plan, 50
Constitutional Union Party, 139
Constitution of United States, 49–57
    amendments to, 53–56
    Articles of, 44–46
    Bill of Rights, 51, 53, 59
    development and ratification of, 49–52
    election of 1864 and northern
        victory, 152–154
    separation and limitation of powers,
        55–56
    supremacy clause, 53
Consumer credit, 244
    in 1950s, 323
Consumer debt, during Reagan
    administration, 359
Consumption patterns
    in 1920s, 247
    in 1950s, 323
Containment

in Asia, 310–311
    emergence of cold war and, 308–310
Coolidge, Calvin, 237
    election of 1924, 259–260
    President of United States, 260–261
Coolidge, William, 210
Cooper, James Fenimore, 95
Cooper, Peter, 163
Coral Sea, Battle of, 304
Cornwallis, Charles, 40–43
Coronado, Francisco Vasquez de, 8
Corporations, 217, 229, 244–245, 175–176
    antitrust policy, 356
    corporate employment during
        1950s, 324
    dominance of big business in
        twenties, 244
    Sherman Anti-Trust Act, 180, 197, 217
Corps of Discovery, **65–67**
Cortés, Hernando (Hernan), 2
Cotton, 106–107, 231, 267, 274, 281
Coughlin, Charles E., 276, 279
Counterculture of 1960s, 337
Court system, establishment of federal
    court system, 60
Cowpens, South Carolina, 42
Cox, Archibald, 348
Cox, James M., 197, 241–242
Coxey, Jacob, 185
Crane, Stephen, 186
Crawford, William H., 88
Creationism, 254–255
Credit Mobilier scandal, 161
Creel, George, 230
Creole Incident, 116
Creoles, 9
Crittenden, John J., 140
Croly, Herbert, 201
Cuba, 287
    Bay of Pigs, 331
    Castro and, 314
    Cuban Missile Crisis, 331
    during New Deal, 287
    Platt Amendment, 196
    revolt against Spain in 1895, 187
    war with Spain and, 129
Cuban Missile Crisis, 331
Cultural developments. *See* Social and
    cultural developments

Cultural nationalism, 81
Cummins, Albert, 197
Currency Act, 32, 190
Curtis, Charles, Vice president of United States, 261
Custer, George A., 162, 174
Czechoslovakia, 234
    German occupation, 290
    Soviets and communism, 309
Czolgosz, Leon, 309

D

Darrow, Clarence, 254, **255–257**
Dartmouth College v. Woodward, 75
Darwin, Charles, 169
Daugherty, Harry M., 257, 259
Davenport, John, 17
Davis, Henry G., 198
Davis, Jefferson
    Compromise of 1850, 128
    President of Confederate States, 140, 143–144
    Secretary of War, 129
Davis, John W., 259, 276
Dawes, Charles G., 259
    Vice President of United States, 259
Dawes, William, 37
Dawes Act, 282
Dawes Plan, 262
Day, William, 195
D-Day, 304
Dean, John W., 347
Deaver, Michael, 356
DeBow, James B. D., 110
Debs, Eugene V., 185, 189, 204, 207, 230, 242, 256
Decatur, Stephen, 73
Declaration of Cairo, 306–307
Declaration of Independence, 38, 45, 48
Declaratory Act, 33
Deere, John, 105
Deficit Reduction Act, 355
Delaware, 38, 40, 23–24, 49, 143
De La Warr, Thomas, 12
DeLeon, Daniel, 209
DeLôme letter, 191
Democratic party
    during Age of Jackson, 87

election of 1852, 128–129
election of 1856, 133–134
election of 1860, 136
election of 1876, 163–164
election of 1880, 168
election of 1884, 174
election of 1896, 184–185
election of 1900, 189
election of 1904, 198
election of 1908, 204
election of 1912, 217–218
election of 1916, 218
election of 1920, 241–242
election of 1924, 259–260
election of 1928, 261
election of 1932, 269–270
election of 1936, 278–280
election of 1940, 292–293
election of 1980, 353–354
    westward expansion and, 174
Democratic Republicans, 132
Dependent Pensions Act, 180
Depression. *See also* Great Depression and New Deal
    of 1819, 75
    of 1893, 185
    panic of 1857, 136
Desegregation, of schools, 321, 340
de Soto, Hernando, 2, 28
Dewey, Thomas E., 292, 316
Diaz, Porfirio, 172, 210
Dickinson, John, 34, 38, 44, 48–50
Dinwiddie, Robert, 27
Divorce, 248
Dix, Dorothea, 125
    life and work of, **99–102**
Doheny, Edward, 258
Dole, Robert, 368
Dollar diplomacy, 202, 208, 210, 221
Dominican Republic, 202, 211, 222, 287
Dominion of New England, 22–23
Domino theory, 339
Donelson, Fort, 147
Doniphan, Alexander W., 122
Donnelly, Ignatius, 189
Donovan, Ray, 356
Dorr, Thomas, 87
Dos Passos, John, 251, 284

Douglas, Stephen A., 126, 128
  election of 1860, 139
  Freeport Doctrine, 136
  Lecompton constitution, 135
  Lincoln-Douglas debates, 136–137, 141
Douglass, Frederick, 100, 157, 182
Drake, Francis, 10
Dred Scott v. Sanford, 134–135
Dreiser, Theodore, 201
DuBois, W. E. B., 220, 231, 249, 209
Dukakis, Michael, 256, 359–360
Dulles, John Foster, 311
Duquesne, Fort, 27
Dutch West India Company, 14

E

Eagleburger, Lawrence, 363
Eagleton, Thomas, 343
East India Company, 35
Eastman, George, 181
Eaton, John, 91
Eaton, Peggy, 91
Economic Advisors, Council of, 314
Economic Recovery Tax Act, 355
Economy. *See also* Great Depression and
  New Deal
  in 1840–1850, 129
  in 1877–1882, 168–170
  in 1882–1887, 175–176
  in 1887–1892, 180
  in 1892–1897, 183–184
  in 1897–1902, 190–191
  in 1902–1907, 199–200
  in 1907–1912, 207–208
  in 1937–1938, 281
  in 1950, 322
  after American Revolution, 46–47
  after War of 1812, 74
  in Age of Jackson, 92–93, 105
  big business, 244
  under Carter administration, 351
  Civil War and, 129–130
  under Clinton, 350–351
  colonial economy in eighteenth
    century, 24
  depression of 1819, 75
  economic advances and social tensions
    of twenties, 242–246

effects of first New Deal, 270–271
expanding economy in 1820s, 77–78
under Ford administration,
  350–351
under George H. W. Bush, 360–361
under Grant during reconstruction,
  162–163
Nixon policy and problems of, 341
panic of 1837, 92–93
panic of 1857, 136
post-WW I, 236–237
Reagan administration and, 359
Eddy, Mary Baker, 170
Eden, Anthony, 313
Edison, Thomas, 168, 187
Education
  in 1877–1882, 171
  in 1882–1887, 177
  Age of Jackson, 99, 111
  desegregation of schools, 316,
    321, 340
  post-Revolutionary years, 177
  in 1960s, 320
  in twenties, 249–250
Edwards, Jonathan, 26
Egypt
  Camp David Accords, 352
  Persian Gulf crisis, 364–365
  Suez Canal crisis, 312–313
Ehrlichman, John, 348
Einstein, Albert, 177
Eisenhower, Dwight D., 269, 304, 318
  dynamic conservatism of, 318–320
  election of 1952, 318
  foreign policy of, 311–314
Eisenhower Doctrine, 313
Election, presidential
  of 1796, 63
  of 1800, 64
  of 1808, 70
  of 1824, 87–90
  of 1828, 89
  of 1832, 92
  of 1836, 93
  of 1840, 93
  of 1844, 117–118
  of 1848, 126
  of 1852, 128–129
  of 1856, 133–134

Election, presidential (*continued*)
  of 1860, 139
  of 1864, 152
  of 1868, 158–159
  of 1872, 162
  of 1876, 163–164
  of 1880, 168
  of 1884, 174
  of 1888, 179
  of 1892, 183
  of 1896, 184–185
  of 1900, 189
  of 1904, 198
  of 1908, 204
  of 1912, 206
  of 1916, 217–218, 224
  of 1920, 236, 241–242
  of 1924, 259–260
  of 1928, 261
  of 1932, 269–270
  of 1936, 278–280
  of 1940, 292–293
  of 1944, 304
  of 1948, 316
  of 1952, 318
  of 1956, 319
  of 1960, 322
  of 1964, 334
  of 1968, 339–340
  of 1972, 343–344
  of 1976, 351
  of 1980, 353–354
  of 1984, 356–357
  of 1992, 366–368
  of 1996, 368–369
  of 2000, 369
  of 2004, 370
Electoral college, 51, 88
Electrical industry, 243–244
Elementary and Secondary Education
  Act, 334
Eliot, Charles W., 192
Eliot, T. S., 251
Elizabeth, Queen of England, 10
Elkins Act, 198
Ely, Richard T., 177
Emancipation Proclamation, 150–151
Embargo of 1807, 70

Emergency Banking Relief Act, 272
Emergency Quota Act, 253, 264
Emergency Relief Appropriations
  Act, 277
Emerson, Ralph Waldo, 97
Employment. *See* Labor
Employment Act of 1946, 314
Encomiendas, 9
Endara, Guillermo, 363
England. *See also* Great Britain
  American Revolution, 31–49
  coming of American Revolution, 31–36
  exploration, 9–10
  French and Indian War, 26–27
  Spanish Armada, 10
  Treaty of 1794, 62
English, William, 168
Enlightenment, 25–26
Equal Rights Amendment, 338
Erdman Act, 190
Erie Canal, 79
Espionage Act, 230–231, 242
Estonia, 234
Ethiopia, Italian invasion of, 289
Ethnic activism, 336
Evolution, 264
Executive departments, establishment
  of, 60
  Ex Parte Merryman, 150
Exploration, Age of
  English and French exploration, 9–10
  Gilbert, Raleigh and first English
    attempt at colonization, 10–11
  Spanish conquistadores, 7–9
  Treaty of Tordesillas, 7
Exxon Corporation, 362
Exxon Valdez, 362

F

Factory system, 79–80, 104, 130
Fairbanks, Charles, 198
Fair Deal program, 316
Fair Employment Practices
  Committee, 282
Fair Labor Standards Act, 281–282
Fall, Albert B., 257–258
Fallen Timbers, Battle of, 62

Falwell, Jerry, 357
Family and Medical Leave Act, 367
Farley, James A., 270
Farm Credit Administration, 273
Farmers' Alliances, 169, 176
Farm Holiday Association, 269
Farm Security Administration (FSA),
    281–282
Farnham, Marynia, 324
Farragut, David G., 145
Farrell, James T., 284
Faulkner, William, 284
Faure, Edgar, 313
Federal Bankruptcy Act, 190
Federal budget
    billion-dollar budget in 1890, 180
    under George H. W. Bush, 360
    during Harding administration, 258
    Reagan administration and, 354
Federal Deposit Insurance Corporation
    (FDIC), 272
Federal Election Campaign Act, 341
Federal Emergency Relief Act, 273
Federal Farm Loan Act, 207, 218, 273
Federal government
    federal and state shared powers, 55
    powers reserved only for, 55
    restrictions on powers of, 56
Federal Highway Act, 243
Federal Home Loan Bank Act, 267
Federal Housing Administration, 272
Federalists, 51
    election of 1800, 64
    Federalists era, 59–60
    Hamilton, Alexander, 61
    during Washington's administration,
        60–61
Federal Land Bank, 218
Federal land policy, 91
Federal Power Commission, 278
Federal Reserve Act of 1913, 216–217
Federal Reserve Banks, 216
Federal Reserve Board, 216, 341, 351
Federal Reserve System, 216, 278
Federal Trade Commission, 217, 244, 278
Federal Trade Commission Act, 217
Fellowship of Christian
    Reconciliation, 288

Feminism. *See also* Women
    in 1877–1882, 171
    in Age of Jackson, 99–100
Ferguson, Patrick, 42
Fermi, Enrico, 306
Ferraro, Geraldine, 356
Field, James, 183
Fillmore, Millard, 128, 134
    President of United States, 128
Film, 187, 231, 244, 286
    in 1907–1912, 210
Finland, 234
Finney, Charles G., 98
First Continental Congress, 36
Fish, Hamilton, 288
Fishing, 77
Fiske, Robert B., 368
Fitzgerald, F. Scott, 251
Five Power Pact, 262
Fletcher v. Peck, 75
Florida, sale of, 73
Floyd, Charles, **66**
Flynn, Elizabeth Gurley, 209
Folk, Joseph, 198
Food. *See* Agriculture
Food Administration, 228
Forbes, Charles R., 228
Force Bill, 91, 179
Ford, Gerald R., President of United
    States, 350–351
Ford, Henry, 243
Ford Company, 208
Fordney-McCumber Tariff, 257–258
Foreign policy
    in 1877–1882, 171–174
    in 1882–1887, 178–179
    in 1887–1892, 181–182
    in 1892–1897, 187–188
    in 1897–1902, 193–196
    in 1902–1907, 202–203
    in 1907–1912, 210–213
    under Carter administration, 352–353
    under Clinton, 368–369
    under George H. W. Bush, 363–364
    Johnson, Andrew, 155–156
    New Deal diplomacy, 286–288
    new imperialism, 171
    under Nixon, 343

Foreign policy (*continued*)
    Reagan's second term, 354–356
    during twenties, 262–263
    Wilson's new freedom policy, 221
Four Power Pact, 262
Fourteen Points, 232
France
    colonization by, 13–14
    exploration, 9–10
    French and Indian War, 26–27
    help in American Revolution, 31–33
    King George's war, 25
    Monroe Doctrine and, 155–156
    War of the Spanish Succession, 25
Franklin, Benjamin, 26, 43
    Constitutional Convention, 50–51
Frazier-Lemke Farm Bankruptcy Act, 274
Fredericksburg, 198
Freedman's Bureau, 154
Freedom of Information Act, 350
Freedom Riders, 329
Freeport Doctrine, 136
Free Soil Party, 126, 129
Free-speech movement, 336
Frelinghuysen, Theodore, 26
Fremont, John C., 122, 134
French and Indian War, 26–27
French Revolution, 61–62
Friedan, Betty, 338
Frobisher, Martin, 10
Fuel Administration, 228
Fugitive Slave Law, 128, 131, 141
Fulton, Robert, 78
Fur trade, 78, 112

G

Gadsden Purchase, 129
Gage, Thomas, 36–37, 39
Galbraith, John Kenneth, 325
Gallatin, Albert, 66
Galloway, Joseph, 36
Galveston, Texas, 197
Gardoqui, 46–47
Garfield, Harry A., 228
Garfield, James A., 168
Garner, John Nance, 269
Garner-Wagner Bill, 268

Garrison, William Lloyd, 100–101
Garvey, Marcus, 249
Gary, Elbert H., 237
Gates, Horatio, 41–42, 45
Gates, Thomas, 21
General Motors, 244, 284, 291, 315
Geneva Accords, 312
George, David Lloyd, 233
George, Henry, 171
George III, King of England, 33, 38
Georgia, 25
    as colony, 25
German immigrants, 144
    anti-German sentiment and WW I,
        230, 238
Germany
    Berlin crisis, 309
    Berlin Wall, 331
    invasion of Poland and beginning of
        WW II, 290
    occupation of Rhineland, 289
    Rome-Berlin Axis, 289
    Tripartite Pact, 295
    Versailles Treaty, 234
    war debt and reparations for
        WW I, 262
    in World War I, 266
    in World War II, 304–310
Gettysburg, Battle of, 151
Ghent, Treaty of, 71–72
G.I. Bill of Rights, 315
Gibbons v. Ogden, 76
Gilbert, Humphrey, 10–11
Gingrich, Newt, 367–368
Ginsburg, Allen, 326
Gladden, Washington, 170
Glass-Steagall Act, 272
Glorious Revolution, 22, 26
Glyphs, 2
Goddard, Robert, 210
Godkin, E. L., 174
Gold, money backed by, 163
Gold, Harry, 317
Goldstein, Robert, 231
Goldwater, Barry, 334
Gompers, Samuel, 176, 192
Good Neighbor Policy, 286
Goodyear, Charles, 104

Gorbachev, Mikhail S., 357, 364, 366
Gore, Al
  election of 2000, 369
  vice president of United States, 369
Gore-McLemore Resolution, 223
Gospel of Wealth, 169
Graham, Billy, 325
Grant, Ulysses S., 144, 146, 158
  in Civil War, 144–151
  corruption under, 160–161
  economic issues under, 162–163
  election of 1868, 158–159
  President of United States, 151–163
Great Awakening, 26
Great Britain. *See also* England
  neutrality in Civil War and, 143–144
  Venezuela border dispute, 187
  War of 1812, 70–71
  Webster-Ashburton Treaty, 116
Great Depression and New Deal
  American response to war in Europe,
    290–291
  criticism of New Deal,
  diplomacy during and road to war,
    286–288
  economic and human effects of, 266
  election of 1940, 292–293
  first New Deal, 270–271
  Hundred Days, 271–272
  labor unions, 283–284
  last years of New Deal, 280–282
  reasons for depression, 265–266
  road to Pearl Harbor, 294–297
  Second Hundred Days, 276–277
  Second New Deal, 276–282
  social dimensions of New Deal era,
    282–283
  stock market boom and crash during
    twenties, 263
  threats to world order, 289–290
  United States neutrality legislation,
    288–289
Great Migration, 16
Great Society programs, 334
Great Sun, Natchez group leader, 3
Greeley, Horace, 140
Green, William, 245, 283
Greenback-Labor Party, 168

Greenback Party, 163
Greenbacks, 149, 159, 163
Greene, Nathaniel, 42
Greenland, 291
  U.S. occupation of, 293
Greenville, Treaty of, 62
Grenville, George, 31–33
Gresham, Walter Q., 188
Grey, Edward, 224
Gross national product, in 1950s,
  322–333
Guadalupe-Hidalgo, Treaty of, 123
Guam, 192, 195
Guantanamo Bay, 196
Guatemala, 313, 172
Guilford Court House, North
  Carolina, 42
Guiteau, Charles, 168
Gulf of Tonkin resolution, 338, 342
Guzman, Jacobo Arbenz, 313

H

Haber, Al, 336
Hacienda system, 9
Hagerty, Thomas, 209
Hague Conference, 209
Haiti, 182, 202, 222, 287
  in 1887–1892, 182
Hakluyt, Richard, 11
Haldeman, H. R., 348
Hale, John P., 129
Half Breeds, 167
Half-Way Covenant, 21–21
Halleck, Henry W., 146–147
Hamilton, Alexander, 49–51
  death of, 69
  election of 1800, 64
  Federalists, 61
  as Treasury Secretary, 60–61
Hancock, John, 34, 51
Hancock, Winfield S., 192
Hanna, Mark, 192
Harding, Warren G.
  death of, 258–259
  election of 1920, 241–242
  President of United States,
    256–259

Harriman, E. H., 175
Harriman, Job, 189
Harris, Joel Chandler, 181
Harrison, Benjamin
    election of 1888, 179
    election of 1892, 183
    President of United States, 182
Harrison, William Henry, 70–71, 93, 115
Hart, Gary, 356, 359
Harte, Bret, 171
Hartford, Connecticut, 72
Hartford convention, 72
Hawaii
    in 1887–1892, 182
    annexation of, 129, 195
    as state, 320
Hawley-Smoot Tariff, 267
Hawthorne, Nathaniel, 96–97
Hay, John, 196
Hay-Bunau-Varilla Treaty, 202–203
Hayden, Tom, 336
Hayes, Rutherford B.
    compromise of 1877, 164, 167
    election of 1878, 168
    President of United States, 169, 172
Haymarket Riot, 169
Hayne, Robert, 91
Haynesworth, Clement F., Jr., 340
Hay-Pauncefote treaty, 196
Haywood, "Big Bill, " 209
Head Start, 334
Hearst, William Randolph, 191
Heller, Joseph, 325
Hemingway, Ernest, 251, 284
Hendrick, Burton, 201
Hendricks, Thomas A., 174
Henry, Fort, 147
Henry, Patrick, 32, 51
Henry Street Settlement, 187
Hepburn Act, 198
Herberg, Will, 325
Herkimer, Nicholas, 41
Herter, Christian A., 311
Hessians, 39–40
Higher education
    in 1882–1887, 177
    in Age of Jackson, 99
    post-Revolution years, 82

in twenties, 249–250
Hijuelos, Oscar, 372–373
Hinckley, John W., 355
Hiroshima, Japan, 306
Hiss, Alger, 317
Hitler, Adolf, 236
    occupation of Rhineland, 289
HIV, 371
Hobart, Garrett, 184
    Vice President of United States, 189
Ho Chi Minh, 312
Holland, 14
    Navigation Acts and, 20–22
Hollywood, 210
Holmes, Oliver Wendell, Jr., Sedition
    Act, 230–231
Homelessness, during Great
    Depression, 266
Home ownership, in 1950s, 323
Home Owners Loan Corporation
    (HOLC), 272
Homestead Act, 148
Homestead strike, 185
Hood, John B., 152
Hooker, Joseph "Fighting Joe, " 150–151
Hooker, Thomas, 17
Hoover, Herbert, 228, 257, 261
    depression policies, 266–269
    election of 1928, 261
    election of 1932, 269–270
    President of United States, 263, 266,
        269, 316
Hoovervilles, 266
Hopkins, Harry, 273, 277, 285
House, Edward M., 224, 233
House-Grey Memorandum, 224
House of Representatives
    Constitution of United States, 50–52
    impeachment and, 158
    required percentages of voting, 64
    responsibilities and duties of, 111–112
    Speaker of, 52, 138
Housing Act, 329
Housing and Urban Development
    Act, 334
Houston, Sam, 114, 117
Howe, Elias, 104, 130
Howe, Louis, 269–270

Howe, Richard, 39
Howe, William, 37, 39–41
Howell, William Dean, 171, 177, 186
Hudson, Henry, 14
Hudson's Bay Company, 113
Huerta, Victoriano, 210, 222
Hughes, Charles Evans, 197, 219, 220, 224, 256, 262, 280
Huguenots, 9–10
Hull, Cordell, 170, 186, 288, 306
Hull House, 187
Human rights, Carter and foreign policy based on, 352–353
Humphrey, Hubert H., 334
Vice president of United States, 339
Hundred Days, 271–275
Hungary, 234, 308
Hunter, Robert, 201
Hurley, Edward N., 229
Hussein, Saddam, 364, 375
Hutchinson, Anne, 16
Hutchinson, Thomas, 35
Hydrogen bomb, 311

Iceland, U.S. occupation of, 293
Ickes, Harold L., 270
Idaho Power Company, 319
Immigrants/Immigration
in 1877–1882, 170–209
in 1892–1897, 187
in 1960, 334
eighteenth-century colonial, 25
Japanese, 221
lack of government policy for, 170
restrictions during twenties, 202
social gospel and, 98, 170
suspension of, from China in 1882, 178
from 1815 to 1837, 102
under Wilson, 220
Immigration Act of 1965, 334
Immunity of Witness Act, 199
Impeachment
Andrew Johnson, 152
Clinton, 366
of judges, 66

Nixon and, 348
Senate and House role in, 369, 56
Income
during Great Depression, 266
during twenties, 283
Income tax, 278
Indenture system, 12
Independent Sub-Treasury system, 118
Indian Affairs, Bureau of, 282
Indian Emergency Conservation Program, 282
Indian Removal Act in 1830, 90
Indian Reorganization Act, 282
Indian reservations, 174
Individual Retirement Account, 355
Industrialization
corporation, 79
expansion of during 1877–1882, 167
growth of unions, 80
labor supply, 80, 91
rise of factory system, 79
Industrial Workers of the World (I.W.W.), 209
Industry
growth of, in Northeast during Age of Jackson, 104
Hundred Days legislation, 277
productivity and prosperity during twenties, 242–233
in Southern states during Age of Jackson, 110
in WW I, 245, 274
Inflation
in 1837, 102
under Carter administration, 351
under Nixon, 341
during reconstruction, 267
Sherman Silver Purchase Act, 180
Insular cases, 196
Interest rates
under Carter administration, 351
Federal Reserve Bank and, 207, 216
Internal Waterways Commission, 199
International Workers of the World, 238
Interstate Commerce Act, 175, 198
Interstate Commerce Commission, 190, 198, 205, 236, 244, 278,
Mann-Elins Act, 205

Interstate Highway System, 319, 323
Intolerable Acts, 36, **48**
Inventions
  automobiles, 208
  in Northern states during Age
    of Jackson, 104
  Wright brothers, 201
Iran
  Iran-Contra, 358, 374
  Iranian crisis, 353
Iraq
  Iraq war, 364–365, **375**
  Persian Gulf war, 364
Irish immigrants, 130
Iron Curtain, 308, **327**
Irving, Washington, 81
Isle of Pines, 192
Isolationism, during 1930s, 288
Israel, 313, **328**
  Camp David Accords, 308
Isthmian canal, 308
Italy, 308
  invasion of Ethiopia, 289, **299**
  Rome-Berlin Axis, 289
  Tripartite Pact, 295

J

Jackson, Andrew, 88. *See also* Jacksonian
  democracy (1829–1841)
  invasion of Florida, 73–74
  President of United States, 89–90
Jackson, Helen Hunt, 174, **213**
Jackson, Jesse, 356, **360–361**
Jackson, Thomas J. "Stonewall," 146
Jacksonian democracy (1829–1841),
  87–123
  Adams administration, 63, 64, 65,
    88–89
  age of reform, 95
  changing emphasis towards states'
    rights, 94
  election of 1824, 87–90
  election of 1828, 89
  election of 1840, 93
  mormons, 98–120
  Northern states during, 87, 88, 110
  organized reform, 98–101

Southern states during, 87, 106, 110,
  111–112
transcendentalists, 97
utopians, 97–98
war on the bank, 92–93
Webster-Hayne Debate, 91–92
James, Henry, 171, 178
James, William, 186, 192
James I, King of England, 13, 15
James II, King of England, 22, **29**
Jamestown, 12, 21, **28**
Japan
  containment in, 308, **310–327**
  gentleman's agreement with,
    in 1907, 203
  Manchurian crisis, 289
  relations in 1878, 172
  relations in 1882, 178–179
  road to Pearl Harbor, 294–297
  Russo-Japanese War, 202–203
  Sino-Japanese war, 187, 290
  Taft-Katsura Memo, 203, 211
  Tripartite Pact, 295
  Wilson early foreign policy, 221–222
  in WW II, 236
Japan Americans, internment of,
  during WW II, 303
Jaworski, Leon, 348
Jay, John, 43, 46, 51, 62
Jay Cooke and Company, 163
Jefferson, Thomas, 38, 53, 60, 61–63, 64,
  65–67, 77, 89
  Bill of Rights, 53, 56
  conflict with judges, 66
  domestic affairs, 67–69
  election of 1796, 63
  election of 1800, 64–65
  international involvement, 69–70
  Kentucky and Virginia resolutions, 64
  as President, 89
  Republican party, 69
  Vice President of the United States,
    63, 34
Jenkins, Robert, 25
Jews
  immigration restrictions, 220, 250
  Ku Klux Klan, 160, 249, 250, 252,
    259, **264**

during twenties, 252, 283
Jim Crow laws, 104
Johns Hopkins University, 177, 215
Johnson, Andrew
    attempt at reconstruction, 155
    congressional reconstruction, 156–158
    foreign policy under, 155
    impeachment, 162
    President of United States, 52, 216
Johnson, Hiram, 198, 206
Johnson, Hugh S., 260, 270, 274
Johnson, Lyndon B.
    election of 1964, 334
    President of United States, 52, 216
    Vice President of United States, 314
    Vietnam war, 337, 350, 352
Johnson, Tom L., 198
Johnson Act of 1934, 288
Johnston, Albert Sidney, 144, 147
Johnston, Joseph E., 144, 145, 146
Joint Chiefs of Staff, 315
Jones, James, 325
Jones, John Paul, 43
Jones, "Mother" Mary Harris, 209
Jones, Sam, 198
Jones, Thomas Catsby, 121
Jordan, David Starr, 192
Juarez, Benito, 156
Judiciary, impeachment of judges, 350
Judiciary Act of 1789, 53, 60

K

Kansas
    Bleeding Kansas, 132–133
    Kansas-Nebraska Act, 132
    Lecompton constitution, 135,
        136, **141**
Kansas-Nebraska Act, 132
Kassarine Pass, Battle of, 304
Kearney, Stephen W., 122
Keats, John, 325
Kellogg, Frank B., 262
Kellogg-Briand Pact, 262, **264**, 289
Kemp, Jack, 368
Kennan, George F., 308
Kennedy, Anthony, 359
Kennedy, Edward M., 353

Kennedy, John F.
    assassination of, 332
    Cuban Missile Crisis, 331
    election of 1960, 322
    New Frontier and liberal revival, 329
    President of United States, 322, 330
Kennedy, Robert F., 330
    civil rights movement and, 335
Kent State protests, 342
Kentucky, 46, 63, 245
Kern, John, 204
Kerouac, Jack, 326
Kerr-McGillicuddy Act of 1916, 218
Khomeini, Ayatollah Ruhollah, 353
Khrushchev, Nikita, 312–313, 331
    Cuban Missile Crisis, 331
King, Martin Luther, Jr., 312, 330,
    331, 334
    assassination of, 335
King George's war, 25
King Philip (Metacomet), 22
Kings Mountain, Battle of, 42
King William's War, 25
Kissinger, Henry, 342–343
Kleindienst, Richard, 348
Knights of Labor, 169
Know-Nothing Party, 130–131
    election of 1856, 133–134
Knox, Frank, 278, 291
Knox, Henry, 60
Knox, P. C., 199, 211–212
Knudson, William S., 291
Korean War, 311
Korematsu v. United States, 303
Kosovo, 368–369
Ku Klux Klan, 160, 252, 259
    during twenties, 250
Kuwait, Persian Gulf crisis, 364–364

L

Labor. *See also* Unions
    in 1887–1882, 174–175
    child labor laws, 200
    corporate employment during
        1950s, 324
    formation of AFL, 283
    Lowell System, 80
    in 1950s, 324

Labor *(continued)*
   strikes in 1919, 229
   during twenties, 245
   work hour restrictions, 274
   in WW I, 229
LaFollette, Robert M., 197, 206, 259–260
Landon, Alfred M., 278–280
Land Ordinance, 46
Land policy, federal, 91
Landrum-Griffen Labor-Management
   Act, 320
Lanier, Sidney, 181
Lansing, Robert, 221, 223, 233
Lansing-Ishii Agreement, 221
La Salle, Sieur de, 13
Latin America
   in 1892–1897, 172, 179, 188
   arbitration treaties, 211
   during twenties, 263
Latvia, 234
Lavelle, Rita, 356
Lawson, Thomas, 201
League of Nations, 234, 289
Leary, Timothy, 337
Lease, Mary, 183
Lee, Jason, 118
Lee, Richard Henry, 38
Lee, Robert E., 138, 144–146, 150–153
Legislative branch, Constitution
   of United States and, 177
Leisler, Jacob, 23
Lemke, William, 279–280
Lend-Lease Act, 293
L'Enfant, Pierre, 65
Lever Act, 228
Levitt, William, 323
Lewis, Henry, 201
Lewis, John L., 237, 245, 283, 315
Lewis, Sinclair, 251, 284
Lewis, Meriwether, **65–67**
Lewis and Clark expedition, **65–67**
Lexington, 36–37
Leyte Gulf, Battle of, 305
Liberalism
   Carter's moderate, 351–352
   Kennedy's New Frontier and revival
   of, 329

New Left in 1960s, 336–337
Liberal Republicans, 162
Liberty Party, 118
Libya, Reagan administration and, 357
Lieberman, Joseph, 369
Liliuokalani, Lydia Kamekeha, 182, 188
Lincoln, Abraham
   Anaconda Plan, 145
   assassination of, 155
   election of 1860, 139
   election of 1864, 152–154
   Emancipation Proclamation, 150
   Lincoln-Douglas debates, 136–137
   plan for reconstruction, 154–155
   President of United States, 143–149
   as war leader, 143–145
Lincoln, Benjamin, 42
Line of Demarcation, 7
Lippmann, Walter, 260
Literary nationalism, 81
Literature
   in 1877–1882, 171
   in 1882–1887, 176–177
   in 1892–1897, 186
   in 1897–1902, 192–193
   in 1902–1907, 201
   in 1907–1912, 209
   during Age of Jackson, 95–96
   children's literature in 1887–1892, 181
   realism, 177–178
   in 1930s, 284–285
   in 1950s, 323
   during twenties, 251
   yellow journalism, 191
Lithuania, 234, 366
Little, Arthur, 210
Little Rock, Arkansas, desegregation of
   schools, 321
Locke, John, 26, 64
Lodge, Henry Cabot, 192, 211, 235, 241
Logan, John, 174
London, Jack, 201
London Economic Conference, 287
Long, Huey, 276
Long Island, Battle of, 40
Longstreet, Augustus, 96
Louisbourg, 25

Louisiana Purchase, **65**, 67, 68, 76, 200
Lovejoy, Elijah, 100
Lowden, Frank O., 214
Lowell, James Russell, 96
Lowell System, 80
Loyalty Review Board, 317
Lumbering, 78
Lundberg, Ferdinand, 324
Lusitania, 223

M

MacArthur, Douglas, 269, 305–306, 310–311
Mackenzie, Alexander, **65**
Macon's Bill No. 2, 70
Madero, Francisco I., 210
Madison, Dolley, 70
Madison, James, 49–51, 66, 70–72
   Constitutional Convention, 50–51
   election of 1808, 70
   Kentucky and Virginia resolutions, 64
   Republican party, 69
   as secretary of state, 66
   War of 1812, 70–71
Magazines, 176–177
Magellan, Ferdinand, 9
Magruder, Jeb Stuart, 347
Mahan, Alfred Thayer, 183, 192
Maine, statehood, 76
Maize, in pre-Columbian culture, 5
Manchuria, 289
Manhattan Project, 306
Manifest destiny, 112–115
Mann, Horace, 99
Mann Act, 209
Mann-Elins Act, 205
Manufacturing. *See also* Industry
   expansion of, during 1877–1882, 168
   in Northeast during Age of Jackson, 104–106
   in Southern states during Age of Jackson, 106
Mao Tse-tung, 311, 345
Marbury, William, 66
Marbury v. Madison, 66, 75
March on Washington, 330–331

Marion, Francis, 43
Maritime shipping, in WW I, 229
Marquette, Jacques, 13
Marshall, George C., 309, 311
Marshall, Thomas, 206
Marshall, Thurgood, 320, 336, 363
Marshall, John, 65–66, 69, 75–76,
Marshall Plan, 309
Mary II, Queen of England, 22
Maryland, 17
   colonial founders, 17
   state constitution, 43–44
Mason, George, 51
Mason, James M., 148
Massachusetts
   Dominion of New England, 22–23
   Massachusetts Bay colony, 15–16
   ratification of Constitution, 17
   state constitution, 43–44
Massachusetts Bay colony, 15–16
Massachusetts Circular Letter, 34
Massachusetts Government Act, 16, 36
Mass production, 79, 104, 283
Mather, Cotton, 23
Matsu, 312
Maximilian, Archduke of Austria, 155–156
Mayas civilization, 1–2
Mayflower, 15
Maysville Road, 90
McAdoo, William G., 215, 220, 229, 241
McCarran Internal Security Act, 317
McCarthy, Eugene, 339
McCarthy, Joseph R., 318
McClellan, George B., 150–152
McCord, James, 347
McCormick, Cyrus, 130
McCulloch v. Maryland, 76
McDowell, Irvin, 145
McFarlane, Robert, 358
McGovern, George, 343
McHenry, Fort, 71
McKinley, William, 180–194
   assassination of, 190
   election of 1896, 184–185
   election of 1900, 189

McKinley, William (*continued*)
   foreign relations in 1892–1897,
      187–188
   President of United States, 188–191
   war with Spain, 190
McKinley Tariff, 180
McNary-Haugen Bill, 260
McVeigh, Timothy James, 371
Meade, George G., 151–152
Meat Inspection Act, 198
Medicare, 334, 360
Meese, Edwin, 356
Mellon, Andrew, 256
Melville, Herman, 96
Mencken, H. L., 251, **255–257**
Mercantilism, 20–21
   drain on eighteenth-century
      colonies, 32
Meredith, James, 330
Mergenthaler, Otto, 176
Metcalf, Henry, 189
Meuse-Argonne offensive, 227
Mexican Americans
   employment during WW I, 249
   during New Deal, 282
   in twenties, 249
   United Farm Workers, 336
Mexican Cession, 120, 123, 126–127
Mexican War, 120–126
Mexico
   Mexican War, 120–126
   Monroe Doctrine and, 222
   during New Deal, 282
   revolution of 1910, 210–211
   Wilson early foreign policy, 221–222
   Zimmerman telegram, 225
Michelson, Albert, 177
Middle class, in 1950s, 324
Middle East, Nixon administration
   and, 343
Midway, Battle of, 305
Mikoyan, Anastas I., 313
Military Reconstruction Act, 158
Miller, Arthur, 325
Minimum wage, 206, 209, 274, 281,
   314, 316
Minutemen, 37
Missionaries, 179

Mississippi River, 3, 8, 27
   explorations around, **65–67**
   Treaty with Spain in 1795, 62
Missouri, 132–135
   statehood, 76–77
Missouri Compromise, 76, 114, 125, 132,
   135, 140
   explorations around, **65–67**
   repeal of, 132
Mitchell, John, 348
Mitchell, John Purroy, 198
Moctezuma, Aztec King, 2
Molasses Act, 24, 32
Moley, Raymond, 270
Mondale, Walter, 351, 356–357
Money
   after American Revolution, 44
   Currency Act, 190
   greenbacks, 149, 159, 163
   Sherman Silver Purchase Act, 180, 184
Monmouth, Battle of, 41
Monroe, James, 182
   Monroe Doctrine, 74, 155–156
   presidency, 74
Monroe Doctrine, 74, 155–156,
   222, 235, 291
   Lodge corollary to, 211
   Roosevelt corollary on, 202
Montevideo Conference, 287
Montgomery, Richard, 37–38
Montreal, 9, 27, 37
Moral Majority, 357
Morgan, Daniel, 42
Morgan, J. P., 175, 199
Mormons
   origins of religion, 98
   westward migration of, 119–120
Mormon War, 120
Morocco, 203
Morrill Land Grant, 148
Morris, Gouverneur, 50
Morrison, Toni, 373
Morse, Samuel B., 104
Moscow Conference, 306
Motor Carrier Act, 278
Mott, Lucretia, 103
Movies. See Film
Muckrakers, 200–201

Mugwumps, 174
Murray, Philip, 315
Mussolini, Benito, 289, 304
My Lai massacre, 341

N

Nader, Ralph, 369
Nagasaki, Japan, 305, 306, 327
Naismith, James, 181
Napoleon, Louisiana purchase, 63, 67–69, 74, 155–156
Napoleonic Wars, 69
Napoleon III, 155, 156
Narragansett Bay, 16
Narvaez, Panfilio, 8
Natchez group, 3
Nashoba, 97
Nasser, Gamal Abdul, 312
National Aeronautics and Space Administration (NASA), 320, 333, 359
National Association for the Advancement of Colored People, 200, 249
National Association of Manufacturers, 245
National Banking Act, 149, 215
National Broadcasting Company, 251
National Conservation Commission, 199
National Cordage Company, 185
National Defense, Council of, 227, 291
National Defense Education Act, 320
National Grange, 169, 176
National Guard, preparedness for WW I, 224, 237, 263, 330, 331,
National Housing Act, 281
National Industrial Recovery Act, 274, 283, 298
Nationalism, 81, 112, 217, 206
National Labor Relations Act, 227, 280, 283, 298
National Labor Relations Board, 227
National Labor Union, 169
National Military Establishment, 315
National Monetary Commission, 207
National Organization for Women, 345, 388
National Origins Act of 1924, 253, 264

National Recovery Administration (NRA), 274,
National Republicans, 89, 93
National Road, 78
National Security Act, 315
National Security Council, 315, 358
National Union for Social Justice, 276
National Urban League, 249
National Youth Administration, 277
Native Americans
  in 1877–1882, 174
  American Indian Movement, 336
  frontier problems of 1794, 62
  under Jackson, 88
  King Philip's war, 22
  during New Deal, 282
  pressuring Indians to move west of Mississippi, 73
  Trail of Tears, 90, 124
Native tribes and new immigrants, in pre-Columbian culture, 4–5
Nativist movement, 130
NATO (North Atlantic Treaty Organization), 310
Natural science, 171
Navigation Act, 20, 21, 22, 32
Navy
  American Neutrality Patrol, 293
  great white naval fleet, 203
  modern, 167
  shoot-on-sight order, 294
  war with Spain, 10, 11, 185, 188, 190, 191, 193, 195
  in WW I, 226–227
Necessity, Fort, 27
Neutrality, American, 223, 293
Neutrality Act
  of 1935–1937, 288, 289
  of 1939, 291
New Amsterdam, 14, 18
Newburgh Conspiracy, 45
New Deal. *See* Great Depression and New Deal
New England colonies
  Dominion of New England, 22
  life in, 19, 20
  Navigation Acts, 22
New Federalism, 340

New Hampshire, colonial founders, 16, 17
New Harmony, Indiana, 97
New Haven, 17
New Jersey
    colonial founders, 18
    Dominion of New England, 22
New Left, 336, 337
New Mexico, 114–115
New nation (1789–1824)
    conflict with judges, 66
    domestic affairs, 67
    educational development, 80
    establishment of executive depart-
        ments, 60
    expanding economy, 77
    Federalist era, 59
    foreign and frontier affairs, 61
    industrialization, 79
    internal development (1820–1830), 74
    internal problems, 62
    international involvement, 69
    Jeffersonian era, 65
    John Adams' administration
        (1797–1801), 63
    Madison's administration (1809–1817), 70
    Marshall court, 75
    postwar developments, 73
    religious life developments, 82
    repression and protest, 64
    revolution of 1800, 64
    statehood, 76, 46
    transportation revolution, 78
    Washington's administration
        (1789–1797), 60
New nationalism, 217, 206, 207
New Orleans, Battle of, 71
Newspapers, 81
    comic strips, 286
New York
    changing from New Amsterdam, 18
    Dominion of New England, 22
    Leisler's Rebellion, 23
    ratification of Constitution and,
        216, 316
New York City, rise of, 79
New York Free School, 81, 99
Nez Perce War, 174
Ngo Dinh Diem, 312, 338

Nicaragua, 221, 222, 263, 287, 358
    in 1894, 185, 188
    Reagan administration and, 358
    Wilson early foreign policy, 221
Nichols, Terry, 371
Nicols, Richard, 18
Niebuhr, Reinhold, 325
Nimitz, Chester W., 305
9/11 attacks, controversial response to,
    371–372
Nine Power Pact, 262, 289
Nixon, Richard M., 37, 313, 318, 322,
    340, 344
    conservative reaction of,
        first term, 340
    election of 1960, 322
    election of 1968, 339
    election of 1972, 343
    foreign policy, 343
    President of United States, 340–343
    Vice President of United States,
        313, 314
    Vietnamization, 341
    Watergate, 347, 374
Non-Intercourse Act, 70
Noriega, Manuel, 363
Norris, Frank, 193
Norris, George W., 260, 288
North, Frederick, 34
North, Oliver, 358
North American Free Trade Agreement
    (NAFTA), 367, 375
North Carolina
    colonial life, 42
    colonial period, 7
    ratification of Constitution and, 316
Northern Securities Company, 199
Northern states. See also Civil war;
    Reconstruction; Sectional conflict
    blacks' role in, 280
    everyday life in the north, 106
    growth in cities, 103
    growth in industry, 104
    immigration, 130
    increase in median age, 102
    inventions and technology, 104, 105
    new market economy, 105
    population growth, 102

problems in urbanization, 99, 103
revolution of agriculture, 105
revolution of commerce, 106
rise of unions, 104
social unrest, 103
women's role in, 103–104
Northwest Ordinance of 1787, 46, 125
Northwest passage, 9, 10, 14, **65**
Nuclear arms
Reagan administration and, 356,
358, 359
reduction under George H. W. Bush,
364
SALT and, 343, 346
Nuclear testing, in 1960s, 331
Nullification, 91, 94, 124
Nye, Gerald, 288, 298

O

Oberlin College, 99
Occupational Safety and Health Act, 341
O'Connor, Sandra Day, 356, 359, 374
Oglethorpe, James, 25
Ohio, French and Indian War, 26
Ohio River, 13, 36
Okinawa, Battle of, 306
Old Age Revolving Pension Plan, 276,
298
Olney, Richard, 188
Oneida Community, 97
Open Door policy, 294, 188, 202, 203,
214
Operation Desert Storm, 365, 375
Oppenheimer, J. Robert, 306
Oregon
settlement of, 118
westward expansion and, 115
Oregon Trail, 118, 119, 120
Oregon Treaty, 119, 124
Organization Act, 282, 316
Organization of American States, 172
Organization of Petroleum Exporting
Countries, 343
Oriskany, Battle of, 41
Orlando, Vittorio, 233
O'Sullivan, John L, 117
Oswald, Lee Harvey, 332

Otis, Elisha, 170
Otis, James, 31, 32, 33
Overman Act, 228
Owen, Robert, 97, 280

P

Pacific, War of, 307
Pago Pago, 172, 182
Paine, Thomas, 38, 48, 82
Palestine, 367
Palmer, A. Mitchell, 237, 238, 241
Panama, George Bush administration
and, 363
Panama Canal, 172, 221, 239, 352, 295
Pan American policy, 182, 188, 222
in 1887–1892, 179, 181
Pan American Union, 172, 222
Panic of 1873, 160, 163, 165, 169
Panic of 1907, 199, 207, 216
Paraguay, 172
Paramount Pictures, 210
Parenting, in 1887–1892, 181
Paris, Treaty
of 1763, 27
of 1783, 43, 49
of 1900, 195
Paris Peace Treaty, 43
Parker, Alton B., 198
Parker, John, 37
Parkman, Francis, 96
Parks, Rosa, 321
Paterson, William, 50
Patrick, Deval Laurdine, 361
Patriot Act, USA, **371–372**
Patroon system, 14
Patten, Simon, 177
Patton, George S., 269, 304
Peace Corps, 332, 345
Peale, Norman Vincent, 325
Pearl Harbor, 178, 294, 296, 297, 299, 327
road to, 294
Peek, George, 260, 270
Pemberton, John C., 151
Pendleton Act, 168
Peninsula Campaign, 146
Peninsulares, 9
Penn, William, 23, 29

Pennsylvania
founding of, and colonial life, 19
state constitution, 43
Pennsylvania Dutch, 24
Pentagon Papers, 342
People's Party, 183
Perkins School for the Blind, 99
Perot, H. Ross, 366
Perry, Matthew, 129
Perry, Oliver Hazard, 71
Pershing, John J., 222, 227
Persian Gulf crisis, 364
Peru, 1, 5, 28, 314, 172
Philadelphia, British in, 41
Philip II, King of Spain, 10
Philippines, 188, 192, 195, 203, 206, 288,
296, 304, 305
independence of, 288
Philippine Sea, Battle of, 305
Phillips, David, 201
Pierce, Franklin, 101, 128
President of United States, 216
Pike, Zebulon, 68
Pinchback, P.B.S., 361
Pinchot, Gifford, 205
Pinckney, Charles, 64, 70
Pinckney, Thomas, 62
Pinckney Treaty, 62
Pingree, Hazen, 198
Pitt, William, 27
Pittman, Key, 288
Pizarro, Francisco, 1
Pizarro, Juan, 1
Plantation system, 106–108, 110
Planter class, 107
Platt Amendment, 196, 214, 287
Plymouth, pilgrims at, 15
Poe, Edgar Allan, 112
Poindexter, John, 358
Poland, 290
invasion of, and beginning of WW II, 290
Political parties. *See also* Democratic
party; Republican party; Whig party
Age of Jackson and, 87, 94, 95
appearance of, 61
nativist movement, 130
in 1850s, 130
Polk, James K., 117
Mexican War and, 120, 121, 123, 125,
126, 144

Ponce de León, Juan, *8*
Pontiac, *29*, 30
Pope, John, 146
Popular sovereignty, 126, 127
Population
in 2000, 369
in colonial eighteenth century, 25, 26
growth in 1790–1860, 102
growth in 1950s, 323
growth of, by 1840s, 129
during twenties, 252, 283
Populist party, 183, 184, 208, *213*
election of 1892, 183
election of 1896, 184, 187
Portsmouth, Rhode Island, 16
Portsmouth, Treaty of, 202
Portugal, Treaty of Tordesillas, 7
Postal Savings Banks, 184, 208
Postmaster General, 220
Post-revolution era. See New nation
(1789–1824)
Potsdam Conference, 308, 327
Pound, Ezra, 251
Powell, Lewis F., Jr., 340
Powers, Francis Gary, 313
Powhatan, 12, 28
Preamble of Constitution
of United States, 52
Pre-Columbian cultures, 1–6
important civilizations of, 1–2
maize in, 5
native tribes and new immigrants
in, 4–5
Preemption Act, 115
Presidential Succession Act, 174, 316
President of United States, office of
cabinet, 215
Constitutional Convention, 50, *57*
Constitution of United States, 49, 52
electoral college, 51, 88, 179
powers of office, 51
requirements for, 94, 154
responsibilities and duties of, 52
Presidents of United States. *See also*
Election, presidential
Adams, John, 34, 43, 59, 63, 64
Adams, John Quincy, 88, 182, 124
Arthur, Chester A., 168
Buchanan, James, 120, 133

Bush, George H. W., 354, 357, 360, 366
Bush, George W., 369, 370, 375
Carter, James Earl, 351
Cleveland, Grover, 174, 179, 183, 192
Clinton, William Jefferson, 366
Coolidge, Calvin, 237, 241, 259, 260
Eisenhower, Dwight D., 269, 304,
    311, 318
Fillmore, Millard, 128, 134
Ford, Gerald R., 348
Garfield, James A., 168
Grant, Ulysses S., 114, 146, 158
Harding, Warren G., 241, 256
Harrison, Benjamin, 179, 183
Harrison, William Henry, 70, 71,
    93, 115
Hayes, Rutherford B., 163, 167
Hoover, Herbert, 228, 257, 261, 263,
    316
Jackson, Andrew, 71, 73, 87, 88, 89, 90,
    91, 94, 114,
Jefferson, Thomas, 38, 53, 60, 61, 63,
    64, 65, 77, 89
Johnson, Andrew, 152, 155, 159, 175
Johnson, Lyndon B., 322
Kennedy, John F., 322
Lincoln, Abraham, 136, 139, 167
Madison, James, 49, 50, 51, 61
McKinley, William, 180, 184, 189
Nixon, Richard M., 313, 318, 322, 340
Pierce, Franklin, 101, 128
Polk, James K., 117
Reagan, Ronald, 351, 354, 357
Roosevelt, Franklin D., 242, 269, 270,
    301, 303, 306
Roosevelt, Theodore, 218, 219, 241,
    270, 167, 188, 189, 190, 192, 197,
    198, 202, 204, 206, 214
Taft, William H., 204
Taylor, Zachary, 121, 122, 126, 127
Truman, Harry S., 314
Tyler, John, 93, 115
Van Buren, Martin, 93, 117, 126
Washington, George, 27, 38, 49, 50,
    51, 52, 59, 171
Wilson, Woodrow, 215, 333, 117
Price Administration, Office of, 291
Prices
    freezes under Nixon, 341

price controls and Truman, 301, 314
    wage controls during WW II, 301
Princeton, 40, 215
Prisons, during Age of Jackson, 87
Proclamation of 1763, 32
Proctor, Redfield, 194
Production Management, Office of, 291
Progressive era (1877–1912)
    economic depression and social crisis,
        1892–1897, 183
    emergence of regional empire,
        1887–1892, 179
    new industrial era, 1877–1882, 167
    reaction to corporate industrialism,
        1882–1887, 174
    regulatory state and ordered society,
        1907–1912, 203
    Theodore Roosevelt and progressive
        reforms, 1902–1907, 197
    war and Americanization of the world,
        1897–1902, 189
Progressive Party
    election of 1912, 205, 206, 217
    election of 1924, 259
Progressive reform movement, in
    1902–1907, 197
Prohibition, 232, 239, 269, 271
    repeal of, 269, 271, 278
Prohibition Party, 189
Prohibitory Act, 38
Prosser, Gabriel, 109
Protestant Revivalism, 98
Providence, Rhode Island, 16
Public Information, Committee on,
    231, 239
Public schools
    in Age of Jackson, 95
    first, 257
Public Utility Holding Company, 278
Public works, during Great
    Depression, 267
Public Works Administration, 273
Puerto Ricans, during 1920s, 249
Puerto Rico, 249
Puget Sound, 119
Pulitzer, Joseph, 177, 191
Pullman strike, 185, 214
Pure Food and Drug Act, 198, 214
Puritans, 15, 16, 17, 18, 19, 21, 22

Puritans (*continued*)
 Half-Way Covenant, 21, 22
 life in the colonies, 19
 at Massachusetts Bay colony, 15, 28, 29
Pyle, Howard, 181

Q

Qadhafi, Mu'ammar, 357
Quakers, 23, 100
"Quarantine the aggressor" speech, 290
Quartering Act, 32, 33, 36
Quasi-War, 63
Quayle, Dan, 360
Quebec, 13, 27, 28, 29, 36, 37, 38
Quebec Act, 36
Queen Anne's War, 25
Quemoy, 312

R

Rabin, Itzhak, 367
Race riots, of 1919, 238
Radical Republicans, 150, 154, 155
Radio, 187
Railroads, 218, 228
 expansion of, 274
 growth of, during 1840–1850s, 106
 Interstate Commerce Act, 175, 198
 in WW I, 228–229
Raleigh, Walter, 11
Randolph, A. Philip, 282
Randolph, Edmund, 50, 60
Randolph, John, 69
Rationalism, 25, 65
Ray, James Earl, 335
Reagan, Ronald, 351, 354, 357
 domestic concerns in first term, 366
 election of 1980, 353
 election of 1984, 356
 President of United States, 216
 second-term domestic/foreign
  affairs, 358
 tax policy, 354
Realism, 178, 209, 284
Recession
 of 1837, 281
 of 1920, 242
 of 1937–1938, 281

Reciprocal Trade Agreement Act, 288
Reciprocity Treaty, 129
Reconstruction
 Compromise of 1877, 164, 166, 167
 congressional reconstruction, 156, 158
 corruption under Grant, 210–212
 economic issues under Grant, 213–214
 election of 1872, 162
 election of 1876, 163
 election of 1868 and fifteenth
  amendment, 158
 Freedman's Bureau, 154, 156
 Johnson's attempt at, 155
 Lincoln's plan of, 154, 155
 Military Reconstruction Act, 158
 Panic of 1873, 160, 163, 165, 169
 postwar life in south, 159
 Radical Republicans, 150, 154, 155
 reestablishing governments in seceded
  states, 154
 Ten Percent Plan, 154
Reconstruction Finance Corporation,
 267, 298, 318
Red Cross Conference, 178
Red Scare, 209, 237, 238, 239, 251, 252
Reed, Thomas B., 179
Reform movements
 abolitionist movement, 100
 asylums for mentally ill, 99
 educating the public, 101
 feminism, 99, 171
 higher education, 81, 99, 177, 250
 prison reform, 99, 200
 progressive reforms in 1902–1907, 197
 public schools, 80, 99, 111, 257, 357
 sources of inspiration, 98
 temperance, 98
Rehnquist, William H., 359
Reich, Charles, 337
Reid, Whitelaw, 183
Religion
 in 1887–1892, 181
 Great Awakening, 26, 29
 post-revolutionary years, 82
 Puritans, 15, 16, 17, 18, 19, 21, 22
 in 1950s, 322, 323
 Second Great Awakening, 82
 in twenties, 262
Religious Toleration, Act of, 16, 17

Reno, Milo, 269
Republican party
  election of 1856, 133
  election of 1860, 139
  election of 1876, 163
  election of 1880, 168
  election of 1884, 174
  election of 1896, 184, 187
  election of 1900, 189
  election of 1904, 198
  election of 1908, 204
  election of 1912, 205, 206, 217
  election of 1916, 218, 219, 224
  election of 1920, 236, 241
  election of 1924, 259
  election of 1928, 261
  election of 1932, 269
  election of 1936, 277, 278, 280
  election of 1940, 292
  formation of, after Kansas-Nebraska
    Act, 132, 141
  Half-Breeds, 167
  Jefferson, Thomas, 38, 53, 60, 61, 63,
    64, 65, 77, 89
  Liberal, 74, 77
  Madison, James, 49, 50, 51, 61, 66, 70
  Radical Republicans, 150, 154, 155
  Stalwart, 167, 168
  during Washington's administration,
    60, 102
Resettlement Administration, 277, 281
Resolution Trust Corporation, 361
Reuther, Walter, 315
Revenue Act, 229, 257, 261
  of 1918, 229
  of 1926, 261
  of 1935, 278
  of 1942, 302
Revere, Paul, 37
Rhode Island
  colonial founders, 16
  ratification of Constitution and, 316
  state constitution, 43
Richardson, Elliot, 348
Riis, Jacob, 192
Rio de Janeiro conference, 202
River traffic, 78
Road building, 78
Roanoke settlers, 11

Roaring twenties
  conflict of values during, 251
  Coolidge administration, 260, 261
  creationism and Scopes trial, 254, 257
  economic advances and social changes
    during, 242
  election of 1920, 236, 241
  election of 1928, 261
  foreign policy during, 262
  Harding administration, 256
  immigration restrictions during,
    220, 250
  Ku Klux Klan, 160, 249, 250, 252,
    259, *264*
  prohibition, 232
Robinson, Joseph T., 261
Rockefeller, John D., 168, 175
Rockingham, Charles, 33
Rodino, Peter, 348
Rolfe, John, 12
Romanticism, 95, 98, 177
Rome-Berlin Axis, 289
Rommel, Erwin, 304
Roosevelt, Eleanor, 270, 282
Roosevelt, Franklin D., 242, 269, 270, 301
  Atlantic Charter, 294, 299, 301
  death of, 303
  election of 1932, 269
  election of 1936, 277, 278, 280
  election of 1940, 292
  first New Deal, 270, 271, 272, 275, 283
  Good Neighbor Policy, 286
  neutrality, 289
  "Quarantine the aggressor" speech,
    290
  road to Pearl Harbor, 294
  second New Deal, 272, 275, 276, 277
  threats to world order, 289
Roosevelt, Theodore, 167, 188, 189, 190,
    192, 218, 219, 241, 270, 278,
  Big Stick diplomacy, 202
  election of 1900, 189
  election of 1904, 198
  election of 1912, 217
  President of United States, 216, 52
  Vice President of United States,
    314, 52
Root, Elihu, 202
Root-Takahira agreement, 211

Rosecrans, William, 151
Rosenberg, Ethel, 317
Rosenberg, Julius, 317
Roszak, Theodore, 337
Ruby, Jack, 332
Ruckelshaus, William, 348
Rural Electrification Administration, 277, 319
Rush Bagot Treaty, 73
Rusk, Dean, 339
Russia, Russo-Japanese War, 202
Russo-Japanese War, 202
Ryswick, Treaty of, 25

S

Sacco, Nicola, 225
Sadat, Anwar, 352
St. Augustine, 10
St. Lawrence River, 4, 9, 13, 25
St. Lawrence Seaway, 319
St. Leger, Barry, 41
St. Louis, World's Fair, 200
Salary Grad Act, 161
Salem witch trials, 23
Salinger, J. D., 325
Salvation Army, 170
Samoan Islands, 182
Sanborn Contract fraud, 161
Sandino, Augusto, 263
Sandys, Edwin, 13
San Gabriel, Battle of, 122
Sanger, Margaret, 239, 248
Santa Anna, Antonio López de, 114
Santa Fe Trail, 78, 114, 120
Saratoga, 40, 41, 48
Saturday Night Massacre, 348
Savings and loan debacle, 361
Savio, Mario, 336
Scalia, Antonin, 359
Schools
    in 1877–1882, 171
    desegregation of, 316, 321, 328, 330
    higher education, 81, 89, 177, 250
    public, 80, 99, 111, 257, 357
Schurz, Carl, 160, 174, 192
Schwarzkopf, H. Norman, 365
Science, in 1907–1912, 210

Scientific management, 243, 176
Scopes, John, **255–257**
Scopes trial, 254, **255–257**, 257
Scott, Winfield, 122, 124, 128, 144, 145
    Anaconda Plan, 145
Scowcroft, Brent, 363
Secession, 127, 134, 135, 138, 140
Second Continental Congress, 36, 38
Second Hundred Days, 277
Sectional conflict
    Bleeding Kansas, 132, 133, 141
    Compromise of 1850, 127, 128, 129, 131, 141
    Dred Scott case, 134, 135, 136
    election of 1848, 126
    gold in California, 126
    Hinton Rowan Helper's Book, 138
    Kansas-Nebraska Act, 132, 141
    Lecompton constitution, 135, 136, 141
    Lincoln-Douglas debates, 136, 141
    manifest destiny and, 83, 112, 115, 117
    Republican Party formation, 141
    secession crisis, 64, 140
    strengthened Fugitive Slave Law, 131
    Uncle Tom's Cabin (Stowe), 101, 131, 141
    Wilmot Proviso, 125, 127
Securities and Exchange Commission, 272, 278, 298
Sedition Act, 64, 67, 84, 230, 231
Segregation
    in government agencies, 220
    in schools, 249, 250, 254, 257
Selective Service, WW II and, 226, 292
Selective Service Act, 226
Senate
    Constitution of United States, 49, 52
    impeachment and, 56
    required percentages of voting, 56
    responsibilities and duties of, 52
Separatists, 15
September 11 attacks. See 9/11 attacks
Serbia, 368
Seven Cities of Cibola, 8
Seven Days, Battle of, 146
Seven Pines, Battle of, 146
Seven Years' War, 27

Seward, William H., 137
  purchase of Alaska, 156
Sewell, Arthur, 184
Sexual revolution, during twenties, 248
Seymour, Horatio, 159
Shakers, 97
Share Our Wealth Society, 276, 279
Shays, Daniel, 47
Shays' Rebellion, 47, 57
Sheen, Fulton J., 325
Sheridan, Philip, 156
Sherman, James S., 204
Sherman, John, 138, 163, 188
Sherman, William T., 144, 152
Sherman Adams Scandal, 320
Sherman Antitrust Act, 213, 217
Sherman Silver Purchase Act, 180,
  184, 213
  repeal of, 184
Shriver, Sargent, 173
Shufeldt, Robert Wilson, 173
Silver, 180
  Sherman Silver Purchase Act, 180,
    184, 213
Simmons, William J., 252
Simms, William Gilmore, 96, 112
Simpson, "Sockless" Jerry, 183
Sinclair, Harry F., 258
Sinclair, Upton, 201, 214
Singer, Isaac, 130
Sino-Japanese war, 187, 188, 290
Sioux War, 174
Sirhan Sirhan, 339
Sirica, John J., 347
Sit-down strike, 284
Sit-ins, 322, 336
Six-Day War, 343, 345
Sixties
  cold war during, 308, 331, 366, 375
  counterculture, 337
  emergence of black power, 334
  ethnic activism, 336
  foreign policy during, 368
  Johnson and Great Society, 332
  Kennedy's New Frontier and liberal
    revival, 329
  new left, 336, 337
  Nixon's conservative reaction, 340

  seeds of rebellion, 325
  Vietnamization, 341
  Vietnam war, 337, 350, 352
  women's liberation, 338
Slater, Samuel, 79
Slavery. *See also* Civil War, causes of
  in colonial world, 19
  concurrent majority, 89, 112
  Constitutional Convention, 50, 57,
    135
  free slaves and voting, 76
  gang system, 108
  as institution, 108, 112, 115
  as labor system, 106, 108, 336
  slaves' reaction to slavery, 109
  slave trade, 108, 127, 128, 209
  in South Carolina, 42, 124
  Southern response to antislavery
    movement, 111
  underground railroad, 109, 127
  urban slavery in Southern city, 108
  westward expansion and, 87, 94, 112,
    115, 124
  Wilmot Proviso, 125, 127
Slidell, John, 121, 148
Sloat, John D., 122
Smith, Alfred E., 259, 261, 276
Smith, Gerald L. K., 276, 279
Smith, Jedediah, 112
Smith, Jesse, 258
Smith, John, 12
Smith, Joseph, 98, 119, 124
Smith, Mary Wells, 181
Smith Act, 317
Smith-Connolly Act, 303
Smith-Hughes Act, 250
Smith v. Arkwright, 303
Social and cultural developments
  in 1877–1882, 170
  in 1882–1887, 176
  in 1887–1892, 181
  in 1892–1897, 186
  in 1897–1902, 191
  in 1902–1907, 200
  in 1907–1912, 209
  during Age of Jackson, 87, 94, 95
  during New Deal, 265
  in 1950s, 322, 323

Social and cultural developments *(continued)*
  during twenties, 283
  during WW I, 188, 189, 245, 252,
    260, 262
  during WW II, 236, 274, 290, 296
Social Darwinism, 169
  in 1877–1882, 170, 171
Social gospel, 98, 170
Socialist Democratic party, 189
Social Security, 277, 278, 280, 298, 316,
    318, 340, 355
  under Eisenhower, 331
  establishment of, 22, 60, 61, 204
Somoza, Anastasio, 263
Sons of Liberty, 32, 48
Souter, David, 362
South Carolina
  in American Revolution, 31
  colonial life, 19
  colonial period, 7, 20
Southeast Asia Treaty Organization, 312
South End House, 187
Southern states. *See also* Ctivil war;
  Reconstruction; Sectional conflict
  classes in, 107
  commercial activity, 110
  cotton kingdom, 77, 106
  daily life, 111
  education, 99, 111
  institution of slavery, 108, 112, 131
  life in postwar, 159
  manufacturing, 110
  response to antislavery movement, 111
  role of women, 103, 111
  voice for change, 110
Soviet Union
  aid to, during WW II, 294
  Bush-Gorbachev summits, 364
  Carter administration and, 351, 356
  cold war during 1960s, 331
  collapse of, and end of cold war, 366
  Cuban Missile Crisis, 331, 345
  emergence of cold war
    and containment, 308
  Iron Curtain, 308, 327
  Khrushchev, 312, 313, 328, 331
  Nixon administration and, 340, 341
  Reagan administration and, 356,
    358, 359

recognition of, 352
  Summit Conference with, 295, 313
  in WW I, 215
  in WW II, 301
Spain
  conquering Aztecs, 2
  conquistadores and colonialization,
    7, 8, 9
  Cuban's revolt against, in 1895, 187
  encomiendas, 9
  hacienda system, 9
  help in American Revolution, 24, 31
  King George's war, 25, 26
  New Spain, 9
  sale of Florida, 43
  Santa Fe Trail and trade with, 78
  Spanish Armada, 10
  Treaty of 1795, 62
  Treaty of Tordesillas, 7
  War of the Spanish Succession, 25
  war with, in 1898, 185, 190, 214
Spanish Armada, 10
Spargo, John, 201
Speakeasies, 253, 254
Speaker of the House, 52, 88, 174, 175,
    179, 205, 316, 367
Specie Resumption Act, 163
Spock, Benjamin, 323
Sports, 181, 250, 285, 286
  during twenties, 250
Squatter sovereignty, 126
Stalin, 307, 308, 310, 312, 328
Stalin, Josef, 312
Stamp Act, 31, 32, 33, 48
Stamp Act Congress, 33
Standard of living
  in 1877–1882, 167, 168170, 171
  rise of, during twenties, 247
Standard Oil Company, 191, 199, 201
Stanton, Edwin M., 158
Stanton, Elizabeth Cady, 100
Stark, John, 41
Starr, Kenneth W., 368
State Department, 317, 318, 123, 186,
    208, 211
State government
  compact theory, 64
  Constitution of United States and,
    49, 52, 57

federal and state shared powers, 55
interstate relations, 53
powers reserved only for, 55
progressive reform in 1902–1907, 197
required percentages of voting, 56
restrictions on powers of, 51
Stead, William T., 189
Steamboats, 163
Steffens, Lincoln, 78
Steinbeck, John, 284
Stephens, Alexander, 140
Stephenson, David, 252
Steuben, Baron von, 41
Stevens, Thaddeus, 155, 160
Stevenson, Adlai E., 183, 318
Vice President of United States,
52, 314
Stimson, Henry L., 291
Stock market
Black Monday, 359
boom and crash during twenties,
263, 264
crash of 1929, 236, 265
Hundred Days legislation, 272, 298
insider trading in 1980s, 361
Stockton, Robert, 122
Stowe, Harriet Beecher, 100, 101, 131
Strasser, Adolph, 176
Strategic Arms Limitation Treaty I, 343
Strategic Arms Limitation Treaty II, 352
Strategic Arms Reduction Treaty, 364
Strategic Defense Initiative (SDI) sys-
tem, 353
Strikes
in 1919, 237
in 1946, 315
sit-down strike, 373
Strong, Josiah, 183
Stuart, J. E. B., 151
Stubblefield, Nathan, 187
Student Nonviolent Coordinating
Committee (SNCC), 322
Students for Democratic Society, 336,
345
Suburbs, 247, 323, 324
growth in 1950s, 247
Suez Canal, 312
Suffolk Resolves, 36
Sugar Act, 32, 33, 48

Summit Conference, 295, 313
Sumner, Charles, 133, 160
Sumner, William Graham, 169, 177
Sumter, Fort, 143
Sun Belt, population growth in 1950s, 323
Supply-side economics, 354
Supremacy clause of Constitution, 53
Supreme Court
Charles River Bridge, 94
Constitution of United States, 49, 52
Dred Scott v. Sanford, 134
Eisenhower appointments, 319
establishment of, 22, 60, 61, 204
George H. W. Bush appointments,
362–363
Marshall court, 75
Nixon appointments, 340
Reagan appointments, 356
Roosevelt and, 221, 241, 278, 282, 294,
Sedition Act, 64, 67, 84, 230, 231
Worcester v. Georgia, 90
Sussex pledge, 224
Sweatt v. Painter, 320
Swift, Gustavus, 175

T

Taft, Robert A., 292
Taft, William H., 204
dollar diplomacy, 202, 208, 210
election of 1912, 205, 206
President of United States, 52, 216, 314
Taft-Hartley Act, 315, 316, 327
Taft-Katsura Memo, 203, 211
Taiwan, 311, 312, 352
Tan, Amy, 372
Taney, Roger B., 134, 150
Tarbell, Ida, 201
Tariffs
Dingley tariff, 186
Fordney-McCumber Tariff, 257
Hawley-Smoot Tariff, 267, 288, 298
McKinley Tariff, 180, 183
Payne-Aldrich Tariff, 215, 208
Protective tariff, 73, 85, 115, 117, 118,
140, 179, 180, 184, 186
Underwood-Simmons Tariff Act, 215
Walker Tariff, 118
Wilson-Gorman tariff, 184, 186

Tax Equity and Fiscal Responsibility
Act, 335
Taxes
Civil War and, 215
income, 216, 228
under Nixon, 341, 348
no taxation without representation,
33, 34
under Reagan, 355
reduction of, during twenties, 215
Stamp Act, 31, 32, 33, 48
Tea Act, 35, 48
Townshend Acts, 33, 34
WW I finances and, 262
Tax Reform Act of 1986, 358
Taylor, Frederick W., 176, 243
Taylor, Zachary, 121, 122, 126, 127
Compromise of 1850, 127, 128, 129,
131, 141
election of 1848, 126
Tea Act, 35, 48
Teapot Dome Scandal, 258, 264
Technology
in 1897–1902, 191
man on moon in 1960s, 334, 346
in Northern states during Age of
Jackson, 87, 88, 110
space exploration under Eisenhower,
286
Tecumseh, 70
Teheran Conference, 307, 327
Television, 323, 324, 325
in 1950s, 323
Temperance, 98, 171
Tennent, Gilbert, 26
Tennent, William, 26
Tennessee, 46
establishment of, 264
Tennessee Valley Authority, 261, 274, 298
Ten Percent Plan, 154
Tenure of Office Act, 158
Terrorism, 252, 369, 370, 371, 372, 375
Tet Offensive, 339, 346
Texas, annexation of, 117, 118, 124
Thames, Battle of, 71
Thayer, Webster, 255
Thomas, Clarence, 362
Thomas, Dale, 12

Thomas, Norman, 270, 280, 293
Thoreau, Henry David, 97, 123
Three-Fifths Compromise, 50
Thurmond, Strom, 316
Ticonderoga, Fort, 37
Tilden, Samuel J., 163
Tobacco, in Virginia colony, 28
Tocqueville, Alexis de, 87, 94
Tojo, Hideki, 295
Townsend, Francis E., 276
Townshend, Charles, 33
Trail of Tears, 90, 124
Transcendentalism, 98
Transcendentalists, 97
Transportation Act of 1920, 236
Treasury Department, 149
Trenton, 40, 48
Tresca, Carlo, 209
Tripartite Pact, 295
Trist, Nicholas, 123
Troy Female Seminary, 99
Truman, Harry S.
election of 1948, 316
Fair Deal, 316
President of United States, 314
Truman Doctrine, 308, 309, 327
Vice President of United States, 314
Truman Doctrine, 308, 309, 327
Truth, Sojourner, 103
Truth-in-Securities Act, 272
Tubman, Harriet, 109
Tugwell, Rexford G., 270
Turner, Frederick Jackson, 183
Turner, Nat, 109, 112, 124
Twain, Mark, 171, 177, 192
Tweed, William Marcy "Boss," 159
Twenties. See Roaring twenties
Two Moratorium Days, 341
Tydings-McDuffie Act, 288
Tyler, Elizabeth, 252
Tyler, John, 93, 105

U

U-2 incident, 313
Uncle Tom's Cabin (Stowe), 101
Underground railroad, 109, 127
Underwood-Simmons Tariff Act, 215

Unemployment
   during Great Depression, 266
   under Carter administration, 351
   march of unemployed, 351
Union Pacific Railroad, 279
Union Party, 139, 152, 279, 299
Unions
   in 1877–1882, 169
   craft vs. industrial, 283
   Democratic party and 1936
      election, 277
   growth of, 80, 283
   growth of CIO, 284
   Landrum-Griffen Labor-Management
      Act, 320
   length of work day, 105
   during New Deal, 283
   radical labor unions, 209, 238
   rise of, in Northern states during
      Age of Jackson, 110
   sit-down strike, 284
   strikes in 1946, 315
   Taft-Hartley Act, 407
Unitarianism, 82
United Auto Workers, 284, 315
United Farm Workers' Organizing
   Committee, 336
United Mine Workers, 237, 245, 283,
   315, 199
United Nations, establishment
   of, 365
United States Constitution. *See*
   Constitution of United States
United States Housing Authority, 281
United Textile Workers, 245
Universalism, 82
Universal Negro Improvement
   Association, 249
Updike, John, 325
Urbanization. *See also* Cities
   in 1877–1882, 170
   growth of cities, 103
   problems of, 99, 103
   rural-urban conflict, 251
   in 1960s, 324
   during twenties, 242
Urban revivalism, 166, 181
U.S. Steel Corporation, 191

U.S. Supreme Court. *See*
   Supreme Court
Utopians, 97, 98
Utrecht, Treaty of, 25

V

Vaca, Cabeza de, 8
Vallandigham, Clement L., 150
Valley Forge, 40, 41, 48
Van Buren, Martin, 93, 117, 126
   election of 1836, 93
   presidency of, 92
Vance, Cyrus, 353
Vanzetti, Bartolomeo, 255
Vaudeville, 234
Veblen, Thorstein, 192
Venezuela, 187, 188, 202, 314, 343
   border dispute with Britain, 72
Vermont, establishment of, 41, 63,
   194, 260, 280
Verrazzano, Giovanni da, 9
Versailles Treaty, WW I, 234, 289
Vesey, Denmark, 109
Vespucci, Amerigo, 7
Veterans
   Bonus Expeditionary Force, 268, 298
   veteran bonus under Coolidge, 261
Veterans' Bureau, 258
Vice president of United States, office of
   electoral college and, 51
   role in Senate, 44
Vice presidents of United States
   Adams, John, 59
   Agnew, Spiro T., 340, 344
   Arthur, Chester A., 168
   Burr, Aaron, 64, 68, 69
   Bush, George H. W., 354, 357, 360, 366
   Calhoun, John C., 71, 89, 91, 112,
      117, 125
   Colfax, Schuyler, 158
   Coolidge, Calvin, 237, 241, 259, 260
   Curtis, Charles, 261
   Dawes, Charles G., 259, 262
   Fairbanks, Charles, 198
   Fillmore, Millard, 128, 134
   Garner, John Nance, 269
   Gore, Al, 366, 369

Hendricks, Thomas A., 174
Hobart, Garrett, 184, 189
Jefferson, Thomas, 38, 53, 60, 61, 63, 64, 65, 77, 89
Johnson, Andrew, 152, 155, 159, 175
Johnson, Lyndon B., 322
Marshall, Thomas, 206
Mondale, Walter, 351, 356
Nixon, Richard M., 313, 318, 322, 340, 344
Quayle, Dan, 360
Roosevelt, Theodore, 218, 219
Sherman, James S., 204
Stevenson, Adlai E., 183, 318
Truman, Harry S., 303, 309, 314
Tyler, John, 93, 115
Vicksburg, 147, 151, 165
Vietnam war, 337, 350, 352
background of, 338
domino theory, 339
end of, 341
escalation of, 342
Geneva Accords, 312
Gulf of Tonkin resolution, 338, 342, 345
student protests against, 337
Tet Offensive, 339, 346
Vietnamization and Nixon policy, 341
Villa, Francisco "Pancho," 222, 239
Vincennes, Indiana, 42
Virginia
early colonization of, 10, 11, 13
indenture system and, 12
Jamestown, 12, 21, 28
Navigation Acts and, 20, 21, 22, 32
ratification of Constitution and, 44, 155, 202
Roanoke settlers, 11
as royal colony, 13, 17, 18, 23
state constitution, 43, 44, 53
tobacco in, 12
Virginia Company, 11
Virgin Islands, 222
Volcker, Paul A., 351
Volstead Act, 253
Volunteerism, during Great Depression, 226, 230
Voting

African Americans, 333, 334
blacks, 54, 158, 159
Electoral College, 51, 88, 179
expansion of electorate in 1824 election, 87
required percentages of, for Senate and House, 56
women, 54
Voting Rights Act, 334, 340, 356

W

Wade-Davis Bill, 155
Wadsworth, Henry, 96
Wages
minimum wage, 274, 281, 314, 316, 318, 329, 206, 209
wage controls during WW II, 301, 341
Wagner Act, 365, 372
Wagner-Steagall Act, 281
Wake Island, 195, 304
Wald, Lillian, 187
Wallace, George, 344
Wallace, Henry A., 270, 292
Wallace, Lew, 171
Walsh, Frank P., 229
Ward, Lester Frank, 177, 186
War Department, 191, 273
War Industries Board, 228, 236, 239
War Labor Board, 229
War of 1812, 70, 72, 74, 85, 89, 112
War of Jenkins' Ear, 25
War of the Austrian Succession, 25
War of the League of Augsburg, 25
War of the Spanish Succession, 25
War Powers Act, 343
War Production Board, 301, 327
Warren, Earl, 319, 332
Warren, Mercy Otis, 81
War Resources Board, 290
Warsaw Treaty Organization, 310
Washington, Booker T., 171
Washington, George, 27, 38, 49, 50, 51, 52, 59, 171
administration (1789–1797), 60
as commander of Continental Army, 52

Constitutional Convention, 50, 57, 135
President of United States, 216
at Yorktown, 42, 43, 48, 304, 305
Washington, Harold, 360
Washington Conference, 262
Washington Heights, Battle of, 40
Watergate, 347
Watson, Thomas, 183, 184
Wayne, Anthony, 62
Weaver, James, 168, 183
Weaver, Robert, 336
Webster, Daniel, 72, 91, 92, 116, 128
Compromise of 1850, 127, 128, 129, 131, 141
Webster-Ashburton Treaty, 116
Webster-Hayne debate, 91
Webster, Noah, 82
Webster-Ashburton Treaty, 116
Weems, Parson Mason, 81
Weld, Theodore, 100
Welfare reform, 367
Welles, Gideon, 145
Westmoreland, William C., 338
Westward expansion, 36, 74, 87
Louisiana and fur trade, 112
manifest destiny and, 112, 115, 117
Mexican War, 120, 121, 123
Mormon migration, 119
New Mexico and California, 114
Oregon country, 113, 117
slavery issue and sectional stress, 115
Texas, 114
Webster-Ashburton Treaty, 116
Wheeler-Rayburn Act, 278
Whig party, 93, 94
during Age of Jackson, 87, 94, 95
disintegration of, 131, 132
election of 1844, 117, 118
election of 1848, 126
election of 1852, 128, 130
Tyler and, 115
Westward expansion and, 87
Whiskey Rebellion (1794), 62, 84
Whiskey Ring fraud, 161
White, Henry, 233
White, John, 11
White, William Allen, 201
Whitefield, George, 26, 29

Whitewater, 368
Whitman, Marcus, 118
Whitman, Walt, 96
Whitney, Eli, 77, 79, 84, 104
Wickersham, George, 204
Wilder, L. Douglas, 361
Wilkes, Charles, 147
Wilkie, Wendell L., 292
William of Orange, 23
Williams, Roger, 13
Wilmot Proviso, 125, 127
Wilson, Woodrow, 177, 198, 206, 215, 333
Congressional Government, 177
domestic problems and end of Wilson administration, 232, 236
early years and implementing new freedom, 215, 234
election of 1916, 218, 219, 224
foreign policy and road to war, 289–292
Fourteen Points, 232, 233, 234, 239
military campaign in WW I, 226
mobilizing home front, 227
new nationalism, 217, 206, 207
road to war in Europe, 223
social issues in first administration, 220
Versailles or Paris Peace Treaty, 234
wartime social trends, 231
Winthrop, John, 16, 17
Witch trials in Salem, 23
Wolfe, Thomas, 251
Women
in army during WW I, 226
colleges for, 177
domesticity during 1950s, 325
education and, 171
first higher education for, 99
liberation movement during 1960s, 346
during New Deal, 265
role of, in Northern states in Age of Jackson, 87, 94, 95
role of, in Southern states during Age of Jackson, 87, 94, 95
suffrage, 217, 220, 231, 236, 239
during twenties, 263, 264
voting, 356, 54
in workforce, 324
during WW I, 215

Women's Christian Temperance
   Movement, 171
Wood, Leonard, 241
Wood, Robert, 187
Woolley, John, 189
Worcester v. Georgia, 90
Works Progress Administration, 277, 298
World's Fair
   in Chicago, 169
   St. Louis, 198
World War I
   American Expeditionary Force, 268, 227
   American neutrality, 223, 293
   America's declaration of war, 225, 226
   armistice, 227, 233, 239
   consequences of, 236
   Espionage and Sedition Acts, 230
   final peace effort before war, 225
   Fourteen Points, 232, 233, 234, 239
   Gore-McLemore Resolution, 223
   House-Grey Memorandum, 224
   major military engagements, 227
   mobilizing home front, 227
   peacemaking and domestic problems,
      1918–1920, 232
   raising American army, 226
   road to war in Europe, 221, 223, 286
   submarine crisis of 1915, 223
   Sussex pledge, 224
   unlimited submarine warfare, 225
   Versailles or Paris Peace Treaty, 234
   war at sea, 226
   women and minorities in military, 226
   Zimmerman telegram, 225

World War II
   American involvement in, before Pearl
      Harbor, 296
   atomic bomb, 305, 306, 308, 310, 328
   declared war begins, 301
   demobilization and domestic policy, 314
   diplomacy of, 221
   home front, 301
   north African and European theatres, 303
   Pacific theatre, 304
   road to Pearl Harbor, 294
Wren, William S., 198
Wright, Frances, 97
Wright, Jim, 362
Wright brothers, 201
Writs of Assistance, 31, 33

X

XYZ affair, 63, 84

Y

Yalta Conference, 307
Yancey, William L., 139
Yazoo Land Company, 75
Yazoo Land controversy, 69
Yellow journalism, 188, 191
Yeoman farmers, 107
Yorktown, Virginia, 42
Young, Brigham, 98, 119
Young America, 112, 129
Yugoslavia, 234, 366, 368

REA's Test Prep Books Are The Best!
(a sample of the <u>hundreds of letters</u> REA receives each year)

(more on front page)